ANDREW SOLOMON

Andrew Solomon holds a PhD in psychology from the University of Cambridge; is a professor of psychology at Columbia University and President of PEN American Center; and is a regular contributor to the *Guardian*, the *New Yorker* and the *New York Times*. A lecturer and activist, he is the author of *Far from the Tree: Parents, Children and the Search for Identity*, which won the Wellcome Trust Book Prize, the National Book Critics Circle Award and many other awards; and *The Noonday Demon: An Anatomy of Depression*, which won the National Book Award, was a finalist for the Pulitzer Prize, and has been published in twenty-four languages. His TED talks have been viewed over 16 million times. A dual U.K./U.S. national, he lives in London and New York.

www.andrewsolomon.com

ALSO BY ANDREW SOLOMON

Non-fiction
The Irony Tower: Soviet Artists in a Time of Glasnost
The Noonday Demon: An Anatomy of Depression
Far from the Tree: Parents, Children and the Search for Identity

Fiction
A Stone Boat

ANDREW SOLOMON

Far and Away

How Travel Can Change the World

VINTAGE

1 3 5 7 9 10 8 6 4 2

Vintage
20 Vauxhall Bridge Road,
London SW1V 2SA

Vintage is part of the Penguin Random House group of companies
whose addresses can be found at global.penguinrandomhouse.com

Penguin
Random House
UK

First published in Vintage in 2017
First published in hardback by Chatto & Windus in 2016

penguin.co.uk/vintage

A CIP catalogue record for this book is available from the British Library

ISBN 9781784700720

Printed and bound by Clays Ltd, St Ives Plc

Penguin Random House is committed to a sustainable future
for our business, our readers and our planet. This book is made
from Forest Stewardship Council® certified paper.

MIX
Paper from
responsible sources
FSC® C018179
www.fsc.org

For Oliver, Lucy, Blaine and George,
who have given me a reason to stay at home

Think of the long trip home.
Should we have stayed at home and thought of here?
Where should we be today?
. . .
Continent, city, country, society:
the choice is never wide and never free.
And here, or there . . . No. Should we have stayed at home,
wherever that may be?

Elizabeth Bishop, 'Questions of Travel'

Contents

	Dispatches from Everywhere	1
USSR	The Winter Palettes	45
USSR	Three Days in August	59
RUSSIA	Young Russia's Defiant Decadence	71
CHINA	Their Irony, Humour (and Art) Can Save China	103
SOUTH AFRICA	The Artists of South Africa: Separate and Equal	141
USA	Vlady's Conquests	177
TAIWAN	'Don't Mess with Our Cultural Patrimony!'	181
TAIWAN	On Each Palette, a Choice of Political Colours	205
TURKEY	Sailing to Byzantium	211
ZAMBIA	Enchanting Zambia	219
CAMBODIA	Phaly Nuon's Three Steps	229
MONGOLIA	The Open Spaces of Mongolia	237

CONTENTS

GREENLAND   Inventing the Conversation   249

SENEGAL   Naked, Covered in Ram's Blood,
             Drinking a Coke and Feeling
             Pretty Good   261

AFGHANISTAN An Awakening after the Taliban   269

JAPAN   Museum without Walls   287

SOLOMON ISLANDS Song of Solomons   293

RWANDA   Children of Bad Memories   305

LIBYA   Circle of Fire: Letter from Libya   321

CHINA   All the Food in China   359

CHINA   Outward Opulence for Inner Peace:
             The Qianlong Garden of Retirement   373

ANTARCTICA   Adventures in Antarctica   385

INDONESIA   When Everyone Signs   397

BRAZIL   Rio, City of Hope   407

GHANA   In Bed with the President of Ghana?   429

ROMANIA   Gay, Jewish, Mentally Ill and a
             Sponsor of Gypsies in Romania   435

MYANMAR   Myanmar's Moment   443

AUSTRALIA   Lost at the Surface   483

AFTERWORD   The Entrance of Brexit and a
             Last Word on America First   493

             Acknowledgements   521

             Notes   527

             Bibliography   571

             Index   601

FAR
and
AWAY

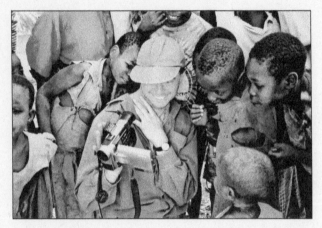

Zambia, 1997 *(Photograph by Luca Trovato)*

Dispatches from Everywhere

W hen I was about seven, my father told me about the Holocaust. We were in the yellow Buick on New York State route 9A, and I had been asking him whether Pleasantville was actually pleasant. I cannot remember why the Nazis came up a mile or two later, but I do remember that he thought I already knew about the Final Solution, and so didn't have any rehearsed way to present the camps. He said that this had happened to people because they were Jewish. I knew that we were Jewish, and I gathered that if we'd been there at the time, it would have happened to us, too. I insisted that my father explain it at least four times, because I kept thinking I must be missing some piece of the story that would make it make sense. He finally told me, with an emphasis that nearly ended the conversation, that it was 'pure evil.' But I had one more question: 'Why didn't those Jews just leave when things got bad?'

'They had nowhere to go,' he said.

At that instant, I decided that I would always have somewhere to go. I would not be helpless, dependent or credulous; I would never suppose that just because things had always been fine, they would continue to be fine. My notion of absolute safety at home crumbled then and there. I would leave before the walls closed around the ghetto, before the train tracks were completed, before the borders were sealed. If genocide ever threatened midtown Manhattan, I would be all set to gather up my passport and head for some place where they'd be glad to have me. My father had said that some Jews were helped by non-Jewish friends, and I concluded that I would always have friends who were different from me, the kind who could take me in or get me out. That first talk with my father was mostly about horror, of course, but it was also in this regard a conversation about love, and over time, I came to understand that you could save yourself by broad affections. People had died because their paradigms were too local. I was not going to have that problem.

A few months later, when I was at a shoe store with my mother, the salesman commented that I had flat feet and ventured that I would have back problems in later life (true, alas), but also that I might be disqualified from the draft. The Vietnam War was dominating the headlines, and I had taken on board the idea that when I finished high school, I'd have to go fight. I wasn't good even at scuffles in the sandbox, and the idea of being dropped into a jungle with a gun petrified me. My mother considered the Vietnam War a waste of young lives. The Second World War, on the other hand, had been worth fighting, and every good American boy had done his part, flat feet or otherwise. I wanted to understand the comparative standard whereby some wars were so righteous that my own mother thought they warranted my facing death, while others were somehow none of our business. Wars didn't happen in America, but America could send you off to war anywhere else in the world, rightly or wrongly. Flat feet or not, I wanted to know those places, so I could make my own decisions about them.

I was afraid of the world. Even if I was spared the draft and fascism failed to establish a foothold in the Nixon years, a nuclear attack was always possible. I had nightmares about the Soviets detonating a bomb in Manhattan. Although not yet acquainted with the legend of the Wandering Jew, I made constant escape plans and imagined a life going from port to port. I thought I might be kidnapped; when my parents were being particularly annoying, I imagined I had already been kidnapped, taken away from nicer people in some more benign country to be consigned to this nest of American madness. I was precociously laying the groundwork for an anxiety disorder in early adulthood.

Running in counterpoint to my reckonings with destruction was my growing affection for England, a place I had never visited. My Anglophilia set in about the time my father started reading me *Winnie-the-Pooh* when I was two. Later, it was *Alice in Wonderland*, then *The Five Children and It*, then *The Chronicles of Narnia*. For me, the magic in these stories had to do as much with England as with the authors' flights of fancy. I developed a strong taste for marmalade and for the longer sweep of history. In response to my various self-indulgences, my parents' usual reprimand was to remind me that I was not the Prince of Wales. I conceived the vague idea that if I could only get to the U.K., I would receive entitlements (someone to pick up my toys, the most expensive item on the menu) that I associated more with location than with an accident of birth. Like all fantasies of escape, this one pertained not only to the destination, but also to what was left behind. I was a pre-gay kid who had not yet reckoned with the nature of my difference and therefore didn't have a vocabulary with which to parse it. I felt foreign even at home; though I couldn't yet have formulated the idea, I understood that going where I would actually *be* foreign might distract people from the more intimate nature of my otherness.

My incipient Anglophilia was nourished by a childhood babysitter. I was a colicky infant, so my mother had sought a helper who could give her a bit of a break one day a week. She advertised the position and set up interviews with likely prospects. One day the bell rang when no one was expected. My mother was surprised to find at the door a middle-aged Scottish woman as wide as she was tall, who announced, 'I'm the nanny. I've come to take care of the baby.' My mother, presuming she had forgotten an appointment, led Bebe back to my room, where I grew calm in seconds and ate my best meal yet. Bebe was hired on the spot; only later did it materialise that she had got out of the lift on the wrong floor and was supposed to be going to the family in 14E rather than to us in 11E. By then, it was too late. For the next decade, Bebe came on Thursdays and made us sherry trifle and told us stories about growing up on the Isle of Mull. As a little girl she had had a purse with three patches on it that read *Paris*, *London* and *New York* and had told her grandmother that someday she would visit all those places. Her grandmother had laughed – but Bebe did visit them all; indeed, she lived in them all.

Like the characters in my beloved British books, Bebe was eccentric and magical – childlike herself, and incapable of exasperation, disappointment or anger. She taught me how to roll my *r*'s. Her sharpest reprimand was the occasional 'Gently, Bentley!' when my brother or I grew raucous. I imagined that everyone in Britain would be similarly delighted by me almost all the time, and that over there, children were served second helpings of dessert at every meal, even if they hadn't finished their vegetables or done their homework.

I was likewise moved by a story of another England, one that reassured me as I thought of those who had perished because they had nowhere to go. Our next-door neighbours, Erika Urbach and her mother, Mrs Offenbacher, were Czech Jews who had secured English entry visas as the Nazis closed in. But their transit visas for crossing Europe did not materialise until after their English papers had expired. They nonetheless boarded the train in Prague. In the Netherlands, an officer tried to eject them, arguing that they would not be admitted in England, but Mrs Offenbacher insisted that they could not be removed because their transit visas were valid. When their ferry landed in Dover, they disembarked and Mrs Offenbacher stood for a full hour watching people proceed through border control, trying to decide which official seemed kindest. Finally, Mrs Offenbacher (who was a beautiful woman, as Erika was a beautiful child) carefully selected a queue. The customs officer noted, 'Your entry permit for the United Kingdom has expired.' Mrs Offenbacher calmly replied, 'Yes. But if you send us back, we will be killed.' There was a long pause while they looked each other in the eye, and then he stamped both passports and said, 'Welcome to England.'

My preoccupation with discovering a foreign refuge was matched by an intense curiosity about the same world I found so threatening. Although England lay at the forefront of my imaginings, I also wanted to know what Chinese people ate for breakfast, how Africans styled their hair, why people played so much polo in Argentina. I read voraciously, immersing myself in Indian fairy tales, Russian folk stories and *Tales of a Korean Grandmother*. My mother brought home a Kleenex box illustrated with people in their native costumes. Believing that everyone in Holland clunked around in wooden shoes and all Peruvians wore jaunty bowler hats, I imagined meeting them all and kept the box after the tissues had been used up. I wanted to visit every country in the world at least once – as though having set foot in China or India met the same checklist parameters as touching down in Gambia or Monaco or connecting through the Bahamas.

Fortunately for me, my mother loved travel. She first went to Europe immediately after the Second World War, when she was twenty-two, when visiting the ravaged continent was considered enough of a novelty that her hometown paper chronicled her departure. Our first significant family trip abroad – to England, France and Switzerland – came when I was eleven, and in the years that followed, we often tagged along on my father's European business trips. He was never particularly interested in new places, but tourism brought out the best in my mother. Before we went anyplace, she would teach us about it. We'd read relevant books, learn local history, find out about the food we were going to eat and the sights we would see. My mother was a scheduler; she would have worked out an itinerary for each day, down to when we'd get up and when we'd return to the hotel. Such precision may sound alarming, but it was actually relaxing, because it meant that we were surprised only by the places themselves. We never rushed. My mother said you should always travel as if you would return; if you thought you were making your sole visit anywhere, you would try to see everything and therefore wouldn't really see anything. 'Always leave something for next time, something to tempt you back,' she said.

Not until high school, though, did I begin to connect these geographical adventures to a sweeping narrative. Mr Donadio, my ninth-grade history teacher, was fond of the orotund phrase: he described various important figures (Ramses II, Pontius Pilate, Catherine the Great, Napoléon, Thomas Jefferson) as standing at 'the crossroads of history'. I envisioned them as brave men and women who disregarded traffic lights, turning sharply left or right where everyone else had planned on proceeding straight ahead. I came to recognise that while such men and women had made choices that reshaped the world, they were, equally, making those choices because of their circumstances. Another teacher insisted that it was impossible to determine whether such leaders were consciously making history or merely fulfilling its demands. I remember thinking in ninth grade that I would like to behold the crossroads of history, with some grandiose adolescent hope that if I could describe what happened at the intersection, I might even affect its course.

In 1980, during my junior year of high school, our glee club was scheduled to perform in the USSR, but the Soviets had invaded Afghanistan a few months earlier, so we were rerouted to Romania and Bulgaria. (My debut solo performance – which was very nearly my swan song, given my sonorous but strident baritone – consisted of my singing the Spanish folk song 'Ríu Ríu Chíu' in a nursing home outside Pleven, Bulgaria's seventh most populous city.) I had never even heard of anyone's going to those countries. Before we left the United States, several teachers and other wise adults advised me that whereas Bulgaria was a Soviet puppet state and a terrible place, Romania had a brave, independent leader, Nicolae Ceauşescu, who refused to obey orders from Moscow. Once we arrived in Bulgaria, however, we all experienced unaffected warmth. Even when our lead soprano, Louise Elton, and I were briefly carried off by a troupe of Gypsies, the mood remained cheerful. In Romania, by contrast, we saw scenes of repression every day that stood in stark contrast to our hosts' attempts to persuade us that their country was free and liberal. A patient tried to wave at us from a hospital window, only to be pulled back fiercely by an army-uniformed attendant who immediately lowered the blinds. Anxious-seeming Romanians approached on the streets and asked us to smuggle out letters for them, but were afraid to engage in conversation. Glowering military personnel could be seen at every corner. We were forbidden to explore in Bucharest on grounds that 'here in Romania, we have no funny nightlife', a remark we took great delight in repeating throughout the rest of the trip.

After we returned, I reported that Bulgaria was charming and Romania, a creepy police state. Everyone who knew better told me how wrong I was. When the regimes later changed, it turned out that the Ceauşescus were not so admirable – that Romania's was quite possibly the most repressive regime in Eastern Europe. That was a good lesson about intuition: places that seem lovely at first glance may actually be sinister, but places that feel sinister seldom turn out to be lovely.

Nearly three decades later, I interviewed Saif al-Islam Qaddafi, son of Libyan leader Muammar Qaddafi. He was in some ways persuasive: beautifully dressed in a Savile Row suit, eloquent in English, socially well connected and gracious in his grand fashion. He was also ominously self-absorbed and a patent liar; his buoyant narrative of Libyan life was so much at odds with what I saw and heard first-hand that it seemed almost like performance art. A few years after my visit, I was invited to a breakfast for Saif Qaddafi organised by a prestigious foreign-policy association. After his twenty-minute oration, each of us was invited to ask a question. I was astonished by the deferential posture of the interlocutors, many of them seasoned diplomats. When my turn came, I said, 'All of what you have promised will happen is the same as what you were promising five years ago, and none of it has so far come to pass. On what basis are we to presume that those promises now have merit?' I was admonished afterward for having been rude to a 'gifted statesman' who represented 'our best hopes for North Africa'. Saif Qaddafi is now imprisoned and wanted for prosecution by the International Criminal Court for crimes against humanity after his disastrous behaviour in the Libyan revolution, during which he announced that 'rivers of blood' would flow if the populist uprising continued. A witness can be of more value than a policy analyst. An amateur witness, free of conceptual bias, sometimes sees the plainest truth. One should never be blinded by tailoring.

The summer after I finished college, I visited my friend Pamela Crimmins, who had landed a job as personal photographer to the American ambassador in Morocco. At the time Morocco had no mobile phones and few landlines, so we had arranged beforehand that Pamela would meet me at the airport when I arrived in Rabat, the capital. It was the first time I'd ventured alone to a place so remote from my life experience. I landed at night, found no one waiting to greet me, and panicked. A man with a decrepit car offered to drive me to Pamela's apartment building, where I started up the staircase, calling 'Pamela!' at every floor, until I finally heard her sleepy voice say, 'Andrew?' In hindsight, the events of that evening were trivial, but I remember my mounting terror at being in a foreign place and not knowing how to take care of myself. I was scared as much by my ingenuousness as by any real sense of threat.

I woke the next morning excited about our plans to tour the country, only to learn that Pamela had been given an urgent assignment. She mentioned that Ahmed El Houmaidi, a driver at the embassy, wanted to visit his aunt in Marrakesh and she suggested that I go with him; we set off by bus the next day. Ahmed's aunt lived on the outskirts of town in a cinder-block house built around a courtyard with a pomegranate tree. She treated a foreigner's arrival as a great occasion and vacated her room to accommodate me.

Every evening that week, the men of the household would walk to the Djemaa el-Fna, the big square in Marrakesh, which is a tourist clot by day and the hub of local social life by night. Some of Ahmed's cousins worked there, so we would all hang out with the magicians, storytellers and dancers as twilight deepened. When we returned to the house, a tagine dinner would be awaiting us. The women, always veiled, would have spent all day cleaning and cooking. Now, they would pour water over the men's hands, then withdraw, returning after we were finished to eat what remained. The house had no running water and no electricity. Ahmed's aunt's one prized possession was a battery-operated radio. Our last day there, she told Ahmed that she wanted to know the words to her favourite song, and since Ahmed's English was unequal to discerning the lyrics, he asked me. 'Your aunt may have a tough time understanding this song,' I replied. 'It's called "Girls Just Want to Have Fun".'

Two years later, because my brother was studying evolutionary biology in college, our family planned a trip to the Galápagos Islands. Included with our boat tickets was a tour of Ecuador. My parents were not interested – and neither were any of the other people joining the cruise. So my brother and I had a guide to ourselves. After touring Quito, we proceeded to Cuenca to explore the Inca ruins at Ingapirca. Our guide warned us of unrest in the area but said he'd be game if we wanted to go. The road was almost empty and we had the ruins to ourselves, interrupted only by the occasional llama. On the way back, we had to stop abruptly because a large boulder was in the middle of the steep road. Seconds later, a bunch of agitated people sprang out from behind a shrub and rushed the car. One slit the tyres; one smashed the windshield; one brandished a gun. The guide suggested we get out, pronto. We were locked inside a shack with our guide while the driver negotiated with the revolutionaries, who had declared their independence because they didn't want to pay taxes. We explained via the driver that, coincidentally, we didn't much like paying taxes, either. The driver apparently told them that the U.S. military could bomb their village and poison their crops, and after about two hours we were released. We shuffled down the mountain until we were able to hitchhike back to Cuenca. I was already a different person from who I had been in Morocco, much less unnerved by a much more alarming incident.

Living in another country is entirely different from travelling through it. I went to graduate school in England and found that even England was a place of unnervingly foreign habits – my fantasies of a spiritual homecoming notwithstanding. Adopting the accent and learning a smattering of different vocabulary was not cultural fluency. I had to master new rules of intimacy and conversation, of dress and comportment, of humour and reverence.

I had been assigned to a college-owned house I was to share with other Americans and a few Australians. The tutor for rooms explained that I would 'certainly feel more comfortable' with my 'own kind'. But I hadn't crossed the ocean to cohabit with my countrymen. My pleas to move were politely but firmly denied; when I persisted, the denial became less polite and more firm. Two weeks into term, I developed a nasty cold and went to see the college nurse, Sister George, who volunteered that the newly laid synthetic carpeting in my house was full of toxins. 'Perhaps you have developed an allergy to your room?' she suggested. Seizing the opportunity, I asked her to mention that implausible likelihood to the tutor for rooms. He called me into his office the next day and said, with an exasperated sigh, 'All right, Mr Solomon. You've won. I've found you a room in college.'

It took a while to comprehend that in England an education was often considered a pleasurable luxury rather than an ambition-driven necessity. I hadn't understood how delicate a hold meritocracy had in a class-riven society. I didn't know why so much food was boiled so long. Neither had I imagined the confidence that accrues to families that had lived and toiled on the same land for centuries; the elegant use of humour to half mask urgent sincerities; the whole country's reassuring habit of permanence. I was amazed by how many of my favourite writers my English acquaintances had not read, and by how many of their favourite poets I had never heard of. We were indeed divided by a common language that was less common than I'd imagined. I loved the universal penetration of pomp and circumstance, and the novel belief that pleasure mattered as much as success. I loved the country's bank holidays and tea breaks. I loved how religion was high-minded and ritualistic instead of judgemental and perpetually reinvented. I was struck by how much more steadfastly the English travelled; indeed, their more immersive model of exploring helped launch me on the course this book documents. I came to love England for other reasons than those that had made me a juvenile Anglophile.

When I finished my first postgraduate degree, I decided to stay in England for a while. I set about sending enquiry letters to publishing houses and magazines, and when my parents visited me that spring, I airily told them that I was looking for a job in London. My father was so angry that he banged his fist on the table of the pub in Grantchester where I'd announced my plans, silencing all the other patrons. He declared that he was forbidding it, and I told him that he was no longer in a position to forbid things. We all revolt against our parents, but it is striking to me in retrospect that I did so in relation to place.

Actually, I had chosen to stay partly to strengthen my bond with my new home and partly to assert that I could exist away from my old one. I was twenty-three, and gay, and preparing to come out of the closet (although I didn't entirely know it yet), and I couldn't do it in New York, where I felt sucked back into a vortex of expectations and assumptions. I needed to break free of America for breathing space – not to be myself, yet, but to figure out what self I was becoming. I confused, as many young people do, the glamour of being an outsider with the liberty to do or think whatever crossed my mind. It was not enough to acknowledge some newfound self; I would create a new persona and be famous for the radical imagination with which I did so. I sported outré clothing that I thought echoed some elegance of a bygone era; I used arch constructions of speech; I was socially promiscuous, accepting all invitations. This exercise in self-definition, though ultimately useful in the way of youthful misadventures, was often irksome to others. What I presumed to be originality often smacked of affectation. I was both presumptuous in expressing my new, English self, and hypocritical in cleaving to my native system of values. I disavowed my privilege and the autonomy it gave me, but I also discounted my turmoil. I manifested my confused sexuality via my ambiguous nationality.

Like many gay people of my time, I rooted myself in a chosen place and friendships. But as time passed, I came to realise that I had an amateur's arrogance in my English friendships and had failed to understand that I had to be someone slightly different to succeed at them. I was charmed by how English my English friends were, and I assumed they would be delighted by how American I remained – but I had chosen to transplant myself and they had made no such choice. I deeply offended several people I loved. Perhaps those friendships would have foundered anyway; I was young, psychologically careless, and enmeshed in the solipsism of burgeoning depression; I also remained single while many old friends married, a difference of experience that made me feel uncomfortably marginal. Today, many of my closest friends are English people who live in New York or Americans who live in London. Displacement becomes a forgiving homeland, a thing held in common with others.

If moving to England was the beginning of my jubilant exile, my removal to Moscow was its apotheosis. My high school glee club trip had been cancelled thanks to the invasion of Afghanistan. The family trip to the Soviet Union we planned some years later was cancelled at the last minute thanks to the Chernobyl nuclear disaster. So much of my favourite literature was Russian that like Chekhov's renowned sisters, I had taken to asking, plaintively, when I would ever get to Moscow. In 1988, I was working for the British monthly *Harpers & Queen* as arts correspondent, and Sotheby's was planning its first auction of contemporary Soviet art. After looking at the advance materials, I had concluded that terrible art was being hyped to wealthy collectors in a scheme of cynical exploitation. I proposed writing a tell-all article about the jet-set tomfoolery of the whole sorry affair.

Then I went to Moscow. My third day there, I had planned to interview a group of artists who had studios in a squat at Furmanny Lane, and my translator failed to show. I didn't want to be rude, so I went to their studios by myself. They indicated that I could hang out for a bit. At first, there wasn't much communication; I spoke no Russian and they spoke no English. A few hours later, someone came by who spoke French, which I speak poorly, so we made some headway; a few hours after that, someone came by who spoke English. But the gift, though I didn't know it at the time, was those hours of being unable to communicate verbally. It gave me time to watch the artists interact. As they showed their work to one another, I saw that they were getting things from it that I wasn't. Later, I learned that the artists had designed their work to appear banal to avoid the unwelcome attentions of the KGB, but had filled it with hidden meanings. The key to understanding those meanings lay in the personal relationships among the artists, none of whom expected to exhibit to a larger audience. The work was full of inside jokes. More important, it reflected a deep mysticism: these artists believed they were safeguarding integrity in the face of a regime that was out to undermine truth itself.

If my translator had come that morning, I would never have recognised any of that. The West was curious about these artists; I soon understood that they were just as curious about the West and lacked a point of reference, all interchange having been forbidden. I entered their orbit knowing a bit about the Western art world, and they wanted the guidance I could provide. Shockingly unmoored from familiarity, I didn't know how to make sense of their world, but they were kind to me as a mutual coherence slowly emerged.

The following summer, I returned to Moscow for a month of research. I remember sitting at Heathrow Airport in a panic. I wanted to see my Russian friends; I had decided to write my first book about them; yet I felt a tinge of that dread of unfamiliarity that had overcome me in Morocco four years earlier. My sense of myself was still fragile and depended on the constant reassurance that only familiarity affords. Everything in Moscow was different: what I ate, where I slept, what we talked about.

I started out living in a dacha with a group of German artists, but ended up camping out somewhat apprehensively in the Furmanny Lane squat. I considered myself an observer but came to understand that my artist friends considered me a participant in whatever was happening – both because lives are changed by being recorded, and because the presence of an interloper is never neutral. More than a hundred artists were living in the building by then. Though there were toilets in various locations, only one bathroom, at the far side of the courtyard, was fully functional. Unlike the artists, I bathed every day. I borrowed a fuchsia terry-cloth bathrobe from the painter Larisa Rezun-Zvezdochetova. Since Larisa is not quite five feet tall, the robe hung rather weirdly on my lanky frame. A Russian documentary, released a few years later, about the art world in that late Soviet period includes overhead footage of my daily trek across the courtyard in Larisa's bathrobe as a kind of punctuation to mark the passing days.

I had gone to Moscow knowing about the darkness of Soviet dominion, but I had not reckoned on the heroic dimension of resistance, nor the sociability that a protracted ideological crisis can engender. These Russians' capacity for intimacy correlated to their society's dysfunction. I had long daydreamed about the power of art to change the world, but I had also always assumed that art was in fact just entertainment. To the Russians, though, changing the world was the prime reason to make art. 'You see,' the artist Nikita Alexeev said to me, 'we have been preparing ourselves to be not great artists, but angels.' Now faced with a Western market system in which they were expected to comply with commercial expectations, some produced work that played well to collectors and museums; some continued to follow their original moral purpose, creating art with little market potential; some renounced art entirely.

Irony had been their best defence from the Stalin years onward, and irony was the armour in which they approached the new world order. The artist Kostya Zvezdochetov had been called up for punitive army service in the early 1980s, one of many Soviets who were excused from military conscription and later drafted; this process attracted less Western attention than a sentence to the Gulag, but served the same function. Kostya found himself among a coalition of thieves and murderers in Kamchatka, the peninsula that lies east of Siberia and north of Japan. His battalion had been ordered to excavate the foundation of a building that had been constructed on melting ice. Kostya, who is physically diminutive, got sick repeatedly;

his superiors finally realised that he was a gifted draftsman and put him to work making propaganda posters. Many years later, at his first exhibition in Western Europe, he reminded me that he had once been sent further east than he had ever dreamed of going or wanted to go, and that he had been put in a room and given paints and supplies and been told to make art, and that he had done so even though he did not agree with the purpose of that art, because it saved him from hard physical labour. Now, he explained, he was further west than he had ever dreamed of going or wanted to go, and once more he had been put in a room, and once more he had been given paints and supplies, and once more he had been told to make art, and once more he suspected that what he was doing supported an ideology to which he did not subscribe – but once more, he would do it if it saved him from hard physical labour.

When my book *The Irony Tower: Soviet Artists in a Time of Glasnost* was published in June 1991, people asked whether there would be a Russian translation; I replied that the Soviets hardly needed a foreigner to tell them about what was happening in their own country. In 2013, however, a Russian edition was published, with an introduction by Kostya. By then the political and artistic landscape of the country had completely changed, and the lives we had led were of historical interest. That made me feel old, but it also made me contemplate the possibility that my adolescent goal of participating in change had come to fruition – that chronicling the changes had inscribed me in them.

In November 2015, I had dinner with one of these artists, my friend Andrei Roiter, and told him about this book, recalling some of the shared history I was putting into it. 'Remember how much hope we had?' he asked. I wondered whether he regretted the dreams that hadn't come to fruition, and he said, 'Even if it turned out to be groundless, the very fact of having felt that hope at that moment determined everything else I have thought, everything I have painted, everything I have become.' We bemoaned the iniquities of Putin's Russia, and he said, 'Even that violence is different because it follows on hope.' As we talked, I came to understand that hope is like a happy childhood; it equips its beneficiaries to deal with the traumas that inevitably ensue. It is experienced as a primal love. My life, relatively apolitical until I went to Moscow, took on the urgency of such embattled integrity when I was there. I did not yet know to call it *purpose*, but the travels described in this book all followed from that exaltation. The feeling of optimism among those Soviet artists was based on what turned out to be largely a fiction – but it was a genuine feeling even if it pertained to an imagined reality. A crushed hope is suffused with nobility that mere hopelessness can never know.

I moved home from London and Moscow when my mother was dying so I could spend the final months of her life close at hand. Leaving New York had given me independence, but my mother's death eviscerated my self-created identity; my independence had required something of which to be independent, and that something had been partly the United States and partly my family of origin. Reckoning with my mother's illness, I concluded that differentiation was overrated. I moved home to be with her and stayed there because I was finally able to accept being more or less American. No one had forewarned me, however, that if you live abroad any good while, the notion of *home* is permanently compromised. You will always be missing another place, and no national logic will ever again seem fully obvious to you.

A year after I resettled in New York, my London solicitor called to advise me that because I had held a British work visa for six years, I could apply to be naturalised as a U.K. citizen. I needed only to meet a dozen criteria. I had always paid my taxes; I had never been arrested for a felony. The final criterion, however, was that I not have spent more than two months outside the U.K. in any of the previous six years, and here, alas, I was in trouble. On a lark, I wrote a letter to the Home Office explaining that I'd been in Russia to research my book and in the United States to care for my mother, but that in my heart I was loyal to the Queen. A bored clerk must have been on duty when my note arrived in the autumn of 1993 because I received citizenship papers by return post.

British citizenship conferred legitimacy on what had previously seemed something of a subterfuge. It allayed some anxiety in me to have dual nationality; I could not only claim two different places, but also be two different people. It seemed to rescue me from the burden of crafting a single identity, from the exhausting attempt to squeeze my contradictory nature into a single narrative. It marked my experiment with foreignness as a success. And it gave me options. I couldn't look at that new passport and not think about my father saying, 'They had nowhere to go.' I had someplace to go, permanently.

The naturalisation papers validated my claim to be a world citizen. Though I would doubtless have continued to travel, I now felt doubly justified in exploring far and wide. Days at home often blur into one another; days in strange surroundings intensify life. Tennyson's Ulysses said, 'I cannot rest from travel: I will drink / Life to the lees'. I cherished travel for the ways it stopped time, forcing me to inhabit the present tense. Augustine of Hippo legendarily said, 'The world is a book and those who do not travel read only one page,' and I wanted to go cover to cover. I set out to see the change I wanted to be in the world.

My friend Christian Caryl, a distinguished political journalist and essayist, moved to Kazakhstan in 1992 to head the country's institute of economics; I went off to visit him there a year later. When I said I wanted to go out to the steppes and meet nomads, he laughed and asked what I planned to say when I met them. While hiking up a mountain at the edge of Alma-Ata (which has since been renamed Almaty), we were caught in a blizzard. After an hour of huddling against the storm, we heard a vehicle approaching and waved it down frantically. The driver took us in; he was drinking regularly from a flask, but we were hardly in a position to complain. When he passed his tipple over to me, I took a swig of what I assumed would be vodka, but it was *spirit* – pure grain alcohol. That single swallow made me temporarily blind and dizzy. Then I passed it over to Christian. Drinking and singing, we made our way down the mountain. When our rescuer asked me what I was doing in his part of the world, I blurted out my line about meeting nomads on the steppes, and he offered to take us to the steppes the following morning. We volunteered to buy the next day's *spirit*.

The nomads (who had become somewhat less than nomadic since Stalin's forced collectivisation) could not have been more welcoming. We sat in their yurt and peppered them with questions. One mentioned that his perceptions of Iran were based on that country's provision of roads and hospitals in the area, while his impressions of the United States were drawn largely from episodes of *Baywatch*, the foreign programme most often broadcast there. He had decided on this basis that Iran was good and America was decadent and evil. Since Kazakhstan is a large and oil-rich country and was then newly independent, I thought this was momentous information. When I got home, I wrote it up and submitted the piece to an editor I knew at the *New Republic*. He called me back almost immediately and said, 'Oddly enough, this is the second proposal I've had this week about Kazakhstan's prejudice in favour of Iran. Something must really be going on there.' I sheepishly called Christian, who acknowledged that he, too, had submitted the story of our day out.

Travelling with my parents when I was younger, I had absorbed the touristic notion that a visitor should come to observe a society, not to engage with it. As a journalist, I quickly became aware of the narrowness of that precept. When I visited a new place, I was usually on the receiving end of enormous generosity from the people I met there, and I didn't see how I could fail to reciprocate. In 1992, a friend and I were in a car crash in Zimbabwe. Our front tyre had blown out on a dirt road, and our car had landed upside down in a thick jungle. We had to get our jalopy back to South Africa. We had been camping and had with us ten days' worth of food as well as many bags of mealie meal, a corn-derived staple of the local diet that we had planned to share with locals if we needed to stay with them. There was no point taking it all back with us. So just after sunrise, we pulled off the road near a collection of particularly shoddy rondavels, and I climbed a steep bank. Several people were rubbing their hands for warmth around a thin fire, and I handed them ten bags of groceries and basked for a moment in their astonishment. Travel entails help both to and from strangers.

I became increasingly concerned with this question of engagement and reciprocity. Any new relationship is disruptive on both sides. Rather than avoiding and minimising this disruption, I began trying to open myself to it. Sometimes the engagement was profound; often, it was happenstance. While I was good at fitting in under anomalous circumstances, I had to acknowledge my differences and accept that others noticed them, too. You can't fit in with people by pretending to be just like they are; you fit in by engaging in a dialogue about your differences, and by putting aside the assumption that your way of life is in any way preferable to theirs.

Because Castro had for many years insisted that Cuba was atheist, then allowed his country to be more moderately secular, and finally met with the Pope in 1996, the celebration of Christmas was still tentative when I visited Havana in 1997. Over the preceding decades, New Year's Eve had become something of a family-centred celebration to make up for Christmas; now, people were just beginning to ponder the notion of more ebullient festivity, and I decided to act on that emergent vigour. Friends and I found an apartment in Old Havana, in a pretty rough area but with twenty-foot ceilings, decorative columns, detailed cornice mouldings, and a balcony looking out over the ancient buildings across the street. If you want to get to know a strange country quickly and deeply, there's nothing like organising a party. At Cuban parties, the dancing starts when the party starts. A gorgeous black lesbian ballerina named Marleni led me to the centre of the room. 'Music is the most important thing there is for me,' she confided. 'It makes me feel things.' We were feeling things anyway: six Brits, two Americans and thirty or so Cubans (diplomats, doctors, artists, television personalities, foundation directors, musicians, hustlers, students), all gathered to celebrate our various ideas of a new beginning. We soon lost our self-consciousness – the mojitos were very helpful – and at midnight, we leaned over the balcony and poured buckets of water into the street to wash away the old year and welcome in the new. Everyone in the nearby houses was doing the same thing, though some people had only sherry glasses and others had barrels of rainwater; someone even poured out a mojito. We loaded a heaping plate of food and a drink to leave outside for the Santeria gods. Then we ate again, and then we danced until dawn, as everyone in the streets seemed to be dancing when we stumbled back home at sunrise. The Cubans loved our party because it was so American, and we loved it because it was so Cuban.

In 1993 I went to South Africa to report on its burgeoning art scene. Before my trip, I had arranged a rental car and bought a road atlas. My plane arrived late, and the airport was all but closed when we taxied to the gate. I was the only person from the flight hiring a car, and I reminded the sleepy man at the desk that I'd arranged ahead of time for one with an automatic transmission. I'm no good with a stick shift under the best of circumstances; South Africa has left-side driving, and I'm none too good at that, either. I was going to be thumbing through maps as I went, and it was an era of carjackings, when you had to be vigilant every time you stopped the car, ready to speed away through a red light in a threatening situation. The rental guy disappeared for twenty minutes, then came back and said, 'Okay, boss, we have one automatic car.' I signed the paperwork and we stepped outside, where I beheld the largest white Mercedes I had ever laid eyes on. So much for fitting in.

It was still illegal for white people to enter the black townships, and when they did so nonetheless, they were usually accompanied by a black person who knew the way around, since there were no maps of these districts. One day I went to Soweto to interview a painter. He met me at the township entry and guided me to his studio; when we finished, he said that the way back out was so simple I could drive by myself. I headed off according to his directions and was getting along rather well until I heard a siren behind me and saw a policeman signalling me to pull over. He came up to my window and announced, 'You were speeding.' I apologised and mentioned that I'd seen no posted speed limit. White South Africans had a reputation for being condescending to black policemen, but I was respectful and apologetic. The policeman said, 'Wait here. I'm getting my supervisor.'

Ten minutes later, another police car pulled up and the supervisor got out and approached my window. 'You were speeding,' he said. I apologised again. 'You're not from here, are you?' he said. 'I'll get my commander.'

After another ten minutes, a third police vehicle drove up. 'You were speeding,' the commander said.

I apologised for the third time.

'Why were you speeding?'

'I didn't know there was a speed limit; it doesn't seem to be posted;

and I am a white foreigner in a gigantic white Mercedes driving by myself in Soweto, which is inherently nerve-racking.'

At that, the commander burst out laughing. 'Don't worry about it, man. We'll escort you out.'

I left in a motorcade, with two police cars in front of me and one behind.

Travel is an exercise partly in broadening yourself and partly in defining your own limits. Travel distils you to a decontextualised essence. You never see yourself more clearly than when immersed in an entirely foreign place. In part, that is because people make different assumptions about you: often, expectations relate to your nationality rather than to the nuances of your manner of speech, the cut of your clothing, or the indicators of your politics. Equally, travel disguises you; one can feel oddly camouflaged and anonymous wrapped in the sketchy preconceptions of others. I enjoy being lonely so long as I am lonely by choice; I can enjoy some place far away and difficult so long as I am missed back home. I dislike social constraints, and travelling has helped me to be free of them.

At the same time, as I learned in the Soviet Union, I was also intensely unsettled by such social anonymity. This anxiety reflects both the difficulty of reading people in other cultures and my illegibility to them. If I cannot figure them out, they probably can't figure me out, either. When you must learn the unfamiliar rules of a new place, you become suddenly callow again. Travel makes you modest; what is prestigious at home can seem irrelevant or ludicrous abroad. You cannot rely on the veracity of your opinions in a country where standards are different. You often cannot understand why something is funny there; you sometimes cannot understand why something is sombre. You question your own standards of humour, solemnity, even morality. Familiar landscapes cushion you from self-knowledge because the border between who you are and where you are is porous. But in a strange place, you become more fully evident: who you truly are is what persists at home and abroad.

Cultural dissonance often provides linguistic hilarity. At a hotel in the Norwegian fjordland, I found a menu that announced, 'Breakfast is available daily from 7:30 to 8:00 a.m. Lunch is available daily from 12:00 to 12:30 p.m. Dinner is available daily from 7:00 to 7:30 p.m. Midnight snacks are available until 10:00 p.m.' One has to admire that thrifty spirit. I was very taken with the room service menu in French West Africa that offered for appetisers either 'Rolled crepes with smoked salmon and egg of lump' or 'Small bags of eggplant toma-to-mozzarella'; for main course, the 'Gratin of Moulds, breadcrumbs with parmesan' or the 'Roasted Captain, Olive Oil Sauce' or the veg-etarian option, 'Indian Jumps of Lentils'. For something sweet to end the meal, the only thing to be considered was the 'Dessert Opera on custard'. In Xi'an, we were introduced to a pianist who explained over lunch that he gave few concerts and supported himself by per-forming at night in a bar. We decided to go to the bar to hear him despite his efforts to dissuade us. With the Chinese gift for lyrical euphemism, a sign outside identified the establishment in English as the SUNSHINE-AFTER-EIGHT FRIEND-CHANGING CLUB. It was a brothel. Whenever a friend has since needed changing, I fantasise a trip back to north-west China, and I remember the young women from the provinces, some defiant and many sad in their flimsy negligees.

Even when one is paying attention, it is easy to become confused in alien surroundings for lack of reference points. In Prague in 1985, my friend Cornelia Pearsall and I studied the only available tourist map and decided that we ought to visit the Jewish ghetto, number sixteen on the map. Expecting squalor, we were pleasantly surprised to find a complex of beautiful apartments, many with spectacular views. Since all the signage was in Czech, we had to work out the narrative for ourselves. Cornelia noted the large number of pianos about, and I explained that the Jewish community in Prague had been highly cultured and artistically accomplished. Only two days later did we discover that the Jewish ghetto was actually number seventeen on our map, and that we had spent the afternoon at Mozart's villa.

Sometimes one simply doesn't understand what one is looking at. I got to know former U.S. secretary of defense Robert McNamara when he was in his eighties. The man behind the draft that had so ter-rified me in childhood had destroyed a country, occasioned a million needless deaths and accomplished nothing. He was now a congenial senior citizen, regretful of the gruesome crossroads of history that he had traversed. He described returning to Vietnam and meeting some of his military counterparts there. The conversation, as he described it, consisted of the Vietnamese asking, 'Why did you do X?' Then McNamara said, 'Well, because you did Y, which meant such and such.' Then the Vietnamese would counter, 'No, no, no, it meant the exact opposite of that! But then you did this thing that was clearly an attempt to escalate!' To which McNamara would comment, 'No, we did that to try to quiet things down, because we thought you . . .' and so on and on and on. McNamara's errors proceeded from his ignorance about his opponents – a problem much exacerbated by the dismissal of Asia experts from the U.S. government and universities during the purges of McCarthyism. Like Cornelia and me in Mozart's villa, McNamara was applying off-base assumptions to a place he had completely misunderstood. Had more than a million deaths not occurred in the Vietnam War, his encounter with his former foes could have been something out of a French farce. To learn a place is like getting to know a person: it is an exercise in depth psychology. You must understand those with whom you communicate to understand the content of their communication. It takes modesty to recognise that your coherence is someone else's incoherence and vice versa. 'We argued in the language of war,' McNamara said to me, 'which I wrongly thought was a universal language.'

Much is made of the difference between tourism and travel. Tourists are said to move about in clusters and to reassure themselves with unflattering comparisons between wherever they are visiting and their homeland. Travellers venture forth because they want to experience a place, not just see it. When Flemming Nicolaisen, a Greenlandic Inuit friend, visited me in New York on his first foreign trip, he seemed uninterested in the Statue of Liberty, the Metropolitan Museum, Broadway shows. He preferred taking my dog for long walks all over town. 'When you came to Greenland,' he said, 'did you want to see the war memorial? Or the museum in Nuuk?' I had to admit that I mostly wanted to be surrounded by the prismatic landscape of ice. He pointed out that the entire population of Greenland would have fit in one of the Twin Towers (then still standing) and said he just wanted to feel what it was like to be in a place with so many people. He was a traveller, and my agenda for him had been touristic.

Authenticity is a traveller's grail. It can be sought, but not planned. When I was twenty-eight, I drove across Botswana with my friend Talcott Camp on the country's one major road; we'd periodically have to stop for a crossing herd of cows. Once, we saw a herd far, far ahead, but no evidence of a cowherd. As we got nearer, we realised that they were elephants. We had already seen elephants in enormous reserves, in their 'natural habitat'. But the legal demarcation of national parks where paying tourists came to observe wildlife introduced a whiff of artifice to our encounters. Chancing on these creatures outside official boundaries was infinitely more transfixing. One was blocking the road, so we had to stop the car. We sat there for nearly an hour. The sun was low and washed the pachyderms in pink light. I've seen elephants in a dozen African and Asian countries, but nowhere else have I experienced such a feeling of revelation.

Two years later, I travelled to the Baltics with my father. In Lithuania, we visited a tiny museum devoted to Vilnius's vanished Jewish population. We were alone in its four rooms except for a couple of babushkas, half-asleep on plastic chairs, who we assumed were either guards or cleaners. Nazi propaganda had blamed the Soviet annexation of Lithuania on Jews, 90 per cent of whom had been slaughtered with the enthusiastic collaboration of local authorities. Lithuanians who tried to help their Jewish neighbours were killed as well. Relatively few Lithuanian Jews ended up in labour camps, but one of the display panels at the museum described the conditions in such a camp and referred to a song the emaciated workers had sung to cheer themselves. My father, a great enthusiast for music, commented on it, and I wondered aloud what the tune had been. From the corner, a thin, reedy voice piped up. It had not occurred to us that the woman in the corner could understand English, nor that she might be Jewish; but now she sang that song of the camp, and we understood that she was not only this room's guard but also its subject. When she fell silent, we tried to talk to her, but she withdrew back into apparent unilingualism and seemed unable to understand what we were asking her. She was one of those who had had nowhere to go, yet had survived.

It is easy to be primitive without being authentic, but nearly impossible to be authentic if you are afraid of the rustic. John Ruskin, the great Victorian essayist, complained that the efficiencies of train travel eliminated the joys of voyaging. 'It is merely being "sent" to a place,' he wrote, 'and very little different from becoming a parcel.' It took me some time to acquire a taste for discomfort. At first, I liked having had adventures better than I liked having them, but bit by bit, I realised that either you have a good time or you have a story to tell, and I ended up being open to either result. As a child, I experienced fairly luxurious travel; as I grew older, I learned to travel with fewer material expectations and discovered that luxury is a mutable concept. When I went to Guatemala City to write about gang life, I found myself one day in the poor neighbourhood of La Limonada. An old man with a herd of goats approached us. 'You thirsty?' asked the teenage felon who was showing me around. When I said I was, the goatherd milked one of the goats directly into a large paper cup, then handed it to me. I have never enjoyed a beverage more.

If we want to avoid learning why the rest of the world at once loves and hates us, it is advisable to stay at home. I remain an American patriot when I am abroad, but I also see my country's failures of dignity, empathy and wisdom. You can't fully interpret the American invective against immigration without visiting centres of emigration and refugee camps. You can't understand the bizarre tyranny of the NRA (National Rifle Association) until you have spent time in other countries (most other countries, actually) where sensible gun laws limit violent crime. You can't discern how far America has lapsed in social mobility until you encounter a society moving towards economic justice. Travel is a set of corrective lenses that helps focus the planet's blurred reality. When E. M. Forster was asked how much time he had needed to write *A Passage to India*, he replied that it was a question not of time but of place. He had been unable to write it when he lived in India, he explained; 'When I got away, I could get on with it.'

Sometimes, these new perspectives are raw, but they are almost always useful. 'All travel has its advantages,' Samuel Johnson wrote. 'If the passenger visits better countries, he may learn to improve his own, and if fortune carries him to worse, he may learn to enjoy it.' I had started travelling out of curiosity, but I have come to believe in travel's political importance, that encouraging a nation's citizenry to travel may be as important as encouraging school attendance, environmental conservation or national thrift. I recalled my high school singing tour in Romania and Bulgaria, when the reality I witnessed seemed so obvious, even though most reports contradicted it. You cannot understand the otherness of places you have not encountered. If all young adults were required to spend two weeks in a foreign country, two-thirds of the world's diplomatic problems could be solved. It wouldn't matter what country they visited or what they did during their stays. They would simply need to come to terms with the existence of other places, and recognise that people live differently there – that some phenomena are universal and others, culturally particular.

Relatively porous immigration serves the same ends. You cannot know your own country if you are unobserved; people from elsewhere help you to reimagine your problems, which is requisite to solving them. We understand them not only by voyaging out but also by receiving those who voyage in. Free passage from home to abroad and free passage for others from their homes to yours abroad are of equal value. Not love, nor work, nor favourable prospects, is a zero-sum game. Sharing good fortune replenishes it. We find our boundaries both through encounters with otherness and through being that otherness. Identity is both contingent and reciprocal.

My forebears suffered from anti-Semitism, but unlike those who died in the Holocaust, they did have someplace to go: the United States. My paternal grandmother's parents were born in Russia and came to New York before my grandmother was born. My paternal grandfather, born in Romania, made his way across difficult terrain to get here. My maternal grandmother came from Poland; my maternal grandfather's parents, from Vienna and Ukraine. Without such liberal opportunities for immigration, I would never have existed. But they have likewise served to keep American culture vigorous. My ancestors crossed the Atlantic for freedom, which has been the

United States' most subsidised export. By investigating places apparently less free than my native country, I learned not only a deeper appreciation of American liberties, but also that my life is less free than I have tended to imagine. Freedom is a slippery concept and entails the option to choose adherence to strict ideologies; a large part of what I have championed constitutes liberalism rather than freedom. Oppressive societies have freedoms that are unknowable here, freedoms shaped by the lack of choice and the battle to achieve dignity in the face of disenfranchisement. When Chinese intellectuals spoke to me of the good that came of the Tiananmen massacre, when Pakistani women spoke of their pride in wearing the hijab, when Cubans enthused about their autocracy, I had to reconsider my reflexive enthusiasm for self-determination. In a free society, you have a chance to achieve your ambitions; in an unfree one, you lack that choice, and this often allows for more visionary ambitions. In Moscow in the 1980s, I became close to a group that called themselves 'paper architects'. Knowing there were no supplies to build to their specifications even if the Soviet bureaucracy had afforded them the chance, they harnessed their architectural training to their imaginations and designed, for example, the Tower of Babel, or proposed whole cities, or suggested a structure for a theatre that might float on the sea. Their creative energies were loosed, but they were always architects, and their discourse – new and conceptualist though it was – used the basic grammar of architecture. No Western architect governed by materials has ever thought so freely.

Freedom is seldom correlated with stasis; it comes in short bursts at times of enormous change. One of its constituents is optimism, which entails the belief that what is about to happen may be better than what is happening now. Change is often heady; change often goes horribly wrong; change often electrifies the air only to evanesce, unrealised. Democratising requires that each member of a population accept the partial weight of decision-making. To many, that idea is appealing in the abstract and daunting when it comes time to vote. When the Burmese author and activist Dr Ma Thida came to New York eighteen months after I interviewed her in Myanmar, she said she was shattered to realise that not only did the government need to change – which could happen quickly – but so did the minds of people conditioned by oppression, which could take an entire generation. In witnessing how people break forth into freedom, I have seen how glorious and hard the shift can be. Of course, after you win your freedom, you must learn to be free; in Toni Morrison's phrase, you must 'claim a freed self'. Many Westerners presume that democracy is the underlying preference of all people, and that it will simply emerge when obstructions are eliminated. (George W. Bush and Tony Blair seemed to operate on this presumption in Iraq.) The evidence does not support this projection.

Freedom must be learned and then put into practise. When I was in Afghanistan in February 2002, my friend Marla Ruzicka arranged for me to speak to three educated, liberal-minded women. They arrived wearing burkas, which they promptly removed, but I wondered why they were wearing them at all. The Taliban had fallen, and the law no longer constrained them. The first one said, 'I always assumed I would be rid of this thing if times changed. But now I am afraid that the change is not stable. If I go out without a burka and the Taliban returns to power, perhaps I will be stoned to death.' The second said, 'I would like to give it up, but the standards of our society have not yet shifted, and if I go out without wearing this and I am raped, they will tell me it is my own fault.' The third woman said, 'I hate this garment and I always assumed that I would give it up as soon as the Taliban was out. But over time, you get used to being invisible. It defines you. And the prospect of being visible again then seems extremely stressful.' So much needs to change within individuals before a change in society ensues.

History is rife with waves of joyful transformation followed by descent into horror. A culture's relationship to its history often reflects the citizenry's sense of agency. Some cultures see history primarily as something that happened to them; others, primarily as something they did. Chronologies of events are often less significant than people's understanding of the relationship between past and present; a revolution may represent both the full realisation of a long tradition and a break from it. Democracy tends to arrive with an aura of revelry, which is partly to do with democracy but partly to do simply with arrival. Witness the Arab Spring, which delighted people in the countries where change was occurring as well as people abroad, many of whom erroneously assumed that whatever would come next must be better than what was being left behind.

The nearly universal fear of extreme change on an individual level sits comfortably beside the heady prospect of change in the vast company of one's fellow citizens. I am susceptible to that little moment of romance when a society on the brink of change falls temporarily in love with itself. I've heard the same people speak of the great hope they felt when Stalin came to power and the hope they later felt when he died; others, of the hope they felt when the Cultural Revolution began and the hope they felt when it ended. The insistence that change is possible is a manifestation of hope. Many societies have reached forward, and for some, conditions really did improve; for others, not. Life in Russia in the twenty-first century is better for the average Russian than it was when the serfs were freed, but not by nearly enough. Afghanistan remains a mess. Iraq and Syria have degenerated from ostensible liberation to vicious bedlam. Libya was much worse under Qaddafi than anyone who hadn't been there could understand, but it would be a stretch to describe its current condition as anything short of disastrous.

Sometimes, however, a great tyranny is dismantled. For all that has gone wrong in South Africa, the downfall of apartheid has renewed the world's faith in decency. Life is better in China, too, than before Deng Xiaoping, though with plenty of room for improvement. Hope is a regular chime of political life; Americans lapse into it every four years, when many of us presume that our one-minute act of self-determination at the polling station might shift history. Walter Pater identified experience, rather than the fruit of experience, as life's goal. Zhou Enlai is said to have suggested that it is too soon to judge whether the French Revolution was a success. But the French Revolution was not only a route to a new order; it was also an event in itself. Moments of shift can be valuable even if their promises are never realised. My lifelong fascination with resilience has often propelled me to places in the throes of transformation. Time has made me more cynical than I used to be; at history's crossroads, changes that seem to be for the better often backfire, while great advancement sometimes goes hand in hand with tragedy. Nonetheless, the feeling of newness and rebirth is significant even when it dawns in a society muddled in perennial uncertainties. Furthermore, change is often the product not of gradual erosion but of burgeoning false starts; transformation arrives only when two or three or ten failed inceptions accumulate into a breakthrough.

Conversely, change prompts immediate nostalgia. A better present does not erase a flawed past, and no past wants for elements of great beauty. A person's ability to remember an expired identity yet live in the present tense contains real valour. In 1993, one of my Moscow friends took me to see an old woman she knew. We climbed seven narrow flights of stairs to reach her cramped, dark apartment. She told me about growing up in a palace in St Petersburg. Almost everyone she knew had been killed in the 1917 revolution. Later, she had lost her husband to hard labour in the Gulag. She had managed to keep only one relic of her aristocratic origins: a teacup of nearly transparent Imperial Porcelain, elaborately painted with a pastoral scene. Because I was an honoured guest, she served me tea in it. I have shaky hands at the best of times and have never wanted less to handle anything than I did that fragile emblem of a vanished life. 'Who knows?' said my friend, who knew the older woman's stories by heart. 'Maybe with glasnost we will live in this way again.' The old woman only laughed. 'No one will ever live this way again,' she said, and urged us to have more of the cake she had baked following a recipe from the tsar's court, with ingredients that she'd stood in lines four consecutive days to buy. That cake and that teacup: what courage she had evinced in her survival, and what passion lay in those last links to who she had been. She was wistful only as most old people are homesick for their youth.

The stories in this book are from the past. They did not predict the future when they were written, and while some of the dreams expressed in them have come to fruition, others have foundered. These are non-agenda-driven accounts of particular places at particular times. Even the most intensively reported pieces do not reflect expertise in their locations. I was in Russia a good bit and have often travelled in China, but I visited Afghanistan for less than two weeks,

Libya for six. I did plenty of research before, after and during these trips and have kept up with many of the people I got to know, but my observations are based on a relative breadth of cumulative knowledge rather than depth of singular knowledge. I can't compete with sinologists or Kremlinologists or Africanists. My art writing has been more about artists than about what they have produced. Complex stories are best told by those who can embrace complexity, and art forces its makers to grapple with social ambiguities and tensions. These reports are in many ways psychological studies rather than political ones, documents of a passing zeitgeist rather than policy papers. I am only a generalist, a collector of experiences, and an eccentric one at that.

Reading through one's assembled work is a humbling, occasionally agonising experience. While these stories reflect a world in flux and development, they also reflect my own flux and development, and I have resisted the impulse to edit them to hew to my current opinions and perceptions. This is what I wrote then, not what I would write today. If it is disappointing to grow old, it is likewise embarrassing to have been young. One is startled by what one did then but wouldn't do now. Having started out from the rather supercilious perspective that the problems of both nations and individuals could be solved, I have come to believe that accepting problems is often wiser than trying to fix them. I have attempted to find patterns in the few things that change – new borders, general progress on civil and disability rights – and the many things that don't – the failure of elections to bring justice, the tendency of power to corrupt. I've tried to become less prescriptive, better at questions and less quick with answers. I used to be sure of transformative revolution, but I still believe in ameliorative evolution. Yet the convictions that now appear naïve motivated some of my investigations of other cultures.

I have revised some of these articles a bit, a few significantly and others not at all. I have used longer versions of a few articles that were cut for length. When I went on assignment to write travel articles on Brazil and Myanmar, I had this book in mind and so did the reporting for longer essays than I'd been commissioned to write. I have eliminated outdated travel recommendations from stories that included them. The articles appear largely chronologically, though

I have attempted to prioritise the chronology of reporting over the chronology of publication. I have moved around a few stories because I did additional reporting after a story was published and wanted to include the newer information. (My comments about the Qian-long Garden, however, are placed in keeping with my visit there, even though I learned more about it in the years that followed.) For each article, I've written a few new paragraphs to provide context both within my experience and in light of ensuing events. I have not annotated the previously published articles, which were fact-checked at the time of publication. I have, however, put together end notes for new material, both to explain where I got the information and to provide resources for those who may wish to pursue these topics further.

I am interested in beauty as well as truth. I started writing for *Travel + Leisure* in 1996 and soon discovered that writing frequently about travel is work, but doing so once a year amounts to a paid holiday. I also realised that most journalists for the magazine wanted to write about a spa hotel in Positano or a resort in Nevis, but that such articles require a visit of only a day or two, while articles on more obscure destinations demand much longer stays and much deeper research. Sometimes, I simply loved these countries and took pleasure in saying why; indeed, saying why often helped me love the places. Holidays without reporting now feel weird to me; they lack the excuse for asking questions. It can be unsettling to shift rapidly from reporting on wars and desolation to reporting on restaurants and touristic sights, but both are elements in the larger project of engaging with the world and so ultimately feed a single truth.

In my two most recent books, *The Noonday Demon: An Atlas of Depression* and *Far from the Tree: Parents, Children and the Search for Identity*, I included reports from far-flung locations: I wanted to understand how narrative changed when context changed. I tailored what I wrote to the books I was working on; here, I've included versions of those sojourns that are of a slightly different shape. When I went on tour to promote my book about depression, I was struck by the variety of attitudes I encountered. In Spain, almost every journalist who came to interview me began the conversation by saying, 'I have never been depressed myself, but . . .' and off we went, as I quietly wondered why these allegedly cheerful people had chosen to interview me in so much detail about mental illness. In Japan, every interviewer commented on his or her own depression but asked me not to mention it to anyone else. On the leading morning TV programme in Finland, a gorgeous blonde woman leaned forward and asked in a mildly offended tone, 'So, Mr Solomon. What can you, an American, have to tell Finnish people about depression?' I felt as though I had written a book about hot peppers and gone to promote it in Sichuan.

This book is contiguous with my work on psychology and family dynamics. I have written two recent books about the inner determinants of difference and identity, but I am equally interested in the outer ones. I grew up in a household in which there was a preferable approach to everything – and I quested after the strength to choose among my childhood principles rather than be obligated to them. Travel taught me how to relate to disparate people with incongruent values, and, thereby, how to be contradictory myself. If I came subsequently to report on mental illness, disability, and the formation of character, that was an extension of my mission to break loose from the presumption that there is a single best way to be. I continue to move between the internal abroad and the external abroad. Each enhances my relationship to the other.

The collective result of my anthologising is a bit of a bildungsroman, a book of my adventures as much as of the planet where I had them. I could never have written it if I were not infatuated with the notion of elsewhere, an ingenuous exuberance that goes all the way back to that long-ago Kleenex box. I've made it to 83 of the 196 recognised countries in the world. I plan a future book of profiles of people to supplement this book of places. But in some profound sense, people are places and vice versa. I have never written about one without the other.

In the quarter century or so covered in this book, the status of gay people has changed dramatically in a surprising variety of countries. Twenty have approved gay marriage as of this writing. Additional countries have passed legislation that provides other protections to gay men and women. In many societies, homosexuality remains a pulsating subculture; like art, it is a window through which to interpret a place.

I used to travel with my sexual orientation incognito, but have been increasingly open about being gay, a mark not just of my own maturation but also of the world's. In some instances, my identity has been more obvious than I realised; in Ulaanbaatar in 1999, I saw a young Mongolian shepherd coming down the street where my hotel was located, leading a flock of fat-tailed, carpet-wool sheep. I stared inquisitively at this spectacle and was astonished when he crossed over and said in serviceable English, 'You are gayboy? I am gayboy, too.' Then he added in an insinuating voice, 'Maybe I leave sheep in hotel car park and come inside with you?' In Ilulissat, my guide sighed that it was not easy being the only gay dogsled-driver in western Greenland (a reflection I remember whenever existential loneliness strikes). At a formal dinner in Delhi, when I asked whether the city had a gay culture, given how many Indians disparaged homosexuality as a 'Western import', my host looked at me as though I had dropped in from outer space and said, 'What do you think this party is?' And in Cartagena de Indias in Colombia in the question session that followed a lecture I gave, an elegantly dressed woman said she'd heard that children of gay parents were better adjusted than children of straight parents and suggested, 'I suppose it is because men and women argue so much.' I revel in the notion that gay couples are above contentiousness. Sexual identity is at the forefront in a wide range of societies; it has become an unavoidable conversation.

My husband and I wed in England in 2007 in a ceremony then called civil partnership, but offering all the benefits afforded to married people in Great Britain. This gave John U.K. immigration rights. I wanted to be sure that he had someplace to go, too. A marriage in Massachusetts (the only U.S. state that had legalised it at that time) would have been called *marriage*, but would have granted us no legal protection. Though liberal society in the coastal United States was more accepting of gay people than was its British equivalent, the law advanced more rapidly in the U.K., reflecting the relative absence of religion from British politics. Two years later, we married, that elusive word *marriage* finally in hand, in Connecticut, where the law now afforded us a new wave of rights to go with it.

Progress on gay rights has hardly been universal. The United Nations Security Council had its first session on LGBT issues in August 2015 to address abuses committed by the Islamic State of Iraq and the Levant (ISIL, also known as ISIS or Daesh). This terrorist group has posted videos of the executions of homosexuals, mostly in Syria and Iraq. In June 2015, ISIL posted photos of a gay man in northern Iraq being dangled, then dropped from a high building in front of a crowd of onlookers. In Iran, homosexual acts are punishable by death; Makwan Moloudzadeh, accused of having committed sodomy when he was thirteen, was executed there at the age of twenty-one even after his alleged victims had withdrawn their accusations. In Egypt, a raid on a bathhouse was staged for television; twenty-six people were imprisoned. In another episode, several Egyptian men were jailed merely for having attended a gay wedding. In Saudi Arabia, gay people are subject to capital punishment; two men found to have had sex there in 2007 were sentenced to seven thousand lashes each and are permanently disabled as a result.

Russia's law against 'gay propaganda' has led to gay men and lesbians being beaten in the streets; many have fled the country. In Kyrgyzstan, police entrap gay men on internet dating sites and subject them to blackmail and extortion; those found guilty of 'propagating nontraditional sexual relations' are subject to a year's imprisonment. In late 2013, India's highest court upheld the colonial-era criminalisation of homosexual behaviour. And twenty-seven African countries have passed antisodomy laws. In Nigeria, gay people can legally be stoned to death, and extrajudicial lynchings of gay people have become common. A Cameroonian was sentenced to three years in jail in 2011 for sending an affectionate text message to another man. Cameroon incarcerates more people for homosexual acts than does any other country, often 'proving' the sexuality of purportedly gay men by having court-ordered medical 'exams' to check the elasticity of their anus, despite the fact that such procedures are illegal under international law and have no basis in science. The president of Zimbabwe refers to gay people as 'filth' and has threatened to behead them. Uganda made homosexual acts a capital offence in 2014, though that law was eventually overturned.

Hasan Agili, a student whom I met in Libya, wrote to me after he had left the country. A friend had borrowed his laptop, called up his search history, then outed him at his medical school. He was bullied so mercilessly that he abandoned his studies and moved to another city. But the threats continued unabated. 'I watched public videos of friends beheaded for being homosexual,' he wrote to me. 'It's just done for me there. I can't go back. I am known and I would be hunted. I can't even tell my family what happened or why I left.' He is now in hiding in a neighbouring country where homosexual acts are illegal, without papers that would allow him to get a legitimate job, in continual fear of being found out, harassed and deported to a country where his life would be under threat.

I have spent considerable time in countries where I was advised to keep my sexual identity secret. My husband-to-be first accompanied me on assignment on a 2002 trip to the Solomon Islands. I was surprised by how difficult John found the situation, but he had devoted many years and much psychic energy to coming out and did not welcome a return to the closet. While we were not facing potential execution in the Solomons, we were repeatedly discouraged from booking a room with a shared bed, or from any overt expression of affection that might be 'misinterpreted' – which actually meant 'correctly interpreted'. John's outrage initially annoyed me. How much of a problem was it to accommodate this nicety of the place we were visiting? Over subsequent years, I came to feel that while observing local standards of privacy was an appropriate adaptation, retreating into dishonesty was not. The line often remains unclear. As I grow older, I have grown angrier at visa forms that ask whether I am married, on which I have to negotiate the reality that at home I am, and in the place I wish to go, I will not be. It feels like having multiple personality disorder. When my book on depression was translated into Chinese, references to my sexuality were removed without my consent. As a mental health advocate, I was glad to be helping depressed Chinese people, but it was disquieting to find my story bowdlerised. Full disclosure would have rendered it impossible for many Chinese people to hear what I had to say, but expurgation meant that others I might have helped were forsaken.

Censorship is hardly restricted to issues of sexual orientation. In 2015, I became president of PEN American Center, an organisation devoted to American and global literature and free expression at home and abroad. PEN champions writers silenced by censorship or oppression, including many who are jailed for the open declaration of views that contradict those of the people in power. Since assuming this office, I receive word daily of violence against writers abroad who are pushing recalcitrant societies towards transition. PEN also monitors restrictions in the United States on writers who feel stymied by surveillance, by racism or other forms of silencing prejudice, by fear of losing jobs or housing, or by those who would close down speech in the name of some ostensibly higher ideal. 'Words are no deeds,' says Shakespeare's Henry VIII, but I would disagree. Hate speech is dangerous: Holocaust deniers or the Ku Klux Klan, for example, sow great darkness, and my time in Rwanda brought home to me how easily propaganda can drive ordinary people to appalling acts. Conversely, the suppression of provocative ideas does not result in social justice, nor is it a constituent of freedom. Open discourse leads to righteousness more readily than enforced control does, no matter how well intentioned. There is courage in refusing the very idea of forbidden statements, and a radical brilliance in saying what is forbidden to make it sayable.

A common moral value is to seek for others the advantages one enjoys, but we fight for global free expression out of more than *noblesse oblige*. 'Until we are all free,' the American poet Emma Lazarus wrote, 'we are none of us free.' The embrace of human diversity implied in Lazarus's words is part of my purpose as a reporter, as evidenced in this book. Every voice that is muzzled deprives those who might have heard it, and detracts from the collective intelligence upon which all of us draw. In 1997, the Burmese Nobel laureate Aung San Suu Kyi asked the American people, 'Please use your liberty to promote ours.' Our liberty is contingent on everyone else's. In fighting to sustain the freest possible expression here and abroad, PEN is engaged not in two separate projects, but in a single campaign for the open exchange of ideas.

I started off as a voyager to ensure I would always have someplace to go and I came to understand that I had to give others a place to go, too. I felt a dramatic sense of disconnection when the first of my Soviet friends came to New York and stayed at my family's apartment (I was living in England, but was home on a visit). The world of the Moscow

vanguard had seemed so removed from my bourgeois New York existence, and finding the radical performance poet and artist Dima Prigov
enjoying a drink with my parents in our living room seemed like a scene
out of Buñuel. It took me some time to recognise that you do not learn
the world by compartmentalising. Nowadays, friends from abroad are
always staying at our house; it's a constant cultural exchange programme.

When I met Farouq Samim on my first day in Kabul, I was prepared for a working relationship with him as my translator and fixer,
but it rapidly became clear that we might be friends. We were together
for fourteen hours a day every day that I was in his country. It was a
frightening time to be in that part of the world; the abduction and
ultimate decapitation of the journalist Daniel Pearl in Pakistan was
unfolding as I transited through Islamabad and Peshawar on my way
across the border. To my surprise, however, I loved Afghanistan, in
part because Farouq so loved Afghanistan and communicated his
passion so compellingly. Farouq had studied medicine in Kabul under
the Taliban, which meant that each day contained many hours of
religious instruction and only a few of medical training. He wanted
to understand how doctors worked in a developed society, so after I
came home, I spoke to administrators at New York Hospital, who said
they would welcome him for a two-month visit to observe procedures.

Then he filed a visa application, with which I attempted to help.
We were repeatedly told that the chance of an unmarried, young
Afghan man getting into the United States in 2002 was virtually
nil. Farouq eventually gave up medicine because he had no chance
to broaden his insufficient education in Kabul and had found his
engagement with foreign journalists deeply rewarding. He won a
media fellowship to study in Canada. Nearly a decade after my visit
to Afghanistan, we succeeded in getting him into the United States.

American policy is focused on security, and the 9/11 hijackers
were Muslims to whom visas had been granted, perhaps recklessly. I
know why Farouq's profile scared consular officers. But I also know
that Farouq had helped many Americans in his homeland, and that
a visit to the United States in 2002 would have strengthened his
positive impression of our country. He would have returned home
with that gospel. He didn't want to emigrate here and he didn't want

to blow up a building. He wanted to be part of the cultural exchange through which peoples come to know one another. I have more recently tried to get my gay, Libyan friend Hasan Agili a visa to come to the United States, where he could finish his medical education and help the sick and the desperate, rather than be deported to face the murderous gangs who await him at home. Such procedures have become no easier. When I was in Libya, the people I met who had an essentially pro-American stance had all studied in the United States, whereas those who were vehemently anti-American had not. This is not to say that a proliferation of student visas issued at the behest of Iowa State or UCLA will solve the world's problems, but only that it's hard to love a place you've never visited. A blanket policy of excluding visitors from 'suspect' countries may ultimately damage our security, by preventing the people who would have spoken the best of us from finding out what there is to admire here beyond *Baywatch*.

After the Paris attacks of November 2015, cultural exclusion was put forward as our best defence, an argument that reached its nadir in American and European attempts to disenfranchise refugees from Syria and Iraq. Leading Republican presidential contender Donald Trump proposed that all foreign Muslims should be barred entry to the United States and that even American Muslims should carry special ID cards. This cruel demagoguery is contrary to our interests. Walling ourselves off from everyone else renders us odious to those who are excluded, providing incentive for them to become radicalised. Quarantining otherness breeds in those others an ignorance of us that engenders hatred, which soon becomes dangerous. It awakens an equally dangerous hatred in us. The central proposition of this book is that circling the wagons is not only impossible in a globalised world, but finally perilous. 'Seek and ye shall find', the biblical adage holds, but seeking is an early casualty of xenophobia. We sequester ourselves not in the well-guarded, imperial palace that American isolationists fantasise but in a festering prison.

The growing worldwide aversion to unifying bodies such as the E.U. is based on tribalism, and tribalism draws on the perception of likeness. It is an archaic, ethnic notion of collectivity that shares ground with racism. Historically, most people have wanted to be ruled by leaders with abilities that far exceeded their own; these days, many want to be governed by someone with whom they can share a pint – by someone like them. They would rather identify with than admire those who lead them. Skill in governance is not seen as a qualification to govern.

'Jerusalem,' sets these lines by William Blake:

> I will not cease from mental fight,
> Nor shall my sword sleep in my hand:
> Till we have built Jerusalem,
> In England's green and pleasant land.

That imagined paradise is not achievable through isolationism. We are none of us entirely independent. That may be dispiriting to those who perceive their identity to be tenuous, but pretending otherwise is counterproductive.

My last book, *Far from the Tree*, deals with the nature of difference within families: how parents learn to cherish children who aren't what they had in mind when they set out to have kids. This book is in some measure about a similar process: embracing alien points of view and ways of doing things. I wouldn't undersell the effort involved. If accepting unlike children is tough, this is tougher. Natural instincts propel parents towards their children; natural instincts propel us away from strangers who are different from ourselves. But that doesn't mean that we have to go down the rabbit hole of affinity groups and 'safe spaces', where people who already share opinions 'protect' one another from the intrusion of other points of view. In forestalling intimacy with the vast and bewildering world, we disenfranchise ourselves, no matter how our might proliferates.

Diplomacy is more often a skill than an instinct. We both engage with other countries because they are our allies and make them our allies through engagement. A capitalist society often defines that engagement in terms of money and military prowess, but those are inadequate models. Like all engagements, internationalism must be a rendezvous of human beings. The import of Japanese technology and Italian fashion has been gratifying; the ubiquity of Coca-Cola speaks on our behalf; and boots on the ground have increased American sway in some beleaguered nations. Yet it is in transnational civilian-to-civilian interactions that we find solutions to our disaffection. 'If one does not understand a person,' Carl Jung wrote in his *Mysterium Coniunctionis*, 'one tends to regard him as a fool.' Both parties lose in that scenario. In national as in personal relationships, it is easier to resolve tensions when you can figure out what the other is thinking. The art and culture and even the cuisines and monuments of other places can help us to do so; the people of those places help us most of all. America uses such soft power for suasion abroad, but often we do not allow ourselves the luxury of being persuaded by others. Travel is not merely a pleasant diversion for the well-to-do, but the necessary remedy to our perilously frightened times. At a moment when many politicians are stoking anxiety, telling people that it's too perilous even to leave the house, there is new urgency to the arguments for going out and recognising that we are all in the game together. The quest for freedom and adventure reflects the imperative of internationalism in these paranoiac times.

I am not suggesting that we can or should eliminate borders or nations, nor that we will one day crossbreed into a single, encompassing citizenry, nor that some Rosetta Stone of cultural values will quell innate antipathies. Enemies often come from abroad, and both early and recent history are marked by plunder and conquest. Belligerence is wired into us, and utopian idylls of nonviolence have never brokered sustainable harmony on a grand scale. Equanimity is not a default trait from which we deviate only by circumstance. Having spent considerable time on the ground with members of the U.S. military, I am grateful to the people who have developed armaments and the people who wield them on our behalf. More than that, I have seen how violence mediates compassion. Peace is most often achieved through intervention, not through ennobled passivity. Concord exists in contrast to aggression, but seldom obviates it.

How, then, to balance these contrary needs: to define an other, to recognise the threat that other might pose, to learn about that other as deeply as possible, and then to welcome that other as much as we safely can? People flee even when they have nowhere to go. As Justin

Trudeau in Canada and Angela Merkel in Germany extend a hand of friendship to refugees, we are reminded how foolish it is to presume that those who come from a land full of enemies are themselves necessarily enemies. Having nowhere to go can be fatal; having somewhere to go is a precondition of dignity; providing somewhere to go is often a canny generosity that benefits both sides.

It's hard to love one's neighbour, and harder to love one's enemy; indeed, the latter is sometimes an exercise of poor judgement. Social animals, we organise according to similarities. Embracing diversity may be an ecological imperative, a societal responsibility, and the ineluctable nature of a shrinking world, but ignoring the differences among people and cultures always backfires. Contrary to liberal expectations, some persuasive research suggests that children to whom race is never mentioned tend to sort themselves according to skin colour, while children to whom the contexts of difference are emphasised are more willing to commingle. We are essentialists who achieve our identity primarily by contrasting it to the unfamiliar character of others. There could be no America without an abroad; if you could demystify the abroad entirely, America as we know it would vanish. But we can segregate by our passports and still strive towards kindness among nations, recognise that the Marshall Plan worked at least as well as the firebombing of Dresden, and support as equals those who lack our advantages. We can separate the urgent need to identify our already existing enemies from the rank folly of making new ones.

After my husband and I had children, we began taking them with us on trips as soon as they learned to walk, because we wanted them to have a sense of the world as a large and varied place overflowing with possibilities. Children are malleable for a short time only, and whatever limits you set soon become their norm. We wanted that norm to include what is surprising, enchanting, uncomfortable, glamorous, disorienting, exciting and weird about travel. They can decide to be homebodies when they grow up, but at least they will know what they are setting aside.

My daughter is eight and my son is six and a half, and both are already excellent travellers. When they were toddlers, people would say, 'They're far too young. They'll never remember Spain.' But we don't have current experiences only for the sake of future memories; adventures have their worth even if they are restricted to the present tense. While I anticipated that George and Blaine might not remember a particular place, I knew that I would remember taking them there, and that they would be shaped by the earliest possible understanding that people have varied customs and beliefs. When Blaine was three, I carried her outside a restaurant to see the sunset over the Place de la Concorde and told her about having seen the same sight with my own mother. 'Oh, Daddy,' she said, 'I'm so happy right now.' A year later, we were on the floor playing with her dolls, and she announced, 'Emma is hungry. She has to go get something to eat.'

I said, 'Well, where would Emma like to get something? Maybe from Central Market?'

'No, I don't think so.'

'Where, then?'

'Paris.'

My son George has shown a particular interest in maps. He studies them for hours on end, tracing where one country abuts another. A New York cabbie announced to us that he came from Senegal, caught the eye of then five-year-old George in the rear-view mirror, and said, 'I'll bet you don't know where that is, little boy.'

George said, 'South of Mauritania, next to Mali and Guinea.' The driver nearly crashed the taxi.

A few months later, we asked George where he'd go if he could go anywhere in the world. He thought for a moment before responding, 'Syria.'

John and I were both alarmed. 'Syria!' we said. 'Why Syria?'

George said patiently, using an expression that has some currency in our house, 'Someone has to tell those people that what they're doing is inappropriate behaviour.'

Travelling with my children offers three primary pleasures. First, their delight in new things kindles my own delight, returning freshness to a ride in a gondola, a Rocky Mountain vista, the Changing of the Guard. Many touristic clichés are overexposed because they are singular and spectacular, and children provide an excuse to enjoy them again. Second, the advantages of travelling make a worthy legacy: I am lucky that I was given the world so early. In passing that gift along, I rekindle my intimacy with my mother; taking my children to faraway places honours her memory. Finally, my children have returned a sense of purposefulness to my travel. I've been to so many places and seen so much, and sometimes it feels like a glut of sunsets and churches and monuments. My mind has been stretched by the world's diversity, and may be approaching its elastic limits. In addressing the minds of my children, however, an urgent sense of purpose is renewed. I do not expect that George will settle the conflict with ISIL, but I think the knowledge he and Blaine and their half siblings Oliver and Lucy are accumulating will broaden their inherent kindness and thus increase the planet's depleted stores of compassion.

I used to think that I was unusually reactive to the thinness of the air in a plane's pressurised cabin. I cry on planes – at the movies I watch, the books I read, the letters and emails I attempt to answer. Those surges of emotion have a quality of abrupt intensity that is most often associated with substance abuse. Sometimes, it's a good trip, and sometimes, a bad one; sometimes, the emotionality is thrilling, and sometimes, deeply distressing. For years, I presumed that this hypersensitivity was affiliated with other physiological effects of altitude, such as the diminished ability to distinguish flavours – a mercy on most airlines. I sought research that would reveal whether more or less blood was flowing to which areas of my brain, how my pulmonary capacity was compromised by the angle of ascent.

Now I've come to believe that departure simply makes me sad, whether it points to someplace I've always wanted to see or to the home I have missed. Though travel can intensify life, it also evokes dying. It is a detachment. I grow anxious at take-off not because of the air pressure and not because the plane might crash, but because I feel myself dissolving. I was brought up to value safety more than comfort, and comfort more than courage, and have spent adulthood striving to invert that hierarchy. Rilke said, 'We need, in love, to practise only this: letting each other go. For holding on comes easily; we do not need to learn it.' As we climb above the clouds, I practise letting go of the place I've come from or the place I've gone. Though I am sustained in these departures by the prospect of arrival, separation always tugs me towards at least momentary regret. Even in that sorrow, however, I know that I failed fully to love home until I went repeatedly abroad and could not appreciate abroad until I had returned home time and again. Valediction is, at least for me, a precondition of intimacy.

The Winter Palettes

Harpers & Queen, 1988

I had often wondered why people who went to Russia seemed to become obsessed with it, and I learned why on my first assignment reporting from abroad, in 1988, when the British monthly *Harpers & Queen* sent me to the USSR to cover Sotheby's groundbreaking sale of contemporary Soviet art. Three years later, I published an expanded account of the same events in *Connoisseur*. Here, I have combined the two articles, reflecting those experiences of exhilarating discovery – not only for me, but also for the artists involved – as our personal and political worlds collided. The encounter described in this article launched me on the path towards my first book, *The Irony Tower: Soviet Artists in a Time of Glasnost*.

'To Brezhnev!' said one of the artists. Since it was nearly sunrise and I was exhausted, I raised my glass of tea without quite registering the name. 'To Brezhnev!' we all chorused, and downed our tea. Only then did it strike me as odd that, in the summer of 1988, we were toasting Brezhnev rather than Gorbachev. It must have been four in the morning, or perhaps five, and the conversation had degenerated; we had left behind Baudrillard and deconstructionism and postmodernism and were making jokes about Japanese tourists. The seven of us were crowded around a small table in a small room, all talking at once, and all greedily attacking the food that one of the artists had made, taking turns with the plates because there weren't enough to go around. Then came this toast, after which someone observed that it had been a good evening of good talk, 'just like in the days of Brezhnev'. I was too unfocused even to ask.

We left the interlinked studios on Furmanny Lane, located, ironically enough, upstairs from a school for the blind, at half past six. Dawn had come to Moscow, and the street seemed incredible. I had been there since eleven the previous morning, and it had taken on that quality of being the sole reality that inevitably comes of protracted debate and total exhaustion. We parted with those words once more: 'To Brezhnev!' Then one of the artists reminded me, 'Be at the station at noon today. We'll see you then.'

I went back to the dubious opulence of my Western hotel. At eleven my alarm sounded like a bad joke, and I peevishly dragged myself out of bed and set off for the train station, wondering all the while what could have possessed me to make this appointment. When I got there, I saw some familiar avant-gardists and, discovering that I was glad to see them, ceased to curse the missed night's sleep and remembered why I'd sat up so late in the first place.

We all went off to a place of bucolic vista, about two hours outside Moscow. Only one person – there were about forty of us – knew where we were going, and even he didn't know what we would find when we got there. We were on our way to an Action, by the Collective Action Group (K/D), and this mystery was part of it all. When we left the train we found ourselves at the edge of a thin strip of woods, and we walked single file, talking in low voices, sometimes laughing, waiting to see what would happen. After the first bit of woods we arrived at sweeping fields of corn, with odd, tumbledown houses beyond them; then came a wood of birches, then a lake surrounded by reeds newly gone to seed, then a pine woods with stolid trunks rising from a smooth floor. Imagine this: all the Moscow vanguard, the many faces of genius and the eager eyes of their acolytes, walking through a forest as still as the first day of creation.

We came into a field with a river running through it. On the river, fishermen in rubber boats were casting their lines and watching –

with some puzzlement but not much interest – the procession of artists. At last we came to a rise, where we stopped, stood in a row, and watched the river. Soon we saw an artist, Georgi Kisevalter, standing by the water. He jumped in, swam across, and disappeared on the other side. We kept our eyes on the spot where he had disappeared. He returned to the water's edge carrying a huge, flat package, leaped in, and swam back. He went to a hill opposite our knoll, where he was joined by the leader of K/D, Andrei Monastyrsky, and another artist. They removed the brightly coloured outer wrapping from the package to reveal a large black-and-white painting. They carefully took out the nails that held the canvas to the stretcher and laid the canvas on the ground. They disassembled the stretcher, which was of complicated design, until they had reduced it to its component strips of wood. They wrapped the wood in the black-and-white canvas and wrapped that in the outer covering. Then Monastyrsky distributed photocopies of the painting to the onlookers.

All the while, on a hill behind us, a bell was ringing in a blue box and no one heard it.

That was the Action. Two hours to get there, two hours back (not to mention the time to go to and from the station), and ten minutes of what I took to be ponderously self-important performance art. We had a picnic by the river afterwards, which should have been jolly, but I was annoyed. I was glad to have seen the woods, and the bread and cheese were dandy, but the rest seemed pure idiocy. Sergey Anufriev, one of the leaders of the Medical Hermeneutics movement, took me aside and explained it in detail, articulating elaborate references to previous performance pieces, art's connections to nature, old and outmoded Soviet aesthetic concerns, and episodes in individual people's lives. When he finished, I had a moment of thinking I understood. By that time, I was too tired to worry about it.

Only later did I understand that I had understood nothing, and that that had been the point. By then, I had begun to realise why we had been toasting Brezhnev, the oppressor, and not Gorbachev, the liberator. Under Brezhnev, as under Khrushchev, the Soviet avant-gardists were unable to exhibit their work in public, so they would hang it in their apartments or studios and invite people to come and look at it. The only people who ever saw their work were other avant-gardists. They were, in their own phrase, 'like the early Christians, or like Freemasons'. They could recognise one another at a glance, and they stuck together through thick and thin, never betraying the members of the circle. They believed that they knew a higher truth than was vouchsafed to the rest of the Soviet people, but they knew also that its time had not yet come. From their circumstances of difficulty, they learned integrity and built a world of mutuality. Though shot through with intense ironies and petty conflicts, this life force still gave their work urgency in a country where, for so many people, all gesture had come to seem futile. In the face of misery they achieved their tightly shared joy, and the constant surprise of such a profound sense of purpose taught them the value of their talent.

That talent was formidable. Their joy may have been considerable, but the passage to it was too fraught to tempt anyone who was incapable of transcendence; moreover, the frustration of battling the all-encompassing Soviet system with an inadequate intellect quickly defeated fools. The Moscow artistic community had no room for the passive observer; the commitment of its members was enormous. Since the experience of their work always depended on the experience of them as people – since the hundred or so individuals who made up the avant-garde were both the creators of Soviet art and its audience – the artists' personalities were key to what they created. Their strong personas are defined in part by the place they fill within the art world, and in part by the proclivities with which they came to the avant-garde, but their genius is, of necessity, that of the painter, the poet and the actor. This curious concatenation makes them compelling, irresistible, implacable and ultimately impenetrable. It is why they combine that rigorous trait of integrity with a sly elusiveness that can all too often masquerade as dishonesty. Their work is full of truth, but all told in slanted language.

Anufriev's description of the Action was a witty lie. I was being cajoled into the belief that what had happened was comprehensible, coherent and straightforward. What had gone on was, in fact, a fascinating comment on the problems of contemporary Soviet art, and at a fairly literal level it was explicable, but it was also an affirmation of the artistic community that oppression had created, a community that felt itself being shaken by freedom. The whole point was that it contained so many references that no one could begin to get them all. The artists in attendance could affirm their places in the avant-garde by getting many of them and could confirm the degree of their secrecy by failing to get the rest. The circle of the avant-garde, suddenly threatened by those who think that being an artist is an easy path to fame and fortune, holds such events to protect its terrible new fragility as loosening restrictions and foreign markets threaten its members' psychic citadel.

I had come to Moscow to attend Sotheby's sale of contemporary Soviet art. The hype surrounding the auction was blinding. Sotheby's was organising the ultimate Moscow tour, a package involving dip-lomatic entertainments, singing Gypsies, endless viewings of rarely seen icons, meetings with important persons, cases of imported champagne and beluga buckshot previously reserved for tsars and commissars. We were going not to a mere auction but to an impor-tant event in the history of East and West. On a drop-dead-smart brochure, the word *Sotheby's* blazed red in both Latin and Cyrillic type against the sienna tones of an ancient map with illegible letter-ing. Charmed though travellers were by the prospect of fish eggs and icons, many were taken aback to discover that this map – the logo of the trip, reproduced time and again in the international press – was actually an old map of Bermuda. 'It's what sprang to hand,' one of the Sotheby's directors told me.

As a for-profit company, Sotheby's had reasons for staging the sale other than an interest in the work of the Soviet avant-garde. It was an opportunity to establish good relations with the Soviet government at the dawn of perestroika, with the possibility of monopoly contracts and other boons down the line. Initially, contemporary art and artists were seen as a means to an end. Although Soviet art had actually been discovered by the West incrementally during the decade preceding the Sotheby's sale, when a few Soviet artists started to get exposure in

Western Europe and New York, the big players in the art game didn't pay much attention.

By the time Sotheby's was revving up for its sale, gallery exhibitions in the West were taking place, notably an installation at Ronald Feldman Fine Arts in New York by Ilya Kabakov. He had created a Moscow communal apartment in which each room belonged to someone driven to obsessiveness by the close quarters. In one room lived the Man Who Never Threw Anything Away, whose space was filled with cards on which tiny items were pasted to boards and labelled: 'lint from my pocket', 'dust from the corner', 'a paper clip', 'an insect'. In another room, the Man Who Flew into Space from His Apartment had rigged a seat in mid-air with four huge springs that ran to the four corners of his ceiling, planning to fling himself into the freedom of the stratosphere. In yet another lived the Man (perhaps Kabakov himself) Who Described His Life Through Characters. Such exhibitions had impelled a few serious collectors of Soviet art, but though theirs was no longer an eccentric taste, it was still a cultivated, obscure one.

Before taking over as director of Sotheby's Europe, Simon de Pury had been the private curator to Baron Thyssen-Bornemisza. Travelling with him to the Soviet Union, de Pury had picked up word of the contemporary art scene there. He also gathered that a great deal of important work by the avant-garde of the 1920s in the Soviet Union remained in private hands, as well as precious eighteenth- and nineteenth-century furniture and objects. He was eager to get off on the right foot with Gorbachev's new government with its policy of glasnost, or openness, so that Sotheby's would be in a favourable position if financial straits pushed the Soviets who owned these treasures into selling them. Lenin had sold some of the best works from the Hermitage Museum to underwrite his new government; perhaps Gorbachev might do something similar. The new art was a glorified bargaining chip. The 'contemporary' sale that I had come to witness included a number of important works from the twenties – including major pieces by Aleksandr Rodchenko, Varvara Stepanova and Aleksandr Drevin. 'Wait and see how long it takes before we have an office in this country saying SOTHEBY'S MOSCOW over the door,' one of de Pury's colleagues remarked. But de Pury soon saw that the contemporary art could be valuable in itself. 'This is all a wonderful, giant risk,' he said to me. 'We know so little about this work we are buying – except that we know it's worth buying.'

The night of the auction, 7 July 1988, brought together people no previous circumstance could have assembled. At six thirty, the Sotheby's tour group began to file into the great conference chamber of the Mezhdunarodnaya Hotel. After stopping at the registration desk to collect paddles, each guest walked to his or her reserved seat at the front of the room. Elton John's manager exchanged pleasantries with the sister of the king of Jordan. A retired baseball player escorted a small bevy of titled Scandinavian ladies. A group of prosperous German women, dressed in red in honour of the host country, engaged in cheery banter with a member of the U.S. State Department. 'Are you really going to buy that one?' someone asked.

'At any price,' came the response, with a chuckle.

A thin woman with diamonds at her throat and an oversize crocodile handbag flipped back and forth between two pictures by two different artists. 'I just can't decide. I can't decide,' she moaned, then asked a neighbour, 'Which of these do you like better?'

Behind the Sotheby's entourage came Westerners who lived in Moscow and powerful, overdressed Soviets, who looked fat and easy among Americans abroad and Western Europeans on holiday. American ambassador Jack F. Matlock was there with his wife, his son, and his son's Russian fiancée. The sons and daughters of wealthy foreign businessmen stationed in the USSR were there. Many missed the habit of Western social events and welcomed this occasion to sport their Adolfo and Valentino. The press was there in spades with notebooks, cameras and TV equipment – not art press flown in for the event but the political press, with all the Moscow bureaus covering this historic moment.

The back third of the room had no chairs. The space, cordoned off by velvet ropes, was crowded with all the rest of invited Moscow, people with cards that were said to have been sold at amasing prices, cards for which we were apocryphally led to believe paintings and even apartments had perhaps been exchanged. The artists in the crowd – many of whom had been part of the Collective Action at the river – stood in whispering knots, only a sideshow at what was properly their own seminal global event. Behind the ropes were the curators of the Pushkin, the friends of the Soviet artists, the other members of the vanguard. Some artists from Leningrad had come; one artist's cousin had made the trip from Tbilisi, over a thousand miles away. People pushed and shifted towards the front of the throng, only to be borne back again on the waves of people pressed against people, crushed, but redeemed in mid-July by the blissful air-conditioning, which was not exactly a staple of Soviet life.

At seven o'clock the bidding began. De Pury, perspiring despite the air-conditioning, was behind the podium, conducting the sale as though he were the master of ceremonies at the greatest show on earth. The early Soviet work far surpassed its anticipated prices; one painting by Rodchenko, *Line*, estimated at $165,000 to $220,000, sold for $561,000.

With Lot 19, the sale of contemporary Soviet art began. The works were listed by the artists' surnames in alphabetical order – alphabetical in the Latin alphabet. So the first was Grisha Bruskin, a tiny, gnarled man who had been at the periphery of things for years, deemed by his peers to be sweet and technically capable but relatively insignificant. All his paintings doubled, tripled, quadrupled their high estimates; then one estimated at $32,000 sold for $415,700.

The artists began to look at one another sharply. They were finally getting to see how people from the West spent money. With casual, almost weary gestures, the members of the Sotheby's tour raised paddles of blanched wood into the air, offering six-figure sums. A difference of $1,000 seemed to move them not at all. Fortunes such as many of these artists had never dreamed were casually handed over for a painting – a Soviet painting. The artists began to understand that changing government policies might ultimately leave them inconceivably wealthy.

After Bruskin came Ivan Chuykov, a highly esteemed elder statesman of unofficial art. If someone would pay over $400,000 for a painting by Bruskin, then surely the work of Chuykov would be worth millions. But his *Fragment of a Fence* failed to reach its low estimate of $15,000, and *Noughts and Crosses* didn't reach its low estimate of $20,000; they barely exceeded their reserves. Thus the sale continued, with high prices that confounded the Soviets and low prices that embarrassed them. Then a remarkably pretty but essentially decorative painting by Svetlana Kopystiyanskaya went on the block; she was a serious woman and a good painter, but not a riveting original, and the bidding for her work was going higher and higher. How could it be? If the vanguard had not been sequestered behind the rope, and if they had understood the ego dynamics of the auction world, they might have noticed a paddle battle. Had they been at the posh official dinner the night before, they might have gathered that Elton John had instructed his manager to bid on the same painting that a glamorous Swiss woman announced that she would have at any price. After that painting realised $75,000, the artists kept repeating, in an uncomprehending drone, 'Does that mean that people from the West think Sveta Kopystiyanskaya is a better painter than Chuykov? Than Kabakov?'

Almost every painting sold. The prettiest paintings, or sometimes the most blatantly unusual works, sold for the most money, which threw the Moscow avant-garde for a loop, instilling a dread that the West might create a canon based on standards totally unrelated to their own. They were deeply upset by some of the bidders they met, whose refusal to engage with a Soviet context seemed to imply an inability to recognise that there was a context at all. At one studio, after listening to a highly theoretical painter give a thirty-minute explanation of his work, a woman who ended up placing one of the highest bids of the sale had asked, 'Do you paint in black and white and grey because it's hard to get coloured paint in this country?'

Though some of the best work was sold to people who understood it, most went to people who were shopping for souvenirs. The sale brought in $3.5 million, more than twice the optimistic estimate of $1.8 million. Simon de Pury hugged Sergey Popov, deputy director of the Ministry of Culture.

As they left the great room, one woman pointed to her catalogue and exclaimed to another, 'I bought this one.' She frowned slightly. 'Or else this one. I don't remember which.'

'Whichever,' said the other. 'As long as you have something to remember tonight by. Wasn't it exciting?'

Thus the artists were brought into the public eye, an unsettling place to be if your work is based on the most extreme form of privacy. Designed to be meaningless, even boring, to the eyes of the KGB, it was created according to standards so secretive that, paradoxically, it would remain incomprehensible to the West long after it became famous there. When an artwork is cut off from its origins, the easiest thing to lose sight of is its irony. Insistence on the multiplicity of truth, in Soviet art, is as political as is painting, because accepting a single official truth is an old Stalinist habit. The nature of elusiveness – rather than the thing eluded – must be the focus of criticism. This is why sociological examination is the most rational way to proceed. It is valid, in short, to applaud the brilliance of disguise; it is comical to applaud the disguise itself. The Sotheby's sale catapulted the artists into an ambivalent relationship to celebrity and fortune that was to undermine their entire system of values.

While the bidders' ignorance was not the fault of the auction house, had the sale been staged less theatrically, some of the souvenir shoppers would have stayed at home. Of course, then the paintings would not have brought such enormous sums. And if the sale had not been such a blockbuster, the Ministry of Culture would have been far less likely to stage in the months that followed other, similar events that would help many more Soviet artists. The ministry, which retained a sizeable part of the takings, suddenly began looking at the once-detested artists with a self-interested kindness now that they had become a prime source of hard currency.

Sotheby's saw all these perspectives. The auction house knew it was tapping a new wellspring of profit, but at the same time it transcended its usual pedestrian commercialism. At the farewell dinner the next night, even the most cynical of the Sotheby's staff – and the most sceptical officials in the Ministry of Culture – appeared to be on the brink of tears. The two sides had long stood in emblematic opposition to each other, and if one accepts that the function of art is ultimately communication, then this sale was itself a work of art, a miraculous engagement. In the years that were to follow, critics, curators, collectors and artists variously credited the auction house with discovering a movement, inventing a movement or destroying a movement. To some extent, all of them were right.

The artists had mixed feelings about the sale and were perhaps unable to see all the motivations and reasons behind it. The day after it took place, they organised a trip on a large boat to protest Western commercialism. The avant-gardists were all there, arguing fiercely, as we sailed to a resort area, about the likely effects of Western commercialism. Then everyone disembarked to walk in the woods, sit in the sand or rent rowing boats or little paddleboats. I ended up in a rowing boat with Viktor Misiano, the curator of contemporary art at the Pushkin, and Zhora Litichevsky, a painter with incredible staying power as an oarsman. Everyone was at play, affirming once again the strength of the avant-garde community. As paddleboats tried to bang into us and laughing people tried to splash us, Misiano would nod towards this or that one and say, 'There is an important Leningrad conceptualist. There is a true Communist painter. There is a Soviet formalist.' Like the Action in the woods, it was a chance to see this madcap community at play, which was a good way to begin to understand their coded work.

Only after the sale did one of its organisers describe to me the first meeting at which Sotheby's had discussed individual artists with the Ministry of Culture. At that time, it was exceedingly difficult to get information about artists, and Sotheby's put forward a list of under-ground artists whose names they had obtained from Western contacts inside the USSR. The culture commissars told the auction-house contingent rather peevishly that every Westerner who came for a meeting brought exactly the same list – and that it could be identified as *exactly* the same list because one of the names on it was of a pianist rather than a painter.

The sale marked a turning point in Soviet art history. In the two years that were to follow the event, some artists who had been dom-inant figures in the avant-garde sank into obscurity. Others grew accustomed to life in the jet set; they were invited to the penthouses and palazzi of collectors and had dinners thrown in their honour in apartments at Trump Tower in New York. Their work came to be mentioned regularly in the press, but even when it was unpopular, they themselves were often popular. They appeared on morning television shows and were profiled in glossy magazines. Their strongest work came to reflect the certainty that the West could understand the will to communicate, if not their specific acts of communication. That they would look forward to a certain celebrity with cautious ebullience never meant they were beyond reflecting bitterly on what was past.

The poetics of meaning for these Soviet artists lies partly in their nostalgia, and it is perhaps a greater mercy than they realise that the tendency to homesickness is among their cultural attributes. When they recognise in their work that a dream realised is also a dream forsaken, they resuscitate both their purity of purpose and the sense of humour that we in the West find so beguiling. Time and inevitable failures have started to restore to these artists the subtle gift for self-reference they employed so effectively in the pre-auction years. In rediscovering their country and their former lives of oppression from a salutary distance, they have rediscovered their original reasons for telling, secretly or otherwise, what they perceive as inalienable truth. The strength of their beliefs convinces us. Truth-telling gives this work its high moral and aesthetic standing – the ultimate gift the artists provide not only to museums and collectors, but also to the world. As these Soviet artists and their body of work move West, how they change will change how we think about art.

––––––––––

Though the work of many artists of the late Soviet avant-garde was commercialised by the West, they soon achieved a degree of visibility in their own country as well. The Russian capital now boasts the Moscow Museum of Modern Art, the Multimedia Art Museum and the Garage Museum of Contemporary Art; the Garage is housed in a lavishly converted fifty-eight-thousand-square-foot former restaurant in Gorky Park, with an atrium that features two thirty-foot-high murals by Erik Bulatov. Artists work in studio spaces in a former power plant in Moscow and in what was once St Petersburg's Smolinsky industrial bread bakery. Independent art schools in Russia include the British Higher School of Art and Design (established in 2003), the Rodchenko School of Art (2006), the Institute Baza (2011) and the Open School Manege/Media Art Lab (2013). The Hermitage was the site of the last Manifesta, an important pan-European exhibition, and the Moscow Biennale is going strong, along with commercial art fairs such as Cosmoscow.

Vladimir Putin's government disdains free expression, however, and Russian authorities frequently ban or close down exhibitions that offend conservatives. The women of the feminist rock band Pussy Riot were imprisoned following a 2012 performance at Moscow's Cathedral of Christ the Saviour; their story captivated the international press, but is only one of many such episodes. The 'art-anarch-punk gang' Voina, 'War', seeks to challenge 'outdated repressive-patriarchal symbols and ideologies'. Voina staged an orgy at the Timiryazev Museum of Biology in Moscow concurrent with the 2008 Russian presidential election. In 2010, five of its members sketched a two-hundred-foot-high phallus on St Petersburg's Liteiny drawbridge so it would be visible from the offices of the Federal Security Service when the bridge was raised. Many members of Voina are currently in prison. Alex Plutser-Sarno, who remains at liberty, said that the locus of the group is behind 'a high, impenetrable wall of the St Petersburg prison', where the artists Oleg Vorotnikov and Leonid Nikolayev are 'slowly fading away'.

Some of the exhibitions shut down in the past decade or so include *Forbidden Art* at the Sakharov Center Moscow (2006), which cost the director his job; *Spiritual Invective* at Moscow's Marat Guelman Gallery (2012), after which the organisers were brought in for questioning; and *Welcome to Sochi*, shown in Perm (2013), of which Putin-loyalist parliamentarian Andrei Klimov wrote, 'The works brought together reminded me of the way Russia was portrayed by Hitler's propagandists, and by Napoléon's flunkeys before them. Goebbels, I'm sure, would be pleased.' Most recently, the Moscow Exhibition Halls Association shut down *Be Happy* at the

Bogorodskoe Gallery, Moscow (2015); and *Being Yourself: Stories of LGBT Teenagers* at Red Square gallery, Moscow (2015). When the organisers of the latter exhibition attempted to show their photos outdoors, the pictures were destroyed and photographer Denis Styazhkin, who is an activist for LGBT rights, and a sixteen-year-old onlooker were detained. Funding for the Moscow Premiere film festival was abruptly redirected to a new 'Youth Festival of Life-Affirming Film' run by one of Putin's cronies. Russian authorities have even tried to impede exhibitions abroad: the minister of culture objected to the public display of pieces slated for the Paris show *Sots Art: Political Art from Russia*, so he prevented them from leaving the country.

Nor is the market easy even for those whose exhibitions don't get shuttered. The proliferation of museums in Moscow notwithstanding, affluent, glamour-besotted Russians generally prefer flashier, more prestigious contemporary Western art to what is produced by their countrymen. Although global prices for Russian contemporary art have stabilised somewhat, the domestic art market has suffered a deep recession. Moscow's three best-established galleries – Aydan Gallery, Marat Guelman Gallery and XL Gallery – have had to reinvent themselves as nonprofits. Vladimir Ovcharenko, director of the Regina Gallery, said, 'Most artists are working in their kitchens as they did in Soviet times.' It is not clear whether, as in Soviet times, they are working with moral purpose.

Three Days in August

New York Times Magazine, 29 September 1991

My first book was about artists in the Soviet Union. They were my subjects, but they also became friends, and I was eager to return to Moscow following publication so that I could spend time with them without interviewing them. I had anticipated a relaxing time, visiting friends in their dachas and talking and drinking into the night, so the dramatic events recounted here came as an ambush. It had been my persistent hope, but hardly my belief, that art and literature were purposeful, and that honing the ability to express difficult truths was a tool in the permanent project of fixing a broken world – that the pen or the paintbrush was indeed mightier than the sword. During those three days in Moscow I came to understand that – at certain times and in certain places – my hope might be true.

———

Monday, 19 August: At eight in the morning, a phone call from Viktoria Ivleva, a photographer, wakes me. 'I'm sorry to call so early,' she says, 'but I think I'm going to have to cancel dinner tonight. You see, Gorbachev has just resigned, and I don't think I'm going to make it to the market, and I have no vegetables in the house.'

My mind is fogged. 'Gorbachev has resigned?' I repeat vaguely.

'Apparently yes. That's all I know about it.'

I am recovering from a party that went on until the small hours of the morning, a typical gathering of Moscow's avant-garde artists. 'All right, Vika, I'll talk to you later,' I say, and go back to sleep. The mood in Moscow in mid-August is so powerfully positive, the attitude towards Gorbachev so nonchalantly dismissive, that his resignation strikes my bleary mind as only another meaningless step in the restructuring of Soviet politics. For more than two years, people have been saying that Gorbachev's time has passed, that he has to step aside for more vigorous reformers. His decision at last to do so is not worth much fuss.

When I do get up, I turn on CNN, one of the benefits of a few top hotels in Moscow, which is reporting confusingly on his disappearance. The word *coup* is mentioned. I look out the window. All the usual vendors are along Rozhdestvenka Street, and the usual crowd is pouring out of the Kuznetsky Most metro station to buy things.

I phone the building at Furmanny Lane that Moscow's vanguard artists have turned into studio space. I have been working and living with these artists for more than three years, communicating in English, French and my minimal Russian, and have just published a book about our adventures together. Larisa Zvezdochetova, a conceptual artist, answers the phone. 'Have you heard what's happened?' I ask.

'So it's true? This morning, at eight, Anton Olshvang called me with this terrible news, and I said to him, "Anton, I am getting very tired of your sense of humour," and I went back to sleep.' At eleven, Larisa received another call, reporting that a friend had seen tanks approaching the Russian Parliament. Concluding that these were just ordinary manoeuvres, Larisa went back to sleep again. 'But when I got up a little while ago, I put on my television, and I saw only Tchaikovsky ballet on every channel, and then I began to be very afraid.' Tchaikovsky ballets had played on every channel when Stalin died – it was the surest sign that something so extreme had happened that there was nothing else to broadcast.

I head for the decrepit building that houses the studios; eight artists are gathered in the small room on the top floor where we go late at night to drink and talk. The birthday of Larisa's artist husband,

Kostya Zvezdochetov, was two weeks ago, and his sometime collaborator Andrei Filippov made 'the biggest Russian flag in the world' for him, because their work deals with the tension between Russian spirit and Soviet bureaucracy. This ten-foot length of tricoloured fabric has been in the corner of the studio for days, and now Kostya wraps it around his shoulders like a shawl.

He has managed to tune in Radio Liberty, the American propaganda and information channel, but the sound comes and goes. We are only half listening; now, as in the days of Khrushchev and Brezhnev, irony is the only way to deal with fear and crisis, so the conversation is quick, the witticisms as sharp and brittle as the news. The artists found out long ago that the way to combat a government that presents lies as if they were the truth is to tell the truth as if it were a joke. Humour became a means of encoded communication, and so long as they made jokes they could be vocal and invulnerable. But today, behind the banter, the artists are building up the courage they will need for whatever is to follow. Soon they will have to drop their habitual obliqueness; this calamity will call for real and palpable action.

Hungry for information, we set off together for the Kremlin and are astonished to find Red Square closed off, its vast acreage empty, tanks and officers guarding the entrance. We press into the crowds and get copies of the written statements that are being distributed by the resistance.

In Manezh Square, just below Red Square, a rally is beginning. Here, too, the centre has been closed to pedestrians. People are gathering to listen to extemporaneous speeches. 'You know as much as we do,' one of the soldiers says to us. 'We were just told this morning to come here. We've had no further orders.' Vladimir Mironenko, a painter, replies, 'It's great that you've surrounded the Kremlin, but your guns are in the wrong direction. All you've got to do is turn them around so that they point towards the Kremlin and away from us, and everything will be fine.' The soldiers laugh.

One speaker says that a resistance movement is building around the Russian Parliament and that Boris Yeltsin is leading the fight against the new junta. 'Elected!' the speaker keeps repeating. 'Yeltsin we have elected!'

The artists shake their heads. 'Yeltsin is a troublemaker, a political animal, and no member of the intelligentsia likes him very much,' one of them says. 'But we may all have to stand behind him in this moment of crisis.'

As we head up Tverskaya, the central boulevard, we stop to photograph one another beside tanks or talking to soldiers. The streets, cleared of cars and mobbed with people, seem almost as though they have been swept clean for a parade.

We run into a friend who says that there is more action at the Parliament. We take the metro to Barrikadnaya station, so called because it is on the spot where barricades were built during the first Russian Revolution – a redundancy that everyone loves. The ordinarily sullen old woman who sweeps the station has taken it upon herself to confront anyone who seems to pause even for a moment. 'Go!' she says. 'Go at once to the demonstration!' Then she moves on to the next lot of people. 'Go! Go quickly!'

We join the flood of humanity spilling down towards the Parliament. It never strikes us, as we listen to speeches delivered from the balcony, that we are swelling the ranks the press will record as protesters. We are all horrified by the emerging picture of the coup and the dangerous profiles of the members of the junta, but we have not gone to the Parliament to protest. We have gone to investigate.

The speakers warn us that the place is to be stormed at 4:00 a.m. and urge us to form human barricades to defend it. 'Will you do that?' I ask my friends.

'If it's necessary, then of course we must' is the answer.

We head towards the river, where there are more tanks, and talk to soldiers. The artists' technique is to engage them in conversation. 'So,' someone will ask, 'you've been in the army a long time? Where do you come from? Ah, my grandmother came from near there. Have you been in Moscow before?' At the end of such a friendly chat – often accompanied by a gift of sausage, chocolate or bread bought nearby – they suddenly bring the conversation around. 'Listen, you don't know what your orders tonight will be,' one of the artists says, 'and I certainly don't know, but I want to tell you that I and all my friends will be defending this building. We'll be sitting outside it. Don't shoot us.'

The soldiers are mostly nervously non-committal. 'We hope not,' they say.

'No, that's not enough. Don't shoot us. If you have problems, if you need to go into hiding from your generals, we will hide you.' Names and telephone numbers are readily exchanged, often scribbled on the back of the Yeltsin statements carried from the Parliament building.

In 1988, when I started to write about Soviet artists, the people I met would ask me not to telephone them from my hotel lest I arouse the suspicion of the KGB, not to use their names in describing certain activities. But now there is no question of anonymity. I say that I may publish something about the resistance and ask whether I should try to disguise identities. 'You must tell everyone in the West, everyone in the world, that I have gone to this fight,' says Yuri Leidermann, an artist. 'You should shout our names from the rooftops.'

At the end of the afternoon, we help build the barricades.

'It is usually the nuisance of Moscow that everything is under construction,' Kostya says. 'But now it will be our salvation: what popular movement has ever had such good materials so readily available? Today, in this place, we will make a real communal work of art.'

It has started to rain, and a woman in high heels asks each of us, 'Excuse me, but do you know how to drive a steam shovel or a bulldozer?' Someone has managed to jump-start the construction equipment, and in the end it has to be manoeuvred by men who have clearly never before driven anything more challenging than a car. The machines push and drag, and we all line up and push and drag, and the barricades begin to take shape. The self-appointed overseer is another woman, with a shrill but commanding voice. Mud-spattered, wet, cold, she stands hands on her hips and shrieks instructions into the fray. T-shirts with Western writing – the words don't matter – are fashionable in Moscow; across this woman's generous figure is stretched I'D RATHER BE PLAYING TENNIS.

We agree to meet at the studios later in the evening. By nine thirty, most of the artists I know best are there, perhaps forty in all. The fun-fair atmosphere has given way to something more purposeful. Andrei takes the tongue-in-cheek flag he made for Kostya and tells us that, should we become separated, we can meet beneath it. As we head for the Parliament, we are upbeat. 'This is the end of the suspense,' Josif Bahkstein, a critic, says to me. 'If we win now, reform has triumphed. If we lose now, we have truly lost.'

We discuss the general strike. 'My refusal to go to the philosophy department of the university,' comments Viktor Zagarev, 'is unlikely to frighten our junta. Today, for the first time, I wish I were an auto worker.' Someone else says, 'If I close my art gallery, it will leave only four people unemployed.'

When, just before midnight, we hear the sound of the barricade being pulled apart, our hearts sink; we go running to the spot and find dozens of people struggling to open a gap in our fortification. 'Come on,' they say. 'Troops loyal to Yeltsin!' We eventually understand that a battalion has defected to our side and rush to join the demolition effort.

It is only a handful of tanks, but we leap on the fronts of them and ride to the Parliament, Andrei waving Kostya's flag, the painter Serioja Mironenko, Vladimir's twin brother, recording the whole thing on video. The soldiers in the tanks say, 'We've come to join you.' Their arrival heightens our uneasiness: this could be the start of civil war. Nonetheless, the joy as they come through is surpassing. The demonstrations have seemed largely symbolic until now, a gesture no more meaningful than a work of politicised art. Suddenly, the force of physical power is with us.

It is cold and starting to rain; I and my group go up to stand in the sheltered plaza outside the Parliament. Some of us have been separated, and we mass again under Andrei's flag. A hundred people loosely associated with the intelligentsia must be here, including some I have never met. 'People complain that there is no nightlife in this city,' one artist says. 'But tonight, every interesting person in Moscow is here, and we'll probably all stay for hours.' Lena Kurlyandtseva, a critic, comes rushing over and says, 'Andrew, you do not know Artyom Troitsky. Artyom, you have never met Andrew. But you have each read the other's book, and I think you must have many questions to ask each other.' We stand in the rain and chat. 'Private and public energy are fused by Soviet underground rock musicians, and that's something Western readers have trouble grasping,' Artyom speculates. 'They're more willing to accept such simultaneity in the work of visual artists.' We might as well be at a cocktail party.

Olga Sviblova has been filming the Moscow art scene for almost four years and is a fixture at every party and exhibition, with her semifunctional camera and her semi-competent technicians. Late on Monday night, she suddenly makes an entrance, elaborately made up and turned out in a black silk miniskirt. She borrows Serioja's video camera and films each artist. Since there is almost no light, she asks us to hold cigarette lighters around the faces of those she is shooting. 'Two years ago,' she says, 'I asked every one of these people whether they thought glasnost might fail, and I asked what they would do if it did. Tonight, I want only to record that they are here, and the attitudes of their faces. It will be the perfect ending for my film – if, of course, the new authorities don't destroy it.'

By 2:00 a.m., we are getting cold and tired and bored, and we agree that some of us should go home so that we can return, refreshed, tomorrow. 'We can't all just live here for the next six months,' Larisa remarks. As we walk towards the barricade where we parked four hours ago, we are accosted by a striking woman with blonde hair and a pale grey coat. She explains that she is helping to inflate a helium balloon to fly over the Parliament and that she wants to attach to its cord the banners of resistance. 'You have the biggest Russian flag I have ever seen,' she says. 'If you will give me your flag, then all the people of Russia will be able to see it and take hope from it.'

Andrei smiles. 'Of course you can have it.' He hands it over. 'Long live Russia.'

What was wholly ironic between Andrei and Kostya, then semi-ironic as the banner of the vanguard – 'And how will we find one another tomorrow?' Larisa asks. 'We will have to meet like tourists from Japan, under a green umbrella' – has become at this moment of crisis wholly unironic.

Tuesday, 20 August: In the afternoon, Viktoria, the photographer, calls me to say that she went to Germany last night, using up her one-exit visa, to deliver film from Monday. 'I wanted to make sure the photos got there. And now I have returned to defend my country. Who knows whether I will ever be able to get out again?'

Kostya stops by my hotel to watch CNN for half an hour. 'It's my flag,' he says when the Parliament building flashes on the screen, the balloon and flag hovering over it. When we get there, a little later, we are in time to hear Yeltsin speak of rallying under the Russian flag, and Kostya and Andrei exchange glances. 'It's our flag,' they remark.

That evening, I have dinner with Kostya, Larisa, Serioja and Kostya's mother, a survivor of hard labour in the Gulag. We drink lots of toasts: to Kostya's mother, to Kostya and Larisa, to me, to freedom, to Gorbachev, to Yeltsin. Kostya doesn't want his mother to know that he is going to the Parliament. We have a whispered consultation and devise a ruse.

I am feeling increasingly uneasy. A curfew has been declared. Driving back to the hotel, I see that the streets are almost empty. In the lobby are men from the military police.

At about 1:00 a.m., Tanya Didenko, a musicologist, calls me. Her apartment, opposite the Parliament, has become a sort of base of operations for many members of the intelligentsia, and throughout the night I check in with friends who have gone there to get warm, have tea or use the phone. 'Who would have thought it?' Tanya says. 'My home has become the public lavatory of the vanguard.' She is organising the women's line, to stand behind the men in the human barricade, and she is also negotiating contact with the outside world. 'Please keep me informed as you get information from your CNN,' she says. CNN keeps saying that its information is not yet available to the crowds outside the Russian Parliament, but as I repeat everything to Tanya, she sends runners down to tell the mob. I hear that there has been one death; she hears that there have been seven. Much of the time, it is hard to tell who has the more accurate information.

There are a few hitches. The phones are going haywire; they work and then stop, cut us off and reconnect us. There is constant clicking. Once, Tanya gets through and asks me to tell her exactly what CNN is saying. I reply that CNN seems to have shifted its reporting away from the Moscow coup and is now going on about a hurricane that is hitting New England. I explain that Hurricane Bob is wreaking devastation on the East Coast. Half an hour later, word is running around the Parliament that Hurricane Bob is coming in from Siberia, destroying everything in its path, and will soon hit Moscow.

At two thirty, Kostya calls to say that he and Larisa and Serioja have been looking for petrol and have been unable to get any. The metro has stopped running, and there are no taxis. So they have all gone home. I make a half-hearted effort to get down to the Parliament, but I am stopped by the military police. So I pace outside the hotel for a while – symbolically breaking the curfew – and then I go to bed.

At four, I later learn, Josif Bahkstein, the critic, wakes from a bad dream, gets into his car, and drives to the Parliament, joining the throng outside the building. 'I met many very attractive young girls,' he says afterward, 'one of whom I will see again in some days.'

Wednesday, 21 August: The day breaks cold and wet. Kostya and Larisa and I go to the Parliament, where we find a damp version of the previous day's rally. We want to see where the men were killed last night – the three fatalities, apparently the only ones so far, occurred at 1:00 a.m. in a tunnel as they attempted to block the observation slit in an oncoming infantry fighting vehicle – so at about noon we head off together towards Smolenskaya. Where the bodies were dragged after the shooting, flowers are scattered; perhaps a hundred people have gathered to speak of the tragedy.

A young man who looks like some early Bolshevik, or like the student from a Chekhov play – unshaven, wire-rimmed spectacles, crumpled cap held in a tense, pale hand – comes running from the barricade. He announces through a megaphone that tanks are approaching and asks for volunteers to come and stop them. Without discussion, we all follow him to the outer limit of the many-tiered system of defences we have built and range ourselves along it. We are prepared for anything, though there have been so many rumours of tanks that none of us really expects to see one.

In fact, they arrive within minutes. I am petrified; facing down tanks has not previously been a part of my job description. But I am also exhilarated by the intense purposefulness of our stance. I have never before had to defend my ideals this way, and though doing so in this instance is frightening, it also feels like a privilege. There is something oddly romantic about our encounter with brutality. The soldier in the first tank explains that they have come to destroy the barricade and orders us to move, adding that they will have to run us down if we do not give way. The man with the megaphone responds that we are holding our ground not in aggression, but to defend the rights of the people. 'We are only a few, but there are tens of thousands at the Parliament, and across all this country,' he says. He speaks of democracy and reminds the young men in the tanks of the terrors of the past. Others join in; Kostya and Larisa both declaim to the drivers. We emphasise that no one can force orders on them. 'If you do this, it is because you have chosen to do it,' says the man with the megaphone.

The soldiers look at one another and then they look at us. We are so wet, so cold, so impotent in all but the courage of our convictions – so entirely persuaded that we speak in the name of righteousness, but so transparently lacking in material defences – that the soldiers might easily laugh. Instead, after staring at us intensely for a full minute, the driver of the front tank shrugs as though he were doing nothing more than giving way to the inevitable course of destiny. 'We must bow to the will of the people,' he says, and instructs us to move aside so the tanks can make U-turns. It takes a lot of space and some time for a tank to make a U-turn.

'Why do you think they are really leaving?' I ask Kostya.

'Because of us,' he replies. 'Because we are here, and because of what we've said.'

All of us – friends and strangers – embrace, then stand and cheer until we are hoarse.

Only after it is over do we feel the particular enthralling mixture of our receding fear and our brush with heroism. Then we decide that we have had enough of bald courage for the moment, and so we collect friends, to whom we enthusiastically recount our adventure, and go back to my hotel, where we have a good lunch and are proud. My visa expires today, so I leave for the airport after lunch. The others are going home to sleep and recover and make phone calls and prepare for the night's vigil.

But that vigil does not come. By the time I check in for my flight, the coup has failed, defeated in part by internal argument and in part by soldiers who deferred to human barricades.

For the artists, this has brought another kind of liberation. Freedom has always been their obsession; in these three days they have had the luxury of physically defending it. 'We won the war,' says Kostya when I speak to him later on the phone. 'You, me and all our friends.' He pauses for a second. 'But it was my flag.'

Young Russia's Defiant Decadence

New York Times Magazine, 18 July 1993

When I returned to Russia two years after the Soviet Union collapsed, the country was changing dramatically with the sudden explosion of personal freedom and new wealth. I was in my late twenties, and found my contemporaries of particular interest because they were capable of accommodating the new order. Old Soviets' sensibilities were mostly fixed in the poisonous system that had formed them; these young people seemed – even more than most young people – to be defining what was to come. Vladimir Putin has since taken Russia in another direction. I read today with particular sorrow the assertion by experts that broader gay rights were nearly an inevitability, an optimistic position that has now been roundly disappointed. But these character sketches speak to the Yeltsin years, when cynicism and autonomy were committed bedfellows.

Travelling in Russia recently as a writer, I came quickly to feel like a spy – not an American foreign agent, but a spy for each emerging social class to the others. Members of the Russian mafia – the organised-crime circle – are fascinated to hear that intellectuals believe the criminal class exerts social influence. The intelligentsia are obsessed with the greed of the new rich businessmen, whom they blame for the end of idealism. A return to the Orthodox Church has left homosexuals worried about repressive neoconservatism; nightclub owners are pondering whether artists who flourished underground can survive in the new daylight. Politicians wonder whether power will devolve to these chaotic elements. Across all these strata, the changes are most evident among members of the younger generation.

Overall, their outlook is harsh indeed. According to an article in the mainstream newspaper *Argumenty i Fakty* in April, 'Young Russian malcontents are considering suicide every second.' One-third want to leave the country. Since 1989, the birthrate has dropped 30 per cent, as discouraged young people choose not to have children.

Even so, some young Russians who fall outside these depressing statistics are plunging ahead with often decadent abandon to find freedom, wealth and power, defying both the timidity and the idealism of the older generation. They have broken up into hundreds of different *tusovki*, a colloquial word that mixes the ideas of 'clique', 'scene' and 'social circle'. In this world, the Wild West mentality of nineteenth-century America mixes with a decadence reminiscent of Berlin between the wars. Only someone from the outside can move easily from group to group, reporting to one what is happening in another. It's a shame that Russians can't do this more easily, because the essential truths about the new Russia lie not in the behaviour or beliefs of any one group, but in the very diversity of visions, opinions and goals now rising from the wreckage of Communism.

Raves, Parties and Nightclubs

We are going to a rave, Kristall II, at the big St Petersburg ice-skating rink. Beforehand, we visit Viktor Frolov, debonair man-about-town, who is loosely connected to the party's organisers. Among those present are a pop singer, a few artists, some models, a film actress and others without clearly defined jobs. The women are all attractive and wearing Western-type make-up and retro-chic clothes. The men have leather jackets. Frolov is an eminently courteous host. Everyone must have several drinks and get high before we go: hashish, now available only for hard currency, is expensive, but whereas it used to be difficult to procure, it is today always available to anyone with money. Some take magic mushrooms, easily found in the woods around Petersburg. Some do cocaine to prepare for the long night. Earlier this year, customs officers seized a shipment of the drug that had arrived in Petersburg disguised as detergent. Television news showed officials confiscating this cargo; three days later, every dealer had it in bulk.

At around 2:00 a.m. we drive to the rink. About two thousand five hundred people are there. There is live music by a visiting Dutch band and relentless, recorded techno music, and an elaborate laser show. Half of the rink has been boarded over to make a dance floor. On the other half, people are skating. In the grandstands, people smoke more hash or pass out on the seats. From the bar in the corner, people buy big cups of vodka. We are on the wrong side of the Neva, and at night the drawbridges go up; we will not be able to get home until they go down again at 6:00 a.m. Everyone agrees that raves are no longer 'in' – no trend can last more than a year – but members of every fashionable *tusovka* have nonetheless come this evening. 'The craze is over,' explains Georgi Guryanov, a painter. 'But there's nothing else to do.'

The mafia contingent makes up 10 to 20 per cent of the crowd. Everyone knows who the mafia people are. They will get a share of the profits from this party; every club or bar or party in Russia pays the mafia between 20 and 60 per cent of its revenue. 'In your country, you have taxes,' someone explains. 'And we have this system.'

The rave scene in Russia began with the First Gagarin party on 14 December 1991, organised by Yevgeny Birman and Aleksei Haas. Held at the Cosmos Pavilion at VDNKh, the ultimate Stalinist temple to the socialist state, it attracted more than four thousand people. 'The First Gagarin was amasing because everyone was so hungry for it,' explains Birman, who has since organised other major parties. 'We're trying to mix the semiotic in this postmodern world and bring these different *tusovki* together. It's about autoeroticism and an absolute beauty code, which we never had in the Soviet period.'

Birman is boyish, exuberant and fun; Haas has a cosmopolitan professionalism and a hard self-assurance. I chat with him in his Moscow apartment near Red Square while his American wife prepares dinner. 'The First Gagarin's budget was twelve thousand dollars,' he explains. 'We had to pay for security, music, DJs, rent, firemen. We gave the mafia twenty per cent' – a low figure, achieved by sharp negotiations – 'and we didn't make a profit. But I proved to myself that these people did exist in Moscow. I went out in my car in the weeks before the party, and when I saw the right kind of people, I gave them invitations. I invited a thousand friends for free. We ran TV ads on the day of the party; they were in English, to select the audience.' The First Gagarin was unlike anything ever before seen in Moscow: lasers bounced off the rich architecture and Western DJs played the latest music.

Haas plans to open a club in the autumn. 'You come in from the provinces to Moscow,' he explains. 'You're ambitious; you're young. What do you see? Success is in the hands of these big mafiosi driving expensive cars, with pretty girls around them. It's dark energy, evil. I want to start a club for light energy, a place for clean people with good bodies and smart minds. You can't win people over to light energy by being a hippie: I want a club for ambitious people with success written all over them. I'm not going to have alcohol there: it makes people retreat into the fog, and our lives are foggy enough. I'm going to have the best sound system and the best music and amasing DJs. And the price will be really low. That's democracy: it's for everyone, for the new Russia.'

I want to see the clubs of Moscow. I mention five names to Vladik Mamyshev-Monroe, a Marilyn impersonator and hero of Russian pirate television. 'Mafia, prostitutes, a few businessmen,' he says. I ask about Diskoteka Lise, the biggest in Moscow. 'Oh, no,' he says. 'Even in America you must have these places, full of heavy, middle-aged Georgian women with bleached hair, blue eyeshadow, and Lurex tank tops, shimmying out of time to old Debbie Harry songs.'

After trying a few dreadful places – at one, three bananas and three drinks cost $95 – I am in despair.

But in mid-April, I go to the painter Sveta Vickers's new, low-budget club in the Hermitage Theatre, where I find members of the artistic-bohemian *tusovka*, with people from television, some actors, painters, conceptualists and intellectuals. A big room in front has tables and chairs where people can drink and talk; the dance floor is in the theatre itself. I run into more than a hundred people I know within my first half-hour at Sveta's; there are no strangers here. 'I would be happy to come every night,' says Tanya Didenko, a musicologist and host of the voguish late-night television music-talk show *Silence Number Nine*. Arisha Grantseva, an artist, is holding court at a table in the corner. Painters come by to say hello, and MC Pavlov, a rapper, drums out time on the back of his chair. I meet a Bulgarian-Swiss performance artist and a Greek architect. I even spot Aleksei Haas on the far side of the room. The club has never advertised; everyone knows of it by word of mouth.

Sveta, at the centre of it all, laughs. 'You know,' she says, 'I have two big advantages over these other people who are running clubs. In the first place, none of them is Jewish! And in the second place, none of them is a mother!'

The pleasure of Sveta's club lies in something Russian that I have never encountered in a club in the West. It lies in visionary, exuberant love, which you feel all over the place, as tangible as the decoration or the music. 'We know how to enjoy,' a young painter says to me. 'We grew up with the image of our parents suffering together. The legacy of that communal pain of the bohemian world is strong in us, and it makes our joy palpable.'

I go with some friends to visit Petlyura for the first time. Near Pushkinskaya, on Petrovsky Boulevard, we come to what appears to be a construction site. One of our party heaves a shoulder against a hidden door, and we enter a large courtyard, dominated by a thirty-foot-high copy of Vladimir Tatlin's Constructivist *Monument to the Third International*. 'This is it,' someone whispers to me. This building, once the home of a nobleman, later divided into communal apartments, is now Petlyura's squat. It is a fine example of Russian nineteenth-century architecture, a pale yellow neoclassical building, appallingly decrepit.

We go into an entryway and down a hallway painted in black with silver graffiti. We knock on a door. It flies open at once, and from within come the sounds of Tibetan monks chanting, and a heavy smell, sweet and acid, of decay and vodka and ethyl spirits. We can see six people sitting around a table and drinking. 'We've come to see Petlyura,' we say.

One of the group, the performance artist Garik Vinogradov, agrees to show the way. We walk through a large dance hall, now empty, to a bar. The walls are covered with a giant collage that includes old Soviet models, Barbara Bush, men in trench coats smoking obscure brands of cigarettes, Audrey Hepburn and the Sistine Madonna. At one end, a blackboard announces prices. Along the walls, instead of banquettes, are broken television sets and small tables. Lounging on one of the televisions is a man about five feet tall, with a Leninish goatee, wearing bright red trousers and a big, shapeless crimson jacket; gathered around him is a hotchpotch of young men and women.

'Come in, sit down,' Petlyura says.

Petlyura's place has become a haven for lost souls. People who have run away from home, have had problems with drugs, are wandering in this new post-glasnost world with no sense of direction, come to Petlyura's and find a community and a way of life. 'Everyone carries on about glasnost,' says Petlyura disdainfully. 'So before we were slaves to the Communists and the KGB. And now to the democrats and capitalists. It's still a hollow sham. My place is an escape from all that.'

Thirty-four people are currently living in Petlyura's place. He was brought up in an orphanage, and this background has served him well: everyone has assigned duties on rotating schedules. The residents must do their share of scrubbing and cooking and serving. 'It's like the military,' Moscow critics say. 'More like a kibbutz,' replies Petlyura. Who can stay and for how long is decided by Petlyura alone. 'They are all my rules,' he says, 'and whoever doesn't like them is free to go elsewhere.' The stalwart of his house is an ethnically Polish woman dwarf of about sixty-five called Pani Bronya, who is always in evidence; her husband, who believes that he is Lenin, stands guard outside.

The second time I go to Petlyura's, Lenin is wandering around the courtyard in uniform. Inside, people are gathering: about a dozen are drinking at the bar. A room next door has been transformed into a 'boutique', and racks of old Soviet clothes are for sale at low prices. The people pouring into the shop are dressed in thrift-shop chic and have a slightly punky manner.

I go to Vinogradov's part of the squat, where I listen to 'experimental' music with a lot of chanting, some black light and incense. Then I go see an exhibition of work by one of the squat's residents who has done a series of paintings called *Untold Fairy Tales*, which show zebras and giraffes floating on icebergs in an arctic landscape. 'I'd never really thought about art,' she says, 'until I came here about two months ago.'

Petlyura's is the best and most interesting of the various squats with *tusovki* and bars and dance halls – but there are many of them in town. Every Wednesday, the Third Path, on the far side of the river, has dancing; I try to go one evening, but am told that it's closed for a few weeks because 'the violence has been getting out of hand'. Violence? 'Mafia hooligans,' the man at the door tells me. I look around at the destruction. 'There's nothing to steal here,' he says. 'We have nothing.' And he closes the door.

The Life of the Mind

Everyone in Russia seems to be starting a magazine. Of the literally thousands of new magazines, mostly made with photocopiers (access to which was restricted under Communism), some are commercial, but most are not. They are about a particular subject – microbiology, business advice, fashion, the arts. Most have a circulation of between fifty and five hundred.

Perhaps the most impressive at the moment is *Kabinet*, the brainchild of a group of Petersburg intellectuals. Each quarterly issue contains several hundred pages of dense philosophical text, translations of Western criticism, satirical essays, and sharp cultural commentary; each is designed by a different Petersburg artist.

I attend a staff meeting of the magazine, held in the Arabian salon of an eighteenth-century palace, where the artist Timur Novikov currently has an exhibition of textile pieces. The lights are low, and Eastern music plays in the background. The editors of *Kabinet* – Viktor Mazin and Olesya Turkina – read aloud a brilliantly provocative dialogue 'in the style of Plato' about Timur's work. The company of twenty-five includes Timur; Irina Kuksinaite, artist, actress, and *Vogue* model, who has just opened an exhibition in a palace nearby; Georgi Guryanov, painter; Yevgeny Birman, organiser of raves, and other intellectual-social trendies.

After the reading, the company smokes hash and drinks Crimean sherry while debating the merits of Mazin's translation of Paul de Man on the Hegelian sublime. Mazin explains to me that he has translated several books of critical theory recently, without thought of publication, because he wants to share them with his friends. Irina Kuksinaite talks about the semiotic distinctions between the German concept of fatherland and the Russian concept of motherland. Others ask me about Lacanian revisionism in America and discuss the validity of the Stalinist apologist Maurice Merleau-Ponty, whom they are translating for the next issue. Then we get onto the subject of the rave that night, who will go, what to wear, and what the music is going to be.

In Moscow, at the end of a dinner party, a young philologist recites Greek futurist poems of the thirties. Another guest responds with Mayakovsky. I say that this is unusual dinner-party behaviour by American standards. 'But how, then, do you sustain an oral poetic tradition?' an architect asks softly.

Rock, Pop and Rap

Throughout the seventies and the early eighties, the lyrics to songs by Akvarium, Kino or Boris Grebenshchikov gave information about a better way of life to Soviet people. Rock music was heroic, the performers closely tied to the intelligentsia. Pop musicians represented official culture; their music was often on the radio, but their popularity was suspect and usually artificial.

I see Boris Grebenshchikov, who is about to release a new album. His records once sold in the millions; he now expects to sell fifteen or twenty thousand. 'It's time for Russian pop now,' Irina Kuksinaite says, 'because all anyone wants is dollars and muscles.'

In Moscow, I spend an evening with Artyom Troitsky, director of music programming for Russian National Television. 'When I was younger,' he says (he is thirty-eight), 'the situation was incredibly simple. They were black and we were white. We stood for vitality and goodness in a society that was flaccid and evil. Young people choose the simplest thing. For us, the simplest thing was to be moral; today, the simplest thing is to live well. In my day, you were marginal because the system gave you no other options, and you expressed your politics with rock. Now, if you want to be in politics, no one is stopping you. It's not forbidden; it's just sickening. But you can't very well sing about that.'

His comments help to explain the vapidity of the new Russian pop. One of this year's most popular songs goes, 'You are a stewardess named Zhanna. You are adorable and wantable. You are my favourite stewardess.' Bogdan Titomir – male sex symbol of Russia, hero of teenyboppers – has a video that features a chorus line of Russian boys dressed in American football uniforms and helmets trying to dance like Michael Jackson. The Russian record industry has been destroyed by economic liberalisation; only the lucky few can afford records, and the profits for singers such as Titomir come from endless concert tours.

The managers for the big pop stars are all tied to the mafia. 'I get bribes pushed at me all the time,' says Troitsky. 'People offer hundreds of dollars to get a video shown once. The man with my job at one of the commercial channels got murdered a few weeks ago. I don't take bribes – it's part of my old-fashioned heroic mentality – so I've only had my life threatened once. The managers drop like flies.'

I have dinner with the rapper MC Pavlov, whom I remember from his days in the rock band Zvuki Mu. Pavlov keeps out of the serious pop scene, but his new band is making videos, and his records are out; his concerts are increasingly popular, and even Titomir has admitted that Pavlov is the only true rap artist in the country. 'I wouldn't mind becoming nationally famous,' he says, 'but I don't want to get into crime. Corporate sponsorship would be good.' Pavlov is for the cultural elite, the supercool; he played at the First Gagarin party.

'Heroic Russian rock,' Pavlov says, 'wasn't for dancing. We wanted to bring some fun into this country. We do some rap and some house and some RnB and some jazz.' MC Pavlov is part of an amalgamated Russian music based on Western ideas, yet unlike anything heard in the West. He is tall with blue eyes and a shaved head, and he is wearing a little square hat and loose-fitting rapper clothes, a few rings, and a few ethnic necklaces. 'We're not from the 'hood. We know that. We're not interested in being political like American rap or Russian rock; we don't want to sing about the unavailability of sausages in the shops. We rap mostly in English because rap in Russian sounds stupid. I kind of make up a language, English words and Russian grammar.'

Pavlov's music is danceable, with strong rhythms and good mixes. He has a kind of plausible funkiness that is not often found in Russia. 'I guess if we have some concerns to get across, they're spiritual rather than political. We're vegetarian, antiviolence, antidrugs, antidrink, into pure souls. We follow the teachings of Buddha. People from the West worry about Russian politics, but we're not up to that yet. First teach the people to be human, then maybe you can start on politics.'

The next night, I have dinner with the Moscow painter Sergei Volkov. 'To see these young people trying to imitate American rappers,' he says, 'is as incredible to me as it would be to you if you went up to Harlem one day and found everyone there dressed as Ukrainian dancers and strumming on balalaikas.'

The Gay Nineties

Gay life in Russia is somewhat better than it was. Even without anti-sodomy laws, 'only those creepy activists actually go and talk about their sexuality all over the place', a gay friend says. 'And they do it only for the attention they get from the West; activism occurs here because Westerners put Russians up to it.'

This seems to be the general view. Even celebrities who are

obviously gay do not admit it in public contexts. The Petersburg artist Timur Novikov has worked on gay subjects for years. Privately, he says that part of the pleasure of homosexuality is its secrecy; interviewed on television, he denies any suggestion that he might be gay. Sergei Penkin, a pop singer who is sometimes called the Russian Boy George, has performed often in Moscow's one gay club; but he, too, on television, says he is straight.

'I don't want to be part of a subculture,' says Valera Katsuba, a St Petersburg artist and photographer. 'I know that's the fashion in the West, but though I may choose to sleep mostly with gay men, that doesn't mean I want to socialise primarily with them.'

This year, James Baldwin's *Giovanni's Room* was published in Russia. The film *Longtime Companion* was shown on television, paid for by a private sponsor. 'I was visiting my family in the small town in Belarus where I grew up,' says Katsuba. 'And we were watching television, and suddenly this film came on. "Look," my mother said, "it's about homosexuals." I was surprised she even knew the word. I asked her what she thought, and she said, "If they're happy, it's all right with me." Ten years ago, no one would have said that.'

Most people here, some straight and gay friends agree, have bigger questions on their minds. 'They wonder if the Russian Federation is about to fall apart,' one offered. 'Or whether the mafia is running the whole country,' said another. 'They fear they will not be able to pay for food next month,' added a straight man. 'Whether other men are sleeping with men – really, no one could care less.'

I spend an afternoon with Kevin Gardner, an American AIDS activist in Moscow. 'There are many gay groups,' he says, 'a special body of gay hearing-impaired, several gay dating services, lots of gay newspapers. You see gay personal ads even in mainstream newspapers. There's a gay theatre group, and there's something called the Rainbow Foundation for the Social Rehabilitation of Gays and Lesbians. Pamyat' – a neofascist group – 'is still very anti-gay, but the tide is definitely towards liberalisation, at least in the big cities. And gays do come flooding into Moscow. But there's still a lot of self-hatred, depression and suicide.'

A friend says, 'I get my sense of community elsewhere. Russians are very romantic people, but we're not really very sexual. Intolerance drives people to suicide, but tolerance isn't going to draw us into this Western fantasy of gay subculture and lifestyle.'

Keeping the Faith

I go to church in St Petersburg, to Izmailovsky Cathedral, which was used as a silo by the Soviet government. It has been cleaned and restored, and services take place there again. The congregation includes a small grouping of young people. 'I come for aesthetic reasons,' one tells me. 'I think our Orthodox religion is very beautiful, but of course I don't believe in it.'

Others do believe. In Moscow, I spend an afternoon with Masha Ovchinnikova, an artist in her late twenties whose work has great religious meaning. 'The church is my life,' she says. 'The only important thing. Pre-glasnost, you had to suffer to belong to the church; only true believers came. Now people are joining in huge numbers. A few are really inspired with faith, but most come because they mistake the philosophy of the church for ideology. They expected ideology as children, knew it from their parents. But they come without understanding, hoping only to be given absolute diktats. It is the tragedy of our church. These people have confused doctrine with totalitarianism.' Such people have also been the first to be won by the tides of American evangelists who have been sweeping across Russia lately, running large, vulgar advertisements, promising answers to the questions of a sick society.

The Orthodox Church excluded itself from Russian politics and life during the Communist period. 'I was baptised at nineteen,' Ovchinnikova explains. 'I had always seen myself as outside of my society: it was a kind of autism. The people within the church had never adapted themselves to social interaction. The new people who have come to the church are mostly those with no economic satisfaction or pleasure in their private lives. They come to the church because the church does not value these things, without understanding what the church does value.'

Some church members make their religion a cornerstone of right-wing nationalism. 'The church must not involve itself in worldly questions,' says Ovchinnikova. 'It is not a political body.' The church encourages the Russian habit of passivity. 'A good life is a gift from God,' says Ovchinnikova. 'It is folly to reach for this yourself.' The church has also bred intolerance and bigotry. 'You will not be saved,' Ovchinnikova says to me pityingly, 'because you are not part of our church.'

The Young Businessmen

The New Capitalists, the young businessmen, bankers and stock-brokers, are visible everywhere. You see them in suits and ties, with their hair neatly cut, looking respectable but non-bureaucratic. It is a new look in Moscow. Few of these yuppies are involved in production, which is still state-dominated and tangled in bureaucracy. 'We only trade and invest,' says Yaroslav Pachugin, twenty-five, an expert financial adviser at the private, profit-oriented Foundation for the Privatization of State Industry Through International Investment, 'moving what already exists from one set of hands to another.'

He adds, 'I earn much more than my parents. That embarrasses me; they are both accomplished professional people. But members of that generation cannot now learn what is necessary to function in capitalist terms. The basic structures of capitalism are no problem for us. We've all caught on about that.' He pauses. 'What we still don't understand, of course, is democracy.' I talk to Igor Gerasimov, who, at twenty-four, is general director of the Inkomtrust, a division of the vast Inkombank. He is responsible for the investment of private funds, which he places in real estate and foreign currency. 'I usually get money to invest for between one and three months,' he says. 'No one trusts the economy enough to let go of their money for longer. So investment in industry and construction is impossible. Also, our inflation is paralysing.

'What I am doing is important. I have a moral duty to continue as a businessman, to help Russia to grow. I could not now choose another way. Of course, I do this also for myself; I'd like a nice apartment, a dacha, a car, maybe even a Lincoln Town Car. But the more I take for myself, the more I help Russia.'

Russia's Rich Are Different

While these businessmen make up a yuppie class, others form a financial aristocracy, the dollar millionaires, the nouveaux riches. At one end of a continuum lie the pure businesses; towards the middle, businesses dominated by the mafia; further up, mafia activity based on business; and at the far end, pure mafia activity. Many of the very rich are at the mafia end of the spectrum, but not all of them. To succeed at the honest end of the spectrum takes an ability to deal with mafia threats, however, since they cannot be avoided.

I go to see Yuri Begalov, who owns, with two partners, Kvant International, a company whose turnover last year, I am told, was $1 billion. He is thirty; I have heard that he is honest and sophisticated. At his office in Profsoyuznaya, a modest enough location, he is wearing a cashmere blazer, flannel trousers, a Hermès tie, and a Patek Philippe watch. His Porsche is parked outside. Initially, we sit in a cramped Soviet-looking room to talk; then we move down the hall to a conference room, where we sit at a large table laid with crisp linen and set with bone china and heavy silver. The staff serves a five-course lunch of refined Georgian food, complete with various wines. Begalov is Armenian, but grew up in Georgia; he has imported an entire Georgian kitchen, housed in the office complex.

'To start a business in this country, you need connections more than you need anything else,' Begalov says. 'So because my partners were both physicists, we set up a firm to specialise in business uses for scientific research. We went wherever our connections led us; any work was okay if it was profitable.' When the Moscow Exchange opened, Begalov saw that this was the next wave of opportunity, and he immediately took out a bank loan (loans were then very new) and purchased a seat. The Moscow Exchange works according to arcane and bizarre rules. 'It was incredibly high risk,' he says, 'and my only real advantage was that I had taken the time to understand Russian business practise and Russian law, which almost no one else bothered to do.'

A Russian sociologist I know says, 'The opportunities in this country are completely wasted on the Russians.' I will hear this sentiment over and over. Begalov followed the move towards privatisation within Siberia, and when he heard that a commodities exchange would open in Tyumen, he bought a seat. Oil was a vastly inefficient state-run industry: state-run wells passed oil to state-run refineries that sold it to state-run factories. Begalov went to the director of a Moscow factory and got a commission to buy oil, then went to the first day of the exchange and bought the oil offered. The members of the exchange telephoned around town to get more oil, and Begalov bought that oil as well, establishing market control.

Begalov became a dominant force in Siberian oil and helped it enter the world market. Initially, his business was not covered by the tax code, and his activity remained wholly unregulated; business law in Russia is so new, so tangled, and so badly constructed that a clever person can still circumvent it. 'I don't worry about whether I'm doing good for this society,' says Begalov. 'It's been relatively easy for me to be successful in this context. There's surprisingly little competition.'

Aydan Salakhova is owner and director of Aydan Gallery. She is in some ways the best that the new Russia has to offer: intelligent, beautiful, sophisticated, knowledgeable, with good contacts in the East and the West. She is herself a talented painter, and her gallery has a sleek, finished quality unusual in Moscow. She shows many of the city's best artists and sells work to informed Russian and foreign collectors. 'I see myself as helping to educate this population,' she says. 'They have money, but often they have no idea what to do with it. They buy cars. They buy apartments. They have showy parties with Gypsy music. And after that, they need someone to show them what is beautiful, how to live well. It's like in your country, only faster. First you get money, then you want power, then you go for taste. Someone has to bring together our cultural riches with these newly wealthy and empowered people. It's a social responsibility.'

I go to an exhibition, at Moscow's Central House of Artists, of the Rinaco corporate collection. Young bankers and artists pass and nod. 'These people need each other,' says the curator, Olga Sviblova. 'Everyone got money and culture from the Soviet state, a kind of forced diet of culture, but now culture is expensive and desirable; people have to interact with each other to get these things.'

'Yes,' says Sergei Volkov. 'The "sophisticated" businessmen now bring on the artists the way the unsophisticated ones bring on the dancing girls.'

A Life of Crime

You cannot get away from the mafia in Russia. Nothing happens without their knowledge and involvement; they are intimately connected to government, business, the military, even the arts. They are as visible as bureaucrats were in the Soviet system: you see their cars – top Western models without licence plates. Most have a slick but sleazy look that is very much their own. The men have broad shoulders and tend to stand with their legs apart and their necks forward, in a pose Russians call 'the bull'. Their women are usually pretty, expensively dressed and completely silent. The Russian mafia is growing at an incredible rate, and more and more young people are choosing to join. 'It used to be fashionable in Leningrad to have an artist for a boyfriend, or a rock singer or a journalist,' says Irina Kuksinaite. 'Now, the attractive girls want mafia boys.'

One of my mafia contacts, a thirty-two-year-old Muscovite, says, 'You know that in our country the government offers no structure or control. Without these things, a nation falls apart. The mafia is all that's holding this country together. We do provide structure, and when we take over a business, that business works. It's noble work. A young man of ambition, someone who wants to have an effect on this society, he'd have to be a moron to think the way to do it is to join the Parliament. If he's smart, he'll join the mafia.'

My contact is extremely charming and helpful. He explains which ethnic mafias (there are seven major ones) dominate which areas and provides a sort of ideological structure within which to understand all mafia activity. He himself 'takes over' companies, puts money into them, and then puts 'good people' in charge of them. 'Of course we all started off as petty criminals,' he says. 'But with time, you move beyond that. The mafia includes most of the smartest people in the country.' He has become a patron of culture. 'It's sometimes hard to know how to spend all my money. And for me it's a great pleasure to move in different circles. Many mafia people get bored by the company of other mafia people, and to move in different *tusovki* – that's our ideal.' The art people are delighted by this patronage.

'We have a lot of fun in the mafia *tusovka*,' he says, 'and we laugh a lot. When I get in trouble, the family helps; I was in prison in Finland, and they got me out. But it has its downside also.' I later learn that his partner was brutally murdered a few weeks ago because of a difference with another ethnic mafia that began when the partner's wife, rather drunk, made insulting remarks at a restaurant.

Another mafia contact has been close to international drug traffic. He is twenty-five, good-looking, tremendously articulate and entertaining. He is an expert at spending money: he puts together parties, buys art for mafiosi, makes useful introductions. He speaks excellent English and has read a surprising range of books. 'The big guys in the mafia like this about me,' he says. 'A few years ago, when organised crime was just getting into full swing, they were a bunch of coarse vulgarians. But then they saw all these American Hollywood movies about the Italian Mafia. *The Godfather* and so on. And they decided that they liked this idea of being hyper-refined and hyper-polite. Though, of course, there is still that common element, mostly doing the dirty work.'

'Killing people?' I ask.

'You've seen a lot of movies, too. Of course there are hit men around, but it's very much out of fashion in sophisticated circles. The same guys who were killing each other a few years ago are now involved in financial manipulation, which is more pleasant and more profitable, white-collar. The killing part of the game – those people are really very unattractive.'

I go out several times with another contact who is part of the Azerbaijani mafia. On our first such evening, we go to an expensive restaurant in a hotel owned by a well-known Western chain. We sit down at the best table with a few heavies; one of them takes out a lump of hash the size of a baseball and starts to roll joints. I am a bit startled. 'Do you think it's a good idea to smoke hash in the middle of this restaurant?' I ask. 'You know, this is a Western hotel.'

He laughs. 'My friend wondered whether you would mind if we smoked here,' he says to the manager, gesturing languidly at the lump of hash.

'Please,' says the manager, looking rather green. 'Have a nice smoke. You do whatever you like.' He stands smiling meekly at us.

At a party a few days later, one of the young mafiosi offers to introduce me to his boss, a plump man with blond hair and a scruffy beard. We have a nice chat about cars. He hopes that what I have been learning is interesting. 'Our mafia is the best,' he says.

'And what do you actually do?' I ask brightly.

His eyes narrow. 'You know, you seem like a very nice guy, and I know about your project here, and if some guys want to talk to you, that's up to them. But I think you should be careful. I would really hate for something unpleasant to happen to you.' He smiles meaningfully.

I have recently heard talk of a Latvian journalist who was researching a story on the mafia when he disappeared; he turned up dead in an alley with seven bullets through his body. This image has not been comforting.

'Now I have a question for you. And I hope you know the right answer.' The boss lowers his voice conspiratorially. 'I have a problem with which someone from the West should be able to help me.' I am overcome with dread; this is how one gets sucked into crime. 'I have terrible trouble with dandruff,' he says, 'and I wanted to know whether Head & Shoulders shampoo from America really works or whether you can send me something else from your country?'

Shortly before I leave Moscow, I have dinner with him. He has decided that I am okay in the wake of my shampoo tips. We discuss politics, restaurants, fashion. 'You've had a good trip here?' he asks. I have. 'You have some problems with people in Moscow?'

'Nothing worth mentioning.'

'You know,' he says with a big smile, 'a hit man in our country costs just twenty dollars. I can arrange this for you if you want.'

I assure him that I do not need such services.

'Well' – he gives me his card – 'here are my numbers. If you have problems in America, you can also call me. A hit man for New York is twenty dollars, plus airfare, plus one night hotel fee.'

The Politics of Change?

The rigidly hierarchical Communist system meant that important positions in Soviet politics could be occupied only by people of advanced years. Younger politicians, whatever their ambitions, operated in the meek language of the bureaucracy, avoiding transgressions, exercising what little power they had in terms dictated by their superiors.

The idea that members of the younger generation can hold mean-ingful positions in Russian politics is still novel. 'Even the strong democrats who say they want change,' says Romuald Krylov, thirty, chief of the department of art and culture for the central district of Moscow, 'are uneasy seeing me in a senior bureaucratic position. They would prefer to find a sixty-year-old man with no interest in art and culture. It's what they're used to.'

That is a hundred times more the convention in national govern-ment. Yegor Gaidar's brief tenure as prime minister demonstrated to the people of Russia that new policies might come from young people. Gaidar's politics were deliberately shocking; the younger generation in Russian politics show tremendous variety in their language and their policies, but they seem to be tired of the idea of utopia. In the West, younger politicians talk of radicalism while older ones are conciliatory; in Russia it is quite the reverse. What is both comical and disturbing, however, is that this move towards moderation seems to come not from a spirit of cooperation, but from a general understanding that the rhetoric of compromise will be the best line to power.

It is impossible to pinpoint the individuals who will be in power in three years' time, but it is possible to look at the character of this generation as a whole, to try to understand what kind of younger people have chosen to enter the political fray, and how, and why. Perhaps twenty-five men under age forty are helping to define the younger voice in Russian politics, and several hundred others follow in their footsteps. The range of their sentiments and abilities can perhaps be grasped by looking closely at three: Andrei L. Golovin, people's deputy and chairman of the Faction Smena–New Politics; Aleksandr A. Kiselev, president of the executive committee of the Russian Movement for Democratic Reform, and Sergei B. Stankevich, counsellor to the president of Russia on political affairs.

Andrei Golovin holds to what he calls a centrist line. Russian politics tends to function in extremist terms, and I am intrigued by the idea of a centrist party. 'Those who call themselves democrats,' he says, 'are radicals, left-wing radicals. Your government supports them because you think that if you don't, the right will take over. But we are really closer to you and to your national interests than are those radicals. When Clinton was elected, I assumed he would see this and understand it; it's so disappointing to us that he continues the paranoiac foreign policies of President Bush. Doesn't he see that Russian, American, and international interests all lie with the centre, with something mediated and controlled? The danger does not come from the red or the blue, but from the fact of extremes locked in battle.'

Golovin, in his mid-thirties, has an arrogance that sometimes borders on condescension, but his arguments are compelling. Five years ago he was a physicist at a research institute. With perestroika, he moved towards government service. He sketches out military, economic and civil policy; his centrism reminds me more of Swedish socialism than of anything else. 'You talk in your country about a stable government that represents the middle class,' he says. 'We at Smena are the government of the middle class.'

I ask, 'But is there really a Russian middle class? Do people in this country want compromise? Who are your constituents?'

'If we were in power, there would be a middle class, and they would want compromise. If we come to power, we'll have support everywhere. And we'll get rid of most of these ruinous economic reforms, to permit the re-emergence of a middle class.'

I point out that within democratic systems this is not the usual sequence of events, that you are supposed to have support before you get elected.

'Well,' he says, 'there is no freedom of the press in this country. The left-wing press is underwritten by our government; and so is the right-wing press, because fear of the right wing drives support to the left. We don't get that kind of media play. It's hard to do dramatic PR for a centrist position; it's not eye-catching. The radicals, Communists and fascists used to be in the same party, and they all have a Bolshevik mentality. We're clean. We were never part of the Soviet bureaucracy. I'm frightened by the movement here towards a sort of Latin American situation, in which power comes from the mob and the government is beholden to illicit special interests.'

Then his expression softens. 'This is a great civilisation.' He gestures out the window. 'We can interact in a civilised fashion. Why should people vote for us? Because we're intelligent and honourable. Print my photo and my biography next to Yeltsin's photo and his biography, and ask yourself who has led a good life, with a commitment to public service, and who is an old Communist, steeped in misguided ideology and corruption? We want to establish reasonable laws. In fifteen years, when I am president, Bolshevism, extremism, will be dead.'

Golovin is eloquent and moving, but he evinces a curious disdain for the realities of his own country. He seems not to understand that you cannot impose civility on an entire society. He talks a lot about pragmatism replacing ideology, but fails to recognise the essential ideological basis for his pragmatism, which was designed to create a pragmatic society where one does not now exist. 'It will take a long time to de-ideologise this society,' he says, apparently unaware that a programme to de-ideologise a society is finally very ideological.

With Golovin's description of the 'radicals' as 'Bolsheviks' ringing in my ears, I go to see Aleksandr A. Kiselev, whose ardent belief in democracy is unaffected. But if Kiselev had been active thirty years ago, he would, unquestionably, have defended the cause of Communism with equal conviction; indeed, he was a big wheel in the Komsomol (the youth organisation of the Communist Party) when he was an adolescent in Volgograd, and the Communist Party was still the Communist Party. When we meet, Kiselev is wearing a powder-blue suit that, eleven sizes larger, might have belonged to Brezhnev; he looks like 'a typical bureaucrat'. He continually answers concrete questions by saying, 'We must have democracy in order for the people to be strong' or 'We must ask the people in what kind of state they wish to live and build accordingly.'

The Movement for Democratic Reform, which he leads, is the remains of the political machine that propelled Yeltsin into power, and it is as close to a political party as anything gets right now in Russia. Kiselev's answers to my questions, especially after Golovin's passionate clarity, feel inauthentic and banal. He batters me with statistics. I ask him whether the majority of the Russian people want democracy at all, of any kind, and he looks puzzled and plunges into the details of last week's parliamentary debate. He has no impulse towards abstract thinking or large enquiries.

Kiselev is one of the advocates of a new constitution; in fact, a new constitution is really his movement's raison d'être. 'We will impose this democratic constitution on the Parliament and on the people,' says Kiselev. 'And then Yeltsin will explain it to the people, and when they hear him explain it, they will understand that it is good.' I comment that this agenda does not accord with existing laws. 'Well,' says Kiselev, 'criticise Yeltsin for breaking the laws if you want, but in fact everyone breaks them. The current constitution is so bad that most people don't bother with it.'

I spend the afternoon with Sergei B. Stankevich, Yeltsin's counsellor on political affairs. Russian politics is unpredictable, but character is distinctive; of these three men, this is the only one who could run a country. He is at the moment unpopular and has severed his ties to various movements that might have helped him to greater success, but unpopular in Russia can turn to popular in hours, and Stankevich has had moments of great popularity. He has recently distanced himself from Yeltsin, though he has kept his Kremlin office and official position. In the past, when Yeltsin has acted strangely and unpredictably, Stankevich has been the one to explain.

Stankevich has neither Golovin's pragmatic idealism nor his pristine record, and he is not free of Communist-type language. He has often been accused of dirty politics and was at the centre of a small scandal last year when a great deal of government money went to an almost non-existent music festival. He is said to have used his influence to get apartments for family members and to arrange other special favours. 'You're seeing Stankevich?' asked a friend from the old underground. 'Make sure you take a bath afterwards.' But Stankevich has a quality of immense competence; sitting in his large Kremlin office, one is lulled into a sense that politics is straightforward. He pursues his political vision with the clear knowledge that his kind of democracy will benefit not only Russia, but also himself.

'The reforms in this country have come in waves,' he says. 'The first was Gorbachev's wave, which began in 1985, peaked with perestroika, and began its downward turn with the election of Boris Yeltsin as president of the Russian Federation. The goals of this first wave were to introduce controlled elections and controlled free speech while preserving the system and retaining Communist Party control. These goals were accomplished. But the leaders of the first wave failed to introduce a new political or intellectual paradigm, and so they had to fall.

'The second wave was Yeltsin's wave, which included such men as Andrei Sakharov, and the goal was to remove Communist ideology from its predominance and to establish basic freedoms: free speech, a free press and a parliamentary system. These goals were accomplished. This wave peaked during the coup in 1991. In 1992, the second wave broke when state control was in large part lifted from the economy. The second wave failed to invent a new Russia, to balance this country's racial, ethnic and religious mix, to achieve the crucial joint goals of being market-oriented and socially responsible. The second wave has been heading downward for a year and a half.

'Now it's time for the third wave, the base for which is already in place. It will begin in earnest with the elections and with the adoption of constitutional reform. The first goal of the third wave will be to establish a constitution and system of rule that allow for cooperation rather than competition among the branches of government. We will create a representative government, so that the republics now acting semi-autonomously will feel that their representatives are involved in establishing national laws and that they are therefore bound by those laws. We will remain socially responsible, but we will take reasonable steps towards economic reform. I think we will accomplish these goals with moderate, conciliatory behaviour, to create a single, strong, united Russia. We have passed the time when you can rule this country by standing on top of a tank.'

This seems a surprising line from someone who is still a presidential adviser – Yeltsin is the one who stood on top of a tank – and I press Stankevich on it. He implies that Yeltsin is undependable, a people's hero but not a professional. 'Yeltsin could conceivably be at the helm for the third wave if he accepts its conditions,' Stankevich says. 'But the third wave must belong in large part to my generation.' The new Russian politics is younger politics. Unlike many younger politicians, however, Stankevich has built his career slowly. He was a great favourite of Gorbachev's and later headed the strategic staff for Yeltsin's political campaigns. When the coup was declared, he flew home from a holiday, went to the Russian White House, and stayed with Yeltsin for all three days.

At the moment Stankevich is veering towards the right-wing Russian Patriotic movement, which is perhaps foolish; he has a non-Russian last name and an extremely intellectual delivery, which will not go down well there. 'He's always been the dark horse,' one Moscow political columnist says to me. 'It's impossible to know exactly how much power he's wielding behind the scenes.' Stankevich says, 'There is not at this moment a single democratic thing in Russia. Nor can there be until the third wave comes in, and constitutional reform is enacted.' What does it mean for a top presidential adviser to the 'democratic' president to speak in this way? 'It's time for the renewal of the political class,' Stankevich continues. The radicals who helped bring down Communism are no longer needed, he explains. 'We're in the most dreadful catch-twenty-two' – it's comical to hear that phrase in a Kremlin office – 'in which the country can function only when we have a new constitution which changes the role and definition of the Parliament; and such a constitution can be passed only by this Parliament, which it will destroy.' So what now? 'Perhaps it will be necessary to proceed outside current laws. Could the leaders of the American Revolution have won by sticking to the laws of the colonies?'

If Golovin had in hand the heartening rhetoric of what is right, then Stankevich has the language of what is necessary. 'How much,' I finally ask him, 'can you change the course of events in Russia, and how much have they taken on a momentum of their own that no elected or appointed official can control?'

'Government in this country,' Stankevich says, 'now and for the foreseeable future – it's without power. All we have is influence. Our goal must be to recognise that, to stop pretending that we have absolute power and to use our influence soundly. And our goal must be to gain power again. We will accomplish that goal.'

In the middle of our conversation, the telephone rings. On a desk in the furthest corner of Stankevich's office is a collection of a dozen telephones of different colours and designs, each connected to a different line. Stankevich walks across the room to answer one of the phones and speaks in his same voice of calm authority for about five minutes. Step by step, he instructs someone – I think it is a relative – on how to fix his car. Again, he has that lulling tone in his voice. Try this. If it doesn't work, try that. It is the day before a national referendum on Yeltsin's presidency, and Stankevich is not – as are some others in the Kremlin – hysterical. His manner says clearly that what will happen at the polling stations in sixteen hours cannot injure him.

The most important new skill these younger men and women have is adaptability: they figure out how to get for themselves what they want faster and better than anyone else. What they do not have is any framework in which to place themselves or their own successes; nor do they have a clear sense of the responsibilities their success may carry. The Soviet Union was dominated by the rhetoric of ideology, until finally ideology itself lost its meaning. When you discuss democracy with the empowered members of the younger generation, they seem to understand it as a euphemism for capitalism, and capitalism they take to be a system in which everyone grabs for himself whatever will be most useful to him. Fifteen years ago, many of these people might have been battling against an establishment that they would have seen as evil. 'Those heroic days are over,' Artyom Troitsky says to me rather bitterly. 'I wouldn't be living heroically if I were part of today's younger generation.'

I spend my last afternoon in Moscow with Vasily N. Istratsov, director of parliamentary relations for the foreign ministry. A sage man in his mid-thirties, he has been pulled from his position as a professor at Moscow University into this high office. Ironical, witty, charming, he has the bearing more of the worldly diplomats in Tolstoy than of the self-promoting men and women I have met. He and I talk about the politicians I have interviewed, many of whom he knows. 'You know,' he says, 'the traditional structure of Russian politics is like a football match. Everyone is on one of two teams, and they are interested in winning by attacking each other. The only thing that changes is the subject of division: this week, pro-Yeltsin is facing anti-Yeltsin, but last week it was something else, and next week it will be something else again. I am a civil servant, a close-up spectator at the match. I watch as the sides align and realign themselves, as the teams re-form, the way they've been re-forming in this country for years. These members of the younger generation, the people you've been talking to – they're not spectators. They're out on the field, playing the game. But they don't have on uniforms. You ask yourself, "Are they with black or with white?" And very soon you understand that they are playing not on the side of black, not on the side of white, but on the side of the ball.'

The real source of the chaos of the new Russia is not the weakness of the police, the dominance of the mafia, the difficulty of constitutional reform, the undependability of Yeltsin, the spiralling inflation, the naïve policies of Western governments in their distribution of aid, the shortage of food or the inefficiency of state-run factories. The problem is the ascendancy, in a society in which everyone was once asked to work for the common good, of a system of values within which everyone has an eye only on his own progress. It inheres in the impossibility of coherence in a country now run on the chance alignments and misalignments of hundreds of thousands of different, singular, individual agendas.

Timur Novikov died of AIDS at forty-three in 2002; Georgi Guryanov died at fifty-two in July 2013 of AIDS-related liver failure. That same year, Vladik Mamyshev-Monroe drowned at forty-three in a shallow pool in Bali – perhaps because he was too drunk to roll over after he fell, or perhaps, as some have suggested, in a staged murder, since he had been a vocal critic of Vladimir Putin.

Petlyura's attempt to build a 'free academy' came crashing down due to poor organisation, but he gained an international reputation, appearing under the auspices of the avant-garde theatre artist Robert Wilson in the United States. In 2000, Petlyura staged a retrospective exhibition about the disappearance of the socialist dream into the new Russia. Pani Bronya, meanwhile, won the Alternative Miss World title in 1998, while Garik Vinogradov became a target of Moscow's powerful mayor, Yuri Luzhkov, in 2009 after making an anagram of the mayor's name to spell *skilful thief.* Valera Katsuba has developed a following in the West, recently doing a portrait series of fathers and sons. Olga Sviblova has become an international celebrity; one artist recently described her to me as having 'a personality like a propeller – always going'.

Boris Grebenshchikov was featured in *Newsweek* as the 'Soviet Bob Dylan'. After a failed attempt to become a U.S. pop sensation, he has gone home to Russia, where he is now called the 'grandfather of Russian rock'. MC Pavlov is actively mourning the loss of his popularity to a new generation of Western-style rappers. Artyom Troitsky has protested against Putin, citing Article 20 of the Russian constitution, which prohibits censorship. Putin scornfully likened the protest symbol, a white ribbon, to a condom; in 2011, Troitsky dressed as a condom for a protest march, mocking Putin.

Yuri Begalov became a partner in a major minerals and oil industry firm and married, and then divorced, a famous television presenter.

In 2009, Aleksandr Kiselev was appointed head of the Russian postal service. In 2013, he resigned from that position and received a payout of more than 3 million rubles. Sergei Stankevich was charged with graft in 1996 and fled to Poland; he has returned to Russia and is a senior expert with the Anatoly Sobchak Foundation.

Russia has no shortage of defiant decadence. *Pravda*, always a government organ, spews nightclub propaganda: 'According to *Forbes*, Moscow has more billionaires than any other city in the world, so you can imagine the level of opulence you'll be able to experience first-hand in some of the nightclubs. This makes the destination a great place for a guys' getaway or the perfect location for the most epic stag parties.' Disdain for social norms is only strengthened as those norms become more rigid. At twenty-four, Avdotja Alexandrova created a modelling agency called Lumpen, which features women with scratched faces, unkempt hair and puffy eyes, on grounds that an 'emotionally inexpressive face, no matter how regular or symmetrical the features, cannot be beautiful'. Sergey Kostromin, who founded a zine called *Utopia*, said, 'Everyone is in search of their own private utopia: satisfactory emotions that might be faked with the help of consumerist society.' Another zine, *Russia Without Us*, was founded by Andrey Urodov as 'a magazine for teens who miss the times they never had the chance to live in'. It's a nostalgia rag for the Yeltsin days. Asked to characterise the scene, one Moscow food critic said, 'Every Moscow restaurant is a theme restaurant. The theme is that you're not in Moscow.'

Pop music continues to be censored. Andrei Makarevich, called 'the Paul McCartney of Russia', found his concerts closed down after he performed for children in eastern Ukraine. Moscow's best-known rapper, Noize MC, accepted a flag from a fan at a concert in Ukraine. 'I sang in Ukrainian, and someone gave me a Ukrainian flag,' Noize said. 'And in Ukraine, it was totally fine.' Weeks later, his shows started to be cancelled; sometimes, bomb squads showed up claiming fictive dangers. Almost all of his performances during a tour of Siberia were blocked; authorities visited his hotels and physically stopped him from playing at alternative venues.

The anti-gay-propaganda law has resulted in innumerable vigilante attacks on gay people. Groups lure gay men and teenagers by professing to want a date, then beat their victims and force them to perform humiliating acts such as drinking the urine of their assailants. These episodes are recorded and posted; hundreds appeared online in 2015. Many victims sustain bone fractures and facial injuries;

some develop anxiety and depression; others are so frightened that they become homebound. Gay people are assaulted on the streets, on the underground, at nightclubs, or during job interviews. The Russian government has refused to prosecute these acts as hate crimes.

Yelena Klimova has been forced to pay enormous fines for trying to build an online resource for gay teenagers. In the spring of 2015, she published an album called *Beautiful People and What They Say to Me*, in which she shows the profile photos of people who have threatened her on social media. A smiling woman holding a bouquet wrote, 'Go and fucking kill yourself before they come for you'; a man whose winsome profile pic shows him with a baby goat wrote, 'Gunning you down, you little bitch, is just the beginning of what you deserve.' The gay activist and poet Dmitry Kuzmin wrote, 'Russia lacks the concept of respect for another person simply because he or she is another person, a unique, independent individual. It is therefore useless to say here: "I'm gay and I have rights."' Kuzmin said that escalating homophobia makes gay people into unwilling radicals. 'As long as the image of the enemy is being concocted out of gays, I must make all my public statements exclusively as a gay man on the battlefield in this war that has been imposed upon me against my will.'

The countercultural status the Orthodox Church enjoyed in Soviet times (though the church even then was complicit with the KGB) has vanished entirely; it now openly enforces Putin's agenda. In 1991, only a third of Russians described themselves as church members; in 2015, more than three-quarters do. At the same time, nearly a quarter believe that religion does more harm than good, and a third of church members say they do not believe in God. Few attend services. The leader of the church, Patriarch Kirill, described Putin's leadership as 'a miracle' and said of the opposition that 'liberalism will lead to legal collapse and then the Apocalypse'. Patriarch Kirill is rumoured to have a personal fortune of some $4 billion and flaunts a $30,000 watch and a penthouse in Moscow. He rents out the Cathedral of Christ the Saviour for commercial functions.

Putin has been photographed repeatedly with the Night Wolves, an Orthodox biker gang. Ivan Ostrakovsky, the group's leader, said, 'The enemies of Holy Russia are everywhere. We must protect holy places from liberals and their satanic ideology. The police can't cope with the attacks. When I came back from serving in the Chechen War, I found my country full of dirt. Prostitution, drugs, satanists. But now, religion is on the rise.' Another skinhead Orthodox gang severely injured a protester who was marching in opposition to the stiff sentence meted out to Pussy Riot, the radical band arrested for performing an anti-Putin prayer in Moscow's cathedral. 'He insulted our sacred, holy things,' they said.

Georgi Mitrofanov, the sole Russian cleric who has demanded that the church acknowledge its historic relationship with the Soviet authorities, has said, 'We lost so many honest people in the twentieth century that we have created a society where imitation and role play are the norm. Before we had people shouting they were building Communism, but they were just using slogans that gave them opportunities. Now a new lot, and indeed some of the old one, shout about "Holy Russia". The words mean nothing.'

Russia's criminal gangs are involved around the world in extortion, human trafficking, drug smuggling, prostitution, arms trading, kidnapping and cybercrime. Both the English prosecutor leading the inquiry into the murder of whistleblowing FSB officer Alexander Litvinenko in London and Spanish money-laundering investigators have concluded that much Russian organised crime is coordinated from within the Kremlin. The Spanish inquiry alleged that Alexander Bastrykin, head of Russia's Investigative Committee, which oversees major criminal inquiries, and Viktor Ivanov, head of Russia's Federal Narcotics Service, associate with criminals. WikiLeaks cables identify Russia as a 'virtual mafia state' that sustains an assortment of criminal organisations: larger ones such as Solntsevskaya Bratva (estimated annual income: $8.5 billion), Bratskii Krug, Tambovskaya Prestupnaya Grupirovka and the Chechen mafia, as well as innumerable smaller ones. Many are run by college graduates who play the system at the most sophisticated level.

Corruption costs the Russian economy as much as $500 billion each year. Freedom House gave the country a 6.75 rating on a corruption scale on which 7 is the maximum score. Putin has invited criminals who have assets abroad to bring them back; in 2015, he signed a law guaranteeing amnesty for such people, who will be protected from criminal, tax or civil prosecution. Even so, an estimated $150 billion left the country that year. 'We all understand that the assets were earned or acquired in various ways,' said Andrey Makarov, chair of the State Duma's budget committee. 'However, I am confident that we should finally turn the "offshore page" in the history of our economy and country. It is very important and necessary to do this.'

Symbolic shows of legal rectitude are staged for the population. Moscow banned imports of European cheese and other foods in retaliation for sanctions. This boycott has had much less effect on its foreign targets than on the Russian people. To show that Russia follows through, state television featured huge machinery destroying over six hundred tons of contraband food. Such theatre is patriotic, perhaps, but in a country where people are starving to death, many Russians found it ostentatiously cruel.

The economy has become one of the most unequal in the world, with just 110 people holding more than a third of the country's wealth. The poverty rate increased by a third between 2011 and 2015. In the same period, half a million people fled to seek economic opportunity abroad. The Russian economy is afflicted by lack of diversification, over-reliance on oil markets, international sanctions, minimal worker productivity, corruption and the lack of incentive to change. Moscow has sponsored large companies under government control, but not small and medium-size independent enterprises (SMEs). In the E.U., SMEs produce 40 per cent of GDP; in Russia, about 15 per cent. This shift out of private enterprise is not economically promising. Oil and gas account for more than two-thirds of exports, which means that every time oil prices drop by a dollar per barrel, Russia loses $2 billion. Ongoing sanctions will reduce the country's economy by nearly 10 per cent. Russian workers remain singularly inefficient. Ian Bremmer wrote in *Time* that while an American worker contributes $67.40 for each hour worked, a Russian worker contributes only $25.90. However, financial training starts early; at VDNKh, a 'young investor school' teaches financial literacy to children as young as eight.

Though over two-thirds of Russians report being distressed by the country's economic woes, the same number approve of Putin's economic leadership, despite revelations in the Panama Papers that show the extent of his gross corruption. Most Russians get their news from state-owned media, which have portrayed the invasion of Ukraine and other acts as part of a 'Russia vs. the West' scenario. 'Putin knows what his people want to hear,' Bremmer writes. 'It's just not clear if he knows how to fix his flailing economy.'

Politics has grown ever more cynical. In 2014, Max Katz, twenty-seven and a sometime poker champion, was elected to the Moscow District Council. His campaign slogan was 'The Moscow District Council is completely useless. It possesses no power whatsoever.' He claimed that he won because he 'chose to be honest'. At twenty-four, Isabelle Magkoeva is both a boxing champion and an unabashed Communist – a face of the new Russian left who publicly describes Lenin as a 'great revolutionary'. At twenty-nine, Roman Dobrokhotov, whose Twitter bio says, 'Revolution is me', has been arrested well over a hundred times. He sent Edward Snowden a letter explaining that since everyone knows that every conversation in Russia is monitored, he would find nothing to uncover in his new domicile.

Opponents of Putin protested after the elections in 2011 and 2012. They were led by Garry Kasparov, chess champion; Ilya Yashin, activist; Left Front leader Sergei Udaltsov; Alexei Navalny, anti-corruption campaigner, and Boris Nemtsov, member of a regional parliament. In 2015, Navalny and Udaltsov were placed under house arrest. Nemtsov was shot in the back as he crossed a Moscow bridge, hours after he posted a Twitter message asking his followers to protest against Putin's activity in Ukraine.

Georgy Chizhov, of Moscow's Center for Political Technologies, said, 'Russians are now divided between "us" and "national traitors." Liberals cannot protest; they would be going against most of society.' Nikita Denisov, thirty-three, who had been an active protester, said, 'We realised that going on these marches was actually useless, even unfashionable.' Yelena Bobrova, twenty-nine, said, 'We took to the streets thinking that we could make a difference, but only met with indifference from not only those in power, but our friends and relatives, too.' So apathy has become a national pastime.

Their Irony, Humour (and Art) Can Save China

New York Times Magazine, 19 December 1993

It can be hard to remember the presumption common into the 1990s that no art of merit was being made outside the West. After I had written about Russia's new generation, my editors at the *New York Times* asked me what I'd like to do next, and I suggested artists in China without knowing whether there were any. I assumed that if so much was happening in Moscow and St Petersburg, something parallel had to exist in Beijing and Shanghai. Work from the USSR had been incomprehensible to Westerners, but the work in China was inaccessible. Because the only art available for viewing internationally was state sanctioned, most critics presumed that everyone was working to Party decrees. Once I had landed the assignment, I panicked, but bit by bit I found introductions to relevant artists, initially via a German conceptualist I'd met in Moscow. Nowadays, half of modern art seems to hail from the People's Republic, and Western exhibitions of Cai Guo-Qiang and Ai Weiwei have been among the most visited in the world.

I have restored some material excluded from the original published version of this piece.

On 21 August 1993, the *Country Life Plan* exhibition was scheduled to open at the Meishugan (National Art Gallery) in Beijing. Though the paintings were indifferent and had to the ordinary eye no hint of political significance, officials ruled that many failed to show the positive side of life in the People's Republic and were therefore unacceptable: only about 20 per cent of the work was approved to hang. The prime mover behind *Country Life Plan*, the artist Song Shuangsong, was furious that the exhibition had been edited. He told friends that on 25 August he would go to the gallery and cut off his long hair, a symbol of his individualistic way of life.

At noon that day, Song, his friends, a professional barber in a clean white smock, a reporter from Shanxi television and I all gathered in the exhibition room. Solemnly, Song spread newspapers on the gallery floor and placed a chair in the middle of them. Chance visitors to the gallery stopped to watch. We all stood in fascinated silence as Song's hair fell lock by lock to the floor. Song faced first in one direction, then in another, holding a serious expression for a while, then grinning and posing. After twenty minutes or so, Song had the chair taken away, and he lay down, cadaver-like, on the floor. The barber soaped Song's face, produced a straight razor, and began to shave him. When his beard was gone, Song sat up for the final attack on his hair. But just as the barber began to cut again, the director of gallery security came in and saw the crowd and cameras. 'Who is the authority behind this behaviour?' he asked, his face tight with rage.

'This is my exhibition,' Song said, 'and I take full responsibility.'

After a brief exchange of hostilities, the director of gallery security stormed out, only to return with threatening-looking minions. You would have thought, to witness the scene, that Song Shuangsong had been caught holding a bomb rather than succumbing to a haircut and shave. Everyone was thrown out of the room. The doors were secured with heavy chains and padlocks. The exhibition was closed down immediately and permanently. Song was led out roughly between two guards.

One Westerner who strayed into the performance turned to me with a shrug and commented on how sad it was that these attempts to fight openly for democracy in China always failed. He had arrived at the popular Western conclusion that an artist who runs up against the state must be working directly or indirectly towards free elections and a constitution. This logic is grounded in a misreading of China and the Chinese. In this case, it missed the point: the haircut had in fact been entirely successful. The Chinese intelligentsia – including the vanguard 'underground' artists, many of whom are or have been active pro-democracy demonstrators – are united in their firm belief that Western democracy in China would be not only a mistake, but also impossible. The Chinese like China. Though they want Western money, information and power, they do not want Western solutions to Chinese problems, and when they protest for democracy, this is a covert way of pushing towards Chinese solutions. In the East, more than one artist emphasised to me, it is customary to ask for what you do not want in order to get what you do.

The very decision in China to act as an individual is radical. It runs against a five-thousand-year history of which the Chinese are intently aware and immensely proud, a history they frequently revise (sometimes violently) but never abandon. The members of the Chinese artistic avant-garde are individuals every one, but individualism carried too far is in Chinese terms ridiculous; artistry lies not in what the Chinese would deem coarse Western-style self-interest, but in balance. What seems to us to be a disowning of the Chinese tradition of uniformity is really more a means of stepping outside of it so as to prod it to evolve. China, despite its problems and cruelties, is highly functional, and that is much more important to the Chinese, even the Chinese intelligentsia, than any Western notion of democracy. Even iconoclastic artists, horrified by Deng Xiaoping's government though they may be, are by and large surprisingly content with how their system works. The acts of defiance of the Chinese avant-garde function legitimately within their system; they are not designed to be interpreted within ours.

What looks radical often is radical, but not always in the ways you think. In Nanjing dialect, the sounds *i luv yoo* mean 'Would you care for some spiced oil?' 'What the West does, encountering our art,' the artist Ni Haifeng said, 'is to think we're saying we love you, when we're only having a private conversation about cooking.'

Soul of the Avant-Garde

Chinese society is always hierarchical; even the most informal group has a pyramid structure. The 'leader' of the Chinese avant-garde is Li Xianting, called Lao Li (Old Li, a term of deference, respect and affection). 'Sometimes it's easier to say "Lao Li" than "Chinese avant-garde",' the painter Pan Dehai said. 'Both mean the same thing.' Lao Li, forty-six, is a relatively small man with an eccentric beard and a quality of intelligent gentleness and considered kindness that sometimes borders on radiance. He is a scholar, highly literate, who knows the history of Chinese art and is informed about Western art.

Lao Li lives in a small courtyard house, typical of old Beijing; it is the heart of Chinese avant-garde culture. Mornings are off-limits since he sleeps until lunch, but in the afternoon or the evening you can always find artists gathered there, sometimes two or three, often twenty or thirty. Everyone drinks tea; at night, occasionally Chinese schnapps. The conversation can be grandiloquent and idealistic, but more often it is simple and even gossipy: which exhibitions have been good, whether someone is going to leave his wife, a string of new jokes.

Lao Li's house has just three small rooms and, like most courtyard houses, no indoor bathroom and no hot water. But once you have arrived at this cosy, comfortable place and crowded onto the banquettes, you can stay for hours. If the conversation goes late, you can even stay over. Once this summer, a group of us talked until almost 5:00 a.m.; miraculously, there was room for all eight and we were so tired by then that we slept soundly. If there had been twenty of us, there would still have been room. Lao Li's house is like that.

It's hard to explain exactly what Lao Li does. Though he is a fine writer and curator, his main role is to guide artists gently to a language in which they can experience and discuss their own work. Wherever I went in China, we spoke about Lao Li: his recent essays, whether it was right for one man to hold so much power, whether he thinks himself more important than the artists he discovers and documents, what kind of women he likes, whether he has changed since his travel to the West last year. 'The artists bring him their new paintings the way children bring homework to a teacher,' said a member of the Beijing art circle. 'He praises or criticises it and sends them to their next projects.' Artists from every province in China send Lao Li photos of their work, asking for his help. He travels to see them, taking with him books and information. 'It's a kind of agriculture,' he said, 'bringing these materials to the provinces to fertilise the culture.' Wherever he goes he makes slides; his archives document every meaningful artistic effort in modern China. When he finds interesting artists, he invites them to Beijing. Through Lao Li, the art world is kept constantly invigorated with fresh blood.

For all his scholarly accomplishments, Lao Li does not sustain a critic's objective distance, and his detractors fault him for this. His response is always as much empathetic as critical, and his pleasure in work comes largely from his sense of moral purpose. Lao Li devotes himself to encouraging those ways of thinking that empower his society. This agenda is higher than, and different from, the interpretive mission of an art critic.

The artists in his circle define themselves as members of the avant-garde; one gave me a printed calling card with his name and, below, *Avant-Garde Artist*. At first, I found the definition bewildering: many of these artists were not, by Western standards, particularly avant-garde. As I talked to Lao Li, I understood that what was radical in this work was its originality, that anyone who cleaved to a vision of his own and chose to articulate it was at the cutting edge of Chinese society. Lao Li is individuality's greatest champion. The quality of his singular humanism is to make way for freedom of spirit and expression in a society that, through its official strictures and internal social mechanisms, does not allow for original thought.

'Idealism?' Lao Li said at one point. 'I hope that a new art can appear in China and that I can help it. Pre-'89, we thought that with this new art we could change the society and make it free. Now, I think only that it can make the artists free. But for anyone to be free is no small matter.'

Some History

'Chinese art rests on three legs, like a traditional cooking pot,' Lao Li explained. 'One is traditional brush and ink painting. One is realism, a concept imported from the West at the beginning of the twentieth century. One is the international language of contemporary Western art.'

The period from 1919 to 1942 brought general disillusionment with traditional Chinese literati, or scholar-artist, ink painting; when Mao Zedong took power, a heroic style based on the Soviet model became the official language of revolution. Not until 1979 did the Stars group initiate the avant-garde movement. It was part of the Democracy Wall movement, which brought together social, cultural and political impetus for change. 'Every artist is a star,' Ma Desheng, one of the Stars group's founders, has said. 'We called our group Stars to emphasise our individuality. This was directed at the drab uniformity of the Cultural Revolution.' The members of the Stars group, who had never trained at official academies, could not show their work, so in 1979 they hung their paintings on the fence outside the National Art Gallery. When police closed down their open-air exhibition, they demonstrated for individual rights.

In 1977, the art academies, which had been shuttered during the Cultural Revolution, reopened, and young artists began to go through the unspeakably gruelling application process, taking their exams over and over for the few places in the Zhejiang Academy in Hangzhou and the Central Academy in Beijing. Between 1979 and 1989, as the Chinese government was liberalising, exhibitions of Western art appeared at the National Art Gallery, and students would spend days there. In China, even those who railed against society wanted the academic formal training that they felt entitled them to speak and think. The Stars had brought in radicalism of content; now, the '85 New Wave introduced radicalism of form. In 1985, five critics, including Lao Li, privately set up *Fine Arts in China*, a magazine that became a voice for new art movements until it was closed down in 1989. These other critics, who were as important as Lao Li, have since either emigrated or lapsed into relative silence.

Many artists during this time signalled their disdain for social norms by ceasing to cut their hair (a radicalism to which Song's haircut performance alluded). Ignoring the prurient repressiveness of Chinese society, they spoke freely of women, did not conceal the details of their personal lives, told dirty jokes. They sat up at night discussing Western philosophers, artists, poets. Much previously unavailable literature was suddenly published, and they read voraciously. Despite their general looseness, however, most had jobs and were painstaking in the execution of their duties. Art they made for themselves, showed with great difficulty and sold only occasionally to 'international friends' (the phrase, beloved of artists, was Mao's euphemism for foreign sympathisers).

As artists took up arms against their society's values throughout the 1980s, they tended to use Western visual language. Some Western critics, looking at this art, have dismissed it as derivative. But that Western language was powerful in China simply because it had been forbidden; the use of it was calculated and meaningful. The artists of the Chinese avant-garde have no more copied Western styles than Roy Lichtenstein has copied comic books or than Michelangelo copied classical sculpture. The form looks similar; the language is imitative; the meaning is foreign.

The last gasp of the exuberant Chinese art movement came just months before the 4 June massacre in Tiananmen Square. In February 1989, the *China/Avant-Garde* show opened at the National Art Gallery in an atmosphere of naïve ecstasy, its symbol the Chinese road sign for 'No U-turn'. Ten years earlier, the Stars had fought to hang their work outside the gallery, but now the critics of *Fine Arts in China* joined with others to put on a monumental exhibition of the most radical work of all the new artists of the Chinese avant-garde.

Many artists thought this show would give their work the official imprimatur it needed to reach the larger population. At the opening, two artists fired gunshots into their installation. Shocked officials closed the exhibition immediately, leaving the dreams of the avant-garde in ruins. Today, some artists have seen 'confidential' memos in government files that say no measures will be counted too extreme to prevent another event like the '89 show.

The closing of the exhibition paralysed Chinese artists; they were discussing the next step when the 4 June massacre took place. Artists and idealists realised that they had no influence on their country's future. The critic Liao Wen, who is Lao Li's girlfriend, has written, 'Today, surrounded by the ruins of bankrupt idealism, people have finally come to an unavoidable conclusion: extreme resistance proves only just how powerful one's opponent is and how easily one can be hurt. Humour and irony, on the other hand, may be a more effective corrosive agent. Idealism has given way to ironic playfulness since 1989. It is hardly an atmosphere conducive to the serious discussion of art, culture and the human condition. People these days find all that stuff irrelevant.'

Some artists emigrated pre-'89; many others, immediately afterwards. Most of the great figures of the old avant-garde have fled the country. Only one member of the Stars group remains in Beijing. Yet the idea of 'No U-turn' goes on. Dozens go to Lao Li's house every evening without fail.

Purposeful Purposelessness

Lao Li has defined six categories for contemporary Chinese art, some of which are more widely accepted than others. Artists complain that his categories are artificial, but the Chinese impulse to order things remains strong, and it is difficult to know how to begin to approach the variety of Chinese art without categorisation. His taste extends more readily to painting than to performance, conceptual work or installation. Of the categories of painting that he has defined, the two that are most discussed, debated and, in the end, accepted are Cynical Realism and Political Pop.

Cynical Realism is very much a post-'89 style. Its primary exponents, Fang Lijun and Liu Wei, and its other practitioners, including Wang Jinsong and Zhao Bandi (who doesn't like to be called a Cynical Realist), all have high-level academic training and are accomplished in photo-perfect figurative painting. The work, brightly coloured and highly detailed, shows people strangely alienated from one another. Fang Lijun paints men without hair caught in disconnected proximity: one is in the middle of an enormous yawn; one grins at nothing; black-and-white swimmers float in a blank sea. The characters are always idle, sitting or swimming or walking around purposelessly. Using sophisticated composition and exquisite technique, Fang depicts an absence of activity that seems hardly worth depicting. The result is often funny, lyrical and sad, a poignant representation of what he calls 'the absurd, the mundane and the meaningless events of everyday life'.

Liu Wei and Fang Lijun are always grouped together artistically and socially. They went to the same academy and have been friends for years. They have a confrontational air: in Fang Lijun this seems like a front, but in Liu Wei it is an authentic streak of hooliganism. Liu Wei is the son of a high-level general in the Red Army, and he usually paints his parents. In the eyes of most Chinese, highly placed army officials live well and are happy; Liu Wei portrays 'the helplessness and awkwardness of my family and of all Chinese people' in hilarious and grotesque pictures. 'In 1989, I was a student,' he said. 'I joined the democracy movement, like everyone, but didn't have an important part of it. After June fourth, I despaired. Now I have accepted that I cannot change society: I can only portray our situation. Since I cannot exhibit in China, my work cannot be an inspiration here, but painting helps to relieve my own sense of helplessness and awkwardness.'

Wang Jinsong conveys this scathing message with almost plastic smoothness. Zhao Bandi's work is subtle, slightly twisted, a series of meticulous and beautifully coloured monumental images of people imprisoned and alone. The Cynical Realist movement is not entirely cynical; the idealism of these artists lies in their portraying a cynicism their society would deny. These works are like cries for help, but they are also playful and roguish, presenting humour and insight as empowering defences. 'I want my paintings to be like a thunderstorm,' Fang Lijun said, 'to make such a powerful impression when you see them and to leave you wondering afterwards about how and why.'

Political Pop is popular with Westerners. Its leading figure, Wang Guangyi, loves money and his own fame, and his work has reached prices in excess of $20,000. He recently rented a $200 hotel room just 'to feel what it was like to live like an art superstar'. Wang wears dark glasses even when he is inside, has a long ponytail, and is always mentioned by other artists as an exemplar of Western values in China. He is at work on a series called 'The Great Criticism', in which he plays on the comical parallels between the publicity Mao once negotiated for his revolutionary policies and the advertising campaigns of prosperous Western interests. The names Band-Aid or Marlboro or Benetton are placed against idealised young soldiers and farmers wearing Mao caps. 'Post-'89, with people so vulnerable,' he said, 'I worry that commerce will harm their ideas and their ability to have ideas, much as AIDS can destroy people's love relationships or their ability to have love relationships. Of course, I enjoy my own money and fame. I criticise Coke, but drink it every day. These contradictions are not troublesome to Chinese people.'

Yu Youhan, in Shanghai, paints Mao over and over, usually overlaid with garish patterns of flowers taken from the 'peasant art' the Chairman loved. Mao mixes with common people or sits at ease on a folding chair; sometimes his face is clear, but sometimes a flower blocks one of his eyes or his nose. One of Yu's recent paintings is a very pop double portrait: on the left is Chairman Mao, applauding one of his own principles; on the right, Whitney Houston applauds her own music. Both are copied from existing photographs, and the similarity is uncanny.

Individualism by the Numbers

Traditional Chinese painters trained by copying their teachers; originality was reserved for old age, when you might make changes so slight that they were almost imperceptible. The history of traditional Chinese art is rich but slow. The avant-garde goes at breakneck pace.

The artists who engage fully with the question of individuality are perhaps the most interesting in China right now. Paradoxically, the New Analysts Group in Beijing, which includes Wang Luyan, Gu Dexin and Chen Shaoping, has decided, as an experiment, to suppress the individual in art. After the '89 avant-garde show, they adopted a resolution stating that members of the group could not sign their work. Shortly thereafter, they established rules of operation. The artists in the group conceive these rules together, pass them by majority vote, and agree to be bound by them. 'Facing the rules, we are all equal,' Wang Luyan explained to me. 'Since we regard the rules as more important than the artists, we express ourselves in a language of regulations. Symbols and numbers best convey our ideas.'

So the New Analysts Group has made up complex formulae to express its inter-relationship; its members use these to produce graphs and charts. One recent piece begins, 'A1, A2 and A3 are individuals before reaching the set quantity, and also stand for the order of action after reaching the set quantity. A1, A2 and A3 set arbitrarily their respective graph for measuring, i.e., graphs A1, A2 and A3. A1, A2 and A3 share a set quantity, i.e., table A.' This kind of deliberately arcane absolutism becomes a playful critique of the Chinese principle of conformity, delivered always in the most serious possible manner. The work, regulated though it may be, is some of the most original I saw in China. 'Originality is the by-product of our cooperating according to rules on which we have agreed,' Wang Luyan said.

They are an odd triumvirate. Chen Shaoping was sent to the mines during the Cultural Revolution and spent twelve years excavating coal; he is now an art editor for the *China Coal* newspaper. Wang Luyan spent the Cultural Revolution being reeducated as a farmer and is now a designer for the *China Transportation* newspaper. Gu Dexin is younger than the other two; he was a worker in a chemical factory until he decided to become a full-time artist.

Mention Song Shuangsong and his haircut performance and these artists shake their heads. 'Imagine growing long hair,' Gu Dexin says, laughing, 'such that people in the market or at the bus station could tell you were an artist!' Their individuality is infinitely more powerful because it is camouflaged. When a recent Western exhibition that included the work of Gu Dexin ended, the packers confused Gu's work with their own packing material and his piece was accidentally discarded. 'I like for my work to be thrown away,' he said. 'There is so much art in the world to preserve and study, and I don't want to clutter further the history of art.' To this, both others nod: non-individuality here is an almost unconscious impulse, opposite to what Chinese artists see as the appalling self-importance and egotism of Western artists.

Zhang Peili and Geng Jianyi, based in Hangzhou, also play with these questions. Hangzhou is a beautiful city, an ancient capital of China, set beside the famous West Lake. Artists have a more relaxed time there than in Beijing or Shanghai: they are less frequently interrupted by international friends or by local dramas. Most Hangzhou artists are graduates of the Zhejiang Academy, and like Ivy League students who remain in Cambridge or New Haven, they have an ambivalent but affectionate relationship to their old student haunts. In the mode of students, they preserve an emphatic connectedness to abstract principles, but they bring a mature sagacity to these abstractions. They think more than artists elsewhere – and perhaps produce less. When I was in Hangzhou, I lived in the Academy, surrounded by students and student work. When I wanted quiet time to talk to Zhang and Geng, we took a boat for the afternoon and paddled around the West Lake, eating moon cakes and drinking beer and looking at the view of mountains in the distance. In the evenings, we would eat seafood and dumplings at outdoor tables set up in small market streets. Once or twice, we were joined at dinner by the artists' old teachers from the Academy. Hangzhou had an atmosphere of sheer delight in art that was quite different from Beijing or Shanghai.

Before the '89 exhibition, Geng Jianyi sent a questionnaire to a long list of avant-garde artists. It went in official-looking envelopes, with a return address to the National Gallery, and purported to be one of the many bureaucratic papers that are an inescapable part of daily life in China. The first questions were standard – name, date of birth, etc. – but then 'What are your previous exhibitions?' might be followed by 'What kind of food do you like?' or even 'What kind of people do you like?' Some of the recipients understood at once that this was an artist's project and gave creative answers with funny pictures, but others, eternally paranoid in the face of bureaucracy, took it seriously and answered every question. For the '89 exhibition, Geng posted these forms.

Zhang's and Geng's identities were transformed after 4 June. 'Before the massacre, there was so much noise,' Zhang said, 'a deafening roar of protest. Then the tanks came and everyone fell silent. That silence was more terrifying than the tanks.' Zhang and Geng made an enormous painting of a massacre victim and hung it by night on a pedestrian bridge. 'Perhaps if you see someone being killed on the other side of the road,' Zhang said, 'you will run across to stop the murderers, without thinking. It was like that.' Fearful after that, they went into hiding in the countryside, expecting all the time to be imprisoned.

Zhang found himself particularly disgusted by the expressionless manner in which China's leading newscaster described the massacre. He decided that whoever determined what this woman was to say decided the fate of the Chinese people. 'The news was so inescapable and this woman so omnipresent that I became obsessed with her, with how everyone in China understood our government through her. I found a connection to her through a friend of a friend of a friend. I asked her whether she would agree, for a fee, to read aloud from the encyclopedia. I needed to find a completely neutral text, one that was neither on her side nor on mine. She asked a lot of questions through the intermediaries, but I fooled her. I said I would use her reading of the encyclopedia entry on water for an exhibition about water, with displays of flowers. And so this woman, who is almost our government itself, agreed to read the text I had selected. It was an experience of immense power, for me, an unofficial artist who had been in danger of being arrested, to be able to manipulate an official symbol in this way. And it showed a lot about the status of money in our society. I couldn't get over how easy it was: it had never occurred to me that I'd be able to do this so readily.'

True to his word, Zhang mounted the exhibition he had described. To an uninformed observer, it was about water and flowers. But to a canny insider, it was an exhibition about commerce, integrity and the manner in which the powerful can be captured by the powerless. 'Humour and irony must be carefully dosed, so that they are part of the form of a work but do not become its content,' Zhang said. 'I have never lost my independence: I have always stood at a certain distance from the events of China. An artist does not opt for such alienation, but once it has happened, it has happened. You cannot resist it.'

'It is not just that our society does not encourage or support indivi-duality,' Geng said. 'We do not allow for it where it clearly exists.' He teaches painting and design at the Institute of Silk Technology. Last year, he suggested that instead of teaching technique the staff should teach the reasons behind that technique. He was allowed to outline his proposals to the staff of the school, who, having expressed interest in innovation, rejected them on grounds that they were incompatible with established teaching standards.

Geng has a gentle lightness of touch. Zhang Peili is much harder, much tougher. Though his work is also often humourous, it has an edge of brutality. 'There has always been anger in my work,' he said. 'I need to make the work, but it does not relieve my anger. It's not like going to the toilet.' Zhang has worked in video, performance and painting. Before the '89 show, he cut up white plastic medical gloves and sent pieces of them to various artists. Some were caked with red and brown paint. The artists who received pieces of apparently bloodied gloves were horrified and bewildered; more and more of these strange packages began to arrive in their households. Then one day, everyone who had been on Zhang's mailing list received a formal letter, explaining that the gloves had been sent at random and spread like a hepatitis epidemic, and that the whole matter was now over. No further gloves were sent.

During the Hygiene Campaign of 1991, when everyone in China

was instructed on cleanliness, when an absurd and patronising bureaucratic language interfered in the most personal aspect of people's lives, Zhang Peili made his classic video *The Correct Procedure for Washing a Chicken*. The video is two and a half hours long. It is appalling and fascinating to watch the sufferings of the poor chicken as Zhang repeatedly covers it in soap, rinses it down, and lays it out on a board. The chicken goes free at the end, but you cannot help suspecting that it will never again be the same chicken. Zhang's flat delivery masks profound empathy; the ethical rhetoric of these government campaigns is revealed through such work in its hypocrisy, shallowness and cruelty.

The installation artist Ni Haifeng lives (in principle) on a remote island off the coast of southern China, but he is among the most sociable figures of the avant-garde scene and is often in Beijing, Hangzhou or Shanghai. Ni is laid-back and humourous, with a broad-ranging if sometimes unfocused intelligence. He is in some ways the freest spirit of all, making art when and as the mood descends, a gypsy king in the avant-garde. Ni receives a teaching salary at the Zhoushan Normal School, but has been relieved of teaching responsibilities on grounds of being 'too weird'. In 1987, he began to paint on houses, streets, stones and trees; he covered his island with strange marks in chalk, oil paint and dye. He has said that he wished to reduce writing to the 'zero level' where it is without meaning. 'When culture invades private life on a large scale,' he said, 'the individual cannot escape being raped. From this viewpoint, my zero-level writing can be taken as a protest against the act of rape. I also want to warn people of the dangers inherent in cultural rape.'

An Artists' Village

In China, your housing is ordinarily provided by your work unit; if you strike out on your own, you sacrifice many protective services and must find yourself a home, which is both expensive and difficult. Officially, you cannot move without government permission. Many avant-garde artists therefore work at least part-time in official jobs; others manage to live just past the edge of legality.

One place they live is the village commonly called Yuanmingyuan, about forty-five minutes from central Beijing. Built by local farmers in the late 1980s, it has dirt roads and a traditional layout: rows of one-storey houses, each with a small courtyard and a tiled roof. There is one toilet shed and one telephone for everyone. Vines grow on some of the houses, and screen doors are always slamming. Nearby are farms and a park. In one direction lie the vast grounds of Beijing University and, in the other, the Summer Palace itself. The first artists here thought it close enough to central Beijing, but sufficiently removed so that they could live in relative peace. Many others soon joined them.

The village is a mecca for Western tourists and journalists. Articles in dozens of countries have described the village as the centre of the Chinese art scene because its blend of freedom and accessibility makes it look like a centre to a Western sensibility. The Chinese are not an immediately open people: many artists of the avant-garde are secretive, elliptical to the point of obscurity and emotionally inaccessible. In contrast, the village artists are easygoing with a casual professionalism in presenting their work. You can wander along knocking on doors and various locals will volunteer to be your guide. The traffic has become so intense that some artists say they have no time to work any more.

With a few notable exceptions – particularly Fang Lijun and Yue Minjun – artists in the village are not particularly distinguished. Many imitate one another, unimaginatively combining Cynical Realism and Political Pop. Most of these artists are only a half step away from jade carvers or other practitioners of cottage-industry handicrafts for foreign consumption. Certainly it is the steady influx of Western money and Western interest that allows the artists to live like this. Mostly, their work is not sophisticated enough to have political meaning, but if they cannot always comment persuasively on freedom, they can live unconstrained personal lives.

'We're part of the post-'89 phenomenon,' the painter Yue Minjun said to me. 'Before '89, there was hope: political hope, economic hope, all very exciting.' Yang Shaobin, another painter, picked up the thread: 'Now there's no hope. We've become artists to keep busy.' Talking to them, you feel that this rhetoric, too, sells well. Cynicism is the fashion in the village, but it is a flattened cynicism, more the stuff of student coolness than of despair.

Missing Mao

One thinks of the Cultural Revolution as a terrible time for intellectuals: many were killed, others sent to hard labour in mines, in factories or on peasant farms. But you do not hear in China the tones of horrified disgust with which Russians speak of Stalin or that Romanians summon when someone mentions Ceauşescu. In avant-garde artistic circles, the love for Chairman Mao is ambivalent but incontrovertible. 'Even those of us who were opposed were believers, at least partway,' Lao Li said late one night over tea. Branded a counter-revolutionary at the beginning of the revolution, he was imprisoned for most of it. 'Mao was a very convincing man, and we intellectuals felt we were sad figures. In the Cultural Revolution, the people thought only of building a pure and perfect society. I disagreed with their particular idealism and fought against it, and would fight against it again, but I can say without hesitation that there is nothing in our commercialist society today that is equal to it. A misguided idealism is better than no idealism at all.'

Zhou Tiehai and Yang Xu, based in Shanghai, call themselves the New Revolutionaries, and they make enormous paintings in the style and spirit of the Cultural Revolution. One of these, recently criticised in the official press as decadent, is two by four metres, painted on newspaper and features an odd juxtaposition of propaganda and commercial imagery with a portrait of Marie Antoinette in a bustier in the middle. The work is covered with slogans such as 'To concentrate the day-to-day phenomena and embody the contradiction and struggle among them'.

'I was nursed on the milk of two mothers,' said Zhou Tiehai. 'One was the woman who carried me. The other was Chairman Mao.'

Zhou Tiehai and Yang Xu dress in superb, matching double-breasted suits and brightly coloured ties; they explain that this conservative costume keeps their political extremism secret. They both are handsome, and eerily young for Mao nostalgia. Their extreme pose may be ironic and certainly borders (intentionally) on the ridiculous, but they sustain it unflinchingly, speaking in the leaden rhetoric of which the Red Guards were so fond. 'Mao taught us to tell the difference between good and evil,' they told me, speaking back and forth as though they were the two voices of a single mind. 'But what has happened? We belittled dancing girls and prostitutes, but now only the most beautiful women can go into these professions. We need revolutionary thinking, to use the socialist spear to hit the capitalist seal. In the past, people were poor but they knew why they were living, and now people are rich but unhappy. We like the sixties, when at breakfast, at dinner, even when we slept, we read Mao's book. These ideas are obscure for Westerners, but they are very accessible to the Chinese people.'

I went to see the painter Yu Youhan in his mother's apartment in Shanghai, a few rooms at the top of the house that once belonged to his family. His father, a banker, was killed during the Cultural Revolution, and he went through re-education after being denounced in school. But when I probed for anger, he shook his head and said, 'When we reject Chairman Mao, we reject a piece of ourselves.' The Hong Kong dealer Johnson Chang, who represents almost all of the artists of the current avant-garde, said, 'It's like an unhappy childhood. You cannot dwell on it all the time and impose it on others, but if you disown it completely, you will be an artificial or incomplete person.'

Fang Lijun does not, in general, care to talk about politics, but late one evening we got onto the subject of Mao. Fang's family used to be landowners, and they had as bad a time as any during the Cultural Revolution. Fang once said he had become an artist because painting kept him busy at home; he could not go out because everyone felt entitled to attack him if the mood struck. 'I will never forget the day that Mao died,' he said. 'I was at school when they announced it, and everyone broke down immediately and began to cry. And though all of my family hated Mao, I cried loudest and longest of all.' When I asked him why he had cried, he said, 'It was in the programme, and we lived by the programme.' And when I asked him whether he had felt sad, he smiled and said, 'That, too, was in the programme.'

The Chinese impulse towards conformity runs deep, and I was repeatedly told that the Cultural Revolution had a luxurious quality for many Chinese people, who did not have to consider what to do, what to say, what to think, or even what to feel. Surely, I said to Fang, you must look back on that period with horror. 'With some horror, yes,' he said. 'But I am glad to have been through that. Younger people are jealous of me. Younger artists are trying to make themselves part of a history that never included them. Do you know, I went on June fourth to Tiananmen Square with a friend? We saw the tanks coming and heard the shots, and he ran away, but I went to the square. Not to be heroic, but because I was drawn there and had to see what was happening. I've always thought that my friend must regret forever having run away. You cannot run away from the Cultural Revolution, either. Maybe it's a very Chinese way of thinking, but I believe you can have a happy present only if you have an unhappy past.'

Ni Haifeng said, 'Of course, many were killed in the Cultural Revolution. But many are killed in every era. These people were seized with a fever and could not see that what they were doing was wrong. They gave up a great deal to join the revolution and kill those they thought had to be killed, and that was courageous. I admire that courage.' Later, we spoke of Tiananmen Square. 'We all demon-strated,' he said. 'And what happened was terrible. But if it hadn't happened – then maybe there would have been civil war in China, with hundreds of thousands of people killed. Maybe the country would have fallen apart like Russia. You cannot say absolutely that what happened there was wrong.'

The performance artist Liu Anping, branded as a leader of the Hangzhou democracy demonstrations, was imprisoned for a year. 'No one at Tiananmen understood or was interested in the principle of free elections,' he said. 'To be free in how and where we live, what we do – that's what we really want. We'd like an end to corruption and to be able to make whatever art we like. But China is too big and too difficult to manage for free elections. We are a xenophobic culture. We are nostalgic for the Cultural Revolution because it was so Chinese. We could never accept Western-style democracy – simply because it is Western. We must arrive at a Chinese solution, and the Chinese solution is never as free as free elections. Nor would we want it to be.'

Zhang Peili, who risked being imprisoned to hang his post-Tiananmen victim painting in Hangzhou, confirmed this view: 'Idealism in the hands of an artist is a splendid thing, so we keep it up; it is our right as artists. But idealism in the hands of a leader is terrible.' The rhetoric of democracy is powerful in some circles in China, but not in literal terms. 'You can't run a country on the basis of a billion opinions,' said Zhang. 'It would be disastrous, and far more people would be killed than are killed now.'

At twenty-six, Feng Mengbo is among the youngest of the circle around Lao Li and has an unusually sharp understanding of the relation between Eastern and Western dynamics. Chinese kids in video arcades play Western games in which they take the part of good guys trying to kill off evil. Feng has suggested that this is not far from the behaviour of young people in the Cultural Revolution, who similarly took a stance as good, blew up anyone they thought was bad, and got lots of points for doing so. He has done static paintings indicative of a series of video games he would like to produce, based on Mao's Revolutionary Model Operas. Another series shows a video game featuring Mao in his customary pose, his right hand extended in a wave of benediction. Feng Mengbo has called the game ' "Taxi, taxi," says Mao Zedong,' playing both with Mao's pose and with the Chinese habit of quoting every word of Mao's as though it contained ultimate truth. In the game, Mao stands by the side of the road with his hand held up while taxis speed past. Mao loses every time because none of the taxis ever stops for him. In the eyes of many Chinese, the Cultural Revolution was like a game, and the new interaction with the West is another version of the same game, and perhaps a less interesting one.

Most of the artists in the Chinese avant-garde are below the age of forty, and so their relationship to the events of the late sixties and early seventies is passive; they were aware of what happened, but insofar as they participated, they did so without understanding these events.

Among the older generation, the avant-garde movement was smaller and more dangerous; almost all its artists have emigrated. Yang Yiping, the sole artist in the Stars group still in China, was the son of a well-placed party member, and when the Cultural Revolution came, he got a position in the army, the safest place to be. Yang stayed in Beijing, doing propaganda paintings for the military and discussing ideology with friends until he recognised the disastrous side of the Cultural Revolution and joined the Democracy Wall movement in 1978.

His current paintings are enormous black-and-white images of young people, their faces suffused with idealism, walking out of the canvas towards the viewer. They are set in Tiananmen Square, and Mao's portrait at the gate of the Forbidden City is always at the centre of the picture. These achingly sad paintings, the colour and mood of faded snapshots, bear witness to a youthful clarity of purpose that seems, in retrospect, almost unimaginable. I stood in Yang's studio and looked for a long time at those shining, almost implausible faces rising above the collars of their Mao suits; then, turning away, I saw a small black-and-white photograph – a young Yang Yiping, wonderfully dashing in his army uniform. I saw in those eyes, too, the unthinking self-assurance of a young person ready to save the world. 'I believed in it all so ardently,' he said. 'And then there was the Democracy Wall, and the Stars.' We stood looking at his paintings. 'That was my youth. I didn't understand what I was doing. Now I'm sorry that I did it – but how happy I was then! I couldn't give it up, nor would I.'

Jiang Wen, thirty, China's leading young actor, is directing for the first time. He has chosen to adapt *Fierce Animals*, one of the bestselling novels in China last year, which is set during the Cultural Revolution. I talked to Jiang Wen on location at a school where he had mixed professional actors with enrolled students. To give the students the feeling of the era, he had taken them for 'indoctrination programmes' in the countryside. It was spooky going from the classroom on the right side of the hall, which has been converted for the film, where everyone wore matching trousers and cloth shoes and the picture of Mao reigned on high, to the classroom on the left side of the hall, where school was in ordinary session, and the kids wore track suits and spoke in or out of turn. Echoing a sentiment that I heard many times, Jiang said, 'People in the West forget that that era was a lot of fun. Life was very easy. No one worked; no one studied. If you were a member of the Red Guards, you arrived in villages and everyone came out to greet you and everyone sang revolutionary songs together. The Cultural Revolution was like a big rock-and-roll concert, with Mao as the biggest rocker and every other Chinese person his fan. I want to portray a passion that has been lost.' He was not blind to lives sacrificed at that time, but neither did he think they were the whole story, any more than romantic war poetry and war movies in the West erase the blood lost in other fights.

I had dinner at the apartment of Wu Wenguang, a filmmaker who recently completed a documentary called *My Life as a Red Guard*. He found five men who had once been Red Guards, interviewed each of them at great length, then edited the footage to show the curious mix of nostalgia and shame and pride and anger that these men felt about their own history. It was a good dinner, with an interesting assortment of guests, including the Cynical Realist painter Zhao Bandi; a director who had just finished doing the first productions of Sam Shepard in Beijing and would soon open his adaptation of *Catch-22*; Ni Haifeng; and various others. I asked Wu Wenguang whether he had felt disdain or horror at the role those Red Guards had played in the murderous history of their era. 'Look around this table,' he said. 'We're all at the cutting edge of new thought in China. We're the avant-garde, the ones who are pushing towards the next wave, believers in democracy, helping to build China into a better society.' I nodded. 'How can we feel disdain or horror? If we'd been born twenty years earlier, we would have been Red Guards, every one of us.'

Old-Timers

In Shanghai, I visited the great scholar Zhu Qizhan, who, at 102, is widely regarded as China's greatest traditionalist brush-and-ink painter. 'In my youth,' he said, 'I studied oil painting also, and it touched and influenced my work, especially the strong colours. I would say of the West that Chinese artists can use it, but for Chinese purposes. A Chinese man can ignore Western art, but he cannot ignore Chinese art. And if he sets out to mix up both forms and both kinds of meaning, he will likely be neither fish nor fowl.'

The Chinese painting tradition is based on the principle of escape, designed to raise the viewer's soul to new heights. Perhaps the greatest difference between Chinese traditional painting – called *guohua* – and avant-garde art is that traditional painting takes you away from your problems, while avant-garde work forces you to look at them. Zhu Qizhan's eloquent and remarkable pictures command the respect of younger artists, but demonstrate how much a departure, both in form and in meaning, the work of the avant-garde represents.

The vogue for realism began in China in 1919, and it thrives today. The work of the most prominent realist, Chen Yifei, is by Western standards too hackneyed for greeting cards. Chen has emigrated to the United States, but the meticulous craftsmanship of his paintings of young girls in turtleneck sweaters playing the flute still exerts its powerful fascination, primarily on Asians; in Hong Kong, his work can fetch $250,000.

I went to see Yang Feiyun, a portraitist of Chen's school. His women, without flutes, have the photographic sharpness and plastic smoothness to which Chinese academic training aspires. 'I was influenced most by Botticelli, Dürer and Leonardo,' Yang said. 'Maybe realism was too good for too long in the West, and artists grew tired of it. I cannot accept the Western way of rejecting the past, or even of rejecting your own past, of starting anew all the time. The pursuit of perfection is more important than choosing many ways. People have said that art has no limit, but this is true only when art stays in its own hemisphere. When West and East meet, art does have limits.'

Why Gilbert & George?

In recent years, China has been increasingly open to exhibitions from the West, which are accepted so long as the West pays for them. For about $25,000, you can take the upstairs rooms in the National Art Gallery for a month and, subject to certain approvals, you can hang whatever you like. Since Robert Rauschenberg broke the ice in 1985, several one-man shows have been sent by obscure artists with sponsorship from their own governments, along with a few international student projects and a big Rodin exhibition, which opened in June.

Gilbert & George, British avant-garde artists, have made a point of exhibiting their enormous, brightly coloured, highly politicised photomontages internationally. Their Moscow show from 1990 is still discussed in Russian artistic circles. That exhibition was organised by a savvy and enterprising Englishman named James Birch; when he said to Gilbert & George, 'Where next?' – they said, 'China!'

By the time of the Moscow show, Russia was in the throes of glasnost, and the decision to show art that, even in the West, has provoked hostile comment for its cultural, political and sexual radicalism – some of it highly homoerotic – fit with a general agenda of 'nothing's too extreme for us.' In China, many things are considered too extreme, and the decision of the Chinese government to host an exhibition of Gilbert & George seems at first glance to be startling. Gilbert & George's last major exhibition was called *New Democratic Pictures*, and though this title was not used in China, the meaning of the work was quite clear to anyone literate in the language of contemporary Western art.

Though Chinese officials were won over in part by Birch's enthusiasm, economics carried the day. Not only did Gilbert & George and their London dealer, Anthony d'Offay, rent the gallery, but they also promised to bring Westerners for the opening, to stage banquets and television presentations, and to pump money into the local economy. According to one participant in the exhibition, the total bill ran close to £1 million. Further, the government was naïve about these images. 'You don't imagine,' said Lao Li in an amused voice, 'that these officials understand what this work is about? It's famous from the West, and that's as much as they know.' Then, the Chinese needed to appear open before the Olympic Games site was chosen. Additionally, with a 'what the West says doesn't affect us' mentality, the Chinese knew that by controlling what happened at the opening they could control the media image of Gilbert & George.

The exhibition was opened with high pomp on 3 September by the British ambassador and the Chinese minister of culture. About

150 people had come from the West; myriad high Chinese officials flocked to the event. Gilbert & George felt that the flowers arranged for the opening were insufficiently opulent, and they went out themselves and bought gorgeous arrangements that bedecked the exhibition hall – to the immense amusement of the Chinese, who knew, as Gilbert & George did not, that these were funerary bouquets. Gilbert & George made a point not only of hanging the exhibition but also of speaking at the opening and at the seven or eight banquets associated with it. They gave interviews to the press and to television. It should be noted that very little of what they said to the press was printed; that the show had, within China, relatively modest publicity; and that the speeches they made were substantially altered and toned down even in simultaneous translation at the events.

The British got in touch with Lao Li, who was given invitations to distribute to artists, but the Chinese avant-garde found the jet-set glamour of the opening obnoxious, imperialist and self-aggrandising. They deplored the tolerant enthusiasm with which Gilbert & George basked in the attention of officials. At the opening banquet, someone looked at them at the head table and described them as 'a pair of blockheads among the rotten eggs'. In the eyes of the Chinese, the opening almost defeated the meaning of the work. It had the same aura of hypocrisy that might be noted if Mother Teresa came on a goodwill mission and spent her whole visit with Donald Trump and Leona Helmsley. The Chinese officials knew that by arranging the opening as they did, they could castrate the work in the eyes of the radical element in their own society.

Most Chinese artists have seen Western contemporary work primarily in books. In the painter Ding Yi's studio, I leafed through a volume called *Western Modern Art*, which included one of Gilbert & George's monumental colour photomontages, which are often twenty feet long or high, reproduced as a scratchy black-and-white plate two inches square. During their tour, Gilbert & George said repeatedly, 'Our art fights for love and tolerance and the universal elaboration of the individual. Each of our pictures is a visual love letter from ourselves to the viewer.' What higher message could there now be for Western art in China? 'I think,' Lao Li said, 'that what is important in this work will get through to the people who are interested in understanding it.' The opening was only like bad static.

East Meets West

'The West tends to equate civilisation, modernisation and westernisation,' Zhang Peili said. 'But it is only in this modern period that the West has arrived at new ways before China has. In past eras, we were the more advanced civilisation.' The Chinese hate the Western habit of taking credit for industrialisation. 'You look at a factory and you say that it's Western,' Bo Xiaobo, a Shanghai journalist, said to me. 'But we've had factories here for a hundred years. Westerners started using gunpowder immediately after they found it in this country, but no one speaks of the American Revolution or the First World War as Chinese. If someone gets in a car and drives or goes to a factory and works, that's not Western life; it's just modern life.'

The West also tends to take credit for all art that is not brush painting. Today, the Chinese employ visual language that was developed in the West. But paper originally came from Asia, and all works on paper are not deemed Asian. Why should every oil painting be called Western? Why is it that the West feels it owns conceptualism, installation, modernism and abstraction? The Hong Kong dealer Alice King, who shows work that uses *guohua* styles in modern ways, asks, 'What is a Chinese painting? Is it any painting made by someone from China? Any painting made by someone who is ethnically Chinese? Or is it a stylistic question? Can a Westerner make a Chinese painting if he uses rice paper and a brush?' Westerners sometimes dismiss Chinese work as derivative. 'We must as artists solve the problems of China, even if they're boring for the West,' said the painter Wang Yin, one of the artists of the Yuanmingyuan village.

Li Xianting pointed out that until Western literature reached China during the Qing dynasty, a great gap existed between Chinese written and spoken language: 'Classical Chinese is a very vague, open-ended language in which much of the content is left to the reader to determine. Only when Chinese scholars read foreign books did they imagine that there could be a direct correlation between the written and the spoken word. After that, our written language took on this Western precision. But it was still the Chinese language; the subjects were still Chinese. If I hand you a recent Chinese novel, you will not say, "But this is in English!" No more should you say that of our art.' One could say much the same thing of Chinese economic and social reform, for which the West, to the intense irritation of the Chinese, seems far too often to claim responsibility. 'Now it's a one-way situation,' the Shanghai New Revolutionaries said, 'with every Western thing and idea in China, and no Chinese ideas or things in the West. It must balance.'

The extent of Western freedom – that natural corollary of democracy – is a subject of constant discussion among the Chinese. Gu Wenda, who now lives in New York and, with Ai Weiwei and Xu Bing, is a leader of Chinese art abroad, told me that while his exhibitions in China had been closed down for 'inappropriate political meaning, something about a code for political secrets', he had found in New York that when he showed work made with traditional Chinese medicines, including a powder made from human placenta, the authorities once more closed down his work, saying something about abortion. For him as an artist, there wasn't so much difference.

Last year, Ni Haifeng won a German arts prize and lived for three months in Bonn, where he befriended local artists. One of them invited him to a potluck dinner and said, 'We were hoping you'd make something Chinese.' So Ni Haifeng made a soup of which he was particularly fond. 'I served it to everyone,' he told me, 'and they all said they loved it. I tasted it last and realised at once that I had done something very wrong. The soup was terrible. At first, I thought everyone was just being nice to me, but people ate many bowls, and I finally understood that they all really liked it. But I felt guilty about having served them bad soup, and so a few weeks later I had everyone to my house, and I made the soup again. This time the soup was perfect. "Well," they said to me, "this is okay, but not nearly as good as last time." And they took very little of it.'

The Chinese are amused by Westerners' inability to understand their cultural standards. One evening in Hangzhou with Zhang Peili, Geng Jianyi and other friends, we got onto the subject of two women from their school who were 'like unsellable goods from an old department store'. Both had found happiness with Western boyfriends. Zhang and Geng described having dinner with the family of one of the boyfriends, whose mother kept whispering that she'd never met a girl 'so beautiful'. 'Our next big export,' they said, 'will be the ugliest women in China. They can all marry attractive rich Americans.' Then they put me through a sort of quiz. 'Look there,' they'd say. 'One of those women is pretty and the other plain. Can you tell which is which?'

Despite the insatiable appetite of Chinese consumers for Western products, the West, in the eyes of the Chinese, doesn't really count. I had dinner one night with the wife of an artist. She said, 'You know, my husband would be furious if I went out for supper with a Chinese man.'

'But dinner with me doesn't matter?' I asked.

'No,' she said. 'Of course not.'

I was similarly struck by the availability of the *International Herald Tribune,* by the fact that many people get the BBC World Service, by the tolerance for Gilbert & George. At first, I supposed that this represented a loosening of ideological barriers; only later did I understand that imported Western ideas cannot really affect anyone, whereas something much slighter in a Chinese forum – a haircut, for instance – could trigger a revolution.

China officially ended its isolationist policies in 1978, but the isolationist mentality lives on. 'We were so cut off for so long,' Zhang Peili said, 'it's as though you are in a dark room and suddenly the curtains are opened. You cannot see the view because your eyes are still adjusting to the light.' The Shanghai artist and critic Xu Hong said, 'People speak all the time of mixing Western and Eastern influences, as though it were like mixing red and blue ink to paint pictures in purple. They do not think of what it means to understand these cultures and to try to incorporate their different ways of thought.' Every artist I met explained why his work was really not as Western as it looked. 'And how can it be Western?'

asked Zhang Wei, a university teacher who lives in the village at Yuanmingyuan. 'Of course, we have come of age in the era of the so-called open-door policy, but we all understand that it is at best a door-ajar policy. And we know that that door will never really stand open, that people will never be allowed to pass back and forth through it as they choose.'

It is difficult for artists to cut themselves off completely from Chinese tradition. The abstract painter Ding Yi lives quietly in Shanghai, where he has produced large, beautifully coloured canvases in which simple patterns are arranged over graphic spaces. He has recently started to produce these abstract paintings on bamboo and paper fans. 'I needed to tie myself to the Chinese tradition,' he said. 'And I wanted simultaneously to make this Western principle less frightening for Chinese people.'

Other artists, meanwhile, are doing work with Chinese media and Western form. Lu Shengzhong studied folk art at the Central Academy in Beijing, and his specialty is paper cutting. Traditionally, a rural woman should be able to cook, sew and cut paper; Lu Shengzhong tells of old women who, having lost all other facilities, can do nothing but cut paper and who express themselves with their elaborate narrative paper cuts. He is a master paper cutter and the author of several books on the subject. In his recent work, he has limited himself to the single form of the 'universal man', and he cuts it over and over in different sizes, always from red paper, to create enormous, mystical installations. Lao Li dismisses such work. Many Chinese find this mixing of peasant tradition and modernism almost unclean. They resent the West's enthusiasm for material that looks so Chinese but is so connected to Western thought. It is as though Lu Shengzhong has prostituted himself and the culture, giving something to the West that they should not have, selling something off too cheap.

A voice of nationalism emerges in the persistent, strong rejection of the West. The Chinese, competitive always, will take from the West whatever they can put to their own use. 'Western culture reigns,' Lao Li said. 'In a past era, Chinese culture was the highest. Right now, the West is in a state of decline and China in a state of ascendancy. Soon, we will cross paths.' Gu Wenda said simply, 'If China had been the strongest after the Second World War, artists of the West would use my language and not I, theirs.'

The matter of China's ruling the world is discussed as routinely in China as though it were already settled. The only matter for debate is when it will happen. Some think it will take only twenty years; some think it could take more than a century. Artists expect their international position to be paramount when China has risen above all other nations. 'I am the guard of God and the voice of God,' the painter Ding Fang, author of terrifying Wagnerian mythological landscapes, told me. 'I create a renaissance of the spirit and spiritual elevation. My work will last forever, as surely as the sun will go on rising; only the blind will not see it. With this work, China will return the spirit to the humans of the world.'

A Dangerous Idea

In the artists' village at Yuanmingyuan, everyone calls Yan Zhengxue the mayor. At forty-nine, he is older than the others and has been in the village longer. Yan does not particularly look like an artist; he has short hair and ordinary clothes. His big ink paintings are decorative and traditional; his manner, unassuming.

On 2 July, Yan took bus line 332 from central Beijing to Yuanmingyuan. He tried to get off just as the conductor closed the door and a minor argument ensued. The conductor was aggressive and Yan was annoyed. At the next stop, the conductor deliberately closed the door just as Yan tried to exit, and so Yan was carried to the last stop, where the conductor accused him of having taken items from his money bag and summoned the police. The area is under the same jurisdiction as the village, so the three policemen who came all recognised Yan Zhengxue as the mayor. He recognised them as the policemen who had closed down an exhibition that artists in the village had tried to mount. Yan said he had never touched the conductor's bag, but the police pulled him out of the bus, beat him and threw him on the ground. Some local residents stood watching, too afraid to interfere.

Then the police dragged him to the station and beat him with electric nightsticks. 'I did not fight back,' Yan said, 'but only kept asking, "Why are you beating me?" But they didn't stop.' We were talking in Yan's small courtyard house in the village, and he produced photographs of himself burned, covered in blood and oosing blisters. 'They hit my groin repeatedly.' He held out a particularly grotesque photo. 'The electric sticks burn badly. They loosened my teeth, and they bruised my chest, back, bottom, head. They told me to kneel down, but I refused and then they beat me even harder. They said, "If you vomit, you will clean the floor with your tongue. We know who you are. Artist, who made you mayor of the village? You have no authority at all."' Then they asked him to sign a confession stating that he had stolen from the bus conductor, and when he refused, they beat him unconscious and dumped him, at midnight, outside the station. At 4:00 a.m., a local resident wrapped him in a blanket and took him to a hospital, where he was treated for bodily injuries and loss of hearing.

A few days later, one of the village artists recounted this story to Wang Jiaqi, a lawyer who ordinarily works in a Beijing property company. Wang immediately contacted Yan: 'I told him this fierce event violated the law. Our central government does not like such petty police violence. I suggested that we bring a lawsuit.'

Yan asked artists to sign a petition protesting his treatment. Fang Lijun was among the first of the Yuanmingyuan artists to sign; Lao Li kept a page of the petition at his home, asking those who visited to sign as well. Some Chinese journalists agreed to write about Yan's lawsuit. As publicity spread, Yan got hundreds of letters from victims of similar violence. 'Some asked how to bring a suit; others warned me that I would meet with a "sudden accident" if I didn't take care.'

Wang submitted papers including photos, hospital documents, Yan's statements and copies of the petition to the courts. 'They agreed to hear our case,' Wang told me. 'We won't get any money and the police won't be punished, but if we can get them to admit that they committed a crime, that will be something. I avoid speaking publicly of human rights and democracy. It's too dangerous. I work on individual cases in legal terms. The Chinese people have no idea of using law to protect themselves; they imagine that laws exist only to constrain them. We want to stand against that.'

As I flipped through the snapshots in front of me, showing Yan Zhengxue's injuries in horrible detail, I said, 'It's funny that I am in China to write about art and about artists and that I have found myself listening to a story about civil rights and personal freedom. It almost belongs to another project.'

'This is a story about art and about artists,' Yan said. 'The police hate me because I am an artist, disobedient, free in what I do. They resent their lack of control over this village, these unregistered people living here without work units, without schedules, with Westerners wandering through. I was a natural target. In this country, you can seek money, have women, drink, and as long as you are registered in a unit, it's okay. But to be an artist' – he gestured at his big ink scrolls – 'this is a problem.'

Wang nodded at this. 'Mr Yan is bringing this suit. He is continuing to disobey convention by pursuing the law. Because he is a strong individual, Mr Yan was beaten badly, and as an individual he is not simply accepting this. Whether we win or lose, I hope we will give this idea to people, that they can protest, that they can find a way to stand up for what they believe, that they can live as human beings.'

I thought again of Song Shuangsong's haircut and I understood then why it had generated so much anger, and I saw in what terms it had been a success. I saw why even that trivial event was, in its way, more dangerous than a bomb. So long as art can assert its own danger, it succeeds. For this whole concept of individuality, this humanism of which Lao Li is the epitome, is something almost unknown in the People's Republic. And if the idea were to penetrate to the vast population of that country, it would shift them towards self-determination. That would be the end of central government, of control, of Communism – it would be the end of China. With luck, this struggle between humanists and absolutists will never stop: for either side to win absolutely would be tragic. Injustice is terrible, but the end of China is also something that no one wants, neither Deng Xiaoping nor Lao Li and his circle.

Acceptance of Chinese contemporary art within the Western art world came more readily than acceptance of Soviet/Russian work. It has coincided with a rethinking of Western cultural history, in which what European and American cultures have exported to Asia is matched by what we have learned from Asia. Asian influence inheres only superficially in a taste for lacquer and porcelain; it resides more profoundly in philosophy. Minimalism and formalism are Asian ideas. Would Fluxus have been possible without Asian traditions celebrating temporality? Having ceased to disparage Asian contemporary art as plagiaristic of modernism, we must now reckon with the idea that modernism was in some ways plagiaristic of Asia. While Western artists learned a bit of technique from calligraphic brushwork, what they mostly took from character-based languages was the metaphoric richness of blurring the line between language and visual representation. Only lately have we acknowledged this debt.

Contemporary art from China, so marginal to Western consciousness when I first encountered it, has since become pivotal to any conversation about contemporary art, and works by Chinese artists have reached astronomical prices. In 2007, the Cynical Realist Yue Minjun set a record for Chinese contemporary art with the $5.3 million sale of his painting *Execution*. It was soon surpassed when a picture by Zhang Xiaogang, whose paintings had sold in 2004 for about $45,000, sold in 2008 for $6.1 million. Zhang Xiaogang's record was exceeded that same year when Zeng Fanzhi's *Mask Series 1996 No. 6* fetched $9.7 million; in 2013, his *The Last Supper* sold for $23.3 million.

Lao Li calls much of this work *Gaudy Art*, a term he made up to characterise the shiny surface and slick appeal of work that demonstrates 'the powerlessness of art to shake the pervasiveness of consumerism'. He has referred to it as 'a self-ironic response to the spiritual vacuum and folly of modern-day China'. Apolitical cynicism abounds. Cao Fei, a prominent artist from Guangzhou, said, 'Criticising society, that's the aesthetics of the last generation.

When I started making art, I didn't want to do political things. It's all been expressed.' The painter Huang Rui said of the new generation, 'They grew up during an economic period. They think economics influences their lives. They don't realise politics can influence their lives even more.'

The Yuanmingyuan artists' village was shut down by authorities in 1993. Lao Li, Fang Lijun and Yue Minjun were among the first to migrate to Songzhuang, a peasant village about twelve miles from central Beijing. Many others soon followed. Town government was pleased to have tax revenue from this influx, but artists soon became embroiled in land disputes with local residents. Other artists set up shop at 798, an abandoned electronic-switching factory in the north-east of Beijing. This became a mandatory stop for art tourists and the cafés and boutiques that follow artistic efflorescence world-wide soon developed. Li Wenzi, a Beijing dealer, said, 'The Yuan-mingyuan Artists' Village was a haven for idealists, for troubled souls seeking freedom and peace. From the very beginning, these other villages have been driven by money.' The government was eager to exploit cultural tourism, but its promotion of these areas pushed up rents, and many artists were soon priced out of 798. The problem was less acute in more far-flung areas, and over four thousand artists now work in Songzhuang, which is only one among more than a hundred artist communities on the outskirts of Beijing.

Lao Li is director of the Songzhuang Art Museum and the Li Xianting Film Fund, which for ten years organised the Beijing Inde-pendent Film Festival. In a 2010 interview, Fang Lijun stated, 'Lao Li was like the sun in the sky, shining down on all of us.' In August 2014, authorities closed the festival the day before it was to open. More than a dozen police arrived to confiscate documents from the festival office; officers detained Lao Li and two collaborators, forcing them to sign papers assenting to the cancellation, then turned off the electricity at the festival venue. They later blockaded the space where the Li Xianting Film Fund had for many years offered a workshop for aspiring filmmakers, which now moved to a secret countryside location. The organisers were bewildered. 'Our main goal is to open our students' minds – to teach them new ways to think about life and cinema,' said Fan Rong, the festival's executive director. 'Nothing we want to do is against the party or the government.'

After bringing his 1993 lawsuit over abuse at the hands of the police, Yan Zhengxue, the 'mayor' of Yuanmingyuan, was sent to a re-education labour camp for two years. He produced some hundred paintings of dark landscapes oosing blood under black suns, each divided by a central vertical line – the result of his attempt to conceal the true themes of his pictures by painting only half at a time. To get them out, he would stuff them into plastic bags, conceal them in his underwear, and then drop them into the vats of excrement that passed for camp lavatories; his children and friends would go there to retrieve them. He has been brought into police custody more than a dozen times since his release. In 2007, he was imprisoned for 'subversion of state power'. He made no art during this two-year sentence. 'I was tired of fighting,' he said. He attempted to hang himself.

Transgender performance artist Ma Liuming was jailed in 1994 on charges of pornography. All performance art became illegal after Zhu Yu displayed a video of his performance allegedly eating a fetus in the 2000 *Fuck Off* show in Shanghai organised by Ai Weiwei and Feng Boyi. Wang Peng, who grew up in a rural village but works in Beijing, knew nothing of the Tiananmen massacre until 2002, when he gained access to software that broke China's internet firewall. He abandoned abstract painting to work with bloodied surgical gloves retrieved from clinics where forced abortions take place. He said that learning of the massacre 'made me want to rip open the most shocking and ugly side of society. It made me realise beauty is not what's important, reality is.' Chen Guang was one of the soldiers at Tiananmen, and the memory of that horror informs his blood-soaked imagery. After he staged a private show at home in 2014, he was taken away by the police, who came to his humble apartment with four armed vehicles. In 2015, Shanghai artist Dai Jianyong was arrested for 'creating a disturbance' after he sent friends a Photoshopped image that showed President Xi Jinping with a moustache and crinkled eyes; he faces five years in prison.

Shipping crates of Zhao Zhao's work were seized by authorities in 2012. After they were taken, he was told that he had to pay a fine of about $48,000, though he was charged with no crime. He would not get his work back in any case, but after he paid, he would be allowed to see it once before it was destroyed. He had no means to raise such a sum. Asked if he was afraid following this incident, he replied, 'I don't want to become cautious.'

Wu Yuren was arrested in 2010 for protesting in Tiananmen Square against the government's seizure of his studio and the studios of several other artists. Many important artists came to his trial, including Ai Weiwei. Wu was released in 2012. Shortly before the 2014 Chinese New Year, Wu Yuren was sent a leaked document. An official notification from the Beijing Domestic Security Department, it instructed officers to act against 'the unsafe, suspect population throughout the city'. They were to keep such people away from central areas. The memo ended, 'Stop the harmful influence caused by people gathering.' The anonymous sender added a note to Wu Yuren, almost a dare, saying, 'If you post this, the government will come and grab you.' Wu Yuren posted the document on his WeChat channel and four hours later, after his post had been shared by many people on WeChat, he received a police invitation to 'a cup of tea'. It was the middle of the night, but he headed out. On the way to the teahouse, Wu was confronted by four police officers and some additional heavies. At the police station, one of the officers said, 'The New Year is coming up, and you're going to be here. We're not going to let you go home.' Wu replied evenly, 'Actually, I'm cool with that. I haven't prepared at all for the New Year's celebration. I'm really behind schedule. This is a great excuse.' This time, insolence worked; he was released a half-hour later. 'My parents of course want me to leave the country or to stop criticising the government,' he said. 'It's something all parents would want. I don't want my own child to live in China, especially under the current circumstances. People of their generation all say that there's nothing you as an individual can do, so stop trying, it's not worth it.'

In 2014, police detained thirteen residents of Songzhuang for 'creating trouble' after Wang Zang posted a picture on Twitter of himself holding an umbrella. The umbrella had become the symbol of Hong Kong's pro-democracy demonstrators. Police confiscated Wang Zang's umbrella and took him into custody; still in jail two months later, he suffered a heart attack following sleep-deprivation torture. 'Despite all these troubles, I think my husband did the right thing,' his wife said. A vast increase in police in Songzhuang immediately followed the arrest. Artists who had been marketing their work to anyone with funds now shooed away potential buyers. The painter Tang Jianying, who also came under increased surveillance, said that Wang's error had been to use the internet. 'Among friends, we can speak freely,' he said. 'But if you speak freely on the web, they'll get you.'

In the spring of 2015, President Xi Jinping said, 'Fine art works should be like sunshine from blue sky and breeze in spring that will inspire minds, warm hearts, cultivate taste and clean up undesirable work styles.' This rather novel description of springtime weather was followed by statements from the State General Administration of Press, Publication, Radio, Film and TV, which expressed its willingness to relocate artists to rural areas so they could 'form a correct view of art', finding opportunities in the hinterland to 'unearth new subjects' and 'create more masterpieces'. The message could not have been clearer. As during the Cultural Revolution, artists who refused to self-censor would be sent into punitive exile.

When I wrote my story for the *New York Times* in 1993, three of China's greatest artists – Xu Bing, Gu Wenda and Ai Weiwei – were living in the United States. The artists I encountered in China spoke of them and I met them when I returned home. Ai – artist, poet, architect, activist – is by far the most explicitly political. The son of a poet exiled during the Cultural Revolution, he gained fame for designing the 'Bird's Nest' stadium for the 2008 Olympics, but enraged authorities by describing the games as a 'false smile' from the Chinese government. Trouble escalated rapidly after he began a 'citizen investigation' into the deaths of thousands of schoolchildren in the 2008 Sichuan earthquake, most at schools that did not meet building code. He catalogued their names and collected and displayed their little backpacks, deeply embarrassing the government. When he attended the trial of another earthquake activist in 2009, he was assaulted by police officers and beaten until his brain bled. He posted a photo of himself with a tube through his skull to relieve the haematoma and a bag with the draining blood in his hand. Disillusioned with Gaudy Art, he wrote in 2012, 'Chinese art is merely a product. Its only purpose is to charm viewers with its ambiguity. The Chinese art world does not exist. In a society that restricts individual freedoms and violates human rights, anything that calls itself creative or independent is a pretense. To me, these are an insult to human intelligence and a ridicule of the concept of culture – vehicles of propaganda that showcase skills with no substance, and crafts with no meaning.'

Ai Weiwei has many detractors within China. 'It's all stunts, phony posturing,' said one curator in Beijing. 'It's not so different from the government's propaganda, but a type that's aimed at pulling foreigners' heartstrings.' Ai said of such critics and artists, 'They always stand on the side of power. I don't blame them. I shake hands, I smile, I write recommendation letters for them, but . . . total disappointment.'

Anger is a corollary of hope, but sorrow is the upshot of despair. Yue Minjun's countless self-portraits, in all of which he is laughing riotously, are perhaps the most recognisable images to come out of China in these past two decades; he cannot keep pace with collectors' demands, and counterfeits of his work are all over Beijing flea markets. Yue Minjun is categorised with the Cynical Realists. But one curator said that over time his works have come to exude 'a sense of melancholy rather than cynicism'. The poet Ouyang Jianghe wrote of his work, 'All immemorial sadness is in this laughter.'

The Artists of South Africa: Separate and Equal

New York Times Magazine, 27 March 1994

I first went to South Africa in 1992, then returned in 1993. Even in that short time, the change wrought by the waning of apartheid was irrefutable, though that gruesome system was not fully abandoned until the first free elections in 1994. South Africa is the redeeming narrative. The art of protest has shifted somewhat as the occasion for protest has been diminished. For some artists, this has proved liberating; for others, extremely difficult.

I had already covered the art scene in both Russia and China and so thought that a South African assignment would call on relatively familiar skills. Soviet Russia or post-Maoist China, however, had essentially two camps: the 'official' circle that benefited from and celebrated the existing power structure, and the counter-revolutionary underground whose members attempted to redeem their own identities from dehumanisation. But in South Africa, the authorities had not limited artists to the production of cultural propaganda, so no body of imagery reinforced the apartheid status quo. All the artists I met – black and white – aspired to a just society, even if they did not entirely agree on how it would look.

My own role was discomfiting. In Moscow, no one had supposed that I was a party member, and in Beijing I was never mistaken for a Red Guard, but in Johannesburg, I was white and therefore incriminated. Allowed to go where black people generally couldn't, I had no claim to innocence. At the least I was a privileged spectator in a country where the majority was brazenly disenfranchised.

This piece had a particularly rough time in the editing process, so I returned to my drafts and notes and reworked it substantially. It felt like cheating to drop the artists who have faded into obscurity, or to call much more attention to the ones who have become superstars. I have therefore tried not to change the perspective from what I perceived then, instead restoring material that was edited out and paring back other passages to reflect my original intentions.

At the first artistic gathering I attended in Johannesburg in the summer of 1993, the talk was all about Barbara Masekela's flight from Cape Town to Johannesburg. Masekela is Nelson Mandela's personal assistant, and one gains access to the great man through her; she is among the most powerful women in the African National Congress (ANC): a bright, tough, accomplished person who stands out in any context for her sheer force of personality. Yet when the flight attendant came through the first-class cabin with the in-flight meal, she served first the white man on Masekela's right, then the white woman on Masekela's left, then the people in the row behind. When Masekela complained, the attendant seemed genuinely startled and apologised profusely, explaining that she 'just hadn't seen you sitting there'. She literally hadn't registered Masekela, as though the upholstery had camouflaged her black face. The white artists with whom I dined argued that while their work couldn't make white people like black people or vice versa, it needed to address this invisibility.

Two weeks later, I found myself with one of the same artists and some of his friends at a beach near Cape Town. The breeze was hot, the sun was fierce, the sea was icy, and the landscape was stunning. We were lying on the sand when an old coloured man (*coloured* was the apartheid catch-all for people of mixed race) approached with a crate of ice cream, so heavy he could hardly carry it. He wore a suit with long sleeves and long trousers, and he was sweating profusely in the sun. 'God, ice cream,' said one of our group. 'Who wants some ice cream?' Of course we all wanted ice cream. 'It's on me,' said someone, and we all chose our flavours, took the ice creams from the man, opened them, and began to eat. 'Eight rand,' said the man, and the one who'd volunteered to treat us all checked the pocket of his shirt. 'Damn!' he said. 'I've only got five rand.' No one else had brought any money to the beach. 'I've got some money in my car,' said one of our company. 'If I see you later, I'll give you the rest.' No one suggested that he go and get the money. No one looked embarrassed. No one apologised. Uncomplaining, the old man picked up his crate and stumbled down the beach in the blasing sun.

The Old South Africa is going strong, even among those who profess to regret it.

But the New South Africa can be equally troubling. I went to the launch of the National Arts Initiative (NAI), which was set to introduce a new era of artistic freedom to the country. Mike van Graan, an ANC member and the general secretary of the NAI, who is coloured despite his Afrikaans name, had arranged a programme attended by noteworthy artists, writers and musicians. He suggested that the proceedings take place in English since everyone there spoke English; but several representatives demanded that the proceedings also take place in their native languages. The whites who were on hand sat nervously and submissively through the long monologues in Zulu and Xhosa, with attentive looks fixed politely on their faces. The representatives who had made this demand had understood the speeches when they were first delivered; they chatted merrily throughout the translations, apparently satisfied to have prevailed. As the translations meandered on, some delegates, obviously bored, simply got up and left. The reckless waste of time, money and energy was stupefying.

Pictures, Concepts and Beads

The conflicting priorities and mutual insensitivities of the South African art world were being played out in microcosm in the National Gallery of South Africa when I was there. Five years ago, the National

Gallery was a dead loss: pictures by Henk Pierneef, the 'great' Afri-
kaner painter, of conquering Boers in lush landscapes hung gloom-
ily beside third-rate works by second-rate American and European
artists. Marilyn Martin, the dynamic new director, swept in like the
west wind and changed all that. The gallery now houses a permanent
collection of work by many of the best artists working in South Africa
along with historical material by the liberal white and radical black
artists of the past forty years.

This is great progress – especially when one considers that in 'free'
Namibia, for example, the national museum shows old pottery alongside models of mating rhinoceroses and dioramas with black man-
nequins clad in 'native dress'. Confusion about what art is and what
its purpose may be can make even the designation *art museum* feel
suspect. At the National Gallery, I found in one room a large installation by the middle-aged, white conceptualist Malcolm Payne, built
up with shopping carts, ancient and new ceramics, light projections,
and a text full of such words as *appropriation* and *deconstruct*. The
piece made no concessions to the possibility that some viewers would
be unversed in the international discourse of contemporary art. In the
room beyond was an exhibition called 'Ezakwantu: Beadwork from
the Eastern Cape'; in the corner sat two Xhosa women, Virginia and
Lucy, who beaded quietly all day unless asked a question through
their translator.

It is fashionable in South Africa to call craft 'art', especially if it's
very good craft. Very good craft is very good craft – not less than
art, but different. 'We have freed ourselves of the shackles of such
Eurocentric definitions,' Marilyn Martin said in a bluntly PC manner – though she holds to the Eurocentric principle of the museum.
Yet the Xhosa beadwork in the museum's gift shop, where I bought
some milk pails, is not an imitation of the work in the museum; it *is*
that work. In contrast, the Pierneef postcard that I bought at the same
time is not a Pierneef, but a representation of a Pierneef. There is good
and bad art, and good and bad craft, and some work that falls between
these categories. This does not mean that the categories are irrelevant.

The presence of Virginia and Lucy in the museum also points
to this unacknowledged distinction. Marilyn Martin insisted that

Virginia and Lucy were there to demonstrate that the historical tradition continues, a point made elsewhere simply by the inclusion of contemporary material. Of course, Martin had not asked a German expressionist to sit all day and paint in the gallery showing German expressionism, nor had Malcolm Payne been invited to sit in the middle of his installation and conceptualise. Putting the ladies in situ was meant to elevate their craft, but it felt only patronising; Malcolm Payne compared it to the nineteenth-century European enthusiasm for putting Hottentots on show for the public.

The Bag Factory and Others

A London-based patron opened the old Speedy Bag Factory to Johannesburg artists in mid-1991; it contains nineteen studios now, occupied by black and white artists. On Fridays, they have lunch together. To many outsiders, this place seems a miniature utopia, where racial barriers have been eliminated, but closer examination shows painfully vivid gaps.

Several of the leading lights of the black art world are at the Bag Factory: David Koloane, Durant Sihlali and Ezrom Legae, as well as younger artists such as Sam Nhlengethwa and Pat Mautloa. The distinctive and poetic styles of such artists as Koloane and Sihlali reflect a courage and self-determination not relevant to the work of white artists. This does not make the black work better (it's often ingenuous), but it does make it different. 'It's very politically correct,' said Sam Nhlengethwa, 'not to write the race of murder victims in the newspapers. But you can always tell – from the names, the place of the murder, how much space it gets in the paper. It may seem gracious not to mention the race of the artist, but you can always tell the difference.' That is to say that while you are advised to treat the art *equally*, you should not treat it *equivalently*.

I was talking to Nhlengethwa at the Bag Factory when one of the white artists burst through the door. 'I've been waiting for you for three hours,' he said to me angrily, though I had said simply that I would be at the building from noon onward and would hope to see a number of people. 'If you don't come now, I'm going home.' No apologies were offered to Nhlengethwa: he was as invisible as Barbara Masekela had been on the plane. I was rather embarrassed by this affront, but Nhlengethwa said, 'Go ahead. I'm in no rush.' When I came back to Nhlengethwa's studio, I apologised for the confusion. 'It's okay,' he said. 'He's really trying. He's a good guy. He's just still a white South African.'

The white artists at the Bag Factory are young, the trendiest crew in South Africa, a trendiness manifest in clothes, mannerisms, reading materials and racial attitudes ('that testosterone-dripping avant-garde', Malcolm Payne called them). Joachim Schönfeldt presents his pieces under the banner of 'Curios and Authentic Works of Art', playing with Eurocentric definitions of 'native' African production. In subtle, funny and disconcertingly beautiful carvings, always made from the wood of blue gums (the most politicised trees in Africa, introduced by settlers to build struts for the mines), Schönfeldt combines an Afrikaans sense of kitsch with a cynical approach to those questions of art versus craft that the National Gallery prefers to finesse. Alan Alborough works with boundaries, crossable and inviolable, and has done a particularly powerful series in which children's games become metaphors for social definition and exclusion. Belinda Blignaut's formalist production makes a point of not engaging with politics. Kendell Geers's art often includes the materials of violence – broken glass, barbed wire, the tyres used for 'necklacing' (the practise of vigilante execution with a burning rubber ring) – and incorporates post-structuralist and modernist conceits. The effect is often powerful and occasionally pretentious. The work of these youngish artists is sometimes too sophisticated; they fail to realise that nothing is more provincial than denying your own provincialism. Their work can feel confused when it tries to fit in with, but misunderstands, the international art world, and derivative when it grasps it more accurately but fails to add much to it.

For someone engaged in political work, Geers can be strikingly insensitive. 'I've had as hard a time as anyone in this country,' he complained when I mentioned oppression. 'It's damned hard to be a white South African, especially if you've grown up without a lot of money and privilege.' Though it can be unpleasant for whites in South Africa to be constantly reminded of others' suffering, to be denied a right to any sadness that is not empathetic, Geers's life has not been as difficult as myriad others' in South Africa; this kind of competitive self-aggrandisement is deeply troubling.

The competitive tension between black and white artists at the Bag Factory is hard to overlook, much as the residents deny it. Foreign critics and curators tend to focus on black artists even though the work of white artists is generally accessible to them and the work of black artists is often more reliant on local context for its meanings. 'It's pretty unfashionable to be white here,' Kendell Geers said. Wayne Barker, who likes to play the enfant terrible, conflates personal, formal and social concerns in highly theatrical and often angry work. He submitted a work to a 1990 drawing competition under the black-sounding pseudonym Andrew Moletsi, and it achieved some renown. He suggested that all white artists should work in this way to break down the existing barriers.

Among the younger Cape Town artists who work in a similar mode to the Bag Factory group, Beezy Bailey – whose captivating, hyper-expressive, loosely conceptual, highly imagined, pink-and-orange-and-green work had had some success but had never entered the top echelon of South African galleries – took Barker's challenge to heart. In 1991 he submitted work to the prestigious Cape Town Triennial. One piece went in as the work of Beezy Bailey, and three others he submitted as the work of Joyce Ntobe, a domestic worker. No one paid much attention to the Bailey work, but Ntobe's work was purchased by the National Gallery. He revealed the ruse only months later. Bailey and many other white artists believe that the buying of black work because it is black does more in the long run to erode black self-esteem than to increase it. Bailey subsequently mounted a 'collaborative' exhibition of work by himself and Ntobe; he continues to promote his work along with that of his black alter ego, claiming that only by trying to live with both a black and a white vision can one be an artist of the New South Africa. The white liberal community was outraged at Bailey's ploy, but many black artists applauded his courage.

I asked David Koloane, who is black, and Beezy Bailey, who is white, how they became painters. 'I'd always liked to draw,' said Koloane, 'but I never knew you could do anything with this. When I was sixteen, Louis Maqhubela moved in across the street from me and said there were people called artists who did drawing and painting and nothing else as their work. We decided we wanted to do that.' Koloane, at sixteen, had never heard of art. Bailey said, 'When I was sixteen, I was seated next to Andy Warhol at lunch, and he suggested I apply to the London art schools.' Lunch on Fridays is all very well, but it doesn't align such differences.

The White Liberal Artists

The older generation of white liberal artists were tireless in the fight against apartheid, always working to build a more equal society. They were the equivalent of the writers who won vast international approbation: Nadine Gordimer, Athol Fugard, J. M. Coetzee. Yet they did not get nominated for the Nobel Prize or its equivalents; indeed, they languished in relative obscurity outside their country's borders. Their heroism continues to be debated, and so does the quality of the art they produced. Visual art is always more oblique than the written word, and while this could be liberating for such artists, it could also muddy their professions of idealism. Apartheid was dismantled primarily for economic reasons, but the white liberal artists did soften a brutal country with their persistent humanity and moral righteousness. Yet they are now often deemed hypocritical for disdaining a system from which they have benefited and then marketing their disdain. Many white South Africans are almost as embarrassed by the label *liberal* as by the label *racist*. White liberalism can have a sense of obligation about it that is antithetical to art.

Throughout the eighties, the cultural boycott, set up by the ANC in exile and enforced by the United Nations, served to undermine the apartheid government's appearance of legitimacy. Under its terms, foreign artists, athletes and academicians were asked not to come to South Africa, and South Africans not to exhibit or compete abroad. The cultural boycott helped speed the demise of apartheid, but while that isolation had devastating effects for both blacks and whites, it had silver linings. Black artists in South Africa would have been largely cut off from European influences even without the boycott, but white artists would have been working internationally, a possibility that was rendered unavailable except to a wealthy few who could afford to travel. 'The cultural boycott helped to cut the umbilical cord to the U.S. and Europe,' Marilyn Martin said to me, arguing that the independence and vitality of the art scene were the immediate consequence of this isolation. 'Of course the cultural boycott was cutting off our own noses at one level,' said Sue Williamson, one of the leading artists of the older generation. 'But it did have the unsought positive effect of increasing our sense of South Africanness.'

Williamson does sophisticated work in which she confronts problematic local history. For a recent piece, she took scraps from District 6 (a rich and diverse coloured area that was swept away because it was too close to white land and had too pleasant a view for the coloureds), encased them in Lucite, and used these bricks to build a small house, a testimony to what was lost. Penny Siopis's mesmerising paintings and collage/assemblage pieces often address women's history and experience and the integrity of the female body. They are strangely overcrowded, full of faces and bodies pressed close together; the power of her work lies in its hidden quality of empathy as much as in its technical achievement and sophisticated intellectual base. She is both a rigorous thinker and the most humane artist in South Africa.

William Kentridge's work is poetic, lucid and eloquent, fully engaged with the situation of South Africa, but refreshingly free of the political self-consciousness that circumscribes the work of so many of these other artists. Kentridge is producing a series of drawings that make up films (or films that require drawings). He does large charcoal sketches, then redraws and erases them, shooting one frame at a time, to make beautiful symbolist parables, free-form, loosely narrative sequences tied both to the horror of the country and to the elusive associations that define human consciousness. They are at once stark and romantic. Kentridge puts together the music for the films, shows them as shorts, and sells off the final states of the drawings. Unlike the Bag Factory artists, he does not try to exaggerate the importance of South Africa above the rest of the world. 'In Venice, we seemed quaint at best,' he said, referring to the Biennale. 'We must figure out how to enjoy and exploit the margins where we live. Johannesburg will not be the next New York or Paris.' In his latest film, a complex dialogue between a white man and a black woman takes place in symbolic terms as they watch from their separate perspectives the creation of the landscape of the East Rand, an area east of Johannesburg that has been the site of extreme violence. Figures appear, are shot or killed and covered with newspapers, then turn into hills or pools of water and become the stuff of which the landscape is made, so that this bleak terrain, so familiar to all South Africans, comes to be not simply a geological phenomenon, but the physical manifestation of an accrual of deaths.

'My work has many polemics and no message; it is not to inspire people to save the country,' Kentridge said. He has a strong ethical viewpoint, but he shies away from persuasion. The inherent danger of confidence about anything is his work's only surety. He is secure in his methods and bullish in his beliefs, but he is the patron saint of ambiguity. His qualm-riven art consistently reverts to a critique of dogmatism, limning the compelling but necessarily fruitless impulse to know. That phenomena are indecipherable does not mean that they are disastrous. Kentridge presumes injustice to be an ineluctable characteristic of the world. One must confront it even if trouncing it remains impossible. He never lapses into the existentialist proposition that everything is pointless; he merely elaborates on the idea that we seldom know or can even guess the point of anything. But beauty is not incidental to him, nor is humour unserious, and questions are worth asking even if they have no answers. 'One of the tasks of the years has been to find strategies to keep clarity at a distance,' he said. Both the melancholy and the exuberance of his work hinge on the impossibility of resolving most human problems.

Malcolm Payne, David J. Brown, Pippa Skotnes and the capable sculptor Gavin Younge are the most highly regarded of the older artists in Cape Town. Among younger artists, Kate Gottgens's kitschy landscapes are full of romance and dread and cleverly play with the South African obsession with fear. Barend de Wet's sculpture and installation are powerful also. Andries Botha is the leading artist of Durban, and his sculptural constructions often express European ideas with African techniques. Botha has been accused by white liberals of having exploited the workers who actually construct his sculpture. He is inept at the rhetoric of liberalism (an Anglo invention more than an Afrikaans one), but two black assistants defended him to me; they said that by teaching in the townships, he had helped them to make art and sell it out in the world.

Jane Alexander's large-scale models of displaced or homeless black men, built in plaster and then dressed in scrap clothing, are eerie, desolate and compellingly human. 'In the New South Africa, there won't be a place for work like mine,' she commented wistfully but not sadly. 'Everyone wants jolly little black men running around and looking utopian. Black artists paint their leaders the way Russians once painted Lenin. White artists will have to move into the background as part of affirmative action. I taught for a while in a coloured school, in part because I wanted to reach out to that population. But I had to give up my job when a coloured teacher came along who wanted it. In the next ten years, my work will go down to the storerooms, even if to you it looks sympathetic to the struggle.' I talked to her about the current politics, the spirit of compromise, the efforts other whites were making, the impetus for change. She smiled quietly and said, 'A large part of the white population is trying to redress the inequalities as quickly as possible because they want to get it over with.'

Townships and Art

The borderlands between sinister social control and admirable attempts at social improvement are confused across South African society. Within the townships, art centres, mostly set up in the apartheid period, provided a venue for residents to make art and music, to dance, to act, and so on. They kept people off the streets, taught them a cottage industry, and let them discover themselves and their talents. Throughout apartheid, art centres also served a second function. It was illegal to organise political rallies or meetings in the townships, but it was not illegal to organise cultural evenings, and so forbidden organisations, including the ANC, would hold art events as a cover for their activities.

The support of art centres was an international priority until

Mandela's release in 1990. Before the mid-seventies, black art activity occurred only at Cecil Skotnes's Polly Street Centre, at a Swedish missionary-run art school for black students at Rorke's Drift, and at the Johannesburg Art Foundation. The foundation was established by Bill Ainslie, a white painter, as a teaching facility where black and white artists could mix. An abstract expressionist, Ainslie tended to teach abstraction, a safe style during apartheid because it was explicitly non-political. With the black artist David Koloane, Ainslie later set up the Tupelo Workshops, designed to advance racial dialogue.

But the dialogue being advanced was more focused on social reconciliation than on creating good art. I went to a Tupelo workshop in Cape Town, and it reminded me of summer camp. Everyone was talking, laughing and having a good time; the smell of paint was heady, the conviviality, stirring. The same result could equally easily have been realised at a cooking class. Meanwhile, as South Africa fell off the top of everyone's 'oppressed' list following the release of Mandela, the money for socially engineered art centres evaporated. Some have now been abandoned; others have been turned into commercial operations. The Alex Art Centre, at the edge of the Johannesburg township of Alexandra, for example, was once funded by idealists abroad, but now it's virtually a shell; the potter's wheels are still there, but the clay is not. On the other hand, the Katlehong Art Centre – in a particularly dangerous township, where big guys with big guns incongruously achieve peaceable fulfilment through weaving, print-making, carving and drawing – sells work to white South Africans, rendering it one of the township's most profitable enterprises.

Black and white students attend Michaelis, the big art school in Cape Town. A few black people also study in the fine arts departments at Wits (in Johannesburg) and at the Natal Technikon (in Durban). The two independent art schools for blacks are Fuba, in Johannesburg, and Funda, in Soweto. But even in these contexts, the questions of art for art's sake and art as a tool of social advancement are muddled. 'We get letters,' Sydney Selepe, who runs Funda, told me, 'from mothers who say, "My son has failed at school, so please make him an artist."' The graphic artist Charles Nkosi described trying to judge candidates who had never drawn anything except in school science classes. Though some students are sophisticated, others arrive without ever having been to a gallery. 'We ask about their dreams,' Selepe explained. 'In this way, we move forward.' Sometimes, in these unlikely places, a true artist stumbles upon a deep calling.

The role of white people in these contexts is thorny. Stephen Seck, the white director of the Johannesburg Art Foundation, said, 'It's a two-phase process: the colonials destroy, and then the patrons help to rebuild. It's been so fashionable to try to retrieve a "true" black identity, as though the work were somehow more authentic before the whites came. Recently, some black students asked me for a class in colour theory – they wanted to be serious oil painters. Is teaching them to do beadwork instead a matter of restoring their identity, or is it the ultimate apartheid gesture of giving everyone their place?' Whites simultaneously tend to diminish the work of black artists by patronising it and to glorify it by sentimentalising it. Most black and most white artists hate the belittling but commercially successful phrase *township art*, with its echoes of art born in a separate, primitive context; even more, they hate *transitional art*, a phrase that appears often in the press, which implies a logical progression whereby black traditions are supplanted by white ones.

'I know exactly where I come from and who I am,' the painter Alson Ntshangase said to me. He had walked over to meet me when he'd finished his shift as a handyman in a white-run Durban hotel and was in white overalls. 'I grew up in Zululand, and I am a Zulu.' He showed me that underneath this immaculate uniform were ordinary Western clothes, and that underneath those was a traditional Zulu loincloth. 'I don't wear it all the time, but when I feel like I am for-getting.' His work, however, marks some departure from Zulu values. 'Show one of my people a basket, and they will know at once whether the grasses have been well dyed. But show them a painting and' – he looked across the room – 'that plastic shopping bag with the bird on it, and they will not be able to see why one image is better or more valuable than the other.' His painting *The AIDS Doctors* shows a doc-tor, a priest and a *sangoma* (witch doctor) all ranged surrealistically around a patient lying in bed. How to make sense of the science, the spirit, and the black and white views of life and death?

White discomfort when visiting the townships can distort the understanding of art made in these areas, whether it is 'township art' or not. Though the danger of the townships was exaggerated by the apartheid government, and though many whites retain a disproportionate fear of them, township violence is unpredictable and people do get killed. The ritual surrounding a white visit is complex. You are well advised to be accompanied by someone known where you are visiting; it is usually best to meet on neutral ground, then let your guide take the wheel. You are never sure whether you are going to make it into the township on the day you had planned, because often enough your guide may warn you that it's a 'bad day'. Your guide takes responsibility for your safety, and you are dependent on his knowledge, connections and radar. Sometimes during a visit to someone's house or studio, the phone will ring and your host, without any real explanation, will say that you have to leave.

The people I met in the townships all understood the effort involved in a visit; I was given a gratifying, perhaps exaggerated, sense of my own courage. Just by coming, they said, I was doing something for them. They knew that someone thought it was worth the trouble to bring me. That decision stood in contrast to their own experience of segregation. 'I was excluded from many places during apartheid, and I am still excluded in many places,' the painter Durant Sihlali said to me as we sat in his house in Soweto. 'And I am not so eager to include all the whites who say in their casual, offhand way that they want to come here. It's my territory here, and I don't bring anyone who I don't like. It's an effort for me to come into Johannesburg and pick someone up, think about their safety all the time, entertain them, and drive them home. I am not going to give my life over to doing it.'

Sihlali grew up under apartheid, but he is educated, self-assured, even diffident, with a rich use of the English language. As a young man in the sixties, he once stumbled upon some white art students and their teacher who had come to the township to paint. He watched them for a long time, then walked up to one and silently held out his hand. The art student handed Sihlali a paintbrush, and Sihlali finished the picture. The art teacher was impressed by his skill. Although Sihlali could not enroll at the school, the teacher invited him to model for them. 'In this way, though I never lifted a brush during class, I was able to learn everything, just by watching and seeing how the teacher criticised the students.'

For years, Sihlali made a living painting and selling seashell souvenirs and commercial signs; in his free time, he created a series of watercolours depicting local scenes. These figurative watercolours address few of the concerns about the nature of representation that occupy contemporary Western artists. But the work of black South African artists, which often focuses on family, history and dreams, must be understood on its own terms. Sihlali's watercolours document a life that the apartheid government wished to conceal. 'My interest was not in beautiful things, but in recording our history,' Sihlali explained. 'They are not an expression of rage; when you tell the truth, you don't become angry. I felt I had to do it. Often it was a race against time. I painted against the bulldozers as a mode of protest, and when I finished painting a house before they destroyed it, I felt that I had won.'

Sihlali's house was in Jabulani – or, as he called it, 'deepest Soweto'. Houses in the township all have metal grilles over their windows, and Sihlali had made art even of these bars at his house, working them as narrative scenes, one showing a mother and child. We left that area and went to see Vincent Baloyi, a sculptor, and Charles Nkosi in the Chiawelo Extension section of Soweto. There we sent some children off to get us beer and sat in the front room talking. In the townships, you do not in general close your door to your neighbours except when you perceive a threat. It doesn't matter if they are drunk or tiresome or if you just don't like them; the house is open to all, and everyone stops to talk. 'So you are in Soweto!' people would say as soon as they saw me. 'You're afraid now?' And everyone would laugh. 'Tell them it's not so bad, not so bad, not so bad,' they would say. Many wanted to know why I was interested in art. Art is the basis of a proud and almost sovereign dialogue that is rare and precious in the townships, that exceeds in its meanings anything you could adduce from the appearance of the work. 'All this about equality and working with white artists,' said Charles Nkosi. 'It's going to take a lot of time. It's like when you get a new hat. For the first time you have it, it's really a nuisance. You just keep leaving it everywhere, you can never remember you have it, and when it's on your head, you feel the weight of it all the time. Even if you used to be cold, the new hat's not easy to start having.'

The painter Sam Nhlengethwa said, 'People look at my work and they ask me, "How can you do such happy pieces out of the township?" In the townships, it's not just war. We have music, weddings, parties, even though people are dying in the next street. When there is violence, people from outside look only at that. That's wrong. I try for a ratio in my art that reflects the reality: thirty per cent violent pictures, and seventy per cent happy, festive gatherings. The other day I woke up and walked out my door and almost fell over a corpse. So that's a part of my reality, and it goes into my art. But I went out to where I was planning to go anyway. That's how my life is balanced.'

I travelled to the Durban township of Umlazi with Alois Cele, a commercial painter who has in the last five years built up a trade in T-shirts, signs and billboard advertisements. Now he is expanding (curiously) into the juice trade. Cele is a bit of a Zulu hotshot; he teaches voluntary workshops in his township and has been approached by people from other townships who would like him to expand that programme. His success and swagger have given him an air of authority. People come to him for T-shirts and other goods, and he tells those people, who often belong to different political parties, when to come back. 'I tell the PAC guys and the ANC guys and the Inkatha guys, all of them, that I'll have the shirts on Wednesday around four o'clock,' he said, 'and then I keep them waiting so that they'll have to talk to one another. They sit there fuming, but they see one another as people, too. You can do everything through the art business.' Cele's ambitions extend well beyond the art world: 'I'll teach people to think for themselves. Zulu people are dangerous because they are illiterate and believe the first thing they're told. They don't want to think for themselves. Zulus always work together; when they cause trouble, they do it together. I want to teach them to be independent! That's the only way.'

Apartheid had four categories: white, black, Indian and coloured. In Cape Town, I went to the coloured township of Mitchells Plain with Willie Bester, who is perhaps the most highly regarded urban, non-white artist in South Africa. Bester was the son of a coloured mother and a black father; he was classed with the coloured rather than with the black population, thanks to letters from his school saying that his behaviour was of a high standard and that he was therefore not really black. Bester joined the police as a young man, 'to fight crime – and so no one would steal my bicycle'. As a coloured policeman, he was supposed to fight the ANC, but when he read ANC literature, he found it moving. 'These weren't the people for me to be attacking. These were *my* people. If they were the Communist enemy, then I knew I was also the Communist enemy.' Assigned to riot duty, he arrived at the station one day to find a floor-to-ceiling stack of slaughtered black youths. 'One of the officers told me to get rid of the blood that was pouring all over the station, and while I was standing there, stunned, someone else grabbed a fire hose and began washing the blood away, because they thought it would look bad if the media showed up. All these policemen were congratulating one another on how many people they'd killed. I went home that night so sick I couldn't move for days.'

The coloured population today has neither the privilege of the whites nor the self-actualisation of many black Africans, and some coloured people cling to the slight privilege they enjoyed during apartheid. They have too much to be blatantly destructive (like a good many black Africans) and too little to live well (like most whites). This population is fearful in two directions rather than one. Bester's powerful collage-assemblages use found materials of the township in juxtaposition with painted images. One work has bits of barbed wire; a copy of the government book categorising the various races; snapshots of a racist attack that, according to official documents, never took place; and a police officer's ammunition belt. 'When I was younger,' Willie Bester said, 'I did pretty things for white men to buy and hang in their houses to help them ignore what was happening outside. Now I am free. Now I do work about real life and the problems of the townships. Now I am working for myself.'

Black Art, Yes; Black Artists, No

Bester's assertion is only half-true. He may be working for himself, but almost all of his collectors are white. Liberals buy his work both because it is good and because buying it relieves their sense of responsibility. In the current climate, work by non-white artists in which they express their suffering is what white collectors want; you can no longer please them with attractive Cape landscapes. This is progress, but it's hardly freedom. Some non-white people express an interest in non-white art, but few collect it; indeed, few take on board the idea of art as a commercial enterprise. Some of Willie Bester's neighbours own and enjoy his work, but when they attended the opening of his big Cape Town exhibition, they could not believe the prices and were bewildered that so many white people wanted to interview, meet and celebrate him. David Koloane's paintings are collected by a few black doctors, and one hangs in Nelson Mandela's home, but this is a small and rarefied audience. Koloane said, 'The area where the Johannesburg Art Gallery is located was a whites-only park. And now it is a mostly black park. The black people like to take snapshots of one another at the gates of the gallery. But none of them ever thinks of going in.'

South Africa has only three important commercial galleries, all white-owned with almost exclusively white clients, showing a lot of black work: the Goodman Gallery (oldest; the flagship), Everard Read Contemporary (hottest, newest, trendiest) and the Newtown Gallery (a bit unfocused). How is a non-white population to resolve this monopoly of control? It is not simply a matter of who has capital, but of who has the will to engage in this commerce. Eighteen months ago, playwright Matsemela Manaka declared his Soweto home a gallery. When I visited, I found his crew patiently explaining to callers what art was; these visitors, though curious, were there more to observe the strangeness of the set-up than to understand the messages of the work. Linos Siwedi has set up shop as a dealer, but though he used to sell from Soweto, he is now working through Johannesburg because the blacks won't buy and the whites won't come into a district they still perceive as dangerous. He's a middleman, keeping track of what happens in the townships, getting the work into the public eye, setting up exhibitions in rented spaces. He even sets up private art tours of the township for rich visitors. Of the white liberals who have taught in the townships, he said, 'They taught people how to make things, but not how to sell them.' But his admirable effort cannot compete with the larger, commercial, white-owned galleries.

Some people feel that even the radical artists of the black consciousness movement have been co-opted by this system. In allowing their work to be sold by white people to white people, they have become complicit in the existing power structure. Fikile Magadlela was long held up as the ultimate exemplar of black radicalism, but he was among the first to be snapped up by white dealers. 'If your work is in an art gallery, it is working for the state,' Malcolm Payne said. 'Fikile, too, wanted to sell.' Fikile was shown at the Goodman Gallery long before the waning of apartheid. Durant Sihlali's work sold well in the galleries of apartheid-era Johannesburg. 'It was incredible to me,' he said. 'The perpetrators of injustice would buy my work and hang it on their white walls without ever noticing that it was telling the story of their cruelty.'

These artists won prizes at art competitions. South Africa has more competitions in more fields than anyplace else on earth, and these, in Payne's view, 'became the most powerful instrument of oppression.' Although Fikile spoke to me about blood and suffering when we met, he spoke as much about his white collectors, and his recent work seemed studied and somewhat artificial. More than one commenter warned that an artist might 'go the same way as Helen' – a reference to the painter Helen Sebidi, whose beautiful work became repetitive after the galaxy of prizes she won from white juries led her to repeat her inspiration rather than renew it. Even as these painters' art of struggle became a commodity, it served to answer their own struggle to survive. Now, township artists are accused of reducing their heritage to pablum for the white market; crossover artists, of working in a 'European' mode.

I knew that the black Durban artist Trevor Makoba had been featured in the South African exhibition at the most recent Venice Biennale, so when I visited his township, I asked him about the allegorical picture that had been exhibited, which depicted a piece of cheese in the shape of South Africa being nibbled from one side by a black mouse, and from the other side by a white mouse. He, in turn, asked me all about the Biennale. Was it really an important exhibition? Would a lot of people have gone to see his work? When I finished describing the show, he said, a bit sadly, 'I'm glad that I have been in this exhibition. But I do wish that they'd asked me first. I would have liked to talk to them about it.'

I was astonished. 'No one asked you whether you wanted to be in Venice, representing South Africa?'

'No. The first I heard of it was the week of the opening.'

South Africa's invitation to the Biennale (after decades of exclusion) sat with government officials for ages before the rushed 'democratic' selection of the artists, whose work was shipped in days. The government paid for bureaucrats to go to the opening, but did not provide tickets for artists. Several white artists bought their own tickets, and when the South African authorities found, to their embarrassment, that they had many white and no black artists in town, they quickly sent tickets to black artists. In most instances these were people who had never travelled across their own country, much less overseas. The sculptor Jackson Hlungwani sent a message saying, 'The radio is good but the message is bad,' indicating that though he might have liked to travel, this was not the way to go about it. He declined to leave his home in Gazankulu. Makoba made a valiant effort, but even with the help of white friends he couldn't get himself on a plane in time. No one seemed able to say what the arrangements would be in Venice, what would be paid for, how the artists would eat. 'The clear implication,' observed Sue Williamson, a white Cape Town artist, 'was this: you are not important; only the fruit of your labour is important. It's what the whites have been saying to the blacks since the start of apartheid.'

Art from Above

In Gazankulu in the late apartheid period, white liberals set up a programme for local blacks to explore their heritage by learning basket weaving. Since the appropriate grasses did not grow locally and none of the local people knew how to weave baskets, the organisers had to import materials and teachers. No one observed that this area was rich in clay and that these people had a tradition of clay modelling. The basket weaving was absurd. It's not that artists in Gazankulu should have to work only in local media, but simply that ignoring the clay and importing grasses is so wasteful not only of resources but also of abilities; it represents a monolithic view of black people that is one of apartheid's ugliest legacies. Art made according to a political agenda dictated from on high is seldom revelatory.

South Africa has no tradition, in either the black or the white communities, of going to look at pictures. In the same way that developments in American ichthyology tend to be of interest primarily to American ichthyologists, art in South Africa is of interest primarily to South African artists. Though art's audience is limited to its producers, as it was in Soviet Moscow, that number is not small, because in the New South Africa, everyone is being encouraged to make art, including many who, left to their own devices, would never consider such a possibility. 'Rural outreach' programmes, big on the liberal agenda, attempt to persuade people far from urban centres to make art. To this end, enterprising individuals have descended on one community after the next with big pads of paper and lots of crayons, or with beads and thread. The work produced through these programmes is touted as highly 'authentic'.

Creation of such work may help the 'artists' to feel better; looking at it may help its audience to feel better. 'The end product is not so important as the process,' Sue Williamson explained, but even the process she vaunts may be dubious. There is a difference between giving everyone the free voice that is the cornerstone of democracy and trying to make everyone speak in a 'free' voice whether they are so inclined or not. Sue Williamson said earnestly, 'Of course all South Africans are particularly pleased with themselves at the moment for having pulled off something that the world had thought was impossible, just when they'd been written off. But our race has denied that other race, and so every one of those people is *important*; everything they have to say is worth saying, and we must listen to *all* of it.' There is no such thing as an adequate response to apartheid, and the urge to white penance is admirable. But the suggestion that everyone is an artist – that every voice must be heard – is in the end a denial of individuality, not a celebration of diversity.

Affirming that everyone is of equal importance, legally and morally, is one thing; saying that everyone has something to say of equal importance is cacophony; you cannot hear a thousand voices at once and understand what anyone is saying. You have to make choices. I saw Helen Suzman, the human rights activist twice nominated for the Nobel Prize, the week after the decision was made that the New South Africa would have eleven official languages. 'I can't bear to think what will be lost in the translation,' Suzman said to me. The urgency of acknowledging diversity should not upstage the imperative for some kind of unity in a national government.

The Politics of It

The ANC's Department of Arts and Culture believes that art should serve the state, that the struggle is not over, that artists must help to establish the new paradise of South Africa. Chairman Mao advanced the same policy when he launched the Cultural Revolution. The non-party-affiliated National Arts Initiative (NAI), set up by artists and writers, believes that art should be publicly funded and that artists should be free to make art that is true to their experience. President John F. Kennedy advanced the same policy when he set up the National Endowment for the Arts. The writer Mtutuzeli Matshoba commented with some dismay, 'While the NAI purports to represent the interests of "art and cultural practitioners", the ANC's main objective is the cultural liberation of the disenfranchised people of South Africa. The ANC perceives cultural liberation not as an end in itself, but as an aspect of national liberation.' Many object to such a mechanistic, propagandistic vision of art, which leaves no place for free expression. Mike van Graan, head of the NAI, complained, 'Those of us who fought alongside the ANC against apartheid thought that now at last we would have the peace to create, to sing, to laugh, to criticise, to celebrate our visions unhindered. We were wrong.' Later, he confessed to me, 'We have literally been instructed to do work about the ANC but that makes no reference to ANC corruption because that gives ammunition to the nationalists.'

Everywhere you go in South Africa, someone is forming a new committee. Whatever it is, its name is an acronym. At the launch of the NAI, which I attended in Durban, voting rights had been awarded to the AWA, AEA, ADDSA, APSA, ICA, NSA, PAWE, SAMES and SAMRO, while provisional voting rights only were the lot of the ATKV, COSAW, FAWO and PEAP. God help you if you go to an arts function in South Africa and don't know what all these things stand for. The endless speeches at an ANC arts din-ner I attended in a Johannesburg hotel were incomprehensible, even though they were in English, because they included such a dizzy-ing, tedious array of such subgroups. This rage for committees is an unfortunate legacy of the ANC. At dinner with Penny Siopis and Colin Richards, deeply committed white liberals, I commented on the problem. Richards put his hands to his head, saying, 'Those committees! Throughout the apartheid period we went to meetings of those committees – mind-numbing, endless meetings, thousands and thousands and thousands of them, hour upon hour upon hour. That was the only way we could show our support. It was a big part of what we could do against apartheid, but, my God, when I think of the number of tedious hours that went that way, it makes me weep.'

In South Africa, people often said to me, under their breath, as though the air were bugged, 'It's ridiculous, I know.' I heard this from rural people, black and white, in the Northern Transvaal; I heard it in the homes of the white bourgeoisie; I heard it from committed liberals; I heard it from township moderates, on great estates, on farms, in the township drinking houses called shebeens. No one in South Africa will publicly acknowledge the absurdity of anything but apartheid, because apartheid is so much worse than whatever is wrong with the country now. But everyone is aware of spending a great deal of time in an absurd theatre of symbolic respect.

The gratuitous complexity of this bureaucracy was often matched by a surprisingly simplistic approach to complex issues. In South Africa, big questions are very much in vogue. What is art? What is democracy? What is freedom? More astonishingly, confident answers to these questions abound. At the NAI meeting, matters that should have taken five minutes to cover took two hours, but matters that have concerned philosophers across the millennia were settled in time for lunch. As the meeting grew longer and longer, because every speech was being repeated in several languages, the head of the Credentials Committee, Nise Malange, stood up and said that because of the added difficulties, 'The Happy Hour will have to turn into something else.' I was sitting next to the white critic Ivor Powell, who said that the headline for his report on this meeting would be just that line: no context, no explanations.

Several white South African artists I met referred to the Pan Africanist Congress of Azania (PAC) as 'black racists'; the PAC motto has been 'One Settler, One Bullet.' This political group is far to the left of the ANC. But when I met Fitzroy Ngcukana, the PAC's secretary for sports and culture, at eleven o'clock at night in a downtown Johannesburg jazz bar, he was much more forthcoming than any of the ANC people with whom I'd met. He was moderate in his views and expansive in his manner. We talked through much of the night. 'People in the arts are free spirits and have the right to every approach,' he said. 'They should do what they want without political control. Black and white artists should be friends, should learn from each other, cross-pollinate. Sectarianism must stop with the arts.'

The Hinterlands

In some sense, the art of South Africa all feels sullied. The work of black artists has been polluted by their reliance on a white market; the work of white artists has been contaminated by their inevitable complicity in an exploitative system. Oppression poisons both the oppressors and the oppressed, who all long for an imagined, highly romanticised innocence, something untouched and genuine, a prelapsarian rightness. Nowhere has that fantasy seemed closer to the surface than in Venda, one of the quasi-autonomous Bantustans where black people lived in ostensible independence with limited rights of self-governance – albeit with no economic means to sustain themselves except handouts from the central South African government.

As you go north from Johannesburg, the landscape of South Africa grows in scale and grandeur, and you begin to feel that you are incontrovertibly in Africa: the vague Europeanising influence that is so powerful in Cape Town and half-successful in Johannesburg seems to disappear. If this area is a hotbed of gross Afrikaans conservatism, that must be because it is so obvious here that you cannot shut out Africa with a high fence or a well-planted garden of foreign herbs and flowers. The closer you get to Zimbabwe, the uglier the white cities are, and the more gratuitous their ugliness seems. I have never been anywhere else so incongruously free of charm as Pietersburg or Louis Trichardt. The road from Louis Trichardt to Venda climbs slowly into the gentle, lumbering hills south of the Limpopo River. It is still the N1, the biggest highway in South Africa, but its many lanes have dwindled to a ribbon of tar with dirt paths forking from either side. There is not much traffic: a few trucks taking goods up to Zim, a few combies (minibuses), an occasional farm vehicle. When you arrive in Venda, you are made quiet by it; an air of mystery and joy and of a dialogue of spirits hovers over Venda the same way an atmosphere of excitement and bustle and urban decay hangs over New York.

The first time I visited South Africa, two years ago, Johannesburg dealers had described Venda as the land of the innocents, where an authentic black culture still reigned, and I thought it might be the missing link that would make sense of my experience of South African urban black and white art. The Venda people have been carving curios for a long time – bowls, animals, little figures – and the new Venda art, suddenly fashionable in the past five years, connects to this tradition. Some of the works are just inflated knick-knacks; some, parareligious objects; some reflect a Western idea of art. The story of their integration into the South African art market is a pretty good parable for the confused but touching cultural interaction that will be the basis of the New South Africa.

There are no road maps of Venda, an area of about three thousand square miles. The artists are not easy to find; most don't have electricity or indoor plumbing, much less a telephone. You just show up and they are usually at home – and usually glad to see you. The artists are all religious, but it's hard to explain what their religion consists of: it is a hybrid of Christianity and a dozen other mythologies, with regular visits from the spirits of the past, a lot of *sangomas*, and a priestess who rules over the nearby lake where your ancestors turn into fish. When you arrive in Venda, you can get initial directions from Elias, the old man who runs the curio shop by the main road. These you must follow up with local directions as you get closer to where you are going.

I went to Venda with the Cape Town artist Beezy Bailey, and we headed off first to visit Noria Mabasa, the only woman among the Venda artists. We turned off the main road at a field of hemp and passed through a village of mud rondavels with pointed thatch roofs; the people all stopped to look when they saw our car. Many of the women wore traditional dress, their breasts bare, their wrists and ankles glittering with hundreds of thin silver bangles, their bodies wrapped in brilliant, geometrically patterned cloth.

We found Mabasa sitting outside with some friends and relations, barefoot, dressed in a blue smock and a multicoloured knitted hat. 'Most of my things are in Johannesburg now, at an art gallery,' she said. 'Too far away.' But a few pieces were still scattered around outside. She carves hollow trunks into rings of people reaching out towards one another, or dancing, their faces turned outward, strangely intricate. Next to her rondavel, Mabasa had built a new house of poured concrete. 'From my art I am building this,' she said proudly.

'It wasn't my choice to make these things,' Mabasa told us. 'I was sick. So sick, terribly sick.' Mabasa shook and hunched over, as if ill. 'And I had a dream, and a terrible old woman came to me in my dream. And I was very much afraid.' Mabasa stood up to imitate the old woman and pointed with one arm rigid. 'She said I must make some figures from clay, for being well. So after this terrible dream I began to make some figures, and I got well.' Mabasa smiled wide. 'Oh, I was so well again, with making these figures. And it lasted, oh, some years.' Mabasa's laugh is like an explosion. 'And then I was ill again. And again this terrible woman came to me in my dream, and she said I must stop to cut my hair. So each time as it was growing, I began to get more strong and more strong with this hair, and I never am for cutting it again.' Mabasa took off her hat to reveal a fibrous topiary of hair that had been neither cut nor combed. 'And then this old woman came a third time and told me to carve, and that it was the last time – if I carved, she would never be coming and bothering me again. When she was gone, I began to carve my dreams, to keep her away. And she has never bothered me again. Now, when it is a strong dream, I begin with making my carvings.' We walked together behind the house; Mabasa picked some mangoes, which we ate. 'Now these people are coming from Johannesburg and they take my carvings away and sell them. I went to Johannesburg, too. Too many people! Terrible place.' She put her hands up to the sides of her head.

Mabasa's work was about to be shown in Amsterdam, and she was being flown out for the exhibition. It would be her second trip out of Venda. She was the only person in her village to have left it. We warned her that Amsterdam gets cold in winter, and that she must take warm clothes.

'It's really? It's really?' She took snuff.

'You know that there is not so much snuff in Amsterdam,' we said.

'No? I will take a big bag of it with me.' She spread her hands wide to show how big and shook her head with the wonder of it. 'Do they have cigarettes? Mangoes?'

We wanted to see the Ndou brothers, Goldwin and Owen. Mabasa said it was too difficult to explain where they were, and after some cajoling she agreed to come with us. Like Mabasa, Goldwin had earned some money, and he, too, had a 'luxurious' concrete house with a battery-operated television. When we arrived, the mother of the Ndou brothers was standing in front of the house. Tall, erect, dignified, she was bare breasted and wore traditional clothes. When she saw the white men coming in their car, she disappeared into her rondavel, next to Goldwin's house, and emerged wearing the house-coat of a domestic servant.

For fourteen years, Goldwin worked on the railway and lived in a township hostel. Then one day, in Venda, he cut down a mopani tree and saw the hard, dark wood at its centre. 'I said to my little brother Owen, "In Johannesburg they are selling some things from this wood for big money."' Each made a carving, and they took them out to the road to sell, and Goldwin never returned to the railroad. Goldwin speaks slowly, but Owen is anomalously slick. The first time I saw Owen, he was wearing a silk jacket; the second time, he was in tartan trousers and Italian-looking loafers. Three thousand years of history seemed to lie between him and his mother. Unlike other Venda artists, Owen was pretty clued in on current South African politics, but he supported no one. 'It's the good thing in Venda,' he said, 'not too much politics, and no one fighting for politics. No violence.' At Owen's house, I saw a painted wooden sculpture of an angel, wearing a dress Jean Paul Gaultier could not have conceived of, her enormous breasts projecting from green accordion pleats. Another recent work is a six-foot-tall rabbit dressed in plus fours holding a golf club, called *Sport for a Gentleman*. Owen has never seen a golfer, or anyone wearing plus fours. And why a rabbit?

We sat in Goldwin's house drinking beer and listened until the sun set to the international news, which came from the mouth of a six-foot monkey he had carved to hold the radio. Though the Ndou brothers' work, often inspired by their dreams, feels ritual in its strangeness, they are making it to sell and do not weep when a dealer comes and takes it away. They have fixed prices, can negotiate rationally, and have even signed contracts.

The next day, we set off to visit Freddy Ramabulana. In this rural community, Ramabulana is an outsider. He lives in extreme poverty and suffers from a disfiguring skin disease. No one wanted to accompany us to see him. A Johannesburg gallery owner had warned us not to touch the children at Ramabulana's place or we could get worms. Ramabulana's carvings are rough, primitive, frightening. His sculptures feature marbles for eyes and glued-on hair and beards. He carves genitals in full detail, then clothes his carvings in children's dresses, torn pyjamas, long, faded shirts. When we arrived, he was kneeling in the dust and gluing the beard on a carving of a man with his hands stretched out in front of him, holding a large rock. We greeted Ramabulana, and he nodded but did not move; we stood for twenty minutes in the hot sun while he finished his work. Then he went inside his hut to retrieve a sculpture of a kneeling man with painted blood pouring over his face and body. He set the figure down, then positioned the new one above it, so that it was bludgeoning the kneeling figure's head with the rock. Killer and victim both stared blankly ahead. Another piece – an enormous, roughly carved penis – lay on the ground, wrapped in a blanket. When we uncovered it, the children all giggled nervously and scampered around us.

Ramabulana's English was almost incomprehensible, but one felt that his Venda was also probably mumbled and bewildering. Bailey had brought some invitations to his forthcoming exhibition in Cape Town, and he gave one to Ramabulana, who studied it closely for a good four minutes. The painting was of two dancing men with teapots for bodies. 'I can carve this,' he said. We had a hard time explaining that it was just a picture for him to enjoy, that we weren't commissioning him.

Later that day we set out to find Albert Mbudzeni Munyai, rumoured to be mad; the last time his Johannesburg dealer had come to see him, Munyai chased him off the property with a panga, a blade like a machete. He lives in the northern part of Venda, and it took us an hour or so to get to the area. 'Munyai? You must go down the hill and past the Zimbabwe Supermarket,' said the woman we asked for directions. 'Then you cross the river, and after the third big tree on the right, you will see him, sitting in the middle of his orchard and singing.' We found Munyai sitting under a metal awning on the far side of the orchard, intent on his carving. When we drew near, he jumped up and welcomed us as though we were the friends of his childhood, embracing first Bailey and then me. He was good-looking and muscular and wore only a pair of shorts, his hair in tiny dreadlocks, his eyes sparkling. 'You are from America?' he asked me, shaking his head with wonder. 'You have come by flying?'

I said that I had.

'Look at you!' He leaned back. 'Like a butterfly!'

Munyai was first encouraged to make art by the Afrikaans sculptor David Rossouw, the first white artist to befriend his counterparts in

Venda. Munyai was the gardener of a friend of Rossouw's. At first they smoked hash together, then created art together; you can see each of them reflected in the other's work. As we talked, Munyai's wife sat beside him, sanding the sort of large spoon found in local curio shops. Munyai was driving scales into the sides of a wooden fish; we carried on a five-way conversation, with Munyai addressing at least as many comments to the fish as to his wife or to us. 'I have to make the sculpture,' he said, 'so the wood won't be burned. It's so beautiful, the wood! My God! I am saving these pieces of wood from the fire.'

I asked him how he felt about selling his work.

'Oh, my dear. It makes me so sad that you ask me this question. My dear, it breaks my heart every time. But I must have some tools for working. The children play more games with three pebbles than with two. But, my dear, these men coming for buying: this money talk is ugly talk.' Later, when we were looking at his work, which combines wood and metal, he said, 'I cannot live with all my work. Thanks to God that these people come and take it away from me! It's too strong for me, too powerful. If I live with it all the time, I am made weak by it.' We wanted to see his sculptures more clearly, but he hesitated to bring them out into the sun: 'You don't know what they can do.'

Munyai sent his wife to fetch a sheaf of papers. 'Can you tell me, please, what is in these papers?' Munyai had won an Honourable Mention in a pan-African competition for indigenous art. The judges declared that this artist, by melding postmodern influences with a traditional African spirit, had successfully synthesised separate schools of art and was therefore a voice of a rising Africa, at once a guardian of tradition and an avowed modernist. Munyai's work was chosen over that of hundreds of other artists. 'It's really?' he asked. 'My God, my dear, it's wonderful!' He looked at me, his head to one side. 'You will go and write about my work for the people in America?' I nodded. He burst out in a long, wonderful laugh. 'Everyone must see it!' he said. Then, serious: 'They must understand it. It's magic work.' He walked us back to the car. He looked at it for a long moment. 'Go on, then, and fly along the ground.'

Our last day in the region, we went down to the neighbouring area of Gazankulu to see Jackson Hlungwani, often identified as the greatest black artist in South Africa. Until two years ago, Hlungwani lived in an Iron Age site on top of a hill, among the great stone circles that mark the site of an ancient citadel. God came to Hlungwani and told him to live there, to make great carvings to His glory, and Hlungwani laid out a sacred ground filled with giant monuments, some of them as high as trees, surrounding a crucifix twenty feet high. Hlungwani became famous all over Venda and Gazankulu for his preaching and his life in 'the New Jerusalem', and for his personal iconography; his strange four-eyed faces, as eerie and intimidating as the heads on Easter Island, seem alive, as though Hlungwani has set free something organic in the trees.

Five years ago, Ricky Burnett came up from the Newtown Gallery in Johannesburg and said he could make Hlungwani famous and send his work all over the world. Hlungwani got excited and told Burnett to take everything, and Burnett took everything. At the end of the retrospective, Hlungwani, enraptured by the adulation he had attracted, gave Burnett permission to sell everything. Hlungwani's work went all over the world, and he became the most famous black artist in southern Africa. But when the great monuments from the New Jerusalem were sold, Hlungwani felt the spirit go out of him. Defeated and lost, he climbed down from his hill and left the stone citadel. Hlungwani says he has been betrayed and curses Burnett; Burnett says he has taken good care of Hlungwani and that if he didn't want to sell the work, he shouldn't have offered it. In 1985 Burnett had staged an exhibition called *Tributaries*, which flew in the face of the received wisdom that South Africa had no artistic activity outside white circles. Featuring artists from Venda and elsewhere, the show began to break down the solid wall between black and white artistic experience. '*Tributaries* was our Armory show,' said William Kentridge. But it can be hard to find the line between amplification and exploitation of these 'authentic' artists.

We found Hlungwani sitting in the shade between the legs of a giant devotional figure, carving a stack of angels. He started to tell us about his vision: 'I'm rebuilding the Garden of Eden.' We expressed interest, and he said, pointing ahead, 'You go up that hill until you see God, and then you will find it just on the other side, among the trees.' On the hill, we found God. Hlungwani had carved an entire fallen tree with a complex many-featured face (dozens of eyes, several noses); in the garden beyond, we found more carvings. Hlungwani told me that I must go and look the snake in the eyes. He sent me to the edge of the hill, where a ten-foot white piece of wood sat on several little wooden props. I looked at the butt end of the wood and came back. 'It's the snake,' he confided, 'and it was in the ground and on the ground. That's where the evil comes from!' he almost bellowed. 'I dug it up and I am keeping it off the ground, and so now there will be peace. Peace in the New South Africa and in the world.'

He brought out two carvings. 'I have something for you, for your spirit. This one is finished.' He showed me an angel. 'It's perfect. This one is not for you.' He picked up the second one. 'This one is not finished. I am giving it to you so you can finish it from your own spirit.' I looked closely at the two angels. 'Use your brain! Give him a face yourself! This angel is full of love! Tell the people in America all about it!'

People in Venda still talk about Nelson Mukhuba. His surviving sculptures are astonishing: graceful and alive, as though the spirit of the wood had been released from it. When the Venda craze was just getting under way, the Market Gallery in Johannesburg offered Mukhuba a one-man show. Everyone in the Johannesburg art world went to the opening, for which Mukhuba himself had travelled down from Venda. Into the room he danced, among the swanky crowd with their glasses of white wine. He was wearing a high-peaked cap and walking on stilts, and from top to bottom, he was almost twelve feet tall. He had brought drummers from Venda, and as they drummed, he danced through the opening, incredibly lithe on his stilts; to add to the spectacle he blew fire from his mouth. The exhibition was a raging success.

A month later, on a sunny day in Venda, Mukhuba took a panga, cut down the trees around his house, killed his wife and children, set fire to his home and all his remaining work, and hanged himself. Some people say that Mukhuba just went mad. Some say that a spirit came for him. Many think that it was a *muti* death, that someone had cursed him. Perhaps it was the chief, who, some people say, was not pleased to see all the money and attention going to Mukhuba. Perhaps it was some other artist. Or perhaps it was the violation of a way of life that occurs when a rapacious market and a naïve artist come into contact. Everyone in Venda still talked about Mukhuba, but no one spoke about the circumstances of his death. In Venda, *sangomas*, witch doctors, are still held in awe. Some are much loved, but those who have misused their powers are stoned to death. 'I am always thinking of Mukhuba,' Mabasa told me, and her big smile left her face for a minute, and she looked dark, and I was suddenly frightened.

On Seeing and Being Seen

Black artists are influenced by white culture just as white artists are by black culture. 'To tell the truth,' David Koloane said to me, 'my first influence was the local movie house, not the African tradition.' Tony Nkotsi has emerged as a remarkable painter by any standard – 'but,' one ideologue I met groused, 'it might as well be white art.' Ivor Powell has suggested that the 'innocence' so many South Africans associate with Venda cannot continue indefinitely, that as the dealers keep going to Venda, the artists there will begin to cater to the market, and the magic will be lost. It will not work, however, for a paternalistic white establishment to set out to 'preserve' the tradition. If it can survive, it will survive; if not, those who have witnessed it will always count ourselves lucky.

'What one is doing in one's own studio doesn't sound like the same question as what is happening in the country, but very often they are the same question,' William Kentridge told me. 'The personal concerns have to be interesting as thoughts outside in the world, and what I contemplate in the world has to have resonance in the studio: there has to be something to make or draw. I work through inversions and transformations.' Those are the inversions and transformations that are central to the work of black and white artists in

South Africa. Politics is front and centre in the minds of most South Africans in this period of new freedoms and new anxieties, but art that is only about the political situation tends to be dull. Sometimes, the refusal of politics can be a noble stand, but often art about artists' internal processes becomes tiresome. Of all the South African artists whose work is both optimistic and pessimistic about both art and social progress, Kentridge is the most coherent. His work is always intensely personal and legibly political.

One rather cold night towards the end of my stay, I found myself in a small house in Johannesburg with a black artist named Paul Sekete. I had been asking him about exhibitions, shows, internationalism. 'I think art should make people happy, not just show them what it's like to be happy,' he said. 'I want to make people happy. That's what we need from art.' It was late, and we were both tired. 'Can you make people happy?' I asked. Sekete reached out one hand and began to tickle me, and I started to laugh. 'You see how easy it is?' he asked. We had been talking about a white conceptualist we both knew. 'That stuff – it's okay, but it isn't art,' he said. 'Such a waste of time. Why do they keep doing it?'

A few days later, I saw the white artist – and his excellent work – and described my evening with Sekete. I got as far as recounting being tickled, and he interrupted me. 'But that isn't art,' he said irritably. 'I thought you were here to write about the damned art scene, not to do more PC quasi-political reporting. If some guy tickled you in New York, would you write it up for an art magazine?'

It should be noted that each of them had given me an invitation to an exhibition where their work was being shown together and had used that invitation to demonstrate the point, close to both their hearts, that the art world had no racial differences, that they shared a vision in which they were all the same. But their showing together did not mean that they wanted the same things out of art, any more than the listing of blacks and whites together in the population registers of the New South African government means they will vote in commensurate ways or for reconcilable reasons. It's slow, frustrating progress from artistic tolerance to aesthetic parity. But remembering how the artists I'd seen upon arrival had decried Barbara Masekela's invisibility to a flight attendant, I was struck by how hard these two artists were looking at each other, even if neither was fully convinced by what he saw.

————————

Riason Naidoo, director of the National Gallery, said in 2013, 'The market today is unrecognisable from what it was ten years ago. It has become more professional; there is more competition with many more commercial galleries, and there are many international museums and collectors acquiring South African modern and contemporary art, which can only be good for the artists. South African commercial galleries are now more visible at international art fairs from Miami to Berlin.' His point becomes only more relevant when one compares the recent past with all I had first witnessed two decades earlier.

As in Russia and China, there is an ongoing problem of censorship. In 2012, the ANC sought to censor a painting by artist Brett Murray of polygamist president Jacob Zuma as Lenin with his penis exposed; it was a reproof of corruption in South African government. In an ANC official statement, Jackson Mthembu announced, 'We have this morning instructed our lawyers to approach our courts to compel Brett Murray and Goodman Gallery to remove the portrait from display as well as from their website and destroy all printed promotional material . . . It is in our view and we remain steadfast in that the image and the dignity of our President as both President of the ANC, President of the Republic, and as a human being has been dented by this so-called piece of art by Brett Murray at Goodman Gallery. We are also of the view that this distasteful depiction of the President has violated his individual right to dignity as contained in the constitution of our country.' Zuma supporters soon entered the gallery and smeared paint all over the image, effectively destroying it. The leader of the Shembe Church, which has millions of congregants, ordered that Murray be stoned to death. Steven Friedman, the white director of the Centre for the Study of Democracy in Johannesburg and a columnist for *Business Day*, wrote that Murray's painting was regarded by many black people 'as yet another example of the contempt in which they believe they are held by white people'. In contrast, Aubrey Masango, a black writer for the *Daily Maverick*, worried that South Africa's rulers 'will hijack misinformed ideas of cultural identity and manipulate the real economic discomfort of the masses to generate sympathy'. Jonathan Jansen, the black vice chancellor of the University of the Free State, wrote, 'I cannot think of a more necessary dialogue that must take place than between these two hard-line positions, but this being South Africa, heat overcomes light. Both corners in their rigid self-righteousness boxed the living daylights out of each other as they came flying out of their corners in this bloody fight.' A decision by the Film and Publication Board to 'classify' the painting as offensive and potentially harmful to children was ultimately overturned.

In 2013, controversy erupted over the removal from the Joburg Art Fair of a painting by Ayanda Mabulu depicting President Jacob Zuma in a manner that the curators thought might offend the fair's sponsors. Explaining his reasoning, the event organiser acknowledged that the decision was provoked by concern over the ability of the fair to attract future financial support: 'I felt that the art fair has a responsibility to the creative economy and the painting could compromise that.' The painting was reinstated after photographer David Goldblatt, the fair's featured artist for that year, threatened to quit in protest. Mabulu said, 'It's not the first time that I've been censored. I find it difficult to witness the same thing that was happening during the apartheid era happening today. It makes it difficult to understand in which direction we are going as South Africans, and artists, if we are going to allow the minority, two people, to decide what's palatable for you people.'

Controversy subsequently arose over the appointment of two white curators for the South African Pavilion of the 2015 Venice Biennale and over their selection of only three women out of thirteen exhibiting artists, including only one black woman. Stefanie Jason of the Johannesburg *Mail & Guardian* noted, 'Can a country whose reputation of butchering foreigners is being streamed around the world afford the further embarrassment of a pavilion in crisis?'

Vlady's Conquests

New Republic, June 1994

Vladimir Zhirinovsky is founder and leader of the nationalist Liberal
Democratic Party of Russia, and served as vice chairman of the State
Duma, or the lower house of parliament, until 2011. The BBC called
him 'a showman of Russian politics, blending populist and nationalist
rhetoric, anti-Western invective, and a brash, confrontational style'.
Howard Amos, writing in the *Guardian*, called him a 'nationalist
firebrand'. A flamboyant, belligerent, crude, obstreperous, inflammatory, racist, sexist, homophobic, authoritarian buffoon, he has grown
no more appealing in the two decades since I wrote this piece.

———

At a recent party in New York with various members of the
Moscow intelligentsia, the topic of conversation was, of
course, Vladimir Zhirinovsky. I was surprised to find that members
of that liberal circle who had first championed Gorbachev spoke of
Zhirinovsky with the sort of good-humoured affection that so many
Americans seemed to have for Ollie North in his heyday. 'You know,'
said one, 'he's just a cynic. Everyone in Moscow is a cynic. Everyone
in New York is a cynic. It's not such an interesting problem.'

Amused by my curiosity about their leading nationalist, the
Russians suggested I join them the following evening to meet Zhirinovsky's New York friends and advisers. At ten at night at the

kitschy restaurant called Russian Samovar on West Fifty-Second Street, I was introduced to several bearish-looking men with broad features and beards, who wore turtlenecks with their dark blue suits. My attempts to discuss Zhirinovsky's anti-Semitism were curtailed by the Unforgettable Eugenia, a seventy-two-year-old woman in a long sequined dress, who wore enormous plastic glasses and sang Russian Jewish folk tunes. 'I spent last month with him,' one member of our group reported between songs, producing snapshots to prove it. 'It's a shame, you know – he's really getting very arrogant, not nearly as funny as he used to be. Famous people always have this problem with their sense of humour.'

I wondered how funny he used to be and said that he seemed strikingly unfunny these days. 'You've been reading the New York papers too much,' one man said. 'Vladimir just likes power and attention. Everyone hated him at school; he was the class clown, and provincial! So he says whatever will make him popular now, but he doesn't believe any of his own rhetoric. He's not like Rutskoi or Hitler or Stalin. It's all a joke, the biggest joke around.' I thought this was pushing cynicism pretty far, but I didn't get to say so because the Unforgettable Eugenia began her grand medley from *Fiddler on the Roof*.

'Let's go somewhere we can talk,' said Zhirinovsky's friends, and they led me to a basement at the corner of Fifty-Seventh Street and Eleventh Avenue, where I found what appeared to be a reproduction of the lobby bar at the Intourist Hotel, circa 1986. A band in navy-blue jackets with yellow piping was singing Beatles songs in Russian. A mirrored ball revolved overhead, and every table had plates of those revoltingly grainy tomatoes and cucumbers I had thought you could grow only in the depleted soil of the steppes.

I asked whether Zhirinovsky was gay, a rumour I'd heard from friends in Moscow. 'He's never very interested in women,' someone remarked. 'And he's always got those good-looking young guards around him.' Someone else knew a male poet who claimed to have had a long-term liaison with Zhirinovsky. The vodka had been going around, so everyone was keen to be helpful at this point. 'If you want to sleep with him, we could probably arrange that for you,' one volunteered. Another shrugged and said, 'It might be fun to write about afterward,' then added *sotto voce*, 'but I know, believe me. I'd think twice about it if I were you.'

I was somewhat distracted by the women who had come to join us, all wearing enormous quantities of turquoise eye shadow, one sporting a floor-length black satin dress and black satin gloves up to her shoulders with jet buttons. Feeling out of my depth in the political conversation, I got up and danced under the mirrored ball to 'All You Need Is Love' and 'Let It Be', making good use of the slow-dance two-step that I had last utilised in high school. When I sat down, I pointed out that even if Zhirinovsky was really an actor and didn't believe his own rhetoric, he might get trapped by it. 'Don't worry,' someone said. 'He won't get enough power to be trapped. He'll just get influence. Russians are too cynical to elect such a cynic.' I expressed relief. 'A cynic like that,' said one of the company, 'could much more easily be elected mayor of New York, even president of the United States.' He slapped his hand on the edge of the table. 'That's why we live here,' he said, and burst out laughing.

'Don't Mess with Our Cultural Patrimony!'

New York Times Magazine, 17 March 1996

In 1995, the Metropolitan Museum was planning a sensational exhibition of work from the National Palace Museum in Taipei, and they were courting press coverage. They anticipated safe, flattering articles about how loans of the first order were being brought over for a spectacular installation. My first draft of this story consisted mainly of a semi-scholarly discussion of Song dynasty Chinese painting, which I had studied in college. When plans for the show began to unravel, my essay had to be rewritten entirely. It ran as a cover story with an image of a landscape painting by the Song master Fan Kuan behind a rope and the caption 'The Chinese Masterpiece You Won't See at the Met'. Although the curator was distressed by that cover, the exhibition was among the most visited in the museum's history. As I'd learned in Moscow and Beijing, controversy can be a great ally of art. If this exhibition was important enough to provoke national protest in Taiwan, it must be worth seeing.

On 20 January, someone under the misapprehension that I was an employee of the Metropolitan Museum of Art hit me quite hard in the jaw. It was my last night in Taipei, and I'd gone with art-world friends for a late drink at an attractive bar near my hotel. On one side of us, some skinny young men with loosened neckties were using mobile phones; on the other, two young women in chic Japanese eyeglasses giggled. Nearby, a guy with jeans and a leather jacket was punctuating his Chinese sentences with snatches of California-style English. It was Saturday, around midnight, and we were drinking beer with salted prunes in it, as is done in Taipei. I was quietly describing my dinner that evening with Chang Linsheng, vice director of the National Palace Museum in Taipei; Maxwell Hearn, the Met's curator of Asian art; Shih Shou-chien, director of art history at Taiwan University, and others.

The guy with the leather jacket, who had overheard me, walked over and leaned heavily on our table. 'Don't mess with our cultural patrimony,' he said in a tone of voice that in America is not usually associated with the phrase *cultural patrimony*. 'We're onto your tricks.' He was speaking loudly, and several people clustered around. They did not strike me as a museum-going crowd.

'You'll never get the Fan Kuan,' one of them taunted. 'You'll never get any of the twenty-seven. You'll be lucky if you get a few Qing bowls.' The mobile-phone users, sensing trouble, had removed themselves to the other side of the room. The young women with the eyeglasses followed.

'The conservation status of works of art is awfully technical,' I said gently. It seemed a harmless enough remark, but I could not have raised the tension more if I had advocated the subjugation of Taiwan to mainland rule.

'You Americans don't know a thing,' a round-faced man breathed through clenched teeth.

Then someone said, 'What are you, a spy from the Metropolitan?' – and socked me in the face.

A friend grabbed my arm. 'Come on, someone just said you *do* work for the museum – there's going to be trouble.' He hurried me out into the damp night.

The conversation at dinner had been about the exhibition of Chinese art from the Palace Museum that was to open at the Met in less than two months. The show was the flower of more than five years of careful negotiation and represented economic, social and cultural cooperation at the highest level. Many museum shows require delicate international diplomacy, but this one was unusually loaded with political meaning. At a moment when the United States was alternately currying favour with China and slapping its wrist over human rights violations, and when China was threatening to force a reunification with Taiwan, which it considers a renegade province, the exhibition would remind an American audience of Taiwan's presence and its increasing hunger for self-determination. The opening date of the Met show – Tuesday, 19 March – would be just four days before Taiwan's first free presidential election, a display of freedom that had already led the mainland to rattle its sabres at almost deafening volume. Moreover, the show would be the greatest exhibition of Chinese art ever mounted in the West, curated to tell the tradition's entire history – a history that is Taiwan's, not China's, to dispense because Chiang Kai-shek took all the pre-eminent monuments, paintings, calligraphy, ceramics, jades and bronzes when he fled to Taiwan in 1949. The Chinese believe that the collection was stolen and should be returned to Beijing.

So, on 3 January, two weeks before the art was to be packed for shipping, the protest movement began. The export of this 'cultural patrimony' – whether China's or Taiwan's – had incensed many people on the island. By mid-month the situation had become a crisis. Whether the art should or would travel dominated the evening news and the front pages of Taiwanese newspapers and became a rallying point on university campuses. Legislators and ministers, poets and painters found themselves in an unlikely alliance against the Palace Museum, in a bizarre but telling display of Taiwan's deep identity crisis. No one could say whether the show – the cornerstone of the Met's season – would be cancelled. Nor could anyone say what the protests meant for the future of Taiwan.

Wen C. Fong, sixty-five, came from Shanghai to Princeton University as a student in 1948, and when the revolution began back home a year later, he stayed on. He is now a professor of art and archaeology at Princeton and chairman of the Asian art department at the Metropolitan Museum. Fong, an imposing but cheerful man, is also a member of Taiwan's Academia Sinica, the island's most advanced institute of higher learning, and enjoys access at the highest levels – the most coveted commodity in Chinese societies. Taiwan's art world is full of his former students, and being in Taipei with his blessing is like being in Oz with the kiss of Glinda the Good glowing on your forehead. Fong's scholarship is sterling, his opinions rigid, his passion exhilarating. When, during an early meeting about the Met show, Palace Museum officials tried to withhold some paintings, Fong suggested that it might be better to do just a ceramics show. The paintings went back on the list.

Fong has made the Met's Chinese collection first-rate, and his seminal book *Beyond Representation* narrates Chinese art history through that collection. He had always coveted the work in Taiwan, so when the Palace Museum loaned a few pieces to the National Gallery of Art's *Circa 1492* exhibition in 1991, he told Philippe de Montebello, the Met's director, 'This is our moment to strike.' Fong went to the National Gallery opening in Washington to press his cause with Chin Hsiao-yi, director of the Palace Museum in Taipei. Chin, who had been Chiang Kai-shek's amanuensis, is now in his seventies and has the stiffly gracious manner of a minor deity. He and Fong have a friendship as carefully tended as a military alliance, within which the terms of the Met exhibition were negotiated. The contracts were finally signed in 1994.

Taiwanese politics caused trouble right from the start. Even though the $6.2 million show seemed an obvious blockbuster, Mobil backed out as a potential sponsor in 1994, worried that any support for Taiwan would offend the Chinese government. In August 1995, under pressure from Beijing, Citibank withdrew its sponsorship as well; Acer America, a subsidiary of the eponymous Taiwanese computer company, pulled out when the protests began.

Protectionism is not unusual in the art world. Popular protests occurred in Mexico against the Met's big Mexico show, in Italy against the Vatican show, in Greece against *Greek Art of the Aegean Islands*. Nor is it unproductive for exhibitions to have diplomatic goals: the Met's 1978 King Tut show ameliorated perceptions of Egypt as that country eased out of war with Israel. For societies whose history transcends their modern reality, artefacts of that history are as potent as weaponry or wealth.

In this case, more than internal Taiwanese politics was at stake: the tenuous relationship among China, Taiwan and the United States had come into play. If Taiwan can sustain order and wealth and democracy, as it seems to be doing, then it becomes a model for democracy in China. American support of Asian democracies advances our foreign-relations goals in China more than economic boycotts or statements about human rights. Though China's militant Taiwan policy has many causes, hatred for that democratic model is a major one. Being the host country for this show would be the perfect cultural complement to our economic support of Taiwan, so the emerging crisis over the show was our crisis as well.

It is impossible to separate the history of the Palace collection from the history of China. Most of the work had political underpinnings when it was made many centuries ago, and it continues, amulet-like, to exert political influence today. Taiwan's Legislative Yuan, or Parliament, understanding the Met exhibition to be a diplomatic matter, allocated $3.1 million to help pay for it. 'Since the current status of Taiwan prohibits its government from making statements about politics to its primary ally – the U.S. – it must communicate with economics and culture,' Fong said. 'Cultural communication is about to rise to the same level as economic.'

Last October, I attended the celebrations for the Palace Museum's seventieth anniversary. The Song dynasty (960 to 1279 AD) is to China what the Renaissance is to the West, and for the anniversary exhibition, the museum had brought out its greatest masterworks by Guo Xi and Fan Kuan. The issues of representation at which the West arrived after the invention of photography – those complex webs of abstraction and uncertainty that were opened up by Cézanne and taken up by Picasso and Duchamp – can be read in these Chinese works from a thousand years ago. The same paintings can be inter-preted historically and contextually; artists of this era invested their work with secret political signals, using painting to communicate what was forbidden. Such painting is also full of a native vocabulary: every tree has its meaning, sometimes multiple meanings: plum trees, for example, can refer to sexual potency among old men or to someone surviving a harsh winter; a plum tree that grows in a back palace courtyard can symbolise a neglected lady whose beauty has passed, or, by extension, a courtier who was favoured but is no longer sought by the emperor. Pine trees are held to be principled gentlemen for staying green all through the winter while other trees change colour. Each season means something, each kind of rock, each enveloping cloud of mist.

This work both reflects and demands a specific, meditative, exalted state of mind. Nearly one thousand years ago, Guo Xi – whose *Early Spring* shows a dynamic feeling of movement and excitement, half fantasy and half reality – wrote, 'It has been said that there are landscape paintings one can walk through, landscapes that can be gazed upon, landscapes in which one may ramble, and landscapes in which one may dwell . . . If one looks with the heart of the forest and the streams, they will be lofty. But if one approaches them with an arrogant eye, they will appear diminished.'

Guo Xi was the court painter for the exuberant new emperor Shenzong, who had come to power in 1067, five years before *Early Spring* was painted, bringing with him dramatic plans – the New Policy – to change China. Early spring is the time of renewal and change, and the painting is an allegory for the political reworking and social reordering of the society: peasants and fishermen are at the bottom of the picture, monks just above, an official on horseback a bit higher than that. It is an entire peaceful but shifting hierarchy revealed in layers. Mists obscure certainty, but at the height of the painting is a perfect clarity, for at the helm of the society was the exquisite conviction of Shenzong. Despite that flattery, the painting is honest, too; it lacks compositional stability, as befits the beginning of a new emperor's reign. Next to Fan Kuan's earthier *Travellers amid Streams and Mountains*, which is dated about fifty years earlier, *Early Spring* looks like an explosion of whim and air.

Nowhere else can you see such works side by side and thereby understand so much of the ethos and aesthetics of dynastic China. The museum where the Imperial Collection is housed opened in Taipei in 1965, though the Palace Museum was officially established in 1925 in Beijing. The seventieth anniversary was celebrated in both Taipei (where the collection resides) and Beijing (where the name *Palace Museum* is used to refer to the Forbidden City); in Taipei, you felt as if you were at the Pope's birthday dinner in Avignon. I was with a New York delegation that included Philippe de Montebello and Wen Fong. We were shepherded into an auditorium for lectures, then to a party. President Lee Teng-hui, the prime minister, and the most important legislators from the ruling Kuomintang (KMT) party were in attendance, but virtually no one from the art world was present. De Montebello called it 'the most peculiar museum event I have ever attended'. The officials whirled around Fong; I could little have guessed what rage against him I was to encounter three months later.

If there were an emperor in Taiwan, he would probably choose to live in the Palace Museum. Situated on a green mountain at the northern edge of Taipei, the hyper-Chinese building reigns over and embraces the city at its feet. If you lean over the carved banister that runs up its 130 marble steps, you can take succour from the gardens below: the pools of carp, as happy as the Taoist writer Zhuangzi could imagine; the pines, emblematic of the Confucian virtue of constancy; the tea-drinking pavilions, crowded with schoolchildren on field trips; and the beautiful rocks, to which young brides come daily to have their wedding portraits made.

The interior, however, is miserable: ceilings oppressively low or pompously high, lighting hideous, installation cases designed for security rather than accessible display, wall labels stunningly uninformative. You cannot linger on these inadequacies, however, because spread before you like a fool's supper is the greatest art of China: Neolithic jades, Zhou drinking vessels, Song porcelains, Qing treasure boxes and, most exalted of all, an astonishing array of Tang and Song painting and calligraphy. This work, accumulated by emperors over more than eleven centuries of dynastic rule, is still called the Imperial Collection. No Western museum has such a concentration of great work, but then, no Western country has a history as relatively uninterrupted and permanently centralised as China's.

The Imperial Collection remained in the hands of the last emperor until he was evicted from the Forbidden City in 1924. The next year, when the Palace Museum was established in Beijing, the collection, unseen by the public for a thousand years, was finally put on display. When the Japanese invaded Manchuria in 1931, however, the collection was sent in twenty thousand wooden crates to Shanghai for safekeeping. It later went to a storage facility in Nanjing, and when the Japanese army was on the verge of taking over the southern capital in 1937, the crates travelled by boat up the Yangtze, by train over the Qinling Mountains, by truck to Hanzhong. Every single object made it to a safe location, despite a sequence of sinking ships and blown-up buildings worthy of James Bond. At the end of the Second World War the collection was returned to Nanjing, still crated, and when the Communists drew near in 1947, Chiang simply took the best with him to Taiwan, storing it in tunnels hollowed out of the side of a mountain.

There the work stayed except for one year, starting in spring 1961, when some two hundred pictures and objects – including Fan Kuan's *Travellers amid Streams and Mountains* and Guo Xi's *Early Spring* – toured the United States in *Chinese Art Treasures*, the show that, Fong said, 'single-handedly created modern Western scholarship in this field'. After seeing that exhibition, J. Robert Oppenheimer, father of the atomic bomb, said to Wen Fong, 'If all were to be destroyed on the earth except what we could fit in a single spaceship, some of these paintings would have to be on that ship.' Four years later, Chiang finally opened the doors of the new Palace Museum in Taipei. Despite having lost China's great cities and most of its population and land, Chiang had retained one great treasure: the Imperial Collection.

People who work at the Palace Museum in Taipei do not leave. They enter it young, their good doctorates barely sufficient to earn entry-level jobs as tour guides. They will grow old within this place, which will be the locus of their social and professional lives. Those lucky enough to become curators will have their books published by the Palace, and directly or indirectly, their books will be about the Palace. They will be trained in the weird history of the collection and allowed into the fabled storerooms, where 99 per cent of the works lie in elegant silk boxes, carved wooden cases, or great metal trunks. They will play on the Palace Museum badminton team. 'It's the last vestige of the Chinese feudal system,' one curator said.

This collection does not travel even within Taiwan, which is why the decision to send its greatest objects – 475 of the world's most important works of Chinese art – to the United States became so incendiary. Among the items scheduled to go to the Met were twenty-seven from the Palace Museum's 'restricted list' of particularly exalted pieces, usually displayed for only forty days every three years. Whereas Americans tend to think of a museum primarily as an educational institution that mounts displays for the public, the Chinese think of a museum as a storehouse that safeguards cultural treasures. Art lovers in China enjoy looking at paintings, but beauty is considered incidental to historical value. Sending Fan Kuan's painting abroad therefore is a bit like lending out the original of the Declaration of Independence or the Constitution.

The art at the Palace Museum hangs with eighteenth-century attributions despite recent scholarship suggesting that many of them are incorrect. 'If they started reattributing paintings, they'd be accused of devaluing the collection!' one Taiwan art scholar told me. 'Imagine the hysteria there would be in the Legislative Yuan if they said a certain work was not really Fan Kuan!' Instead, scholars at the Palace reattribute work in secret ways. In the Chinese tradition, important paintings hang in the autumn; if you see a Fan Kuan in spring, you know that Palace authorities believe it is not by Fan Kuan. The phrase *This work is not characteristic of the artist's style* in a label also signifies reattribution. One of Wen Fong's major negotiating triumphs was permission to hang work at the Met with his own attributions.

On 2 January, the Palace opened a preview exhibition of the works destined for New York. 'We thought we should exhibit this material so that people could see it; then we would show it again on return so they could see it was the same work in good condition,' said Chang Lin-sheng, the museum's pellucid deputy director and the force behind Chin's throne. The preview included everything going to the Met except the twenty-seven items on the restricted list. A label on the wall explained that since these pieces had just been displayed for the seventieth anniversary, they did not need to be exhibited again now. Had this statement been more diplomatically phrased, it was to be pointed out, perhaps the protests wouldn't have happened.

The restricted list has little to do with fragility. Scrolls must be remounted every few hundred years but are otherwise stable. Rolling and unrolling, however, must be done with care. At the Palace, this service is performed mostly by old soldiers who came over with Chiang and were retired as 'technicians'. One senior technician in particular tends to create strain marks. ('He likes to do a final twist and hear them go *ieieiek*,' said one horrified scholar.) The restricted list includes early works that were at one point being unrolled five or six times a week for examination. In the mid-1980s, Chin made up the restricted list to have an official excuse for refusing to accommodate visiting scholars. But the implication is that the pieces might vaporise if someone breathes on them, and the wall label at the preview reinforced that paranoia.

On 3 January, as Chin escorted the vice director of the Legislative Yuan through the exhibition, a self-described 'irate art lover' named Tang Hsiao-li, a young woman with the sinister gleam of obsession that one sees in old footage of Red Guards, began yelling about fragility. 'If Director Chin had been polite to Miss Tang, instead of ignoring her, perhaps this wouldn't have happened,' one observer said later. 'But Director Chin is Director Chin.' Tang, who felt that art too fragile to hang in the Palace Museum should not leave the country, called around town, and on Friday, 5 January, the *China Times* quoted her invitation: 'Please wear black and come and sit quietly at the Palace Museum to protest fragile paintings going abroad, starting Saturday morning at 10 a.m.'

Saturday the sixth was a radiant, sunny day, and crowds gathered. ('If it had rained,' one curator said, 'perhaps this wouldn't have happened.') Tang had rallied most of the people who would become key players in the conflict, including several former Palace Museum employees who had left 'under a cloud', as is said there; a few people with personal grudges against Fong or Chin or both; and some genuinely concerned citizens. Chu Ko, an artist who previously worked at the Palace, wrote in the *China Times*, 'I am absolutely astonished that these extraordinarily fragile paintings should be allowed to go.' His Palace connection gave him great credibility. Shia Yan, an oil painter, also wrote an inflammatory article; he had learned to mistrust the United States when a New York gallery dealt with him shoddily. Estimates of the number of protesters ranged from sixty to four hundred; dramatic photos showed up the next day on front pages throughout Taiwan. 'Lending these works of art is tantamount to betraying our ancestors,' said the poet Kuan Kuan, subsequently photographed at the base of a pillar, positioning himself for a hunger strike.

By Monday, 8 January, politicians had seized the stage. Chou Chuan, the whip of the opposition New Party, dropped in on Chin with a dozen reporters in tow. She also brought Chu Hui-liang, who at the time still worked at the Palace (and was the star of its badminton team), had recently earned her doctorate from Princeton (advised by Fong), and had just been elected to the Legislative Yuan. Chu suggested to Chin that he replace the originals with high-quality reproductions. 'How can you, a museum-trained person, even suggest this?' asked Chin, but he got short shrift in the press. The same day, protesters gathered outside the Control Yuan, which monitors the branches of government. By now the Ministry of Education had been given responsibility for the Palace matter. In the Legislative Yuan, opposition party leaders banned the twenty-seven restricted items from export and called a public hearing for Wednesday, 10 January, to consider how to proceed.

James C. Y. Watt, a Hong Kong–born Chinese scholar who works under Fong, dislikes confrontation. He had come to Taiwan to oversee the preparation of condition reports and the packing of artwork. Now he found himself in the middle of a scandal. At the public hearing in the Legislative Yuan, he was the first speaker. As he ascended to the podium, the lights of ten television cameras blinded him, and the protesters, who had packed the building, began screaming expletives as he tried to speak. 'Shameless! Shameless! You're crazy!' they heck-led. He talked decorously about the Met's commitment to cultural exchange. No one listened. When Watt stepped into the corridor, a reporter collided with a protester; they ended up in a fistfight from which Watt narrowly escaped. 'I felt like I was stuck in an Ionesco play,' he said later.

By this time, de Montebello said, the museum had 'a war room in New York'. He and Fong and Emily K. Rafferty, the Met's vice president for development, stayed up most nights phoning Taiwan for news. Judith Smith, Fong's special assistant, consolidated infor-mation and wrote up detailed daily reports. The team drafted letters to government officials and protesters – anxious letters, conciliatory ones. Some were sent and some were not. Every day Fong planned and cancelled a trip to Taiwan; it was ultimately decided that his presence there would only further inflame the protesters. De Mon-tebello reached Chou Chuan, the New Party whip, 'but she had no sympathy for our cause', he said. 'For her it had become a matter of politics, the drama to be magnified for political ends, like [former senator] Jesse Helms on Robert Mapplethorpe, a populist stance that distracted voters from the real issues of the country.'

On Saturday, 13 January, protesters gathered at the Chiang Kai-shek Memorial Hall in Taipei. They had written slogans on strips of gauze and tied them around their foreheads, and they carried huge banners. The politicians present included one independent presidential candidate, who suggested that the leaders of the ruling KMT were exploiting their control of the Palace collection to reflect glory on themselves. Some young people, to whom democracy was new, seemed drunk on the power of protest. A surprising number of angry young men and women burning with Chinese nationalism had shown up. 'We won't grovel before the West,' said one. 'We get the work forty days every three years, and you get it for a year? And we pay half the expenses of the show?'

Aware of the growing anger, Fong declared in an open letter to the Ministry of Education that he would forfeit two of the top three paintings in the show, asking only for Guo Xi's *Early Spring* because it was on the cover of the catalogue (which had already been printed).

To Fong and Director Chin, all the fuss felt like politicised senti-mentalism. 'My grandmother or my maiden aunt would also say, to expose this is to destroy it,' Fong would later concede about the Palace collection. 'But the time for such mawkishness is past.' The increasingly hostile Taiwanese press quoted him as saying, 'quite arro-gantly', that he would cancel the show if more work were withdrawn. 'It wasn't a matter of my cancelling,' Fong said, 'but of there being no show with the cuts they'd proposed.'

In the Met's war room, de Montebello and the others 'made lists of what we could not live without', he said. 'We were willing to accept a show that was quantitatively reduced, but not one that was typologically reduced. No single major category of objects could be missing. It was necessary that the show sustain its goal of presenting a transversal history of Chinese art, that we not be forced to elimi-nate the Tang, Song or Yuan dynasties from our presentation, that the curatorial vision be left intact. But being too pious in this matter would not have been public spirited. It was important that we not in our disappointment cancel a remarkable show. One day I thought our chances were at sixty per cent; the next day it was thirty per cent.'

The Met's press office, which had been organising expensive pre-view trips to Taiwan and printing colour brochures, descended into hysteria. Interviews were forbidden and information was given so much spin as to become implausible. Attempts to control journalists could hardly have been more stringent during the Cultural Revolu-tion than they were in January and February at the Met.

At another protest, on 17 January back in Taipei, the rumours flew: the Metropolitan Museum would lock the Chinese treasures in its basement and send back cleverly made copies; President Clinton would give the art back to the mainland; the U.S. Congress's guar-antee of protection for foreign cultural treasures was no more reliable than the diplomatic relationship with Taiwan that it had terminated in 1978. 'Neither at the Met nor elsewhere in the West do you know how to treat work on paper or silk,' one protester told me. When a Chinese friend of mine countered that the Met's studio for the conservation of Asian art operates at a much higher standard than the Palace's, people screamed insults at him. 'This work is much too

sophisticated for you,' another protester said. 'People in your country couldn't understand or appreciate it. Sending it is just a waste.'

The Ministry of Education formed a committee to investigate the
whole fiasco. At a big rally on Thursday, 18 January, demonstrators
wrapped themselves in a petition with twenty thousand signatures that
had been gathered in a single day at Kaohsiung University. Particular
rage was directed against committee members associated with Fong –
though it would have been difficult to form a qualified committee free
of Fong-trained scholars. Fong was still being advised to stay in New
York. 'You can do nothing but wait,' he was told by a friend on the
committee. 'I hope there will still be a show to save by next week.'

I was standing in the crowd outside the investigative committee's
first meeting when a television camera suddenly pointed at me. 'I'm
told you've actually met Wen Fong,' a journalist said. 'Is he really as
we understand him to be: greedy, arrogant, selfish and mean?'

By 20 January, when I met Chu Hui-liang, the new New Party
legislator, she was expressing regret over the debacle: 'I worried about
sending *Travellers amid Streams and Mountains* – I thought they
were being irresponsible. People need to know what a "restricted list"
actually means. But I didn't intend that the whole show be destroyed.'
Within the high walls of the Palace there was frustrated sadness.
'What is wrong with these people?' asked the Palace Museum's Chang
Lin-sheng, who was handling the day-to-day trauma of the protests.
I had had to sneak into her office, since she was avoiding interviews;
she looked tired. 'Don't they have jobs? Don't they have anything
to do all day besides march up and down out there with inaccurate
slogans?' The phone rang. She talked fast for forty-five minutes, her
tone conciliatory and irritable. 'Wen Fong,' she said when she hung
up. 'I told him I can't help him any more.' She picked up a copy of
a popular magazine with *Travellers amid Streams and Mountains* on
its cover. 'I suppose it's something that now everyone in the country
has heard of Fan Kuan, when recently this population couldn't be
bothered to see our seventieth-anniversary exhibition. The truth is,
we all worried about sending Fan Kuan. Maybe one or two others
are best left here, as the *Mona Lisa* stays at the Louvre. But for the
rest – people should see it. How can the people be so suspicious

of us? Don't they understand how much we love that work? We're all fragile. Should we never leave home again?'

Fong used a different analogy: 'You don't stop eating because you might choke.'

The investigative committee and its subcommittees decided to reconsider every object, not just those on the restricted list, and protesters threatened legal action against the Palace Museum. De Montebello's backdoor approaches and 'corridor diplomacy' did not seem to be working. Neither he nor the director of the American Institute in Taiwan, our de facto 'ambassador' there, was ever able to reach the minister of education. To those in power in Taiwan, the strong wishes of the Metropolitan Museum were of little interest, and the Met, realising that posturing would not protect the show, lapsed into relative silence. But Fong remained confident: 'The government has to be seen to be responsive to the people. So pieces would be withdrawn. But if the whole show is cancelled, the government will appear to be helpless in the hands of some hysterics. Such a display of weakness would run contrary to their interests.'

Still, the Met's situation was getting scary. The packing was already a week behind schedule, and the exhibition cases the museum had commissioned couldn't be built because no one knew what would go in them. The reserved cargo space on planes had been forfeited. Acer had withdrawn its $1.5 million sponsorship, and now the protesters were trying to halt the Taiwanese government's financing. The standard greeting in Taipei art circles was: 'What news from Wen today?' But it had become clear that there was nothing that Wen Fong or anyone else in the United States could do.

Towards the end of January, reports of new Chinese threats to Taiwan pushed the art controversy off the front pages. On 23 January, the committee announced a compromise that left all sides frustrated: twenty-three items, including several landmark pieces, were withdrawn, and nineteen other important works were restricted to forty days of display. Then the Met bravely decided to start packing without financial guarantees for one of the most expensive exhibitions in its history (although insurance and transportation costs were somewhat reduced by the exclusion of key priceless works).

'We told the board of trustees we would be picking up the gap of $1.5 million left by the withdrawal of corporate sponsors,' said Rafferty. 'We also said there was a possibility that the $3.1 million from Taiwan would not come through. It was a gamble – $4.6 million from our operating budget wouldn't have closed down the museum, but it would have been devastating.' De Montebello asked wryly, 'Whom should it make anxious to have the work here and the money not?' In the end, Taiwan's Foreign Ministry came through.

So *Splendors of Imperial China* will open at the Met after all, but without thirty-six of its crowning splendours. Sadder even than the absence of *Early Spring* or *Travellers amid Streams and Mountains* is that the elegant narrative coherence and balance of the planned exhibit has been substantially undermined. It is still, however, in many ways the greatest exhibition of Chinese art ever staged in the West, and the work will be displayed and lighted a thousand times better than it has ever been at the Palace. It may also be the last show of its kind: given the frenzied protectionist sentiment during January's fracas, much of this work is unlikely to leave Taiwan ever again.

The unrest in Taiwan was strange for two reasons. First, Taiwan is hardly anti-American. An enormous number of Taiwanese travel to, and study in, the United States. Much of the population speaks English, and the occasional bar fight about Fan Kuan notwithstanding, as an American you tend to feel at home in Taiwan more easily than in almost any other East Asian country. Seven of Taiwan's seventeen cabinet members hold PhDs from American universities. Taiwan is the world's third-largest purchaser of American armaments, our eighth most important trading partner. 'The educated population here is as much American as anything else,' a young artist told me.

The second reason the protests were so surprising is more subtle and important. Taiwan has been in turmoil for a long time, and particularly in the past five years, about whether or not it is China. The 'one China' policy is the most pressing political issue of the day: Will Taiwan at some point be reunited with the mainland – by force or otherwise – or will it eventually declare independence? The official stance of mainland Communists and Taiwan's KMT is that Taiwan is a province of China; both Taipei and Beijing claim to be valid rulers of China. To the casual Western observer, the situation seems ludicrous. Taiwan has a separate economy, political system and educational system; citizens carry Taiwanese passports. But Chinese nationalism is deep-seated. Some Taiwanese like to feel that they are part of a great nation and not, as one essayist wrote, 'citizens of *another* piddling South East Asian provincial hole-in-the-wall country'. To many Taiwanese with close ties to the mainland, declaring independence would be like cutting off their own arms.

Not that the mainland will countenance independence. Since President Lee Teng-hui of Taiwan visited the United States in June to deliver a speech at Cornell, China has conducted ever-grander 'standard military exercises' on the shores opposite Taiwan and in the sea off the island's northern coast. So Taiwan, under constant threat from the mainland, must toady both across the strait and to the West. That the United States withdrew its ambassador in 1978 still provokes rage. There's Taiwan – a peaceful democracy that the United States doesn't recognise because we do recognise another country with a terrible human rights record, with which we do less than half as much trade, and which snubs us in its foreign and domestic policies.

Taiwan's identity struggle fed the Palace protests. During the seventieth-anniversary celebrations, I encountered more people in Taipei art circles who wanted to disavow the Palace than who praised it. Though the Palace has always attracted tourists, most locals have avoided it – because of its forbidding air, because Taiwan has long been indifferent to art, and because the museum is, according to many Taiwan intellectuals, 'alienatingly Chinese'.

A powerful ethnic tension exists within Taiwan today between the 'mainlanders' (also called the '1949ers'), who came over with Chiang and their progeny, about 20 per cent of the population, and the 'Taiwanese', whose forebears settled there earlier. This ethnic tension is perplexing inasmuch as both groups are Han Chinese, all tracing their roots back to the mainland; the indigenous aboriginal population is tiny. But Chiang's forces arrived with the air of conquerors, and from 1949 until the end of the brutal 'Chiang dynasty' in 1987, the mainlanders of the KMT ruled, and the ethnically Taiwanese, despite controlling much land and wealth, were treated as an underclass.

Chiang's government, still claiming to rule mainland China, and filling its legislature with representatives from every mainland district, was corrupt. But over the past nine years, the country has transformed itself with remarkable fluidity into a functional democracy with a highly educated population (the literacy rate is more than 90 per cent, which in a character-written language is astonishing), enormous national wealth (including one of the largest per capita cash reserves in the world) and open elections. The legislature no longer professes to represent all of China.

'The Palace Museum is a nice place, but it's too Chinese and insufficiently Taiwanese,' said Chen Shih-meng, deputy mayor of Taipei and former secretary general of the Democratic Progressive Party (DPP). The DPP, one of two major opposition parties, stands overtly for independence. 'Whether Chiang Kai-shek took that material rightfully or wrongfully, I don't know, but we need a Taiwanese place to complement the Palace Museum. We deserve to understand ourselves as Taiwanese. I was taught that I was a part of a Chinese culture to which I never truly belonged. We must raise the consciousness of our next generation. We must help them towards cultural freedom from the mainland.' Then, as is typical given the tense politics of Taiwan, Chen fused the topic at hand with the more essential matter of independence: 'The leadership here says that to avoid irritating the mainland, they must speak with creative vagueness. This vagueness, meant to confuse Beijing, confuses the people of Taiwan more than it does the enemy. If China uses military force, we will counter-attack. We could destroy their economic zones incredibly fast. We will not win by pitching threats against Chinese military experts, but if we use our military capacities to sow fear among the economists, we can divide that leadership to triumph. We must make our plans clear to the mainland. Developing a native cultural awareness is a part of this policy. The Palace Museum does not enable such objectives.'

Chang Lin-sheng of the Palace Museum said of those who would advocate an autonomous Taiwanese art, 'These are rootless people.

Did you know that the aboriginal tribes the localists love so much have no word in their language for art?' She paused dramatically. 'Democracy is not good for art.' She wrung her hands and laughed. 'Communism is worse. Capitalism is a good approximation of an imperial system and is very good for art. There is no Taiwanese culture. It's not like the racial problem in the U.S. – we are all Han people, and our culture was at its greatest in imperial courts.' The Palace Museum, she insisted, was the best answer to the Taiwanese search for dignity.

The greatest landscapes of the Song dynasty will not be on view in *Splendors of Imperial China*, but masterpieces of calligraphy and later painting will be. It is fashionable to note the failure of Western medicine to reconcile the mind-body split, and to look to the East for holistic cures. The Western division of word and image, sundering literary and artistic history, is no less troubling a split. It does not exist in China, where the character is at once a verbal representation and a visual language, and where the components of a painting are almost as iconic as literary vocabulary. Calligraphy is still the hardest of the Chinese arts for most Westerners to grasp: language is not metaphor but object, and what is signified is to some extent the process of signification. The writing and the content are harder to dissever than the dancer from the dance. It can be epistolary and spontaneous, with an ink trace that is entirely expressive, or it can be formal and ritualistic.

Visitors to the Met will see Huaisu's *Autobiographical Essay*, a self-congratulatory drunken celebration of cursive forms, dated 777. In it, Huaisu explains that he writes best when inebriated. As he grows drunker, the text becomes less literary, but the quality of the calligraphy is exalted. The characters flow into one another as the brush charges forward, making fluid patterns of line – rhythmic, pulsing, almost erotic. Zhao Mengjian, writing in the thirteenth century, said that Huaisu 'grasps his pen grandly like a frightened snake, rings it about roundly, and yet is very strangely spare'. Huaisu himself wrote, 'Good calligraphy resembles a flock of birds darting out of the trees, or startled snakes scurrying into the grass, or cracks bursting in a shattered wall.'

Every student of Chinese art studies Su Shi's *Poems Written at Hangzhou on the Cold-Food Festival* of 1082 as the apotheosis of calligraphy, and the most powerful part of Wen Fong's masterful catalogue for the Met's exhibition is his close reading of this work. An essayist beloved of Emperor Shenzong (to whose first triumphs *Early Spring* alludes), Su Shi became a policy critic at court, narrating contemporary problems through historical analogy. Given a series of provincial appointments, he became increasingly concerned about the life of the people and petitioned the court constantly to reduce taxes. This enraged the emperor's chief adviser, and in 1079 Su Shi was convicted of having slandered the emperor and was banished to Huangzhou. He became a poet, turned to Buddhism, and wrote some great classics of Chinese literature, including *Ode to the Red Cliff*, to which later artists often alluded when they wanted to make indirect criticisms of government. His poems were disseminated throughout China by his powerful friends, and in exile he became a hero of the intelligentsia and the cultural elite, until in 1084 he was finally invited back to the court – only to be banished again a few years later.

At the height of his exile, Su Shi wrote *Poems Written at Hangzhou on the Cold-Food Festival* – a notion of spring almost opposite to Guo Xi's:

> Since coming to Hangzhou,
> Three Cold-Food Festivals have come and gone.
> Each year I wish to prolong the springtime,
> But spring departs without lingering.
> . . .
> All in secrecy spring is stolen and wasted,
> Wreaking vengeance in the middle of the night.
> How does it differ from a sickly youth
> Up from his sickbed, his hair already white?
> . . .
> Dead ashes blown will not stir to life.

The calligraphy is a study in balance and line, each character shaped and angled, the brush moved with an exquisite self-assurance and constancy. This is not the madly exuberant curling writing of Huaisu; it is as graceful and intricate in its structure as the branching of a tree. Su wrote, 'My writing swells up like ten thousand gallons of water at the wellhead, erupting through the ground, spilling over the flat valley, and running unchecked for thousands of *li* a day.'

Su Shi dismissed realism – which would obsess Western artists for the next eight hundred years – as 'the insight of a child'; he also rejected art that served the state. Western art of the Middle Ages remains intensely formal, but Su Shi's calligraphy bespeaks an almost expressionist realm of the personal. His is an art of process and artistic transformation, and as a viewer you are invited to join him in his journey. *Poems Written at Hangzhou on the Cold-Food Festival* is sad but also redemptive, for what is revealed is the struggle to know a self. Nine hundred and fourteen years later, its ashes, blown, still stir to life.

Splendors includes several important Yuan paintings. Yuan painting is somewhat harder for a Western audience to understand than Song painting. The Yuan painters were striving for complete simplicity of style and subject, the imagination given free rein within tight confines. The painter Wu Zhen spoke of 'flavour within blandness' when he rejected the theatricality of Song styles.

Huang Gongwang created the long hand-scroll *Dwelling in the Fuchun Mountains*, between 1347 and 1350. Song artists had risen to the peak of naturalistic representation, hiding the brushstroke by using washes; they wished to delete themselves graphically from their work. Huang's brushstrokes, like his sentiments, are everywhere apparent, as if he were writing the letters of his own heart.

Also coming to the Met is Emperor Huizong's *Two Poems*, a fine example of his 'slender gold' calligraphy. Done more than three centuries later than Huaisu's piece, it stands in sharp contrast to it. Scholar James Cahill writes, 'Each character, occupying its assigned space, exhibits order and stasis, as if engraved in stone.' Huizong was an incompetent emperor, ambitious about building great public gardens and vague about running the country, but he was a glorious patron and practitioner of the arts. 'Only through creativity,' he wrote, 'does one's merit remain behind.'

Splendors reflects and includes the merit of Chinese emperors, which sometimes lies more tangibly in paintings and calligraphy than in political achievement or military conquest. Wen Fong's catalogue, significantly titled *Possessing the Past*, is in some ways an embarrassment to the Met. The cover shows Guo Xi's *Early Spring*, which is not in the exhibition. The copyright page thanks Acer for the corporate sponsorship it withdrew. And the text refers at some length to work that will probably never be seen in this country, all of it illustrated in glowing colour. ('Well, at least you have your book,' de Montebello told Fong when it looked as if the show would miscarry altogether.) Still, the book uses techniques of connoisseurship to narrate a thousand-year evolution of the idea of painting and calligraphy, balancing social and formal art histories. It explicates the force that won these Chinese masterpieces their canonical position and the force that canonical position has afforded them.

Possessing the Past also seems to tell over and over the story of what happened in Taiwan in January, because this disaffection between a beleaguered population and an autocratic elite has recurred across many dynasties of Chinese rule. 'How much high Chinese culture is there in China?' Fong asked me one evening this winter. 'It's all Western. So much has been lost and forgotten by Chinese people in the last hundred and fifty years. What they still have is so precious, but being proud of your heritage and having the will to understand it are two different things.'

Some protesters in January spoke of the need for an exhibition in Taiwan of European art, as grand as *Splendors*, that would include everything from the Venus de Milo to *Guernica*. They might want to call such an exhibition *Escaping the Past*, because traditional Western art looks mostly forward (neoclassicism and postmodernism notwithstanding) while traditional Chinese art tends to look back. Emphasis on the future is a point of contention in Taiwan's politics, and the Palace Museum symbolises the case against novelty. Exhibitions there tend not to propose new ideas so much as to reveal old ones.

In fact, the surging New Party, which led the protests, advocates eventual reunification, an ultimate means of possessing the past.

The battle over the Palace Museum collection suggests that the next struggle may be over the terms of unification rather than about the sort of wide-eyed independence that has swept Eastern Europe. Like most historical art exhibitions, *Splendors of Imperial China* is about the past. More than most others, it may be about the future as well.

Beginning in 2002, the National Palace Museum underwent extensive renovations, making it more visitor friendly and more earthquake-proof. It reopened in December 2006 with an exhibition that included a Song dynasty landscape loaned by the Metropolitan Museum of Art. The renovations have captured a newly engaged audience; more than 5 million people visited the National Palace Museum in 2014, and a new southern branch opened in Chiayi County in 2015.

In 2009, China loaned Qing dynasty relics for display in Taipei. In a reciprocal expression of goodwill, National Palace Museum director Chou Kung-shin subsequently refused to exhibit two sculptures allegedly looted from the Summer Palace outside Beijing at the end of the Second Opium War. In spite of this, the Taiwan Palace Museum has refused all loan requests from museums in the People's Republic of China out of fear that Beijing may refuse to return borrowed art. Loans worldwide are extended only where national law forbids the seizure of disputed property.

Public protest remains vital in Taiwan. In 2013, the White Shirt Army made its first appearances. A movement of Taiwan's youth, it has refused to take a position on reunification with China. 'We don't support any side or leader,' said Liulin Wei, the thirty-year-old who initiated the movement by posting a note accusing the government of abusing its citizens. 'We are for civil rights, common values, democracy. And we made it very simple to join. You just put on a white shirt.' Weeks later, a quarter of a million white-shirted youths marched in Taipei. 'People our age are too busy and too turned off by politics,' said Liulin. 'But they do care. We just have to make it easier for them to be involved.' Though that movement seems to have faded, in March 2014 hundreds of young activists, dubbed the Sunflower Movement because of the blooms they carried, occupied Taiwan's Parliament building in an unprecedented protest against a trade pact aimed at forging closer ties with Beijing. The question of unification or independence continues to spool out bewilderingly in a context of calculated vagueness.

———

On Each Palette,
a Choice of Political Colours

New York Times, 4 August 1996

I became deeply enmeshed in Taiwan's complex politics and soon discovered the country's vivid contemporary art scene. I had assumed that Taiwanese new art would be a lesser version of Chinese new art, but what I found was something more interesting than that. The artists I had encountered in China survived an oppressive society via fantasies about freedom; the artists in Taiwan lived in a more free society under constant threat of oppression. Unfortunately, I later found, while everyone in New York wanted to know what was happening in China, few people wanted to know what was happening in Taiwan. The mainland artists have developed a huge international audience, while the Taiwanese artists, many of them equally interesting, have a much smaller place in the international art world.

———

In 1985, Taipei had fifteen galleries; now it has more than two hundred. Most sell decorative oil paintings in a kitschy impressionist style for bourgeois decorating, but a good number of more serious places exhibit engaged contemporary work in various so-called Western, Chinese, and nativist Taiwanese styles. Taiwan under dictatorship knew just what it was: the Nationalist government of China in exile. Taiwan under democracy cannot decide to what extent it is Chinese, independent, or westernised. The re-election of President Lee Teng-hui confirms the country's commitment to what our State Department calls 'creative ambiguity.' This crisis of identity is reflected in – and, two high government officials told me, partly caused by – the country's increasingly conflicted art.

You can almost say that to do traditional Chinese brush painting is to support the right-leaning New Party, which favours reunification with the mainland; to do conceptual art is to ally yourself with the left-leaning Democratic Progressive Party (DPP), which favours independence; to do oil painting (almost all dreadful by Western standards) is to tie yourself to the ruling centrist Nationalist Party or Kuomintang (KMT).

The Taipei Fine Arts Museum, the enormous museum of contemporary art of Taiwan, is a city entity, so its new director was appointed by the DPP mayor of Taipei, who has recently announced plans to build two more museums dedicated to Taiwanese art. At a banquet given by the museum's director, I was seated next to the director of exhibitions, Lee Yulin, a young woman of singular grace who moves easily between official circles and the world of contemporary artists. I asked her to help me with introductions to a few artists. 'I'm DPP,' she said. 'I'll help you if you'll put forward the case for an independent Taiwan in your article.' A week later, I was seated at a banquet next to Chou Hai-sheng, chief editor at Taiwan's leading art publishing house. 'I'll make introductions to our great Chinese artists,' he said. 'I was there the day the New Party was founded,' he explained.

In Taiwan right now the term *ben sheng ren*, 'people of this province', refers to the ethnic Taiwanese; the term *wai sheng ren*, 'people from outside', refers to mainlanders who came over in 1945 and their progeny; and the newly voguish term *Taiwan ren*, 'people of Taiwan', is the politically correct term that may save the day. Much of Taiwan's art is about these three modes of self-definition.

The heart of the avant-garde art world in Taiwan is an artist-run gallery called IT Park, founded in 1988 by five friends who felt the need for an alternative space. It is three upstairs rooms, a small, sun-drenched terrace, an office and a little bar. About forty artists are associated with IT Park, two of whom actually run the place day to day. Artists drift in to look at one another's work or just to see one another. The conversation is easy, casual. Most of the IT Park artists have studied in the West – at Cooper Union in New York, the École des Beaux-Arts in Paris, and similar institutions. When I stopped in, Dean I-mei, a young conceptualist, was showing a mitten made with a raised middle finger; this in-your-face piece, he said, had been knitted to his specifications by his mother. At lunch, he showed me a canvas with two nearly identical watches nailed to it, both bought in Chinatown in New York. One has the mainland flag for a face, the other, the Taiwan flag. *Made in Hong Kong* is the title. 'Culturally I am Chinese but politically I am not,' said the erstwhile art critic J. J. Shih one night as we sat with our drinks on the balcony at IT Park. Another artist, who calls himself Tchenogramme, put it this way: 'I am an international citizen and a Taiwan localist.' The question of whether their art is Taiwanese and why dominates conversation among these artists.

In the seventies, much art embraced the peasant culture of Tai-wan and represented the distinctive features of the landscape: 'In the seventies, politics was using art; in the late eighties, art started using politics,' explained another young artist, Tsu Ming. 'In the seventies, our localism reflected our insecurity around the time we were thrown out of the United Nations; now, our Taiwanism reflects our self-con-fidence as we move towards complete freedom and great prosperity.' As Lynn Pascoe, until recently director of the American Institute in Taiwan and thereby the U.S. 'ambassador' to Taiwan, explained to me, 'In 1964, Taiwan graduated from aid; then it rapidly graduated from a rural to a handicraft to a technical economy. For a brief period the rural-handicraft side of the society was its basis, and now it's a sentimental matter.'

Artists such as the IT Park crowd, educated in the West, have more sophistication than they know what to do with. 'Some of us are breaking with Chinese culture; some are breaking with Western culture; some are breaking with their entire past,' said J. J. Shih.

'There is underground xenophobia against the West and overt xeno-phobia against China. But localism is not really nationalism.' Tsong Pu, one of the founders of IT Park, said, 'Artists make work about Taiwan's politics, but their definition of and notion of a political art was learned in American art schools.'

Like most vanguards, this one is full of frustration. The difficulties of 'becoming international' often seem insurmountable. 'Artists are struggling for a Taiwanese vision, but the struggle is never the subject of the work,' Dean I-mei said. 'That's why the work isn't interesting to the rest of the world.' Chen Hui-chiao, an artist who makes for-malist-minimalist installations with needles and steel and water, said, 'Don't look at my work and think about Taiwan. Just look at it. It's just art.'

The contemporary art market in Taiwan is weak right now, and about 90 per cent of galleries operate at a loss. 'The problem,' explained Lily Lee, director of the Gallery Association and owner of the Dragon Gate Gallery, 'is that prices became very inflated at the dawn of the museum era, when the Taipei Fine Arts Museum was established and everyone began fussing about Taiwanese art. And then it turned out that the secondary market was unpredictable and that our art hadn't really gone international. Chinese people don't like this kind of unstable investment.' So while the development of a contemporary-art world is key to Taiwan's continuing struggle for cultural identity, the manufacture of art is increasingly marginalised by its unprofitability.

A five-minute cab ride away from IT Park is the New Paradise, another artist-run space. The New Paradise is nonprofit, windowless, in a basement, with no chic coffee bar and no balcony for philos-ophers to sun themselves. The audience here is even smaller and more self-referential, the work even more sophisticated and isolated. In one piece, all the clocks are set at 2:28, lest we forget the two-two-eight events (the Taiwan massacres of 28 February 1948), heroic background to Taiwanese nationalism.

As Lee Yulin of the Fine Arts Museum and I set out to see her boldly Taiwanese artists, we talked about the delicate pragmatics of an independent Taiwan that would be born of the vision of artists.

'Taiwanese orthodoxy rejects the Chinese past, but our new identity will in fact be half discovered and half created,' she said. 'We cannot throw away the Palace Museum and our Chinese heritage, for that is an important part of modern Taiwan. The problem is to include our Chinese past but also distinguish ourselves from it. Culture is a thing that accumulates; you can't just start a new culture right now. It has to be based on the past.'

In the studio of Wu Tien-chang, we discussed what he calls 'the passenger mentality of the KMT'; that the Nationalist government came to Taiwan only to pause before reconquering the mainland. 'Everyone comes here expecting to go away again,' he said. 'We have no superhighways because the KMT didn't think it was worth building them because they expected to leave as fast as possible. This island is full of fancy buildings made of plywood. Nothing has a real base, no real roots. We in Taiwan are so accustomed to this fakeness that we accept it as real. We have to change that.' He gestured at his *Self-Portrait as a Sailor*, the colours eerie, the light artificial, the scenery hilariously kitsch. 'Everything in my work is fake because that reflects the social reality of this island.'

Later that night, we sat in a garden – we were outside the congested centre of Taipei, and this one-storey house looked as if it had materialised out of a scroll painting – with Huang Chih-yang and his wife, watching the moon rise over the city and drinking tea and eating pumpkin seeds. His work is hauntingly beautiful, employing the techniques of Chinese brush painting to make conceptual installations. 'When I was beginning art school,' he explained, 'I decided to study Chinese art because to me at that young age all Western art looked the same. I knew I wanted to do something new, and I didn't think there was anything new to be said in Western media.' *Maternity Room*, one of his most spectacular pieces, has more than a dozen hanging lengths of rice paper with life-sized ink pictures of skeletal figures, their sexual organs exaggerated and aestheticised, half-human and half-monstrous. 'Why is it thought that to be modern and to be Chinese are artistically alien ideas? I am after the truth of this mad, mixed society,' he said.

I went with the editor Chou Hai-sheng to see Shia Yan, one of the great old men of art in Taiwan, an oil painter whose work looks derivative and banal to the Western eye but whose retrospective at the Taipei Fine Arts Museum last year was a blockbuster. 'An artist learning Western art has a plan to improve Chinese art with Western,' Shia Yan said. 'This philosophy only damages the tradition and does not reconstruct it at all. Perhaps at best it is possible to bring together Chinese feeling and Western form.'

Another day we went to see Hsia I-fu, who paints landscapes in which only the trained Chinese eye can see corrupting traces of Western perspective and some non-traditional contrasts between wet and dry brushwork. 'Western painting you go to when you are feeling quiet and it makes you excited,' he said. 'Ink painting you visit when you are excited and it makes you calm. Ink painting is closer to religious experience: like a meditation, it purifies the mind. My work itself is not Chinese, not Taiwanese, but from the heart: for in our hearts here, what most of us really want is to be calm; and what you from the West want, and what these young avant-garde artists and DPP people want, I think, is to be excited.' He paused and looked around the room. 'Elections; bombing raids; do we need art to excite us, too?'

———————

Two years after I wrote this article, in 1998, the Taiwan Domestic Airport was closed down temporarily after missiles were fired by a citizen of mainland China who had arrived in Taipei just days earlier. Estimates range, but the official figure for the number of missiles involved in the incident stands at two hundred. Residents of northern Taipei were surprised but 'not unduly alarmed', according to one local report, by the flashes of intense light and the terrific noise. No injuries were reported. The closing of the airport had been negotiated in advance by the Taipei Fine Arts Museum, and the missiles had been fired by Cai Guo-Qiang, an artist then based in New York, in a performance for the opening of the Taiwan Biennial. His project, *Golden Missile*, was one of many radical works in an increasingly politicised approach to art in Taiwan.

Sailing to Byzantium

Travel + Leisure, July 1997

I was seriously depressed in 1996 and nearly unable to travel. But I had accepted an assignment – my first for *Travel + Leisure* – so I dragged myself off to the eastern Mediterranean coast. There I discovered a valuable truth: while exercise, medication and psychotherapy are the most effective treatments for depression, a truly enchanting holiday can help, too. The Turkish coast was gorgeous; my travelling companions were delightful; the weather was impeccable; and I got better. I mentioned the experience in *The Noonday Demon.*

The ostensible purpose of the trip was to learn painting. On the first day, I said to Susannah that I couldn't paint. 'Nonsense,' she said. 'Everyone can paint. You've never had proper instruction and I will change all that.' At the end of our first day, she said, 'You're right. You can't paint. Perhaps you should try photography.'

E leven amateur artists had signed up for the sailing adventure, and we were meant to learn painting. Every morning, we were out of our cradles within minutes of waking, endlessly rocking to the mild swell of the wine-dark eastern Mediterranean, the same sea first called 'wine-dark' when nobler men dwelt on the earth and sang their warrior songs. Up on deck we would find bread and fresh butter, feta and olives, and cups of good strong Turkish coffee. The youngest of the crew served our meals. His name was Ibrahim, and he called us 'sir' or 'madam', and he was always at one's elbow just when one wanted honey or yogurt or Anatolian cherry preserves. Usually the sun was quite high by then, and the light soaked the air. Some people complained of having had too little sleep and too many of the captain's special cocktails, but mostly there was only happiness that it was another day on the *Arif Kaptan B.* None of us minded getting up early, which, had you known us under other circumstances, you would hardly have believed. We hardly believed it.

After we had sated ourselves, the engine would start up or the sails would be hoisted, and we would journey along the contours of the land, following them as if they belonged to a lover's body whose every curve we needed to know. Tom Johnson, managing director of Westminster Classic Tours, would tell us which of the old men on the piers were café owners in competition with one another, or about how new houses in traditional styles had been built 'just there' (he would point) on foundations from the fourth century BC. Meanwhile, Andrew Hobson, an Oxford University classicist dedicated to preserving knowledge of the great early civilisations in a world divorced from its own origins, would tell us about events that were taking place when those foundations were laid. These shores seemed so busy with ancient history that they could hardly contain the present; when you looked at them, you saw their past. We talked about this as we smoked Turkish cigarettes and finished our coffee, reclined on pillows, rubbed sunscreen on one another's backs, and began to turn the seaworthy colour of our captain and crew.

Then came the morning painting lesson. We were amateurs but keen, and the lessons were made for us. Susannah Fiennes is all sensibility delivered in a voice of sense; she sees the world with a precise but passionate eye. Her one-woman show at the National Portrait Gallery in London was praised for both its expressive accuracy and its austere poignancy. Looking herself like a Gainsborough – her face a perfect English pink, her clothes fluttering in the wind, a large straw hat held on with a frayed white satin ribbon – she would teach us the vocabulary of primary colours and their opposites, of suffused and diluted tones, of rich washes and negative space. 'Saturated colour is freedom from grey,' she would say as she set us up with our palettes and watercolour paper. Her voice would lift as she directed us towards all the forms and tones that are hidden along the coast of Lycia (an ancient region in south-west Turkey) and in its monuments. She could be forceful.

'Did Charles ask you for advice when you were painting together?' one of us asked Susannah, who has, at royal invitation, accompanied the Prince of Wales to paint during his state visits.

'No,' she said, 'but he got some anyway.'

Sometimes she read aloud from a book about colour theory, or from Cézanne's letters. She would instruct, 'Painting must analyse the natural world and still be subjective.' All of us, under her tute-lage, learned to see anew. 'Look at the beauty of that shape,' she'd say, 'where the sky is between those two peaks.' She once exclaimed, 'Look at that! It's not really a nose at all; it's the most remarkable broken triangle of light!' – which rather alarmed the bashful cook, who until then had been sure it was a nose: his rather comely one.

Then we would go ashore to see some historic place or pull into a bay to swim in water so transparent you could scarcely tell it from the light (but it was a bit more alizarin, Susannah would explain). We breathed in sharply when diving from the height of the deck because we were always overwhelmed at first by the depth of that sea; but then suddenly we would find that it was not overwhelming at all, and we would swim past one another or tread water holding hands or splash up onto some deserted beach or bit of rock or play at being sea monsters. One of the women had a pink bikini that she had bought in Saint-Tropez, and though the rest of us had nothing of the kind, we all felt equal in the common, salty, clear element. You could swim once around the boat, or you could swim a mile to an inviting rock. It was delicious: so sweet and so cold.

We were usually damp when we sat down to lunch. We noted the colour contrasts of the salad and drank the local wine; sometimes the women put flowers in their hair, and we told one another our best stories, our intimacy quick and authentic. Perhaps this can happen only when you are in Lycia and the weather is fine, the youngest of you is only twenty-four and the eldest over eighty, each of the mahogany-panelled cabins has its own shower and bathroom, the boat is eighty-five feet long and has blue sail covers, and a red Turkish flag the size of a carpet flies at the stern. It is most likely to happen when the cost of going hasn't been high, and two classicists and a painter are with you at all times. It happens when you have all taken off your watches and do not put them on again for eight days. It happens when most of you have read too much Evelyn Waugh, have pondered but never fully understood both Aeschylus and Matisse, and can identify immediately most episodes of *Absolutely Fabulous*.

'Listen! What is that? I think it's the bird we were talking about yesterday, that rare Anatolian eagle,' said someone.

We were all silent for a moment.

'That's Venetia's alarm clock,' someone else said.

And so it was, that time, but overhead birds were flying and crying as though they, too, thought the simple fact of this day and this light warranted celebration.

After lunch, worn out by the morning's exertions, we would lie in the sun on big blue mats at the bow of the boat, and usually we would sail on to yet another wonder. Later we would have tea and biscuits and halvah and then disembark for the day's site. Once it was a Greek theatre built into the hillside, and once it was an eerie necropolis of the ancient Lycians, where the wealthy had had themselves placed in rock tombs that would last forever. We examined the inscriptions in the lost language of Lycia, and Andrew Hobson told us about modern efforts to break the code. Tom Johnson puzzled out the Greek epitaphs and translated them for us as we climbed with him to hear what funny things had happened on the way to a polis here, an acropolis there. Near Demre, Tom showed us where Gelasius the nut seller had carved his name into a theatre wall, to claim a prime position at the top of the stairs in the main vomitory. Tom led us to the altar in Arykanda where the ancients worshipped Helios in the fifth century BC; and he sat with us beside the tomb of Archemdemos, son of Ermapios, in Üçağız.

Nothing was behind wire. Once or twice we had to pay an entrance fee at a famous site, but mostly the ruins we visited were empty, with wild thyme and clover growing between the stones. As we scrambled around, we felt as if we were the first travellers in these virgin realms of gold. It was the ancient world as it was discovered by the Romantics, and not the Disneyland museology of Pompeii or the scrubbed self-importance of tourist-trodden Delphi. Like the Victorians Sir Charles Fellows and Captain Spratt, we came upon the magnificent Roman theatre at Myra and saw the church of St Nicholas and the spectacular integrity of Arykanda, where Alexander the Great conquered and where Hadrian dallied. At the stadium there, a shepherd stumbled through with his flock; two old women in head scarves moved on to tilled fields below; and we were the only other human beings. Each place we saw was magnificent in its decay, and we felt how the mighty must once have looked on all this and despaired. We regarded it more humbly, carrying on with our watercolours but leaving no further marks on so rich a palimpsest.

The hills we painted were everywhere purple with blossom, and the red-roofed village houses were weighted with bougainvillea. No one had ever been more free from grey than we were as we sat here or there, recording our impressions of the crenellated rocks, while Susannah looked over our shoulders. 'I want to see what the form of that pediment makes you feel,' said Susannah. 'Think from the edges in.' Our work was quick, sketchy, expressive.

Then we would leave, perhaps to see another tomb with a view; or perhaps if we were near a village, we would sit in a bar and drink aniseed-perfumed raki. We might buy kilims and postcards and old Armenian silver belts, or we might run into some local who was a friend of Tom's or of a crew member's and climb with him into hidden streets where women with a few gold teeth were doing laundry and cooking, and where men, fat with success, sat smoking and playing backgammon. 'A man without a belly,' our captain, Hasan, told us, 'is like a house without a balcony.' Sometimes the chaps in our party went to see the village barber, who would shave us with a straight razor, massage our faces and shoulders, and comb and oil our hair. Consuming plates of Turkish delight back on the boat, we balconied ourselves like some sultan's palace, then went swimming in the lingering twilight, our paintings strewn about the deck.

Usually around nine, we sat outside again. The sun would at last be setting, and Ibrahim would bring us more wonders from the kitchen below: roasted meats and spiced chicken and stuffed aubergine. When the moon was up, we played charades or told stories, and we drank more raki, and talked more about art or lapsed into epigrams and aphorisms, everyone's wits sharpened by our intense pleasure. On the night of the full moon, we turned off all the electricity; the crew put orange peel on the candles to scent the air, and Andrew Hobson picked up *The Iliad* and read us the narration of Hera's seduction of Zeus. Then we went for a midnight swim, splashing one another with luminescent water. Even the crew joined in the fun: the captain did a belly dance that put us all to shame.

'Listen,' someone said in the small hours. 'You can hear the bells the goats are wearing. They're awake, too.'

We were all silent for a moment.

'That's the ice jingling in Jasper's glass,' someone else said.

So it was, that time. But in the light of the moon we did see the goats, wild goats without bells, climbing up and down the hills. That night, most of us slept side by side on the foredeck, waking up suddenly when rosy-fingered dawn touched us and turned the stones all around an unsaturated pink. We drifted back in and then out of sleep until Ibrahim brought our coffee.

Always, there was the dancing; it seemed that we were perpetually dancing, old and young alike. Some evenings we would go out to the small bars of the port villages and dance with the swashbuckling locals to music as old as the hills, our shoulders thrown back and our arms raised as we went in a ring. Tom was a champion Bodrum *efe* dancer, and he taught the men of our group these local traditional steps ('You have to make it look very high testosterone,' he explained encouragingly). In Kaş, some of us ventured to a provincial disco, where Turkish windsurfers and scuba divers were rocking to Rod Stewart while their women gyrated like latter-day Salomes high on Olivia Newton-John.

But most of all, there was the dancing on board. After breakfast, and again after lunch, some of us would nap while others, listening to music on a cassette player or imagining it in the sounds the wind made as it touched the cliffs, would twirl along the main deck. Susannah, wearing one of her trailing dresses, would laugh as someone dipped her over the bow so that her hair hung down towards the sea, and the crew would peek out from the main saloon. In this world of teak and sailcloth, we fancied ourselves bacchants.

During a sudden rainstorm one hot day, we all rushed out and stood with the water streaming down our faces, halfway between dancing and swimming, sliding on the deck while, on one of Tom's tapes, a Turkish man sang in a throaty voice about his burning, burning love. It seemed that, though we had a concentration of that respect for irony that is the essence of English humour, we had somehow left ashore ironic distance from our immediate circumstances. This was the first and only odyssey, and everything we did on that boat seemed more real than our real lives, at least for the moment. And if we thought of the long trip back, we no more imagined that we might have stayed at home and contemplated Lycia than did Alexander the Great, who first touched these still-unspoiled shores in 333 BC.

_____

Enchanting Zambia

Travel + Leisure, February 1998

I had first visited Zambia in 1992, and I returned in 1997. Zambia
has since become a popular destination, but it was well off the beaten
track in the 1990s, and though this safari was at the rough end of the
spectrum, it allowed the photographer, two friends of mine and me
to see the fierce beauty that can inhere in feral wilderness.

_____

A few years ago, I spent a month driving with a friend through
southern Africa. Our plans were vague and our knowledge thin
until one night in Botswana, when we eavesdropped on a bearded
man with an air of sublime safari competence, solicited his advice,
and rewrote our itinerary. But we had little opportunity to apply our
new certainties. Two days later we overturned our car on a rough road
in Zimbabwe, bringing our trip to an abrupt and ignominious end.
For five years I fantasised about returning to southern Africa, and
last July I finally set off to explore Zambia with two good friends, a
photographer and the bearded man himself, Gavin Blair.

We wanted a country that was challenging, obscure and fresh;
interesting, beautiful and not dangerous. We wanted a place with
good game viewing, as well as access to local culture. In Zambia, the
former Northern Rhodesia, Gavin said we would feel as though we
were discovering an Africa still unknown to the masses who have

inundated the parks in Kenya, northern Tanzania and South Africa. During two weeks there – aside from three days on what passes for a highway – we saw a total of eleven other vehicles.

A white Zimbabwean, Gavin Blair is licensed as a guide in three countries and is familiar with back roads and rare species in several others as well. He knows the Latin names for most plants you may see, the mating seasons of insects and the spoor of every animal. He can fix a car, your binoculars, the broken wing of a bird and the injured feelings of people bickering around the fire.

Gavin collected us at Mfuwe Airport, a small landing strip with good access to north-central Zambia's parks, and drove us to South Luangwa National Park. His beautiful wife, Marjorie, was waiting for us in camp. An able cook, she can make a bed quickly, has a sharp eye for game and is also a distinguished French-horn player who travels to Britain for three months each year to play with the Glyndebourne Touring Opera. She clearly prefers animals to all people except Gavin.

We started early the next day, when the animals make the most of the cool; ate a picnic lunch under a huge baobab tree; and stayed to see the emergence of the predators, who hunt by twilight. All four of us were at that naïve stage when every animal seems marvellous and we paused to look even at pukus, reddish antelope that are as common in Zambia as fleas on a mangy dog. We saw crocodiles and watched hippos going down a slide of their own making to settle happily in shallow water. We saw a hyena eyeing a herd of zebras. Best of all were the elephants, which, like huge ballerinas, tiptoe through the mud, letting their feet go flat only when they are standing on solid ground. A long history of poaching has made local game wary of humans. Nonetheless, one young bull elephant held his ground heart-stoppingly close to us, and we observed him for a half-hour while he used his trunk as though it were a telescope seeking out stars in the mud.

On the second day we saw our first lion. Glinting and deliberate, she stalked a young puku frozen in terror. No dance of seven veils was ever more calculated in its dynamics, more petrifyingly irresistible. That day we also saw wildebeests that looked like grumpy old men on an expedition, a tall and lovely kudu, waterbuck and hundreds of willowy impalas. We watched giraffes preparing to mate: the male gargles the female's urine to see whether she is in season. We wondered at those whimsical long necks and huge eyes, invented on God's most playful day.

After exploring the river area of South Luangwa, where game is thickest, we headed for the escarpment that rings the Luangwa Valley. Driving conditions were rough: we had to ford rivers, and sometimes the road became so faint that it disappeared. Mostly we sat on the vehicle's roof, bouncing, ducking low-hanging branches, getting too much sun, spotting occasional animals and many new plants. One of those jolts bounced my wallet out of my back pocket, but since we doubted we'd ever find it, we went onward. We traversed lowlands infested with tsetse flies, which was awful, but we also picked and ate marula plums in fertile valleys and dissolved the powdery contents of baobab pods on our tongues.

It was afternoon by the time we reached the escarpment. Up we drove, on a road so steep it seemed the vehicle might fall off the face of the rock. When we got to a really deep pothole, we stopped to fill it with stones so that we could keep going. On and on we climbed, through bush that was both lush and desolate, and then suddenly, when we were thinking we couldn't stand it any more, we were on top, and the landscape we'd been in since our arrival was spread beneath us like a map, as broad as the horizon. It was clear and orderly and miniaturised, as if we were seeing it through memory and not our eyes.

Gavin had warned that it would be a long day's drive. The road north of the escarpment was so riddled with holes that you had to weave around its lesions. 'The only ones who go straight,' Gavin observed, 'are the drunk drivers.' We were cantankerous and hungry by the time we reached a lovely Tudor cottage with climbing roses, a formal garden and a picket fence that announced our arrival at Kapishya Hot Springs Lodge. A rather fey white man wrapped in a cotton sarong called a *kikoi* came trotting down the path. 'Well, well, well,' he said, 'I'd really given up on you, quite given up. But do come in, come in.' He was the proprietor, Mark Harvey. A group of villagers holding oil lamps was standing behind him. 'Ernest,' he said to a helper, 'get the luggage in and have them warm supper.' Turning to us, he went on, 'There's just enough time for a dip before dinner.'

We were shown to the rather basic little guest cottages; then Ernest led us to a pool a few hundred yards away. Its bottom was covered in white sand, and a few steps hewn out of the living rock descended into the water. Clouds of steam were rising from the surface, and through them a single palm tree was silhouetted against the almost-full moon. We took off our clothes and slipped into the water, and never before have I had such an exhilarating feeling of the day washing away. The warm, warm water bubbled up through the sand, and our eyes were cleaned of Luangwa's hot, bright landscapes by the silver light that penetrated the steam. Afterward we sat beside a bonfire, where we had gin and tonics, ate shepherd's pie, and listened to Harvey's story of the house called Shiwa Ngandu, which his grandfather had built. We went to Shiwa Ngandu in the morning. It is not colonial Africa; it is non-Africa, a corpulent Victorian mansion in immense English gardens. To walk through the gardens, still half kept by loyal servants but essentially rather dilapidated, was to find a dream of England being consumed by the voracious jungle appetite of Africa. Beneath blossoming vines that covered fussy arbours, we looked out to the mountains and the splendour of a far lake, the slight movements of game in the bush.

Amused and spooked, we soon pressed on westward towards the Bangweulu Swamps. A small road led through dozens of villages of thatched mud-and-brick huts. We learned that a vehicle passed this way only once in a few weeks. The people, dressed mostly in African fabrics, would stop whatever they were doing and run to wave to us. Children would dance and sing, and some did jigs in our wake. As one of our party remarked, this must be what daily life is like for the Queen of England.

At lunchtime we stopped in a village, and since English is the national language of Zambia (there are thirty-five tribal languages), we could communicate easily. A twenty-year-old, Willie Momba, invited me into his one-room house, took me to see his fields (one guava tree, six scallions, four rows of sweet potatoes and two rows of tomatoes), and introduced me to his wife. He had one cherished possession, a camera, but he'd never had any film, so I gave him two rolls.

By afternoon, the villages had become smaller, poorer and closer to the road. Near sunset, Gavin turned (at random, it seemed) onto a vast plain. Twenty minutes later we came upon a causeway, and after another half-hour we reached camp. Around us in every direction for miles stretched the uncharted mire, foggy and shapeless in the night and full of strange sounds and animal cries. Never have I been anywhere else that felt so like the end of the earth. We went to sleep early and had strange dreams.

At dawn we set out with four local guides, broad-smiling men, barefoot but with hats, who had a mystical sense of direction. We sought the shoebill, the most elusive bird in Africa. Through bits of shrub we trekked, and when we came to water, we poled or paddled across in small boats. As we went on, the ground around us got spongier and the morass wetter. Then we came to the floating earth. In this weirdest place of all, the thick grasses had matted their roots together and held soil tightly in them, but beneath were stretches of mucky water. Though it looked like an ordinary field, it gave and shifted underfoot; you sank a few inches with each step. It was like walking across the top of a bowl of soup covered in clingfilm, or strolling on a plush-covered waterbed.

Passionate now to see the shoebill, we went on, eventually arriving where the floating earth could not bear our weight. We sank in up to our knees, sometimes to our waists. We finally found our object: a creature out of James Thurber, a prehistoric bird that came into the world not long after the pterodactyl left it, with a beak like a giant clog stuck absurdly on the front of its head. We saw three shoebills; then, muddy and content, we trooped back and took long showers. We spent the afternoon looking at skinks scuttling about camp, feeling like the only people in all the universe.

That evening we drove along the causeway a few miles, past fishermen's reed huts you could blow down with a huff, and onto the floodplain that lies beside the swamp. Flocks of wattled cranes performed mating dances there; beyond them were red lechwe antelope, five thousand in a herd. Gavin set the throttle, so the vehicle could drift along at about ten miles per hour, and joined the rest of us on the roof. As we were slow and steady and lumbering, the animals were not so afraid; we passed through the way a baggage cart negotiates a crowded airport. Back at camp, Marjorie made dinner. When she brought out bananas flambé for dessert, we heard gales of laughter from the staff. Tears rolling down their faces, they told us that the lady had set our dinner on fire.

Leaving the Bangweulu Swamps was like passing back through Alice's looking glass. Along the road we had taken two days earlier, we once more waved at dancing children. In one village, Willie Momba called to us from the side of the road. He produced a box tied up with string. 'I've been waiting for you to come back. I wanted to give you these sweet potatoes.' He presented what must have been a third of his harvest. 'I was so glad to meet you.' After some protest we accepted his gift. He stood in the road and waved at us until we were out of sight. We felt privileged to have visited this world. These people's poignant generosity, the intense interest they showed in us and their unaffected good humour were as fundamental to our experience of the country as the impeccable weather.

Further from the swamps, the houses became bigger and were set back from the road, and the people seemed more prosperous. Perhaps they had seen more foreigners, because they waved more sedately from further away. By mid-afternoon we came upon a sign, bright blue letters on white: TURN RIGHT TO THE PALACE OF CHIEF CHITAMBO. A hundred yards on was another sign pointing THIS WAY TO THE PALACE OF CHIEF CHITAMBO. We drove past a school and a dirt field with children bouncing balls. The largest sign yet announced YOU ARE APPROACHING THE PALACE OF CHIEF CHITAMBO. PLEASE REMOVE YOUR HAT AND GET OFF YOUR BICYCLE. Beyond low gates was a small square of well-kept English-looking grass, in the middle of which stood a tall flagpole. At the far side of the green were three identical low white buildings and some scattered sheds.

Beneath a tree could be seen the legs of a deckchair, most of which was obscured by an enormous newspaper. The newspaper descended to reveal a spry man in camping shorts. 'You are welcome to my palace,' said the chief in a plummy accent. He led us to his office, where he told us the history of the Chitambe tribe. He was committed to land conservation, he told us, and he rode around on his bicycle each year to visit every one of his ninety thousand subjects.

Drinking the Coca-Cola he had given us, we told him how beautiful Zambia was, and how kind his tribesmen had been to us, and a little bit about America. The chief passed a guest book for us to sign. Outside, he showed us around the grounds. The three low buildings were for his three wives; he spends a week with one, a week with the next, and a week with the third. When we mentioned our practise of having only one wife and living with her full time, he asked, 'Don't you end up arguing a lot?'

The chief had his picture taken with each of us under the flag. As we were leaving, he explained, *sotto voce*, that it was customary to leave some small trinket after such a meeting. We gave him a few dollars for his education fund. Then one of us offered a hat she had planned to give to a child, a sort of squashed tennis hat made of bright plaid with large figures of Bert and Ernie from *Sesame Street* sewn on the front. Chief Chitambo put on the hat, and when he had it adjusted perfectly, we took a group picture. We piled back into our vehicle, and the chief, like Willie Momba, stood in the road and waved until we turned a corner and were out of sight.

By the time we arrived at the small Kasanka National Park, the moon was full and the valley smelled of flowers. Gavin woke us the next morning before sunrise, and we climbed a tall, rickety ladder into the highest branches of a tree. As the sun lifted the steam, we saw herds of the rare sitatunga antelope. Gavin had brought a thermos; we drank tea and munched biscuits and heard the first birdsong. One of us had to fly out that day, so we headed to Lusaka. It was a sad day, and a long one, too.

Lusaka is an ugly city: dirty, crowded and smelly. We stayed outside town at a plush lodge: our rooms had modern light fixtures, hot water came out of the tap whenever you turned it on, and there was even a swimming pool – all quite welcome after the swamps. When I headed to my rondavel after dinner, I found it surrounded by zebras, grasing on the verdant lawn. When I slowly approached, they stepped not more than three feet aside. I stopped at the door and looked at one, and she returned my gaze. If you have spent a week looking through binoculars and craning your neck to see animals properly, such sudden intimacy is heady. The zebra and I stared curiously like strangers on a train; then, as though she had found out all she needed, she turned and trotted off.

The next day, the sun was dipping by the time we reached northern Kafue National Park. We collected firewood in a low gorge and arrived at our campsite in near darkness. Gavin asked us politely not to help set up camp, as we would only be in the way, so we took a bottle of wine down to the river and watched the stars come out. If I had to choose one favourite Zambian park, it would be Kafue. The animals were not so different from the animals elsewhere, nor were the trees, but things were somehow especially elegant, as though nature had been in a landscaping mood when she put it all together. We saw our first leopard there, as sensual and spotted and diffident as we'd anticipated. We saw cheetahs. For three more days we drove through Kafue's hills and took long afternoons for walking, reading and writing postcards. Then we drove south half the length of Kafue, arriving at twenty-five-mile-long Lake Iteshi-Teshi. We climbed onto the boulders, where the rock hyraxes, or dassies, little mammals with rodent-like features, gathered to sun themselves. Lake Iteshi-Teshi was primeval, like the world's inaugural day, with hippos, zebras and one boat: a little canoe making its way across the middle ground like a detail added by a sentimental painter.

The next day we headed into the nearly abandoned southern part of Kafue. The herds of animals – five hundred buffalo together, even more impalas, troops of wildebeests – looked surprised to see us. We saw a hundred pelicans roosting in an acacia tree, its leaves completely white from their droppings. We followed the turquoise flight of a lilac-breasted roller. Finally we came to a clearing in which the sun focused itself bright, an enchanted place. Beneath a spreading mopani tree, Gavin and Marjorie pitched camp. We watched the moon rise and had honest talks while the fire burned down to firefly embers.

In the morning we drove through more wilds, stopped in Livingstone to shop, and then crossed into Zimbabwe at Victoria Falls. At our hotel there, I found my wallet waiting for me. A worker in Luangwa had found it and managed to reach American Express, which had obtained my itinerary and facilitated delivery. My cash was all there.

That night we put on whatever crumpled but presentable clothes we found in the bottom of our suitcases and headed off to the Victoria Falls Hotel for supper. There was a band; there was dancing; we ordered from menus and drank champagne toasts to the bush. When, in the morning, we said goodbye to Gavin and Marjorie, we had that slight pang of an intensity ended, the same feeling I had had when I left college – that things might be otherwise and fine but would never be quite like this again.

———————

One of the liabilities of writing about places off the beaten track is that in doing so you help beat new tracks. Tourism in Zambia has reached unprecedented highs in the twenty-first century. But this seems like a social good: the only effective defence against poachers, logging and everything else that destroys big game is an infrastructure that supports animal protection, and tourism is often the engine of such safeguards. Since my visit, falling copper prices have made Zambia more reliant on tourism; the elimination of yellow fever has made the country more attractive to visitors. It's easy to romanticise neglected places, but that neglect is often deadly for the people who live there.

Phaly Nuon's Three Steps

The Noonday Demon, 2001

I did not go to Cambodia to learn about mental illness, but to study the architecture of Angkor Wat. My first night in Phnom Penh, I sat next to someone to whom I mentioned my depression research, and he mentioned Phaly Nuon. I told him that I'd love to interview her, even if it meant losing a day touring up north. During the interview he helped set up, I realised that I couldn't write about depression without the cross-cultural perspective that subsequently became a defining theme of my book. The following passage from *The Noonday Demon* is slightly expanded to stand on its own.

When I went to Cambodia in January 1999, I wanted to see its architectural marvels, but I also hoped to understand how people lived in a country emerging from inconceivable tragedy. I wondered what happens to your emotions when you have seen a quarter of your compatriots murdered, when you yourself have lived in the hardship and fear of a brutal regime, when you are fighting against the odds to rebuild a devastated nation. I wanted to see what happens among the citizens of a nation when they have all endured almost inconceivable traumatic stress, are desperately poor, and have little chance for education or employment. The despair psychology of wartime is usually frenzied, while the despair that follows devastation, numb and all-encompassing, more closely resembles the depressive syndrome that afflicts the West. Cambodia is not a country in which factions fought brutally against factions; it is a country in which all the mechanisms of society were completely annihilated. It was like visiting that part of the Antarctic ice sheet over which there is no ozone at all.

During the 1970s, the revolutionary Pol Pot established a Maoist dictatorship in Cambodia in the name of what he called the Khmer Rouge. Years of bloody civil war followed, during which a fifth of the population was slaughtered. The educated elite was obliterated; the peasantry was regularly displaced; many were taken into prison cells where they were mocked and tortured. The entire country lived in chronic fear.

Most Cambodians are soft-spoken, gentle and attractive. It's hard to believe that Pol Pot's atrocities took place in this lovely country. Everyone I met had a different explanation for how the Khmer Rouge could have come to power there, but none of these explanations made sense, just as none of the explanations for the Cultural Revolution, Stalinism or Nazism makes sense. In retrospect it is possible to understand why a nation was especially vulnerable to such regimes; but where in the human imagination such behaviours originate is unknowable. Such evil is both contiguous with the ordinary evil of all societies and so extreme as to comprise its own law. The social fabric is always thinner than we care to acknowledge, but it is impossible to know how it gets vaporised. The American ambassador told me that the greatest problem for the Khmer people is that traditional Cambodian society has no peaceful mechanism to resolve conflict. 'If they have differences,' he said, 'they have to deny and suppress them totally, or they have to take out knives and fight.' A Cambodian member of the current government told me that the people had been too subservient to an absolute monarch for too many years and didn't think to fight against authority until it was too late.

People cry easily in Cambodia. The words of the American ambassador were in my ears each time I witnessed a smiling Cambodian abruptly begin to weep, without any apparent middle ground or transition. During numerous interviews with people who had suffered atrocities at the hands of the Khmer Rouge, I found that most preferred to look forward. When I pressed them on personal history, however, they would seem to regress before my eyes, slipping into an agonised past tense. Every adult I met in Cambodia had suffered such traumas as would have driven many of us to madness. What they had endured within their own minds was at yet another level of horror. When I decided to do interviews in Cambodia, I expected to be humbled by the pain of others, and I was humbled down to the ground.

Phaly Nuon, winner of the Figaro Prize for Humanitarian Service and a sometime candidate for the Nobel Peace Prize, has set up an orphanage and a centre for depressed women in Phnom Penh. Her success with these women has been so enormous that her orphanage is almost entirely staffed by the women she has helped, who have formed a community of generosity around her. If you save the women, it has been said, they in turn will save other women, who will save the children, and so via a chain of influence you can save the country.

We met, as Phaly Nuon had suggested, in a small, disused room at the top of an old office building near the centre of Phnom Penh. She sat on a chair on one side, and I sat on a small sofa opposite. Like most Cambodians, she is relatively short by Western standards. Her black hair, streaked with grey, was pulled back from her face and gave it a hardness of emphasis. She can be aggressive in making a point, but she is also shy, smiling and looking down whenever she is not speaking.

We started with her own story. In the early seventies, Phaly Nuon worked for the Cambodian Department of the Treasury and Chamber of Commerce as a typist and shorthand secretary. In 1975, when Phnom Penh fell to Pol Pot and the Khmer Rouge, she was taken from her house with her husband and children. Her husband was sent off to a location unknown to her, and she had no idea whether he remained alive. She was put to work as a field labourer with her twelve-year-old daughter, three-year-old son and newborn baby. The conditions were terrible and food was scarce, but she worked beside her fellows, 'never telling them anything, and never smiling, as none of us ever smiled, because we knew that at any moment we could be put to death'. After a few months, she and her family were packed off to another location. During the transfer, a group of soldiers tied her to a tree and made her watch while her daughter was gang-raped and then murdered. A few days later it was Phaly Nuon's turn to be killed. She was brought with some fellow labourers to a field outside town. Her hands were tied behind her back and her legs roped together. After she was forced to her knees, a rod of bamboo was tied to her back, and she was made to lean forward over a mucky field, so that her legs had to be tensed or she would lose her balance. When she finally dropped of exhaustion, she would fall forward into the mud and drown. Her three-year-old son bellowed and cried beside her. The infant was tied to her so that he would suffocate when she fell: Phaly Nuon would be the killer of her own baby.

Phaly Nuon told a lie. She said that she had, before the war, worked for a high-level member of the Khmer Rouge, that she had been his secretary and then his lover, that he would be angry if she were put to death. Few people escaped the killing fields, but a captain who perhaps believed her story eventually said that he couldn't bear the sound of the screaming child and that bullets were too expensive to waste on executing her quickly, so he untied Phaly Nuon and told her to run. Her baby in one arm and the three-year-old in the other, she headed deep into the jungle of north-eastern Cambodia.

She stayed there for three years, four months and eighteen days. She never slept twice in the same place. As she wandered, she picked leaves and dug for roots to feed herself and her family, but food was hard to find, and other, stronger foragers had often stripped the land bare. Severely malnourished, she began to waste away. Her breast milk soon ran dry, and the baby she could not feed died in her arms. She and her remaining child just barely held on to life through the period of war.

By the time Phaly Nuon told me this, we had both moved to the floor between our seats and she was weeping and rocking back and forth on the balls of her feet, while I sat with my knees under my chin and a hand on her shoulder in as much of an embrace as her trance-like state would allow. She continued in a half whisper.

After the war was over, Phaly Nuon found her husband. He had been severely beaten around the head and neck, resulting in significant brain damage. She, her husband and her son were all placed in a border camp near Thailand, where thousands of people lived in temporary tented structures. They were physically and sexually abused by some workers at the camp and helped by others. Phaly Nuon was one of the only educated people there, and knowing languages, she could talk to the aid workers. She and her family were given a wooden hut that passed for comparative luxury. 'While I went around, I saw women who were in very bad shape, many of them seeming paralysed, not moving, not talking, not feeding or caring for their own children,' she said. 'I saw that though they had survived the war, they were now going to die from their depression.' Phaly Nuon made a special request to the aid workers and set up her hut in the camp as a sort of psychotherapy centre.

She used traditional Khmer medicine (made with more than a hundred herbs and leaves) as a first step. If that did not work sufficiently well, she would use occidental medicine when it was available, as it sometimes was. 'I would hide away stashes of whatever antidepressants the aid workers could bring in,' she said, 'and try to have enough for the worst cases.' She would take her patients to meditate, keeping in her house a Buddhist shrine with flowers in front of it. To seduce the women into openness, she would begin by taking three hours or so to get each to tell her story. Then she would make regular follow-up visits to try to get more of the story, until she finally got the full trust of the depressed woman. 'I wanted to understand very specifically what each one had to vanquish,' Phaly Nuon explained.

Once this initiation was concluded, she would move on to a formulaic system: 'I take it in three steps. First, I teach them to forget. We have exercises we do each day, so that each day they can forget a little more of the things they will never forget entirely. During this time, I try to distract them with music, or with embroidery or weaving, with concerts, with an occasional hour of television, with whatever seems to work, whatever they tell me they like. Depression is under the skin, all the surface of the body has the depression just below it, and we cannot take it out; but we can try to forget the depression, even though it is right there.

'When their minds are cleared of what they have forgotten, when they have learned forgetfulness well, I teach them to work. Whatever kind of work they want to do, I will find a way to teach it to them. Some train only to clean houses or take care of children. Others learn skills they can use as they care for orphans, and some begin towards a real profession. They must learn to do these things well and to have pride in them.

'And then when they have mastered work, at last I teach them to love.' I wondered aloud how one teaches such a skill. 'Well, I actually teach them that by way of manicures and pedicures,' she said. I raised an eyebrow. 'In the camp, I built a sort of lean-to and made it a steam bath, and now in Phnom Penh I have a similar one, a little better built. I take them there so that they can become clean, and I teach them how to give one another manicures and pedicures and how to take care of their fingernails, because doing that makes them feel beautiful, and they want so much to feel beautiful. It also makes them give up their bodies to the care of others. It takes a lot for a woman who has been so wantonly and violently injured to extend her hand or foot, to trust a relative stranger to come at her body with a sharp implement. When they learn not to flinch, it rescues them from physical isolation, and that leads to the breakdown of emotional isolation. While they are together washing and putting on nail polish, they begin to talk, and bit by bit they learn to trust one another, and by the end of it all, they have learned how to make friends, so that they will never have to be so lonely again. Their stories, which they have told to no one but me – they begin to tell those stories to one another.'

Phaly Nuon showed me the tools of her psychologist's trade: the little bottles of coloured enamel, the steam room, the sticks for pushing back cuticles, the emery boards, the towels. Grooming is one of the primary forms of socialisation among primates, and this return to grooming as a socialising force among human beings struck me as curiously organic. When I remarked on that, she laughed and told me about monkeys she had seen in the jungle. Perhaps they, too, were learning to love, she remarked. I told her that I thought it was difficult to teach ourselves or others how to forget, how to work, and how to love and be loved, but she said it was not so complicated if you could do those three things yourself. She told me about how the women she has treated have become a community, and about how well they do with the orphans now in their care.

'There is a final step,' she said to me after a long pause. 'At the end, I teach them the most important thing. I teach them that these three skills – forgetting, working and loving – are not three separate skills, but part of one enormous whole, and that it is the practise of these things together, each as part of the others, that makes a difference. It is the hardest thing to convey' – she laughed – 'but they all come to understand this, and when they do – why, then they are ready to go into the world again.'

———

Phaly Nuon died on 27 November 2012, from injuries sustained in a car accident. Her funeral took place over seven days and was attended by thousands of people, many of whom had been children at her Future Light Orphanage. Hundreds of children who lived there mourned her as their mother.

The situation of the mentally ill in Cambodia is still bleak, and continues to be aggravated by forced displacement and human trafficking. PTSD is ubiquitous. The suicide rate is nearly three times the world average. Yet despite the citizens' fragile mental health, the care system is abysmal; roughly one in three mentally ill people is kept in a cage or tied down with chains. Most mentally ill Cambodians neither seek nor receive help. Only 0.02 per cent of the Cambodian health budget goes to mental health. Only the Khmer-Soviet Friendship Hospital provides inpatient treatment, and Cambodia has a mere thirty-five trained psychiatrists to serve a population of 15 million. In the spring of 2015, one Cambodian province proposed that mentally ill people be rounded up, sent to pagodas and cared for by monks to recover their 'beauty and order'.

The Open Spaces of Mongolia

Travel + Leisure, July 1999

My mother used to indicate the obscurity of some destination – where an uncle she didn't much want to visit anyway was domiciled, where a college she hoped I wouldn't attend was located – by saying, 'That might as well be in Outer Mongolia.' Perhaps that is why Mongolia became for me a symbol of the remote. Often, I've imagined some place to be very exotic only to arrive and find it disappointingly familiar, but Mongolia was emphatically another place and seemed to have lingered in another time. The gorgeousness of Mongolia is a shimmering presence that stays with you as you traverse the country.

I came down with terrible food poisoning in the Gobi Desert. I was travelling with a colleague who decided halfway through the trip that he had had enough and headed home. By chance, I stumbled upon a college acquaintance who was living in Ulaanbaatar; after a brief conversation, I invited her to join me, and she jumped at the offer. She spoke excellent Mongolian and knew enough to contribute a steady stream of insights, but not so much as to be bored by what we saw.

We took the thirty-six-hour train ride (rather than the two-hour plane ride) from Beijing to Ulaanbaatar. On the way my travelling companions and I saw much of the Great Wall and some of Hebei and Shanxi provinces in north-central China. Then we passed through the endless flat monotony of Inner Mongolia, an autonomous region of China. In the next cabin was a twenty-year-old Mongolian Buddhist monk (he joined the monastery when he was eight) who had been studying in India and was returning home for the first time in five years. He was sharing his quarters with a German management consultant, and next to them were a twenty-one-year-old graduate student of Russian from North Dakota and a retired English teacher from Cleveland. A Polish novelist who wore five wristwatches was in number 5. In the next car were an outrageously beautiful French couple who didn't speak to anyone and some Hare Krishnas from Slovenia who were trying (unsuccessfully) to convert us all. After two days we arrived in Ulaanbaatar, capital of independent (aka 'Outer') Mongolia.

Mongolia is one-sixth the size of the United States, with a population of about 2.5 million. Most of its people are nomadic, living in wood-framed felt tents and herding sheep, goats, yaks, camels, cattle and horses. They do not have paved roads. They do not in general use electricity or own cars. They practise Tibetan Buddhism; in fact, the Mongolian ruler Altan Khan coined the title *Dalai Lama* more than four hundred years ago. Many temples and monasteries, despite seventy years of Communism, are thriving.

Though Mongolia has a literacy rate of almost 90 per cent and an impressively well-informed population, outside the cities the way of life is much as it was at the turn of the first millennium. The country has important copper and gold mines and is the world's leading source of cashmere, but it remains largely immune to modernisation and industrialisation. After almost eighty years as an 'independent' buffer state between Russia and China, Mongolia has recently established democracy, and in the last election, despite the limited number of polling stations and the vast distances between them, more than 90 per cent of the eligible population voted.

From Ulaanbaatar the guides and I drove three-quarters of the way towards Kharkhorin before setting up our first night's camp in a big field near a *ger*, one of the low-slung tent-like structures in which Mongolians traditionally live. In the morning, we woke to the sound of horse traffic. I sat up, pulled aside the flap of my tent, and saw a tall man wearing a long side-buttoned coat of blue velvet, tied at the waist with a yellow silk sash. I stumbled into wakefulness, half-dressed, and followed him to the *ger*, where he gave me cheese and butter and a slice of fresh bread. Such hospitality is automatic in this nomad country, and endlessly delightful to a Western visitor. I tried his horses, provoking amused delight from the little boys and girls, who from the age of four know how to ride and at six move more self-assuredly on their mounts than I can walk. An older child, perhaps sixteen, came to look at our car and gestured to the inside of the door with the bemused air of an action hero on an alien space-craft. I showed him how one could rotate the handle to make the window go up (he thought this amasing); and I showed him how if you push down the lock, people can't open the door from the outside (he thought this hilarious).

We arrived in Kharkhorin on the first day of its Naadam cele-bration, a festivity of sport that takes place from 11 to 13 July every year. The number of horsemen we saw heading across the roadless countryside and the bright colours they wore told us which way to go even before we had spotted the first of the distant pavilions. As we came closer, we picked up on the crowd's excitement. The jockeys had set out near dawn, and more than two hundred horses galloped in the morning's race. At least six hundred others stood in rows, and the spectators sat astride their mounts the way Western audiences sit in grandstands. Everyone was eagerly waiting for the first glimpse on the horizon of the winning stallion. The men and women mostly wore long robes, called *del*, often of velvet or brocade, tied at the hip with silk sashes of brilliant yellow, crimson or green. Saddles were ornamented with silver, and many riders had silver crops and chatelaines. Colourful hats, some trimmed in fur, crested in points like steeples. A few hotshot adolescents who had drunk too much *airag* (Mongolia's specialty: fermented horse milk, which is what one might call an acquired taste) were riding fast, and from time to time the crowd had to part before them. Children and the elderly were pushed to the front, while the rest of us on foot strained to see over their heads. The air rang with speculations, greetings, family arguments and plans.

At last the first horse came through, and the cheering erupted. We parted to make way for an endless line of runners-up, all bearing jockeys ages four to seven. They cantered through the crowd and slowed only in the distance. Ribbons flew from the bridles. The winner was taken to a nearby field, where a lama in a flowing robe and a yellow, pleated hat blessed him in the name of the Buddha. Everyone was laughing, some began singing, and the joy was for old and new friends alike. We received invitations – translated by our guide – from every Mongolian we met: come into our tent, have some of our *airag*, have a piece of fried dough, some cheese. They struggled to communicate over the language barrier, swore brotherhood with us, gave us their hats to try on, taught us words of exuberant Mongolian.

The next morning, closer to town, we watched the wrestling. Silk tents were pitched in a great circle on a greensward. Cavalry kept the crowd more or less in order, though periodically spectators rushed forward and threatening words were exchanged. The judges sat under a blue canopy adorned with white sacred symbols. Music played loudly; people jostled one another for good views or shady spots. One by one, the wrestlers came out in long leather *del*, paraded past the cheering crowd, then removed their coats to reveal hand-embroidered wrestler's garb. Each solemnly performed an eagle dance around a judge, then slapped the front and the back of his thighs (*thwack! thwack!* and *thwack! thwack!*). Next, partners began sparring according to ancient rules, striving not to touch the earth except with their feet and the open palms of their hands, while forcing their opponents, with a hair-raising mix of weight and precision, down to the ground.

Nearby, the archers were competing, firing slender arrows over a long meadow. The men shot from a back line; the women, in white silk, stood a few feet closer to the targets. On another field was a pick-up game of polo. Small stands sold cakes, carpets or radios. The hillside that formed the backdrop for the events was a wash of colour: the revellers had pitched a small village there. The smell of meat cooking on open fires mixed with scents of curdled *airag* and the wild thyme that the wrestlers were trampling. I could have lived five years on the hospitality the Mongolians offered. I photographed one man who looked particularly noble in his saddle, and he swept me up onto his horse. From that lofty height I watched the sport as his friends asked me questions and gave me cow's-milk liquor.

We left the Naadam, and as we travelled deeper into Övörkhangai Province (Kharkhorin is on its northern edge), the paved roads stopped. Imagine the worst dirt road you've driven. Now envision the worst stretch of that road; now that worst stretch in the rain; now that worst stretch in the rain immediately after an earthquake. You see in your mind's eye one of the better roads in Mongolia. We crossed muddy fields where it was impossible to see the road, and we forded rivers when our driver thought the bridges looked unstable. It was rough going, and more than once we had to get out to push our car – or to assist others whose cars had given up.

But despite the wild jolting, the magnificence of that drive will stay with me forever. The great hills were nearly mountains. There were, however, no trees; and grasing animals had cropped the lush grass so low that it was as smooth as a golf course. A brook flowed through the bottom of a valley, and yellow flowers bloomed all around. Slender columns of smoke came from a *ger* here and there. Herds feasted on the vegetation: yaks and cows and sheep and goats and even the occasional stray camel from the Gobi, and astonishing numbers of horses running free. There were no predators and no hiding places; the feeling was of sublime peace.

Every so often a herdsman would come into view, smoking a pipe, watching his flock; children played and laughed by the water's edge. Women emerging from their *gers* surveyed the scene with satisfaction as they arranged trays of cheese on their roofs to dry. Eagles circled overhead in deliberate patterns, while smaller birds flew lower. Marmots darted from their holes and scampered in and out of sight. Here were innocent stretches of earth that had been neither exploited nor deliberately preserved. I have never encountered a terrain that was at once so magnificent and so unthreatening; no evidence of the monstrous force of nature was here, but only the golden, the light, the perfect.

Of all the animals of Mongolia, I loved the yaks most. Large and inept, with vain faces and a gratuitous leg-obscuring fringe similar to what you'd find on a Victorian sofa, they moved with the disgruntled self-assurance of old ladies elaborately done up in tattered versions of bygone fashions. A few spry creatures waved their absurd fluffy tails in the air like parasols or darted daringly across the road, mad great-aunts with spring fever. Most of them eyed us dubiously, offering no threat but preserving an air of mild disapproval. They liked being photographed; they would gaze straight into the camera and blink flirtatiously.

Almost none of the land in Mongolia belongs to anyone; it never has. You may drive over any part you want; you may pitch a tent wherever you like. A herder in the Gobi Desert said to me, 'When I move my *ger*, I feel the exhilaration of possibilities and freedom. I can go anywhere, put my house anywhere, take my flock anywhere, except maybe some few little places where they built a city.' He stopped for a moment to pour me tea with camel's milk. 'Tell me, is America also a free country?' For the first time in my patriotic life, I found that question difficult to answer. One-third of Mongolians live below the poverty level, but when I talked about the American dream, that herder said, 'Why would a son want a different life from his father's?' I asked about his young children, who were playing underfoot. 'I am sending them to school,' he said, 'and if they want to be politicians or businessmen, that is up to them. I went to school and I chose to remain a herder; I hope they will make that choice also, because I can imagine no better life.' The fashionable wisdom is that capitalism has won out over communism, but I left Mongolia persuaded that these two systems had never been opposites, that the real opposite of both is nomadism, a way of life that can be as close to joyful anarchy as humankind will ever reach.

We stopped several times for petrol as we travelled south towards the Gobi. The desert starts gradually: bit by bit the plants become sparse, and then the land flattens. The smooth, glorious grass fades away. We drove for hours and hours across Dundgovi (Middle Gobi) Province, which was dull and bleak. Then we came to Ömnögovi (South Gobi), where the sand was even and yellow, and vegetation almost entirely absent. An hour or two later we arrived at one of the Gobi 'forests', full of plants with thick stems and thin leaves, like old driftwood stuck in the sand and decorated with rocket. After that, the real desert began: flat, without ornament of any kind, and vast, vast, vast.

We spent the night at the Bayanzag – a region known as the Flaming Cliffs – where great crumbling formations of limestone, bright red and warm gold, frame and reframe the desert around them. The wind brayed at us through tunnels carved into the cliffs. In the distance we could see snowcapped mountains. Fossils were everywhere, as though the dinosaurs hadn't bothered to clean up when they moved on to their next campsite.

The guides, the photographer and I decided to spend that moonless night with some camel herders, so we simply stopped at their *ger* and introduced ourselves. The camels of Mongolia don't spit at you as Arabian camels do. They are curious creatures that turn to follow you as you pass. Their two humps are topped with tufts of long fur. When they lack water, their humps droop like ageing bosoms. At night, they howl – an eerie sound, like the spirits of purgatory crying out.

I liked the herders at once. There were a brother and sister and their spouses, none older than twenty-five; their parents, who'd recently departed after a long visit, were encamped within a day's ride. The couples readily answered our questions. So I learned that camels are easier to take care of than sheep; your flock will not mix with others. You let the adult camels roam during the day, but you stay with the babies and yearlings and guide them home in the evenings. The mothers return to be with the calves, and the males follow them, so the herd stays together. Camels yield good wool and can manage with infrequent meals. About five times a year, the herders pack their *gers* onto their camels to seek better grasing land.

We had by then learned basic *ger* etiquette, so we knew that men sit on the west side and women on the east, that you are always given something to eat and drink, and that it's rude not to try what you are given. Usually you get milk tea, made with tea, salt, sugar and whatever milk is on hand (this time, camel milk), and often you get *airag*. The herders made us soup from dried mutton, and we added some onions and potatoes we had brought from UB. These items were new to them. The onions they liked; the potatoes they found 'disgusting', complaining that they 'had the texture of dirt'.

At night, a *ger* is usually lit by a single candle, and in the flickering light we talked until it was late and the children started dropping off on the floor. Not wanting to take the only beds in the *ger*, we returned to our tents just outside.

The next day the rain began. It seemed unfair that there should be heavy rain in South Gobi Province, where the annual precipitation is about five inches. It seemed particularly unfair that it went on for three days, making the road we took as we headed back towards Ulaanbaatar virtually invisible and barely navigable. It seemed utterly unfair that our tents were not waterproof as guaranteed and that none of us ever quite dried out. And it seemed cruelly unfair that I had got sick from something I had eaten at the Naadam and that it was now kicking in with a vengeance. I felt as though I were a dry-clean-only item in a mobile washing machine. We got stuck twice. We jacked up the vehicle, checked the tyres, tore up nearby plants, and established traction by laying the branches underneath. I had just finished reading the manuscript of a friend's novel, and its pages did well for getting the wheels re-engaged. The earth might as well have been made of marshmallow.

For the first half of our trip we enjoyed camping and driving and staying in a different place every night. But now we'd had enough of it, so a friend and I flew north to stay in Khövsgöl Province for the rest of the trip. It's hard to write about Khövsgöl in a fittingly superlative tone after having described Övörkhangai's very different beauty. We took a bumpy four-hour jeep ride to Khövsgöl Lake National Park. Having a national park in the middle of Mongolia is like having an urban development zone in midtown Manhattan, but in principle it means that hunting is forbidden, which explains why the wildlife is particularly plentiful there. Khövsgöl Lake contains three-quarters of Mongolia's fresh water; it is enormous, lovely, dark and deep. On its banks are fields of wildflowers so brilliant you might think you were looking at a shoreline of butterflies. All around the lake are steep mountains. There are no buildings with foundations anywhere. Each morning we decided whether to take a boat ride or go hiking or ride horses or ride yaks (which no one who had a horse would ever choose to do except for the novelty of it).

I'd heard of the Mongolian reindeer people, the shamanist Tsaatan, and had always wanted to meet them. The five-hundred-odd members of this race keep far from the beaten path; anthropologists and devoted travellers often have to ride three or four days through the woods north-west of the park to find them. We were in luck, however: a Tsaatan child had spent the night nearby, and he agreed to lead us to his cousins. We were told it was an hour's drive and then a three-mile walk. We had not fully understood that it was a three-mile vertical walk, but we climbed gamely with our seven-year-old guide and a few relatives he had gathered in the valley – assimilationists who had turned to goatherding. We followed a mountain stream that runs into the lake. As we ascended, the view opened up behind us. From time to time the boy would point out a bear's cave or an eagle or a deer.

After about three hours of hiking we found ourselves above the tree line, and on the crest of the mountain we could just make out an *ortz* (one of the conical tepees the Tsaatan inhabit) and a herd of animals. Soon we were at the encampment of the reindeer people. In their dwelling we were given the usual warm welcome, reindeer-milk tea, some nasty cheese and fried biscuits. ('Cooked in reindeer fat?' I asked the oldest woman. She reached behind a cabinet. 'We prefer sunflower oil these days,' she said, showing me the bottle.) Along the side of the tepee were various practical hooks made from antlers, and a few reindeer-skin bags. We asked about a small bundle, hanging opposite the door, of feathers, ribbons, dried flowers, a duck foot and part of an antler. We were told that it was a magical device, and they made clear that further questions about it were not welcome. The boy who had brought us said that his mother was a shaman.

Then we went outside to see the animals: three snow-white reindeer and twenty-seven brown ones. I'd always thought of reindeer as inhabiting an eternal December; these had shed their heavy winter coats and seemed happy with the afternoon sun. They came over to rub their noses and heads against us. Their antlers were furry and sensitive, and we soon discovered that they loved to have them scratched. The father in the Tsaatan family saddled one up and let me try it out. Reindeer sway as they trot, and an amateur rider's natural impulse, upon feeling he is about to slide off, is to grab on to the thing in front of him – which is, alas, their antlers. Doing so, as I found to my chagrin and to the Tsaatan family's immense amusement, jerks back the reindeer's head and sends him running. Reindeer are a great deal faster than you think.

I was glad to return to Ulaanbaatar, which is a funny, mixed-up city, with grand neoclassical Russian buildings, Buddhist monasteries and grim housing from the Communist era. Throughout the city, people have a wry, ironic view of the Cold War government, whose monuments are ubiquitous. In one museum, a Turkish restaurant has opened under the eighty-foot-high mosaic of Lenin. When I walked in, I saw two signs: one on the wall that said WORKERS OF THE WORLD, UNITE! and the other on a freshly whitewashed stand that said DRINKS HALF-PRICE BEFORE 6:00!

In 1931, a third of Mongolia's male population lived in monasteries, and the nation's wealth was concentrated in Buddhist holy places. Stalin's thugs destroyed almost all of these, but a few remain. The most splendid is the Gandan Monastery in UB, the biggest monastery in Mongolia, at the centre of which is a Buddha almost a hundred feet tall, enclosed in a tight-fitting pagoda. Dozens of monks in long robes offer prayers inside and outside, and the aura of peace is strong even with the crowds of noisy tourists shoving through. I ran into my friend the monk from the Beijing train, and he greeted me with warm smiles and talked excitedly about his family.

We had also visited the great monastery in Kharkhorin, named Erdene Zuu, which felt more ancient, less touristed, more hallowed. The monks there, ages six to ninety, strolled through the unkempt courtyards in long red robes; inside the temples others chanted prayers, beat drums and lit candles in front of golden Buddhas carved by Mongolia's great seventeenth-century king and sculptor, Zanabazar. Worshippers made offerings and pressed their foreheads to images of the divine, then turned the prayer wheels. For $2, you could get the monks to recite special prayers for you and your livestock.

The essence of Mongolia outclasses the sights; anywhere in Mongolia (outside Ulaanbaatar) you can see what you need to see, which is an innocent landscape and an immutable culture. Afterward, if you especially want to explore the Gobi or Khövsgöl or find some yaks, you can go ahead and do that, too. In China, people take a curious nationalist pride in the idea that no foreigner will ever penetrate the complexity of their society. Russians believe that their despair is a state no Westerner can attain or affect. Mongolians, however, seem gloriously clear about their place in the world and are delighted if you want to join them there. You get a feeling in Mongolia not simply of history, but of eternity.

Nomadism is declining in Mongolia; intense recent migration means that half the population now resides in Ulaanbaatar, many in vast shantytowns that ring the city. A fifth of the country lives below the poverty line. Though Mongolia remains a democracy, riots have occurred lately over election fraud, and former president Nambar Enkhbaya has been convicted of corruption and sent to prison. The environmental situation is getting sadder. Mining operations and overgrasing combined with global warming are leading to wide desertification and a significant loss of plant density. Many animals, hunted for Chinese medicine or for their pelts, are at record low numbers.

But meaningful progress occurs, too. Modernity comes in fits and starts. The National Solar Ger Electrification Programme seeks to equip nomads with portable, renewable sources of electricity. In 2011, the UNESCO World Heritage Committee designated Naadam as an Intangible Cultural Heritage of Humanity. Among the many shifts that reflect the move away from the Communist past, I found it particularly charming that the Lenin Museum has been turned into a dinosaur museum.

Inventing the Conversation

The Noonday Demon, 2001

Greenland is not terribly far from the United States or Europe, but few Americans or Europeans go there. In this place of transcendent beauty, a traditional way of life and modern technology are delicately balanced. If your country had to be colonised, you might choose Danish overlords. The Danes have invested heavily in infrastructure, medical care and schooling. However, residents of the planet's least densely populated nation speak Greenlandic, an Eskimo-Aleut tongue, as their first language and Danish as their second – which does not equip them particularly well for the global economy.

In a quest to examine diverse cultural constructions of depression, I visited the Inuit peoples of Greenland – in part because depression is pervasive among them, and in part because the culture's attitudes towards it are distinctive. Depression affects as many as 80 per cent of Greenlanders. How can one organise a society in which depression occurs so widely? Greenland is integrating the ways of an ancient society with the realities of the modern world, and transitional societies – African tribal communities that are being folded into larger nations, nomadic cultures that are being urbanised, subsistence farmers who are being incorporated into larger-scale agricultural production systems – often have high levels of depression. Even in the traditional context, however, depression has always been common among the Inuit, and the suicide rate has been high (though it dropped by nearly half with the introduction of television); in some areas, about one in three hundred people commits suicide each year. Some might say that this is God's way of indicating to people that they shouldn't live in such a forbidding place – yet most Inuit have not abandoned their ice-bound lives to migrate south. They have adapted to tolerate the difficulties of life within the Arctic Circle.

Before I went to Greenland, I had assumed that the primary issue there was seasonal affective disorder (SAD), which is depression resulting from a lack of sunlight – a particularly acute vulnerability in a place where the sun barely makes its presence felt for a full three months. I had anticipated that everyone would dip in late autumn and begin to improve in February. That is not the case. The prime suicide month in Greenland is May, and though foreigners who move to the northern part of Greenland get depressed during the long periods of darkness, the Inuit have adapted over the years to seasonal shifts in light. Springtime is an instigator of suicide in many societies. 'The richer, softer and more delectable nature becomes,' the essayist A. Alvarez has written, 'the deeper that internal winter seems, and the wider and more intolerable the abyss which separates the inner world from the outer.' In Greenland, where the springtime shift is twice as dramatic as in a more temperate zone, these are the cruellest months.

Life is hard in Greenland. The Danish government has instituted universal free health care, education, even unemployment benefits. The hospitals are spotless, and the prison in the capital city looks more like a bed-and-breakfast than an institution of punishment. But the forces of nature in Greenland are unfathomably harsh. One Inuit man who had travelled across Europe said to me, 'We never made great art or built great buildings, the way other civilisations did. But for thousands of years, in this climate, we survived.' It struck me that this was quite possibly the greater achievement.

Greenlandic hunters and fishermen struggle to catch enough to feed themselves, their families and their dogs, and sell the skins of the seals they eat to pay for the repair of sleds and boats. They have a high rate of freesing, starving, injury and loss. During the three-month period of relative darkness, hunters dressed in trousers of polar-bear fur and coats of sealskin must run beside their dogsleds to forestall frostbite. Many survive the winter on *kiviak*, which is made from fermented auks buried for eighteen months in a fatty sealskin, then consumed raw. My Greenlandic friends assured me it was no more repellent than blue cheese. Forty years ago, these people lived in igloos. If you've never been inside an igloo, you cannot fathom how small they usually are. The only sources of warmth are a seal-fat lamp and the body heat of the occupants. Sewn into clothes for the winter, the denisens of an igloo would lie partly on top of one another. Now they live in Danish-style prefabricated houses with just two or three rooms because the cost of heating in a land with no readily available source of fuel – Greenland has no trees – is prohibitive.

Inuit families are large. For months on end, a family of twelve people may stay unremittingly inside their own house, usually gathered in one room. It is simply too cold and too dark for anyone to go out except the father, who goes hunting or ice-fishing once or twice a month to supplement the stock of dried fish from the summer. This forced intimacy offers no place for complaining, talking about problems, anger or accusations. In igloo days, having a fight with someone with whom you would have to be in immediate physical contact for weeks on end was impossible. Even now you must share rooms and meals for months. If you storm out, you go into a climate in which you will surely die. As one said, referring to the old days, 'When you got angry or upset, you would just turn your head and watch the walls melt.' The extreme physical intimacy of this society necessitates emotional reserve. Some people who live close to the old ways are storytellers, especially about hunting escapades and near escapes from death. Most are tolerant. Many laugh readily. Others are silent and brooding. But no matter their personality, almost none speaks of his or her feelings. The distinctive features of Greenlandic depression are not direct results of the temperature and light; they are the consequence of this taboo against talking about yourself.

Poul Bisgaard, a gentle, large man with an air of bemused patience, was the first native Greenlander to become a psychiatrist. 'Of course if someone is depressed within a family, we can see the symptoms,' he said. 'But we do not, traditionally, meddle with them. It would be an affront to someone's pride to say that you thought he looked depressed. The depressed man believes himself to be worthless and thinks that if he is worthless, there is no reason to bother anyone else. Those around him do not presume to interfere.' Kirsten Peilman, a Danish psychologist who has lived in Greenland for more than a decade, said, 'No one tells anyone else to behave. You simply tolerate whatever people present and let them tolerate themselves.'

I went in June, in the season of light. Nothing could have prepared me for the beauty of Greenland in June, when the sun stays high overhead right through the night. We took a fisherman's small motorboat from the five-thousand-person town of Ilulissat, where I had landed in a small plane, southward towards one of the settlements I had selected in consultation with Greenland's minister of public health. Called Ilimanaq, it is a place of hunters and fishermen with a total adult population of about eighty-five. No roads lead to Ilimanaq, and no roads traverse it. In the winter, the villagers travel across the frozen terrain by dogsled; in the summer, access can be gained only by boat. In the spring and autumn, people stay in the settlement. At the time of year when I went, fantastical icebergs, some as large as office buildings, flow down the coast, grouping near the Kangerlussuaq ice fjord. My guide and I crossed the mouth of the fjord in a small motorboat, navigating among the smooth, oblong shapes of older ice that had turned bottom-up, and chunks of broken-off glacier that were corrugated with age and curiously blue – our boat humble in the face of such natural majesty. Some ice refracted the light from the sun, which was permanently perched on the horizon. As we progressed, we gently pushed aside the smaller icebergs, some the size of refrigerators, others like floating dinner plates. They crowded the water so that if you let your sight line follow the remote horizon, you would have thought we were sailing through unbroken sheets of ice. The light was so clear that there seemed to be no depth of field, and I could not tell what was near and what was far away. We stayed near the shore, but I could not distinguish the land from the sea, and most of the time we were canyoned between mountains of ice. The water was so cold that when a piece of ice broke off the lip of an iceberg and fell in, the water dented as though it were custard, reclosing itself into smoothness only a measurable few seconds after it was split. From time to time, we'd see or hear a ringed seal plopping itself into the frigid water. Otherwise, we were alone with the light and the ice.

Ilimanaq, built around a small natural harbour, has about thirty houses, a school, a tiny church and a store, which gets supplied about once a week. Each house has a team of dogs; dogs far outnumber the human residents of the place. The houses are painted in the bright, clear colours that the locals adore – Turkish blue, buttercup yellow, pale pink – but they hardly make an impression on the vast rocks that rise behind them, or on the white sea that stretches in front of them. It is hard to imagine a place more isolated than Ilimanaq. The village does have a phone line, however, and the Danish government will pay for helicopters to airlift local people in a medical crisis if weather permits a landing. No one has running water or water-flow toilets, but there is a generator and so some houses, and the school, have electricity, and several have televisions. Every house has an inconceivably beautiful view. At midnight, when the sun was up and the locals were asleep, I would walk among the silent houses and the sleeping dogs as if I were in a dream.

A notice had been posted outside the store a week before I came, asking for volunteers to discuss their moods with me. My translator – a lively, educated, activist Inuit woman who was trusted in Ilimanaq – had agreed, despite misgivings, to help me persuade the reserved local people to talk. We were accosted, somewhat shyly, the day after we arrived. Yes, they had some stories to tell. Yes, they had decided to tell them to me. Yes, it was easier to talk about these things with a foreigner. Yes, I must talk to the three sage women – the ones who had started this whole business of talking about emotions. Everyone wanted to help, even when that help involved an alien loquaciousness. Because of the recommendations that had been sent ahead for me, and because of the fisherman who brought me in his boat, and because of my translator, they made me part of their intimate community while granting me the courtesies due a guest.

'Ask no open questions' was the advice of the Danish doctor in charge of the district that included Ilimanaq. 'If you ask them how they feel, they won't be able to tell you anything.' Nevertheless, the villagers knew what I wanted to know. They did not usually give answers of more than a few words, and the questions had to be as concrete as possible, but even if the emotions were not available to them linguistically, they were clearly present conceptually. Because trauma is a regular part of the lives of Greenlandic people, anxiety after trauma was not uncommon; neither was a descent into dark feelings and self-doubt. Old fishermen told me stories of their sleds going underwater (a well-trained dog team will pull you out – if the ice doesn't break further, if you don't drown first, if the reins don't sunder), and of going miles in subzero temperatures in wet clothes; they talked about hunting when the ice was moving and the thunder of its sound made it impossible for one man to hear another, and you felt yourself rising up as a chunk of glacier shifted position, not knowing whether it would soon turn over and plunge you into the sea. And they talked about how, after such experiences, it had been difficult to keep going, to wrest the next day's food from the ice and the darkness.

We went to see the three woman elders. Amalia Joelson, the midwife in the village, was the closest approximation of a doctor in town. She had had a stillborn child one year; the next year, she gave birth to a child who died the night after it was born. Her husband, mad with grief, accused her of killing the child. At that time she could hardly bear to know that she would deliver the children of her neighbours, but could have none herself. Karen Johansen, the wife of a fisherman, had left her native town to come to Ilimanaq. Shortly afterward, in rapid sequence, her mother, her grandfather and her older sister died, all of different causes. Then her brother's wife became pregnant with twins. The first twin was stillborn at five months. The second was born healthy but died of sudden infant death syndrome at three months. Her brother had one child left, a six-year-old daughter, and when she drowned, he hanged himself. Amelia Lange was the minister in the church. She had married young, a tall hunter, and she had borne him eight children in rapid succession. Then he had a hunting accident: a bullet ricocheted off a rock and his right arm was split halfway between the elbow and the wrist. The bone never healed, and the break line would bend like an extra joint if you took his hand. He lost the use of his right arm. A few years later, he was just outside the house during a storm and was blown by a strong wind. Without his arm to break his fall, he broke his neck and has since been largely paralysed from the head down. His wife had to care for him and move his wheelchair around the house, to bring up the children and to hunt for food. 'I would do my work outdoors and cry the whole time while I did it,' she recalled. When I asked whether others had not come to her when they saw her weeping at her work, she said, 'They did not interfere so long as I could do the work.' Her husband felt he was such a burden to her that he stopped eating, hoping to starve himself to death, but she saw what he was doing, and seeing it broke down her silence, and she pleaded with him to live.

'Yes, it is true,' Karen Johansen said. 'We are too physically close to be intimate. And we all have so many burdens here, and none of us wants to add our burdens to the burdens of others.' Danish explorers of the early and middle twentieth century found three primary mental illnesses among the Inuit, described by the Inuit themselves. These have now largely died out except in very remote locations. 'Polar hysteria' was described by one man who had suffered it as 'a rising of the sap, of young blood nourished by the blood of walruses, seals and whales – sadness takes hold of you. At first you are agitated. It is to be sick of life.' A modified form of it exists to this day as what we might call activated depression or a mixed state; it is closely related to the Malaysian idea of 'running amok'. 'Mountain wanderer syndrome' affected those who turned their back on the community and left – in earlier times, they were never allowed to return and had to fend for themselves in absolute solitude until they died. 'Kayak anxiety', the belief contra reality that water is filling your boat and that you will sink and drown, was the most common form of paranoia.

Although these terms are now used primarily historically, they still evoke some of the conflicts of Inuit life. In Uummannaq, according to René Birger Christiansen, head of public health for Greenland, a spate of complaints recently came from people who believed they had water under their skin. The French explorer Jean Malaurie wrote in the 1950s, 'There is an often dramatic contradiction between the Eskimo's basically individualistic temperament and his conscious belief that solitude is synonymous with unhappiness. Abandoned by his fellowmen, he is overcome by the depression that always lies in wait for him. Is the communal life too much to bear? A network of obligations link one person to another and make a voluntary prisoner of the Eskimo.'

The women elders of Ilimanaq had each borne her pain in silence for a long time. Johansen said, 'At first, I tried to tell other women how I felt, but they just ignored me. They did not want to talk about bad things. And they did not know how to have such a conversation; they had never heard anyone talk about her problems. Until my brother died, I was proud also not to be a cloud in the sky for other people. But after this shock of his suicide, I had to talk. People did not like it. In our way, it is rude to say to someone, even a friend, "I am sorry for your troubles."' She described her husband as a 'man of silence' with whom she negotiated a way to weep while he listened, without either of them having to use the words that were so alien to him.

These three women were drawn to one another's difficulties, and after many years they spoke to one another about shared feelings of anguish. Joelson had gone to the hospital in Ilulissat for training in midwifery and had learned there about talking therapies. She found comfort in her conversation with these other two women, and she proposed an idea to them. It was a new idea for that society. In church one Sunday, Lange announced that they had formed a group and wanted to invite anyone who wished to talk about problems to come and see them, individually or together. She proposed that they use the consulting room at Joelson's place and promised that such meetings would remain confidential. She said, 'None of us needs to be alone.'

In the following year, all the women of the village, one at a time, each unaware of how many others had taken up the proposition, came to see them. Women who had never told their husbands or their children what was in their hearts wept in the midwife's delivery room. And so this new tradition began, of openness. A few men came, though their ideal of toughness kept many away, at least at the beginning. I spent long hours in the houses of each of these three women. Amelia Lange said it had been a great insight for her to see how people were 'released' after talking to her. Karen Johansen invited me in with her family, gave me a bowl of fresh whale soup, which she had said was often the best answer to one's problems, and told me that for her, the real cure for sadness was to hear of the sadness of others. 'I am not doing this only for the people who speak to me,' she said, 'but also for myself.' In their homes, the people of Ilimanaq do not talk about one another. But they go to their three elders and draw strength from them. 'I know that I have prevented many suicides,' Johansen said.

Confidentiality was of the utmost importance; a small settlement has too many hierarchies that cannot be disrupted without making problems far greater than the problem of silence. 'I see the people outside who have told me their problems, and I never bring up those problems or ask in a different way about someone's health,' Joelson said. 'Only if, when I say politely, "How are you?" they begin to cry, then I will bring them back with me to the house.'

Depression is a disease of loneliness, and anyone who has suffered it acutely knows that it imposes a dread isolation, even for people surrounded by love – in Greenland, to some degree, an isolation imposed by the impossibility of being alone. The three women elders of Ilimanaq had discovered the wonder of unburdening themselves and of helping others to do the same. Different cultures express pain in different ways, and members of different cultures experience different kinds of pain, but the quality of loneliness is infinitely plastic. Those three women elders asked me about my depression, too, and sitting in their houses and eating dried cod wrapped in seal blubber, I felt them reaching from their experience to mine. When we left the town, my translator said this had been the most exhausting experience of her life, but she said it with incandescent pride. 'We are strong people, the Inuit,' she said. 'If we did not solve all our problems, we would die here. So we have found our way to solve this problem, this depression, too.' Sara Lynge, a Greenlandic woman who has set up a suicide hotline in a large town, said, 'First, people must see how easy it is to talk to someone, then how good it is. They don't know that. We who have discovered that must do our best to spread the news.'

Confronted with worlds in which adversity is the norm, one sees shifting boundaries between the accurate reckoning of life's difficulty and depression. The families I visited in Ilimanaq had in general made their way through tribulation by observing a pact of silence. An effective system for its purpose, it saw many people through numerous cold, long winters. Modern Western belief holds that problems are best solved when they are pulled out of darkness, and the story of what has happened in Ilimanaq bears out that theory, but the articulation is limited in scope and location. Let us remember that none of the depressed people in the village talked about their problems with the objects of those problems, and that they did not discuss their difficulties regularly even with the three women elders. It is often said that only a leisured class in a developed society falls prey to depression; in fact, that certain class is distinguished merely in having the luxury of articulating and addressing depression. For the Inuit, depression is so minor in the scale of things and so evident a part of everyone's life that, except in severe cases of vegetative illness, they simply ignore it. Between their silence and our intensely verbalised self-awareness lie a multitude of ways of speaking of psychic pain, of knowing that pain.

The problem of depression in Greenland remains acute; suicide is the leading cause of mortality there, accounting for a full tenth of all deaths. The overall rate has held steady since 1980 despite programmes designed to reduce it; the rate among younger people is escalating, often tied to alcoholism and domestic abuse. The suicide rate for 2014 was 78 per 100,000 inhabitants. In 2015, Astrid Olsen, who works to reduce suicide in Ilulissat, explained that she and her colleagues had ceased to use the word *imminorneq*, which loosely translates to 'taking one's own life', and had started to use *imminut toqunneq*, which means 'to kill oneself'. The new term more vividly evokes the reality of suicide as a form of murder, and evokes the emotional trauma that suicide can inflict upon a community. 'It was as if a huge, heavy blanket lay over the whole town,' she said. 'We had to lift that blanket off.'

In 2009, Greenland voted for and received self-rule. It is no longer a colony of Denmark's as it was when I was there. Huge strides have been made with the establishment of hydroelectric power, which allows more of the population in settlements to live comfortably. Despite this cheering progress, the primary news from Greenland is that it is melting: in 2015, the Jakobshavn Glacier lost a piece of ice the size of Manhattan, an event so dramatic that it could be seen from space. Areas that were solid ice when I was in Greenland are now farms. Comparing photos I took in 1999 to photos sent to me since, my heart breaks. The loss of that landscape of ice is not merely an environmental catastrophe, but also a cultural one.

Naked, Covered in Ram's Blood, Drinking a Coke and Feeling Pretty Good

Esquire, February 2014

I remember thinking even as I was having this experience that I'd tell the story for the rest of my life. A detailed version went into *The Noonday Demon*, but when it came time to recount the experience for the storytelling organisation the Moth, I had to condense it and make it punchier. A transcript of the live version was included in the group's first anthology, *The Moth*, then picked up by *Esquire*. There's more information in the original, but the thrust and context of the experience are here. I've cleaned up some of the phrasing from the oral version. Though *Esquire* ran the piece only in 2014, I've placed it here in the book in keeping with the time I visited Senegal in 2000.

I'm not depressed now – but I was depressed for a long time. I lived with blinding depression and had long stretches when everything seemed hopeless and pointless, when returning calls from friends seemed like more than I could do, when getting up and going out into the world seemed painful, when I was completely crippled by anxiety. When I finally got better and started writing about recovery, I became interested in all the different treatments for depression. Having started as a kind of medical conservative, thinking that only a couple of things worked – medication, electroconvulsive therapy and certain talk therapies – I gradually changed my mind. I realised that if you have brain cancer and you decide that standing on your head and gargling for half an hour every day makes you feel better, it may make you feel better, but the likelihood is that you still have brain cancer, and without other treatment you're still going to die from it. But if you have depression and you say that standing on your head and gargling for half an hour makes you feel better, then you are cured – because depression is an illness of how you feel, and if you feel great, then you're no longer depressed.

So I began to open up to alternative treatments. I researched everything from experimental brain surgeries to hypnotic regimens. People wrote to me constantly because I had been publishing on this subject. One woman wrote that she had tried medication, therapy, electroshock treatments and a variety of other approaches and had finally found what worked for her. She wanted me to tell the world about it. It was 'making little things from yarn', and she sent me numerous examples, as well as a photograph of herself in a room with two thousand identical teddy bears. Not that obsessive-compulsive disorder is the same as depression, but, hey – she'd been miserable before and she was pretty happy now.

As I was doing this work, I also became interested in the idea that depression has pitched up not only in the modern, industrialised West, as people tended to assume, but also across cultures, and across time. So when one of my dearest friends, David Hecht, who was living for a little while in Senegal, asked, 'Do you know about the tribal rituals that are used for the treatment of depression here?' I said, 'No, I don't – but I would like to.' And he said, 'Well, if you come for a visit, we could help you do some research.'

So I set off for Senegal, where I met David's then-girlfriend-now-ex-wife, Hélène. She had a cousin whose mother was a friend of someone who went to school with the daughter of a person who actually practised the *n'deup*, the ritual David had mentioned, so she arranged for me to go and interview this woman. I went off to a small town about two hours outside Dakar and was introduced to an extraordinary, old, large priestess wrapped in miles and miles of African fabric printed with pictures of eyes. She was Madame Diouf. We spoke for about an hour, and she told me all about the *n'deup*. At the end of our interview, feeling rather daring, I said, 'Listen, I don't know whether this is something you would even consider, but would it be possible for me to attend an *n'deup*?'

And she said, 'Well, I've never had a *toubab*' – the local word for 'foreigner' – 'attend one of these before, but you've come through friends. Yes, the next time I perform an *n'deup*, you may be present.'

And I said, 'That's fantastic. When are you next going to be doing an *n'deup*?'

'Oh, it'll be sometime in the next six months.'

'Six months is quite a long time for me to stay here in this town, waiting for you to do one,' I remarked. 'Maybe we could expedite one for somebody, move it forward? I'll pitch in.'

'No, it really doesn't work that way,' she said with a tone of mild apology.

'Well, I guess I won't be able to see an *n'deup*, then, but even so this conversation has been so interesting and so helpful to me. I'm a little sad about leaving here not actually getting to see one, but I thank you.'

'Well, I'm glad that you could come. I'm glad it was helpful . . . but there is one other thing. I hope you don't mind my saying this.'

'No, what? What is it?'

'You don't look that great yourself. Are you suffering from depression?'

I hesitated. 'Well, yes. Depression. Yes, I suffer from depression. It was very acute. It's a little better now, but I still do actually suffer from depression.'

'Well, I've certainly never done this for a *toubab* before, but I could actually do an *n'deup* for you.'

'Oh!' I said. 'What an interesting idea. Well, um, yes, sure. Yeah, absolutely, yes, let's do that. I'll have an *n'deup*.'

'Good. I think it will help you.'

She gave me some fairly basic instructions, and then I left.

My translator, Hélène, the aforementioned then-girlfriend-now-ex-wife of my friend David, turned to me and said, 'Are you completely crazy? Do you have any idea what you're getting yourself into? You're crazy. You're totally crazy. But I'll help you if you want.'

First, I had a shopping list. I had to buy seven yards of African fabric. I had to get a calabash, which was a large bowl fashioned from a gourd. I had to get three kilos of millet. I had to get sugar and kola beans. And then I had to get two live cockerels and a ram. So Hélène and I went to the market with David and we got most of the things, and I said, 'But what about the ram?'

Hélène said, 'We can't buy the ram today. What are we going to do with it overnight?' I saw the sense of that.

The next day, when we got into a taxi for the two-hour drive to the *n'deup*, I said, 'What about the ram?'

Hélène said, 'Oh, we'll see a ram along the way.' So we were going along and going along, and there, indeed, was a Senegalese shepherd by the side of the road with his flock. We stopped the cab, got out, negotiated a bit, and bought a ram for seven dollars. Then we had a little bit of a struggle getting the live ram into the trunk of the taxicab. But the cabdriver seemed not at all worried, even when the ram kept relieving himself in the trunk.

When we got there, I said to Madame Diouf, 'Well, here I am. I'm ready for my *n'deup*.'

Now, the *n'deup* varies enormously depending on a whole truckload of signals and symbols that come from above. So we had to go through this whole shamanistic process to figure out my *n'deup*. I still didn't know much about what was going to happen. First I had to change out of my jeans and my T-shirt and put on a loincloth. Then I sat down, and I had my chest and my arms rubbed with millet. Someone said, 'Oh, we really should have music for this.'

I said, 'Oh, great.' And I thought, yes, drumming, some atmospheric, wonderfully West African sort of thing.

Madame Diouf came out with her prized possession, a battery-operated tape player, for which she had one tape: *Chariots of Fire*. So we listened to *Chariots of Fire*. I was given various shamanistic objects to hold with my hands and drop. I then had to hold them with my feet and drop them. Madame Diouf's five assistants had all gathered around. They would say, 'Oh, this augurs well.' 'This augurs badly.' We spent the morning like this. We'd started at about eight o'clock, and at maybe about eleven, eleven thirty, they said, 'Well, now it's actually time for the central part of the ritual.'

I said, 'Oh, okay,' and drumming began – the drumming I had been hoping for. There was all of this drumming, and it was exciting. We went to the central square of the village, and I had to get into a small, makeshift wedding bed with the ram. I had been told it would be very, very bad luck if the ram escaped, and that I had to hold on to him, and that the reason we were in this wedding bed was that all my depression and all my problems were caused by my spirits. In Senegal you have spirits all over you, the way you have microbes in the developed world. Some are good for you. Some are bad for you. Some are neutral. My bad spirits, I was told, were extremely jealous of my real-life sex partners, and we had to mollify the anger of the spirits. So I had to get into this wedding bed with the ram, and I had to hold the ram tightly. He, of course, immediately relieved himself on my leg.

The entire village had taken the day off from their work in the fields, and they were dancing around the ram and me in concentric circles. As they danced, they threw blankets and sheets of cloth over us, so we were gradually being buried. It was unbelievably hot and completely stifling. Along with the sound of these stamping feet as everyone danced around us, the drums got louder and louder and more and more ecstatic. I thought I was just about to faint or pass out. At that key moment, all of the cloths were suddenly lifted. I was yanked to my feet. The villagers pulled off the loincloth that was all I was wearing. The poor old ram's throat was slit, as were the throats of the two cockerels. Madame Diouf and her assistants plunged their hands into the blood of the freshly slaughtered ram and cockerels and rubbed it over my entire body. It had to cover every inch of me; they rubbed it through my hair and across my face and over my genitals and on the bottoms of my feet. It was warm, and when the semi-coagulated parts were smushed over me, the experience was peculiarly pleasurable.

So there I was, naked, totally covered in blood, and they said, 'Okay, that's the end of this part of it. The next piece comes now.'

And I said, 'Okay,' and we went back over to the area where we had done the morning preparations.

One of them said, 'Look, it's lunchtime. Why don't we just take a break for a minute? Would you like a Coke?' I don't drink Coke that much, but at that moment it seemed like a really, really good idea, and I said yes. So I sat there, naked and completely covered in animal blood, with flies gathering all over me, as they will when you're naked and covered in animal blood. And I drank my Coke.

When I had finished the Coke, they said, 'Okay, now we have the final parts of the ritual. First you have to put your hands by your sides and stand very straight and very erect.' Then they tied me up with the intestines of the ram. Its body was hanging from a nearby tree, where someone was butchering it. They removed some of the organs and reserved the head. Another man had taken a long knife and he slowly dug three perfectly circular holes, each about eighteen inches deep. I stood around trying to keep the flies out of my eyes and ears.

Then I had to kind of shuffle over, all tied up in intestines, which most of you probably haven't done, but it's hard. They had divided the ram's head into three parts, and I had to put one in each of the holes; you can drop things in there even when you're tied up. Then we filled the holes and I had to stamp on each one three times with my right foot, which was a bit trickier. And I had to say something. What I had to say was incredibly, strangely touching in the middle of this weird experience. I had to say, 'Spirits, leave me alone to complete the business of my life and know that I will never forget you.' And I thought, 'What a kind thing to say to the evil spirits you're exorcising: "I'll never forget you."' And I haven't.

Various other little bits and pieces followed. I was given a piece of paper in which all of the millet from the morning had been gathered. I was told that I should sleep with it under my pillow and in the morning get up and give it to a beggar who had good hearing and no deformities, and that when I gave it to him, that would be the end of my troubles. Then the women all filled their mouths with water and began spitting it all over me – a surround-shower effect – rinsing the blood away. It gradually came off, and when I was clean, they gave me back my jeans. Everyone danced, they barbecued the ram, and we had dinner.

I felt so up. I felt so up! It had been quite an astonishing experience. Even though I didn't believe in the animist principles behind it, all of these people had been gathered together, cheering for me, and it was exhilarating.

I had an odd experience five years later, when I was in Rwanda working on my subsequent book. In a conversation with someone there, I described the experience I had had in Senegal, and he said, 'Oh, you know, we have something that's a little like that. That's West Africa. This is East Africa. It's quite different, but there are some similarities to rituals here.' He paused. 'You know, we had a lot of trouble with Western mental health workers who came here immediately after the genocide, and we had to ask some of them to leave.'

'What was the problem?' I asked.

'Their practise did not involve being outside in the sun, like you're describing, which is, after all, where you begin to feel better. There was no music or drumming to get your blood flowing again when you're depressed, and you're low, and you need to have your blood flowing. There was no sense that everyone had taken the day off so that the entire community could come together to try to lift you up and bring you back to joy. There was no acknowledgement that the depression is something invasive and external that can actually be cast out of you again.' He paused meaningfully. 'Instead, they would take people one at a time into these dingy little rooms and have them sit around for an hour or so and talk about bad things that had happened to them.' He shook his head. 'We had to ask them to leave the country.'

———

Senegal has fewer than fifty psychiatrists to serve a population of 14 million, and almost no other doctors who have any training in psychiatry. Western-style mental health services are available only in Dakar, and not in rural areas. Nonetheless, the attitude towards those with mental illnesses is accepting in Senegal, with family members involved in care and with communities helping, for example, to feed people with mental illness who are unable to tend to themselves.

While trained psychiatrists used to separate themselves from traditional healers, the lines are now breaking down, and collaboration has become commonplace. In psychiatric hospitals in Dakar, elements of the *n'deup* are often incorporated into group therapy, held in a traditional group circle. Animist healers are often called in to help with especially difficult cases.

As the number of Senegalese immigrants to the United States increases, there are calls for mental health treatments that are specific to the Senegalese understanding of the spirit world. No resolution of psychiatric illness can occur without deep cultural respect. The blanket assumption that modern medicine is right and that ancient ritual is mere superstition is increasingly understood to be a poor model for mental health treatment. According to William Louis Conwill, who pioneered academic study of the *n'deup*, 'Without openness to Lebou beliefs and culture, it would be easy to dismiss *n'deup* spirit possession as mere suggestibility and the ritual slaying of animals as primitive superstition. *N'deup*'s rituals open the door between the physical world of cause-and-effect that Western health professionals typically promote, and the world of spirits who protect the Lebou from illness and catastrophe. Without acknowledgement of the true believer's world and the power of the *n'deup* priestess, the counsellor working with Senegalese immigrants in the U.S. might view *n'deup* as nothing more than "smoke and mirrors", thereby rendering the counsellor's efforts futile.'

An Awakening after the Taliban

New York Times, 10 March 2002

I was in New York on 11 September 2001. Having often rushed headlong towards danger, I found myself hiding out in my house for a week and then taking the first plane out. I had grown up in New York, and a physical attack on the city wasn't among the fears I nurtured into adulthood. When it happened, I felt like Samson after the haircut. Later, I was ashamed of my paralysed disengagement. It was too late to volunteer in lower Manhattan, but it was not too late to help understand the war in which we'd entangled ourselves.

The most successful piece of modern diplomacy is the Marshall Plan, and I believe that if we had invested the money squandered on a pointless invasion of Iraq on rebuilding Afghanistan, we would now have a secure ally in Central Asia. Remember that 1960s Afghanistan was a centre of liberalism where women wore miniskirts. Of the many brief upsurges of buoyancy on which I have reported, no other has seemed so exalted or has been so swiftly and brutally dashed.

This article, though based on the *Times* story I had been assigned, also includes some details from a story I did for *Food & Wine* about our final dinner.

The reopening of the National Gallery in Kabul in February 2002 took place in the dark. The electricity was out again, a casualty of war, and no one could get the gallery's generator to work. A certain grimness lingered in the air. More striking than much of the art was a special display of the ripped-up drawings and broken frames left by the Taliban, lest anyone forget. Yet the mood was hopeful, victorious, even joyful. Presiding over the ceremony, Hamid Karzai, the leader of Afghanistan's interim government, spoke emotionally of the gallery as the locus of 'great hope and brightness', where Afghan culture could come out of hiding. 'This is more, so much more, than the reopening of a museum,' he declared, toasting the moment with a cup of tea. Then, with great delight, he watched Dr Yousof Asefi perform an act of sweet triumph.

Asefi is an artist who, at great personal risk, had disguised the figures of human beings in eighty oil paintings at the gallery by applying a veneer of watercolour paint over them. He had thus saved the pictures from destruction at the hands of the Taliban, who had forbidden representations of the human form as sacrilege. Now, as an assortment of ministers, journalists, artists and local intellectuals looked on, Asefi, scrubbed up in a starchy new suit, approached a painting, dipped a cloth in water, and began washing the watercolour away, revealing the original figures beneath, still intact. There was applause all around.

I had come to Afghanistan to see what remained of the country's culture after the depredations of the Taliban and the devastation of war. I was astonished to find, amid the bombed-out ruins of Kabul, an artistic community that was not merely optimistic but exuberant. Everyone I talked to had extraordinary stories to tell about the Taliban era, but members of this community had survived that time surprisingly well and were taking up much where they had left off. You would think from the Western news reports that Kabul is populated only by desperate peasants, many of them warlike, and government bureaucrats and soldiers. In fact, Kabul also has a population of cultured, soigné Afghans, some of whom stayed through the Taliban years, some of whom have flooded back into the country from self-imposed exile.

But the beginning of a renaissance is not taking place only among a small elite. The Union of Artists, closed by the Taliban, quietly reopened three months ago and has already attracted more than three thousand members countrywide, including two hundred women. 'Our future depends on these people,' Karzai told me. 'We need to save our culture and bring it forward, make a new culture of Afghanistan. This is at the top of our agenda.'

Afghan women have been slow to give up the enshrouding burka, to Westerners the most potent symbol of the Taliban's oppression. During a two-week visit to Kabul in mid-February, I spotted no more than a dozen women showing their faces on the streets, and none showing their hair, despite the lifting of the ban. Their clinging to the garment points to a deep cultural basis for this concealment. But while the emergence of women has been slow and ambivalent, the recent proliferation of art – high, low, traditional, new, Western, Eastern – shows how suddenly free urban Afghans now are.

Contrary to the Taliban's propaganda, the prohibitions against art were never based in Islam. 'The very idea is ridiculous,' said the minister of information and culture, Said Makhtoum Rahim. 'There is no religious justification for such laws.' Nancy Hatch Dupree, a leading Western expert on Afghan culture, calls the restrictions 'total claptrap, entirely political'. Abdul Mansour, director of Afghanistan television and former president of the cultural ministry, said, 'They said it was religion, but it was just a combination of thuggery, profiteering and fulfilling the agenda of the ISI.' He was referring to Pakistan's intelligence service, then underwriting the Taliban. The ISI, he said, 'wanted to see the weakest possible Afghanistan'. He continued, 'And Pakistan is jealous. Pakistan is a new country, a fake country, with no history. While we – we have a splendid history.'

Rahim said, 'Afghan culture has been destroyed many times. By Alexander the Great. By the British army. In the thirteenth century,

Genghis Khan attacked Herat and killed everyone. Sixteen people were out of town for various reasons, and they returned to find that their city no longer existed. First, they wept. But then they decided to rebuild, and though they were just sixteen, Herat rose from the ashes. We will do it again. We want to export a message of love and cooperation for all the world, and to show our great art, so that people understand this is not just a country of warlords and battle.'

Strikingly, in its early days the Taliban supported art and was involved in programmes of cultural preservation. Only later in the regime, when the terrorist group al-Qaeda and foreign agents had begun to wield most of the power, were the anti-art policies established and many of the most beautiful objects in the country, some two thousand national treasures, wantonly destroyed. The Taliban's purpose was to wipe out Afghan identity so that nationalist resistance to the new regime would be weak. Unlike Soviets or Maoist Chinese, who interfered with the arts in an effort to eliminate whatever history could not be used to construct patriotic propaganda, the Taliban worked towards annihilation. The whole idea of being an Afghan was to be eradicated. This programme required interference not only with intellectuals and artists but also with ordinary people and their ordinary pleasures. 'They succeeded in destroying about eighty per cent of our cultural identity,' Rahim says. 'The Soviets had already done their damage; they wanted to turn a thousand years of history into nineteenth-century Marxism. But the Taliban wanted to destroy everything.'

Gathering Around TVs

Television, illegal under the Taliban but reborn in early 2002, is the most popular means of disseminating new ideas and values, though the country's only station's equipment is dilapidated and many shows have to be shot several times because of poor-quality video and cameras that fail. Mansour has brought in professors for programmes about the history of Afghanistan stretching back to 1000 BC. There are also music and art programmes, showings of old Afghan films and recitations of new Afghan poetry. Afghans are hungry for this material;

after five years without television, large groups of viewers in Kabul gather around sets that are often hooked up to car batteries when power fails, as it does most nights.

Guardians of Art

Many of Afghanistan's best artists use traditional media, such as painted miniatures, which originated in Afghanistan and are central in the country's artistic history. The leading miniaturist, Hafiz Meherzad, encloses figurative scenes within exquisite borders of gold leaf and ground-rock pigments. Meherzad said he had been 'too tired to emigrate' after the mujahideen took over in the post-Soviet power vacuum and thought that he could continue his work quietly during the Taliban's reign so long as he didn't show it publicly. But when his neighbours cried out that the Taliban were searching everyone's house, he panicked and buried all his work. It was largely destroyed by the earth's moisture. His sense of cultural responsibility is acute. 'I do not believe in innovation in this field,' Meherzad said. 'If you make changes in this work, you will destroy even the past. You in America can innovate because your past is safe. Here in Afghanistan, we need to secure our past before we begin to create a future.'

The Taliban found it hard to attack calligraphers, whose work was holy; but it held them in considerable suspicion, and men such as Ismail Sediqi kept a low profile. He stopped making beautiful images of his own poems, with lines such as 'I am a treasure within a ruin.' Instead, he became 'a simple scribe' who wrote verses from the Quran. Even here, however, he found room for sedition: he often copied out the opening verse of the holy book, which announces – contrary to the restrictive practises of the Taliban – that God is the God of all men. 'Innovation?' he said. 'Well, I sometimes put modern make-up on the beautiful face of the classic forms.'

Asefi, who has become a potent symbol of cultural rebirth in Kabul, was unable to leave Afghanistan during the Taliban period, which started in 1996, because of family obligations, and he made only landscapes, bare of human or animal figures, and 'unrepresentative in any way of life in Afghanistan'. The pressure and the fear gave him psychiatric problems that continue to haunt him. Now he is returning to those works and adding the figures he always envisioned. 'If the Taliban had lasted five more years, they might have destroyed our culture,' he said. He is grateful for the American military intervention: 'By liberating us, you saved our history as well as our present lives.'

Underground Poets

Afghanistan is a country of poets. Shir Mohammed Khara ran an underground poetry movement under the Taliban. He met with other poets who had memorised their poems so that they could discuss them without running the risk of being found carrying them. Whenever they gathered, they carried copies of the Quran so they could tell Taliban agents that they were having a prayer meeting. A number of poets have allied themselves with the newspaper *Arman* (*Hope*).

'We could not mirror our Taliban-era society,' the poet Mohammed Yasin Niazi said. His colleague Abdul Raqib Jahid added, 'Under the Taliban, I tried simply to write poems that would relieve people of their tension.' Their new poetry is enthusiastically nationalist.

Niazi wrote:

> We saw the results of the work of the ignorant.
> Now we should be rational.
> It is time for open windows
> Through which the sun shines.

Jahid wrote:

> Communism and terrorism wanted to swallow Afghanistan
> But the knife of liberty cut their throat . . .
> I just want to tell you the story of liberty
> As politely as possible.

Other poets, however, express deep bitterness. Achmed Shekib Santyar wrote:

Epitaph

On the biggest escarpment,
On the sharpest peak,
With bold letters,
Etch this,
The message of a futureless generation:
That in childhood, instead of mothers' mercy, we
received the rough talk of soldiers;
And in youth, instead of pens, we got guns in our hands;
And in age, instead of rest, we went out begging.
Don't blame us.
We could do nothing for you.

Close Call for Filmmakers

In 1968, with support from Hollywood, Afghan Films was established. It made a dozen or so films a year – documentaries and features – until the Soviet invasion and the mujahideen, when things slowed down. Under the Taliban, they stopped entirely. The Taliban burned more than a thousand reels when they took Kabul. 'They started doing it here in the office,' said Timur Hakimian, head of the company, waving a hand in front of his face. 'You can't imagine the smell. Since it was asphyxiating them as well as the rest of us, they went to the stadium and made a public spectacle of their bonfire.' Fortunately, Taliban censors didn't know the difference between prints and negatives; what they burned was mostly replaceable, and the negatives, hidden elsewhere, survived. 'Unfortunately, we were unable not only to use our equipment during these years, but also to clean or maintain it,' Hakimian said. 'Much has been destroyed not by abuse, but by neglect. If we could get the equipment, we're ready to roll again.'

Hakimian is a drily humourous and sophisticated man who has

travelled to film festivals around the world. He served for many years as president of the Union of Artists, a position he has now reclaimed. Because he had made a film whose narrator accuses the Taliban of being against culture and Islam, he went into hiding during their ascendancy. 'There was good reason to be afraid!' he told me. 'If these people could blow up your World Trade Center, they could blow up little me! I feel lucky to be alive at all.' He got a friend who worked as a cleaner in the security department of the Taliban to remove and burn his file, and he attributes his survival to this act.

Dozens of men and three women have approached Hakimian about playing in films again. The great actress of pre-Taliban films was Zamzama Shakila, usually just called Zamzama, a gorgeous woman whose physical presence was particularly alarming to the Taliban. She wanted to stay in Afghanistan despite the Taliban; she gave up acting, and her husband (also an actor) sold clothes in the street. But Taliban agents hunted them down, and in one attack by fundamentalists she took five bullets and he took seven, one of which is still embedded in his skull. They survived and fled to Pakistan. For years she managed by singing for weddings in Peshawar. The day Kabul was taken, they came back. 'I was so thirsty for my country,' she said.

She wore the burka for her trip back into Afghanistan; when she arrived in Kabul, she took it off and burned it in the street. She is one of the few women to go without cover today. 'I hear women talking as they pass me, saying they admire my shedding my burka,' she said. 'I confront them and say, "Take yours off. Nothing terrible will happen." Sometimes they throw off their burkas there, and we walk in the street together. Someone has to start this tendency.' Zamzama complains that while Afghan men stare, American soldiers in the Special Forces units are the ones who are obnoxiously aggressive. 'I say to them, "You are worse than the terrorists. You are making life impossible for Afghan women. Cut it out."'

In the dilapidated offices of Afghan Films, Zamzama explained, 'The old crowd is coming together. Of course, actors are more liberal than others, and in these offices we meet each other and shake hands.' She became emotional, held my arm. 'In our happiest dreams we didn't see this.' Since Afghan Films has no equipment, Zamzama keeps her family going by acting in two weekly television programmes. 'I'm ready to do comedy now,' she said. 'Romantic comedy.'

Hakimian is sceptical: 'The women newscasters on TV still wear head scarves; the country barely accepts that they show their faces. If you can't show a woman's hair, how can you show her in a boy's arms?' But Zamzama countered, 'No fighting films. We've seen enough guns in our real lives. People should enjoy the new Afghan films.' She gestured extravagantly. 'It's time for fun, fun, fun.'

Music Breaks a Silence

While cultural resurgence in all the arts is strong, it is most striking in music. A long-silenced country, where women could be arrested for humming to their babies, where it was illegal even to clap your hands, is suddenly full of every kind of music in every place.

I went to a wedding where the band was playing in a very un-Western 'Western style' – what for Afghanistan would have been Top 40 if anyone had been counting. A member of the groom's family had died a short time earlier, and there is supposed to be no music after such a death; but the bride protested that there had been enough years of silence to cover a thousand family deaths. The band included an electric guitar, a drum machine and a Soviet-era synthesiser; the irregular electricity meant that all the instruments kept going on and off, and the performance was undistinguished, but people were overjoyed by the music. They spoke of little else. My favourite song had these lyrics:

> Sweetheart, put on your make-up and perfume.
> Be beautiful.
> Your eyes are like a deer
> Your lips, like a pomegranate flower,
> And your height, like a tree.
> Oh, I am going to my sweetheart
> And I don't know whether to go
> In a Datsun, a minivan, or a Land Rover.

The progenitors of up-to-the-minute Afghan pop are somewhat more urbane. Baktash Kamran is as close to a pop star as you'll find in Afghanistan – good-looking, twenty-three years old, a bodybuilder, a reinterpreter of music from the seventies and creator of new material. On the several occasions when I met him, he wore a leather jacket with an American flag on the back. During the time of the Taliban, he dug out a secret underground basement room, where he practised music, far enough down so that they couldn't hear him. He was an adolescent and a provocateur who was jailed four times: for keeping his beard too well trimmed on one occasion and for having an electric piano on another. He claims he was singing as he escaped.

The first singer to have his own concert on Afghan television after it was reestablished, Kamran showed me the object that he calls his pride and joy: a high-tech Yamaha synthesiser that he brought into the country from Pakistan when the Taliban still controlled the south. 'I couldn't bring it across the legal checkpoints,' he explained, 'so I tied it to a donkey and he and I climbed the mountains between Afghanistan and Pakistan together. Then I wrapped it in a shawl and carried it to Kabul in a taxi.'

Asked about relations between the sexes, the subject of his songs, he said they were getting closer, but added that he had never felt excluded by the burka. 'It's easy to fall in love with a pair of shoes,' he told me. 'Or the way someone's fabric moves.' He has written songs about that.

While this scene is brewing, music is also reentering the lives of people for whom it is a more profound enterprise. On Thursdays, the eve of the Sabbath, the Chishti Sufi people of Afghanistan, Muslim mystics, are gathering once again for the ritual that the Taliban so long denied them. I went to a recently reestablished *khanqah*, a Sufi holy building, in Kabul. The ceremony took place in the poorest part of the city, down a long alley of bombed-out buildings. I climbed a small staircase of mud bricks into a hidden upper storey where about eighty men were seated on old carpets strewn across the floor. The walls were graffitied with phrases from the Quran, and the light came from candles and one electric light, which went on and off according to its whim.

The men had faces from outside of time: craggy and bearded,

though some were quite young, and aflame with the ceremony. They wore traditional Afghan dress, heavy woollen shawls wrapped completely around them. On a raised platform, about a half-dozen instrumentalists were playing strange lyrical music and incanting verses, repetitive and mesmeric. Periodically one would stop, and someone else would take his place. The crowd swayed and shifted to the music, and some intoned nasally with the singers. A young man with a battered teapot crawled around serving everyone tea from the same eight cups. The ceremony went on all night. It was dizzying; time lost its meaning. Sometimes someone would get up and dance or sway ecstatically. The voices would rise and grow thick in the air. Then the tune would become increasingly rapid, the rhythms more urgent, until it broke, and a new tune would make its slow way forward. It felt sacred and as ancient as the seven hundred years that it has been practised by Sufis in Afghanistan.

I had the fortune to meet Afghanistan's most distinguished classical musicians, who have been brought together by the enterprising director of music for Afghan television, Aziz Ghaznavi, himself a popular singer of the pre-mujahideen period who has toured in the United States. 'Of course, practise makes perfect,' Ghaznavi said, 'and during the Taliban period none of us could practise. We lost so much. After five years of not singing at all, I was afraid to hear my own voice, and it was a very scary moment, to sing again for the first time.'

To an untrained ear, classical Afghan music sounds somewhat like Indian classical music, but it uses instruments that are indigenous to Afghanistan – the sarinda, the *rabab* and the *richak* – as well as the tabla and sitar and harmonium. The Taliban insisted that musical instruments be destroyed, so only those that people managed to hide have survived. One man I met had kept his sarinda in the middle of his woodpile, where it passed for fuel, throughout the Taliban period, knowing that any neighbour who spotted it could betray him, should he so wish. 'In recent months, we have been starting over with these warped, broken instruments,' Ghaznavi explained. 'There is only one instrument maker in Afghanistan, and he is now fixing all the broken instruments; he has no time yet for new ones.'

For family reasons, Ghaznavi could not flee Afghanistan during the Taliban rule. Life was incredibly difficult for anyone whose whole life was music, and he became depressed because of unsatisfied yearnings. He went to a doctor and said he would go crazy without music in his life. The doctor suggested that he listen to the one kind of song that even the Taliban couldn't make illegal. So he bought his first birds and fell in love with them. He now has more than fifty pigeons in a coop behind his house. When I called on him one afternoon, I was ushered into his light-purple living room to sit cross-legged on the floor and eat candy while Ghaznavi and a friend tried out some new harmoniums they had just acquired. The sound of the multiple harmoniums playing in this lavender room in which many pigeons were flying around was surreal, and the weirdness was not mitigated by the presence of Ghaznavi's son, the all-Afghanistan weight-lifting champion, who sat in his *shalwar kameez*, traditional tunic and trousers, flexing his stupefying biceps when he was not refilling our teacups.

The practise rooms at the television station are always full, despite being unheated and without amenities. When I went there the first time, Ghaznavi directed me to some particularly talented musicians. A few had recently returned from Pakistan and Iran, but others had spent the Taliban years in Kabul. One, Abdul Rashin Mashinee, caught by the Taliban playing a sarinda, was told that they would cut off his hands if they ever found him playing again. He spent the dark years working as a butcher, but, he says, 'I practised my instrument diligently, every night in my dreams.'

The group kept breaking off to apologise to me for the cold and for not having their full ensemble present. 'There should be eleven of us, not six,' they said. They said that I seemed to appreciate music, and wondered if they could find their friends and get together so I could hear them all. I said I'd be delighted and invited them to my place for the next afternoon at five.

My Dinner in Kabul

I was living for the time being in an old al-Qaeda house that some friends had rented in the fashionable Wazir Akbar Khan area, where we had full-time translators and drivers. I had heard that we would have a cook, but dinner my first night in Kabul was a lovely surprise. We had spicy little meatballs in rich sauce, a wonderful rice dish, crisp fried potato cakes, and fresh Afghan bread. When I expressed astonishment, a friend explained that we had nabbed the best chef in Kabul, and that everyone who came to dinner at our house tried to poach him away. Qudratullah arrived every day at 7:00 a.m. to make us breakfast, produced a hot lunch for us at midday and prepared dinner for us every night.

One wonder of wintertime Kabul was the markets. In this ruined city, the stalls, surrounded by Taliban-era graffiti on bullet-pocked walls, held a profusion of local foodstuffs: pomegranates and oranges, all sorts of nuts and dried fruits, fresh meat (sometimes disorientingly fresh), spices and grains in sacks, a lot of cauliflower, the largest and most vividly coloured carrots I've ever seen (some nearly purple), aubergines, onions, potatoes and different kinds of sweets. While the greatest assortment could be found in the food bazaar near the river, I saw rich displays even in the poorest neighbourhoods. People had no electricity, no plumbing, no heating, sometimes no roof, but they had food. Qudratullah was able to get the best ingredients, and when friends would stop by, there was always enough to eat; he had an Afghan capacity to expand meals to accommodate whoever came. So it seemed natural when I'd invited the musicians over to offer them dinner at our house, where we had not only excellent food, but also that rarer Kabul commodity, heat – in this case, from a woodstove.

I had stopped by UNESCO that day and met with its living-culture expert, who was planning a music festival but had yet to meet any musicians, so I invited him to our concert. I checked in with Marla Ruzicka, the blonde liberal who was staying at the Agence France-Presse house, and I invited her and her translator, who had done a favour for me the day before. I invited all the people who worked at our house – translators, guards, and so on. Scott John-son of *Newsweek* said he thought Antonia Rados from German TV might like to come, and I was pleased. When some people from the *Washington Post* stopped by, we thought it would be a mistake not to include them. I invited a filmmaker I'd interviewed the day before. And so the numbers began to creep up.

When I told Qudratullah we had company coming, he said he'd need some extra money to buy food and some more extra money to buy plates and a bit of further extra money to get someone in to help in the kitchen. I said I thought there would be about thirty of us, and he asked for $200.

My estimate, it turned out, was wildly off. Between the musicians and the house staff and some other people we'd met, we had a good twenty or so Afghans, and the foreigners had all brought friends. By the time we had dinner at about seven thirty, there were between fifty and sixty people. Qudratullah, praise be upon him, produced enough food so that all were fed. We had *qabili pilau*, Afghanistan's national dish, a sweet rice pilaf; roast leg of mutton, cooked until it was falling off the bone; roast chicken; *borani*, a flavourful aubergine dish made with yogurt and garlic; *sabzi qorma*, an Iranian dish of meat stewed with spinach; salad; and *firni*, an Afghan pudding made with cornflour. Of course we had flat Afghan bread.

My plan had been to hear the musicians for an hour or so, but they were so happy to have an occasion and an audience that they played on and on and on. We all danced to this exotic music and ate and danced and ate. Ghaznavi sang for us. In Afghanistan, women and men don't socialise together; even at a wedding, women and men celebrate in separate halls. Our Afghan guests, all men, showed us how they dance in a circle. The Westerners joined in, and showed the Afghans how Western men and women dance together. The music got more and more exuberant.

'My goodness,' said the UNESCO operative. 'There *is* music in Afghanistan after all. I will have a festival, I will!'

'Why not eat more? There is more!' said my translator, Farouq Samim. 'Let's eat until every plate is clean!'

'Do you think this is getting out of control?' asked Scott Johnson, who had official responsibility for the house. I had to admit it was.

At nine o'clock, someone showed up with a bottle of whiskey, which in a Muslim country, where the law forbids alcohol, was the equivalent of showing up with pot at an American party. There was a lot of giggling, and a few of the Afghans made rapid progress towards inebriation. The next morning, I was to teach Farouq the word *hangover*.

Kabul has a 10:00 p.m. curfew, so the party guests began filing out at nine thirty, but the musicians lived too far away to make the curfew and so stayed over. They played and played, and at 2:00 a.m. we were all still sitting together, and the sitar and the tabla were diverting us with gentle, lyrical late-night music. The brief performance we'd planned went on for more than ten hours.

Under the Taliban or during the first phase of the American-led invasion, it would have been unthinkable to throw a party in Kabul. The situation was sober and sad. But though the city bears the terrible scars of its recent history, it is full of people longing, at last, for a little bit of pleasure. Afghan hospitality is legendary, and one thing that was painful to many Afghans about their country at war was that they had no opportunity to extend their hospitality to foreigners. I went to Afghanistan ready for hardship, and I did see horrible things. But I also felt a warmth and a sense of pride that lay not only in the reform of government but also in the return to small satisfactions, so long denied, now so easily and openly and generously shared. There is a kind of joy that can be known only by people who have grieved deeply; happiness is not only a quality of its own but also an effect of contrast. The Afghans were so pleased that we liked their food and music; it seemed that we were accomplishing a diplomatic purpose simply by sharing *pilau* and *borani*, by dancing together to the sarinda and the *rabab* and the *richak*. Our evening was in its own way as ecstatic as the Sufi ceremony. Every note was swollen with fulfilled longing. I have never heard anything else like it.

———

Innumerable Afghan and some two thousand five hundred American lives have been lost and hundreds of billions of dollars have been spent in the Afghan War. At this writing, nearly ten thousand American troops remain on Afghan soil. Dominic Tierney wrote in the *Atlantic* in 2015, 'The popular narrative was once about saving Afghans. Now the focus is on getting American soldiers home, and Afghans have disappeared from the story.' That abandonment is cruelly felt in Kabul. When I recently saw Farouq, we talked about our experiences in 2002, and he said, 'Yes, you were there in those beautiful days – in the time of hope. All of that is gone now.'

Zakia Zaki and Sanga Amach, television journalists, and Shaima Rezayee, a music video show host, are among the female artists murdered because they appeared on television, hoping to liberalise attitudes towards women. When the performance artist Kubra Khademi strolled through Kabul in a suit of armour with exaggerated breasts and buttocks, she received death threats and had to go into hiding. Some women artists have fled the country. But many others have been emboldened. In 2006, several women artists founded the Centre for Contemporary Art Afghanistan. Munera Yousefzada, who founded Shamama Contemporary Arts Gallery in Kabul, said, 'Before I opened the gallery, I felt like I was trapped at the bottom of a well and nobody could hear my screams. Now they can hear me, and they can hear the other women whose paintings hang on the walls.'

In parallel, Turquoise Mountain was established to revive traditional crafts such as woodworking, calligraphy, miniature painting, ceramics, jewellery and gem-cutting. Berang Arts was founded in 2009 by participants in the first Afghan Contemporary Art Prize competition to support contemporary artists in Kabul; they transformed a Kabul apartment into a contemporary arts centre. Professor Alam Farhad, director of fine arts at Kabul University, said that in 2001 his department had eight students; it now has over seven hundred and has to turn away applicants. The artists grapple with complex questions of identity. One, Ali Akhlaqi, said, 'In my opinion, Kabul is a cursed city of night, which has no comfort, and its day enjoys no light. There is nothing real here.' But Shamsia Hassani, a graffiti artist who often paints on semi-destroyed buildings in land mine–infested neighbourhoods, described Afghanistan as a 'newborn baby' and said, 'I want to colour over the bad memories of war on the walls and erase war from people's minds.' Azim Fakhri said simply, 'My feeling is accept what you can't change, but change what you can't accept.' Kabir Mokamel has made an 'artlords' project (the name is a play on 'warlords') and paints on the barricades outside government buildings in Kabul. In 2015, he put a gigantic pair of eyes on the walls that surround the National Directorate of Security, to remind government agents that they, too, were being watched.

Marla Ruzicka, who did such brave work for disenfranchised people and who was my friend, founded the Campaign for Innocent Victims in Conflict (CIVIC), then died in a suicide car bombing on the Baghdad Airport Road in 2005.

Museum without Walls

Travel + Leisure, June 2002

By the time I travelled to Benesse Island, I had chronicled the infiltration of Asian art into Western consciousness. If Americans and Europeans had begun to appreciate contemporary Chinese art, how would people in the Far East make sense of the art being produced in the West? They had acknowledged our influence sooner than we'd acknowledged theirs, but there were sure to be issues of translation in either context.

Modern art has its pilgrims. As soon as I could, I went to Bilbao to see Frank Gehry's Guggenheim. I have driven across the desert to visit the Chinati Foundation, set up by Donald Judd in Marfa, Texas, and I have even dragged myself to Târgu Jiu in southern Romania to see Brâncuşi's *Endless Column*. I hope to visit Roden Crater in Arizona, where the light and space artist James Turrell has spent more than twenty years transforming a natural volcano. My most recent such voyage was to Benesse House on Naoshima Island, a spectacular art complex in southern Japan that seems to invite intellectuals on honeymoon, Zen souls seeking tranquil inspiration and passionate idealists ready for a moment's quiescence.

To get there, you take a train from any southern Japanese city to the Inland Sea and then board the ferry that plies an archipelago known as the 'thousand islands'. This is some of the least developed land in Japan; fishermen live the same way they have lived for hundreds of years – rowing out each morning to try their luck, worshipping at unremarkable yet lovely shrines (which I could see from the ferry's deck), hanging out their nets to dry overnight.

After about an hour, we reached the island of Naoshima and the simple village of Honmura, where we were met by a driver from Benesse House. As we traversed the island's scrubby landscape, it was hard not to notice here and there some strangely anomalous things: a gigantic fibreglass pumpkin at the end of a dock, or a forest of carved rocks surrounding a hot tub, or a sort of enormous salad bowl on a brick plinth down by the sea. We ascended a steep incline to find a building so cleverly integrated into the landscape that one could drive by without seeing it. This is Benesse House, the centre of the Benesse Island complex, and home to one of the world's great private art collections.

Tetsuhiko Fukutake, head of Benesse Corporation, a large textbook-publishing company, fantasised about building a museum where he could share his collection with people who genuinely wanted to experience it – but he did not like crowds or ostentation. So he came up with the implausible idea of building his museum on an island in the Inland Sea. After his death in 1986, his son set up a campsite furnished with yurts, which is still in use, and recruited one of Japan's leading architects, Tadao Ando, to design a museum that would incorporate ten guest rooms. Ando visited in the rain, fell in love with the site, and set to work, half carving and half constructing the building into the face of the island. In 1992, the doors of Benesse House opened, and in 1995, the Annex, with an additional six rooms, was completed.

Benesse Island is not just a museum. It is certainly not just a hotel. It is a synthesis of the two. It reminds me of the Buddhist monasteries where, for a small fee, you can stay with the monks to contemplate the world as they do, eating their food and living in graceful seclusion, neither monk nor tourist. The rooms at Benesse Island are not fancy, but they are comfortable and elegant and have good art; mine featured signed Keith Haring works on paper. Each room has a wall of glass, so that nothing seems to lie between you and the sea. Meals are served in a dining room that is part of the museum, and there, too, you are surrounded by art, with a few striking arrangements of flowers always, and more of that amasing view. The food is excellent and complex: meals of many labouriously crafted components, delicate and flavourful, all served in equally well-crafted ceramic dishes.

Tadao Ando's museum building is a study in simple geometries weighted against one another. The basic structure is a spiral in poured concrete (which seems to be a muted homage to the Russian Constructivist Vladimir Tatlin), with a rectilinear wing in rough stone that houses the guest rooms. The whole thing is built into the hillside. To reach the Annex, at the top of the hill, you get into a cable car and are carried on an angle up to a wonder of fountains, a great central pool and a radial arrangement of rooms. The style is powerful but not grand. Below the museum proper are exhibition spaces for large works of art. Part of the place's charm is that it's hard to tell where the museum ends and the natural landscape begins. Wild grasses grow uninterrupted over the roof of the building, and art is displayed partly in the museum, partly in semi-museum-spaces, and partly on the open seashore. Benesse is not a place for boundaries.

The museum has works by about two dozen artists, including Jasper Johns (his 1968 *White Alphabets*), Bruce Nauman (the giant neon *100 Live and Die*) and Cy Twombly (a gorgeous chalklike scribble). There are also commissioned pieces by another dozen or so, including Kan Yasuda (meditative giant disks called *Secret of the Sky*), Jannis Kounellis (a work of rolled lead and driftwood and ceramics, positioned against a window like some industrial obstruction to the view), David Tremlett (wall paintings) and Richard Long (a stone circle on the floor mirroring a painted circle on the wall). There is in general one work by each artist; taken together, they form a miniature survey of late-twentieth-century art. My particular favourite is a series of photos by Hiroshi Sugimoto that look at first glance like multiple prints of a single ocean view, but are in fact of different oceans. They are hung on the museum's terrace so that if you sit in one of the chairs provided, the horizons of the photos line up with the actual horizon, and the sea you are gasing at lines up with the seas of the photos. The effect is ineffably magical.

Around the museum, scattered in various outdoor spots, are works and installations by Yayoi Kusama (the giant pumpkin), Alexander Calder (a standing fulcrum mobile that shifts with the wind), Dan Graham (*Cylinder Bisected by Plane*) and others. You can peruse the catalogue and go on a treasure hunt, but it's nicer just to walk around, trying to guess who made the various pieces and what they mean, then checking the catalogue to see if you were right and what you missed. I loved Walter De Maria's giant reflective globes, in which you can see yourself and the whole of this landscape. And there's Cai Guo-Qiang's *Cultural Melting Bath*: in the early evening, you can lie in a Western-style hot tub filled with medicinal herbs and experience cosmic harmony while you watch the sunset through the filigree shapes of giant scholar's rocks (the craggy stones that Chinese literati once used to remind themselves of the landscape's rough splendour).

While you have to find the outdoor installations yourself, you are given a guide to the ones in the town of Honmura. A few old houses there, externally much like all the others, have been restored with special care. Inside you'll find neither cooking pots nor futons rolled back for the day but, rather, room-size installations known as the Art House Projects. The James Turrell house, restored in collaboration with Ando, mixes traditional, Zen and modernist elements. You walk into darkness, feel your way to a bench, and sit for at least ten minutes before your eyes are able to discern, glowing out of the void, five rectangles of blue light, a cobalt intensity breaking the blackness and throbbing away from and then closer to you. It's pure meditation. The Tatsuo Miyajima house is flooded with water, and under the water, numbers in red and green on a series of LEDs change constantly, creating an effect that is eerie and haunting and unbelievably beautiful – at once primitive and futuristic. Visitors tread on a thin walkway around the edge. Several other Art House Projects are under construction.

As you wander through the village to see these installations, stopping also, perhaps, at the town's two shrines, the locals nod and smile. They like the art in their town; moreover, they seem to like the smartly dressed visitors from Tokyo and New York who have become familiar to them. Unlike many experiences of contemporary art, this one is warm. Here, the intellect, the senses, and the heart all find their satisfactions.

Since my visit, the Benesse Art Site has expanded considerably. The museum complex now encompasses nearby Teshima and Inujima Islands and includes three new museums on Naoshima, all designed by Tadao Ando. The Chichu Museum houses five paintings in Monet's *Water Lilies* series, as well as work by James Turrell and Walter De Maria; the Lee Ufan Museum is dedicated to the work of the Korean minimalist; and the Ando Museum celebrates the architect. Benesse Art Site continues to commission artists to design its guest rooms. Janet Cardiff and George Bures Miller are currently at work on a double suite. The Teshima Art Museum, an artistic collaboration between artist Rei Naito and architect Ryue Nishizawa, opened in 2010 as part of the Benesse expansion. Teshima Island also hosts Christian Boltanski's project *Les Archives du Coeur*, and the Teshima Yokoo House, a residence transformed into gallery and exhibition space. Inujima Island, third in the developing archipelago, now has its own museum, located in the remains of a copper refinery; the Seaside Inujima Gallery, featuring the work of Fiona Tan; and the Inujima Art House Project, five gallery spaces created largely of recycled materials. Interviewed by Lee Yulin about the larger Benesse project, its founder said that he had sought to create 'an island of dreams for children'.

Song of Solomons

Travel + Leisure, August 2003

I will admit that part of the lure of the Solomon Islands was the name. When I made the reservations to go, I joked that I was leading a trend in eponymous travel. But I was tempted also by the sense that in its obscurity the destination preserved some kind of authenticity, whatever authenticity is. My second day there, I went to board a local flight and found that it had been cancelled and that I'd have to go a day later. When I asked what the problem was, the desk clerk explained that the pilot had converted that morning to Seventh-day Adventism and could no longer fly on the Sabbath.

Among the fantasies I have always harboured is one of the South Seas. While some people who dream of this corner of the world want lavish Tahitian resorts, I wanted desert islands untouched by the ravages of modernity and sky-blue seas with only an occasional canoe or school of dolphins to break the surface. I wanted to meet men and women who would be hungry for my news and generous with theirs. I wanted to be something between Captain Cook and Robinson Crusoe. I was very young when I first heard of the islands out there that had my name, and I was thrilled to discover that the Solomons were about as remote as anywhere else on earth. I wanted to go; I can't remember not wanting to. In *Moby-Dick*, Herman Melville wrote that these islands, though charted and explored and visited, remained terra incognita.

The Solomons, just east of Papua New Guinea, are a chain of almost a thousand islands, many tiny, a few quite large, about a third populated. The country covers more than 520,000 square miles of sea and receives about four thousand tourists a year. There are at least a hundred local languages and dialects; the lingua franca is pidgin, though many people speak English because the islands used to be a British protectorate. Traditional life and ceremonies are called *custom*: custom dances, custom bride prices, custom skull caves, and so on. Missionaries Christianised the islands at the turn of the nineteenth century, and almost everyone attends church services, but Christianity has not supplanted local beliefs and rituals. The Solomon Islands were long notorious for head-hunting and cannibalism, and on my first day in the capital city, Honiara, I stopped in a shop to ask about some pointy objects and found out that they were nose bones – to be worn through a pierced septum.

The islands are perhaps best known in the West as the site of the major Second World War Battle of Guadalcanal, in which the native population helped Americans defeat the Japanese who were trying to build an air base there. The country, one of the world's poorest, has no overclass; subsistence affluence is the rule. Economic and power structures in the Solomons are dominated by the Malaita people, and strife between them and other populations is ongoing, but such violence has on no occasion affected visitors.

The four of us – a friend from high school, Jessica; her husband, Chuck; my boyfriend, John, and I – flew into Honiara and met with our trusty agent, Wilson Maelaua, who was to get us through every difficulty these remote islands could throw our way. I had chosen to start with the island of Makira because Chuck had introduced me to Roger James, who was coordinating Conservation International's operation there. Makira supports more single-island endemic birds than any other island in the Solomons, and CI is working to protect its interior rainforests. Local landowners have established a plan for forest management under the guidance of CI and other nongovernmental organisations, which entails showing the villagers how the protection of the land serves their own interest as well as that of the world. Roger married a Makira bushwoman and has made a life more local than the locals'. 'If you want total immersion,' he promised me, 'I'll give you total immersion.'

Soon after we landed in Makira, we set off for the highlands, accompanied by Roger, a posse of local guides, carriers for our baggage and John Waihuru, the *bigman* (pidgin for 'man of status'), who was the expedition leader. We meandered through the valley for some miles, then came to the first of sixteen river crossings. We walked against the current through water up to our waists while the carriers balanced our rather substantial suitcases on their heads. From there we began the climb upward through the rain forest. As we scrambled along a path invisible to the untrained eye, each of us was helped by our own guide: gentle, steady and – amasingly – barefoot.

One thing you should know about the rainforest: it rains a lot there. We kept under mild skies for some time, but then the storms began – cascades, avalanches of water that drenched us within seconds. Our way grew muddy and slippery, and each of us clung to his or her personal guide. We seldom fell because we were in good hands, but we were always on the brink of falling, and the water beat into our faces, at one particularly inopportune moment washing out one of my contact lenses. We ached from the climbing and the slipping and the chaotic feeling that we didn't know where we were or where we were going; from the river crossings when the current came up to our shoulders; and from the weight of our wet clothes. In the middle of the day, in the middle of the worst rain, John Waihuru announced, implausibly, that we were stopping for lunch. This seemed a ludicrous proposition, but as we watched, he and the other locals dragged sticks from the jungle, pulled down enormous fronds, and erected a shelter with a floor of banana leaves. Palms were quickly woven into plates, and within five minutes we were able to sit down on logs, dry off, eat and recover from the morning's climb.

We made it to a halfway house where we would spend the night: a lean-to of dry leaves that felt impossibly luxurious after our long day. Another day of trekking brought us, near nightfall, to Hauta. The villagers who had not been part of our trekking party, some twenty-five people, lined up to shake our hands. Aside from Roger, we were the first foreigners they had seen in more than two years.

Hauta was situated high in the mountains, with a commanding view, beside a fresh stream. The houses were made of leaves, and opposite the *bigman*'s hut, where we were to stay, was an almost equally large hut for the village pig. We went to the stream and washed off days of mud, then toured the garden plots where villagers grow taro, cassava and sweet potatoes, the staples of local life. We had dinner in the shared kitchen hut by the light of the sunset and a fire that burned in a circle of stones. The villagers have metal blades on their knives, but aside from that, life in the bush is much as it must have been a thousand years ago with one exception: ramen noodles. These seem to have taken the Solomons by storm; for nearly a month, we had everything with ramen noodles: ferns with ramen noodles, cabbage with ramen noodles, taro root with ramen noodles, sweet potatoes with ramen noodles, green papaya with coconut and ramen noodles, even rice with ramen noodles. Having lived through the trip, I would sooner eat dirt than encounter another flavour packet. But that first night, I had not yet learned to deplore them, and though the food was not good at least it had the advantage of newness.

After dinner, we sat in a big communal hut with a small lantern on the floor and learned, to the locals' immense amusement, to chew betel nut, a skill I hope never to use again. Betel is a mild intoxicant to which most Solomon Islanders are attached; you chew it until it gets soft and then dip a rolled pepper leaf into mineral lime to potentiate the pulp. The nut makes your mouth water, and you spit a lot as you chew it. It also turns your whole mouth a lurid red; chewed regularly, it makes your gums recede and your teeth fall out. If you're not used to it, it can also give you a horrendous stomach ache. It makes you dizzy. The lime can easily burn the roof of your mouth. It was a late eight o'clock by the time we had stopped spitting and curled up on the floor of our hut and drifted into deep, captivating sleep.

The next morning, we were led across the stream. On the far side, spear-wielding men in loincloths jumped out of the bush, yelling savagely, and we nearly jumped out of our skins; this, we later learned, was part of the traditional ceremony performed for even a local guest.

Just beyond the spear-bearers, a group of village men were waiting for us, and in double file they led us into the village, playing bamboo panpipes, bent at the waist and swaying with the music. The sound was a cross between a steel drum's and a bassoon's; the movement, primal Martha Graham. They led us through an esplanade of ferns, up to the higher part of the village, where the women put on each of us a necklace of seeds and a headband of flowers, inviting us to sit on a sort of porch attached to the biggest hut. The music got richer and wilder. Big pipes in the central clearing, some seven feet tall, were propped on wooden stands, and the villagers played these as if they were a giant vibraphone, with the soles of rubber flip-flops for mallets.

The villagers asked what we wanted to see. We wanted to know how they built a hut, so they gathered sago palm leaves and showed us how to fold them over rods of wild betel-nut wood and sew them with rattan and layer them to form a roof or wall. They showed us how to rub *gahuto* sticks to start a fire, how to weave traps from *aohe* roots, and how to make a pudding by grinding up smoked *ngali* nuts in a giant pestle and mortar, mixing them with taro, stuffing it all into the central part of a bamboo rod, and roasting it in a fire. Finally, they showed us how they carved the rough but elegant wooden bowls from which we had been eating. We stayed the afternoon learning all these things and trying to imitate, in our appreciation, what might be local etiquette. If I had come in search of another world, I had found it.

Back at our hut, hens were trying to lay eggs on our sleeping mats, and when we had straightened that out, we ate eels caught that day (with ramen noodles). After dinner, we were preparing to go to bed when we heard the sound of music again. It's hard to say that any of what we had seen was artificial; greeting ceremonies are so rare that they are partially reinvented on each occasion, and no foreigners had come to Hauta in a long, long time. But this sudden playing at night was completely spontaneous. Someone had felt like music, and the mood had spread. The pipers came to our hut with their instruments and played under the full moon, with the women singing at the back in chorus, and we listened for perhaps an hour to this abrupt beauty, so festive, so strange. Then they asked whether we had music in our culture, and when we said we did, they wanted to hear it. Suddenly we were the exotics. After a hurried consultation, the four of us decided to sing 'Oklahoma!' and 'Jamaica Farewell' and 'America the Beautiful'. They asked whether we had other kinds of performance in our culture. Maybe dance? So Jessica and I stepped down, and to the eerie music of bamboo pipes in a clearing in the rainforest under a springtime moon, on the uneven ground at the top of a mountain, we did swing dancing; and when we did a dip at the end, we got hoots and hollers, and the music ramped up, and the mood lasted, miraculous as loaves and fishes.

We spent two days coming back down. While the carriers took the same steep route we'd followed on the way up, to keep our belongings dry, we took a gentler one that involved, however, more river crossings, including one swim across deep rapids (in our clothes – there was no way to keep anything dry). By this time we had become close to our guides and talked to them about all kinds of things, trying to answer all their questions and explain our lives: what big cities were like, and why we had all spent so many years in school, and the rules of football, and why we didn't know anything about farming. One of the party had brought along his panpipes and played as we descended, and the birds called to one another through the rain.

When we reached the shore, we went out for a walk without our guides, and along the beach we offered candy to children, who ran away as soon as we talked to them. 'Hi!' we kept saying as we distributed the sweets, only to discover later that *hi* means 'copulate' in the local language (in which the word for 'father' is *mama*). Then we had another brief comedy: in this tropical land, no one thinks of sunbathing, and when one of our party lay down on the beach, villagers assumed he must be fighting the chills of malaria and came to provide remedies.

Following our sojourn on Makira, we chartered the Solomons' only real yacht, the thirty-five-foot catamaran *Lalae*, to take us island-hopping. After a week of jungle climbing and mud and sleeping with chickens, the immaculate white of the boat, the homemade chocolate cake, the attentive service and the always-full basket of fresh fruit were a revelation. The boat is built for fishing, and I caught a large barracuda the one time I threw a line overboard. Our dashing captain, Steve Goodhew, a veteran of the Australian Royal Navy, caught an eight-foot marlin and a host of smaller fish.

Our first port of call was a swimming-with-dolphins resort being built on Gavutu Island under the auspices of a rather tough Canadian animal behaviourist. We were greeted with the resort's custom dancing. The male performers wore loincloths – the local word is *kabilato* – and the women, grass skirts and tops made of seashells, and all had armbands with long grasses stuck in them (John called them the Scallion Dancers). Here I ran up against the constant problem of the would-be adventurer: by and large what you discover has been discovered before, and even people doing the same thing they did a thousand years ago are not really doing the same thing if a veneer of self-consciousness has been added to the enterprise. These performers were proud of their performance and it was all correct to their tradition, but after that spontaneous night in the mountains, we were spoiled, and this practised exhibition tilted too much towards the Hawaiian nightclub show. In the capital, we had gone to the Miss Solomon Islands beauty pageant, which featured gyrating women wearing grass skirts made of shredded pink plastic bags and bikini tops of coconuts and string – which was comical and rather endearing because it had an absurdist element, but it was also a little sad. This felt sad, too: an enactment of tradition rather than tradition itself.

So we were all the more delighted when we got to Loisolin, on Pavuvu, where Steve had made arrangements the month before on our behalf. The islanders had been excited by the prospect of greeting us; though they were known locally for their dancing and, living on the coast, had met some foreigners, no tourist had ever come to their village before with the express objective of seeing them. When we arrived, the entire population was waiting onshore. A few launched canoes and circled our boat; then the spear warriors rushed out into the surf and yelled madly and made the usual friendly, threatening gestures. When we came ashore, little girls out of Gauguin put garlands of frangipani around our necks, and we were welcomed by the chief, who wore a remarkable headband of densely packed possum teeth. A bamboo band played harmonies more sophisticated than those we'd heard in the jungle. Then each of us got a coconut from which to drink, and a leaf basket with a whole lobster, a slice of taro, coconut pudding, cassava pudding, fresh fish, two further kinds of taro with slippery cabbage (a slimy, local green) and hard-boiled megapode eggs. As we ate, a few young women fanned us and our food with large leaves to make sure that no flies came our way.

Meanwhile, some forty villagers, many covered in body paint, performed a sequence of complex dances that ranged from the mesmeric to the passionate, the humourous to the mournful. It was as if the George Balanchine of the South Pacific had been working on Pavuvu. The women, in grasses and shells, did a poetic welcome dance in which they imitated the motion of the waves; the men leaped about like young rams. The rhythms were multi-layered, almost syncopated, and then lyrical and sweet. At the end, they asked us to show them something from our culture, and when Jessica and I did our swing-dancing number, they cheered and cheered and wouldn't let us stop until we were completely exhausted.

In the long afternoon light, when we and they could dance no more, we set sail and passed great schools of flying fish that soared above the water for five hundred feet; a pod of about two hundred dolphins that came and played all around us, in such numbers that they seemed to be waves, suffusing the air with exuberance; terns and frigate birds and brown boobies; and perfect little islands like the ones in children's books, dome-shaped, living-room-size, uninhabited, and bedecked with five perfect coconut palms. Occasionally we saw fishermen in dugout canoes waiting to spear fish. We were caught in an endless postcard, a Pacific arcadia, and we sang and talked and drank local beer on the front deck.

Many of the smaller islands in the Solomons are coral atolls, and these are concentrated around the Marovo Lagoon, the world's largest island-enclosed lagoon, which may soon be protected by UNESCO. Marovo was described by James Michener as the eighth wonder of the world and was the object of our sailing trip. Over four days, we stopped at various isolated spots in the lagoon for snorkelling, including Uepi, where the variety and density of species outclasses that of the Great Barrier Reef. I saw huge schools of chromides, black-tipped reef sharks and grey whale sharks, a dozen kinds of parrot fish, various wrasses, including the endangered Maori wrasse, angelfish, squirrelfish, clown fish, hawksbill turtles, eels, butterfish, a manta ray, foul-looking groupers, giant clams with fluorescent pink and lavender mouths that closed when you approached, needle-nosed gars, many-spotted sweetlips, mudskippers, lionfish, black-and-blue sea snakes, electric-blue starfish. It was an underwater safari.

To me, though, the fish were almost secondary, because the coral of the living reef looked as though Buckminster Fuller, Max Ernst, and Dr Seuss had collaborated on it. There were long, pink- and blue-tipped asparagus, a thin damask-rose lace that a Spanish lady might have worn to church, expanses of olive-coloured stiff scrub brushes, gorgonian fans, lurid striped erections, vaulting mauve domes, voluptuous yellow hydrangeas, orange dreadlocks and fields of embossed purple grosgrain. Strange things rotated like lava lamps on turntables, and the mimosas of the sea seemed to recoil at our approach. By the time we got out, we were dizzy with colour and sheer variety. Every day we sailed; every day we dived into the water; every day we saw wonders beyond all imagining.

After our immersion in the Melanesian culture of the Solomons, the nation's primary culture, we wanted to see some of its Polynesian life. We left our beloved *Lalae* in Honiara and flew to Rennell, the largest of the Solomons' Polynesian islands. Our guide, Joseph Puia, packed us into his car and we headed for Lake Tegano, the biggest freshwater lake in the South Pacific and a UNESCO World Heritage Site, stopping from time to time so that Joseph could machete with astonishing speed and assurance through trees that had fallen across the road.

The lake is dotted with islets of giant mangrove and pandanus and is home to a multitude of endemic flora and fauna, including unique birds and orchids; it also contains nine U.S. planes downed during the Second World War (two of which we could see when snorkelling). Because a U.S. military base had stood by the lake during the war, locals still welcome Americans. Despite the best efforts of obtrusive missionaries, the lake people believe that the spirits of the dead travel as shooting stars to meet God beyond the eastern shore.

In our large, motorised canoe, we saw the famous sunrises over the water, visited the cave where the legendary lake octopus was said to have lived, and saw another cave that Joseph described as 'formerly a residential accommodation' – villages have not existed very long on Rennell. We encountered flocks of glossy swiftlets, frigate birds, terns, cormorants and ibis; as you approached their island rookeries they took to the skies by the hundreds, wheeling like a beautiful reworking of Hitchcock. We visited Circumcision Island, inhabited by the only South Pacific tribe to endorse the practise. We were thirsty, so our boatman shimmied up a tree, threw down fresh coconuts, and brought us limes with green skins and bright orange flesh, a 1960s fashion from the kingdom of fruit. We saw flying foxes, a species of fruit bat, both in the air and hanging in trees like the devil's Christmas ornaments. We both saw and ate coconut crab, a local species that takes thirty-five years to mature.

Alas, we did not get off the island as planned; the flight was cancelled for five days because of weather, and we spent those rainy afternoons in the depressing guest room of the island's missionary centre. We resisted the call to the local version of evangelical Christianity – John, by reading *Moby-Dick*; I, by writing this article about the wild and gentle new reality we had come to love.

A period of civil unrest followed our visit, but all seems to have calmed down again politically. A decade after its nomination, the Marovo Lagoon is still under consideration for designation as a UNESCO World Heritage Site. While this matter was tied up in endless bureaucracy, the Solomon Islands were ravaged by earthquakes and consequent tsunamis in 2007, 2013, 2014 and 2015. Like Greenland, this area is feeling the effects of global warming:

coastal erosion, inundation and saltwater intrusion are all on the rise. One province relocated its capital, Choiseul, because of rising tides – the first township in the Pacific to take such measures. The new site was constructed before residents were moved there in phases. The World Bank sent $9.1 million to the Community Resilience to Climate Change and Disaster Risk in Solomon Islands Project (CRISP) as part of a relief package for warming-induced problems. Some recent research indicates that these areas may face an additional challenge: shifting tectonic plates may be pulling the islands down at the same time that rising seas lap higher on their shores.

Children of Bad Memories

Far from the Tree, 2012

On the tenth anniversary of the Rwandan genocide, I visited the new memorial in Kigali, built by the Aegis Trust, a British company that specialises in genocide commemoratives. Unlike most other buildings in Rwanda, the structure was air-conditioned; its stagey displays felt as though they had been put together by someone previously engaged in dressing shop windows. The wall texts were stirring and the photos horrifying, but the glitzy aesthetic reflected the national urge to dissociate from events of the too-recent past. The exhibits presented the numbers of casualties in keeping with President Paul Kagame's Tutsi-centric estimates, which differ widely from those of international observers.

The purpose of my trip was to talk to women who had been raped in the genocide. The memorial treated the events of 1994 as coolly historical, but these women were still living them ten years on. It was as though no time had elapsed at all.

The Rwandan genocide drew on a long history of ethnic strife in the country. The Tutsi arrived in Rwanda at some disputed date, apparently after the Hutu were settled there, and established themselves as feudal overlords. The colonising Belgians preferred the tall, slender Tutsi herders to the short, dark, wide-nosed Hutu farmers and declared the Tutsi, who made up only 15 per cent of the population, the natural aristocracy, granting them privileges denied to the Hutu. These policies engendered fierce hatred. Towards the end of the colonial period, the Belgians fell out with the Tutsi monarch and transferred power to the Hutu. After independence in 1962, the Hutu ruled, periodically attacking the Tutsi. Ethnic battles throughout the following quarter century sent many Tutsi into exile in Uganda and Congo. They then asked to return.

When the Hutu government wouldn't allow them to come home, they organised an army – the Rwandan Patriotic Front (RPF), under the leadership of Paul Kagame – that engaged in border skirmishes. In 1993, the UN brokered a peace accord between the Hutu government and Tutsi rebels; hard-line Hutu, however, did not welcome the idea of power sharing. In late 1993 and early 1994, the visionaries of the Hutu Power movement began organising the mechanisms for genocide. They assembled mobs of impoverished and disaffected youth, building up a force called the Interahamwe, which means 'those who fight together', and taught the gospel that the Tutsi were an inhuman enemy – 'cockroaches' in their parlance. They established Rwanda's first private radio station, Radio Mille Collines, to preach messages of hatred. They stockpiled arms: some guns, but mostly machetes and knives. They systematically edged moderates out of government.

The genocide in Rwanda began on 6 April 1994, after the plane of President Juvénal Habyarimana was shot down. In the one hundred days that followed, eight hundred thousand Tutsi were killed. Unlike the Nazi-perpetrated Holocaust, where the killings were clinical, systematic and remote, the Rwandan mass butchery was hands-on. The killings were committed by the Interahamwe and farmers, mainly with farm implements. But killing was hardly the total of that time's violence. A Rwandan proverb says, 'A woman who is not yet battered is not a real woman.' The culture's underlying misogyny was easily stoked by ethnic propaganda; rape was an explicit tool of the *génocidaires*. Tutsi women, according to the announcements on Radio Mille Collines, wanted to seduce the Hutu men away so that they could end the Hutu race. Many Hutu perceived the slender, regal Tutsi women as haughty and were determined to teach them a lesson.

The men raped not only to humiliate and shame their victims, but also as a way of killing; many of the men were HIV-positive and were encouraged by their leaders to infect as many Tutsi women as possible. They raped to satisfy their own curiosity; they raped to traumatise these women; and they raped because it was a slower and more painful way of killing. They raped out of odium and desire. According to one propaganda slogan, they wanted these women to 'die of sadness'. One woman recounted having a foot soldier in the murderous youth brigades back her up against a wall and then take his knife to her vagina, cutting out the entire lining of it, and hanging the gory tube of flesh from a stick outside her house, saying, 'Everyone who comes past here will see how Tutsi look.'

At the end of a hundred days, the genocide stopped when Tutsi RPF insurgents seized Kigali, the capital. Most of the Interahamwe fled to Congo, where they continued to wreak terror in refugee camps. Kagame entered office as the new president with much cant about building bridges. Instead, he installed a largely Tutsi power structure – exactly what the Hutu Power movement had feared – with the tacit approval of the rest of the world. Kagame periodically orders raids into the Congo camps; some twenty thousand people have been killed in reprisals since the war ended. The Hutu again live under a largely Tutsi regime and feel enslaved by a loathed minority, while the Tutsi hate the Hutu for having murdered their families. Rwandans are defined by the traumas they have witnessed, received or inflicted. In official interviews, Rwandans say, *'Plus jamais'* ('Never again'), but in private, most of the people I met said another eruption was only a matter of time.

As many as half a million women were raped during the genocide. About half the Tutsi women who survived had been raped; almost all of them were HIV-positive; and they gave birth to as many as five thousand rape-conceived children. These children are called *'les enfants de mauvais souvenir'*, or 'the children of bad memories'; one writer called them the 'living legacy of a time of death'. Ninety per cent of the women in one study said they could not love the child of someone who had killed their family. A woman who had attempted to drown herself under these circumstances and been saved by a fisherman said, 'I could not even die with this baby inside me. It was a curse that kept haunting me.' One woman who had been married off to a rapist, as often happened, said, 'To be taken as a wife is a form of death. There's no death worse than that.' Because Rwandan society blames the women, these pregnancies were 'rejected and concealed, often denied, and discovered late', according to Dr Catherine Bonnet, who has studied the Rwandan rape problem. Godelième Mukasarasi, a social worker, expounded, 'The women who have had children after being raped are the most marginalised. People say that this is a child of an Interahamwe.'

Abortion is essentially unobtainable in Rwanda, but some women self-induced miscarriage in the postwar chaos. Some – no one knows how many – committed infanticide. Others left their rape babies on church steps; the country is peppered with orphanages. Since the women who abandoned their children could not be identified, the women I saw were the ones who had kept their children. The children for whom they were sacrificing themselves served as reminders of their trauma. To love the child who results from violation is almost divine – especially because for most of these women, that violation was only one in a constellation of traumas: loss of family; loss of social status; loss of the societal structures that had once seemed secure; loss of any feeling of stability or constancy; loss of health to HIV. When I went to meet these women and their children in the spring of 2004, their children were nine, and therefore old enough to resemble their Hutu fathers. I went to see how one learned to love such children or reconciled oneself to caring for them without love.

Rwandan society is hostile to these women and children. Some were castigated by their families and community; some hospitals wouldn't treat them. As half-castes, the *enfants de mauvais souvenir* are accepted by neither Hutu nor Tutsi. 'Some women were forced by their families to give up the child,' explained Espérance Mukamana, whom I met in Kigali, where she works for Avega, the widows' organisation in Rwanda. 'In the beginning, it was hard for these women even to see their children as human beings because they are considered children of evil. Most of these women never find true love for their children. They love them enough to survive, but no more. You have to motivate the mothers, repeating again and again that the child is blameless. It's hard for them to see the child as innocent; it's impossible for them to see themselves as innocent.' All had faced financial struggles; deemed unmarriageable, most were struggling to feed themselves and their offspring.

Professor Jean Damascène Ndayambaje, head of the Department of Psychology at the National University of Rwanda in Butare, explained that it was considered a disgrace for a woman to have allowed herself to be raped rather than killed. 'Can one say that one of these things is better than the other?' he asked. 'Our society does not say so. All the shame goes to the woman.' He described how one woman had to be physically restrained while doctors performed a caesarean because she had clenched her vaginal muscles tightly in a last-ditch attempt to prevent the birth. When the doctors brought her the baby, she began ranting and was placed in a psychiatric hospital. 'There are whole mental wards full of such women,' Ndayambaje said. Professor Jean-Pierre Gatsinzi, head of the School of Journalism and Communication at the National University, pointed out a major cultural change, in which a strong bond between mother and child was no longer presumed. 'It is a new society we live in,' he said, 'with different rules. One must recognise that rape and war are both traumas, and that these women experienced both traumas simultaneously. Rape in war is a crime against humanity; it's a lot worse than ordinary rape.' While any rape can be profoundly traumatic for its immediate victim, wartime rape is an attack on social norms and more profoundly traumatises the society in which it occurs.

Mukamana explained, 'Traumatised mothers are harsh and cold to their children, even abusive. The children know that their mothers don't love them, but they don't know why. They speak and their mothers don't listen to them; they cry and their mothers don't comfort them. So they develop strange behaviours. They themselves are cold and restless. Because they receive so little love at home, they go out on the street and follow strangers.' Many of these children have been given darkly evocative names: one child was named Inkuba, or War. Another was Little Killer after his father; another, Child of Hate. Alphonsine Nyirahabimana, who also works with this population at Avega, said, 'I have always wondered how any of these mothers can love their children. For some, Christianity has played a big role, and they succeed by praying. Others see the bright part of their situation; one said, for example, "I was raped and my family was murdered and I have this child who came out of horror, but at least I don't have HIV." But most are without family, desperate, and hopeless. They come to Avega and talk to one another. No one can forget what happened to them, so they might as well remember together.'

Some women form associations and stand up for their rights. Some have gained enough strength from this group identity to compensate for their loss of traditional social position. Professor Célestin Kalimba, head of the history department at the National University, said that a new Rwandan feminism has been among the accidental side effects of the genocide. 'So much of the male population is either dead or in jail,' he said, 'and women have to step into major roles. Post-genocide, women can inherit property, which was not possible before. Before, men had multiple wives. Now they sign a contract in the church when they marry, swearing that they will be monogamous. The situation for women is better now than it has ever been in Rwanda.' Some mothers who endured forced pregnancy have struggled towards a new society – if not for themselves, then for their castigated children.

Most encounter only disenfranchisement. One woman explained to me that a man came and killed her family, including her husband and three children; took her in sexual slavery and kept her for three months; then fled when the RPF forces came. She gave birth to a son, and though she developed AIDS, her son remained healthy. Rwanda has few social networks outside of family; you need relatives to survive. Knowing she would soon die, she worried that her son would be all by himself, so she tracked down the father of her son in jail and decided to foster a relationship with him – so her son would have someone after she was gone. When we met, she was making the father daily meals and taking them to him in the jail. This man had raped her and slaughtered her children. She could not speak of what she was doing without lowering her eyes and staring fixedly at the floor. No new Rwandan feminism had touched her life.

In Kigali, I met with Beatrice Mukansanga, who had a face like a Picasso mask, and Marie Rose Matamura, who was young and sweet looking. Mukansanga had no clear memory of what happened to her in 1994; she remembered being repeatedly raped and waking up pregnant in a hospital some weeks later, but she didn't know how she had spent the war. Sometime during the genocide, her leg was chopped off. Her husband and two children had disappeared in the genocide, 'all lost, all gone', she said. At the end of the atrocities, she was pregnant and HIV-positive, but did not know who her rapists were. She said, 'The baby died in me and was removed.' Whether she had induced the miscarriage was unclear. When she went back to her town of Nyanza, she found that everybody she had known was killed, so she came to Kigali. 'I have a terrible time at this time of year, around the anniversary of the genocide, at the start of the rainy season,' she said. 'I have horrible nightmares. I am living always with the feeling that I will die at any time.' She was angry that government health programmes were available only to those with connections; she had developed full-fledged AIDS, but when she tried to obtain medication, the health workers laughed at her. 'They help those who are well enough to help themselves,' she said, 'and leave the rest of us to die.'

At thirty-four, Marie Rose Matamura narrated the events of her life in an even monotone, with an air of complete resignation. When the genocide began, she fled to her church, but militias soon arrived and, with her priest's consent, killed almost all the people gathered there. She and her sister escaped only to be seized by a Hutu man from the Interahamwe who claimed them as his wives. Many militia would force women into sexual slavery, cynically using the word *wife* to euphemise a multitude of sins. There were no marriages, and there was no guarantee of protection. All the term meant was that these women had been taken on as the object of repeated sexual assault and lived in a man's quarters. Matamura's acquiescence to her captor did not obviate her hatred of him. 'He would just go walking around the neighbourhood raping the ladies,' she said. 'At any time he could force me to accept his friends; I was raped by many others. He told me that he had given me HIV so he didn't have to waste time killing me.'

Matamura's captor fled when the Tutsi forces approached; weak and desperate, Matamura and her sister, both pregnant, remained in his house. Matamura's sister died of AIDS on Christmas Day 2001. Matamura took on her sister's son and has brought him up with her own daughter. Matamura had begun to develop skin lesions and feared that her neighbours recognised them as a symptom of AIDS; she was too afraid to have the children tested for HIV. 'I don't know who will take care of the children when I die,' she said. 'I go from door to door, asking people if they have dirty clothes to be washed. I braid hair for rich Hutu women with husbands. I feel so sad that I will die – not sad for myself, but for the children. I, with my incurable disease, am the only one they have.'

Matamura described trying to protect her children. 'For me, the world is just full of hatred, and I am always afraid; I just want to lock myself in the house and see no one. But I make sure the kids are not worried. I don't want to have them asking me why I am so sad, so lonely. The boy has a hot temper, but I make a particular effort with him because he must feel that I am his mother now. I can see the picture of Hutu militia in their faces, but I can't hate my own child or my sister's, though I never forget where they came from. They ask me sometimes, "Who is my father?" and I tell them that they don't have a father, that they never did. Someday, I will have to tell them the truth. I think all the time about how I will do it and make up the speeches. I will tell them how to behave correctly and what to do if someone tries to rape them. I fear what they will become with me. I fear what they will become after that, without me.'

Marianne Mukamana had a good life before the genocide. She loved her husband, a construction worker, and their daughter, who was then five years old. Early on, the *génocidaires* came for her husband. They said, 'We will kill him and then return for you.' She never saw or heard of him again. She tried to run away with her daughter but had no place to run, and neighbours, fearing for their lives, refused to give her refuge. Hoping to save her daughter, she went in despair to the military base and said, 'I am here for you to do to me what you want,' and because she was beautiful, they took her as a sex slave. Over the weeks that followed, she was kept at the base and raped constantly and by many different men. They told her that she would end up being killed. When the RPF arrived at Kigali, her captors took her on a massive forced march to Gisenyi; when the RPF finally took Gisenyi, she was set free and headed back to Kigali with her five-year-old.

All of her family was gone save two brothers. When she realised she was pregnant, she planned ways to get rid of the baby. 'I wanted to throw her away when she was born,' she recalled. She was now HIV-positive; the child was, too. In the years that followed, Mukamana often felt a surge of loathing when she looked at this daughter, who was a constant reminder of what Mukamana desperately wanted to forget. She could not love this second daughter as she loved the first. She fantasised about finding the child's father and giving her to him, but she had been raped so often that she didn't even know who the father was, and the candidates had in any case disappeared with the rest of the Interahamwe and were probably either dead or in the Congo. 'And thank God it wasn't a boy,' she said, 'because that love would have been even harder. Boys inherit property at twenty-one; since girls have no rights, they pose fewer problems.' But she resolved that she would teach herself to love her two children the same. 'Another heart came in me,' she explained. 'She was my child, the seed of my womb, mine also, and I felt I had to take care of her for a while.' When I met Mukamana, she told me that she felt exactly the same about both her daughters. But she said she would still like to give the younger one away.

The two girls often faced confusion. The elder one was pure Tutsi and looked it; the younger had dark colouring and Hutu features. Neighbours said that they couldn't possibly be full sisters, but Mukamana kept the truth from them. 'Meanwhile, I try to harmonise these two children, to make them as much alike as I can,' she explained.

'And I tell my younger daughter that she is a Tutsi, not to pay attention to the people who tell her she is Hutu. I try to talk to them a lot like that, to make them feel loved.' The older girl still spoke of her father. 'I remember that day people came to our house and he went away,' she said. 'And he never came back. I saw him going but I never saw him returning. Where could he have gone?' The younger girl asked all the time, 'Tell me about my father,' and even, 'Why are you alone, and not with my father?' – but Mukamana kept silent. And the younger girl would say, 'One day, I will meet my father.' These remarks suggest that they knew they had different fathers, but they didn't know why that was a taboo subject with their mother.

The two girls were competitive for their mother's love. The tradition in Rwanda is that the youngest child is the most beloved, and for Mukamana it was hard to embody that expectation. 'I will die of AIDS, and my older daughter will be left alone,' she said. 'The reason is in the rape that made my younger daughter. How to know that without being angry? But both are mine. And as my younger daughter grows up, I can look at her most of the time without rancour. It gets easier with the passage of the years. I try not to think of the past, because I am afraid of it, and I also don't think of the future, because now I know better than to have dreams.'

Small, wide-eyed, mousy and sad, Marcelline Niyonsenga maintains the posture of an importuning child, looking up anxiously as if waiting for someone's permission to go on living. She was nineteen when the war began, visiting family in Kigali when their house was attacked. Her uncle and brother were killed, and she was left with her uncle's child. The next day the militias came back and took Niyonsenga out of the house. She escaped and found a family with whom to hide. The head of that household threw out his wife and forced Niyonsenga to become his sex slave. She stayed hidden all day, creeping out at night to find water, always afraid of being killed. After two and a half months, the man announced that he was tired of her and threw her out. She was gang-raped and reluctantly found refuge with a businessman who took her to Congo. When she learned that

the war was over, she begged to go home, but she was pregnant, and
her husband had decided to keep her and the child, saying, 'Tutsi
woman, if I let you go, you will tell the story of how I took you, and
I and my family will be killed.' She waited months for a day when
he was away on business. She grabbed three thousand Congolese
francs (about $5) and persuaded a taxi driver to take her to Rwanda,
where the United Nations High Commissioner for Refugees took
her in. Her damaged uterus had to be removed after the birth of her
daughter, whom she named Clémence Tuyisenge.

Since the war, Niyonsenga keeps house for her brother, who lost
his wife. She wanted to bring up her brother's son and her daughter
together, but her brother wouldn't let Niyonsenga's AIDS-infected
daughter into his house, so the little girl lives with Niyonsenga's
mother. Niyonsenga sees her once a week, sacrificing living with her
daughter in order to care for her brother and his son; they are men
and must have someone to attend to their needs. At least her brother
did not abandon her, Niyonsenga said; sometimes, he even gave her
money. Whenever Clémence was sick – and she was often sick with
opportunistic infections – Niyonsenga remembered where the child
came from. And when Niyonsenga herself was sick, she thought of the
man who infected her. Clémence's body already had erupted in blisters
her mother called 'pimples'. Whenever Clémence became feverish, her
grandmother would bring her to Niyonsenga, who would take her to
the hospital. When they were both healthy, Clémence and Niyonsenga
would laugh together. When Niyonsenga was sick, Clémence would
curl up next to her. On balance, Niyonsenga felt it would be preferable
for her daughter to predecease her, and yet she is also deeply reliant
on the companionship her daughter affords. 'People pity me because I
have this *enfant de mauvais souvenir*, but she is the light of my life,' she
said. 'To be slowly dying like this without even the comfort of a child
would be a thousand times worse. I am dying, but I am not alone.'

The deadness that afflicted many of the women I interviewed had
not touched Alphonsine Mukamakuza; she would be laughing one
minute and racked with sobs the next, constantly fiery with emotion.

She lived in a mud hut on the outskirts of Kigali, furnished incongruously with an aeroplane seat and two broken wooden chairs. The only light came through a crack between the roof and the wall. In spite of this poverty, she was impeccably dressed in a long cotton print dress and matching head wrap. She did not want her neighbours to know for sure what she felt they had already guessed, that her son was a child of rape, and so while we talked, her nephew stood guard outside, chasing off would-be eavesdroppers.

Mukamakuza was twenty when the genocide began. She thought that the barbarism had broken out only in her village, so she fled to relatives in a neighbouring village. The killing had started there, too, so she and her relatives decided to seek refuge across the border in Burundi. They were near their destination when shooting broke out. Mukamakuza kept running as the rest of her family was gunned down behind her. She bolted into a house, where an old woman said, 'You are safe here. I will hide you.' That night, the old woman's son came home, saw this beautiful woman, and told her that he would make her his wife. For three weeks he raped her repeatedly, telling her that her death was coming soon. She did all she could to stay in his favour; he was both her enemy and the man without whose attentions she would surely have been slaughtered. He brought around other Interahamwe who sometimes raped her while he watched.

A month after the end of the genocide, Mukamakuza realised that she was pregnant. After her son, Jean-de-Dieu Ngabonziza, was born, she tried to give him to her brother, but he would have none of it. She took Jean-de-Dieu with her into a new marriage, but made sure he knew that he was an unwelcome burden, beating him mercilessly and occasionally throwing him out of the house. If they went out in public, she would say, 'Call me your aunt. Never call me your mother.' Meanwhile, her ostensible consort beat her day and night. He said, 'If you want to be with me, get rid of that child. I don't want to see him.' Finally, she summoned the courage to leave and moved to the slum where I found her. 'And then,' she recalled, 'I saw that my boy was all I had. And sometimes he would laugh, despite everything, and it was when he laughed that I began to love him. But he does not look like me, and when he does something wrong, it reminds me of those rapes. He goes to school, and I hope he will learn there about the war. In the end I will have to tell him about his origins, and there will only be more tragedy for us.'

Christine Uwamahoro's proud, erect carriage was not typical of the violated women I met in Rwanda. She was eighteen and living in Kigali when the killing started. 'Secretly or publicly, it didn't matter which, the militias would break into the house, and while one was stealing, the other was raping, and then they would switch. They would give us all kinds of orders: put up your hands, kneel down, stay where you are. One held me up at gunpoint and said, "Undress and lie down, or I'll kill you." But he didn't kill the family. He came back again and again, and each time he raped me, and then my father gave him money to go away. I was saved by God's grace.'

The family finally fled, but soon came to a bridge with a roadblock. They sat by the side of the road for two hours, waiting and watching as other people were slaughtered. As dusk fell, one of the Interahamwe approached with a murderous look. They ran, but Uwamahoro's mother faltered, and Uwamahoro's brother went to help her. Over her shoulder, Uwamahoro saw them both being chopped up with machetes. Uwamahoro herself got a gash in her arm, the scar of which is still visible today; she isn't sure whether it came from falling or whether she got slashed with a knife, because her memory of the whole episode is so blurred. Uwamahoro and her father managed to walk sixty miles to the city of Gisenyi, hiding by day and stealing quietly along the road by night, but the killing had spread there, too, so they walked another few miles into Congo.

On this final leg of their journey, they met another band of Interahamwe. 'Look!' someone called. 'They are Tutsi! They must die, by any means!' They hid for a day in a large bush with two other families; they feared a crying baby with one of them would attract attention, but the baby had tuberculosis and died while they were huddled there. Uwamahoro's arm had become infected and was swollen and painful. They finally reached Goma, where they waited out the war. Uwamahoro feared that she had become infected with HIV, but couldn't bear to find out and still doesn't know. She had been advanced in her studies, but she never returned to school. She hated finding out she was pregnant, and she hated the baby and gave her to her father so she would not have to see her. Even ten years later, the child's existence filled Uwamahoro with sadness and reminded her that her life was ruined; though Uwamahoro visited her sole surviving sister every day, she visited her daughter once a month at most. The little girl is angry and hot tempered, Uwamahoro said. Whatever the girl wants, she wants it now, right away, and if she doesn't get it, she flies into a temper and will refuse to talk for two days at a time in her rage.

Unlike most women with *enfants de mauvais souvenir*, Uwamahoro remarried. Her new husband is a polygamous Congolese man who keeps another wife. 'I couldn't marry a Rwandan after what had happened, not even a Tutsi,' she said. 'I couldn't bear to be touched by a Rwandan man. At first, I tried to hide my history from my new husband, but eventually I told him all about it, and he has been very kind. When I get sad, he takes me out for a walk. When I have flashbacks and bad dreams, which happens often, he reminds me that I could have been killed, and he comforts me. I love my daughter more and I am a better Christian since I got together with this man.' He even proposed that the rape-conceived child live with them, but Uwamahoro didn't want that. 'I have a new daughter, eight months old, from this marriage,' she told me. 'It's a struggle not to play favourites. I know my older daughter would like to live with me, and my father says that she needs a mother's love. It's important to keep reminding myself that the kid is innocent. I pray hard for love. Slowly by slowly, I love her: she is my daughter, who spent nine months inside me; but it's always hard.'

I sometimes ask interviewees, especially those who seem profoundly disenfranchised, whether they want to ask me anything. The invitation to reverse roles helps people feel less like experimental subjects. In Rwanda, these mothers' questions tended to be the same: How long are you spending in the country? How many people are you interviewing? When will your research be published? Who will read these stories? At the end of my interview with Uwamahoro, I asked whether she had any questions. 'Well,' she said a little hesitantly, 'you write about this field of psychology.' I nodded. She took a deep breath. 'Can you tell me how to love my daughter more? I want to love her so much, and I try my best, but when I look at her, I see what happened to me and it interferes.' A tear rolled down her cheek, but her tone was almost fiercely challenging when she repeated, 'Can you tell me how to love my daughter more?'

Only afterward, too late to tell Uwamahoro, did I marvel that she did not know how much love was in that question.

Since Paul Kagame took power in 1994, Rwanda has had a stable political environment and an average of 8 per cent annual growth of GDP. The poverty rate is down by nearly a quarter. Child mortality has been reduced by two-thirds, and enrollment in primary schools is almost universal. The World Bank ranked Rwanda as one of the easiest countries in the world for starting a business.

But Kagame's regime is accused of assassinating opposition leaders and journalists, mass murder of civilians in Rwanda and abroad, invasion and exploitation of natural resources in the neighbouring Democratic Republic of the Congo, and political suppression of the Rwandan people. Only Sudan and Syria have higher levels of political exclusion than Rwanda. The government has shuttered independent newspapers and barred opposition parties from registering for elections. An opinion leader in the *New York Times* has described it as a 'country on lockdown'. In 2015, Kagame persuaded Rwanda's high court and legislature to relax presidential term limits, ostensibly by 'popular demand', thus paving the way for a permanent presidency. The United States and other governments asked that he show an example for the region by relinquishing his post in 2017 after two seven-year terms. Kagame has expressed displeasure at such foreign interference, but has set up a referendum process on the question, which is almost certain to pass. Given the history of assassinations of those who have come out too strongly against Kagame, the Rwandan opposition said they could not find a lawyer in Rwanda who was willing to bring a suit against the president.

My friend Jacqueline Novogratz, who has worked in Rwanda

since the 1980s with her Acumen foundation, described talking to a friend there who said, 'This culture is about lying. We all lie, all the time, to everyone. It's the only way to survive here.' Jacqueline said, 'Do you lie to me?' Her friend said, 'I don't know. We lie so much that I can't even tell when I'm lying any more. I don't know when I am lying to you; I don't know when I am lying to myself.'

Circle of Fire: Letter from Libya

New Yorker, 8 May 2006

Qaddafi's regime was extremely secretive, so while his terrorist foreign policy was deplored widely, the ludicrous humiliations of daily
life in Libya went largely unchronicled. A month in Libya felt like a
decade. Many other countries where I'd worked required complicity
in Kafkaesque bureaucracy and some featured random violence, but
in no other was so much public and personal energy devoted to such
pointless enterprises.

Here's a story they tell in Libya. Three contestants are in a race
to run five hundred metres carrying a bag of rats. The first sets
off at a good pace, but after a hundred metres the rats have chewed
through the bag and spill onto the course. The second contestant
gets to a hundred and fifty metres, and the same thing happens. The
third contestant shakes the bag so vigorously as he runs that the rats
are constantly tumbling and cannot chew on anything, and he takes
the prize. That third contestant is Libya's leader, Colonel Muammar
Qaddafi, the permanent revolutionary.

Libya is about the size of Germany, France, Italy and Spain combined, but its population, just under six million, is roughly the same as
Denmark's. Oil revenues make Libya, per capita, one of the wealthiest
countries in Africa, yet malnutrition and anemia are among its most

prevalent health problems. It is an Islamic country where alcohol is illegal and most married women wear the hijab; it is a secular country where women are legally allowed to wear bikinis and Qaddafi is protected by a phalanx of gun-toting female bodyguards. The version of socialism promulgated in the mid-1970s by Qaddafi's political manifesto, the *Green Book*, is honoured; the country is in the throes of capitalist reform. The head of the Libyan Publishers' League says that the books most often requested in his store are the Quran and Bill Clinton's *My Life*. Then, of course, there's the official line that the country is ruled by its citizens through Basic People's Congresses, and the practical reality that it is ruled by Qaddafi. Libyan officials must far outstrip the Red Queen in her habit of believing six impossible things before breakfast.

For Americans, there's an even more salient contradiction. A regime led by a man President Reagan dubbed 'the mad dog of the Middle East' – a regime that throughout the 1980s sponsored such groups as the IRA, the Abu Nidal Organisation and the Basque ETA and was blamed for the explosion that, in 1988, downed Pan Am Flight 103 over Lockerbie in Scotland – is now an acknowledged ally in America's war on terror. Libya's governing circles are beset by infighting between those who think that this alliance is a good thing and hope for closer ties to the West and those who regard the West with truculent suspicion.

Qaddafi came to power in 1969, at the age of twenty-seven, when, as a junior military officer, he helped stage a bloodless coup against the pro-Western King Idris, who had been installed by the Allies after the Second World War. Now Qaddafi claims that he has no formal role in Libya and is simply an avuncular figure dispensing wisdom when asked. Yet Libyans are afraid to say his name, except in official contexts, where it meets with predictable cheering. The general euphemism is 'the Leader'. Informally, people refer to Qaddafi as the Big Guy or the One, or just point an index finger straight up. Saying 'Qaddafi' aloud is thought to invite trouble. So is questioning his sometimes absurd policy proposals. He once insisted that families use only one bar of soap a week. On another occasion, he proposed that currency be eliminated in favour of barter. 'He believes in desert culture, even though the desert has no culture,' one cosmopolitan resident of Libya's capital, Tripoli, told me. 'He is trying to take life to its childhood.'

The name of Qaddafi's second-oldest son and possible successor, Saif al-Islam al-Qaddafi, is seldom spoken, either. The inner circle refers to Saif, who is one of eight children, as the Principal, but he is also called the Son, the Brave Young Man, Our Young Friend and the Engineer. The relationship between father and son is a topic of constant speculation. The Principal holds no title and, in keeping with his father's decree, maintains that the position of Leader is not hereditary. He does, however, sit comfortably close to power. The Leader, for all his opposition to royalty, looks a lot like a king, and the Principal is his crown prince.

Saif's role is to be the face of reform, 'to polish his father's picture', as one prominent Libyan writer suggested to me. His academic papers at the London School of Economics, where he is pursuing a doctorate in political philosophy, are said to show a solid grasp of Hobbes and Locke. He founded the Qaddafi International Foundation for Charity Associations, which fights torture at home and abroad and works to promote human rights. He appears to be committed to high principles, even though real democratic change might put him out of the political picture. One of Saif's advisers told me that Saif would rather be the first elected head of the Libyan state than the second unelected leader of the revolution, but that he could go either way.

'Qaddafi claims that he is not the Leader, and Saif claims that he is the opposition, and they are both liars,' said Maître Saad Djebbar, an Algerian lawyer who has worked on Libyan affairs for many years. Others see a personal agenda. 'The Leader is a bedouin from the desert and simply wants power and control – he is content to rule a wrecked country,' the expatriate poet Khaled Mattawa told me. 'But his sons are urban; they have travelled, studied abroad, learned sophistication. They go falconing in the Gulf states with the princes of royal families. They want to drive BMWs and rule a country that is accepted in the panoply of nations.'

Saif's office is in Tripoli's tallest and fanciest tower – a hulking glass building topped by a gigantic circular apparatus that was intended as a revolving restaurant but neither revolves nor serves food. The foundation's suite is modest and sparsely furnished, and its staff members appear to be the busiest people in Libya, bent over computers, talking simultaneously on several phones, surrounded by papers. The walls are covered with posters for Saif's causes: one shows a man with his face wrapped in barbed wire, with the caption 'International Campaign Against Torture: Middle East Area: Libya the First Station'.

Saif, however, is usually elsewhere. I met him last autumn in Montreal, where he was opening an exhibition of his own paintings. These are rendered with expressionist enthusiasm in a variety of familiar styles and may feature images of horses, desert skies, the face of the Leader or one of Saif's beloved pet Bengal tigers. Saif has bestowed his pictures on urban centres from Paris to Tokyo, where they have been received as documentary curiosities, like the personal effects of the last tsarina. Whether the primary function of these exhibitions is political, social or artistic is never discussed.

We met at the Sofitel, which had given over the top floor to Saif and his entourage. Various deputies and advisers had gathered in a large, nondescript suite. When he came in, everyone sat up straighter. Though Saif tries to be intimate and casual, his presence, even his name, makes other people formal. He wore a well-cut suit and moved with grace. At thirty-three, he is good-looking and hip, with a shaved head, and he speaks intelligently, though with the vagueness about self and reality that afflicts royalty and child stars, and that comes from never having seen oneself accurately reflected in the eyes of others. He has more than a trace of the paternal charisma, but it has yet to harden into genius, incoherence or his father's trademark combination of the two.

When I asked why Libya was not proceeding more rapidly toward democratic reform, Saif said, 'In the last fifty years, we have moved from being a tribal society to being a colony to being a kingdom to being a revolutionary republic. Be patient.' (After centuries of Ottoman rule, Libya was occupied by Italy between 1912 and 1943.) But, like his father, Saif relishes extravagant pronouncements and soon proposed that Libya give up its entire military.

'The whole faith and strategy has changed,' he said, looking to his courtiers for nods of agreement. 'Why should we have an army? If Egypt invades Libya, the Americans are going to stop it.' During the Reagan years, he said, Libya was 'expecting America to attack us anytime – our whole defensive strategy was how to deal with the Americans. We used terrorism and violence because these are the weapons of the weak against the strong. I don't have missiles to hit your cities, so I send someone to attack your interests. Now that we have peace with America, there is no need for terrorism, no need for nuclear bombs.' Saif dismissed any comparison between the terrorism that Libya had sponsored in the past and the kind associated with al-Qaeda. 'We used terrorism as tactics, for bargaining,' he told me. 'Mr bin Laden uses it for strategy. We wanted to gain more leverage. He wants to kill people. Fundamentalism in Libya – it's always there, though not so strong as in the 1990s.' Saif did not mention that in the 1990s his father's security forces routinely imprisoned fundamentalists.

Religious extremists had 'created a lot of problems in Libya', Saif said. 'They tried to destabilise the whole society. But not any more. Now they are weak. But the threat is there, the potential is there.' Saif noted that three Libyans had been involved in suicide bombings in Iraq last year. 'They are being recruited by Zarqawi,' he said, referring to the Jordanian-born leader of al-Qaeda in Iraq, 'who wants to create cells and attack American interests in Libya – oil companies, American schools, and so on. It's a disaster for us because we want the American presence. There aren't so many of these extremists, several dozen, but even that in a country like Libya is a big headache.' As for American security interests, he said, 'We are already on your side, helping the American war on terror. It's happening, and it's going to happen.'

Saif's rhetoric may beguile his Western admirers, but to the hard-liners in Libya's government it remains anathema. Saif, for his part, refused to acknowledge the substantial Libyan opposition to reform: 'Maybe there are three or four citizens like this. Not more.'

That was the most outlandish of his declarations. An American congressional aide who has worked closely with Saif accurately described him as 'eighty per cent sophisticated'. Saif's prospects will depend not upon his profile abroad but upon his ability to orchestrate support at home. Despite his political presence in Libya, his father's legacy will not easily be assumed; there are too many competitors for the next generation of power. But Saif is a canny fellow. 'The Principal knows that one secret of leadership is to see where the parade is headed,' one of his advisers told me, 'and rush in front of it before it gets there.'

In 2004, two decades of American sanctions came to an end after Libya agreed to pay compensation to the Lockerbie families and renounced weapons of mass destruction. (Saif, who has spent a good deal of energy trying to rehabilitate Libya's image in the world, was involved in both negotiations.) Since then, the great question in Tripoli has been how deeply reform will penetrate a country that has been largely isolated for decades. Within the government, the fighting is bitter. The National Oil Company (reformist) and the Department of Energy (hard-line) are in constant conflict, as are the Ministry of Economics (reformist) and the Libyan Central Bank (hard-line). Since Qaddafi makes the ultimate ideological decisions, the spectacle calls to mind the worst aspects of multiparty democracy, albeit without parties or democracy.

According to Ali Abdullatif Ahmida, a Libyan expatriate who chairs the political science department at the University of New England, in Maine, Qaddafi 'plays his biological son Saif el-Islam against his ideological son Ahmed Ibrahim'. Ibrahim is the deputy speaker of the General People's Congress, and the most public of an influential conservative triumvirate that also includes Musa Kusa, the head of Libyan intelligence, and Abdallah Senoussi, who oversees internal security. Ibrahim has declared that the United States, under orders from President Bush, has been 'forging the Quran and distributing the false copies among Americans in order to tarnish the image of Muslims and Islam'.

The infighting helps Qaddafi moderate the pace of change. 'He thinks reform should come "like a thief in the night", so that it is hardly noticed,' one family friend said. In some areas – notably with respect to civil liberties and economic restructuring – the rate of change is glacial. 'What's the hurry?' A. M. Zlitni, the country's chief economic planner, asked when we spoke, with the careful blandness that Libyan officials affect to avoid affiliation with either camp. 'We are not desperate.' In other areas, change has occurred with startling speed. Although the country is still afflicted with the legacies of its two colonial powers – Byzantine corruption and Italian bureaucracy – it has opened up to international trade with dispatch: foreign goods are for sale, even if few Libyans can afford them. You can buy Adidas sneakers and Italian shoes, along with local knock-offs such as a brand of toothpaste called Crust. In bookstores once devoid of English-language titles, you can find editions of *Billy Budd*, *Invisible Man* and the works of Congreve. The private sector is back in force. Hundreds of channels are available on satellite TV, and internet cafés are crowded. One senior official said, 'A year ago, it was a sin to mention the World Trade Organisation. Now we want to become a member.' The editor of *Al Shams* (*The Sun*), a leading state-owned paper, described a newsroom policy shift from 'expressing struggle against the West to advocating working with foreign countries'.

'Qaddafi understands the tribal structure and has the ability to play one person against another, one group against another,' one Libyan official explained. 'He's a strategic genius. He is doing with the reformers and hard-liners what he has done with these tribes, playing the pro-Western element against the anti-Western element.'

For a foreigner, there's no better illustration of the push-me-pull-you quality of the new Libya than the process of getting in. An application for a journalist's visa that I submitted last year went nowhere, although the Libyan representative to the United States assured me steadily for five months that the visa was nearly ready. (When I met with Saif in Montreal, he volunteered to take care of it, with no evident results.) Next, I joined an international party of archaeologists who had been promised entry – but as we were waiting to board a Libyan Arab Airlines flight in Rome, we were abruptly denied access to the plane. One source in the Libyan government told us that the Ministry of Immigration had recently moved and our papers had been mislaid. Another said that the head of the visa section had sabotaged files during the move. A third said that the story about the move had been floated as an alibi; the Leader had decided not to let in any Americans. Indeed, a tour group from the Metropolitan Museum arrived by ship in Tripoli in October and was not allowed to dock; the next month, five other ships met the same fate.

As a dual national, I applied using my British passport, again as a member of the archaeologists' delegation, and, as advised, wrote on the form that I was Anglican. Finally, I received a document marked 'sixty-day invitation', though no one knew whether that was sixty days from the date of the letter, sixty days from the date the visa was stamped in my passport, or sixty days from the date I entered the country. I called the Libyan consulate in London every day about my visa. In the morning, there was no answer. In the afternoon, some-one answered and said that consular services were available only in the morning. I flew to London, where the consular officer explained that I could enter Libya anytime in the next forty-five days for a stay of up to ninety days. I arrived at Tripoli Airport in mid-November. Through a Libyan travel agency, I had arranged for a car at the air-port, and just as I'd joined a nearly motionless line for immigration, a man from the agency came by with my name on a placard and walked me straight through; the immigration officer never even looked to see whether I matched my passport. 'Your visa expired – you were sup-posed to enter within thirty days,' the agency man said. 'Fortunately, the guy at immigration is a friend, so it wasn't a problem.'

It was an apt introduction to a country where the law is always open to interpretation and personal connections are the principal currency. I was in as a British Christian archaeologist rather than as an American Jewish journalist, but I was in. I promptly went to the International Press Office, where I declared my journalistic pur-pose, and where the man in charge lectured me for thirty minutes about why Libyan democracy was better than American, the terrible untruths that American journalists had heaped on Libya, and Amer-ica's imperialist tendencies. Then he volunteered that the officials I'd wanted to speak to would be too busy for me, and that I shouldn't have come.

This was standard procedure. Last April, after months of planning, the Council on Foreign Relations, in New York, sent an august delegation – including David Rockefeller, Peter G. Peterson, Alan Patricof and Leonard Lauder – to Libya, with appointments to meet both Muammar and Saif Qaddafi. After they arrived, they were told that the Leader was unavailable and that the Principal had made a scheduling error and was on his way to Japan.

Officials in Libya seldom say no and seldom say yes. Libyans use a popular Arab term: IBM, which stands for *Inshallah, bokra, moumken*, or 'With the will of God, tomorrow, maybe'. All plans are provisional, even at the highest levels of government. You can see the head of the National Oil Company with an hour's notice; you can also spend weeks preparing for an appointment that never materialises.

I requested a meeting with the prime minister, Shukri Ghanem, before I went to Libya and every day for three weeks while I was in Tripoli. On my last day, I was in the middle of a meeting when my mobile phone rang. 'The prime minister will see you,' someone said.

I said that I hoped he could see me before I had to leave.

'The prime minister will see you now.'

I began, 'Oh, okay, I'll get my tape recorder –'

'He will see you right now,' the voice interrupted. 'Where are you?'

I gave the address.

'A car will pick you up in three minutes.'

The drive to the prime minister's office was terrifying, as most Libyan driving is. Tripolitans seem to think that traffic lights are just festive bits of coloured glass strewn randomly along the roads, and they rebel against tightly regulated lives by ignoring all driving rules, blithely heading into opposing traffic on the far side of a two-way road, turning abruptly across five lanes of streaming cars. 'No shortage of organs for transplant here!' a Libyan acquaintance remarked during one excursion. The driver dropped me at the wrong building. It took two hours of calls and confusion to reach my destination.

Dr Shukri, as he is called by those close to him and by those who

FAR AND AWAY

pretend to be close to him – he has a PhD in international relations from the Fletcher School at Tufts – had a portly grandeur. With a neat moustache and a well-tailored suit, he exuded an effortless cosmopolitanism that seemed more conducive to facilitating Libya's re-entry into the world than to winning over the hard-line elements at home. When I arrived, he was sitting on a gilded sofa in a room furnished with Arabic reimaginings of Louis XVI furniture, before many trays of pastries and glasses of the inevitable mint tea. In the Libyan empire of obliquity, his clarity was refreshing, and his teasing irony seemed to acknowledge the absurdity of Libyan double-talk.

I mentioned that many of his colleagues saw no need to hasten the pace of reform. This was clearly not his view. 'Sometimes you have to be hard on those you love,' he said. 'You wake your sleeping child so that he can get to school. Being a little harsh, not seeking too much popularity, is a better way.' He spoke of the need for pro-business measures that would reduce bureaucratic impediments and rampant corruption. 'The corruption is tied to shortages, inefficiency and unemployment,' the prime minister said. 'Cutting red tape – there is resistance to it. There is some resistance in good faith and some in bad faith.' Nor was he inclined to defer to the regime's egalitarian rhetoric: 'Those who can excel should get more – having a few rich people can build a whole country.' Qaddafi's *Green Book* decrees that people should be 'partners, not wage workers', but it is not easy to make everyone a partner, the prime minister observed. 'People don't want to find jobs. They want the government to find them jobs. It's not viable.'

The civil service, which employs about 20 per cent of Libyans, is vastly oversubscribed; the National Oil Company, with a staff of forty thousand, has perhaps twice the employees it needs. Though salaries are capped, many people are paid for multiple jobs, and if those jobs are overseen by members of their tribe, failure to show up is never questioned. On the other hand, because food is heavily subsidised, people can get by on little money, enabling them to refuse jobs they consider beneath them. Heavy labour is done by sub-Saharan Africans, and slightly more skilled work by Egyptians.

'We have a paradoxical economy, in which we have many

330

unemployed Libyans' – the official unemployment rate is almost 30 per cent – 'and two million foreigners working,' Ghanem said. 'This mismatch is catastrophic.' The combination of an imported work-force with high domestic unemployment is typical of oil-rich nations, but the problem is especially urgent in Libya because its population is growing rapidly – it is not unusual to meet people with fourteen children in a single marriage. Roughly half the population is under the age of fifteen.

The prime minister's views on Islamic militants were close to those expressed by both the Leader and the Principal: 'Radical fundamen-talism is like cancer. It can strike anyplace, anytime, and you can't predict it, and by the time you discover it, it has usually spread too far to be contained. Is there such fundamentalism here? I honestly don't think so. But it could be hatching quietly, unseen by us all.' The predominant form of Islam in Libya is Sunni Mālikī, a relatively supple creed that is remote from the fundamentalisms espoused by the jihadis. Some Libyans, though, have pointed out that condi-tions that seem to have bred terrorism elsewhere – prosperity without employment and a large population of young people with no sense of purpose – currently prevail in the country.

The prime minister was more circumspect on the prospects for U.S.–Libyan diplomacy. 'We would like a relationship, yes, but we do not want to get into bed with an elephant,' he said, laughing, and spreading his hands wide in a gesture of innocence. 'It could roll over in the night and crush us.'

I mentioned public statements he'd made about being unable to bring about reform when he had to work with a cabinet assembled by Qaddafi and asked about the constraints on his authority. Ghanem assumed the air of one confiding a great personal truth: 'My ministers are like my brothers' – he wrapped his hands around his knee – 'I didn't choose them.' He paused and added with a smile, 'My father chose them.'

At the centre of Tripoli lies Green Square. Now mostly a car park, it is one of those vast, anonymous spaces that military regimes favour.

East of Green Square lie the surviving Italian colonial buildings. To the west is the old city, a warren of tiny streets and shops crowned by the ancient Red Castle, which houses a distinguished archaeological museum. In front is an esplanade beside the sea. The modern city stretches out in all other directions, with some neighbourhoods of private villas, and many of Soviet-style housing developments; it reflects both the optimism and the shoddiness of more recent Libyan history.

I was invited to the opening of a special exhibition on volunteerism, in a tent in Green Square. Addressing a gathering of a hundred or so people, an official said that tribute had to be paid to the greatest volunteer of all: Colonel Muammar Qaddafi, who, unlike the American president, does not draw a salary but out of 'love and honesty' graciously consents to rule. 'There is one God, and Muhammad is his prophet, and Qaddafi is his modern incarnation!' someone in the crowd cried. Such public avowals are of a piece with the billboards you find throughout Libya, showing a beaming Qaddafi, as triumphant and windswept as Clark Gable. Those billboards are the first thing a visitor notices; the second is the ubiquity of litter. Wherever you go – including even the spectacular ruins of the Hellenistic and Roman cities of Cyrene, Sabratha and Leptis Magna – you see plastic bottles, bags, paper, chicken bones, cans: a film covering the landscape. 'It's how the people of Libya piss on the system,' one Libyan academic told me. 'The Leader doesn't actually care about this country. Why should we keep it beautiful for him?' It is the most arresting of the country's many paradoxes: Libyans who hate the regime but love Libya cannot tell where one ends and the other begins. You can take this as a tribute, by way of inversion, to the state ideology.

In the early seventies, the Leader, disappointed by his countrymen's lack of revolutionary fervour, withdrew to the desert to write the *Green Book*, in which he advanced his Third Universal Theory as superior to capitalism and Communism. Individuals were to own their homes; other land was to be held in common. In 1977, he issued a Declaration of the Establishment of the People's Authority, launching the Jamahiriya, or 'state of the masses', and the Libyan system of 'direct democracy', in which the country is 'ruled' by the People's Congresses: what the *Green Book* calls the 'supervision of the government by the people'. The Great Socialist People's Libyan Arab Jamahiriya – memorably abbreviated as 'the Great SPLAJ' – was born. The *Green Book* proposes that, to avoid internal disputes, every nation should have one religion, but it makes no mention of Islam. Qaddafi claimed that his manifesto enshrined the basic tenets of the Quran (freely equating, for instance, the Quranic notion of almsgiving with his redistributive social-welfare policies), and that it therefore had the status of Sharia. His relation to Islam has two aspects: he draws upon it to buttress his authority, but he is hostile to the Islamists because he will countenance no rivals to that authority.

The two radical decades that ensued – televised public hangings, burnings of Western books and musical instruments, the sudden prohibition of private enterprise, intense anti-Zionism, official solidarity with terrorist and guerrilla groups – met with sharp international disapprobation. Libya's rogue status allowed Qaddafi to consolidate power and play protector of his besieged population, a role in which he excels.

One Libyan in early middle age who had lived in the United States until September 11 and who missed America spoke of what was wrong with Qaddafi's Libya and then said, 'But I wouldn't be where I am without the revolution. They paid for my education, sent me to America, and gave me a life I wouldn't have dreamed of without them.'

In part, that reflects the extreme poverty of pre-revolutionary Libya. The Jamahiriya benefited from the dramatic increase in petroleum prices that began in the seventies, and from the more aggressive revenue-sharing deals Libya imposed on foreign oil companies, so that oil earnings in the mid-seventies were roughly ten times what they had been in the mid-sixties. Oil money made possible major investments in education and infrastructure. The literacy rate in Libya has risen from about 20 per cent, before Qaddafi came to power, to 82 per cent. The average life expectancy has risen from forty-four to seventy-four. More than eighty thousand kilometres of roads have been built. Electricity has become nearly universal.

And Qaddafi has become, for most Libyans, simply a fact of life. Three-quarters of Libya's citizens have been born since he came to power. During that period, the cult of personality has sparked and dimmed in a way that has a certain congruence with the phases of Soviet leadership: a heady moment of Leninist-style revolution when many people believed in the ideals; a Stalinist period of cruel repression and deliberate violence; a long Khrushchev period of mild thaw; and now a Brezhnev-style period of corruption, chaos and factionalism. Many of Saif Qaddafi's admirers hope that he will prove to be the reforming Gorbachev of the story.

That an essentially repressive society can be characterised as being in the midst of reform reflects just how grim things used to be there. In Tripoli, I heard stories about life inside prison from many people whose only offence against the Jamahiriya was to be critical of it. In 2002, a former government official who publicly called for free elections and a free press was jailed; he was released in early 2004 – only to be sent back to prison two weeks later for criticising the regime to foreign reporters. There is no opposition press; an internet journalist who had published stories critical of the government spent several months in prison last year on trumped-up charges. 'Social rehabilitation' facilities – effectively, detention centres – are supposedly for the protection of women who have broken the laws against adultery and fornication, some of whom are in fact rape victims rejected by their families. A woman in these compounds can leave only if a male relative or fiancé takes her into his custody.

More widely covered is the case of five Bulgarian nurses who were accused in 1999 of deliberately infecting 426 children in a Benghazi hospital with HIV. The nurses were tortured until they confessed, then sentenced to death in May 2004. Among people outside Libya, the accusations seem bizarre and concocted; among most Libyans, it's taken for granted that the children were deliberately infected and that the Bulgarians are the likeliest culprits. (Whereas Western investigators have blamed the infections on poor sanitation, a Libyan doctor close to the case maintains that only children on the ward where the convicted nurses worked were infected, and that the infections ceased when the Bulgarians left, even though sanitary conditions in all the wards remain far from ideal.) Saif has said that the convictions were unjust, a brave stand given how important it is that he not appear to be capitulating to Western pressure. 'Sure, the Big Guy let Saif say the nurses were innocent – to see how it would play,' a junior government official explained. 'And it played badly.' A few months later, Qaddafi reaffirmed the hard line, declaring that the infections were caused by 'an organisation aiming to destroy Libya'. Negotiations with the Bulgarians are ongoing, however, and Libya's supreme court has granted the defendants a new trial, which is to begin in May. (NB: They were finally extradited to Bulgaria in 2007, where they were pardoned.)

Qaddafi is no Saddam Hussein or Idi Amin. He has been brutal and capricious, but he has not killed a large part of his own population. It is illegal to slander the Leader and Law 71 makes a capital offence of any group activity opposed to the revolution, but this rule has been less strictly enforced lately. Libya has signed the UN Convention against Torture, and the minister of justice has said that he will bring Libyan law in line with international human-rights standards. Some of this is window dressing. 'They closed the People's Prisons, where all our political prisoners were,' one Tripolitan lawyer told me. 'And what happened? The political prisoners got reassigned to other prisons.' The foreign minister, Abdurrahman Shalgham, told me with pride that four hundred policemen had been arrested for human-rights abuses – then admitted that none has been found guilty.

Last year, Omar Alkikli, a highly regarded fiction writer who was a political prisoner for ten years in the seventies and early eighties, sued the Libyan government for excluding former prisoners from the Libyan Writers' League. 'I lost, and I knew I would lose,' he said. 'But I made my point.' Hasan Agili, a medical student at Tripoli's Al-Fateh University, told me, 'Okay, they've fixed maybe four per cent of our serious problems, but I guess it's something.' An official in Benghazi said, 'The laws that were made of stone are now made of wood.'

Few Libyans are inclined to test what civil liberties they may have. Giumma Attiga, a human-rights lawyer and one of the founders of Saif's Qaddafi Foundation, said, 'The fear is very intense, very deeply ingrained. The highest official could tell people to speak freely and openly, with every guarantee that it was safe to do so, and the words would stick in their throats.' In fact, it is a felony entailing a three-year prison sentence to discuss national policy with a foreigner, and although such offences have been less frequently prosecuted recently, most Libyans speak of these matters anxiously. The atmosphere is late Soviet: forbidding, secretive, careful, albeit not generally lethal. I was asked not to mention names on the phone or in email. Several people asked me not to write down their phone numbers, lest my notebook be 'lost'. 'I am speaking from my heart,' an outspoken woman told me. 'Carry it in your head.'

Surveillance is pervasive in Libya. I was warned that the cabdriver who had been helping me get around was reporting to the security services, and I understood that my mobile phone conversations were not to be considered private. All the same, I was surprised when a press officer questioned me about shades of meaning in a personal email I had written home a few days earlier. Someone from Saif's office called me indignantly one day and said, 'You were heard in the hotel unfairly saying that you were unhappy with the help we've given you.'

One night, I had dinner with a bureaucrat who complained about local politics. He told me that he had been questioned at length after a recent conversation with a foreigner. 'Our interrogators were trained in brutality, cruelty and sneakiness by the best – people from Cuba, East Germany, Syria, Lebanon and Egypt,' he explained.

When we had finished our meal, the waiter cleared all our dishes, then came back and redeposited the sugar bowl.

'What's with the sugar?' I asked the bureaucrat.

He gave me a bleakly mischievous look. 'The other one ran out of tape.'

For the most part, when Libyans talk of democratisation they envision not elections but more personal privacy, greater educational opportunities and expanded freedom of speech. '*Democracy* here is a word that means the Leadership considers, discusses and sometimes accepts other people's ideas,' said Zlitni, the chief economic planner. Qaddafi views electoral democracy as the tyranny of 51 per cent – he has memorably written that citizens of Western-style democracies 'move silently towards the ballot box, like the beads in a rosary, to cast their votes in the same way that they throw rubbish in dustbins' – and recently announced, not for the first time, that Western democracy was 'farcical' and 'fake'. He declared, 'There is no state with a democracy except Libya on the whole planet. Countries like the United States, India, China, the Russian Federation, are in bad need of this Jamahiriya system.'

For most Libyan pragmatists, political reform is about changing the mechanisms of Qaddafi's control, not about relaxing it. One government minister told me, 'In most European countries, there are many parties, and in the U.S. only two. So here it is only one! It's not such a big difference.' Even reformers seldom express much enthusiasm for electoral democracy. Most aspire to a sort of modernising autocracy: their ideal is closer to Atatürk or the Shah of Iran than to Václav Havel. 'There are no democracies in the Arab world,' said Ahmed Swehli, a young businessman who had recently moved back to Libya from England, where he was educated. 'We aren't going to go first. What we need is a really good dictator, and I think Saif al-Islam might be just that. And maybe he'll be that and be elected, too, though I can't think why he'd bother.' Others are less cynical about electoral democracy as an ideal, but no more hopeful about its implementation.

One reason that many Libyans are leery of elections is their fear that, in a highly tribal society, the larger tribes would win control and everyone else would be squeezed out. Less intimate and specific than families, tribes are a second layer of identity, stronger for some people than for others. Especially among the less well educated, groups based on kinship and descent – tribes and their various subsets (subtribes, clans) – provide both a social network and a safety net: members of your group will get you a job or help you if you have money problems or mourn you when you die even if they didn't like you much while you were alive. 'Better Qaddafi, a tough leader from a minor tribe, than one who represents his own tribe a hundred per cent,' one Libyan intellectual said.

Meanwhile, the Basic People's Congresses provide at least a theatre of political participation. They are open to any Libyan over eighteen and meet for a week or two, four times a year. In principle, you can discuss anything at a Congress, though an agenda is set from above. When in session, the 468 Basic People's Congresses meet daily. Afterwards, a brief report is sent from each Congress to a Central Committee. (Libya is committee heaven – there is even a National Committee for Committees.) A typical Congress includes about three hundred members. Most educated people who are not trying to climb the political ladder do not go. The format is town hall with touches of Quaker meeting and Alcoholics Anonymous.

The Basic People's Congresses were in session while I was in Libya, and I repeatedly asked, in vain, to visit one. Then, by chance, I mentioned my interest during an interview with the director of the National Supply Corporation (NASCO), which administers the subsidies that are a mainstay of the Libyan economy; he said a meeting would be held at its offices at noon and invited me to attend.

I had hoped to sit quietly in a corner; instead, I was escorted to the front row, and someone scurried in to serve me tea. A voluble woman made an impassioned speech asking why Libya imported tomato paste when there was enough water to grow tomatoes. A discussion of tomatoes ensued. The officials introduced issues of economic reform. My interest was more in the session's dynamic than in its content, so I was paying scant attention when my translator shifted from phrases such as 'openly traded equities' and 'reallocation of subsidy funds' to something about how 'we are lucky to host a prominent American journalist' – and just as I was registering this new topic, he said, 'who will now address the Congress on the future of the U.S.–Libya relationship,' and I was handed a microphone.

While each of my sentences was being translated into Arabic, I had a fortunate pause in which to think of the next, so I gave a warm and heartfelt speech, saying that I hoped we would soon see full diplomatic relations between our countries, that I had loved meeting the Libyans and hoped they would feel similarly welcome in the United States, and so on. I received a protracted ovation, and thereafter every speaker prefaced his remarks with kind words about me. I was just settling into the comfortable glow of new celebrity when my translator said, 'We have to go now,' and took me outside, where three journalists from *Al Shams* wanted to interview me. We wandered through fairly predictable territory, and then they asked my opinion of Qaddafi's efforts to broker peace in Darfur. (Qaddafi has publicly met both with rebel leaders and with the Sudanese president, Omar al-Bashir.) I said that anyone working on that situation deserved support. I also said that Qaddafi's opposition to terrorism would appeal to Americans.

The following day, *Al Shams* ran a nearly full-page story with three large photographs of me at the Congress, under a double-banner headline that said, 'The World Needs a Man Like Muammar Qaddafi to Achieve Global Peace', and, below, 'The American People Appreciate Muammar Qaddafi's Role in Easing the Pain Inflicted by September 11th'. The morning that the piece was published, I received my long-awaited invitation to the Qaddafi compound.

A minder from the International Press Office called to tell me that I was in for 'a surprise' and that he would pick me up at my hotel at 4:00 p.m. At the International Press Office, near Green Square, I joined some twenty other 'international' journalists, all from Arab countries, and talked about why Qaddafi might want to see us. I was solemnly told that one never knows what the Leader wants: 'One comes when asked.' Finally, at about six forty-five, a minibus appeared. We drove twenty minutes and then stopped by a vast concrete wall, at the perimeter of Qaddafi's compound. The car was searched and we were searched, and then we drove through a slalom course of obstacles and another security gauntlet before being ushered into an immense tent with a lavish buffet. Within the next half-hour, four hundred or so people piled in, many in traditional robes.

One of my new journalist friends said that 'the event' was about to start, so we went over a knoll and into a polygonal structure with exposed rafters, which bore some resemblance to a rec hall at a summer camp. Hanging on the walls were sayings of the Leader's in huge Arabic and English type ('The United States of Africa Is Africa's Future' and 'One African Identity'), flanked by poster-size photographs of Rosa Parks. It was the fiftieth anniversary of her refusal to move to the back of the bus, and that, we finally understood, was the occasion for the gathering. At the front of the room, on a dais, stood a gigantic Naugahyde armchair with three microphones beside it. A man in medical scrubs came out and swabbed down the chair and the microphones with gauze pads, to protect the Leader from infection.

Some African-Americans were seated in the row in front of us. I introduced myself to one, and he dourly explained that he was Minister Abdul Akbar Muhammad, the international representative of the Reverend Louis Farrakhan, who had been in Tripoli earlier but had returned abruptly to the United States for health reasons. Qaddafi has long been one of the Nation of Islam's funders.

Then the speeches began. The speakers stood at a lectern off to the side, keeping the dais free for Qaddafi. The first was a former deputy minister of foreign affairs. 'We Libyans cannot accept the prejudice of Americans against Africans,' he began, to applause. 'Those who were seven or eight when Rosa Parks was being shoved to the back of the bus are now fifty-seven or fifty-eight and are leaders of the United States. They still carry this mentality. The new generation inherited this, and it is still going on.' He worked himself up into rhetorical paroxysms, as though Jim Crow laws were still in effect. 'We must fight the hatred of America for Africa.'

When he stepped down, Abdul Akbar Muhammad took the lectern to speak about American racial injustice, mentioning that, under segregation, blacks and whites had had to use separate hammams, or public steam baths (a detail previously lost on me). 'We cannot count on the Zionist-controlled American media to tell our story,' he said. 'Zionists in the U.S. won't show how the leader of the Al-Fateh revolution is in sympathy with us and us with him.'

The Leader never emerged, apparently having decided that, if Farrakhan wasn't making an appearance, he wouldn't, either. Still, the event reflected his fixation on establishing Libya as more an African than an Arab country (even though most Libyans are contemptuous of black people, who do the manual labour that Libyans disdain and are blamed for all crime). Qaddafi's early dream of pan-Arab unity fizzled, and when other Arab nations observed the UN sanctions against Libya in the nineties, while many African countries did not, he turned southward. By African standards, Libya seems wealthy and functional; Arab nations, even North African neighbours, have little affection for Qaddafi. He has backed groups opposed to the Saudi regime, and Libyan agents were implicated in a 2003 plot to assassinate the crown prince of Saudi Arabia. (Saif suggested to me that the Libyans were hoping, in his coy phrase, for 'regime change' but didn't necessarily know that their Saudi partners intended physical attacks on the royal family.)

Qaddafi always sleeps in a tent, true to his bedouin roots. When he went to Algeria recently, a local cartoon showed a tent pitched at the Algiers Sheraton. One man is saying, 'Let me in, I want to go to the circus!' The other says, 'There's no circus here.' The first rejoins, 'But I was told that there's a clown in that tent!'

For modernising reformers such as Shukri Ghanem, Libya's major problems are poor management and isolation, and the solutions are better management and global integration. 'The world has changed,' as Ghanem put it, 'and, like other socialist states, we recognised that we had limited means and unlimited needs.' The internet and satellite television – the dishes are so ubiquitous that landing in Tripoli is like descending on a migrant storm of white moths – have brought further pressure for reform by making that larger world visible. 'The change has been inevitable since *Oprah* came on our televisions,' a leading Libyan poet said to me ruefully. What Libyans mainly relate to, though, is the standard of living in other oil-rich states, as displayed on Al Jazeera and other Middle Eastern channels. Libya seems dusty and poor in comparison, and they wonder why.

Earnings from oil exports account for about 80 per cent of the national budget. In the heyday of Libyan oil production, the country produced 3 million barrels a day. That number has dropped to 1.7 million, but the National Oil Company plans to get it back up to 3 million by 2010. Libyan oil is of high quality, low in sulphur, and easily refined. Libya has proven reserves of about 40 billion barrels of oil, the largest in Africa, and may have as much as 100 billion.

Several major oil companies have ranked Libya as the best exploration opportunity in the world. The Libyans have lacked the resources to conduct extensive explorations themselves. In the fifteen years since foreign companies left, Libya's extractive resources have been seriously mismanaged. 'If Dr No were trying to muck up the Libyan oil economy,' a British adviser to the Libyan government said, 'there is nothing he could think of that hasn't been done.'

Still, oil money continues to make possible Libya's subsidy programmes – the socialism in the Great Socialist People's Libyan Arab Jamahiriya concept. NASCO pays twenty-six dinars for a 110-pound bag of flour and sells it to bakers for two dinars; you can buy a loaf of bread for two cents. Rice, sugar, tea, pasta and petrol are also sold for a fraction of their cost. Economic reform will involve scaling back these subsidies (which currently amount to about $600 million a year) without impoverishing or starving people – which is all the more difficult given that wages have been frozen since 1982. Meanwhile, little credit is available in Libya: no Libyan-issued credit cards can be used internationally; no financial institution meets international banking standards.

'The oil absorbs all the mistakes, of which there have been many,' one Libyan official told me. 'The oil money means that there is stability, and it makes the country easy to run. It's this little country with all this oil – it's like if you decided you wanted to open a 7-Eleven and you had a billion dollars to back it.' The oil is a curse as well as a blessing. The SPLAJ system has produced a population unhampered by a work ethic. Libyans work five mornings a week, and that's it – assuming that they have jobs. 'If they were willing to take jobs in, say, construction, there would be jobs for them,' Zlitni said sternly. 'But we're a rich country, so the youngsters don't want to work hard.' Economies based on resources such as oil generate few jobs unless they diversify. Many university students I spoke to were convinced that, for all the talk of reform, their talents would remain unexploited. 'When I finish my MBA, chances are that I won't be able to get a job,' one complained to me. 'The whole country runs on oil, not on employment. The wealth doesn't come out of anything you can get by working hard, which I am prepared to do, but what's the point?'

'If we hadn't had oil, we would have developed,' the minister of finance, Abdulgader Elkhair, told me. 'Frankly, I'd rather we had water.'

For him, and for aspirants to Libya's emerging private sector, the main outrages are the sclerotic ministerial bureaucracy and its endemic corruption. The nonprofit organisation Transparency International gives Libya a Corruption Perceptions Index of 2.5, ranking it lower than Zimbabwe, Vietnam and Afghanistan. The Heritage Foundation's 2006 Index of Economic Freedom ranks Libya 152nd out of 157 countries evaluated. 'You need twenty documents to set up a company,' Elkhair told me, 'and even if you bribe all the right people, it will take six months.'

One day, I sat in bumper-to-bumper traffic with a Libyan human-rights activist who gestured in despair at the roadworks and said, 'They dig it up and close it and dig it up again, for enormous sums of money every time and with no other purpose. This corruption makes me late for my meetings. Necessary things are not done here, and unnecessary things are done over and over.' I met the previous head of the National Cancer Institute, described to me by other doctors as the best oncological surgeon in the country, who had been removed from his job to make way for a friend of the Leader's. The displaced doctor is now working at a small clinic without essential equipment. The administrator who served under him sells fish at a roadside stand nearby.

'Qaddafi is very happy to have corrupt people working for him,' a Qaddafi insider said to me. 'He'd much rather have people who want money than people who want power, and so he looks the other way and no one threatens his total control of the country.' (Tribal loyalties, which intersect with simple cronyism, also play a role here: Qaddafi has filled many high-level military and security posts with members of his bedouin tribe, the Qathathfa, along with members of a large tribe to which the Qathathfa have long been allied, the Warfalla.) A Tripoli lawyer added, 'Corruption is a problem, and sometimes a solution.'

I attended the opening of a United Arab Emirates trade fair in Tripoli, which was held in a tent and was full of international goods presented with a smile. You could get samples of everything from medication to cookware and industrial equipment, and a select crowd of Libyans passed through with shopping bags. Many business cards were exchanged. 'Look, this country is so rich you can't believe it,' Ahmed Swehli, the English-educated businessman, told me, glancing around. 'Right now, it's like we're the kids of the richest man in the world, and we're in rags. The corruption, the bloat, is impoverishing.'

Compounding the problem of graft is a shortage of basic operational competence. I went to a session of a leadership training programme in Tripoli, organised by Cambridge Energy Research Associates and the Monitor Group, two American consulting firms that are advising the Libyan government. The foreign organisers had been determined to include the people they thought had the strongest leadership potential, but some local officials wanted to choose on the basis of connections. The compromise was neither wholly meritocratic nor purely corrupt. To some in the group, capitalism was still a novelty; others were ready for corner offices at Morgan Stanley. They role-played. They made speeches through crackly microphones under gigantic portraits of the Leader. Some described sophisticated financial instruments and drew flow charts; some talked of 'leveraged buyouts' and 'institutional investors' and 'a zero-sum game'. On the other hand, one participant, dressed in a shabby suit and a bright tie, was asked how he would fund a construction project, and he replied vaguely, 'Don't banks do that?' Another was surprised to learn that international backers usually expect interest or profit sharing in return for risking their money. Libyan business, it's clear, will be led by people of impressive competence and by people of no competence.

At the end of the conference, the prize for the best presentation went to Abdulmonem M. Sbeta, who runs a private company that provides oil and marine-construction services. He was suave and cultivated, with darting, lively eyes. 'We need not leaders but opposers,' he said to me afterwards, over an Italian dinner in the Tripoli suburbs. 'Everyone here has had a good model of how to lead. But no one has ever seen how to oppose, and the secret to successful business is opposition. People want prosperity more than emancipation, but, in any case, social reform can be achieved only through economic development.'

But does Qaddafi wish to teach his subjects to oppose him? An expat businessman told me, 'Qaddafi is afraid that the emergence of a wealthy class might inspire a so-called Second Revolution.' Wealth is a relative term; by world standards, the wealthy people in the country are the Qaddafis, and if anyone else has truly substantial assets, he's smart enough not to show it. In the meantime, the Leader's vagaries have kept Libya's elites off-balance, sometimes in almost absurd ways. In 2000, Qaddafi lifted a longtime ban on SUVs, and prosperous Libyans went out and imported Hummers and Range Rovers. Three months later, the Leader decided that he had made a mistake, and he outlawed them again, leaving a large number of privileged Libyans owning vehicles that it was illegal to drive. 'You can tell if you've reached the top,' a young Libyan told me, 'if you listen to a lot of conversation about SUVs rusting in the garage.'

'Don't say *opening*,' the foreign minister, Abdurrahman Shalgham, said, waving his hands in protest, when I asked him about the new Libya. 'Don't say *reintegrate*. Libya was never closed to the world; the world was closed to us.' But the cost of Libyan paranoia has been an isolation that feeds this paranoia and keeps Libyans in the fold of the Leader. The idea of a world that wants to engage with Libya is dangerous to Qaddafi's hegemony. 'America as an enemy would cause him trouble,' said Ali Abdullatif Ahmida, the political scientist. 'But he doesn't want America as a friend, either.'

Relations between Libya and the United States remain shadowed by history. Qaddafi's most vigorous opponent was President Reagan, who in 1980 closed the Libyan embassy, then suspended oil imports, then shot down two planes over the Gulf of Sidra, where the United States disputed Libya's sovereignty. Ten days after the Libya-linked bombing of a West Berlin nightclub frequented by American servicemen, in 1986, Reagan bombed Tripoli and Benghazi, dropping ordnance on Qaddafi's compound in an apparent attempt to assassinate him. Qaddafi claims to have lost an adopted daughter in the raid. 'His grip on power was sliding and then there was the bombing and it united the Libyans behind him,' one Libyan official told me.

The total isolation of Libya began in 1991, when the United States and Britain indicted two Libyans suspected of involvement in the downing of Pan Am Flight 103, and the French indicted four Libyan suspects in the 1989 explosion of the French airliner UTA 772 over the Niger desert. Libya refused to surrender any of the suspects, and the following year, the United Nations approved economic sanctions. Only in 1999 did Libya allow the Lockerbie suspects to be brought to trial, under Scottish law, in The Hague. (A financial settlement was reached that year with French authorities as well.) The Scottish court convicted one of the suspects and acquitted the other. Libya long denied any wrongdoing but eventually accepted that it had to admit to it, as a pragmatic matter, though Libyan officials see it as a forced confession. Qaddafi never accepted personal guilt.

The Lockerbie question, a closed book to most Americans, was brought up repeatedly while I was in Libya. One official said, 'I can't believe the Libyans at that time could have pulled off something that big. Something that stupid – that is completely believable. But not something that big.' Western investigators continue to argue whether Libya had direct involvement in the event. Initial inquiries suggested that the bombing was the work of the Syrian-led Popular Front for the Liberation of Palestine–General Command, a terror group funded by Iran, and both a former Scottish police chief and a former CIA officer later submitted statements claiming that the physical evidence inculpating Libya had been planted. Because of such problems, Robert Black, the QC and Edinburgh law professor who helped set up the trial, told the *Scotsman* this past November that the Lockerbie verdict was 'the most disgraceful miscarriage of justice in Scotland for a hundred years' and would 'gravely damage' the reputation of the Scottish criminal-justice system. The case is under consideration by the Scottish Criminal Cases Review Commission. Because Libya supported foreign terrorist groups, though, the regime could have been implicated even if it was not the main author of the disaster.

In recent years, U.S. diplomatic relations with Libya have warmed slightly. In 1999, the United States agreed to the suspension of UN sanctions, but not its own, which it renewed in August 2001. Then came 9/11. Qaddafi condemned the attacks, called the Taliban 'godless promoters of political Islam', and pointed out that six years earlier he had issued a warrant for Osama bin Laden's arrest. In August 2003, the Libyan government pledged to deposit $2.7 billion in the Bank for International Settlements, in Switzerland, to compensate the families of those lost on Pan Am Flight 103. Four months later, after secret negotiations with a British-led team, Libya agreed to renounce its WMD (weapons of mass destruction) programme, and American sanctions were eased.

Qaddafi had made similar overtures to both George Bush Senior and Bill Clinton but was spurned – in part, according to Martin Indyk, who was Clinton's assistant secretary of state for Near Eastern affairs, because Libya's weapons programmes were not considered an imminent threat. This contention has been borne out. Mohamed ElBaradei, head of the International Atomic Energy Agency, described Libya's nuclear programme as 'at an early stage of development' – many of the centrifuges had evidently never been uncrated. But John Wolf, who as George W. Bush's assistant secretary of state for nonproliferation played a key role in dismantling Libya's programme, maintains that something of real value was secured – more by way of information and evidence than by the removal of a present threat. 'The Libyans had the design of a nuclear weapon, sold by the A. Q. Khan network,' he told me, referring to the former head of Pakistan's nuclear-weapons programme. 'Libya's decision to turn over not only equipment but also the documentation, shipping invoices, plans, et cetera, provided a treasure trove of materials that were instrumental in establishing the credible case that mobilised countries against implicated individuals and companies abroad. We would not have been able to convince many of these countries or the IAEA (International Atomic Energy Association) of the cancer-like nature of the festering A. Q. Khan network without that documentation. The information that enabled us to break up the network was critical.'

After the 2003 agreement, President Bush said that any nation that gave up WMD would 'find an open path to better relations' with the United States and that 'Libya has begun the process of rejoining the community of nations'. By late 2004, the United States had revoked the travel ban to Libya, established limited diplomatic relations, and lifted many remaining trade restrictions. What Saif calls 'this cocktail of problems and sanctions' had, it seemed, been largely addressed. Certainly the Bush administration was eager to see American companies compete for oil-exploration rights in Libya, and it has facilitated economic engagement. But issues such as the 2003 anti-Saudi plot and the affair of the Bulgarian nurses have stalled the entente, and Libya remains on the State Department's list of state sponsors of terrorism. Until the country is taken off the list, the United States must vote against IMF and World Bank loans to Tripoli, and substantial sanctions remain in place.

'It's almost the same as during the embargo,' the head of the National Oil Company said. Libyan hard-liners point out that U.S. officials have acknowledged that no act of terrorism has been linked to Libya in years, and they complain that while Tony Blair, Jacques Chirac, Gerhard Schröder and Silvio Berlusconi have all visited Tripoli, the United States has sent no one above the under-secretary level. The United States has no official consulate in Libya; Libyans who want visas apply in Tunisia, and the United States does not grant them freely. Libyan reformers who thought that settling Lockerbie and renouncing WMD would allow the resumption of normal relations talk about 'receding goalposts'.

David Mack, a former high-ranking U.S. diplomat who has served in Libya, told me, 'It's been useful to us to be able to engage in intelligence exchanges with Libya; it's quite clearly been useful to them.' He pointed out that the United States had agreed to list the dissident Libyan Islamic Fighting Group as a terrorist organisation and got it banned from Britain, where some of its members had been based. 'Having made all this progress,' Mack said, 'if we now just let things drift, inevitably there will be relapses.' So while the Bush administration holds up Libya as a role model for disarmament – 'If Libya can do it, Iran can do it, too,' John Bolton, the U.S. ambassador to the United Nations, has said – some policy analysts think that the administration has done too little to promote that example. Ronald Bruce St John, a Libya scholar at Foreign Policy in Focus, observes that America's priority has been to control WMD and get support for the war on terror; Libya's priorities are the rationalisation of commercial and diplomatic relations. American goals have been met; Libyan goals have not. In Tripoli, hard-liners seethe that Libya gave away the store, while the reformers feel undermined.

The reformers' own diplomatic efforts have had limited success. Representative Tom Lantos, Democrat, of California, and Senator Richard Lugar, Republican, of Indiana, both have visited Libya, where they met with Saif, Shukri Ghanem and Qaddafi himself, and have taken an optimistic view. 'Qaddafi has clearly made a hundred-and-eighty-degree turn,' Lantos said to me, 'and we are turning around the aircraft carrier that is U.S. policy.' But when Lantos sought a cosponsor for the United States–Libya Relations Act, which was meant to strengthen bilateral relations, nobody was interested. Mack said, 'We need to show the world, particularly governments like Iran and North Korea, that there is an alternative paradigm for dealing with the United States, and much to be gained by having a normal relationship with us,' and suggested that American interests would be served by improved relations with an Arab leader who opposes fundamentalism and has substantial oil reserves.

'Deep down, the Libyans think the U.S. will not be satisfied with anything short of regime change,' one of Saif's advisers said. 'And deep down, the Americans think that if they normalise relations, Qaddafi will blow something up and make them look like fools.'

Everywhere I went in Libya, opposition to U.S. policy was tempered by enthusiasm for individual Americans. Among the older generation of Libyans, the reformers were eager for news of the towns where they had once studied, in Kansas, Texas, Colorado. (Most of the hard-liners I met had never visited the United States.) Because the pariah experience has been a lonely one, many Libyans hoped for improved relations with the outside. I spent a morning with the human-rights lawyer Azza Maghur, a striking woman with cascading hair and a warm laugh who had just returned from a humanitarian conference in Morocco. Her father was an important figure in post-revolutionary Libyan politics, and this has given her leeway; she seemed almost oblivious of the constraints that keep most Libyan women in head scarves and at home. I asked her how she felt about the United States, and she told me that it was hard for her to be pro-American in the wake of the news reports about Abu Ghraib and Guantánamo. 'You cannot imagine how we worshipped the idea of America.' She looked down at the floor, as though she were talking about a relative who had recently died. 'We wanted nothing more than to be with you: this rich, fair democracy. But now we ask, "Who is giving us this lesson of freedom?" I mean – if you caught your high priest in bed with a prostitute, would you still count on him to get you in the door of heaven?' Maghur is still hoping to show her young daughter the United States. She said that at least once a week, her daughter asks how things are going between Libya and America, and Maghur says, 'It's going, sweetheart.' And her daughter wonders, 'So can we visit Disneyland yet?' And Maghur has to say, 'Not yet, sweetheart, not yet.'

For a culture that is politically and socially underdeveloped, Libya has a surprisingly active intelligentsia, who view their society with tenderness and irony. People I met and liked invited me out repeatedly and introduced me to friends and family. I went to a birthday party at the house of one such Libyan; his wife cooked a feast, and we stayed up half the night with their children, watching movies. The day before I left, friends took me out for late-night tea and gave me full traditional Libyan dress – a long shirt, an embroidered vest and a little black hat – as a going-away present.

The social life of Libyans is essentially private. Tripoli is latticed with wide highways; petrol is subsidised, and because there are no bars or clubs and few cinemas or theatres, the most popular pastime is driving; people cruise around for hours. The privacy of cars enhances their charm, but mostly the Tripoli highways, busy through the night, provide diversion for citizens desperate for entertainment or novelty. When they aren't driving, most Tripolitans socialise at home rather than in cafés, partly because of the absence of women and alcohol in public places.

I had my first drink in Libya after a friend called an army colonel and asked, 'Do you have any pomegranate seeds?' (It is wise to use euphemisms in police states.) He did, and we drove to the outskirts of a small city, to a large white house with a long veranda, beside a dirt road. In the Libyan way, the house was built of concrete and painted white, but it was beginning to show signs of wear. We sat on a wide, bright-coloured banquette under fluorescent lights in an enormous room. The place was decorated with souvenirs from Central Asia, where our host had trained, including many carvings of bears with fishing rods. We listened to a medley of Shirley Bassey hits played on the zither and took turns smoking from a five-foot-tall hookah. The colonel, a beaming, extroverted Libyan of sub-Saharan ancestry, served the local home brew, 80 proof and rough enough to remove not just fingernail polish but quite possibly fingernails as well, on a table covered with a lavishly embroidered cloth and laden with Fanta and Pringles. The atmosphere was reminiscent of a high school pot party. I asked my friend how he would feel if his sons drank, and he laughed, replying, 'It's inevitable.' Then I asked about his daughters, and he grew serious: 'If my daughters were drinking, I would be very, very upset – furious, in fact. Because, if people found out that they had been drinking, they would think they might also be sexually active, and their marriage prospects would be shattered.'

I met a Libyan woman who worked for Alitalia, a job that she loved but that she felt no Libyan husband would tolerate. 'I have to choose between a marriage and a life, and I have chosen a life,' she said. 'Most women here choose a marriage. It's a question of taste.' The restrictions are a matter not of laws – on issues such as gender equality, the laws are more progressive than in most Arab countries – but of social norms.

Qaddafi accepts such customs, but he frequently describes his own society as 'backward' (his favourite term of disapprobation); one Libyan intellectual complained to me, 'If you listen to his words, you will agree that he hates the Libyan people.' While Qaddafi represses the democratising forces from the left, he is far more brutal with the Islamist ones on the right. Indeed, most of the regime's political victims in the past few decades have been members of Islamist groups that he has banned, including the Muslim Brotherhood. Libya's Islamic institutes, almost fifty of them, were shut down in 1988. When clerics protested Qaddafi's 'innovative' interpretations of the Quran and his dismissal of all post-Koranic commentary and custom, Qaddafi declared that Islam permitted its followers to speak directly to Allah, and that clergymen were unnecessary intermediaries. A year later, he likened Islamic militants to 'a cancer, the Black Death, and AIDS'. As if to vex Hamas, once a beneficiary of his largesse, he has even argued in recent years that the Palestinians have no exclusive claim to the land of Israel and called for a binational state – he dubbed it *Isratine* – that would guarantee the safety of both Palestinians and Jews, who, far from being enemies of the Arab people, were their biblical kin. ('There may be some objections to the name,' he allowed, 'but they would be unhelpful, harmful and superficial.')

'You ask us, "Why do you oppress the opposition in the Middle East?"' Qaddafi said in March, speaking via satellite link to a conference at Columbia University, dressed in purple robes and seated in front of a map of Africa. 'Because, in the Middle East, the opposition is quite different than the opposition in advanced countries. In our countries, the opposition takes the form of explosions, assassinations, killing . . . This is a manifestation of social backwardness.' On this point, at least, the hard-liners and the reformers tend to converge. Foreign Minister Shalgham told me, 'The fundamentalists represent a threat to your security. They represent a threat to our way of life. They are against the future, against science, the arts, women and freedom. They would drag us back to the Middle Ages. You fear their acts; we fear the ideology behind those acts. Okay, read the Quran for an hour a day, and that's enough; if you don't also study engineering, medicine, business and mathematics, how can you survive? But people have figured out that the tougher your Islam, the easier to find followers.'

The fear of radical Islam helps explain why authorities cracked down so forcefully when, in February, protests erupted in Benghazi over the Danish cartoons of the prophet Muhammad and the decision of an Italian cabinet minister to wear a T-shirt featuring those images. Eleven people were killed by the police, and violence spread to at least two other cities in the eastern part of the country, where Qaddafi's hold on power has always been relatively weak. Saif gave local voice to international opinion, saying, 'The protest was a mistake, and the police intervention against the demonstrators was an even bigger mistake.' His father, too, repudiated the 'backwardness' of the police response, but mainly wanted to insist that the riots hadn't arisen from Islamic fervour, much less from discontent with his regime. Rather, they were spurred by anger at the history of Italian colonialism. (More than a quarter of a million Libyans – perhaps a third of the population – are estimated to have perished as a result of the Italian occupation, many in concentration camps.) 'Unfortunately, there could be more Benghazis', or even 'attacks in Italy', if Rome didn't offer reparations, Qaddafi warned, saying that he would be mollified if Italy were to build a highway across Libya, for some three billion euros. The Italian foreign minister, Gianfranco Fini, said that this was 'a not too veiled threat', adding, 'We have already said that we want to put the colonial past definitely behind us in our relations with Libya. We maintain this position in a clear and transparent way. We expect a similarly coherent position from the Libyan leader.'

When I read this statement to a Libyan acquaintance, he burst out laughing and said, 'Good luck, Mr Fini!' Expatriate opposition leaders have claimed that Qaddafi staged the riots to extract concessions from Europe, but that they escalated out of control. In Libya, the issue was widely seen to be economic – a disgruntled population of unemployed youth needed an outlet for their anger.

The most immediate sequel to the riots was the dismissal of Prime Minister Shukri Ghanem. (He was given a post at the National Oil Company.) I had already heard rumours in Tripoli that Ghanem was going to lose his job in a cabinet reshuffle; the openness that seemed so refreshing when we met had not pleased the Leader. 'He made three basic mistakes,' one Qaddafi adviser said to me. 'First, he associated reform with his own name and complained publicly about the Leadership. In Libya, if you want to accomplish things, you make yourself invisible, you sublimate your ego. Second, he thought that a strong position with the West would guarantee his hold on power and didn't understand that the West counts for very little here. Third, he failed to win over the Libyan people; he never seemed to be concerned about their suffering . . . In the street, there is relief that he is gone – though there is no affection for the alternative.' Ghanem's successor was the taciturn hard-liner Baghdadi al-Mahmoudi. 'For the Leadership, it will be easier to make economic adjustments now that the reform will come clearly and directly from the Leadership and not be seen as admissions that the Leader was wrong, as concessions to some kind of competition.'

The change of prime ministers was a reassertion of Qaddafi's power: more tumbling of the rats. Several ministries – including oil and energy – were shaken up, with people removed from jobs they had held for decades. The U.S. State Department's decision, in late March 2006, to keep Libya on its terrorism list both reflects the problem and contributes to it and has outraged Libyans in and out of power.

Because Ghanem's strong suit was supposed to be his ease with Western powers, his failure to get Libya removed from the U.S. terrorism list helped ensure his replacement by a hard-liner. Baghdadi al-Mahmoudi has been described to me as financially corrupt but wily, calculating, and extremely industrious. He is 'a technocrat out of the Revolutionary Committees who works hard to glorify the Leader's policies', a Libyan American academic said. 'Will reform slow? Well, Shukri Ghanem talked a good line about reform but accomplished so little that there's not much backsliding to do. Mahmoudi realises that economic reform has to move forward and will do that for the Leader. He has absolutely no interest in political or social reform, and he will leave it to the Leader to have a relationship with the West.' It has been suggested that, with the appointment of a hard-liner, some of the infighting will subside.

'Ahmed Ibrahim's power will wane, too,' one of Saif's advisers told me hopefully, referring to the deputy speaker of the General People's Congress. Saif will be his own man: 'He's old enough to carry that off.'

'We call the world close to the Leader "the Circle of Fire",' one Libyan intellectual said. 'Get close and it warms you up; get too close and you go down in flames. The Circle of Fire includes both reformers and hard-liners; Qaddafi likes the chaos that creates.' The man spoke with irony, almost disdain, yet he was not above warming himself at the fire. The class of educated Libyans – which includes poets, archaeologists, professors, ministers, doctors, businessmen and civil servants – is tiny. Given the way that tribalism intersects with class alliances and political identities, social relationships exist in Libya among people who in a larger society would probably be kept apart by mutual opposition. Political enmity is often cross-hatched with social amity. In Tripoli, I had dinner at the home of the poet and physician Dr Ashur Etwebi, who spoke passionately of the injustices of the Qaddafi regime in both its absolutism and its new capitalism. 'He has to go,' Etwebi said. 'This colonel has eaten the best years of my life, poisoned my soul and my existence, murdered the people I loved. I hate him more than I love my wife. He and his government and everyone who has anything to do with him must go. Enough is enough. We have no souls left. Do not let yourself be fooled by this talk of reform. What kind of reform is it when this man is still sitting in Tripoli? I cannot say it to you enough times. He must go. He must go. He must go.' A few minutes later, when I mentioned a high-ranking member of the regime whom I hoped to interview, Etwebi said, 'Ah, he was here for dinner earlier this week.' He added with a shrug, 'I don't agree with him, but I like him.'

The cosiness between the authorities and many of those who railed against them continually surprised me. Some of this was simple pragmatism, but not all; it was more intimate than that. A person's network of loyalties and connections was never predictable. I had a drink (of non-alcoholic beer) in the Tripoli planetarium with a professor who had previously claimed that the prime minister and Saif got drunk together and raped the country – and they were the good guys. We had joked about the government's inefficiencies, and he had said darkly that no one who wasn't Libyan had any good reason to endure such chaos. He had asked how I could hold on to my sanity when I was dealing with government offices.

Now he was beaming. 'Hey, I've been given a job with the ministry.' He raised a hand up over his head in a gesture of pride and triumph.

I was surprised that he was so eager to join a regime that he loathed.

'Well,' he replied, 'it also happens to be the only game in town.'

Of the many lessons I've learned against optimism, none other has been so bitter as Libya's descent into chaos following Qaddafi's ignoble end. The problem, it would seem, was not that the West supported the overthrow of Qaddafi. The problem was that we did not seek to ascertain or shape what would ensue. The elimination of a great evil achieves little without some coherent good to fill the vacuum. The murder of U.S. ambassador Christopher Stevens, Foreign Service information management officer Sean Smith and two CIA contractors in Benghazi on 12 September 2012, came as a rude awakening to just how dysfunctional Libya had become. Hillary Clinton, then secretary of state, was criticised for having denied requests for increased security in Benghazi, where she wished to maintain a low profile, apparently as a misguided show of faith in the incipient Libyan democracy. Since then, militants from ISIL (also known as ISIS or Daesh) have captured Qaddafi's home town of Sirte and slaughtered Christians there. Armed conflicts have emerged in Benghazi, Derna, Tripoli, Warshafana, the Nafusa Mountains and other areas. In the south, the Tuareg and Tebu ethnicities are slaughtering each other. People from sub-Saharan Africa flood through the uncontrolled desert borders hoping to cross the Mediterranean and settle illegally in Europe, usually under the supervision of human traffickers. Amnesty International maintains that among the hundreds of people assassinated by Islamist groups are atheists, security officials, state employees, religious leaders, agnostics, activists, journalists, judges and prosecutors. There is no functioning legal system. Even my closest friend from Tripoli, Ashur Etwebi, who wanted to help build the new Libya at almost any cost, has fled with his family to Norway. Hasan Agili has gained UN refugee status – though not a residence visa or a work permit – in Lebanon. Those who can get out, no matter how much they love their country, are out. This misery is Qaddafi's legacy; he had so destroyed his society that no human structures were left to sustain government without him.

In the primitive south of the country, tribal warfare is unbridled; in the anarchic north, kidnapping is a commonplace. The elected government – the House of Representatives (HOR) – which enjoys international recognition, has fled Tripoli and taken refuge in Tobruk, in the eastern area of the country. A competing government primarily of Islamists – the General National Congress (GNC) – has declared itself in Tripoli, which means Libya has, in the words of the French foreign minister, 'two governments, two parliaments, and complete confusion'. The influence of the Islamic State is growing, and the UN's attempts to form a GNC and HOR 'unity government' will surely strengthen the Islamists, whose predecessor, the Libyan Islamic Brotherhood, lost roundly in the last two elections. The West supported the overthrow of elected Islamists in Egypt; the West now supports a role for Islamists in Libya, where they have never been elected. General Khalifa Haftar, the renegade who leads the HOR army, has threatened to form a third government wing of his own under the banner of Karama (Dignity), focused primarily on the fight against Islamists.

Wagging his finger like a disappointed nanny, Saif Qaddafi warned as the revolution against his father began in 2011, 'There will be civil war in Libya . . . We will kill one another in the streets.' Now such killing is rampant. Saif himself, wanted by the International Criminal Court for crimes against humanity, is imprisoned in Zintan; his captors have amputated the digits he used when reprimanding his country's citizens. Though he was sentenced to death in the summer of 2015 by GNC-controlled courts, he is unlikely to be executed anytime soon; he is a useful bargaining chip for those who hold him. Indeed, the whole sentencing appeared to be a gesture of defiance by the GNC against the international community that wants Saif Qaddafi sent to The Hague. In August 2015, pro-Qaddafi demonstrators took to the streets for the first time, chanting, 'Zintan, Zintan, free Saif al-Islam.' From a distance, that old horror had begun to look attractive, especially to anti-Islamists in Benghazi, Sebha and Tripoli.

All the Food in China

Travel + Leisure, October 2005

Pleasure comes at a cost, and I gained eleven pounds on this month-long eating trip. At the end of our sybaritic stay, during a foray to the trendy 798 area of Beijing where many of my artist friends had studios, my partner, John, and I stumbled on a boutique with an elegant mandarin jacket in its window display. I asked the saleswoman, 'Would you have that in my size?' She looked at me with a respectful expression and said extremely politely, 'Ah, no. I am so sorry. We make clothes for thin people here.'

Before my first trip to China in 1982, I was warned that the food would be terrible, and it more than met expectations: greasy, gristly, dismal, prepared with that brutal indifference Communism seemed to celebrate, and served up grey and ugly. Hong Kong, Taiwan and Singapore kept alive the Chinese culinary tradition, three tiny candles standing in for the greatest bonfire in the world. By the early nineties, the situation was somewhat better, as long as you stuck with simple things or ate in people's homes. In the past five years, Chinese cooking has risen phoenix-like from the ashes, and divine food is now to be found in the country's unnumbered restaurants. It is hard to understand how the Chinese have retained some semblance of sanity in a country so utterly transformed, because the China of today is as dissimilar to the China I first visited as Oz is to Kansas. Where miserable-looking people in tattered uniforms once tilled depleted fields while unconvincing workers celebrated the Communist state in unbearable factory performances, one now finds a level of efficiency and sophistication in the cities that leaves me feeling that New York is quite nearly a provincial backwater. Of course legions of peasants still labour in poverty, but the advances in China have spread through a broader swath of society than those in Russia. The improvement in the food reflects a profound social transformation: what was once reliably unpleasant is now often thrilling. While these changes are most obvious in Beijing's and Shanghai's smartest restaurants, they can also be found in country inns and at street dumpling stands.

I had the good fortune to do a culinary tour with the fashion designer Han Feng, who is warm and glamorous and sparkling with life, and who led us to both the fanciest restaurants in China and the best street food imaginable. 'You won't believe it,' she said on our second day in Shanghai as we drew near to Jia-Jia Juicy Dumplings, in the old Yu Yuan district, a grungy-looking stand where a huge meal costs about a dollar. Seated on plastic stools on the pavement, we gorged on dumplings filled with soup and pork, shrimp, or hairy crab (a regional delicacy). You dip them in rice vinegar with ginger, and when you bite down, first the warm soup floods your mouth, then you experience the smooth skin and the rich meaty filling. Mobs descend on the place in all sorts of weather, and the eight women who work there are crowded so close together that you wonder how they can move their arms. A great steamer sits outside, piled high with bamboo baskets, watched over by a woman whose face is constantly shrouded in vapour. But everyone smiles and laughs. 'How can this be so good?' Han Feng asked us, glowing with pride.

She was the inventor of our trip – and it took some considerable inventing – and she is also the inventor of herself, as miraculous and unlikely as modern China in all its glory. Han Feng left the People's Republic in 1985 to move to New York, but has recently taken a Shanghai apartment, relocated her production to her homeland, and started dividing her time between the two countries.

Shortly after I published my article about Chinese artists twelve years ago, I was invited to a dinner in New York at which my host told me, 'One of my friends is bringing his new girlfriend tonight. She's Chinese and doesn't speak much English. I put her next to you since you've been there recently.' Han Feng and I began dinner with stiff attempts at conversation in a language we only half shared. I volunteered news of my recent research. 'I don't know much about contemporary art in China,' she said. In a vague attempt to keep the conversation from dying, I related some of my adventures. I wasn't sure how much was getting through, but at some point I mentioned Geng Jianyi, and she sat up suddenly and said, 'Geng Jianyi from Hangzhou? Really, really good-looking, about our age?'

'Yes, that's the one!'

'I dated him in high school and I never knew what happened to him!'

She came from a country of a billion people; I'd been there. How could we not have someone in common?

Since then, I've learned that Han Feng knows most of the world's interesting people, and I've been lucky to be invited to the divine dinners she cooks at home and those she organises in Chinatown, where one runs into Jessye Norman, Lou Reed, Susan Sarandon, Rupert Murdoch, Anthony Minghella or, just as likely, her wisecracking upstairs neighbour or the fur buyer who once paid her a compliment. Her satisfying, throaty laugh makes every evening feel like a celebration. Han Feng is profoundly international. 'I love wherever I am and whatever I'm doing,' she once said to me. She arrived in the United States as 'a Chinese peasant potato', as she says. 'Some people climb staircase of success,' she told her then husband. 'I take express elevator.' Soon she met someone who wanted to back her design activities and promised to make her rich and famous. 'I said, "Maybe we can forget about famous and concentrate on very rich."' Since then, she has developed a private label that has been sold at Bendel's, Takashimaya, Bergdorf's and Barneys; designed opera costumes for the English National Opera and the Met, and made a line of clothes for the Neue Galerie in New York. She is an international style icon who has been the face of Christian Dior in China and has graced the covers of American magazines.

After her divorce, she had a long-term relationship, which ended when her boyfriend said he wanted to move in. 'I can't believe it! I say, "Move in? Move in? I don't have that kind of closet space!"' Most people fall in love with Han Feng if they get half a chance. The king of Morocco has commissioned her to make many of his clothes, and she has been a regular guest at his palace. 'I stay there and see all the pomp and circumstance,' she confided, 'and I think how glad I am to live a simple life!' It's the most high-powered simplicity I've ever encountered; whatever kind of potato she was when she left China, she's become an orchid of the first order.

We started in Shanghai, where my favourite place was the YongFoo Élite, brainchild of a local decorator who leased the former residence of the British consul and spent three years and $5 million restoring the space, furnishing it with antiques and replanting its gardens, giving it the aura of the old Shanghai: decadent, lavish and sophisticated. While we rhapsodised about the sweet shrimp, the fish fried with pine nuts and the quail's eggs roasted with octopus and pork, our Chinese friends were impressed by the romaine salad – an exotic touch in such a setting. Dessert is not always Chinese cuisine's strong point, but the crisp date pancakes with sesame seeds were both tangy and sweet, as if they were already nostalgic about the rest of the meal. After dinner there, we went to a jazz club that felt like a speakeasy and met up with artist friends. Later, we headed off to the perennially fashionable Face Bar, where we met a Chinese doctor friend of Han Feng's, who took my pulse and prescribed a health regimen even as we lounged on opium beds drinking hot brandy toddies; the next day, I found myself being whisked off to the acupuncturist.

Ordering in Chinese restaurants is an art. In New York, Han Feng will spend half an hour talking to a Chinatown waiter about what she wants. If saints are usually represented with their primary attributes, then Han Feng should be painted with a menu. She reads the pages as if they were poems – poems in need of editing – and seems to inspire the kitchen with her particularity and fervour. She enquires about the freshness of ingredients and tries to balance the meal so that it has hot, cold and tepid dishes; spicy and mild tastes; fish, meat and vegetables; heavy flavours and lighter ones. Each meal needs to be conceived as a whole. The Chinese spend a larger proportion of their income on food than almost any other nationality. In his great book *Food in Chinese Culture*, K. C. Chang talks about 'food as social language' and 'food linguistics'; in dynastic China, you respected a visitor by cooking a dish yourself even if you had servants; you honoured ancestors with food sacrifices. The food is the society.

The best food in China is not necessarily in the splashiest places. Crystal Jade is in a Shanghai mall and looks like it, but the Cantonese dim sum there is divine – fried potato dumplings that melt in your mouth; roasted skin of baby pig, duck and chicken; shredded daikon with dried shrimp layered in a kind of filo pastry. Across town at Jade Garden, the throbbing bass beat from the nightclub downstairs obtrudes, but not enough to diminish the lotus root stuffed with sticky rice or the tea-smoked duck, which is to waterfowl what Lapsang souchong is to Lipton.

On New Year's Day, we drove to Hangzhou, where Han Feng grew up. According to a Chinese saying, when you die, there is heaven; but when you live, there is Hangzhou. The city lies beside the West Lake, where pleasure boats travel from island to island, and the sun glints off the urban skyline on one shore and elegant, tall pagodas on another. A typical local dinner includes *chou doufu*, or 'stinky tofu', which tastes like elderly athletic socks left through a muggy summer in a dank locker and then boiled in sour milk; a street hawker of *chou doufu* was recently arrested for violating air-pollution laws. It is an acquired taste I have yet to acquire. We headed to the gala opening of the new Hangzhou Opera House and afterwards, unready to call it a day, indulged in a late-night foot massage: our feet were soaked in Chinese herbs, pounded with rubber mallets, rubbed with heated salt, and kneaded in every conceivable direction. We drove back to the hotel at 2:00 a.m. in absurd bliss.

The following day, we went to lunch at Longjing, a tiny establishment with just eight tables arranged in private pavilions around a beautiful garden in the middle of a tea plantation. This was Chinese cooking so refined that some of its particular triumphs were lost on our inexperienced palates. We had twenty-two dishes: rare delicacies such as steamed turtle wrapped in lotus leaves; a broth of locusts and old duck (old ducks are supposed to warm you up in winter), which sounds rather bizarre but was in fact glorious; a rich, delicate soup called Heroes' Soup in honour of the fish in it, which are boiled alive; fatty pork slow-cooked for four days and served with eggs; and braised venison. We had quenelle-like fish balls, made by nailing a fish to a plank, scraping the flesh off one layer at a time so that it becomes completely soft, beating the resulting mush with cold water into a foam, then poaching it. 'Making that is hard like hell,' Han Feng said, 'and no one has ever done it better, even for an emperor.'

We drank the fresh local Longjing tea, for which the restaurant is named, while a violin prodigy, winner of the Paganini Competition and part of Han Feng's extended circle, gave a sweeping virtuoso performance, at once precise and passionate and thrilling. Han Feng took us to the Ming-era Guo Family Garden at the west end of the lake, less touristy than some other Hangzhou parks and magnificently restful. Later we visited the Zhiweiguan restaurant. Where Longjing served up food that was exotic to a Western palate, rare and understated tastes impossible to conceive outside of China, Zhiweiguan was so glitteringly splendid and yet so wholly accessible that it could sustain a hopping trade on New York's Upper East Side. For one dish, the chef cut a single, narrow eleven-foot-long strip of pork (like a continuous ribbon of apple peel), spiralled it into the shape, more or less, of a stepped pyramid at Chichén Itzá, and roasted it. At the table, the server unwound it, cut off short pieces, and wrapped them in spinach pancakes. A whole chicken stuffed with garlic had been wrapped in thin paper and then encased in salt before baking – the meat was almost implausibly juicy.

Few foreigners go to Shaoxing, and it is hard to understand why. The canals are romantic and dreamy, and the Qing dynasty houses are built right down to the water; the windows are adorned with carved wooden screens, and women kneel beside the water to scrub laundry; the canal boats are as intimate as gondolas, and the boatmen use their feet to push the big oars. You can always see the grand pagoda on the hillside just beyond the city, and on the day we were there, someone was listening to Beijing opera at high volume, and the music echoed down the byways. To get to and from the canal boats, you travel by bicycle rickshaw through winding, enigmatic streets too narrow for cars. We ate at Xianheng and had several variations on *chou doufu*, some palatably mild. I took more eagerly to another local fermented specialty: Shaoxing rice wine. We also had aubergine with a peppery okra-like vegetable, and caramelised-pork buns, sweet and rich. For dessert there were sticky rice cakes with black sesame seeds, an almost bitter flavour, and honey. Han Feng led the toasting, and we felt ready to burst with food, alcohol and pleasure. We realised that we were having an average of twelve dishes at each meal, and that we were having two meals a day, and that we were going to be in China for twenty-one days, which meant that by the time we left we would have tried more than five hundred dishes. We took some deep breaths.

For the Chinese, there are two great cuisines – Sichuan and Cantonese. Travellers know Cantonese because it is the cuisine of Hong Kong, but Sichuan province is still off most tourist maps. Sichuan natives talk about peppers the way other people talk about sports teams. Their cuisine makes Mexican food seem bland, but the heat is layered and complex, the different kinds of hot spices mixed and remixed, toasted and fresh, soaked in different agents to create a range of intense pleasure and exquisite pain. The trademark Sichuan pepper is *hua jiao*, which is in fact not a pepper at all, but the dried fruit of the prickly ash shrub. Amasingly potent, it makes your mouth numb, but it is a wonderful numbness. You can feel it setting about its anaesthetic work as soon as you taste it, yet at the same time it seems to make your taste buds somehow more intensely awake. It's almost as if whatever you're eating has been stewed in cocaine. Strange and distressing at first, it becomes an object of longing.

We had lunch at My Humble House, a very unhumble restaurant

in Chengdu in a park surrounded by bamboo groves and waterways. The style is upmarket modern Chinese, with giant scholars' chairs, a silk-draped four-poster bed on which you can loll, pools of carp, halogen lights and tables scattered with silk rose petals. The food is Chinese fusion – incorporating the influence not of Western food, but of the multiple branches of Chinese and South-east Asian cuisine – so, for example, the traditional Cantonese shark's fin soup is made here with the addition of creamy pumpkin.

Sichuan is justly famous for its teahouses. Most Chengdu businessmen leave their offices in the afternoon and conduct business over tea. Women go to play mah-jong, gossips to gossip, children to play. We went to Yi Yuan, the most beautiful teahouse in Chengdu, in a restored Ming garden with a dozen courtyards, reflecting pools, pavilions, walkways, gaming tables, great sculpted lake rocks and bridges framed by pines. We sat at a table next to some Buddhist monks and drank perfumed tea.

On entering China Grand Plaza for dinner, I felt as Marco Polo must have at the gates of the Forbidden City. Here in what I had foolishly thought was the middle of nowhere was dazzling opulence. You walk through enormous doors into a vast lobby, where a pianist is playing Chopin on a concert grand, and see porcelain and furniture that could easily be in one of the world's better museums. China Grand Plaza includes an art gallery, a spa with three gigantic heated pools and a bevy of gorgeous masseuses, two karaoke bars (one of which has a glass ceiling in which fish swim), four restaurants, and hotel guest rooms. The feeling is of extravagant elegance with a touch of *Goldfinger*.

A member of staff, in black with white apron and gloves, stands before each of the doors down a long, vaulted red-lacquer hallway. We were ushered into one of these private rooms, which make up the haute Sichuan restaurant; there is no communal space. Amid burnished Qing candle stands and expressive Ming calligraphy, we were given fresh tea and glasses of *baijiu* (Sichuan brandy), which burns like wildfire all the way down. We had 'husband and wife' (spiced beef and pork lungs), and jellyfish with coriander, and then a light consommé of fresh worm herb, which, famous for its health-giving qualities, sells on the open market for as much as $2,000 a pound;

food and medicine are not clearly distinguished in China. Floating in the broth was a poached soufflé of bean curd and chicken. Abalone came over bricks of crisped rice. Kung Pao chicken was full of the freshest *hua jiao*. Halfway through dinner, a dancer came to our room to do a private 'face-off'. In this old Sichuan tradition, a sequence of brightly coloured cloth masks is worn in layers. As the dance unfolds, the dancer pulls a hidden string and one mask after the next is revealed. After dinner, we were offered Cuban cigars and a bottle of 1988 Château Lafite Rothschild, but, choosing our indulgences, had massages instead.

Chengdu is the great unsung city of China. In addition to incomparable food, it has wonderful sights: a panda-breeding centre, where you can see the animals up close, including the adorable new cubs; the Wenshu Monastery, with its chanting monks and holy processions; and, a two-hour drive away, the 233-foot-tall Leshan Grand Buddha, carved into the Lingiun Hill rock face in the eighth century AD to subdue the violent confluence of two rivers. It is the largest Buddha in the world – its big toe is twenty-eight feet long.

We went native that night: Sichuan hot pot. Hot pot restaurants abound in Chengdu, and a local friend led us to Huang Cheng Laoma, where two burners are built into the middle of each table, allowing us to have one cauldron chock-a-block with chillies, and one with a mild broth of chicken and sea horse. We ordered some twenty trays of stuff to cook in them, including sirloin steak, chicken, alligator livers, bamboo pith, bamboo-pith fungus, Chinese spinach, sausage, freshwater and saltwater eels, five kinds of mushrooms, Sichuan ferns, fresh lotus root and slivers of beef throat. Whatever we cooked in the spicy soup we dipped in sesame oil with onion; whatever we cooked in the mild one we doused in a salty herb sauce. After dinner, we went to another teahouse to see Sichuan opera – a cavalcade of face-off, puppetry, dance, dexterous clowns performing folktales, acrobatic stunts, magic tricks and masked flame-blowers.

Beijing residents, prohibited from debating who would be the best Party leader, have instead turned their critical attention to a more pressing question: who makes the best Peking duck? There are many details to consider. Is the preparation too refined or flashy? Is the skin too fatty or dry? Is it cooked over apple wood or apricot? Is the sauce bean- or fruit-based? Should the skin be dipped in sugar? How should the duck be carved? We went duck hunting seven times. Among the restaurants that cater in good part to Westerners, we liked Commune by the Great Wall and Made in China; among those more for the locals, we preferred Xiangmanlou. Commune by the Great Wall is a hotel composed of villas by leading contemporary architects. From each villa, you can climb up to the Wall and walk along a pleasantly unrestored section that is yours alone. We had the restaurant's traditional Peking menu, which includes fried shrimp balls, duck soup, braised cod, dumplings and the duck.

Made in China is in the Grand Hyatt, so you certainly don't feel as if you're discovering someplace obscure; you could be in L.A. or New York. Nonetheless, the wisdom in Beijing is that it's the city's top restaurant, and everything we had there was delicious. We ate shrimp boiled in green tea, and poached chicken with spicy peanuts. The duck skin had separated entirely from the duck; it was crisp and firm and unfatty, but not brittle. The pancakes were papery thin, and the sauce was made from sweet beans mixed with honey and sesame oil, then reduced to a satisfying thickness.

Xiangmanlou has no frills, though it is clean and pleasant, and the bill for six people would barely have covered sandwiches in New York. Beijing families crowded every table. The duck skin here is divided – the best is put on a special plate, and the 'hard skin' is served separately. The duck is fattier than at Made in China, but in a sinful way, like foie gras. A soup of duck bones follows. We had fish, too, brought to us flopping around in a basket before its execution.

The best Beijing street food is the *jianbing*, and the best place to get it is the stalls outside the Baoguo Temple complex, now a flea market. The seller first spreads batter on a wide iron griddle to make a crêpe with spring onions in it; then breaks an egg over the top and spreads it around so it cooks into the batter; then flips it over and slathers on bean sauce and chilli sauce; and finally wraps the whole thing around a piece of sweet fried bread. It's steamy and fresh and eggy and starchy and delectable.

To vary our massage addiction, we tried out a late-night ear massage. The Beijing place was like a comfortable hospital – extremely clean, and the massage girls wore nurses' hats. Before a statue of the Buddhist goddess of mercy, Guanyin, a variety of offerings had been made, including a high-calorie health drink – in case mercy was getting a little thin on the ground.

We celebrated and mourned our last night in Beijing at the ultra-high-concept Green T. House, with its chairs upholstered in feathers, revolving coloured lights, exhibitions of contemporary art, rocking horse in the corner, mirrored tables, and so on. The scene is very sceney, screamingly cooler-than-thou. The menu is an absurdist document, the poetry of which, already strained in Chinese, becomes endearingly ludicrous in English: 'A Little Caviar Sashimi with Unimaginable Sauce' or 'Mystic Beef Rolls Stuffed with Enoki Mushrooms and Mozzarella' or 'Bliss upon Cuttlefish' or – my favourite – 'Erotic Dance by Six Mushrooms around a Lonely Chestnut.' The food is somewhat less impressive than the titles, but the models smoking long cigarettes and the young hipsters with amasing haircuts are unparalleled.

For twenty-one days, we ate Chinese food at every meal, except for one night, in Beijing, when beloved American expat friends threw a dinner party for us at their apartment. They had borrowed the chef from the French embassy, and he did a terrific job. But Western food tasted strange after the alluring flavours of the Orient. Having to cut things up seemed vulgar and tedious; the buttered fresh vegetables seemed to lack imagination; and the beef, though cooked to perfection, seemed sort of chunky and bland. It was hard to switch back. We had culinary jet lag and all the familiar things felt wrong for a little while. Like scuba divers, we had to come up gradually to avoid getting sick as the atmosphere changed.

'Food comes first for the people,' says an ancient Chinese proverb, and foodie culture has blossomed in China as hedonism has grown less stigmatised. The average Chinese citizen spent more money on food in 2015 than at any time in the past, and food TV shows such as *A Bite of China* have soaring ratings. Nearly two-thirds of Chinese mobile-phone users consistently photograph their food before eating, then share these photos through food-oriented apps and social media; fluency in food culture is deemed a mark of sophistication. The China Cuisine Association has asked UNESCO to place the country's cuisine on the Intangible Cultural Heritage List. Demand for premium and organic foods keeps increasing. Recent research has found that people who eat spicy food all the time live substantially longer; though the exact causality is unclear, the study has been warmly received. Torrents of fabulous new restaurants have opened for wealthy Chinese and Westerners; in Shanghai alone, five recently made the list of Asia's Best Restaurants.

In the meantime, however, increasing pollution of soil and water in China means that some food products are corrupted. Nearly a fifth of China's arable land is contaminated. Other foods are adulterated; three hundred thousand babies were sickened by milk powder that contained melanine; bean sprouts were found to have been treated with toxic chemicals to make them look shinier; flour with dangerously high aluminium content was found in dumplings and steamed buns; rice was full of cadmium and other heavy metals; and pork that had been infected with phosphorescent bacteria was identified by consumers because it glowed in the dark in their kitchens. Vinegar contaminated with anti-freeze killed Muslims at a Ramadan meal in 2011, while fake eggs made of plaster, wax and slimy additives turned up in provincial markets. In 2013, a raid on a food-storage facility turned up chicken feet that had been frozen in 1967; they were being bleached to sell as fresh. In 2015, pork from diseased pigs was approved by bribed regulators. As many as one in ten meals in China uses recycled oil, often from the drains beneath restaurants.

Though increasingly strict laws are intended to address these concerns, they are inconsistently enforced, and many Chinese express scepticism, believing, for example, that much of what is touted as organic is not so. A preponderance of wealthy Chinese consume imported fresh foods they believe are less likely to be compromised –

the market for imported fruit alone is nearly $10 billion. Some organic farms inside China have been set up exclusively for the politically connected and will not sell to common people.

At the same time, the incursion of Western fast-food restaurants means that many people are overeating unhealthily. While the consumption of salt has always been extremely high, Chinese people are eating more and more fats, and while rice sales have gone down, intake of corn products has skyrocketed. Purchasing of packed, processed foods is higher than in the United States and brings in nearly $250 billion a year. Obesity is rising sharply, and about 12 per cent of Chinese have diabetes, giving China the world's largest diabetic population.

Outward Opulence for Inner Peace: The Qianlong Garden of Retirement

World Monuments: 50 Irreplaceable Sites to Discover, Explore and Champion, 2015

I spent time in the Qianlong Garden and the Juanqinzhai, in Beijing, during my 2005 food trip to China. I had made frequent visits to the Forbidden City, but never to this refined and intimate area of it. I had studied Chinese art history in college and was interested in the period during which this garden was conceived and built; I had studied architectural conservation, too. I had become a trustee of the World Monuments Fund and had sought to learn more about the challenges of preserving the garden structures. As WMF's fiftieth anniversary approached, I was asked to write an essay about one of its historic preservation projects, and I selected the Qianlong Garden.

Preservation issues are of concern worldwide, but in China, the erasure of the past to make way for a supposedly better present and future has been pursued with a particularly troubling gusto. I am all for a better present and future, but I don't believe that destroying the past is a good means of getting there.

The central axis of the Forbidden City was designed to impress and intimidate; the Juanqinzhai (Jwen-t(ch)in-JAI), or Studio of Exhaustion from Diligent Service, built by the Qianlong Emperor in the 1770s for his retirement, is intended to coddle and caress. Clandestine though it may have been to the masses, the Forbidden City was public to its privileged visitors, an architectural rendition of the emperor's immutable being; the Juanqinzhai promises an almost lonely privacy. Most great monuments are for civic consumption, but the Qianlong Emperor built the Juanqinzhai and surrounding garden for himself, envisioning a lodge that would allow him to live according to his habits but free from his responsibilities. However, nothing about the Juanqinzhai is modest; a refined discretion nuances its opulence. If the Forbidden City is a grand sculpture, this is a jewelled object. As a linchpin uniting heaven, man and earth, the emperor enacted a formal, immutable self, but the Juanqinzhai acknowledges the passage of time; for all its sumptuousness, it humanises those who enter it.

When I first went to China in 1982, the streets of Beijing still consisted mainly of *hutong*s, long alleys of traditional courtyard houses. Down those narrow byways, anxious people in Mao suits bicycled at lackadaisical speed, keeping a deliberate distance from foreigners. The city was dusty and decaying. Luxury, that corrupting anti-communist idea, was essentially non-existent. In the Qing dynasty, the area that now constitutes Tiananmen Square consisted of a walled, north-south corridor surrounded by government buildings. In the 1950s, inspired by Moscow's Red Square, authorities bulldozed those buildings to create the empty expanse of Tiananmen as we now know it. The square turned barren, brutally austere and insufferably grandiose, a place where the pomp of the Communist state could be paraded before a meekly awestruck populace. In the middle of this dilapidation incongruously rose the Forbidden City, long revered as the ultimate stronghold of power, where the most prosperous rulers in the world had once held their hidden court. Of course, Buckingham

Palace is rather grander than the houses across the street from it, and the Louvre puts the rue de Rivoli to shame. But I have never, before or since, encountered so immediate and stark a contrast as that between the Forbidden City and Deng Xiaoping's Beijing.

The Forbidden City was built in just fourteen years through the efforts of a million workers and is the largest unified complex of wooden buildings in the world. The wood is rare and precious, and every yellow (the imperial colour) ceramic roof tile glorifies the emperor. The Forbidden City was the seat of government for six hundred years, for twenty-four emperors in the Ming and Qing dynasties. When our astutely political chaperone showed us through in 1982, he attempted to condescend to the values it embodied, but he couldn't entirely eliminate the wonder in his voice as he described the life that had once unfolded there. In the outer court, we felt the aloofness of the imperial rulers of China; nothing about these buildings was designed to offer comfort. In the inner court, even the emperor's apartments proved to be forbidding manifestations of imperial station. The whole set-up reflected the inherited wealth and exploitative prerogatives of aristocracy that the country had officially rejected. Our minder was more comfortable with the militarism of the Great Wall than with these palatial quarters, but he recognised that the buildings' conceptual grace and superb proportions represented the apogee of something brilliantly Chinese – that they constituted part of his cultural heritage.

At that time, we neither saw nor heard of the Qianlong Emperor's retirement gardens, the landscape at the far end of which the Juan-qinzhai stands. The site was too intimate for the burgeoning crowds of tourists, and no one in China then had the skills requisite for its conservation, but the decades of its neglect also suggest an element of purposeful disregard. Although the Communists accused the Qing dynasty of exploitation, those emperors had represented total authority, a legacy that Mao and his successors gamely sustained. The pavilions of the retirement garden signify lavish materialism and rarefied intellect and were thus utterly anathema to Maoism. The larger Forbidden City remained at the heart of Chinese command, and the sizeable portrait of Mao that still hangs over its entrance gate was a potent sign of his enduring authority. In contrast, the retirement garden was a luxurious place of repose for an emperor to pamper himself with solitude after giving up power – and the latter-day rulers of China were not interested in a life after power. Nor were champions of collective action interested in the meditative sequestration of an individual.

I returned on numerous occasions to the Forbidden City, but I didn't learn of the existence of the retirement garden until 1999. The buildings there, including the nine-bay Juanqinzhai, had been ignored so utterly as to have suffered little looting or destruction. The Qianlong Emperor had delivered a sort of early preservation edict, commanding that the garden be maintained in perpetuity as a retreat for retired emperors, but since no other emperors retired, it became the beneficiary of benign neglect for the remaining decades of the Qing dynasty. Over six hundred years, the princes' residences and concubines' quarters were rebuilt numerous times – but not the Juanqinzhai. This is the only spot that has the complete vision of one emperor. A dowager empress lived there for a little while, and some members of the court had birthday parties there. Pu Yi, the last emperor, added a painting to the complex. Otherwise, it stood empty, then was locked up in 1924 and used only as storage space by Palace Museum staff focused on the public areas of the Forbidden City. When it was unlocked in 1999, as the Palace Museum began to prepare itself for the Olympic bid, it was a time capsule – one of the few survivors of the attack on history that was China's twentieth century. It was weathered, faded and a bit decayed, but it retained its integrity, and conserving it would require little of the guesswork that has plagued interventions at other historic Chinese buildings.

The Qianlong Emperor, the sixth ruler of the Manchu Qing dynasty, ruled officially from 1735 to 1796, though he effectively reigned until 1799. He was noted for his brilliance as a child, anointed over his brothers for his sobriety of demeanour, his learning in literature and philosophy and his ease in human relations. He was a man of towering ambition, China's equivalent to Louis XIV, Catherine the Great or Emperor Franz Josef. He expanded China's borders and became the wealthiest man in the world; at the height of his rule, China held a positive balance of trade with the West. The author of more than forty thousand poems, he was an impeccable connoisseur with wit, elegance and artistic talent on his side. But he also oversaw the burning of books and the torture and execution of writers whose work displeased him. Qianlong styled himself in later life as 'the old man of the ten perfect victories' – and indeed he had consolidated Qing rule and increased the size of China by a third; at his death, his country's population had grown more than 20 per cent.

Qianlong was the grandson of the Kangxi Emperor, the longest-serving ruler in Chinese history. As a matter of respect, Qianlong was determined not to overshadow his grandfather's reign, and with this in mind he envisioned retirement – the first emperor to contemplate such a step. For a meaningful disengagement from the machinery of state, he wanted a garden, which he envisioned as a marvellous landscape of sculpted rocks and pavilions. He undertook the project when he was in his early sixties, though he would not consider retirement until he reached eighty-five, one year short of his grandfather's dominion. The design and construction of his own quarters there, the Juanqinzhai, occupied the emperor from 1771 to 1774; its decoration took another two years. During this period, he handed off most matters of state, allowing corruption to infiltrate his court. After Qianlong's death, his son-in-law Hashen was forced to commit suicide because he had accumulated so much illicit wealth. Qianlong's sixty-year rule was the most stable in the world, which allowed for great prosperity, but also engendered cultural stagnation. China was bypassed by modernity and the early glimmers of industrialisation. In the period following Qianlong's rule, foreigners came into China, and overspending on wars and putting down rebellions impoverished the court.

The Juanqinzhai project manifests Qianlong's blend of finesse, brilliance and decadent laxity; he built this precious sanctuary as an artistic diversion and never spent a night in it. Though he entered his so-called retirement in 1796, he effectively reigned until his death three years later, refusing to move out of the emperor's quarters or relinquish his authority.

The retirement garden reproduces the basic imperial processional structure. Its main buildings evoke the primary edifices of the larger complex, with similar public courtyards preceding private ones. Its almost two acres were meant to encapsulate the overall structure of the 180-acre Forbidden City. It was also intended as an outsize version of a scholar's garden, adapting subtle landscape principles from the southern gardens of Suzhou, Yangzhou and Hangzhou for grand purposes. It would not be a classic scholar's rockery, nor a locus of imperial magnificence; it would blend the contemplative poetry of one with the stately ambition of the other. For Europeans, mountains represent the terrifying sublime, but for the Chinese, they represent paradise, the geography of the enlightened. The garden evokes such a geography.

This is a winter garden, intended for use during the months when the emperor remained in the Forbidden City. The complex is divided into four courtyards on a north–south axis. This arrangement ensures that the visitor does not experience the space as long and narrow, but rather as a sequence of near squares. Narrow gates – the complex is entered via a curved path through a slit between two rockeries – provide a human scale. To its twenty-seven structures, the emperor gave names that signalled his hopes for the place: one enters through the Gate of Spreading Auspiciousness and passes through, among others, the Hall of Fulfilling Original Wishes (one of the tallest buildings in the Forbidden City), the Building of Extending Delight, the Belvedere of Viewing Achievements and the Supreme Chamber of Cultivating Harmony. The emperor himself not only named such buildings, but also was the primary designer of the garden. The Lodge of Bamboo Fragrance is conceived as a book; its ornament is entirely calligraphy. Many of the original furnishings were made of rootwood, a costly technique valued by emperors but intended to show disregard for human refinement in favour of the Buddhist ideal of unalloyed nature.

The divide in China between court intrigue and the life of scholars, which is central to any study of the country's culture, had been recorded since the Warring States period (475 to 221 BC) and was refined into an often deliberately awkward aesthetic for those outside the court during the Northern Song dynasty (AD 960 to 1127). Though scholar-painters, often banished for their criticisms of the government, produced paintings and poems in miserable exile, it was widely accepted that their work was of greater consequence than the showy, decorative work of the court. Indeed, paintings and calligraphy by many of the scholars who had been ejected from the capital later entered the Imperial Collection. Literati aesthetics define Qianlong's garden project, informed by his travels to inspect the southern territories of his realm. The rockeries, plantings and waterways at the retirement garden, all constructed on a flat piece of land, evoke the mountain landscapes of southern China as portrayed in Song and Ming paintings. The meandering nature of the classical scholar's garden had succumbed in the Ming period to the symmetries of northern taste. In the Qianlong garden, Suzhou's surprising vistas and winding paths have been brought into Manchu discipline, but some of that easy wandering has been re-engaged in a concise, synthetic form.

The life envisioned for the Juanqinzhai was solitary, as befits the literati ideal of contemplation; the elegant building bespeaks cultivated seclusion. 'Exhausted from diligent service,' Qianlong wrote, 'I will cultivate myself, rejecting worldly noise.' The richly ornamented theatre that occupies much of the interior has only one seat. But despite this literati conception, the construction of the Juanqinzhai reflects Qianlong's ebullient profligacy; even the building's framing timbers are polished hardwoods. The eastern five of the Juanqinzhai's nine bays contain the emperor's living quarters, ranged over two levels, and include sleeping and sitting platforms in sixteen separate spaces. This flank features an entire wall of *zitan*, the purple sandalwood beloved of emperors, then exceedingly rare and now nearly extinct. Large jade cartouches are set into screens. Double-sided embroidery, that rare Suzhou art, was employed in the fabrication of 173 translucent interior windows. On the lower face of the wall are scenes of deer amid woods. The background consists of patterned *zitan* marquetry, over which a foreground of carved inner-bamboo skin (*tiehuang*) is applied. The upper storey shows a scene of peacocks, magpies and phoenixes realised with the same methods and materials. Other parts of the screen are ornamented with bamboo-thread marquetry, a labour-intensive means of achieving a variegated, patterned background for surface-mounted ornamentation. These techniques, usually employed for small decorative objects, here are translated onto vast surfaces – the only known instance of such architectural application. The lacquer work in the building is likewise of unique complexity and scale. Porcelain wall insets show the sophistication of a precious vase; wall panels are inlaid in azurite, jade, jasper and other semi-precious stones. The handmade wallpaper is impressed with mica and then printed in malachite. The interior includes one of the largest cloisonné objects ever produced, a hanging pair of couplets in the emperor's own hand. Qianlong was involved every step of the way. The archives record his request that a particular doorknob be replaced with cloisonné, as indeed it was.

The Juanqinzhai is notable for its embrace of foreign influences. Qianlong imported enormous mirrors, which would have been an unspeakable conceit in eighteenth-century China. While the cabinets in the Juanqinzhai are ornately Chinese, their asymmetry shows Japanese influence. The exterior windows are glazed with European glass, and the use of glass in the throne has a kind of occidenterie parallel to the distorted version of China evident in Western chinoiserie. The four western bays of the Juanqinzhai, which contain the theatre with its stage and throne, boast latticework that has been faux-painted on hardwood to resemble the more ephemeral, less durable speckled bamboo. The walls and ceiling are covered in spectacular *trompe-l'oeil* paintings that make use of the foreshortening and single-point perspective developed in Renaissance Italy. They were heavily influenced by the work of Giuseppe Castiglione, a Jesuit painter, missionary and imperial adviser who lived in China from 1715 until his death in 1766 and was known by the Chinese as Lang Shining. The murals may incorporate elements painted by Castiglione, though the Juanqinzhai project was undertaken after he died. The ceiling is particularly seductive, with its depiction of a bamboo trellis groaning under the weight of a spectacular wisteria in full bloom – a joyful symbol of many generations of offspring. The wall murals represent a garden, extending the outside aesthetic to the interior. Here, painted peonies would have continued to bloom, skies to remain summer blue through the long, cold Beijing winters. The murals were painted on silk, using Chinese pigment in a Western style applied in keeping with a Chinese aesthetic. The Chinese influence on Western art during this period has been much pondered, but this entangled reciprocity, though less frequent and perhaps less profound, also warrants notice.

Qianlong liked the fantasy of being a hermit in the mountains. The Juanqinzhai clearly reflects the ambivalent nature of such fantasies. He saw no discontinuity between being the richest man in the world and leading an ascetic life. He claimed to want to be known as 'the man with nothing to do' – but he never pursued such leisure. It is a sign of imperial decadence at every level to pour enormous resources into keeping choice awake for the sake of choice itself, rather than because you want to make such choices. The pleasure of this garden of contemplation was its construction rather than its inhabitance; he built it to impress himself. Yet the content of the garden suggests a deep commitment to Buddhist precepts. Confucian thought suggests that in order to rule, an emperor had to be an enlightened being, and the garden complex expresses the aspiration to enlightenment, a place where Qianlong could seek the humbleness of his human consciousness, apart from his status as emperor. He appears to have felt that his Buddhist goals were his ultimate ones.

The Manchu Qing subscribed to Tibetan Buddhism rather than the Chan Buddhism that had been more popular in China. The Manchus were allies with the Mongolians in the seventeenth century, and the Dalai Lama conferred a living Buddha status on the Manchu rulers in the mid-1600s. Tibetan Buddhism is more orthodox, as far from Chan Buddhism as Catholicism is from Protestantism. It is focused on compassion towards others, rather than on an inward journey to find enlightenment within the self. Qianlong had been brought up alongside a living Buddha, a Mongolian named Rolpai Dorje, who came to live in the court and was educated with Qianlong. He became the Qianlong Emperor's Buddhist mentor, teacher and guide. Identified as a descendant of the bodhisattva Manjusri, Qianlong made extended visits throughout his life to the holy sites at Mount Wutai, where a lock of Manjusri's hair was said to reside. Qianlong may have escalated into decadence in his later years, but he also aspired to mental cultivation, and the garden is full of spots for meditation and contemplation. The vision behind it, though expensive, is extremely spiritual. Qianlong meditated daily; he built many temples; he had many Buddhist images created. The notion of opulent Buddhism may sound oxymoronic to some Western ears, but it is the guiding principle here. The Tibetan aesthetic is evident in the garden.

Westerners have often perceived the decoration of the buildings and the structure of the garden as separate things, the natural and the man-made, the inner self of thought separated from outward action. These Cartesian dualities do not parse in Qianlong's sensibility; the interiors of the Juanqinzhai are all made with views of what lies outside them, and there is no such thing as 'house' or 'garden' – only a single complex. Man, being made by nature, makes only a further show of nature.

It is never easy to form a human portrait of a Chinese emperor. The godlike aspect of these men enters the public record, and the personal is usually so well hidden from view that it can be difficult to know whether it existed. The Qianlong Garden helps. In it, one begins to sense that this emperor was a person, and not just the supreme instrument of an absolute power structure. He had his own interests and personality and desires – spiritual or otherwise. Qianlong was in many ways a romantic; his first wife died at forty, but he wrote her letters in the form of poems until he died.

Received opinion in the West has often suggested that Chinese aesthetics reached an apex in the late Song and early Ming dynasties, declined through the early Qing, and then reached a nadir post-Qianlong. The quality of the craftsmanship at the Juanqinzhai sometimes exceeds the quality of the taste, as opulence upstages subtlety. Many Western connoisseurs prefer Chinese monochrome and minimalism, and some feel that even work from the reign of the Yongzheng Emperor, Qianlong's father, is more refined than this. But Qianlong represents the full efflorescence of Qing taste, and many contemporary Chinese revel in riotous pattern and golden enamel, preferring such exuberance to austere discipline. 'If Qianlong were alive today,' one scholar said, 'he would be wearing Versace.' At a time when Westerners are 'discovering' Victorian architecture and mid-century modernism, Qing monuments should be valued before they are past saving.

In 1998, I went to see the Garden of the Palace of Established Happiness in the Forbidden City, which was then being rebuilt in part under the aegis of the delightfully named Happy Harun. That garden, roughly contemporaneous with the Juanqinzhai, had burned down in 1923 and was being reconstructed on the basis of images and the surviving plinths of buildings. One of the workers there described how the Chinese minister of culture had come to visit the work and had said, 'All the wooden structures are beautiful, but the stone is in terrible condition and should be replaced.' The worker explained that the stone was what survived of the original buildings, and that it was being conserved accordingly. The minister of culture said, 'Would you wear a new suit with old shoes?'

That attitude meant that the restoration teams for the Juanqinzhai had their work cut out for them: shifting the sensibility of reconstruction to one of conservation. To complicate matters further, the techniques used in the Juanqinzhai were so refined as to be beyond the skills of living craftsmen. For example, the building made some use of a stiffened, lacquered gauze for which the technique is lost (though the same technique was used in Han dynasty shoes and Song dynasty hats); we can reproduce its appearance, but not the thing itself. The World Monuments Fund introduced the protocols through which scientific technique and microscopy could help determine most of the original processes used to achieve an effect or finish; this allowed for those processes, often involving many layers of ornament, to be reproduced with precision. The conservation of the Juanqinzhai has had to blend Eastern and Western concepts, aesthetics, techniques and materials, as the original building and grounds did. Long-lost crafts had to be reinvented and relearned, then squared with modern technologies. It took science to understand the vanished techniques and science to reconceive them, though the execution was a matter of extraordinary finesse.

In upscaling miniature techniques, Qianlong's craftsmen had devised new sub-layers to support them. Conservators accustomed to working on small objects had to figure out how to expand restoration practises they developed for snuffboxes and other small works of art to be viable on large architectural surfaces. The governors of southern provinces were contacted in a quest to locate skilled artisans, who came from Anhui, west of Nanjing, and Zhejiang, south of Shanghai. The conservators working on the project felt that the paper used in the restoration should be of Chinese manufacture, so an expert paper-maker from England came to train Chinese workers in a technique originally invented in China. All of the work had to be done within the walls of the Forbidden City to avoid the risk of sending out an original and getting back a masterful copy. Partly on the basis of experience its faculty gained on this international collaboration, Tsinghua University's Cultural Heritage Conservation Center now offers a postgraduate degree in Architectural Conservation for Wood Structures and Historic Interiors and Furniture. This is the first advanced degree available in the conservation of historic Chinese interiors and wood furniture.

The garden and its structures, built so an emperor could play at being a hermit-philosopher, do not show how he lived, given that he never lived there. Rather, they show how he thought: it is how he wanted paradise to look. It is an essay about the end of life, a musing on what it means to grow old. In its immoderate poetry, luxurious appointments and baroque austerity, it expresses the ambiguities of power and detachment. Marie Antoinette was given to simulating ingenuousness with her shepherdess's crook at her Hameau in Versailles about the same time the Qianlong Emperor was building the retirement garden, but what seems like affectation in her points to a genuine idealism in him. On the cloisonné plaque that hung in the Juanqinzhai are the emperor's words: 'Purity and order in the mind on tens of thousands of issues are to be held in one heart.' An emperor's life entails the chaos of an unruly realm; the retirement garden was to be the place where so complicated a life could be made lucid, yet remain undiminished.

Adventures in Antarctica

Travel + Leisure, November 2008

Disaster tourism is a dubious trade in taking people to see vanishing places before they are lost – though the hope is that letting people see them will inspire those people to fight to save them. Antarctica is acutely vulnerable. As huge pieces of it melt and the temperature of the sea changes, the world's ecosystems are thrown into crisis. It is always more shocking to see a great man fall than a lesser one; that is why we read the tragedies of history so closely, and why the heroes in Shakespeare are so often kings. Antarctica is a mighty emperor about to dissolve.

It would have been worth noting, when my husband and I signed up for the *Nimrod* Centennial Expedition to Antarctica, that Sir Ernest Shackleton's pole-seeking *Nimrod* expedition had been a failure, and that venturing south under his name might be tempting fate. But we were trying to do only what he had accomplished – in fact, only part of what he had accomplished – and not what he had aspired to do. With a hundred years of technological advancement, we anticipated that we would easily reach the hut he had built at the edge of the Ross Sea, meant to last one winter a century ago but still standing, testament to his high standards and to a climate hostile even to the microorganisms that cause rot.

Before we launched at 4:00 p.m. on New Year's Day 2008 from the same berth in Lyttelton, New Zealand, that Shackleton had used at the same hour on 1 January 1908, we were blessed in the Anglican church where Shackleton's party had prayed and sang the hymn they had sung, with its Cassandra refrain, 'O hear us when we cry to Thee / For those in peril on the sea'. A substantial public had gathered, including descendants of Shackleton's crew. A brass band played; Samoyeds whose forebears had pulled Shackleton's sledges barked as the crowd waved us off; and we were escorted to sea by the very tugboat that had pulled the *Nimrod*.

Tied onto the upper-deck railing of our vessel, a small banner – the sort a launderette might use to announce its grand opening – read SPIRIT OF ENDERBY, in accordance with our voyage's promotional material. Gigantic Cyrillic letters on the hull, by contrast, proclaimed the boat as PROFESSOR KHROMOV, as did the lifeboats, the maps and the equipment on board; we entered and left ports as *Professor Khromov* because that was in fact the name of the ship. *Spirit of Enderby* was a flight of the enthusiastic imagination of Rodney Russ, owner of Heritage Expeditions and our trip leader. The same advance material had referred to a 'refurbished Russian ice-class ship'. The word *refurbished* had suggested rather more intervention than the installation of industrial blue carpet throughout a Soviet research vessel from 1983 – but we had not come for opulent cabins, and the spartan accommodations seemed, then, to be part of the macho bravado of our enterprise.

The first attraction on our month-long itinerary, two days later, was the Snares, some of the sparse scatter of subantarctic islands between New Zealand and Antarctica. The Snares pulse with such dense birdlife that every path disrupts nesting or breeding grounds, so we toured in Zodiacs and saw the charming endemic crested penguins. Back on board, my partner, John, and I mingled with the other forty-six passengers, including two other Americans, one Canadian, one guy from Costa Rica and a smattering of New Zealanders, Australians, white Zimbabweans and Namibians, and Brits. Sailing onward, we ran into forty-foot swells, which made me feel like a washcloth endlessly stuck in a tumble dryer; the *Professor Khromov*'s ice capacities, we learned, meant a loss of stability in rough seas. We figured out how to wedge our possessions so that the sound of laptops smashing into cameras was muted by sweaters and thermal underwear. Even in the relative safety of your cabin, your head would at times ram into one end of your bunk, compressing the neck, then your feet would ram into the other and compress the knees. I had hoped to lose weight, not height, during an athletic adventure in challenging climates.

Enderby Island, the first shore stop, stayed mercifully fixed in one place, as islands tend to do. The entire landmass is covered in scrub: forests of flowering shrubs; other thick, prickly plants that cling to the cold, hard earth; and a variety of tufted grasses that were beautiful to view and hard to navigate. We saw a stupefying array of birds, including skuas, several species of albatross, and the occasional yellow-eyed penguin. We came across Hooker's sea lions everywhere, and you could see why they were called lions: they were the size of refrigerators, with ruffed collars, and if you came too close to them – as you sometimes did given all the undergrowth – they would lift up their heads and roar. Something about their decision to skip the beach and plop themselves in the thickets was surreal, as though they were trying to trick you into believing that they were properly land animals. They would periodically raise themselves up on their four flippers and walk labouriously across the grass, ponderous and deliberate as old donkeys.

More rough seas led us two days later to Macquarie Island, a nature reserve with a small research station that allows only a few hundred visitors a year. Its shoreline is carpeted in wildlife: royal, king, gentoo and rockhopper penguins, as well as elephant seals. The penguins gather around you curiously, and if you hold out a hand to one of the royals, he will nibble on your finger. Using their flipper-like wings primarily to gesticulate, nodding back and forth to each other as they ran around, the penguins looked like commuters milling about Grand Central before their departure track has been announced, some of them moulting like elderly women in moth-eaten fur coats. More than two hundred thousand breeding pairs of king penguins live at one end of the island, packed in conditions that make

Tokyo look roomy. The seals tended to plop on top of one another, forming the sort of pyramids that high school cheerleaders perfected in the 1950s. The young ones had inconceivably sweet faces with huge, liquid eyes; the older males had long, knobby, trunk-like noses, wobbling and battle scarred.

We had passed through the Roaring Forties and Furious Fifties of latitude, a circumpolar storm belt, and now we were ready for the protracted crossing of the Southern Ocean, where no substantial land-masses slow the winds whipping around the globe. Rodney held a com-petition to guess when we'd see the first iceberg; the ship's bird expert counted off species at sea; and the immanence of the seventh continent was great in us. Shackleton attracts Gurdjieff-like devotion, and the ship was awash in experts on polar exploration. The waves gradually gave up the bright, rough quality they'd had in the subantarctic; the water grew thick and sluggish, almost like the muscles of a slow-moving colossus rippling under taut skin. On 12 January, we found ourselves in a jigsaw puzzle of floating pack ice, the dark lines of the water sketching through snow-dusted shards like a great black spiderweb.

The ice fragments measured up to twenty feet across, in shapes that suggested an eagle, a Volkswagen Beetle, an emoticon, a relief map of Spain. Most climates have sunlight and shadow or else a neutral grey, but here we found an amplified, shadowless ice-white like a strobe. Some of the older ice wore an apron of turquoise just below the waterline, and a few of the icebergs had refracted pockets of cerulean. Elsewhere, much of what is beautiful can be seen in a glance, but what strikes the visitor to this area is the hostile, exquisite, primitive vastness of it, which you can interpret only by entering it. The world ends in ice. Russian crewmen stood at the prow looking out for thick obstructions, and the first mate directed us accordingly to port or starboard; the captain reviewed navigational charts from the bridge. The boat would ride up a little on the finer, floating ice, then the weight of the hull would bear down and the ice would crack open. Late that afternoon, we were all called onto the foredeck for mulled wine as we crossed the Antarctic Circle.

Heading south at about 180 degrees longitude, where seasonal currents usually facilitate passage through the Ross Sea, we entered the endless daylight of the antarctic high summer, and we stayed up that night and the next, many of us, until 2:30 a.m. to take it in. The morning that followed, 14 January, we woke to bad news. At a 'briefing' in the airless lecture room in the ship's bowels, Rodney announced that the pack ice was thicker than expected, and that we had turned around at 3:00 a.m. to retrace our course so we could attempt to re-enter the ice further east. 'The boat could have made it through the way we were going,' he said to us, 'but we face a hundred and fifty miles of pack ice and were going just three knots.' My rudimentary maths showed that this meant it would have taken us two more days to get through, and I wondered about the wisdom of losing a day going backward, but lack of experience rendered me mute. Dmitri, the captain, spoke next. 'This boat not icebroker,' he said in his affectingly poor English. 'This ice too much.'

Someone voiced our collective fear: 'Is there a chance of our not getting through at all?'

Rodney's face was ashen. 'I have made thirty-six trips to the Antarctic, and I've always got through.' He spoke as though his oldest friend were standing him up for a dinner he had organised in its honour. When we went on deck, those great expanses of sea ice that had, when we'd first seen them, given us such joyous anticipation of the frozen world we had come to explore were now brooding and unwelcome barricades to our advance. Whereas we had once felt glee at the soft *ka-thunk* of the boat heaving against them, we now felt constant concern that we were in an icy cul-de-sac, stopped short of the tantalisingly proximate Ross Sea. Our sunny exchanges took on a forced quality, like comments about fine weather in a POW camp. Over the next day, we lived in a strange bunker-afloat mentality. We went down regularly for briefings in the lecture room, and Rodney would tell us what looked good in the ice maps, and Dmitri would tell us what looked bad, and some passengers would champion making a go of it and some would champion giving up.

The ship followed an iceward course at 178 degrees. At bedtime the third night following, the ship was rising up and sinking down on the ice, but we woke in a motionless vessel and obediently trooped down to the lecture room yet again. Rodney had been staying up until

3:00 a.m. every night to try to seduce or bully Dmitri into sticking the course; Dmitri wanted to go to bed by 3:00 a.m., and the passengers were out of the way by then, and so that was the ritual hour of the journey's failures. To the casual observer, the ice we had been going through seemed much of a muchness, and the boat seemed to go through it now faster, now slower, but steadily. But once more at 3:00 a.m., the captain had declared the ice impassable. Rodney acknowledged that it was atypically dense for the season, but emphasised that the ship could do it. The captain, who had a distinctively Russian ability to be uncommunicative and melodramatic at the same time, said that the ice was 'still too much' and shrugged. He said, 'I try hardly', which we feared might be more accurate than 'I try hard', which is what he had intended to say. It seemed we would not get through.

Rodney's eyes filled with tears as he explained how hard it was for him to fail, as though his situation warranted the primary sympathy. At first everyone was terribly British and stiff upper lips were kept and socks were pulled up, but many passengers later admitted to crying in their cabins that day, as if the warm saline of their tears could melt the frozen brine in our way. A few ascended into sanctimonious homilies about how inspiring it was to be reminded that one couldn't always get what one wanted from nature. Then someone asked the obvious question: If we were not going to Antarctica, what exactly were we going to do for the next fifteen days? Rodney said he hadn't really thought about it. 'What do you want to do?' he asked. It was folly to offer a vote to a group of travellers who were neither united nor informed. Before long, desperate and obscure proposals were flying around the room.

The *Professor Khromov* filled up with contagious sadness. It was not a grand or opulent trip, but it was an exceedingly expensive one to which people had made very profound commitments. Conrad's family had saved for eight years to give him this trip as a fiftieth birthday present. Lynne, who had done a previous trip with Heritage, had persuaded her husband and five of their friends to join this great adventure. Nick's mother had asked him on her deathbed to take the little inheritance she could leave and spend it on his childhood dream of visiting Antarctica. Greg had used up all his holiday and some unpaid leave, and would not have time off again until 2009. Lauren had given up her retirement and worked an entire year to pay for her trip with Stephen. And the cool kids – Dean, José, Glenn, John and Carol – were professional crew on high-level yachts and had signed up for this expedition three years earlier, exhausting their savings. There was something Shakespearean about the disappointment, and nothing could be done about it. The British tendency to make the best of a bad situation butted up against the American habit of pursuing impossible dreams. The British and New Zealanders tended to think we had been given lemons and had best make lemonade. The Aussies, Americans and Africans thought we had been given lemons and might as well throw them at the authors of our frustration.

The first night after the surrender, only a few of us stood sentinel to look at the endless expanses of sea ice. Yet in a way, it was hard to believe how disappointed we all felt to be in this strange world. Out on the deck, I was lost in the wonderment of where we were as much as in the sorrow of where we weren't, because the so-called midnight sun had made a spectacular debut at about ten o'clock and gilded a mackerel sky over the hummocky meringue of the furrowed ice. There were mammals and seabirds to see, and we vied to document them with our many digital cameras – the rare Ross seal and the common Adélie penguins alike. The Adélies were scattered, one here and four there, and sat complacently on their islets of sea ice until our boat was almost upon them, then belly-flopped into the water. The snow petrels circled us, resembling, when the sun caught their white feathers, images of the Holy Spirit in Northern Renaissance paintings. If you stood on the metal steps so that you could lean over the prow, you could catch your own prismatic reflection in the shiniest bits of broken ice before the ship sundered them. The air itself was a purifying tonic.

Yet some churlishness in us couldn't be satisfied with the permanent light of the white nonworld in which we were hopelessly adrift, short of our last continent and outside of time. It is true in general, but especially true of travel, that people are thrilled with anything extra and distraught about anything expected and missed. You may never have heard of the pudding-toed tree chameleon or the Cloister Court of St Yvette, but when your guide tells you that you've been privileged with a rare sighting of the lizard, or that you are catching the nunnery open at the whim of the sisters, you are elated. When the opposite happens, you feel not just disappointed but betrayed. You curse yourself for having spent so much money on an experience you're not having. You resent in advance the refrain that will begin, 'Well, actually, we didn't get there.'

Our hopes radically reduced, we lined up a day later for a Zodiac cruise around Scott Island, a seldom-visited outcropping of rock north of the thickest pack ice. Thrillingly, we saw a predatory leopard seal – they have been known to attack humans – sunning himself, looking like a cross between a sea slug and a dinosaur. At that after-noon's briefing, Rodney said he thought ice might be clearing to the south and proposed that we wait near Scott Island a day or two, on the chance that we could still make it through. Even the atheists went to bed that night thick with prayers. We found a fragile camaraderie in staving off despair, as though going through this experience were forging soldiers' bonds among us, though also with a creeping *Huis Clos* feeling that we could not escape one another.

At a time when the environment is under siege and ice shelves are famously dwindling, something about the dwarfing scale of the landscape was reassuring. All of us had come fearful of the greening of Antarctica, and what we found was relentless frozen serenity. Hoping that we would stay the course and break through to the continent, we were still awestruck and humbled by the majesty around us, and while we prayed the thick ice would vanish out of our ship's course, we hoped it would not vanish from the earth.

The following day, we stayed close to Scott Island and waited some more. The terrible briefings were getting to be like consciousness-raising sessions of the mid-1970s at which each participant got to say his or her piece while the others gritted their teeth. Rodney now focused on how long it would take us to get out of the Ross Sea if we got in, but trouble returning seemed less alarming than not getting in at all. I began to understand those historic explorers who wanted to reach the poles so much that they trekked into uncharted territory not knowing if they would ever return, losing limbs to frostbite, dis-appearing into crevasses or whiteout storms. Dmitri now announced that getting through the ice would take several days, that we'd have to come back through the same ice, and that we no longer had sufficient time for the round-trip. Rodney said, unconvincingly, that the captain was right.

People were both shattered and outraged. Now the problem was time, after all these days had been expended on so much back-and-forth. Rodney had thought that we could get through. Dmitri had refused to go. We had been pawns in a contest of personalities. What nature does, one accepts with some degree of grace. What human cupidity has caused makes one furious. If the message had been conveyed to us that the problem was truly the ice, we would have accepted it, but the manner of bungling incompetence and personal conflict made it hard to swallow. That night, up on the bridge, Ian observed that we were going only nine knots, 'as this boat was built more for comfort than for speed'. Mary said, 'I'm not sure it was built for either, really.' That was about the size of it. A number of people on board were reading *The Worst Journey in the World*, the brilliant account of Robert Falcon Scott's fatal expedition of 1910–13, and we began referring to the *Nimrod* Centennial as 'the second-worst journey in the world'.

We still had two weeks left. We would go west to hunt icebergs, then head back to New Zealand via the subantarctic. So far, we had been on solid ground four times, and the intrepid adventurers on board were going stir-crazy. I have always hated being cold, but for those imprisoned days, shivering on deck was oddly thrilling, and I relished that touch of frozen numbness in my fingers and at the tip of my nose. The cold was antarctic even if we didn't have the continent under our feet; it physicalised our brief kinship with the penguins and seals and whales. To reassure ourselves that we had gone somewhere, we tossed off new vocabulary: grease ice and pancake ice, frazil ice and hummocky ice, tabular bergs and bergy bits, first-year ice and multi-year ice, and brash ice and sastrugi. It's not the Inuit who have a hundred words for snow; we do.

We eventually reached icebergs. Many looked almost avant-garde; we saw the Frank Gehry iceberg and the Santiago Calatrava iceberg and the endearingly old-fashioned Frank Lloyd Wright iceberg, not to mention various Walmart and IKEA icebergs along the way. They put to rest the common wisdom that snow is white: snow is blue, with white reflections glinting off it in certain light, except that it is sometimes green or yellow, and very occasionally striated with pink. Caught in its glacial heart is the dense snow that absorbs all but the bluest light, that glows as if neon fragments of the tropical sky had been trapped in a southbound gale and transported here. The last tabular iceberg we approached marked our final farewell to the fantasy of Antarctica that had brought us together. It was the most beautiful we had visited, and the largest, and while we were close to it in our Zodiac, it calved a slab the size of a walk-up apartment, which plunged into the gelid sea with a roar worthy of the Fourth of July.

Among the islands of our funereally slow return, Campbell Island was a joy. The royal albatross nests there, and a group of us were privileged to see a rare changing of the guard, when the male comes to relieve the female from sitting on their egg, so she can fly out to sea and get food. After half an hour of affectionate mutual grooming, the female cautiously stepped off the nest and the male settled in for his long shift. Even the tour's ornithologist had never seen this ritual before.

Otherwise, our strategy consisted largely of approaching an island to take in the view of its hills, then climbing the hills to look at the view of the boat, then returning to the boat for a last look at the hills. Rodney would charge ahead, leaving his older clients to struggle over steep and muddy ravines unassisted. People were crossing off the days: not that the islands were uninteresting, but Heritage offers tours of the subantarctic that last as little as a week and cost about $5,000 per person. This trip, by the time we had paid the various extras, had cost the magazine that sent us more than $40,000 for a double cabin, not including airfare to New Zealand or unreimbursed time away from work.

We waited for Rodney to propose at least a partial refund, or even to give us an open bar for one night, but it never came. When I confronted him, he said, 'This trip has cost me as much as if we'd made it through.' That last evening, the weather was inconceivably lovely, and we stood in that bright warmth, so opposite to our purpose, and were depressed as hell by the clear blue sky, the shimmering water, the gentle beauty of the summery New Zealand shore.

We were like foreign visitors who had dreamed all their lives of seeing New York City and set off with that goal only to end up stuck in downtown Newark with no way home for a month. Disappointment had surged in waves. There was the initial shock. Then there was a lulled feeling that one couldn't stay upset indefinitely, and the very real pleasure of seeing more than a hundred species of birds, some two dozen mammals, and a sea's worth of ice. Finally, there was the sensation of getting off that boat without having done what we'd set out to do – a feeling of rage, failure, gullibility, self-blame and doubt. We had boarded the vessel with the hopefulness of youth rekindled in us, and we came back with the disaffection of age.

Initially, we had viewed the informality of Heritage Expeditions as unpretentiousness and relished the aura of discovery that Rodney conjured. The *Nimrod* Centennial had turned into a disaster because a real problem in nature had coincided with equally real amateurism. We later learned that another boat, the *Marina Svetaeva*, faced with the same ice at the same time, had changed course and made an Antarctic landing in Commonwealth Bay. There was something lovely and fresh about Heritage's bluster, something almost heartbreaking in the feeling that we were all in this together. We never quite felt that we were tourists who'd purchased services; we felt like strangers who had met in friendship and agreed to hold hands and stride boldly into the world's greatest remaining wilderness. Travelling this way has a potent romance, but also risk, and for us, alas, the risk outstripped the romance. Had we reached the great white bottom of the world, I would have loved the very qualities that, in our failed trip, I deplored. Still, we had witnessed kinds of beauty that few men have seen. We held that warm happiness against the hard ice of our regret.

The sea ice that impinged on our trip has become even more abundant as glaciers continue to break up, making it increasingly difficult even for scientists to reach their research stations. Ice blockages are exacerbated by the fierce wind that results from the depletion of polar ozone, the increase of greenhouse gases and the temperature differential caused as the tropics warm faster than Antarctica. Those winds drive relatively warmer water up under glaciers, causing them to melt. Structural characteristics of certain glaciers of West Antarctica render them particularly vulnerable; degeneration of the West Antarctic ice sheet will likely raise sea levels by at least four feet in the near future, a process NASA describes as 'unstoppable'. Meanwhile the Totten Glacier in East Antarctica is taking on warm water through two gateways. The glacier holds back land ice three-quarters the size of Texas; if it melts, sea levels could rise by a further eleven feet.

On 24 March 2015, a record-high recorded temperature of 63.5 degrees Fahrenheit was logged at Esperanza Base on the northern tip of the Antarctic Peninsula. New varieties of fungi are cropping up in Antarctica, buoyed by such warmer temperatures; the number of fungal varietals could be up by a quarter by the end of the twenty-first century. Such fungi could support an onslaught of invasive species. Warmer weather has made Antarctica an attractive destination for king crabs, which may pose significant risk to other sea animals that lack defences against them. Melting glaciers deposit iron in the water, which is good for phytoplankton, which is in turn good for penguins, but which also significantly disrupts the ecosystem.

The ban on polar mining established by the Antarctic Treaty expires in 2048. The Chinese have already built four research stations on the frozen continent and are working on a fifth. China is harvesting vast quantities of krill from Antarctic waters. Liu Shenli, the chairman of the China National Agricultural Development Group, said, 'The Antarctic is a treasure house for all human beings, and China should go there and share.' China has recently signed a five-year accord with Australia that permits vessels to refuel before continuing south; that pact will enable the Chinese to harvest sea life, exploit the continent's abundant oil and mineral resources, and obtain fresh water from icebergs. Anne-Marie Brady, a professor of political science at the University of Canterbury in New Zealand, said, 'China is playing a long game in Antarctica,' adding that the wish to initiate mining operations there has been broadcast 'loud and clear to domestic audiences'.

When Everyone Signs

Far from the Tree, 2012

Nicholas Evans, an Australian linguist I met in 2006 when we were on a shared fellowship programme, told me about a village in Bali where a hereditary strain of deafness had led to the development of a deaf-normative culture, and I had long wanted to visit. After the frustrations of our Antarctica trip, John and I were pleased to stop in Bali on the way home so that I could pursue this research.

When I described Bengkala as an idyll in *Far from the Tree*, some readers supposed I was enthusing about the primitive lives of noble savages. I would never want to gloss over the struggles of people in villages such as this one. It is utopian only from a disability-rights perspective. Deaf people the world over experience social exclusion; a society in which everyone can sign responds to a common dream of shared fluency even if that idyll is circumscribed by the toil of subsistence farming in an impoverished locale.

In the small village of Bengkala in northern Bali, a congenital form of deafness has persisted for some 250 years; at any time, it affects about 2 per cent of the population. Everyone in Bengkala has grown up with deaf people and knows the unique sign language used in the village, so the gap between the experience of hearing and deaf people is narrower than perhaps anywhere else in the world. I found that where deafness is commonplace, it is not much of a handicap. Deaf and hearing people marry each other freely, and people are essentially as happy with a deaf child as with a hearing one.

Bengkala is also known as Desa Kolok, or Deaf Village. When I went in 2008, forty-six of the village's two thousand residents were deaf. I met hearing parents with deaf children, deaf parents with hearing children, deaf families with deaf parents and children, deaf or hearing parents with a mix of deaf and hearing children. It's a poor village, and the general education level is low, but it has been even lower among the deaf. The only education for deaf people supplied by the government was in a signed version of Indonesian, and the only school for the deaf in Bali was in the capital, Denpasar. Signed Indonesian uses an aural grammar to dictate a sequence of signs; people whose grammar is primarily visual find it difficult to learn. Kanta, a hearing teacher in the village, introduced a programme in 2007 to educate the deaf of Bengkala in their own sign language, Kata Kolok; the first deaf class had pupils from ages seven to fourteen because none had had any previous formal education. They were learning fingerspelling for Balinese words and were also working on numeracy.

The life of villages in northern Bali is based on a clan system. The deaf can both participate in and transcend their clans; for birthdays, for example, they invite their own clan as well as the deaf alliance in the village, while hearing people would not invite anyone outside their clan. The deaf have certain traditional jobs. They bury the dead and serve as the police, though there is almost no crime; they repair pipes in the often-troubled water system. Most are also farmers, planting cassava, taro and elephant grass, which is used to feed cows. Bengkala has a traditional chief who presides over religious ceremonies; an administrative chief chosen by the central Balinese government to oversee government functions, and a deaf chief, traditionally the oldest deaf person.

I arrived in Bengkala with the Balinese linguist I Gede Marsaja, born in a neighbouring village, who has studied Kata Kolok in depth. We climbed into a canyon where a river rushed under a two-hundred-foot rock wall. Several deaf villagers were waiting for us by the water, where they farm rambutans. Over the next half-hour, the rest of

Bengkala's deaf arrived. I sat on a red blanket at one end of a large tarp, and the deaf arranged themselves around the tarp's edge. People were signing to me, confident that I could understand. Gede translated and Kanta provided further assistance. I quickly picked up a few signs, and when I used them, the entire group broke out in smiles. They seemed to have multiple levels and kinds of signing, because when they were signing to me, they were like a bunch of mimes and I could follow their narratives clearly, but when they were signing to one another, I couldn't figure out what they were saying at all, and when they were signing to Gede, they were somewhere in between. Some of the hearing people in the village sign better than others, and while Kata Kolok has an exact grammar, purely iconic signs can be strung along without grammatical overlay for people who are not fluent.

The Kata Kolok sign for *sad* is the index and middle fingers placed at the inside corners of the eyes, then drawn down like tears. The sign for *father* is an index finger laid across the upper lip to suggest a moustache; the sign for *mother* is an upward-facing open hand at chest level supporting an imaginary breast. The sign for *deaf* is the index finger inserted into the ear and rotated; the sign for *hearing* is the whole hand held closed beside the ear and then opened while it is moved away from the head, sort of like an explosion coming out of the skull. In Kata Kolok, positive words usually involve pointing upward, while negative ones involve pointing downward; one villager who had travelled told the others that the raised third finger is a bad word in the West, so they flipped the sign and now use a third finger pointing down to indicate *horrendous*. The vocabulary is constantly evolving, while the grammar is fairly static. This language probably took on rules, as many signed languages do, over decades; second-generation language is always more sophisticated and ordered than first-generation.

Local hearing farmers do not have an enormous vocabulary, and neither does this sign language, in which about a thousand signs have been identified by scholars, though deaf people clearly know more signs than that and can combine them to achieve additional meanings. For Western members of the educated classes, intimacy usually resides in mutual knowledge, and that knowledge is advanced when language unlocks the secrets of the other mind. But some people are less given to articulation: people for whom the self is expressed in the preparation of food and in the ministrations of erotic passion and in shared labour in the field. For such people the meaning embedded in words is secondary, an adjunct to love rather than its method. We had come into a society in which language was not the necessary precondition of familiarity for the hearing or the deaf, nor the primary medium through which to understand and negotiate the world.

When we finished lunch, fourteen men put on sarongs, and two women donned fancy, lacy, nylon blouses. Like most deaf people, they could feel the vibrations of the drum, and their dance included movements that seemed to flow from their mimetic language – you could tell when they were dancing about being on a boat, and when they were smoking, and when they were running away. Each woman individually would invite one of the men to dance. One invited me, and I went for it; she hung flowers around my neck as we danced. Then the women remarked that they were all getting hot and tired, as it was incredibly humid, so they stopped. The men offered to show us the martial arts they use as the village security agents. I was interested in the way they mixed signing and the deployment of their hands and feet as weapons. One young man, Suarayasa, resisted joining in the theatrics until he was shamed into it by his mother, and the whole time he was demonstrating his abilities, he was also signing repeatedly, 'Look at me!' It was fierce but playful.

The women gave everyone a Sprite, then the men proposed a dip in the river, so we walked down through the elephant grass and hot peppers and went skinny-dipping. The rock wall rose steep above us, and long vines hung down, and the deaf men swung on them. I did somersaults in the water, others did headstands, and we set bait to fish for eels. Some would swim underwater until they were right beside me and then shoot up out of the current. They continued to sign to me, and the communication was exuberant, even joyful. It seemed possible, in that sunset light, to contemplate this as an idyll for the fluent communication it entailed, despite the poverty and disability of the people whom we were visiting.

The next day, Kanta translated from Kata Kolok into Balinese, occasionally addressing me in his limited English; Gede translated Kanta's Balinese into English, occasionally signing in his limited Kata Kolok; and the deaf Bengkala villagers addressed me directly in animated sign. Communication in this linguistic jumble was established through sheer force of collective will. It was hard to ascertain even the numbers of deaf and hearing people in individual families because everyone had different ideas about what was meant by family: all the male relatives? All the adults? All the people sharing a kitchen? What one could ask was limited because many grammatical structures couldn't be translated. For example, Kata Kolok has no conditional tense nor any sign for *why*; the language has no categorical words (such as *animals* or the abstract notion of *name*), only specific ones (such as *cow* or someone's actual name).

We first talked to the family of Pinda, who currently had two wives and had divorced two others. He was father to two living children, a daughter by Ni Md Resmini and a son by another wife; three children from his previous marriages had died. His wives and children were all deaf. Pinda said, 'I don't like the hearing people here. If I ask them for money, they always refuse.' Pinda was vain and wanted to have his picture taken incessantly, but warm, too, and he laughed readily. He said he loved Resmini because she cut grass all day for the cows and never talked. 'Hearing people talk too much,' he explained. Resmini said, 'I always knew I wanted to marry a deaf man, but I never cared whether my children could hear or not. With a hearing husband, my deaf daughter will probably be richer, and with a deaf husband she will end up fighting like I do. Having too much of a common language with your husband is not an advantage. It makes everyone too emotional.' Pinda seemed to take an obscure pride in this prognosis. 'The deaf, if there is something wrong with the wife, he is kicking her out straightaway,' he said. 'If she's been too friendly with another man, she's kicked out without questions. I would never marry a hearing woman. And I want my son to marry someone deaf as well.' It became clear that it would be harder for him to dominate the family with a hearing woman.

I met the family of Santia, the deaf son of hearing parents, and his wife, Cening Sukesti, the deaf daughter of deaf parents. The two had been childhood friends. Santia was somewhat slow, whereas Cening Sukesti was vibrant, lively and intelligent. Cening Sukesti chose to marry him because his hearing parents owned enough land for them to work. She said, 'If you are deaf, you are deaf. If you are hearing, you are hearing. That's simply how it is. I've never been jealous of hearing people. Life is no easier for them. If we work hard, we will get money, too. I take care of the cows and I sow the seeds and I boil the cassava. If I lived in another village, I might want to be hearing, but I like it here, and here it doesn't matter.'

Three of their four children were deaf. When their son Suara Putra was nine months old, hearing friends observed that he could hear. He began to sign at eleven months, though he came to feel more fluent in speech. As a young adult, Suara Putra often translates for his parents. He'd never want to give up his hearing or his signing: 'I have two where most people have one,' he said. But he maintained he could have been equally happy being deaf. Half his friends were deaf and the other half, hearing; 'I don't count them that way,' he explained, 'because it's all the same to me.' Nonetheless, he said, 'I think my parents like having one hearing child. Yet I'd have less tension with them if I were like them.' Cening Sukesti said that Suara Putra signed even better than his deaf siblings because spoken language had made him more comfortable expressing complex ideas.

Their deaf son, Suarayasa, who had been signing while doing his martial arts moves the day before, told us that he had deaf and hearing friends, but that he really liked getting drunk with deaf friends. 'Deaf people my age don't go to school,' he said, 'so they have time to work, so they've got money and buy the drink.' Alcohol abuse is more frequent in the deaf community in Bengkala, and a number of deaf young men showed me with pride the scars from their drunken fights. Suarayasa's deaf grandmother said he had to get his drinking under control and shook her head when he said he was going to marry a hearing girl. I asked him why, and he said, 'All the deaf girls already turned me down. They don't like my drinking, even though I never vomit.'

An older couple, Sandi and Kebyar, lived with their two deaf sons, Ngarda and Sudarma. Ngarda's hearing wife, Molsami, came from another village, and when she realised she was pregnant by Ngarda, she thought she'd better learn to sign. 'I worry about the difference between a hard-working husband and a lazy one,' she said. 'Hearing or deaf doesn't make very much difference.' Ngarda was glad to have four hearing children. 'We already have many deaf people here,' he said emphatically. 'If all of us are deaf, it's not good.'

Sudarma took the exact opposite position. He is married to a deaf wife, Nym Pindu, and said he would never have married a hearing woman. More than anyone else I met in Bali, he seemed to take the positions associated with Deaf politics in the West. 'Deaf people should stick together,' he said. 'Hearing to hearing is good, and deaf to deaf is good. I wanted deaf children and I want to live among deaf people.' All three of his children are deaf. Sudarma is a big drinker, with scars to show for his brawling.

We were supposed to have started the day by visiting Getar, the deaf chief of the village, and his sister, Kesyar, but Getar had been called out in the morning to fix some pipes, so we talked to them the next day. At seventy-five, Getar is not only still fixing pipes but also, when he has some money, making regular visits to the brothel in the neighbouring town, about which he told us in some considerable detail; on his last visit, he had had three 'girls' for thirty thousand rupiah (just over $3). The number of deaf in Bengkala fluctuates; Getar said that when he was born, the village had only six deaf people – though he subsequently explained that by *people* he meant 'adult men', and that if he included women, he could remember eleven deaf villagers. He communicated frequently with hearing people, and his signing was iconic; it lacked the elegance of Cening Sukesti's or the punch of Sudarma's.

Getar married once only. His wife bore him five children, then died from eating too much jackfruit. His children were all deaf; four of the five survived infancy. His primary responsibility as chief was to order jobs for members of the deaf alliance. 'There are pipes to be fixed. There is a security job,' he explained. 'The big boss comes to me, and I decide who will do the jobs. If there's a death, the family will come to me, and I will decide who will dig the grave. For each job, the person who does it gets most of the money, but some money is also kept to go into the collective deaf-alliance fund, and every six months we slaughter a pig – or some pigs if we can afford it – and the meat is divided equally among the deaf people.' Getar told me that choosing who gets which job is political, since everyone wants the jobs that pay well. 'I keep a record of who has done each job so I can show that the decisions are fair,' he said. 'If someone is hungry and needs the work, then I'll give it to him. If someone hasn't had a job for a long time, I give them a chance.' When the other deaf people sign to Getar, they use more polite, formal signs; he, in turn, uses those forms of address with hearing people. Getar had not been the object of prejudice, but he spoke with longing about the freedoms of younger deaf people. There were more of them, he thought, and their lives were easier. Now they were even going to school.

After our long days of interviews, Cening Sukesti invited us to come out to their farm. It was raining, but Santia shimmied up a tree and brought us fresh coconuts, and we had mealy corn and heavy cassava. There were a lot of jokes with innuendo; Cening Sukesti chuckled as she explained that she had refused sexual favours to Santia until he had finished building their new hut. The deaf alliance had an attractive ease to it, a ready and embracing intimacy. When I asked about prejudice against the deaf, they all agreed that there was none in the village. They all had hearing and deaf friends and could mingle at will.

In Bengkala, people talked about deafness and hearing much as people in more familiar societies might talk about height or race – as personal characteristics with advantages and disadvantages. They did not discount the significance of deafness nor underplay its role in their lives; they did not forget whether they were deaf or hearing and did not expect others to forget it, either. But they considered it within the realm of ordinary variations rather than an aberrance and a severe disability. The deaf alliance in Bengkala is extremely free in every sense except geography; their freedom is predicated on a linguistic fluency shared only in their village. I had gone there to investigate the social constructionist model of disability and found that where deafness does not impair communication, it is not much of a handicap.

———————

Kata Kolok appears to be unique among sign languages for the deaf in that it is used by more hearing people than deaf people. But it is threatened as deaf teenagers from Bengkala are increasingly sent to boarding school, where they learn Indonesian Sign Language (ISL). Many marry deaf people from other parts of Bali and use ISL instead of Kata Kolok; in recent years, eight deaf individuals from Bengkala have moved to other parts of Bali or Australia. Even if non-Bengkala spouses are deaf, the marriages are unlikely to produce deaf children, since individuals from outside Bengkala do not possess the recessive gene that causes deafness there. Since 2005, no deaf children have been born to parents who use Kata Kolok, so no new transmission of the language from deaf parents to deaf children has occurred. As the number of deaf people in Bengkala dwindles, so, too, will the communicative utility of Kata Kolok.

Rio, City of Hope

Travel + Leisure, October 2011

I went to Rio de Janeiro in 2010 for *Travel + Leisure* to report on how the city was changing in the lead-up to the World Cup and the Olympics. The central question was the shifting dynamic between the privileged and the impoverished. I addressed the subject in the published article, but conducted a deeper investigation that finds voice in this expanded version.

A t a time when much of the world is in some form of decline, Rio de Janeiro is the view looking forward; it can feel like the capital of hope. The wave of change owes something to the booming Brazilian economy, something to the discovery of offshore oil, something to the energy brought to the city when it was chosen for the 2014 World Cup finals and the 2016 Olympics, and most of all to the dramatic reduction in crime. All of these changes are elaborately intertwined. Rio has not achieved the placidity of Zürich or Reykjavík, but just as every small joy feels like rapture after a depression, the improvement in Rio has an aura of fiesta that those tranquil towns will never know.

A great many cities sit beside the sea, but no other integrates the ocean as Rio does. You can imagine San Francisco located inland, or Boston minus its harbour, but to imagine Rio without the waterfront is like imagining New York without skyscrapers, Paris without cafés, L.A.

without celebrities. The landscape has an almost Venetian urgency. 'If you don't go to the beach, you don't know anything that's happening,' said the artist Vik Muniz. 'No matter if you have Twitter or a cell phone, you have to go to the beach every day from four o'clock until sundown.' Beaches are inherently democratic; when you socialise in public wearing only a bathing suit, money loses its copyright on glamour. Though the beaches in Rio remain considerably segregated by class, because the colour of your skin and the brand of your bathing suit and sunglasses mark your status, much of what you show at the beach is your body, your skill at volleyball, your aura of cool. The social implications are significant. It takes effort to be a snob in Rio.

The topography has dictated another social anomaly. People of privilege live in the flat seaside areas, which are not prone to land-slides, in the Zona Sul (the Southern District), which encompasses the famous beaches of Copacabana, Ipanema and Leblon. Those neighbourhoods are punctuated by abrupt hills, which have been set-tled by the poor over the past century or so. Although home to nearly a quarter of Rio's population, these steep districts, known as *favelas*, do not appear in detail on most maps of the city and historically have lacked utilities, garbage collection, closed sewers and police protec-tion. Even in the exclusive Zona Sul, you are never more than five minutes from a favela. Muniz said, 'You're sitting in Saint-Tropez surrounded by Mogadishu.'

Building inside the favelas is unregulated, and when the rains come, houses collapse. Walled off from the city proper, these gang-dominated enclaves have been the setting of endless violence. Most cities have slums, but in many – including many others in Bra-zil – these are on the outskirts of town or in a single, contained enclave. Rio's favelas are dotted all through the city like the chocolate chips in a cookie. The city's peculiar geography is such that shanty-town gunfire is audible even in the most affluent neighbourhoods. The social distances in Rio outmeasure the geographic ones.

Much of Brazilian culture originated in Rio's favelas. Samba evolved there, and the new funk music, too. Many soccer stars hail from the favelas, and some of Brazil's famous models. Carnival in Rio – the biggest pre-Lenten festival in the world, with two million people a day partying in the streets – depends largely on the 'samba schools' of the favelas, which compete to put on the most glittering displays. French aristocrats never say that France would be nothing without the slums of Paris, and most upper-class Italians are embarrassed by the Mafia; hip-hop culture notwithstanding, most Americans opt for the suburbs. But in Rio de Janeiro, those who have privilege admire those who don't. José Maria Zacchi, one of the architects of change in Rio, told me that in nineteenth-century Brazil, little distance separated the manor house and the slave quarters, and not much has changed in that regard. 'The educated upper middle class loves to mingle with the people, loves it,' the poet and critic Italo Moriconi said. 'It's part of the Carioca culture.' (The word *Carioca* refers to people or things from or of Rio.) Yet Brazil remains one of the most unequal societies in the world – a place, as the anthropologist Lilia Moritz Schwarcz said, of 'cultural inclusion and social exclusion'.

Carioca pride began its slip in 1960, when the capital was moved to remote Brasília and the government functionaries skipped town. Previously a federal district on the order of Washington, D.C., or Mexico City, Rio was folded into the surrounding, undeveloped state for administrative purposes. Business shifted increasingly to São Paulo; Rio was deindustrialised. Violence from the favelas threatened rich and poor. Wealthy people employed private security forces, drove bulletproof cars, and stopped wearing jewellery. Drug gangs fought one another and an incredibly corrupt police force. The gangs sometimes put their enemies into towers of tyres and set them on fire – a method of execution known as the microwave oven, similar to the South African atrocity called necklacing.

Some policemen moonlighted in private militias, protection organisations within favelas and slums that were hard to distinguish from the gangs they theoretically controlled; Moriconi referred to the 'promiscuous relationship between police and crime'. In 2008, Philip Alston, the United Nations special rapporteur on extrajudicial, summary or arbitrary executions, said, 'A remarkable number of police lead double lives. While on duty, they fight the drug gangs, but on their days off, they work as foot soldiers of organised crime.'

In 2008, 1 in every 23 people arrested by Rio de Janeiro's police force was killed by police or by others in custody before making it to trial – a striking statistic considering that the ratio for the United States is 1 in 37,000.

Luiz Eduardo Soares served briefly as national secretary of public security under President Luiz Inácio Lula da Silva, commonly known as Lula, who ruled from 2003 to 2010. Soares instituted a programme to enter poor areas with respect. 'We were there offering a public service, not invading,' he told me. But policing is a local issue, and it was hard to change problematic procedures and attitudes with a national policy. 'When you give a policeman discretionary authority to kill, you're also giving him authority to sell life,' Soares said. 'He can say to the suspect, "I can kill you. That won't cost me anything. But I can also not kill you. How much would you give me?"' It does not take long for such behaviour to become organised. Favela residents armed themselves heavily. Innocent people were injured and killed in the crossfire, and life expectancy was short. In the Zona Sul, street crime became ubiquitous. Upward of a thousand people a year were killed by police in Rio and São Paulo alone, a significantly higher number than that for the whole United States. The chief of special operations of the Rio police was indicted for corruption. 'If you were poor, you were scared of the police; if you were rich, you were sceptical of them,' said Roberto Feith, Rio's leading publisher.

Given the centrality of sports to the Brazilian psyche, it's no surprise that the World Cup and the Olympics should have inspired Rio's leadership to attempt a change. After decades of internecine quarrelling among their administrations, the mayor of Rio, the governor of the state of Rio de Janeiro and the federal government of Brazil began to work in sync. In 2008, Rio's secretary of security, José Mariano Beltrame, introduced the UPP (Unidade de Polícia Pacificadora, or Pacifying Police Unit), a new force of younger, ostensibly uncorrupted officers under the aegis of the military police rather than of local bosses. 'We need fresh, strong minds, not a Rambo,' said UPP commander Colonel José Carvalho at its start.

Since the programme began, the favelas have been invaded one by one almost as acts of war. Beltrame announces his plan before entering each favela, giving drug dealers a chance to flee; his focus is on eliminating guns rather than on closing down contraband-distribution networks. He enters forcibly, using airpower, the army and the marines. Once the rout is over, police establish a UPP Social, a sort of Marshall Plan intended to install or upgrade education, sanitary services, legal electricity and cable television, and job train-ing. The police stay on to protect the citizens of the favelas, rather than to protect the residents of the Zona Sul from the favelas. Pre-Beltrame, the reactive police presence established sporadic domin-ion in response to particular acts of violence; now, the UPP aims to cultivate a proactive peace. Previous programmes sought to bulldoze the favelas; current ones seek to reform them.

During the dictatorship of the sixties and seventies, police officers received a pay raise for every 'enemy' they killed in the favelas. The new regime has turned that incentive on its head, declaring that even criminals have human rights. UPPs have been established in only sixty-eight of Rio's eleven hundred favelas, but Beltrame started with some of the toughest ones and nearly three hundred thousand people are already living in pacified areas. Ultimately, the goal is for all the favelas to be neighbourhoods within the city, rather than isolated entities. When I asked Beltrame how long it would take to pacify the rest of the favelas, he replied that the problem was finding enough honest police officers.

Conservative forces had long averred that crime could be suppressed by escalating use of force; previous efforts in the favelas were essentially conquests, with the entire citizenry treated as enemy combatants, so extrajudicial killings were considered casualties of war. The more lib-eral perspective was that violence was the product of a flawed social structure and would evaporate only if injustice were redressed; that point of view generated limp social programmes and a proliferation of NGOs. The right was troublingly violent, and the left, troublingly complacent. The genius of Beltrame's agenda is that it satisfies both sides. The right is thrilled because crime is down; the left is thrilled because social justice is advanced. The rich are safer, and the poor are richer. Beltrame told me that he had fired a vast number of police for corruption, but he emphasised that the police were 'only one element in the larger project of public security'. Soares said, 'Half the regular police force is corrupt; another thirty-five per cent are indifferent; and fifteen per cent care about injustice. Now that fifteen per cent are in ascendancy.'

The residents of the favelas were highly suspicious of members of this new police force who claimed their purpose was to serve rather than to oppress. Gradually, the favela dwellers have begun to say that they feel safe in their own homes. As the tension between residents and police has de-escalated, the police have come to feel safer, too, and some have voluntarily stopped carrying heavy guns. The police neutralise the geography by demolishing bunkers, patching gun holes and removing gang-related graffiti. The first day after a pacification, the governor of the state of Rio de Janeiro arrives to tell residents that he's got an eye on what's happening to them. There are still drug dealers inside the favelas, but most people no longer bear arms, and the random violence that has taken so many lives has been radically diminished. Gangsters driven out of one favela have a hard time setting up shop in other gangsters' territories. Many find themselves with nowhere to go but jail. Gang fighting among arms and drug interests – the Red Command and the Terceiro Command are the largest – no longer takes place on the streets of pacified favelas; the Red Command's *patrão* (commander) complained, 'It is fucking up our lives. It's affecting our business badly.'

Beltrame told me that the primary issue was transit. 'The state failed to provide the favelas with schools, electricity, water, sewage or day care, or to enforce simple contracts such as alimony on grounds that they couldn't go in there,' he said. 'Once people can pass in and out of the favelas, all those services become obligations of the state.' He envisioned the UPP Social as the next logical step, one that had to be conceived differently from the forced pacification. 'The troops that landed on Normandy did not rebuild Europe,' he said. 'The UPP has ended a dark empire of the drug lords, a sort of dicta- torship, and now the people can rebuild.' Ricardo Henriques, head of the UPP Social, said that people need a new kind of relationship to replace the one they've had with crime. 'You need to construct a civil society,' he explained. Beltrame added that favela residents who used to aspire only to be big shots within their communities now had an infinity of other possibilities. 'The UPP is opening curtains to a world outside that they didn't know existed, much less that they could be part of,' he explained. 'The police presence grants them the opportunity to transform their own lives, which they didn't have before.'

Some of the people in the favelas contend that the pacification process is just more of the same terrifying violence – not so unlike conditions under the gangs and drug lords. When I met with Colonel Robson Rodrigues da Silva, who has implemented the primary UPP plan and formed the new police force, he said, 'Of course, the first phase of pacification is repressive; we make many arrests. But the second phase is the opposite. We researched what the police and the favela population have in common, and as we are a Christian country, we figured out that the family is it. So the officers were taught always to build a good relationship with children.' In one neighbourhood, police dispensed chocolate Easter eggs. In another, they have been teaching kids to fly kites – an especially potent symbol because children enlisted as lookouts used to warn gang members that the cops were coming by pulling their kites from the sky. The police have created sports competitions at which children from several favelas come together to play; each wears a T-shirt emblazoned with the name of his or her community. Before pacification, this would have been impossible; rival gangs would have killed one another.

Rodrigues proudly showed me drawings made by schoolchildren, some depicting police playing soccer or dancing. 'Every drawing has the sun shining,' he pointed out. 'We looked at drawings done before, and every one with police in it was dark.' The police ask community members about their particular needs; it's what Colonel Rodrigues calls 'soft social control'. He added, 'We will not be a city without violence. We'll be a city with normal violence. We know the plan is working because people in the favelas have started to report petty crime to our police. That's the trust we are trying to establish.' Some police are taking theatre classes to learn how to modulate their voices and demeanour to communicate authoritatively but without aggression. Others have been cynical about such tactics; one complained, 'What's next? Ballet?' But Rodrigues contended that the work has helped the police hone their attention, perception and speech. Geniality is an art.

Rodrigues himself attends funk parties in the favelas. Hip tourists stay in favela hostels, a few of which have achieved high levels of chic. Travel companies sell favela tours, 'like a safari,' Moriconi said, 'in open vans,' and the new Museu de Favela is one of the most dynamic spaces in Rio. But tourism in the favelas can often feel voyeuristic rather than engaged, and many favela residents find it stigmatising and patronising. They don't want to be photographed by visitors exploring the picturesque side of misery and crime.

In the past two years alone, the rate of bullet wounds in Rio has declined by half; the murder rate is now lower than that of Washington, D.C.. The changes do not always go smoothly, but this is clearly a moment of transformation. The popular press thrives worldwide on stories of crime and disaster, but this government has made serenity into headline news. Beltrame told me that so many people have benefited from the UPP that they simply would never allow the old system of gang rule to resurge. 'Any politician who chooses to end the pacification will lose too many votes. It will be impossible,' he said. 'People's lives have improved too much.' The real success of the UPP has been to lessen the role of fear in the social economy. Graham Denyer Willis, a British expert in the developing world who is on the faculty at Cambridge University, notes that the purpose here was to 'decrease the distance – spatial, social and psychological – between citizens and the state'.

Nonetheless, the plan for sustained occupation of the favelas by the UPP can seem infantilising, suggesting that without a visible security force, residents will revert to criminality. Christopher Gaffney, an American professor of urban planning who lives in Rio, said, 'The cheerleaders for the UPPs are saying, "Well, the UPPs are here, we've got rid of the armed drug traffickers," but they don't say, "We've substituted one armed force for another." And that's all they've done without creating mechanisms for a civil society to flourish.'

The psychoanalyst Marcus André, who treats well-to-do Cariocas for high fees and favela residents for free, told me, 'I was tired of being afraid of the favelas; and it turns out they were tired of being afraid of us, too. We had a fantasy of who they were, and they had an equal one about us. When you finally cross the wall, you resolve paranoia on both sides.' When he began working in the favelas, a teenage girl asked him why he'd come. 'I came to learn from you,' he said. She laughed at him and replied, 'You must be very stupid if you need to learn from us.' He hopes to foster self-esteem in such long-disenfranchised people. He takes his own children into even the unpacified favelas. 'There is some danger,' he said, 'but the danger of growing up with that fantasy paranoia is worse.'

André Urani, a leading Brazilian economist and author of *Rio: The Turning Point*, told me that at the end of the eighties, among 188 countries recognised by the International Monetary Fund, only one had a more closed economy than Brazil, which was Myanmar. It's worth remembering that democracy is only twenty-six years old in Brazil; the consumer society is even newer. Urani noted, 'The absence of meaningful economic activity undermined everyone's self-esteem and resulted in huge decadence in economic, political and social terms.' Fernando Gabeira, a popular Brazilian politician and author, said, 'Since the dictatorship, Brazil has become steadily more present in the world, and the world has become steadily more present in Brazil.' That reciprocal presence has called out new competencies and skills. Artist Vik Muniz said, 'Evolutionarily speaking, human beings aren't good at much. We don't have great vision, we're not very fast, we don't have big fangs, and we're not particularly strong. We can dominate the other animals only because of our ability to organise. Somehow, we forgot that in Rio.'

There is a great need for organising, and a great need for organisational tools. Rodrigo Baggio works to bridge Brazil's digital divide by collecting donations of old computers and setting up community centres in the favelas to provide technical training. Less than a third of Brazilians have internet access, compared with nearly three-quarters of people in the United States. Baggio's work began long before pacification, but he's stepped it up since then. 'You are taking away the jobs they were training for, as drug dealers,' he said. 'You have to give them some other opportunities to pursue instead.' That analysis makes humanitarian sense; it makes economic sense, too.

Maria Silvia Bastos Marques, the most successful businesswoman in Brazil, took over the National Steel Company in 1999 – no mean feat for a woman in a Latin country. She was offered the National Oil Company, but turned it down, and at fifty-five, she is overseeing the business side of the Olympics. She emphasised that while credit for the turnaround in Brazil tends to go to Lula, the process really began with his predecessor, Fernando Henrique Cardoso. The 1980s and the early nineties were a time of appalling inflation. 'Rich people don't suffer so much with inflation; their houses and cars go up in price to keep pace,' Bastos said. 'But for poor people, who depend on the money they get each week to live on, it's a tragedy; the job that paid them enough to feed their family last week doesn't pay enough to do it this week.'

Even for someone of her stature, the high inflation rate meant chaos. She would work out her company budget for the year, and two months later it had become meaningless. 'No one could make plans,' she sighed. Once Henrique had inflation under control, however, planning began to happen. 'It changed the whole mentality of Brazil,' she said. The pacification in Rio, in her view, was part of a larger arc of change. She told me that she had always driven a bulletproof car, but that she had recently bought a car with windows that roll down. Her children had never been in such a vehicle before, and they loved it.

The Olympic plan has been controversial. Bastos worked to renegotiate Brazil's international debt with the IMF in the early 1990s, which spurred internal economic recovery, and she believes that the Olympics will provide a similar 'occasion to get our house in order'. Eduardo Paes, mayor of Rio, told me, 'The word *Olympic* refers to something that is hard to achieve. Look, Barcelona was reborn from the Olympics; Athens was nearly bankrupted. It's not easy, what we need to do. The way I see it, we can let the Olympics use the city, or the city can use the Olympics to achieve permanent goals.' Some poor citizens question the decision to build a system of commuter trains to Barra da Tijuca, the wealthy district that first elected Paes to office. The layout seems designed to reinforce social stratification rather than ameliorate it. Many people are being evicted from their homes – nineteen thousand families in one year – to make way for the new lines.

'We should plan according to the needs of the city, not the needs of the games,' Gabeira said. 'Calling them plans for the games means that everything can be rushed through without democratic review.' Actor and activist Marcus Vinícius Faustini said, 'If the pacification of the favelas is really just a ploy to attract more tourist dollars for the Olympics, then it will blow up horrifically. The displacement of citizens is a disaster. There is already evidence that the building plans for the games are mechanisms of social control.'

Favela residents do not pay property taxes, and some middle-class voters resent this. As services increase, such taxes seem inevitable. Purified water and reliable electricity will come with water and electric bills. 'As soon as the neighbourhoods stop being dangerous,' Faustini said, 'the residents become subject to all the commercial exploitation that is routine in prosperous cities, but that they are too inexperienced to resist.'

Some favela dwellers have occupied the same house for three generations, and it seems unrealistic to insist that it's not their property. Others settled in only last year, and it is not a foregone conclusion that they should have squatter's rights. If you grant people ownership of favela houses, will they sell off their land to rich people who want to take advantage of the views? Many favelas enjoy extraordinary vistas; some look over the city of Rio, across to the statue of Christ the Redeemer, and out to sea. In any other city, people would bankrupt themselves for such panoramas. Some favela dwellers pay rent, which has already escalated where UPPs have been established. The prevailing view among most middle-class Cariocas is that the favelas must be preserved; many dislike the idea of seeing all the poor people exiled. I asked everyone I met inside the favelas whether they wanted to move to a 'better' neighbourhood, and the only ones who did were relatively recent emigrants from other parts of Brazil. Favela natives wanted to fix up the world they loved. Though Batan is a favela in the north-western end of town – the really ugly, poorest part, far from the beach – one of the kids I met there said, 'If you could bottle the joy in this place, you could sell it in the Zona Sul.'

Some argue that the whole UPP programme serves as a Band-Aid for the World Cup and the Olympics; that it will surely disintegrate from lack of funding once those events have taken place, with huge budget cuts in 2017; and that if or when the gangs return, anyone who has cooperated with the UPP will be targeted for retribution. In 2010, two years after the UPP was launched, the United Nations Office of the High Commissioner for Human Rights found that nothing was being accomplished by the programme, complained of its strong-arm, militaristic tactics and criticised the idea that 'occasional violent invasions can bring security'. The Geneva Conventions apply to war, but not to a state's policing of its own citizenry. While the military is trained to kill, police in most countries are trained to arrest instead; policing is not soldiering. Any confusion about the line between those two roles leads to abuse. Fear of corruption persists. 'Corruption is never one-sided,' Bastos said. 'Someone has to be willing to pay and someone has to be willing to receive, and we have to address both sides.' The question remains to what extent the UPPs protect the upper class and to what extent they really improve life in the favelas. Security is a military achievement, and safety is a social one. Security may be achieved through violence, but safety requires peace. Is the UPP helping to create safety, or is it really focused on security? Even a benign police action can degenerate into military occupation, especially in a country so recently freed from dictatorship.

I attended a meeting in the recently pacified favela of Morro dos Prazeres at which community leaders from that area and neighbouring districts met with an impressive array of government representatives. City administrators had suspended garbage collection during the rainy season because the steep streets became unsafe for trucks. The favela residents didn't want their garbage left rotting in the streets for months. Some residents' plumbing had failed, so they had to fetch water in buckets. 'Is anyone in Santa Teresa fetching water in buckets?' someone asked ironically, referring to a prosperous area that bordered his favela. Rio has no coherent programme for universal sanitation that could be fully implemented before 2025.

The electric company had installed meters on some streets but programmed them incorrectly, so some people were being charged for others' electricity. The utilities worked where the police set up offices, but not elsewhere. The government had closed a day-care centre that didn't conform to legal requirements, and as a result, some children had nowhere to go when their mothers went to work. Plans had been announced to demolish structurally unstable houses on steep hills prone to mudslides, but nobody had figured out where to house the displaced occupants. People had been searched for arms coming in and out of their own neighbourhoods just because they were young, male and dark-skinned. The social UPP programme was having a rocky start.

Nonetheless, when someone stood up and said, 'Despite all that, we used to fear the police, and now we respect the police,' the crowd of three hundred cheered. Erik Vittrup Christensen, who works for the UN's human settlements programme, UN-HABITAT, in Rio, said, 'Acknowledgement is the oxygen here.' One teenager I met in Batan said, 'I thought I would spend my whole life feeling abandoned, that if I wanted education, health, money, culture, I'd have to leave, and now I think I can stay and have those things.' Another said, 'My cousin was killed by the old police, and now, the police of Batan are my friends; one is giving me classes in capoeira [a Brazilian martial art] and another in music. For him, music is just for listening; for me, it's a chance to save my life.' But he was still afraid of what might happen in his future, after the Olympics, 'after the novelty wears off for these police'. As he pointed out, the same old problems were happening a thousand feet away in another, unpacified favela, 'and they could come back here easily'.

People in Rio with lighter skin unquestionably have an easier time. Officially, Brazilians define themselves as members of one of five races – *branco* (white), *preto* (black), *amarelo* (yellow), indigenous and *pardo* (brown), which a local demographer translated, roughly, as 'et cetera'. When asked to describe themselves, however, a wide sampling of Cariocas provided 136 different descriptions of their own race. Here, race is explicitly conflated with privilege. At one gathering I attended, a journalist pointed across the room and asked, 'Who's that black man over there?' The black people being asked said, 'He's not black; he's our leader.' The leader himself then said, 'When I was black, my life was harder.' In a recent survey, Brazilian city dwellers claimed to notice more racism in small towns than in urban areas; conversely, people in small towns claimed that there was no racism where they lived, but a lot in the big cities. Everyone perceives the problem, but no one claims it. In one survey of São Paulo residents, 97 per cent claimed they were not racist, but 98 per cent said they were closely related to someone who was racist. Self-knowledge is nowhere a widespread commodity.

Marcus Vinícius Faustini left the favelas to become an actor and returned with loudspeakers mounted on his car to announce as he drove through the poorest areas that he would teach theatre to students. He has enrolled two thousand young people in educational and vocational programmes. He believes that the middle class's attraction to the favelas traps the favela residents. 'It's not fair to say that if you're born in the favela, you can express yourself only through funk music or samba,' he said. 'The favela dwellers should have the option to express themselves with Beethoven if they wish.' He points out that the government supports capoeira classes in the favelas, but not courses in marketing or business. He acknowledged that the pacification process was intended to make favela life less chaotic. 'But who defines what chaos is?' he asked. Life works in the favelas because of organic, patched-together systems that serve people's needs. 'If you resolve chaos by destroying what functions, the ramifications can be very alarming,' he said. His own dream is that after he teaches favela kids all the things they don't know from the outside world, the outside world will come in to learn from the favela. 'What the UPP gives them won't have any meaning,' he said, 'until they are allowed to give something back.'

Cíntia Luna, a community leader in Fogueteiro, walked me through her favela at sunset. She pointed out a half-built edifice that had been designated ten years earlier as a school. 'I checked all the records,' she said. 'The school was funded every year; they paid for teachers, lunches, supplies. But the doors were never opened. Where do you think the money went?' I wondered whether such suspicions of treachery had made her a cynic about the pacification. When I asked her, she put a hand on my arm and said, 'Don't say anything for a moment.' We stood in silence, then she explained, 'There was never a moment when you could hear the wind like this. You'd have heard shooting, yelling all around us.'

Despite all that danger and disruption, she maintained that the neighbourhood was peaceful, in its way, even before the police drove out the gangs. 'Everybody knows everybody, and we have a mellow speed of life,' she said. 'We were never afraid of the gangs, who were actually much more efficient about getting the electricity fixed or providing services than these city offices we now have to call. But we were afraid of the conflict between the gangs and the police. So now the people in the Zona Sul are happy not to have our gangs, and we are happy not to have their corrupt police. It's only a compromise, but it gives us all a better quality of life.'

Brazil was primarily a colony, then a dictatorship, and despite occasional brief intervals of electoral government, the idea that it belongs to its own people began to take root widely only in 1988. 'Every institution had to adjust to democracy,' Soares said. 'First the political institutions, then business, then culture. The police, however, we inherited from two centuries of brutality: the time of slavery, the dictatorship. This is the last change.' He described going into the favelas with Lula during his first presidential campaign. Lula said to Soares, 'I want to talk about health care, education, employment, and all they want to talk about is the police!' Soares said he told Lula, 'Because that has to do with whether their sons will come home alive. You have to be alive to want to fight for a job or an education; you have to be alive even to get sick and want treatment.'

Programmes to improve the favelas are nothing new; one Brazilian aid worker quipped to me that there were more NGOs than people in Brazil. But for the first time, people from the favelas are starting their own public service organisations. Luiz Carlos Dumontt and Dudu de Morro Agudo founded Enraizados, which is devoted to 'cultural militancy'; its website gets more than six hundred thousand hits each month. Dudu is a rapper who teaches kids to produce music and videos as a way of enticing them away from gangs. Enraizados artists also make graffiti murals to beautify otherwise grim neighbourhoods. The operation has established a street library: you find a book on the road, log on to the website stamped opposite the title page, and make a note of where you found it, whether you liked it, and where you're leaving it so someone else can find it. Thus the books circulate through the favelas.

Fernando Gabeira is famous for having kidnapped the American ambassador to Brazil in 1969 as part of a protest against the dictatorship; the adventure was the subject of a bestselling book and the 1997 movie *Four Days in September*. In 2008, Gabeira lost the Rio mayoral election by less than 1 per cent. When I sat with him in a pavement café, passing cars stopped to honk appreciation. 'These UPPs are succeeding in conquering and the politicians are celebrating,' he said, 'but are they celebrating the people they've conquered?' Gabeira averred that the long-standing scenario described by police as a conflict between justice and crime had actually been a conflict between two kinds of crime, with the police trying to appropriate the drug dealers' profits and power. 'Security is an impression as much as it is a reality, however,' he explained. 'If people think things are better, they are better. The rich people are happier now, and so are the poor people. That's already quite a success.'

Cariocas are fiercely opinionated about the rejuvenation of historic sites in the frenzy of construction leading up to the World Cup and the Olympics. The Maracanã soccer stadium is being either ruined or saved. The Theatro Municipal has just been fully restored for its centennial; modelled on the Garnier in Paris, it is where Arturo

Toscanini made his conducting debut, and also hosted Sarah Bernhardt and Igor Stravinsky. The theatre holds nearly two thousand five
hundred people and is sold out most nights for programmes of opera,
ballet and classical music. On Sundays, tickets are available for one
real (about twenty-five cents), and the theatre is mobbed with visitors
from the favelas. On the theatre's birthday, 14 July, the public is invited
to come for free, and the theatre is open all day. Luciana Medeiros,
Rio's leading music critic, said, 'The change in crime, you might not
think of it as affecting the life of culture, but with these changes in Rio,
everybody wins. When I was a kid, one of the most symbolic things
was that the street was so dirty. All of a sudden, everybody takes care.'

When I went to meet the mayor in the baroque city hall, half
the people there wore flip-flops. Rio is a casual place. But casual
is not frumpy. While most cultures have created fashion and then
found models to show it off, Brazil produced models and then started
making fashion to clothe them in. 'Our models come out of the
favelas with this amasing natural elegance,' said Sergio Mattos, who
owns one of Rio's biggest modelling agencies. 'They need to look
good with their clothes on. But for Rio's beach culture, they have to
look good with their clothes off. We have the world's only fashion
industry without eating disorders.' Brazilians have a keen sense of
beautiful bodies, and almost no sense of unbeautiful bodies. The
great-looking people wear skimpy swimsuits (including some called
fio dental: dental floss), but people who are old and fat wear equally
tiny suits without self-consciousness. Brazil is singularly devoted to
the aesthetics of sensuality. One young woman I met in a favela confided that she spent a third of her income on hair-care products. 'My
hair is the only beautiful thing I own,' she said, 'and I am going to
parlay it into the rest of my life.'

Italo Moriconi said that when he was growing up in Rio, every
intellectual's identity was as a Brazilian, but that increasingly people
hold an international identity and a strong local identity, founded in
pride about Rio de Janeiro and its transformation. The city's street
life has been reborn now that the streets are relatively safe, and whole
neighbourhoods are given over to the fun between dusk and dawn.
The centre of nightlife is the glamorously seedy downtown historic

district of Lapa. As at the beach, the streets teem with rich and poor alike, though some of the nightclubs are expensive. In the small hours, music pours out of every other door; the calibre of decor and the quality of musicianship are unrelated, so you have to pause and listen before choosing where to go. Many of the venues seem both historical and transient, as though they were built to be temporary but survived into permanence. I decided one night to check out what appeared to be a tiny chapel, its walls crowded with devotional images, only to find that it was a bar, presided over by a middle-aged transgender woman who had moved to Rio from the neighbouring state of Minas Gerais. She offered us a liqueur from her home state, redolent of cinnamon, and told us howlingly funny tales about figuring out her gender identity on a farm in the jungle. It's not only the sun that's warm at this latitude; friendship happens fast in Rio, and you continually find yourself in intimate conversation with people you've just met. They, in turn, eagerly introduce you to their friends – some of whom they've just met themselves – and after a few nights, you are juggling invitations to parties, dinners, rainforests.

One such new friend invited us to an early-evening samba party. People often gather to play music informally; anyone can bring an instrument and join in. Ours was in a downtown area where it attracted both businessmen on their way home from the office and favela residents on their way to clean those offices. Musically and socially, improvisation was the style. The musicians stopped only once, to announce that the smell of marijuana might bring in the police. Two ample women from Bahia were frying *acarajé*, delicious fritters of seafood and black-eyed peas, and the local bar was serving *caipirinhas* in plastic cups. Rio is not Rio without a soundtrack; music salts all the other senses.

Vik Muniz has made a career out of examining these ironies. The film *Waste Land* shows how he befriended garbage-pickers who lived on what they could find in a vast dump outside Rio, and eventually made them partners in his art. 'You meet somebody in New York, and they say, "What's your name?"' he said. 'And the second question is "What do you do?" In Rio, you get, "What's your name? What do you *like* to do?"' Several people I met quoted Antônio Carlos (Tom)

Jobim, the musician who wrote 'The Girl from Ipanema', who once explained, 'Living in New York is great, but it's shit; living in Rio is shit, but it's great.'

The popular talk-show star Regina Casé received me in her extravagant mansion, wearing a flowing caftan, at least five pounds of jewellery, and a cosmetics counter's worth of make-up. 'I've been to North America and to Europe,' she said. 'You have a pine woods. You have a grove of oak trees. Have you been in our Atlantic rainforest? We have a hundred kinds of trees, everything is growing on top of everything else, it's all competing for the sun and the water, and somehow it all survives, more lush than anywhere else in the world. That's the social structure of Rio, too. Just as our Amazon is providing the oxygen for the world, we make social oxygen here. If you don't learn to integrate your societies the way we've integrated ours, you're going to fail. In America, you have a lot of problems, a lot of injustice, a lot of conflict. You try to solve the problems.' She threw up her hands in mock horror. 'In Rio, we invite all the problems to a big party and we let them dance together. And we're inviting the world to come here and dance, too.'

―――――――

In August 2014, four years after I reported this story, I spent a few days in Rio. By then, UPPs were serving some 1.5 million people living in or near almost forty favelas, at staggering cost. Nine thousand police officers had received training to decriminalise and reinvigorate the favelas; in 2016, that number is expected to exceed twelve thousand. From 2009 to 2014, gang and police killings in the pacified favelas fell by half, and rates of other violent crimes dropped even more dramatically. The *New York Times* reported that students in the pacified favelas were performing twice as well as the average Rio student.

Despite this progress, the Institute of Social and Political Studies found that nearly half of Rio's favelas remained under the control of vigilante militias; more than a third were in the hands of drug gangs; and fewer than one in five had a UPP presence. Between

2011 and 2013, the Police Ombudsman's Office received nearly eight thousand complaints of police violence including assault, rape, torture and murder – yet only eighteen officers were sanctioned as a result. A recent Amnesty International study found that on-duty police officers were responsible for 1,519 homicides in Rio over five years – nearly one out of every six of the total homicides registered in the city. In most instances, the UPP Social charged with providing medical, sports and educational services simply failed to materialise.

The report *Exclusion Games*, issued at the end of 2015 and compiled primarily by NGOs, chronicled abuse of children's rights and basic civil liberties in the lead-up to the 2016 Summer Olympics. It noted an increase in police violence as the pacification programme wobbled, and charged that more than four thousand families had now lost their homes while another two thousand five hundred were under threat of similar displacement. Further, it reported the disappearance of several street children in episodes of so-called social cleansing. The Rio government has disputed some of these allegations.

Then there is the matter of Amarildo. On 14 July 2013, a construction worker with epilepsy named Amarildo de Souza, who lived in the Rocinha favela, was seen entering the local police station. He was never seen coming out. He was classed as 'missing' for two months, until enormous demonstrations across Rio with thousands of people chanting 'Where is Amarildo?' finally led to an investigation. Ten officers, including the head of Rocinha's UPP, were accused of torture – including electric shocks and putting the man's head in a plastic bag – and then concealing his corpse.

In April 2014, Douglas Rafael da Silva Pereira, a dancer, was beaten to death by the police. A resident of his favela later said, 'This effort to pacify the favelas is a failure; the police violence is only replacing what the drug gangs carried out before.' In 'pacified' Santa Marta, people complained of escalating tension. The *Washington Post* reported that at least ten gunfights had taken place at police bases in pacified favelas. After the period of relative peace, this mounting animosity between police and gangsters generated an increase in murders, arson and revenge killings. A Rocinha resident, Cleber Araujo, said succinctly, 'It feels like we're in a war.' A

Pew Research Trust study found that in 2014, Brazilians trusted the police less than they had four years earlier. When police battalions arrived to rout out the gangs that controlled the Maré favela, even law-abiding residents found their houses invaded and their possessions destroyed; police helicopters fired indiscriminately. In 2015, Atila Roque, the head of Amnesty International Brazil, said that the whole plan was 'backfiring miserably and leaving behind a trail of suffering and devastation'. Many believe that the pacification programme will be defunct as soon as the Olympics are over. Asked how long it would take for the gangs to resume their position, one favela resident said, 'They will run into each other on the way out.'

I visited Vidigal, recently pacified at the time, with Márcio Januário, a playwright, actor and dancer. Januário is black, heavily tattooed, openly gay and widely beloved; to walk through Vidigal with him is to be greeted every ten steps. He works with children and adults in Vidigal to put on plays. When I saw him, he was fresh from a performance of *Romeo and Juliet* set in the favela and performed in what he calls Favelese – the psychological language of the slums – with his Free Minds theatre company. Vidigal, which occupies a hill right above Ipanema beach and next to Barra da Tijuca, has the best views in Rio. Januário complained that the price of everything had skyrocketed with pacification. Many people had already sold the houses where they had lived for generations for what seemed to them a lot of money – but he said they would never find comparable houses because prices continued to escalate as middle-class purchasers bought into the favela adventure. Vidigal now has poor and rich areas, and these populations seldom interact. When I asked Januário whether he would ever consider relocating, he scoffed. 'I have to be here,' he said as we sat in his spare, attractive studio apartment. 'When it gets too expensive for me, I will leave Rio completely.'

Vidigal has terrible schools and few services. Januário, who volunteers in the schools, said that the kids aren't interested in education because the teachers aren't interested in teaching. He works with between thirty and forty students each year, many of whom go on to university. 'When I began this project seven years ago, a teacher said to me, "You're crazy! This school is for dummies. Poor black people don't need theatre."' Januário contended that people capable of so much fun were capable of learning. 'When they wake up,' he said, 'they open their eyes and say, "Where are the lions? Let's fight them." You just have to change which lions they are after.' I asked whether people were less afraid within the favelas, and he said, 'It's normal to us to live in fear; it's not so hard as it would be for you. Violence is a culture, and there are a lot of people who like violence. Don't assume we all want peaceful lives.' Like many favela residents, he was not only unimpressed by the whole idea of pacification, but also dubious of the problem it was intended to address.

In Bed with the President of Ghana?

New York Times, 9 February 2013

My friend Meri Nana-Ama Danquah's wedding brought me to Ghana. The traditional ceremony began when a representative of the groom's family said to a representative of the bride's, 'We have seen a beautiful flower growing in your garden, and we wish to pluck it.' In keeping with tradition, the two families threw challenges back and forth, which seemed to ritualise the complex ambivalence parents often feel at their children's marriages. But they also kept breaking into song. It felt as though they were simultaneously battling and celebrating. The presentation of the dowry didn't feel, as I'd anticipated, like a commodification of the bride. It felt respectful, less as if they'd bought my friend than as if they'd offered a tribute in acknowledgement of her worth.

When my husband-to-be and I met the Ghanaian politician John Dramani Mahama at a friend's wedding near Accra eight years ago, I liked him immediately. I kept up with his fortunes mostly through mutual friends and was happy to learn in 2009 that he had been elected his nation's vice president. When I read a draft of his trenchant memoir, *My First Coup d'État*, in 2010, I volunteered to introduce him to some agents and editors in New York. Many people in the developed world expect African political leaders to be either terse and political or bloated and ideological. The surprise of John Mahama's book is its tender humanism, and I thought it would go a long way towards breaking down prejudice in the United States. I blurbed the book when it was published last July; I am thanked in the book's acknowledgements; I hosted a party to celebrate its publication; and I conducted an interview onstage with John Mahama at the New York Public Library on 10 July 2012.

On 24 July, the Ghanaian president, John Atta Mills, died, and John Mahama stepped into the presidency; in December, he was elected to another term. In late January 2013, the Ghanaian press suddenly exploded with references to Mr Mahama's relationship with me. 'President John Dramani Mahama has been fingered to be in bed with one Mr Andrew Solomon, a gay lobbyist,' blared one unfortunately worded report. Another announced, 'Andrew Solomon reportedly gathered a few affluent people from the gay community to raise campaign funds for President Mahama with the understanding that when President Mahama won the elections, the president would push the gay rights agenda.' I was reported to have paid $20,000 for copies of the book.

The occasion of these revelations was Mahama's appointment of a woman one newspaper called the 'fiery human and gay rights advocate, Nana Oye Lithur' to head the newly established Ministry of Gender, Children and Social Protection. In confirmation hearings before a parliamentary committee, Lithur averred that 'the rights of everybody, including homosexuals, should be protected', thus provoking a firestorm. I was presumed to have pushed through her nomination, even though I had in fact never heard of her. The argument that Lithur was selected not for her formidable skills but because of a foreign devil dovetailed with the continuing position among some Africans that homosexuality is an import from the decadent West.

I have neither the ability nor the inclination to meddle in foreign elections, and I paid not one red cent for the book John Mahama inscribed to me. The only way I may have influenced him on gay rights was by welcoming him into the household of a joyful family with two dads. It is deeply unsettling to be implicated in a national scandal, to know that my attempts to be kind and helpful to someone would become his millstone.

On Friday, 1 February 2013, the president's spokesman said that President Mahama didn't know me. On Saturday, the president called me to apologise. On Sunday, the government issued a statement that Mahama and I know each other, that I have never made a campaign contribution or persuaded anyone else to do so, and that President Mahama 'does not subscribe to homosexualism and will not take any step to promote homosexualism in Ghana'. I am not sure what is involved in promoting homosexualism, but I am pleased to know that a cordial friendship with me does not constitute such an act.

The situation of gay people in most of Africa is deplorable, and the double-talk from the Ghanaian administration has done little to assuage valid concerns. In the wake of this brouhaha, I have received hundreds of letters from Ghanaians via my website and Facebook. Half are from gay people about how dire their situation is. One said, 'I am tired of this humiliation and embarrassment. I don't know whether if I am a gay I am not a living being. I have tried to pretend to be what they wanted. I need your word of advice and help. Sorry to say I feel like committing suicide. My tears are dropping so badly that I have to end my email here.'

Some others come from angry people who make harsh threats about what will happen to me if I ever return to their country: many are cruel; a handful, frightening. I am unused to being so hated. But more are from straight allies, of whom there appear to be legions. One woman complained, 'Men are deceiving me too much, so I want to join your LGBT please.' Another declared, 'I wish God has blessed me like you. I am not a gay but I respect and love so so much. May you live to always help mankind.' A surprising number come from priests and other clerics who announce that they believe all people are equal in the eyes of God, thank me for my advocacy, and say they will tell their congregations to accept and love instead of judging and castigating.

By curious coincidence, this whole matter arose while I was in

India promoting a book that deals in large part with how any condition may go from being perceived as an illness to being lived as an identity. It draws on my experience of such a transition for gay people in the United States. When I first visited India, some twenty years ago, the only obviously gay people were destitute and marginalised. On my second trip, in the late 1990s, I met a subculture of rather soigné gay men, but their faces flushed whenever the thing we had in common was acknowledged. At the Jaipur Literature Festival in February 2013, the 'gay panel' in which I participated attracted more than a thousand people, many of whom complained of hideous prejudice in India – but who were emboldened to object publicly to the problem in a tone that anticipated its ultimate resolution. There were many, many straight allies there as well.

In Ghana, the articles that attacked President Mahama for knowing me referenced 'the raging national debate on gay and lesbian rights' in Ghana. That there is such a debate – even if it's a debate about whether to lynch us – is meaningful progress. That local propagandists can plausibly suggest that the president of a West African country is in the hands of gay lobbyists reflects an evolving world. I hope that President Mahama will seize this occasion to take a leadership role in the region on LGBT rights. That so many people from his country wrote to me when the scandal broke indicates that many are thinking through these issues. I hope the time is not far off when to know someone like me will be less of a liability and more of an asset.

––––––––––

The bizarre saga recounted in this article continues. My name appears in nearly every piece about gay rights published in Ghana and is invoked by homophobes from Accra to Zabzugu as an emblem of the evil that stalks their country. Meanwhile, heartbreaking letters continue to flood my inbox. In the summer of 2015, a rumour surfaced in the Ghanaian media suggesting that I had somehow figured in the death of former president John Mills, as part of a nefarious conspiracy to install my man John Mahama, 'to pave way for the spread of lesbianism and homosexuality into the country' – this despite President Mahama's continued unwillingness to show support for gay rights. Mahama has had little contact with me in the years since the original accusations were levelled.

Another recent story in the Ghanaian press described a Legon lawyer's ecstatic vision that I would soon experience a profound religious conversion. One report held, 'A Law Lecturer at the Faculty of Law at the University of Ghana, Moses Foh-Amoaning, has prophesised that renowned gay activist, Andrew Solomon, who is an alleged friend of President John Dramani Mahama, will one day become a pastor. "Andrew Solomon will be called Pastor Andrew Solomon one day," he said. The Law Lecturer told Atinka AM Drive that the gay crusader will soon get closer to God.' Another article on the topic said of Foh-Amoaning, 'According to him, the forces behind the recent legalisation of same-sex marriage in the United States of America [USA] is unfortunate – he also cited renowned gay advocate, Andrew Solomon, as chief propagator – but "God will meet him [Andrew Solomon] at a point and hit him to change."' I haven't been hit yet, but rather look forward to the encounter when it comes.

In January 2016, another Ghanaian story said, 'Citing the president's association with the acclaimed gay rights activist Andrew Solomon to buttress his point, the Ningo Prampram parliamentary aspirant said President Mahama will do anything for money. "If President Mahama can collect gay money to run his campaign, then he will soon mortgage Ghana to anti-Christ to win the 2016 elections," he fumed.'

I wonder whether I might collect interest on the mortgage when it is realised.

Gay, Jewish, Mentally Ill and a Sponsor of Gypsies in Romania

New Yorker, 7 July 2014

When this article appeared on the *New Yorker* website, it instantly attracted comments – hundreds of comments, mainly from incensed Romanians. I had gone to their country for the publication of *The Noonday Demon* there. The publisher was generous, the press was flattering and my Romanian friends were impeccably hospitable, but I encountered prejudices that troubled me deeply. In the few years since, I've received many more letters about this article, and in this protracted aftermath, many Romanians have grown more accepting of its arguments. While this essay has continued to attract attention, most of my Romanian correspondents are writing in response to my books, primarily to seek advice because they suffer from depression or have a disabled child.

I n my teens, I asked my great-aunt Rose where in Romania our family had come from. She claimed that she didn't remember. I said, 'Aunt Rose, you lived there until you were nineteen. What do you mean, you don't remember?' She said, 'It was a horrible place and we were lucky to get out of there. There's no reason for anyone to go back.' I begged her to tell me at least the name of the place.

She gave me an uncharacteristically steely glare and said decisively, 'I don't remember.' That was the end of that.

My paternal grandfather – Aunt Rose's older brother, a farm labourer – had preceded her to the United States when he was sixteen, fleeing pogroms and generational poverty. He was processed at Ellis Island and settled in New York City, where he brought up his family under financial duress, only just able to feed his children. He nonetheless ensured that my father got a good education, and my family has lived in relative prosperity ever since. I've often wondered about the life my grandfather left behind. My forebears presumably had enquiring and capacious minds much like mine, my brother's and my father's, and I have pondered what it would be like if we lived in a society that provided little scope for social mobility.

My friend Leslie Hawke moved to Romania fifteen years ago and founded an NGO, OvidiuRo, to teach Roma (Gypsy) children. I joined its board of directors in part because I saw a parallel between the oppression of my Jewish ancestors and the oppression of the Roma. We had bettered our lives through access to education outside Romania; they might better theirs with access to schooling in Romania.

When a Romanian publisher bought the rights to *The Noonday Demon: An Atlas of Depression* last year, it reignited my curiosity about this ancestral place, and I signed on for a promotional tour. I saw an elegant circularity in the contrast between my destitute grandfather's departure and my return as a published author. A second cousin I had unearthed on Facebook said that she thought we hailed from Dorohoi, a small city about 250 miles north of Bucharest, near the Ukrainian border. An amateur genealogist friend offered to do further research, and she located papers confirming that the family had indeed come from Dorohoi. My grandfather and two of his brothers had sailed steerage from Hamburg in 1900, sending for their parents and siblings four years later.

My publisher had worried that Romanians might not be ready to talk openly about depression, but the zeitgeist had shifted more than they had guessed. Romania's greatest living writer, Mircea Cărtărescu, agreed to write an introduction and to participate in the book launch. Even before I arrived in Bucharest, the book was a bestseller, and my first two days there I was interviewed on all three major television networks, on Romanian National Radio, and in many leading newspapers. A large crowd squeezed into a capacious bookstore for the inaugural event, and *The Noonday Demon* went into a second printing the next day. Everyone treated me kindly, and I was impressed by the high level of intellectual and political discourse I encountered.

But all was not to go as smoothly as planned. Before I arrived, Leslie had been in touch with Florin Buhuceanu, who leads a Romanian gay-rights organisation called ACCEPT. Leslie's friend Genevieve Fierau had a connection to the Central University Library, a spectacular building in central Bucharest with an impressive lecture theatre that was opened in 1914 by King Carol I. They agreed that this would be the ideal place for me to speak to Bucharest's LGBT community. Genevieve arranged a meeting for Leslie and Florin with the library director, who, after what they characterised as a cordial hour-long discussion, confirmed that the hall was available, and that she would be delighted for the lecture to be held there. Florin thanked her for her courage in supporting an LGBT organisation, signed and returned the contract, and posted details about the event on Facebook.

Romania had cleaned up its act on gay rights when the United States appointed an openly gay ambassador, Michael Guest, who served from 2001 to 2004, during the administration of George W. Bush. But prejudice remains deeply embedded in Romanian culture, and Putin's homophobic shadow, which falls long in Eastern Europe, has not helped matters. In early June 2014, the Romanian Chamber of Deputies defeated a bill that would have granted legal recognition to gay couples, with 298 votes against and only 4 in favour. That same week, the library director phoned Genevieve, accused her of lying about the nature of the lecture, and said that the library would never have agreed to host an event in which gay identity was to be discussed. Thereafter, she did not return either Florin's or Leslie's multiple messages.

ACCEPT scrambled and found a smaller, less centrally located venue for the lecture at the National University of Theatre Arts and Cinematography. After I spoke there, the question-and-answer session lasted nearly an hour. Many of the questions pertained to my family life: what it was like to have a husband and children; how it felt to find acceptance from my father and in a wider social context, a situation as unimaginable to them as my life of relative affluence would have been to my great-grandparents. Several attendees said that they dreamed of emigrating someplace where they could find such acceptance. Too many described severe depression as a result of social oppression, and several alluded to the change of venue for my lecture as an example of such persecution. While it was hardly comparable to a pogrom, the incident helped me imagine what it might have been like for my family to belong to a group that their countrymen found repugnant.

The next day, Leslie and I drove seven hours to a horse farm in the northern Moldavian highlands, where we stayed overnight, eating rustic food and drinking homemade blackberry brandy. In the morning, we picked up one of the few remaining Jews in the region, who runs a sideline in genealogy, and proceeded to Dorohoi. It was haunting to look at the gently rolling landscape on our approach and think of my grandfather and his grandfather seeing those same hills. Life seemed to have changed little in the elapsed century. Farmers in oxcarts were going about their labour, and women in head scarves were hoeing the fields by hand. Their faces had the cracked skin that comes from brutal summers and winters in close succession. We followed a long dirt road up to Dorohoi's Jewish cemetery, locked behind a tall metal fence. A man who lived nearby had the key, and for about $5 each he let us in, explaining enthusiastically, 'I am not Jewish, but I like Jews.'

The cemetery had been profoundly neglected – like virtually everything else near Dorohoi. A lowing cow wandered among tombstones swathed in nettles. Leslie spotted the first Solomon grave. Soon we found more – many those of people born after my grandfather had emigrated. It's impossible to know whether these belonged to my relatives, but the Jewish community was never enormous (the county has about four thousand five hundred Jewish graves), so it seemed plausible that these namesakes were my relatives. I put pebbles on some of the graves, following the Jewish tradition of placing a stone instead of laying flowers. I thought about these people who could have left but didn't. We went into the funeral chapel, which was just a small barn with a Star of David on it, where we saw an old horse-drawn hearse.

One of the graves had an inscription memorialising the Solomons who had died 'at the hands of Hitler'; many of those dead had first names familiar from my own extended family. A memorial at the centre of the burial ground commemorates the five thousand Jews who were taken from the area, never to return. I heard Aunt Rose saying, 'We were lucky to get out of there.' I had hoped she might not be entirely right: that this wellspring of my family would be at least picturesque, that I'd have a surprising sense of identification with the place. I didn't know how despondent it would make me to imagine being trapped in what still looked like a reduced life, with none of the intellectual excitement of Bucharest anywhere apparent. I've reported from war zones and deprived societies for decades, but they have always seemed profoundly other, and this felt shockingly accessible. I could have been born here and lived and died like this.

As we left, we passed five sour-cherry trees, tall at the edge of the cemetery, and we rushed over to pick their ripe fruit. The dark red juice stained my hands, and I wondered who in my family might have stood beneath these trees and relished the same taste, so sharp and so sweet. I thought of how my own children would have scarfed down those cherries if they had been with me. I suddenly understood that my forebears had been children, too, in their day – that this place had been visited not only by the old men with beards whom I'd pictured as my ancestors, but also by boys and girls who would have climbed the trees to reap the plenty of their upper branches.

On the way out of town, I looked at the local peasants and thought that if some of their forefathers had not burned down the houses of such as my forefathers, mine wouldn't have left. I considered what had happened to my family within two generations, and what hadn't happened for them, and instead of feeling outraged by the history of aggression, I felt privileged by it. Oppression sometimes benefits its victims more than its perpetrators. While those ravaging others' lives exhaust their energy on destruction, those whose lives are shattered must expend their vigour on solutions, some of which can be transformative. Hatred drove my family to the United States and its previously unimaginable freedoms.

The conditions in the Roma settlements to which Leslie took me next made Dorohoi look like East Hampton. Where the subsistence farmers of northern Romania ate simply, the Gypsies of Colonia were going hungry; while the farmers lived relatively short lives, the Gypsies showed obvious signs of chronic illness. The peasants may not have had modern plumbing, but the Gypsies had none at all; they defecated in the surrounding pasture, and the place stank to high heaven. At this writing, as a result of OvidiuRo's work, fifteen hundred Roma children are getting the early education that might help them break out of poverty. I met some of those children, bright-eyed and full of fun, and hoped they could escape growing into morose teenagers and glassy-eyed adults like those who sat around Colonia in the squalor.

On the way back to Bucharest, I received a call from Duane Butcher, the chargé d'affaires at the U.S. embassy (the de facto ambassador, given that we did not have an ambassador to Romania at the time). He wanted to know what had happened concerning the library kerfuffle. A Facebook post I'd written about the incident had been picked up by a wire service and was being widely reported in the national media. He said that he would be writing an official letter about the matter to the Romanian government.

ACCEPT soon issued a press release that quoted Florin Buhuceanu saying, 'A human-rights organisation militating for LGBT rights in Romania cannot access a lecture hall in the most important library in Bucharest? An illustrious American writer and journalist should not speak about sexuality and identity in a cultural institution? Books written by gay authors, foreign or Romanian, will be disregarded in an academic and literary setting because of the sexual orientation of their authors?' Remus Cernea, a member of Parliament, told the press that he had asked the education ministry to punish the people responsible within the Central University Library. (After being called out on the floor of Parliament and in the media, the library officials made a ludicrous claim that ACCEPT had made a 'bad approach'.)

That night, I had been scheduled to engage in a public, forty-minute conversation with Cărtărescu at the New Europe College in Bucharest, a gathering place for the urban intelligentsia. Fifty or sixty people had been expected, but we found perhaps three hundred filling the seats, crowding the aisles and spilling into the hallway. The beginning of our conversation was predictably affable, but twenty minutes in, Cărtărescu said, 'And now I want to apologise personally for what happened to you at the library. I hope you know that these backward views do not represent the mindset of all Romanians.' The audience burst into rambunctious applause. 'We can only hope your other experiences in Romania have shown you the true hearts of our people,' Cărtărescu said, to further applause. Our talk ended up running for nearly three hours. I signed another two hundred books afterward, and their owners all expressed contrition. The last in line was Cernea, who said, 'The legislation for recognising civil unions failed, as you know, but there were three days of debate about a topic no one would have thought to discuss a year ago. Please give us a little bit of time. Our politicians are more conservative than our society.'

How did Romania relate to Jews, to the mentally ill, to gay people, to Gypsies? Many of the groups I represent in one way or another have attracted prejudice there at some point (as they have at other times, in other ways, in my own country). I had not intended to set off a scandal, nor had I anticipated my resonant sadness at this aspect of the six-day trip. I had likewise not imagined the surges of joy beneath those cherry trees and at New Europe College. The supporters of social liberalisation in a conservative, deeply religious country do not constitute the mainstream, but neither do their opposites. Romanian is a Latin language, and Romanians blend the warmth of Italians with the combative spark of Slavs. Various Romanians pointed out that, because my grandfather was born there, I could get a Romanian passport, and some asked me to do so. I'm contemplating it. I understand why Aunt Rose characterised Romania as a horrible place we were lucky to escape, but it's also a wonderful place and I'm glad that I returned.

I learned in 2015 that Andrei Rus, the professor who had arranged for my lecture to take place in the National University of Theatre

Arts and Cinematography, had come under attack from the Ethics Committee there. His contract was terminated for 'ruining the University's image' with his 'gay propaganda and homosexual agenda' – which is particularly striking given that he is not gay himself. His colleagues asked that I write a letter of support for him, which I did; in the end, he was sanctioned but not fired.

Myanmar's Moment

Travel + Leisure, November 2014

My assignment for *Travel + Leisure* was to describe Myanmar's most fascinating sights and most luxurious lodgings. I had recently been elected president of PEN American Center, an advocacy organisation supporting freedom of expression, which gave me access to a group of writers who were forming a PEN centre in Myanmar. So my month in the country long known as Burma seesawed between luxury river cruises and interviews with ex-political prisoners. The contrast was not as extreme as it sounds; the luxury was far less opulent and the prison alumni far more upbeat than one might have imagined. This essay examines Myanmar's social, political and economic life in greater depth than was pertinent for *Travel + Leisure*.

I had anticipated a time of hope in Myanmar. In the eighteen months prior to my visit in January 2014, eleven hundred of the country's political prisoners, including the most celebrated ones, had been released; censorship of the media had eased; limited parliamentary elections had taken place, and most international sanctions had been lifted. Foreign investment was beginning to invigorate the economy. Opposition leader Aung San Suu Kyi, winner of the 1991 Nobel Peace Prize and an icon of courage in the name of justice, had been freed in 2010 after two decades under house arrest and was campaigning for the presidency; her National League for Democracy (NLD) party had finally won seats in the legislature. The country seemed to be progressing economically and socially.

What I found instead was an extremely cautious neutrality. No one denied that things were better, but no one thought things were fixed. The exuberance of transition was tempered by the majority Buddhist philosophy of a people who had seen too many guttering flickers of hope extinguished. The population had been optimistic, perhaps, in the lead-up to independence in 1948; they had been optimistic again in 1988, when student uprisings promised a new justice; they had even had a streak of optimism during the Saffron Revolution of 2007, when thousands of monks rose up against the government only to be brutally crushed. By 2014, the people had eliminated such buoyancy from their repertoire of attitudes, and they were merely waiting to see what might happen next.

Neither were they bitter about their painful history. I had anticipated that former political prisoners would rant about their appalling treatment while incarcerated, but few of them did. Many said they were grateful for their experiences. In prison, they had had time to develop their minds and hearts, often through meditation. Most had set out knowingly to do things that would land them in jail, and they had marched to their cells with heads held high. When they were released, their heads were still held high. The writer and activist Ma Thanegi, who spent many years in jail because she had been Aung San Suu Kyi's personal assistant, told me that the best way to oppose the regime was to be happy in prison. 'It's like spitting in the face of the military,' she said. 'They wanted us to be miserable, and we were not going to oblige them.' If they could be happy there, then their punishment had failed, and the regime had no power over them. As she explained it, their adamantine cheer was both a discipline and a choice.

In 1993, the writer, activist and physician Dr Ma Thida was sentenced to twenty years for 'endangering public serenity', contact with illegal organisations and printing and distributing illegal materials. Her health deteriorated drastically in prison; she developed pulmonary tuberculosis and endometriosis. At her sickest, she weighed less than six stone, had a continuous fever, vomited constantly and could barely drink water or walk more than a few feet. Then her liver began to shut down. Ma Thida had been allowed to keep a supply of medicines to treat other prisoners, but the prison doctor confiscated them when she sought to treat herself, on grounds that she might use them to commit suicide. Only after she began a hunger strike did he relent. Kept in solitary confinement, Ma Thida begged for a companion, even a murderer or a thief, but her request was denied. She was not allowed paper or pencils; in six years, she managed to write only three short stories using smuggled implements. 'But I still owned my body and mind,' she said. 'So I treated this as time to learn how to get free from the circle of life. In this way, I could find total freedom.' When her captors asked what she wanted, she said, 'I want to be a good citizen. That's all. Nothing more and nothing less.' She noted the incomprehension on their faces. But her jailer eventually said, 'Ma Thida, you are free, and we are not.' Upon being released in 1999, she said to him, 'Thank you for this time in prison.' She refused to thank him for releasing her. She clung to the prospect of writing about her prison experience, knowing that her books might be read only by censors, but even to make those functionaries understand her perspective would count for something. Now that her prison memoir is a Myanmar bestseller, she can inspire the younger generation to resist. 'My imprisonment therefore becomes totally positive,' she told me.

She was at pains to point out that the reforms in Myanmar had been instituted by the military government, and she viewed them cynically. 'We Burmese show tremendous grace under pressure. But we also show grievance under glamour, and the fact that these reforms have begun to unfold does not change the deep problems in this society that we learned to see so clearly while we were in prison. What's really changed here is not the laws, not even the enforcement of the laws; what has changed is awareness. People are aware of their rights and use them to make demands and argue. That is the full measure of progress.' This was no small matter, in her view; more important than the next president was the population that president would lead.

Under the military junta, people were frequently jailed for their beliefs, but only after they had expressed them in public. Opinion was never as tightly controlled in Myanmar as in North Korea or Saudi Arabia. 'It's always been a pleasure working here compared to Cambodia, for example, where the intelligentsia is restricted,' said Vicky Bowman, a former British ambassador. 'Here, the intelligentsia has always been visible. Sometimes it's been in jail; sometimes it's had to wait to publish. But it has always been around.'

Although the generals who seized power in 1988 kept the borders largely closed, the attention of the outside world remained vital to their opponents. 'Please use your liberty to promote ours,' Aung San Suu Kyi famously said in 1997. The opposition no longer needed that outside amplification so urgently by 2014. There was a great deal of parsing this change among the people I met and a great many attempts to quantify it. The poet and activist Maung Tin Thit quipped that people who used to be arrested secretly for their radical views would now be arrested publicly. The artist Aye Ko, a leader in the 1988 uprising and later a political prisoner, said, 'I won't believe this government until they are out of power.' The comedian Lu Maw drew upon his reserve of catchphrases to characterise the ostensible reforms. 'Snakes shed their skin, but they are still snakes,' he told me. 'From 1952 up to now, same military. Only a new uniform every so often. Now, same guys but without the uniform.'

Ko Minn Latt, the young, dynamic mayor of a township in Mon State who hopes to run for Parliament, said, 'As the people get less frightened, they get more angry, because it's safe to be angry now. Ten per cent are busy with religion, ten per cent with getting rich, and the other eighty per cent are furious. But problems built during the last sixty years can't be solved within three. This is a "distorted democracy" – not only because these changes are led by the military government, which is still in power, but also because the people don't yet know how to function in a democracy.' Still, he believed that the leadership had become too attached to their newfound status on the world stage to relinquish it; reform now afforded the ego boost once achieved through the brutal exercise of power.

Moe Satt, an independent art curator, told me that Burmese artists had begun to talk about postmodernism. 'But how can we make postmodern comments on a pre-modern society?' he asked. 'There's a lot of catching up to do first.' He felt that many Burmese artists and intellectuals were unready to create work from the vantage of authority. 'We resist the end of pressure,' he explained, commenting on how artists can do their best work under oppression, be it political oppression or market oppression. Nay Phone Latt, who served four years of his twenty-year sentence for blogging about the Saffron Revolution, said, 'The people are not accustomed to taking responsibility; they imagine it will be done for them. If there's not yet democracy here, that is not only the fault of the generals.'

Even the partial and flawed reforms, however, have made for palpable change. Author and presidential adviser Thant Myint-U said, 'For ordinary people, especially the bottom fifty per cent, daily life is not much better at all. But the country was based on fear, and now the fear has been taken out of the equation.' Sammy Samuels, a Burmese Jew who owns a travel agency called Myanmar Shalom, said, 'Two, three years ago, every time I come back from the United States, I am so scared at the airport even though I have nothing on me. The immigration officer starts asking, "What were you doing there?" Now, they've start saying, "Welcome back."' Even pessimists do not predict that things will slip back to the previous level of oppression; they worry about how reform might stall, not about how it might regress.

As the government began loosening its reins, people developed absurdly high expectations that foreign investment would pour in, new airports would be built, and everyone would become wealthy. A friend commented to a cabdriver on how bad the roads were, and the cabbie said, 'If Aung San Suu Kyi is elected, this will all be paved.' In reality, the absence of basic services continues to impede authentic progress. Many have been disappointed to realise how slow development is anywhere. The Burmese call the internet the *internay* – *nay* being the Burmese word for 'slow' – and the web is accessible to only about 1 per cent of the nation's 60 million people. 'Nothing works here,' said Lucas Stewart, literature adviser to the British Council in Yangon. 'Everything breaks. Everything has been illegally bought so it's all second-hand, broken crap from China and Thailand. Skype doesn't work here. It takes a day to download a three- or four-minute video clip.' A recent survey showed that mobile-phone usage was lower in Myanmar than even in North Korea or Somalia, though the price of a SIM card has recently come down from over $1,500 to less than $15. Most cars are second-hand Japanese models outfitted with right-hand drive, even though traffic regulations are set up for left-hand drive. Automobiles are still unaffordable for most people, but much less out of reach; the streets, long empty, are now often choked with traffic.

Many great wars and revolutions are catalysed: the assassination of Franz Ferdinand started the First World War; the kidnapping of Mikhail Gorbachev heralded the demise of the Soviet Union; Mohamed Bouazizi set himself afire in Tunisia and launched the Arab Spring. The reforms in Myanmar seemed to materialise out of the blue. There is no consensus about the reasons for these changes, no agreement about why they happened at the precise time they did. They were not the consequence of a groundswell, but a top-down affair, a controlled process of reconfiguring national policy. U.S. ambassador Derek Mitchell said, 'Myanmar might have had a Tiananmen-like moment of voices coming up from the ground in 1988 or even 2007. But now it's a bureaucratic move from on high.' He added that the regime could probably have limped along for a while, just as the Soviet Union might have persisted if Gorbachev hadn't started to dismantle it. Openness can sometimes seem like the best option even to dictators.

The junta has claimed that liberalisation is a seven-step process initiated in 2003, so it is possible that, like Gorbachev's glasnost, the loosening was started by people who did not realise how far it would go. The final step on the 2003 road map was to vest power in a new government – but it was supposed to be a government of the military leaders' choosing. President Thein Sein, who assumed power in 2011, is the first leader of Myanmar who has avoided the taint of corruption. 'They erroneously chose a good guy instead of a corrupt one,' Ma Thanegi said. 'So now they have to live with the consequences.'

Some Burmese feel that international sanctions were the

triggering factor, impoverishing the country and isolating its rulers. As Myanmar became noticeably poorer than neighbours such as Cambodia and Laos, and dramatically more so than Thailand and Singapore, its leaders lost face, and their choke hold on the country became less attractive even to them. Many people were chronically malnourished; according to UNICEF, one in four Burmese children is underweight and about a third have stunted growth. Many lack reliable access to clean water. The crushing of the Saffron Revolution of 2007 was widely covered by the foreign press, blackening the junta's already dismal international image.

Perhaps most significantly, global isolation had made the country dangerously reliant on China, which in a long and contentious mutual history has never prioritised Myanmar's interests. One government official complained to me of expectations that the Burmese would supply their Chinese overlords with drugs, prostitutes and a venue for gambling. The Arab Spring had been instructive, too, and the junta may have thought it better to initiate concessions than to wait until the restive population became ungovernable. Members of the junta and their 'cronies' – the corrupt businessmen, many ex-military, who have profited under the regime – had witnessed the pathetic demises of Muammar Qaddafi and Saddam Hussein; they apparently preferred to go the way of Suharto's circle in Indonesia, who had retained their wealth and influence even after he finally ceded power in 1998. No military regime goes permanently unchallenged, and a gradual exit can forestall a harrowing one. As the writer Pe Myint drily put it, 'The leaders know that the people can lose several times, but the ruler can lose only once.'

Myanmar's isolation, though it has come at a steep price, has preserved the mystical inwardness of the country's Buddhist majority. Shwedagon Pagoda is among the holiest sites in the land, and people come from near and far to worship at it. The generals are said to have embellished the central stupa with many tons of gold – not gold leaf, but thick plates of solid gold – and receptacles full of jewels hang near its apex. Many Burmese maintain that the pagoda is worth more than the

Bank of England. Incongruous in the modernising city of Yangon, it stands momentous and transcendent, the St Peter's Basilica of Theravada Buddhism. Golden stupas glitter in the sun wherever you go in Myanmar. In the shadow of these hallowed towers, peasants labour in rough conditions. One local mordantly remarked to me that the country is rich, but the people are poor.

For many, life seems to have gone on largely unchanged for centuries: peasants, oxcarts, the same staple diet and simple clothes, the same glittering pagodas, gilded in the richer towns, merely painted in the poor ones. Nothing ever happens when it should; it's amasing that the sun sets on schedule. The country strikes an uneasy balance among this past way of life, still extant in the present; a present life of nascent contact with the outside world and the stirrings of reform; and a fully imagined future of democracy and prosperity about which many people spoke as though it were both incomprehensible and inevitable.

Tourists, who bring in a large share of Myanmar's official revenues, come to marvel at historical relics that its citizens often undervalue. Thant Myint-U observed that no one in Myanmar had ever had a pleasant experience living in a building over thirty years old. Some seven hundred significant structures have been demolished in the historic centre of Yangon over the past fifteen years. Many of the grand colonial buildings that remain belong to government ministries, but in 2005, the government decamped to Naypyidaw, leaving their fate uncertain. Those that are privately owned are often encumbered with lawsuits, rent-controlled tenants and non-resident rights holders (including defunct government agencies), creating a legal mess for any prospective preservationist.

Myanmar was a British colony until 1944, known as Burma until 1989. The British occupied part of the territory in 1824, then cobbled the multi-ethnic country together as a buffer for the Raj in India, expanding to the country's current borders by 1885. The colonial administration ruled the various ethnic groups directly, demanding only loyalty to the crown. Burma became a major battleground between the Allies and the Japanese in the Second World War, and the country lost hundreds of thousands of civilians. Military hero General Aung San – the father of Aung San Suu Kyi – forged a pact of ethnic unity as a means to gain independence from Great Britain, but promised the ethnicities regional autonomy if they would support him, assuring them that they could withdraw from the federation after a decade if they were unhappy with the centralised government. Then Aung San was assassinated even before independence was granted in 1948, and a dysfunctional democracy emerged. The Karen, the Shan and the Kachin ethnic groups declared their independence. All wanted to break away from this artificial country that had not, they felt, fulfilled its promises. In 1962, the failed democracy collapsed in a bloodless coup led by Ne Win, former head of the Burmese army. He controlled the country for a generation of entrenched isolation and economic mayhem under the banner of socialism. By the mid-1980s, Ne Win, in power too long, resorted to increasingly brutal tactics, with intense censorship, pervasive graft, and oppressive control: citizens had to register everywhere they went.

The 1988 student uprisings, in which Aung San Suu Kyi first emerged as a significant figure, sought to replace Ne Win's autocratic version of socialism with democracy. They were galvanised by a fight in a tea shop during which a student was killed by police. The students were young and inexperienced, however, and after several months of burgeoning protests during which Ne Win resigned, the military responded with a violent crackdown (believed to have been orchestrated by Ne Win), indiscriminately killing students, monks and even schoolchildren. Students had led the uprising, so the new military government restricted education, believing that uneducated people were easier to rule. They thereby dismantled one of Asia's fine educational systems, with literacy at the time approaching 80 per cent. Initially, universities were shut down; then private and missionary schools were shuttered as well. In 1990, the country held its first free elections, in which Aung San Suu Kyi's NLD won a landslide victory, but the military refused to relinquish control.

A country that the British had left with reasonably well-managed institutions had morphed into one with no human infrastructure, no legal infrastructure and only a dilapidated physical infrastructure. There was no education, no health-care system, no railway service. Once-maintained roads, bridges and railways soon deteriorated to near impassibility. This police state relied on a network of informers. Tea shops where students had once gathered were targeted by military intelligence. Fortunately, informers were fairly easy to spot: members of the military were the only ones who regularly wore socks, to keep their boots from rubbing against their feet. A knowing eye could identify even snoops in sandals by the rings around their ankles.

The so-called 88 Generation always remained active; some set up radio stations in neighbouring countries to keep opposing viewpoints in circulation. The spirit of protest never disappeared, and after another two decades of subjugation, discontent boiled over with the Saffron Revolution in 2007, after which a quasi-democratic constitution was introduced in 2008. It is in some ways an admirable document, but it contains deeply troubling clauses. One stipulates that the military is guaranteed 25 per cent of the seats in Parliament, while another blocks any changes to the constitution unless they are supported by more than 75 per cent of the parliamentary vote. This creates a broad military veto. There is popular debate about how exactly the constitution should be changed, though there is broad agreement that the role of the military should be reduced and that government processes should be more democratic. Can the constitution be amended to enshrine rights for ethnic minorities? Can the military veto be restricted? Can urgent environmental issues be addressed? How should the constitution be enforced? At least four hundred laws remain on the books that contradict the basic rights it establishes.

Nor has education recovered from the systematic attack it endured, though literacy has improved in recent years. The government now pays young people to study, but many still choose not to do so. Most schooling is focused on rote learning, and most teachers can be bribed, given their measly official salary of $60 a month. Progressive teachers complain that it is nearly impossible to teach critical thinking to students who have never heard of dissent. The urban university campuses were reopened as institutes of higher learning only in 2014. 'In a democracy, the people are the key players,' Nay Phone Latt commented, 'and if they are not educated, how can they fulfil this function?' Ko Minn Latt, the ambitious mayor in Mon State, became involved in politics after seeing a seventh-grade schoolgirl shot down by police in 1988. 'I was at first one of the activists. I want this and I want this. No compromise, no discussion,' he said. 'What I am trying to do now is to help people to become democrats.'

The country that is now Myanmar has rarely focused its military power outward; it could never stand up to China or India, the leviathans between which it is sandwiched. The military's main preoccupation is securing the borders with Bangladesh and Thailand and quelling the various ethnic militias that have doggedly struggled for generations to gain autonomy. Burmese exiles interviewed in camps in Thailand some years ago said they wanted only to return home, no matter what the government did or said. These days, popular sentiment holds that the junta leaders should apologise, but need not stand trial or be punished. The generals can see that sentiment is moving in the direction of accountability, and they react with a not entirely irrational paranoia.

American Buddhist monk Alan Clements interviewed Suu Kyi in 1995 for his book *The Voice of Hope*. Clements wondered how she would reconcile the Buddhist idea of forgiveness with the need to punish oppressors. She said that if the generals would confess to their crimes, it would be easier to forgive them. The result was an immediate crackdown. No South African-style 'truth and reconciliation committees' will be forming anytime soon in Myanmar. Everyone understands that the generals will walk away only if their bank accounts are secure. 'They're old and they don't want to go through the effort of looking after the country again,' Ma Thanegi said. 'They're not interested. In fact, they were never interested. At this point, I don't care if they are not punished. It's a luxury to punish them, and we don't have that luxury.'

The government of Myanmar, long based in Yangon, was moved abruptly in 2005 to the brand-new planned city of Naypyidaw, about two hundred miles north in what had previously been wilderness. The United States had built a highly fortified embassy in Yangon after the September 11 attacks and declined to move to the new capital. I attended one demonstration in Yangon, the organisers of which – having obtained the requisite permits – were protesting the requirement to obtain permits to demonstrate. The crowd was angry and their message was clear, but the government officials and legislators at whom it was aimed would neither hear nor see it. Naypyidaw is a city of government functionaries, largely out of reach of the radicals in Yangon and Mandalay. This geographical buffer protects the government from its own people.

More than a quarter of Myanmar's gross domestic product comes from natural resources. Major corporations have begun to invest there: consumer-product manufacturers such as Coca-Cola, Pepsi and General Electric; financial-services companies such as Visa and MasterCard, and extraction companies such as ExxonMobil and Chevron. Businesses without so much leverage are wary of Myanmar's persisting violence, lack of governmental transparency, erratic policy and unreliable utilities. Many skilled people left the country after 1988, creating a vacuum of competence. Some hundred thousand Burmese professionals are living in Singapore alone, working as construction supervisors, accountants, dentists and doctors. Without them, foreign companies struggle to set up shop, but likewise, until foreign companies begin operations, many emigrants have no incentive to return. Foreign governments are also hesitant in this uneasy dance. As Derek Mitchell told me, 'The international community has dealt with Myanmar as a cause, and now has to deal with it as a country.'

Political activists in Myanmar posited that a third of the people in the government, including Thein Sein, were reformers; a third still favoured military strong-arming; and a third were on the fence. 'If you make the wrong choice in this environment, you lose big,' Mitchell observed. Thein Sein has never been a heroic figure, but he has pushed back against hard-liners; one of his associates told me that he wanted to make the changes irreversible. Since 2011, he has met with Suu Kyi numerous times, but onlookers believe she doesn't trust him. 'She is extremely decisive, and she often treats his cautiousness as indecision,' one diplomat said. 'She didn't hope for the compromise she has been handed; she hoped for a revolutionary reversal.' The popular narrative in Myanmar speaks of 'The Lady and the hunters' – of Suu Kyi and a corrupt military. Ma Thanegi characterised the stereotype as 'the beautiful-victim-and-the-thugs story that has served her so well'. Once Thein Sein reined in the hunting, The Lady had to sully herself with politics, even before achieving official power. That imperative was not entirely welcome.

Turnout for the 2012 by-election had been huge. Everyone I met agreed that if a proposed election were held in 2015, the hint of self-determination would ensure an avalanche of voting. The urgency of that excitement echoed what I had heard in South Africa in the lead-up to the pivotal 1994 elections, for which millions of people waited in line for three days to vote. In Yangon, however, I heard near-unanimous concern that the election would be rigged. Suu Kyi's NLD seemed destined for victory, but members of Thein Sein's Union Solidarity and Development Party (USDP) appeared to be banking on the very real possibility that the NLD might prove incompetent at governing, and that – as in Korea, Taiwan and Mongolia – overthrown oppressors might reorganise and win in elections. Among the most surprising reformers in the ruling party has been Shwe Mann, speaker of the Parliament. When he took that role, it was assumed that he would endorse the military agenda as his predecessors had. Instead he sought to transform Parliament into a forum for actual debate and refused to hew to edicts from on high. But Shwe Mann told Derek Mitchell, 'We tried socialism; we tried a military government; both failed. We believe democracy will make us strong. If the people don't have a voice in their affairs, it will be an unstable country, and no one will invest here.' Suu Kyi, by then a member of Parliament, formed an alliance with him, by which he effectively acknowledged that the only path to long-term relevance was to stick with her.

It's hard to overstate the status of Daw Aung San Suu Kyi (*daw* is a term of respect, Aung San is her father's name, Suu Kyi is her given name, and she is commonly called simply 'The Lady'). 'She is not treated like a rock star,' Derek Mitchell averred. 'She's treated like the Second Coming.' Her father spearheaded the revolution and masterminded the multi-ethnic pact through which Burma achieved independence from the British; after his assassination, he achieved mythic status. Suu Kyi was raised by her mother, Khin Kyi, first in

Rangoon (now called Yangon), then in India and Nepal (where Khin Kyi was successively appointed ambassador).

Suu Kyi received her degree from Oxford University in 1969. After a brief sojourn in New York, she returned to the U.K., eventually marrying Michael Aris, a British fellow student at Oxford, with whom she had two children. By happenstance, she was visiting Burma to care for her hospitalised mother when the 1988 uprising began, and after a few weeks, she gave her first speech, asking for 'unity'. When the revolution was squashed, she banded together with some of her father's former acolytes in the pro-democracy movement and made a sacrificial decision that took on the shimmer of revelation: to stay in Myanmar rather than return to England to be with her husband and sons. Commanding more and more attention, she was put under house arrest a year later, and won the Nobel Peace Prize in 1991. Although she was released from 1995 until 2000, after which her house arrest was reinstated, she was never permitted to travel freely. These circumstances contributed to her aura of virtue, and she has proven to be perceptive and charismatic. I have never met anyone who was unimpressed after meeting her. Thant Thaw Kaung, who works with her, said to me reverently, 'You cannot find another such person in the whole world.'

Although most Burmese who are not beholden to the junta would like Suu Kyi to be president, Myanmar's constitution is designed to frustrate such hopes. Clause 59F forbids anyone married to a foreigner, or whose children are of foreign birth, from running for office – a prohibition inserted specifically to exclude Suu Kyi. When I was in Yangon, the question of whether 59F would be repealed was a constant topic of conversation. Any election in which she is not allowed to participate is sure to seem hollow in Myanmar and internationally. Conversely, her election would serve as a magnet for international aid and economic revitalisation, but she has remained tangled in constitutional bureaucracy. Many expressed concern that she had not built a team of experts nor designated a second-in-command. NLD insiders have fretted that the stubbornness that allowed her to survive for so long under house arrest, apart from her family, does not serve her so well now.

She looks to other people's ability to help her cause rather than seeking intimacy. I did not meet anyone who felt he or she had a personal relationship with her. Burmese entrepreneur Misuu Borit described her as having a 'kind of lonely style'; others said she seemed unable or unwilling to build the trusting human relationships that are required of a leader. 'She keeps her own counsel. Everything runs to her,' Mitchell said. 'It's an authoritarian structure in that way.' A British diplomat pointed out that the next Parliament might include more pro-democracy seats, but would have fewer members with experience as public servants. 'They were in jail, and since they came out, they've been running tea shops,' she said. 'Bright, good intentions, courageous, but to run a government?' The NLD was officially registered as a political party only in 2012, though it counts core members who were involved long before registration. 'How fast can you recruit all the smart people?' Borit asked. 'You can't make a baby by making love with nine women and waiting one month. These things take time – and if you have no money, it doesn't make the recruiting any faster.' Others echoed that sentiment.

The constitutional barrier to Suu Kyi's eligibility for election reflects larger problems with the country's legal system. Robert San Pe, one of her legal advisers, mooted the question of whether to institute common law or civil law – the concern being that there may not be enough case history for common law. San Pe notes that many badly drafted laws are being rushed through the legislature. In 2013, Shwe Mann built a vast research library and hired fifteen hundred new parliamentary staff, but research efforts were stymied by the impossibility of locating information in an uncatalogued collection organised by donor, rather than by author, title or subject. Laws are drafted in Burmese, with no official translations; foreign investors find themselves subject to regulations they cannot understand. One can find street vendors selling English translations of the investment laws to desperate foreigners at traffic lights in Yangon.

'Our people do not trust the courts; we do not believe in justice as delivered by the courts,' Suu Kyi has said. The constitution was ratified in September 2008, when Myanmar was reeling from Cyclone Nargis, which had killed some 140,000 people less than six months before. A recent joint committee was established to consider revising the constitution. Lawyers insisted that it must be easier to amend, and that the mandate reserving one in four legislative seats for the military should be scrapped. They objected to the lack of checks on the power of the president during a state of emergency. The president appoints both the chief justice and the rest of the Supreme Court, and the members need not have any legal background. The 109-member committee for revision of the constitution has invited suggestions from ordinary citizens, and more than forty thousand have poured in.

Ma Thida argued that constitutional reform would be required for Suu Kyi to run; that such reform would require the cooperation of the junta; and that if the junta enacted this reform, she would emerge as part of their plan rather than their fierce opponent. 'She saves them,' Thida said, and seemed pleased at the thought that Shwe Mann might run against Suu Kyi.

Myanmar has two primary paranoias: that it will be overrun by China and that it will be overwhelmed by Bangladesh's 160 million Muslims and those within their own territory. Many Burmese Buddhists – like anti-immigrationists in Europe and the United States – contend that Muslims don't assimilate. In Burma, the complaints are that they keep their wealth to themselves (though most are impecunious), engage in moneylending, and, worst, take several wives to build an eventual majority that might sweep away the Buddhists. The Burmese do not like darker-skinned people, so racism comes into play as well. Racism is acceptable at almost every level of society in Myanmar. For example, in 2009, Myanmar's consul general in Hong Kong wrote to his whole staff that the Rohingyas' dark complexions made them 'ugly as ogres', unlike the 'fair and soft' Burmese.

Muslim descendants of Bengali settlers – many of whose families have lived in Burma for over a century – mostly live in Rakhine State. Although they identify themselves as Rohingya, they are referred to as Bengalis by nationalists who would label them foreigners. 'The Burmese don't understand that this attitude, rather than saving them, will ruin their society, their reputation and their ability to develop,'

Mitchell said. 'They would say that the issue over Rohingyas and Muslims is an issue of national identity. And I say, "You're right. What kind of country are you going to be? Are you going to be one based on lawlessness and violence against a whole category of people because you distrust them, or are you going to respect due process, humanist values, all the things that we thought you were fighting for?"'

Myanmar is extremely religious, and most young men serve time as monks. Wealth is concentrated ostentatiously in the pagodas. The fear that Buddhism is in danger permeates the culture. Many consider Myanmar and Sri Lanka the last two bastions of Theravada Buddhism in a world dominated by Christianity, Islam and Hinduism. According to this narrative, although Buddhism was born in India, invader Muslims destroyed its classical context, uprooting the faith from its homeland. (Many Buddhists did, in fact, flee Mughal India for Tibet.) As Thant Myint-U explained, 'The Burmese self-identity is rooted in the idea that this is a bastion of the true religion and nowhere else in the world is.'

The Burmese state now known as Rakhine was known as Arakan as recently as 1989. Once an ancient and powerful coastal empire, Arakan had counted Muslims among its inhabitants since at least the seventeenth century. It was then conquered by the Bamar, the dominant Buddhist ethnicity for whom Burma was named, in 1784. It was sparsely populated at the time of the British conquest forty years later, consisting primarily of forests and marshes. The British granted plots to settlers to clear, importing Bengali immigrants to labour there. After this first modern Muslim migration into the region, northern Arakan became predominately Muslim. The early twentieth century witnessed a growing sense among Buddhist Burmese that British colonisers and Chinese and Bengali immigrants were thriving across the colonial state while they were being exploited. During the 1920s, a new wave of arrivals shifted the demographics further. Two million Indians a year immigrated to Rangoon, the globe's largest current population shift; the capital was 80 per cent Indian by the end of the decade. Since many resident Indians had fought for the British against Burmese independence groups, nationalists asserted that anyone except the ethnic Bamar, or Burmese, was a foreigner, even if born in Myanmar.

After the 1947 partition of India, a separatist group of Muslim guerrilla fighters seeking union with Pakistan drove many Buddhists from the north of Burma, stoking outrage. Their uprising was put down fairly quickly, and since the mid-1950s no further Muslim insurgencies have occurred. Many Burmese allege that the Rohingyas have links with al-Qaeda and other terrorist groups; in fact, some Rohingyas did fight with the mujahideen in Afghanistan against the USSR during the 1980s, and for the Taliban later on, though in negligible numbers. Although descended from Bengalis, most Rohingyas have no claim to Bangladeshi citizenship; although born in Myanmar, they remain without a country as long as Myanmar classifies them as aliens. Without national identification cards, they have no access to education and live in unrelenting poverty. Since the recent liberalisation began, some of the two million Buddhists living in Rakhine have subjected the nearly as numerous Rohingyas to pogroms, setting fire to neighbourhoods, villages and mosques in broad daylight.

The first recent outburst against the Rohingyas, in June 2012, was triggered by the rape and murder of a Buddhist woman, allegedly by Rohingya Muslims. The next round, later that year, sprang from extremism and political expediency stoked by the Buddhist monk Ashin Wirathu, who exhorts his followers to 'rise up' and 'make your blood boil' to quash a supposed international Muslim conspiracy to destroy the 'golden Burmese' way of life. In sermons, interviews and a logorrhea of online postings, he refers to Muslims as *kalar* (the Burmese equivalent of 'niggers'), 'troublemakers' and 'mad dogs'. Pamphlets distributed at one sermon warned, 'Myanmar is currently facing a most dangerous and fearful poison that is severe enough to eradicate all civilisation.' In the Western press, he has been compared to Hitler. Wirathu initiated the 969 movement to mark stores and houses and even taxis where Muslims are unwelcome. The name of the movement played on Muslims' use of the number 768 to identify stores that sold halal meat – which Wirathu labelled an act of separatism (although halal grocers never excluded non-Muslims). Practically every taxi in Myanmar displays a 969 sticker; one driver ranted to me that the fact that Muslims may take more than one wife proves that Buddhist women were being abducted and forced to bear Muslim children.

While the paranoia is absurd, the basic concern can be tied to historic events. Muslims forced Buddhists out of Afghanistan a thousand years ago; the Taliban more recently destroyed ancient Buddhist holy sites in Pakistan; and radical Islamists have denounced Burma's 'savage Buddhists' to encourage Indonesia's acceptance of Rohingya refugees. Relaxed censorship means that marginal opinions are more openly circulated, to incite prejudice as much as to promote pluralism. Nay Phone Latt said, 'Some think that the lifting of censorship is a mandate to insult one another.'

Wirathu and his camp have waged an aggressive campaign on Facebook. In Myanmar, those who do not have internet access get their news from those who do. Allegations go viral even among those who have never seen a computer. Wirathu had been sentenced for inciting hatred, but was freed in 2012 under the general amnesty and went straight back to his rabble-rousing, claiming that the new freedom of expression had made his crusade legal. Monks in Rakhine began to distribute pamphlets asking Buddhists not to associate with Rohingyas. Neither the government nor, significantly, Aung San Suu Kyi has denounced the genocidal stirrings in Rakhine. It appears clear that doing so would imperil votes.

As Rohingya neighbourhoods in Rakhine towns have been burned and looted, Rohingyas have been moved to refugee camps, where they live in appalling conditions. A sixty-year-old Rohingya teacher described seeing a student she had taught and liked setting fire to her home. Rakhine Buddhists suspected of doing business with Rohingyas have had their houses burned down. The hospital in Sittwe, capital of Rakhine, has only ten beds for Muslims. In the city's overcrowded camps, medical attention consists of one doctor visiting once a week for an hour. Ambassador Mitchell described seeing children dying from easily curable illnesses.

Internecine violence has also broken out in the Rohingya camps. One UN aid worker said he had observed rape, incest and alcoholism among these desperate people, though the violence from guards was far worse. Many are starving; some have seen their children killed. The camps are mostly in low-lying areas that flood during the summer monsoon, when it rains more than three feet a month; even in

January, when I visited, they were muddy and squalid. Because these camps are adjacent to the Rohingya neighbourhoods, many refugees can see their former homes and their mosques from them; the old Muslim ghetto is now cordoned with barbed wire. Many Rohingyas have fled Myanmar, but no neighbouring country wants to give them asylum, so a good number are dying on overloaded boats as they seek a safe port. Their desperate wanderings have become an international crisis. Meanwhile, the price of fish in the province has doubled, given that half the fishermen are in detention camps. Likewise, no lower-wage workers are available to harvest the rice paddies.

The conflict triangulates among the Bamars, the Rakhines and the Rohingyas. The Bamars believe they are the natural rulers of an empire that includes the Rakhines; the Rakhines, mostly Theravada Buddhists, believe they should have dominion over the Rohingyas. The Rakhines, whose ancestral Arakan empire encompassed much of Burma, hate the Bamars almost as much as they do the Rohingyas. Theravada Buddhism, like many ideological doctrines, claims religious and racial superiority, but it was also the basis for the Saffron Revolution, which proposed that the military government had violated the precepts of Buddha *sasana*, or righteous moral rule. Suu Kyi uses Buddhist rhetoric in her speeches and draws on Buddhist ideals in her quest for democracy. Her politics and her religion are inseparable. In what appears to be an electoral calculation, she has refused to condemn the mistreatment of Rohingyas outright. What would be the place of Muslims in such a vision?

Western aid organisations have tried to help the Rohingyas, but Rakhines have often impeded aid. The Rakhines are poor, and scarce resources do not engender amicable relations. Rakhine State is the second least developed in Myanmar, and many people don't have access to latrines or clean water. To function at all, global charities have had to assure a kind of parity, even though the Rakhines live freely while the Rohingyas languish in camps.

Though the Rohingyas are experiencing the worst of it, rage against all Muslims has escalated. Most of Yangon's construction companies are Muslim-owned, and Buddhists have started refusing to hire them. Mandalay, the country's second-largest city, has seen anti-Muslim riots. When I was in Myanmar, curfews had been imposed in areas of Yangon with sizeable Muslim populations. 'We had gangs in cars going down the streets near where I live warning the Muslims that they would be killed. People were cowering behind locked doors,' said Lucas Stewart, who works for the British Council in Yangon, and who called the 969 movement 'nearly a terrorist organisation'.

The Muslims in Myanmar can be divided into four categories. Bamar Muslims settled in the area some twelve hundred years ago; on ancient monuments, historians have found inscriptions to Muslims who served the early kings. Horse traders, artillery soldiers and mercenaries who arrived in the sixteenth and seventeenth centuries assimilated into this group. Second are Chinese Muslims in the north-east, who trace their origins mostly to Yunnan Province and are descended from Turkic settlers from Mongol times onward. Third are those whose nationality changed when Arakan was subsumed into Burma by the British. Fourth are the immigrants from India or Bangladesh over the past two hundred years. 'There is ethnic prejudice, and there is religious prejudice from the monkhood,' Thant Myint-U said. 'They affect the same people, but for somewhat different reasons.'

Schoolmaster Aye Lwin, who won gold for his country overseas as a volleyball player on Myanmar's national team, is the leader of the Bamar Muslims. An elegant man, he lives in a pleasant apartment in central Yangon. He believes that the violence in Rakhine State has been incited by entrenched interests that oppose the slackening government control. 'There are people behind a screen who are trying to undermine democratisation,' he said, 'because if there is full-fledged democracy, there will be rule of law. Rule of law will have repercussions on the current ruling class. Crime is happening every day, rapes are happening every day, but these people manipulate it into a religious conflict. They could have nipped the burning of houses in the bud; they could have constrained the hate speech. But nationalism can be used to exhaust people's energy; it slows down the reform process.'

Misuu Borit pointed out that people in poverty reproduce fastest all over the world, and that while minority population growth was driving majority prejudice, majority prejudice was likewise driving minority population growth. Then a rumour that a Buddhist woman had been raped and murdered by Muslims kindled genocidal episodes. Rape has been used throughout history as an impersonal act of aggression in ethnic, religious and nationalist wars, and Borit finds it sinister that these cross-ethnic rapes have received so much attention, especially given the 'shameful' lack of police interest in rape among the Bamar or the Rohingya. 'Someone is cooking something between the Muslims and Buddhists,' she said. 'When things spin out of control, the rulers call in the army and say that they are "saving the country" and we are the weaklings. They make that true.'

Ma Thida sees a more profound, generalised resentment finding expression in the anti-Muslim atrocities. 'The generals did not discriminate in their cruelty,' she said. 'It was a democratic cruelty.' She believes that people who never believed that the law was intended to protect them are taking their revenge on authority itself. 'So this Muslim situation is not simply communal violence nor religious violence nor racial violence,' she said. 'It's a manifestation of something deeper: of undemocratic violence.'

It is a five-hour boat ride from Sittwe, where I had seen the burned-out neighbourhoods and the camps, to Mrauk-U, Arakan's imperial capital from 1430 to 1785. In this northern part of Rakhine, the shadow of religious hatred seemed almost implausible. My first morning in Mrauk-U, I got up at four forty-five and drove through the eerily darkened byways of the impoverished town to the foot of a small mountain with steps carved into it. Mornings in Myanmar often find bewitching mists hovering over the valleys and around the hills, delineating what is small and close, and what is large and far. Temples and other monuments that look about the same size on first glance can be differentiated in scale by the blurring of their edges, which indicates greater distance. Visitors are enjoined to see all the great sites at sunrise, given the aesthetic appeal of the mists.

After a Rakhine breakfast of fish soup with rice noodles and a lot of spices and condiments, I went to visit some villages in the nearby state of Chin. The Burmese king used to take beautiful women for his harem; to protect themselves, according to legend, Chin women began tattooing their faces with lines like spiderwebs to make themselves ugly to the Burmese, a custom that continued long after the threat had abated. Perhaps as a result, the most easily accessible Chin villages are inundated with tourists, and tattooed women pose for thousands of photographs. Here, a few miles from the border with Bangladesh, people from various ethnic groups seemed hardly aware of the crisis faced by the Rohingya. In a country with such poor communications infrastructure, radicalisation spreads in fits and starts, bypassing whole districts. We didn't see a single 969 sticker there.

There are more than a hundred ethnic groups in what is now Myanmar, and they have a long history of violence in the myriad shifting empires of the region. The students of 1988 proved to be nearly as ruthless as the junta that defeated them, staying rigid in their demands, building their own prison camps, and engaging in torture. The nation's myriad partisans have an often unnerving relentlessness. But Theravada Buddhism points towards an implacable serenity, and that, too, was manifest in most of the activists and artists I met. At their suggestion, I headed across the country and visited the Golden Rock, among the country's holiest shrines. High up a steep mountain, the sprawling site was mobbed with pilgrims, monks and nuns. Street foods and ingredients for traditional medicines were being hawked everywhere: porcupine quills; a goat's leg soaked in sesame oil; bunches of dried herbs. Many people were sleeping on bamboo mats or in makeshift tents. Thousands upon thousands of candles flickered, the hum of chanting was ubiquitous, and the air was heavy with incense and the redolence of food offerings. Young couples come here not only out of piety, but also for the chance to interact in the anonymity of the crowds. Flashing LED displays festooned the buildings, even the animist shrines. If I were to say that it made Grand Central Station at rush hour look like a meditation retreat, I'd be underselling the chaos. Yet for all of that, it felt peaceable.

The Golden Rock itself is an extraordinary sight: a boulder, nearly round, twenty feet in diameter, balanced on the edge of the mountain as if on the verge of plummeting. Legend holds that it remains on its precarious perch thanks to three hairs of the Buddha. The entire rock is covered in gold leaf, to which pilgrims keep adding, so that in some places the gold is an inch thick and stands out in lumps. Atop the rock, far out of reach, is the Kyaiktiyo Pagoda. The gold orb glows at sunrise, in afternoon light, at sunset, in the floodlit night-time. When the light changes, the effect shifts subtly, but it is never less than awe-inspiring. I climbed under it, stood beside it. From every vantage, one feels the fragility of its odd balance, the drama of its massive heft, and the tranquillity that holy places can achieve. It was both miraculously exciting and strangely reassuring. Like any great landscape, it holds the viewer's attention even if he or she is not praying.

Myanmar has some half million monks and a large population of nuns – at least one per cent of the country is in holy orders, and many others have served in the past. Most boys spend a while as monks, then return to their families. Even a casual visitor will pick up a bit of Buddhist arcana. To wit, the six types of religious structure are the pagoda or stupa (or *zedi*), a solid structure that often contains a relic; the temple, a hollow, square building for worship; the cave, which serves as a meditation centre for monks; the ordination hall; the monastery, where monks live; and the library, where the Buddha's scriptures are kept. Most figural monuments of the Buddha are made with a base of brick, or occasionally limestone, and covered with plaster and lacquer. The standard policy is to fix the plaster and lacquer as they fade or chip, which results in Buddhas that look newly reupholstered, without any patina of age. The eleventh-century reclining Buddha at Thaton, recently restored, looked as if it had been fashioned on Tuesday by a pastry chef.

Wherever you go in Myanmar, you are in a former capital – a place where some ethnic group reigned for a while. Bagan was the capital from the ninth to the thirteenth centuries. That was the era when it became fashionable to build pagodas and temples, and noblemen competed with one another to construct the grandest and most splendid, while poorer people built more modest structures. The detritus of that spiritual one-upmanship is a twenty-six-square-mile plain festooned with 4,446 religious monuments. It's impossible to understand this trove through photographs, because its power lies in its sweep. We walked among the pagodas; we drove among them;

we climbed one of the temples to watch the sun set; we surveyed the whole gloriously littered landscape from a hot-air balloon. Even in person, it's hard to compass the scale of Bagan's Plain of Temples. It's bigger than Manhattan, more than eight times the size of the estate of Versailles. Some of the buildings have been poorly restored by the junta, others are dilapidated but still coherent, and countless others lie in ruins. Whichever one you are looking at, you see a thousand more over its shoulder. If one feels exalted by the Golden Rock, one is humbled by Bagan, for both what it was and what it is.

Issues of faith are a constant conversation, and many secular experiences are filtered through Buddhism. San San Oo, a psychiatrist in Yangon whom I met through friends, had been told repeatedly that Burmese people healed themselves through Buddhism and didn't need her ministrations. She tried to explain that therapy might help people brutalised under the regime to emerge from post-traumatic stress disorder, but they insisted they would transcend it only through religious practise. San San Oo uses hypnosis and had finally managed to build a practise by characterising hypnosis as a means for someone else to raise you to a meditative state. She told me she felt certain that it had the same brain-wave profile. Her husband, the artist Aung Min, who had been a provocateur before the reforms, said, 'The Buddhist way means that anger is bad; it upsets emotion and thinking, causing only negativity and destruction. But I was so angry. So I did four months of hypnosis, and my anger diminished. It's just deep meditation.'

While Buddhism predominates and Islam follows behind, other faiths are also in evidence. There is a significant Christian population, and there are even a few Burmese Jews. Sammy Samuels is descended from Iraqi Jewish merchants who came to Yangon in the nineteenth century and set up business selling Burmese tea and rice to India. They established the city's synagogue, a Jewish school and a cemetery, and they married Buddhist women who converted to Judaism. By 1919, some three thousand Jews were in Myanmar. After 1969, most of the community migrated to Israel or the United States, but not the Samuelses. Every day, Sammy's father goes to the synagogue to greet visitors from abroad; the minister for religions attended an interfaith service there. Burmese independence came the same year as the establishment of the state of Israel, creating an unlikely connection. The Burmese prime minister was the first head of state to visit Jerusalem after independence. Moshe Dayan and David Ben-Gurion have visited the Yangon synagogue. Even under the junta, Myanmar sent students to learn agriculture in Israel. Now the Jews find themselves championing the cause of the Muslims because both are beleaguered minorities uneasily united against Buddhist fundamentalism. Aye Lwin said, 'We always were brothers, Muslim and Jews here.'

The Rohingya situation is separate from, albeit related to, armed conflicts waged chronically by several ethnic insurgencies that seek to establish a federal system in which they would enjoy greater autonomy. The Muslim problem proceeds from sectarian, demographic and religious tensions; the armed conflict, from minority nationalism. 'You can have one or two civil wars in a country. Here, there are seventeen going on,' Mitchell said. All of the contentious ethnic groups want the right to elect their own legislatures, and to teach in their own languages. In 2014, the government pushed for a nationwide cease-fire as a precondition for preliminary all-party peace talks. The agreement that was reached stipulated that future negotiations would include ethnic political and social leaders, not just military chiefs; and that those subsequent talks would address nondiscrimination, constitutional changes to support more ethnic/regional control, a more accountable security sector and the clearance of land mines. 'They are willing to leave the central government in charge of defence, currency and international trade,' explained Win Min, a presidential adviser, 'but they want to control education, social sectors, fisheries, transportation within their own state. And they want to get tax money from the natural resources extracted in their territories.'

Myanmar's ethnic conflicts are also ideological. At the height of the Vietnam War, the Cultural Revolution and the Khmer Rouge, the threat of escalating guerrilla warfare was terrifying to many Burmese. The military was eager to expel the remnants of Chiang's Kuomintang army from mountains near the Chinese border, fearing an invasion.

At the same time, the Burmese military was fighting the Communists who opposed the regime. On several occasions, leaders of various ethnic groups sided with the Communists just because doing so gave them combined fighting strength. Thant Myint-U, who is also involved in peace negotiations, pointed out that Myanmar's military government had justified itself by exaggerating 'a half-century-old counterinsurgency campaign on autopilot'. Ma Thanegi said, 'Since independence, there have been so many insurgencies, fighting not only the central government but also one another, that it's a wonder they can keep things straight and not shoot their own people.'

The past few years have seen little sustained fighting, though skirmishes erupt when the government enters a contested territory to regain control of a road, build a dam or establish dominance in a lucrative mining operation. British colonial rule never fully penetrated these remote, rugged areas, and infrastructure is as scarce as political stability. Some militias aim to defend local people against profiteers; others demand taxes from villagers. Other self-styled forces pursue their own business agenda; the three-thousand-strong Mong La National Democratic Alliance, for example, is led by a former Chinese Red Guard accused of running gambling and drug rings and trading in endangered wildlife. In Kachin, 120,000 people remain in government prisons because of their ethnic activism or sympathies; recent video footage shows the Myanmar army bombing Kachin trenches. The jadeite mines of Kachin produce several billion dollars a year, but little of that money trickles down to the Kachin people. In the Karen region, the average villager makes less than $1,000 a year and can see that Karen people a mile away on the Thai side are making $10,000.

When I travelled to Mon State, Kyi Zaw Lwin, a local politician and teacher, told me that he could not advance because he was only half Mon and therefore trusted by neither the Mon nor the Burmese. His mixed ethnicity far outweighed his politics, his experience or his education. The Mon once had a kingdom comparable in scale to Thailand, but they were conquered by the Burmese in 1057 – and they still want their original kingdom back. Individual states already have parliaments, so components of federalism are in place. But how much power should those parliaments have? And should they represent everyone in the state, or just the dominant ethnic group? The consensus is that the central government should share power with regional lawmakers, but to what extent remains in contention.

Thant Myint-U believes that a peace deal is closer than at any time since 1948. Presidential adviser Win Min agrees that the level of trust between the ethnic fighters and the Myanmar army is exceptionally high. But Ko Minn Latt expressed grave concern that, with the nation as a whole unready for global competition, autonomous states were not ready to contend with such large neighbouring economies as those of Thailand or Cambodia. The defining question is whether Myanmar can democratise without fragmenting into impotent pieces. How does the central government support a range of ethnic identities without losing a unifying, national one? How, indeed, can a national identity be forged that does not feel like a vestige of the generals' artificial one? Many Myanmar-watchers fear a devolution similar to the splintering of the former Yugoslavia into long antithetical, warring republics.

The Buddhist emphasis on forgiveness is not without its ramifications here. There is, once more, little talk of retributive justice; moving on is more important than holding people to account. Win Min spent years in the jungle after the 1988 uprising; then he went to the United States to study, then moved to Thailand, where he became a professor. When he was invited to advise the new Burmese government, his family warned him that the regime might be using him to create an appearance of reform, but he yearned to be part of the changes he had hoped for. 'We're not at take-off yet,' he said. 'It takes time.'

Literary tea shops where writers gather for performances and readings have sprung up all over Yangon and Mandalay. 'There's a short-story tea shop just over there,' one local told me as we strolled through Yangon. 'Detective writers and mystery writers go to the one next to the stop at the Macon Building. The poets go to Thirty-Seventh Street, and the novelists go to one on Thirty-Third Street.' Such events would have been impossible five years ago. Censorship under the junta was applied most rigorously to politics, religion and nudity. According to Tin Win Win (who goes by the pen name Ju), depictions of poverty were also prohibited, since they were thought to show the country in a bad light. You had to secure a licence to publish a book, which first had to pass a prepublication review. In 2012, the head of the censorship department announced on national television, 'If it is going to be a true democracy, we have to abolish censorship.' These days, as Ma Thanegi noted, 'Any news of any unfairness anywhere, it's in the papers. We have never before seen such a situation. Even if nothing is done, at least we know.' Journalists long precluded from criticising the government now do little else.

Thant Thaw Kaung, a leading publisher and foreign-book distributor, sold an English-language encyclopedia in 2007. A friend pointed out a paragraph-long entry for 'human rights'. Thant withdrew the whole encyclopedia, collecting all copies that had been delivered to stores, lest someone higher up notice and send him to jail. He now distributes his books in English more widely and has set up travelling libraries to bus books in Burmese into villages.

The government department overseeing book publication, previously called the Press Scrutiny and Registration Department, has been rechristened the Copyright and Registration Department. Although books are no longer censored line by line before publication, the department reviews them after publication, and those that are too broadly critical of the government or military are taken out of circulation. A bestselling author in Myanmar may sell up to a hundred thousand copies of a title, but few foreign books are translated into Burmese. Most writers concentrate on short-form prose and poetry for magazines. Blogging is achieving some reach. But Ma Thida suggested that writers had internalised the spirit of censorship, and that it would take a generation before anyone would write with authentic freedom. She has started a magazine and a newspaper and has exhorted younger writers to expand their scope, arguing that freedom withers if it is not exercised. Her publications touch on long-standing hot-button issues such as ethnic conflicts, and fresher terrain such as women's, gay and disability rights.

Nay Phone Latt decided in 2007 to inform expatriates about

what was happening in Myanmar by starting a blog, a platform then subject to neither censors nor editors. Because Myanmar had no functioning internet, he did his blogging from Singapore. He never criticised the government directly; he wrote short stories and poems full of metaphor. One told of a tiger that came to a village, entered a pagoda and decided to stay. The villagers believed that wild animals belonged in the forest, and some wanted to kill the tiger. The daughter of the village chief said that the problem was not the tiger, but the place where it had installed itself. But no one could get it out of the pagoda, so they lived in constant fear. 'Magazines published these stories because the censors didn't know what I meant,' Nay Phone Latt explained.

When he returned from Singapore just before the Saffron Revolution, he organised the Myanmar Blogging Society so journalists could learn how to file dispatches from Yangon that might reach the outside world. He believes that reporting from inside the country was key to the reforms that came in subsequent years. The government arrested Nay Phone Latt after someone found cartoons disrespectful of the regime in his email inbox. He explained that anyone could send anything to his inbox without his approval, but his inquisitors did not believe him. He was interrogated for ten days, during which he was not allowed to sleep, was often beaten, was sometimes tied up, and was taken from place to place blindfolded, so that he didn't know where he was or who the people questioning him were. 'In a military regime, inside the prison and outside the prison are not so different because the whole country is like a prison,' he said.

Sentenced to more than twenty years' incarceration, he was first sent to Yangon's notorious Insein Prison, where Ma Thida had also done time. Once he was transferred to a lower-security prison in Rakhine, he was allowed to write letters to his family. Again he resorted to metaphor to describe what he saw. 'It's a very, very good place to concentrate,' he said. 'We had the right to read. And my parents came to me every month and brought books. I was never sad. My narrow cell was just like a little library.' He invited other inmates to his cell and taught them English or read to them; he taught them about computers, though there was no computer there. He dictated new stories to his parents, who published them under a pseudonym. After the 2012 general amnesty, he published his *Prison Letters*.

Nay Phone Latt said none of the political prisoners he knew had been afraid during their confinement. 'Imprisonment made us stronger and more educated; prison is our university. There I learned never to focus on the long future. I learned to focus on the present.' Even now, he maintains, the government controls freedom of expression by law. 'Not by pressure, by law. We can write, but sometimes they try to sue the journal, the editor and the writer.' He pointed out that the Electronic Transition Act, under which he had been sentenced, remains on the books, though it has been amended to mandate shorter prison terms. The decision of which rules to enforce rests with the military. 'We are not so safe,' he said. The chilling effect on journalists is strong.

Censorship empowers artists by implying that free expression is both immensely potent and profoundly dangerous. Censorship is a gesture of fear, and fear invests its objects with authority. Htein Lin was among the leaders of the 1988 movement when he was in law school. During the crackdown, he fled to a refugee camp in India. In 1992, India normalised relations with the military government of Myanmar. Though India still claimed to support democracy in Myanmar, members of the All Burma Students' Democratic Front soon fled India to camps in the Myanmar jungle near the Chinese border. A grim clash worthy of *Lord of the Flies* ensued between the new arrivals and those already ensconced in the camps. Htein Lin and about eighty others were accused of being informers, tortured and then locked up by their comrades. Ten died from infections after their fingers were chopped off. Fifteen were executed by their former student comrades. 'You cannot get out of the jungle,' Htein Lin said. 'You get wet and you will never be dry again. You are sinking into the ground every step you take. Where is the food? You cannot get the malaria out from your body. Then the leeches. When you are sleeping, they get into your softest spot and you wake up to feel them sucking blood from your eye.'

He eventually escaped the jungle and finished law school. Then in 1998, his name appeared on a secret list of people planning a demonstration, and all of them were sent to jail. Htein Lin was sentenced to seven years. Compared with the jungle, prison was easy. He had learned to draw in India, and in prison he befriended one of his guards, a man who had never heard of paintings. Htein Lin volunteered to make one for him, so the guard returned with some house paint. Htein Lin extracted the wick from a cigarette lighter and used it as a brush. The prison had no toilet paper, and inmates used strips torn from discarded prison uniforms to clean themselves. Htein Lin saved half of his allotment, and on those banners of abraded white cotton, he painted some of the most haunting images ever to come out of war. Htein Lin used a bottle cap, a piece of glass, a carved bar of soap and an old fishing net to create monotypes. A syringe from the prison hospital was adapted to draw fine lines.

One guard mistook Htein Lin's abstract painting for a map of the prison, intended to facilitate escape, so all his art was destroyed; he began again. He would produce some three hundred paintings during his seven years of confinement. Over time, Htein Lin's guard brought several other sentries into his confidence, explaining that their charge was a great artist. When all the insiders were on duty at the same time, the paintings were spirited away and smuggled to his family. A friend approached the British ambassador, Vicky Bowman, and asked her to look after the collection. She agreed to do so and fell in love with Htein Lin through his art; soon after his release, they were married. He exhibited his paintings in Yangon in 2005. He invited the guard who had obtained art supplies for him to view the work, and they drank a toast to their collaboration. Htein Lin talked to me about the role of art in formulating a new ideology. 'In prison, I met many politicians and lawyers,' he said. 'They all became poets and songwriters there.'

When I met Htein Lin, he was assembling an installation called *A Show of Hand*. He had tried to contact as many as possible of Myanmar's three thousand former political prisoners (that official tally is believed by many to be too low) so he could make plaster casts of their hands. By the time I visited his studio, he had accumulated about two hundred. Plaster is used to fix what is broken as well as to constrain it, and that duality held great metaphoric strength for him. Ma Thanegi said he could cast her hand as long as she could choose the position in which she posed it – and held up her middle finger to the authorities who had put her behind bars. Htein Lin said, 'No wonder you are not dead.'

Other artists relate to politics more circuitously. Wah Nu told me that her family used to produce handicrafts to sell to tourists. Among their most popular items were carved busts of Aung San. After 1988, they ceased to produce them and hid those they had already made. When Wah Nu and her husband, Tun Win Aung, started to exhibit after 2012, they set up a gallery in which Aung San's last speech, which the socialist government had broadcast endlessly as propaganda, played on a loop in a room with dozens of the Aung San busts, no longer illegal. The installation was both nostalgic and ironic, at once reverent of Aung San and mocking of the cultish way his name is used to signify everything good about Myanmar – much as Chinese artists have played with the image of Mao. Of course, every reference to Aung San is also a reference to his daughter. 'Aung San Suu Kyi cannot change us,' Tun Win Aung said. 'I hope she will be elected, I will be very happy, but I don't expect her to change me. We are corrupted by having lived under this government, and now we must learn how to be honest and innocent.'

When I met Maung Tin Thit in Mandalay, he seemed weary. Another of the 1988 activists, he had managed not to get arrested until 1998, when police searched his apartment, found a private note-book of poems, and were particularly incensed by this one:

> The street in front of the house needs the illumination
> of the shining moon.
> I don't own the street.
> But if I don't go on this street or road, I cannot reach
> my home.
> To purify my mind, I may need to clean up the street.

For those few lines, he served over seven years. He has been working on a book about the oil and gas pipeline that runs from Rakhine to China, just the sort of righteous-minded investigation that the regime still punishes. 'Before I went to prison, I was given to excitement and anger, and my poems drew from those emotions,' he said. 'But in prison, as I meditated, I came to understand that anger accomplishes nothing. This new work is not based in anger. And now I am not afraid to go back to the prison, because I learned how to live there.'

Ma Thanegi has also written a book about her jail time, *Nor Iron Bars a Cage*. 'I had no interest in politics at all,' she said. 'But in '88, it was young students out on the streets marching, and they were being shot down. I felt so guilty, so I joined in. Then Aung San Suu Kyi came out to speak, and a large group of us went to the middle of a muddy field to hear her; there were crickets and little frogs jumping all over. We took plastic bags to sit on, and we waited two hours for her to arrive. The sound system was so bad we couldn't hear a thing. I'd seen Aung San Suu Kyi in my school when I was in the fifth grade, and she was in the second. So I mentioned that and we talked in English. On the spur of the moment I said, as others did, "Anything we can help you with, please tell us." The next day she had somebody call me. I knew immediately that I was going to be facing guns and going to jail. I had to be sure that I would not come apart at the seams; to be dignified is an Asian criterion of good breeding. So I thought about whether I could keep my dignity, and I said, "I'm ready."'

A few years later, Ma Thanegi publicly opposed the sanctions Suu Kyi supported, accurately predicting that they would enable the generals to establish monopolies and line their own pockets. She anticipated that the generals would rape forests of their hardwoods and deplete mines of their jade, leaving little for generations to come. 'There is not one tree left,' she said. Suu Kyi denounced Ma Thanegi as a traitor, but Ma Thanegi went to jail regardless, because of their association. She maintains that her ties to her jail friends are deeper than blood. 'This afternoon I was with one of our friends from jail, at one of our houses,' she told me. 'All the young jailbirds and all of us, having lunch and just talking. Some

I haven't seen since then, but when we meet again after twenty-five years, it's like it was yesterday.'

Misuu Borit, also known as Yin Myo Su, is one of Myanmar's most successful businesswomen, progenitor of the country's most charming hotels, and leader of its restaurant culture. She said she found meditation completely impossible: 'I can't go to a place where people tell me to do nothing but concentrate. I tried it when I was little, but your legs go completely numb, you can't feel anything any more, and you get bored. My grandmother's way of meditation is cooking, and that's my kind of meditation.'

Borit's parents had a small guesthouse near Inle Lake. When she was a child in the 1970s, her father would welcome the guests, her mother would cook for them, and Borit would perform as a dancing clown. In her high school in 1988, she began to attend political meetings but was afraid to tell her parents about them. One day, she came home late, and her father demanded to know where she had been. She had to answer a direct question. 'He said, "Go take a shower and eat, and then we will go together back to the centre where the students are meeting." He was not punishing me; instead, he was joining me. That's how my father became a politician. And I ended up campaigning for my father, and I cast my first vote for him.' After he was elected in 1990, Borit obtained her first passport and went to study hotel management in Switzerland.

In the post-'88 era, some 85 per cent of previously elected officials went to prison, many for long terms; Borit's father served only two years. He told the family not to inform Borit; he wanted her to finish her studies abroad. But a friend sent a letter that said, 'Sorry about your dad.' Borit had one aunt in Yangon with a telephone, and when she called to ask what had happened to her father, her aunt hung up. So she knew it was serious and headed home. When she walked in the door, her mother screamed at her to go back, lest she worry her father more. 'It was kind of cruel, but it was her way of protecting me,' Borit said, 'and she was right, because in those days, the generals were scared of everything. Knowing someone had been abroad and come back was suspicious. Three nights I spent with my mum, and they came to look for me.' Her mother hid her, and the next day, on her nineteenth birthday, she fled to Thailand, where she nearly starved before making her way back to Europe, to a French hotel school where she worked for her room and board. Five years later, she finally returned home and saw her father. He was done with politics and had set up a twenty-five-room hotel, and she joined him there.

Borit slowly expanded her family's landholdings. She now has a small hotel in Mrauk-U; a guesthouse by Inle Lake up north; a forty-five-acre farm; and a school for hotel management, organic farming and traditional arts. She employs more than two hundred full-time staff. She also founded the Inthar Heritage House, retraining local artisans in historical building techniques so they could help construct a museum of traditional crafts. She has filled it with her grandparents' furniture and antiques accumulated as her neighbours opted for new, factory-made items from China. Inthar Heritage House also encompasses a breeding centre for Burmese cats – previously long vanished from Myanmar – and the best restaurant in the country, which serves delectable renditions of her grandmother's recipes, including the national dish, *lahpet*, a salad of fermented tea leaves mixed with chillies, sesame oil, fried garlic, dried shrimp, peanuts and ginger; it's rather caffeinated and best not eaten near bedtime. Her guests sometimes marvel at how everything is homegrown and handmade, but she points out, 'We were always farm-to-table because there wasn't anyplace else to get anything for the table.'

Inle is a gorgeous, shallow lake where the locals have for many years lived by fishing. They stand up in their boats and paddle with one leg to keep their hands free for their nets. It's a spectacular sight: they stay tall and move with astonishing grace, in a kind of serpentine full-body undulation. You go by boat to visit the lake's many shrines, numerous pagodas, picturesque villages and an abandoned temple complex, now overgrown. There are a famous floating market and some less touristic markets along the shore where weavers produce cloth from the fibres of lotus roots.

In 2011, Myanmar had two hundred thousand visitors; in 2012,

1 million; in 2013, nearly 2 million; in 2014, over 3 million. Above Inle's eastern shore, a gash in the landscape marks the beginning of a construction project that will triple the number of hotel rooms around the lake. The area's rickety infrastructure can in no way support such a deluge of visitors. The lake itself is silting up because of unsustainable farming practises, and the narrow waterways around it are already crowded. The beauty of the lake – indeed, the beauty of all Myanmar – is partly a consequence of its long-term inaccessibility. It is becoming accessible at such speed that there may soon be nothing to access.

In early 2014, many writers and journalists were arrested. After staff at *Unity Journal* reported on the construction of an alleged chemical-weapons factory, the CEO and four journalists were sentenced to ten years' hard labour, later commuted to seven years. More than fifty others were arrested for protesting those convictions. While Aung Kyaw Naing, a former bodyguard for Aung San Suu Kyi, was reporting on the conflict between Karen rebels and the Burmese army in Mon State, he was taken captive by the army and killed in custody. Another journalist was jailed for a year for 'disturbing a civil servant on duty' and trespassing after attempting to interview an education official about a scholarship scheme at a new government school in Chin State. Laws require that newspapers be registered, but the government withholds registration capriciously, so newspapers publish unregistered until they annoy officials, whereupon they get shuttered. Four newspapers were closed down in Chin State in the autumn of 2014. When the *Bi Mon Te Nay* printed an erroneous statement from an activist group claiming that Aung San Suu Kyi had formed an interim government, three reporters and the two publishers received sentences of two years each. Htin Kyaw was sentenced to thirteen years for disrupting public order because he organised a protest march in Yangon.

In the ranking of countries for freedom of the press, Myanmar's status has steadily improved. It was 169th out of 180 countries in 2011; 151st in 2012; by 2013, it had been promoted to 145th. But Dave Mathieson, senior Myanmar researcher for Human Rights Watch, noted that two hundred people had been detained in 2014, including peaceful protesters, journalists, and activists. Yanghee Lee, the UN's special rapporteur on human rights in Myanmar, reported to the General Assembly that the government continues 'to criminalise and impede the activities of civil society and the media', meting out 'disproportionately high' sentences. The writers, artists and other intellectuals I interviewed in Myanmar had all been released under article 401 of the Code of Criminal Procedure, which allows only *conditional* pardons: they risk having to serve out the remainder of their sentences if they displease the government.

Ma Thida said, 'We are beginning to see how surveillance has changed not only the writer's thinking, but also the society's thinking. You cannot trust one another. And when people cannot trust one another, it's very easy to manipulate them. So the society itself is not yet ready for democracy.' She hadn't expected that the 'reform government' would bring quick freedom, so, like Nay Phone Latt, she wasn't particularly surprised by the backsliding. But she has had to revise her expectations about the recovery of Burmese society: 'Now I see that what we have been missing is a collective dream. Our history is of fighting against oppression: colonialism, the socialist regime, the military regime. We totally forget about what kind of society we truly want to live in. We can only hope for a new generation that has a wider view.'

The Burmese shake their heads on hearing news of journalists being detained, but they have made their peace with worse. The lack of tremendous optimism in the wake of significant positive change is less remarkable than the equanimity and obdurate quietude that prevail among even those with little hope of better personal fortune. The Burmese had not so much optimism, but neither much pessimism – perhaps a cultural expression of Theravada Buddhist ideals. Despite the lack of a collective dream, the collective character is surprisingly robust: an apotheosis of patient endurance that does not guarantee reform, but that constitutes its very essence.

The Rohingya crisis escalated in the lead-up to the 2015 elections. The 969 movement expanded with the introduction of Ma Ba Tha, the

Patriotic Association of Myanmar, which professes to defend Thera-vada Buddhism. Wirathu is one of its prominent members. Persecution by Buddhist radicals has driven many Rohingya to flee, and those who stay face brutal conditions at home and in refugee camps. These people have nowhere to go. An American group filed a lawsuit against President Thein Sein accusing him of genocide. The radical Buddhists attempted to sway the election in favour of Thein Sein's party and failed in that ambition, but they are hardly likely to disappear.

The NLD has shown no interest in helping Muslims. Following the elections, a high-ranking party leader, U Win Htein, said, 'We have other priorities.' Despite the fact that most of the Muslims have been in Myanmar for generations, he explained, 'We have to deal with the Bangladesh government because almost all of them came from there,' adding that they should be 'returned'. The NLD did not put forward any Muslim candidates, and for the first time since independence in 1948, the new Parliament has no Muslim members. Muslims have, however, expressed hope that the NLD will provide rule of law, and that with rule of law, their rights will be better respected than they have been previously.

Since the official dissolution of Myanmar's ruling military junta in 2011 and the relaxation of restrictions on private publications the following year, 32 daily newspapers, some 400 weekly journals, and about 350 monthly magazines have hit the presses, but many have since closed. Thein Sein's rhetoric of reform has been belied by the escalating curtailment of press freedom under his quasi-civilian administration. Although many journalists have been released from prison, the laws under which they were convicted remain intact.

Reporters and publishers have continued to be convicted of vague crimes such as 'inciting unrest'. Official prepublication censorship has given way to widespread self-censorship. Reporters who value their freedom have learned to shy away from controversial topics. Any attempt to investigate government corruption, the situation of the Rohingyas, ongoing conflicts with ethnic groups, rapes committed by soldiers, displacement caused by economic development projects or the lethal aspects of burgeoning Buddhist nationalism represents an invitation to surveillance, harassment and prosecution – if not by the government, then by aggrieved vigilantes. The new NLD government will have much work to reverse the damage done, both to unjustly persecuted individuals and to the country's fledgling independent press. But some of the change may be out of their hands, as penetration of internet access on smartphones has leaped forward in the country, with many people getting their news from Facebook.

Constitutional reforms that would have allowed Myanmar's pro-democracy leader Aung San Suu Kyi to run for the presidency were blocked, but failed to prevent an NLD electoral victory in November 2015. Popular support for Aung San Suu Kyi had not dimmed since her party's triumph at the polls in 1990. Her extended house arrest and the constitutional manoeuvring designed to bar her from assuming the presidency served only to reinforce the impression that her ascendance was inevitable. The voting was so decisive that the generals declined to challenge it. Nonetheless, the military is still guaranteed one-quarter of seats in the legislature, giving it an effective veto. The interior, defence and border security ministries remain under the aegis of the military.

Whether The Lady can be as effective at ruling as she was at opposing remains to be seen. It cannot be predicted whether a leader inclined to keep her own counsel to such a degree will succeed in delegating responsibilities to others. This icon of democracy has already asserted that while she is not president, she will rise 'above the president' who 'would have no authority' – an erosion of the office that has been denied to her. She has spoken of the constitution disparagingly, calling it a 'very silly' document. While the constitution is highly problematic – not least because of clause 59F, which bars her from the official leadership of the country – such disregard for the processes by which bad laws are resolved smacks of authoritarianism.

Time will tell whether a party consisting largely of individuals with no experience in government can succeed in running a country; how the military and its moneyed allies will respond to policy changes that reduce its leaders' economic advantage; and how a new Burmese government will address the country's persistent interracial violence and the inhumane exclusion of lifelong residents from citizenship.

Lost at the Surface

The Moth, 2015

This book starts with my travels as a child and concludes with my travel with a child. It begins with a dawning lust for adventure and ends with reservations about that impulse towards bravado. Intimations of immortality give way to the certainty of mortality. I grew up.

I was a frightened little boy. I did not like fast rides at amusement parks or scary movies or anything that was strange and unknown to me. I became anxious easily. When I was six, Mindy Silverstein's mother took us both out for a bingo night and I was so nervous that I threw up and she had to bring me home. When we visited Uncle Milton and I was sent out to play with my tough cousin Johnny, I had a panic attack and ran back inside to my parents. Like many other frightened children, I lived in books instead of reality. I watched nature programmes on TV and was especially captivated by Jacques Cousteau's documentaries about life under the sea. I loved other people's escapades, but I didn't want my own.

When I was twelve, my mother took me out to lunch and, apropos of something I have long since forgotten, she ventured that I missed a lot by not being more adventurous. 'But, Mom!' I said. 'I just ordered eel for lunch!' She replied gently, 'Being an adventurous eater is not the same as being an adventurous person.'

I decided to become adventurous through sheer will. Unlike the majority of people, who grow steadily more cautious as they get older, I've become less and less constrained in adulthood. I've gone sky-diving and hang gliding; I've reported from war zones and disasters; I've faced the sometimes brutal exposure that accompanies being outspoken about my inner life.

Learning to scuba dive seemed like a good idea when I landed the assignment to traverse the Solomon Islands. A German friend was visiting us in New York prior to the trip, and we agreed to take scuba lessons together in a public pool on East Ninetieth Street, but then couldn't make all the given dates. We nonetheless decided to try an open-water dive, for which we drove to a flooded quarry in Pennsylvania that had been festooned, rather creepily, with old school buses, so that candidates for diver certification would have 'wrecks' to look at. We'd also have something to think about: drowning children. Misunderstanding our brute of an instructor, I plunged in before I was supposed to, and he ordered us out of the water and walked off the job. We went home having spotted only one submerged bus.

On our honeymoon, John and I travelled to Zanzibar. Our wedding had left him feeling terrifically upbeat because it had been joyful; it left me feeling incredibly down because it was over. Our first night in Zanzibar, he said, 'I can't stop thinking about our wedding,' and I said, 'Neither can I.' He said, 'I can't stop thinking what a beautiful, perfect, joyous experience it was, with so many of our incredible friends cheering us on.' I said, 'I can't stop thinking that it would have been better if we'd put Nicky at table five instead of table six.' John decided that I needed some distraction to bring me out of my evident funk, so he suggested we do the week-long scuba course offered at our hotel. I went along with it because there didn't seem much else to do in a Zanzibar resort, but all the complicated diving equipment intimidated me profoundly. It had taken me three tries at a road test to get my driver's licence – after which my mother said that the only reason the inspector had passed me was because he was afraid that if he didn't, he might have to get in a car with me again. I am dyslexic and could not tell my left side from my right until I got the wedding ring. Jacques Cousteau had made it all look so effortlessly graceful. Now I struggled to learn the names of the various pieces of breathing apparatus and safety gear, and to figure out how to assemble them.

Then we had to practise what to do if our air supply failed.

I am good in the face of any crisis that allows me at least a half-hour of thought. I can determine a strategy and negotiate my way through complicated situations. I've managed to get myself out of police custody in East Berlin, to analyse my way through a bewildering maze of bewildering treatments for unnerving depression, to master the baroque logistics involved in making a family as a gay person. But I am not good at hand-eye coordination or any other split-second instinctual response, and the prospect of having to find my diving buddy and share his air hose when I couldn't breathe on my own, thirty feet underwater, made me as nauseated as I was at Mindy Silverstein's bingo night.

Nonetheless, I learned to dive, and in the years that followed, I went diving whenever we were in a place conducive to underwater sightseeing. I had long aspired to see the much-vaunted Great Barrier Reef in the Coral Sea off Australia's north-east coast. So when I was invited to give the opening speech at the Sydney Writers' Festival, I brought John and our son, George, and we arranged a reef visit. My dearly beloved Australian friend Sue Macartney-Snape, a brilliant cartoonist who sketches people's surface oddities to reveal their most hidden depths, had encouraged me to come to the festival in the first place. With her uncanny knack for putting friends together, she had introduced me to new chums in Sydney, organising multiple celebrations during my visit. I persuaded her to join us at the reef even though she didn't care to scuba dive, and she generously offered to stay with George, who had just turned five, while we went off on our expedition. Most of the nicer hotels near the reef don't allow children – which, given that they are essentially beach resorts, verges on obnoxious. Orpheus Island is one of the few that does, so to Orpheus Island we went.

Our first full day at the pleasantly laid-back hotel, John and I selected our equipment – the inflatable buoyancy-control device (BCD), which helps one rise to the surface, the air tanks, the regulators through which we'd be breathing, our extra weights to be strung along a nylon belt, and so on – and hopped on the hotel's commodious motorboat. Sue and George, already building sandcastles, waved us off. We were joined by the divemaster and a soft-spoken man from Maryland travelling with his ebullient college-aged daughter. She announced that diving was her favourite recreational activity; when she was far from the sea, she confessed, 'I spend way, way too much time in aquariums.' She and her father had made hundreds of dives together, and she proceeded to describe most of them.

The boat took us first among small islets and then well out into the open sea – far enough from land that we couldn't see any – before setting anchor so we could descend one by one along the anchor line. The divemaster warned that this area had strong currents and reviewed the dive plan: we'd go down, allow the current to carry us a bit, then be picked up where we surfaced. This arrangement was presented as advantageous on grounds that we'd be able to cover a good distance and see a great deal without exerting too much energy.

Things got off to an inauspicious start. The man from Maryland's regulator was not working and he couldn't breathe through it. Fortunately, he discovered the defect immediately, and he simply hoisted himself back onto the boat to sit out the dive. I was too preoccupied to be unnerved that the hotel staff had sent a guest on an open-water dive with malfunctioning equipment. Down I gamely went. The coral was pretty, though not remarkable, and the fish were colourful, but not nearly so numerous and various as what I'd seen snorkelling at the mouth of the Marovo Lagoon in the Solomons a dozen years earlier. The muscular current had stirred up sand and sediments, so visibility was impaired. The aquarium girl saw a squid and waved us over using the appropriate hand signals for 'come look' and 'squid', but we were too late. The sudden dimming of light indicated that the sun had just slipped behind a cloud. Because I'm always nervous underwater, I breathe much more heavily than adept divers do, so my air gauge hit the red zone much faster than the others'. I showed my gauge to the divemaster, who asked in hand signs whether I was all right to go back up and reboard the boat on my own, and with an emphatic okay sign, I indicated that I was. Up I went, making a decompression stop along the way.

The usual diving protocol is that you surface and wave an arm in the air, then the dive boat comes and picks you up. When I bobbed to the surface, I saw that the current hadn't carried us as far as it had seemed thirty or forty feet below. Cheerily, I waved my hand over my head. The youthful captain was looking vaguely in my direction, and I waited for him to motor over. But the boat just sat there. So I waved again, a bit more vigorously. Still the captain stared my way with a glassy expression, and still I continued waving, now using both arms. I raised my mask and took the regulator out of my mouth and tried to shout, but the wind was blowing straight into my face and I knew he couldn't hear me over the wind and choppy water. I thought of that 'whistle for attracting attention' that is always mentioned on airplane life jackets.

Now remember that a person normally feels exhausted after a dive, and that the Australian sun is fierce, and the waves were not insignificant, and the current was forceful. So I really needed to get out of the water. Channelling late-night television, I tried a Tarzan yell. The captain then walked around to the other side of the boat, which left me staring at a blank prospect.

When I faced into the wind towards the boat, the waves broke over my head. I'd not previously understood how anyone could drown while wearing a life jacket, but as I pumped up my BCD, I realised that I couldn't keep myself oriented towards the boat without achieving unwanted hydration of my pulmonary and digestive systems. It was nature's version of waterboarding. So I turned away from the boat, twisting my body every few minutes to check whether the captain had come back into my view, in which case I would be in his. I waited, and I waited, and I waited, and after about ten minutes, he finally came back and once more appeared to be looking right at me. By now, my waving was worthy of Cirque du Soleil – both arms oscillating rapidly over my head, back and forth and front and back and sideways. I even tried using my flippers to jump partway out of the water, like a sort of flying fish with arms. The captain gazed calmly in my direction for a few minutes, then resumed his little peregrination around the deck.

When you do scuba training – be it in Pennsylvania or in Zanzibar – you get a great deal of tutelage about what to do if your air fails, learn signs to alert your divemaster to what's wrong, and memorise techniques to compensate for a wide variety of potential errors, failures and dangers. But you don't get any advice about what to do on the surface if you have somehow become invisible.

The current was carrying me away from the boat, so I tried to swim into it. Even with my strongest freestyle stroke I didn't make any headway, and I soon realised that I couldn't swim into the waves, especially loaded down with the air tanks and weight belt, and keep breathing unless I kept my mask on and used the remaining air from my tanks. I'd come up to the surface in the first place because I was running out of air, and I needed that air not only to breathe but also to stay afloat, because my BCD was leaking slightly, and I had to keep reinflating it. What about my diving weights? The advantage to keeping them on was that they slowed the rate at which I was drifting away from the boat. The disadvantage was that they likewise slowed my swimming and might be increasing the drag on my ever-deflating BCD. I tried to awaken my logical mind and make a decision, but despite more than a half-hour to think about it, I had no idea what to do. The others had to be on board by now, getting ready to come look for me. The divemaster, despite the lack of landmarks, knew where I'd surfaced. I'd gone in only one direction: that of the current. It couldn't be so hard to find me. I kept the weights on, figuring that the closer I was to the boat, the easier I'd be to find.

Then there was nothing to be done but to let myself drift with the current and conserve energy, my face away from the wind and the boat, surrounded by the limitless sea.

Finally, I heard a reassuring sound. The boat's engine fired up. I breathed a great sigh of relief, spun around, resumed my Olympian waving – and watched as the boat chugged into gear and set off in the opposite direction. Away from me, speeding into the horizon.

Now I was alone at sea, with nothing but water and sky in every direction. There was no one to wave to, nothing to swim toward. For the first time that morning, I thought, 'People die this way.' I assumed that the current was sweeping me further out to sea. I remembered that the Pacific Ocean is a rather large body of water; I remembered that there are sharks in it – most of them harmless, but some, aggressive. My bobbling little head seemed a small target for whoever might ultimately come out to search.

Sometimes I felt scared stiff; sometimes I thought that I'd be fine so long as my BCD worked and I could simply float for a day or two. I'd never fully imagined drowning, and I wondered how long it would take and how painful it would be. I couldn't bear the possibility of being unable to breathe, though I dimly remembered that some people who had been revived after nearly drowning had said the experience conferred a certain semi-final peace. I speculated how long the remaining air in my tank would keep me afloat. I was so tired; I wondered whether I would eventually fall asleep even floating in the sea.

Then I heard the voices of my parents. I envisaged my father saying, 'You took this risk so you could see exotic fish?' I could hear him suggesting that I try spending way too much time in aquariums instead. Not a cloud scuttled across the sky, and I imagined my mother, who had died twenty-five years earlier, chastising, 'This is why you should always, always wear sunblock.'

The waves seemed to be growing. If I drifted out beyond the reef, I'd be rolling in huge swells, and I wouldn't keep my head above water for long.

Sometimes I tried to swim again, just for something to do, and then gave up again.

And no one came. And another twenty minutes passed. And forty minutes passed. And an hour passed.

I felt sorry for John, who would be worrying on board. I envisioned John and Sue explaining to George what had happened. I thought about my daughter Blaine, who was in Texas with her mother, and I felt crestfallen that I might miss her growing up; I was so curious about who my children would become. I thought of Oliver and Lucy, our older children, who lived in Minneapolis with their two moms. I had accomplished much of what I'd always wanted from life: love, children, adventure, a meaningful career. I was grateful for the life I'd had, even if I wasn't going to have much more of it. I thought that my disappearance might kill my father, and I regretted his pain. Mostly, I worried that my children might feel I had abandoned them, and I felt guilty about that – guilty and terribly sad. I wondered whether they would remember me.

I mused, 'These may be my last thoughts. I should be thinking something important.' But I couldn't think of anything important to think. My mind drifted to Shakespeare and the great philosophers, but I didn't have any new insights. I tried to get my life to flash before my eyes, but all that was flashing were the squinty prismatic colours caused by too much time in the sun on the sea. I considered my last words, even if no one was around to hear them. I couldn't come up with anything profound or witty to say to the waves. I found myself dwelling on my favourite Winnie-the-Pooh story, 'In Which Piglet Is Entirely Surrounded by Water', when a frightened Piglet misses Pooh and thinks, 'It's so much more friendly with two.'

I was glad that John was safe and that he would be able to care for George and Blaine, and I was sorry he wasn't with me – both, at once. By that time, I'd been trying to stay afloat for about an hour and a half. I was sunburned to a crisp and felt a little feverish. I seemed to have swallowed gallons and gallons of seawater.

I had never felt so alone.

I remembered the literary trope that we all die alone, no matter how we die.

I tried to enumerate what I had planned to do with and for my children. My own life wasn't flashing before my eyes, but their lives were. I've never been good at the present moment, so I once more took refuge in planning an unplannable future.

I felt my own insignificance; I felt the smallness of man. I felt how little it mattered, really, whether any one person lived or died.

My reverie was punctured by a voice on the wind – a voice that sounded eerily like John's – shouting, 'Help! Help!' I tried to shout back, but the wind still stymied me. Then I heard another voice. It dawned on me that the other three must be in the same situation I was. Because I was downwind, I could hear them, but they couldn't hear me. Judging by their voices, we were far from one another and from the boat. But perhaps the divemaster knew the answers I didn't.

On the horizon, I suddenly saw a boat, though I wasn't sure it was our boat.

Something that resembled a giant pink breast, perhaps five feet tall, came into view, heading towards the now clearly discernible boat. Perhaps the voices, the boat and the breast were mere hallucinations. The boat, which was beginning to look clearly like our boat, moved towards the pink breast, and they appeared to merge. Then the boat headed in the direction from which the other voices had arisen. It stopped for a few minutes.

And then it began to move towards me.

Never in my life have I greeted any lover with the joy I felt when I grabbed the dive ladder. I climbed up shakily and collapsed into John's arms.

John had had a difficult experience, too, but quite different from mine. He was with two other people, one of them a divemaster, and they had surfaced about forty-five minutes after I did. They had faced the same dilemma of being unable to get the attention of the boat captain. They had taken turns trying to swim to the boat, but it always had motored elsewhere before they could reach it. Once, John got within about fifty feet of it. The pink breast was actually an emergency balloon the divemaster had been carrying. Later, I wondered how anyone who knew such a thing might be needed could have let a novice such as me return to the surface alone. The divemaster had inflated the balloon when she spotted the boat, then swum with it until the captain finally saw it and motored over to pick her up. Once on board, she had pointed the boat towards John and the aquarium girl. All the while they were stranded, John had assumed that I was already back on board; he became frantic when he learned that I was unaccounted for. But the divemaster had heard me trying to holler back to John and pointed the ship accordingly. I'd been afloat for nearly two hours and had drifted several miles.

Only after I climbed aboard did I begin to get angry: at the boat captain, at the divemaster, at the hotel management. But I also felt so grateful to be alive, and it's hard to be angry and profoundly grateful at the same time. I hugged John; I hugged the aquarium girl; I hugged the divemaster; I hugged the man from Maryland, slightly to his dismay. The boat captain tried to make cheery conversation, to which I replied in what John later described as my 'Linda Blair voice', a guttural growl like that of the demon-possessed little girl in *The Exorcist*.

You actually can be grateful and angry at the same time.

While I was adrift, thoughts of my children had occupied me. It's not that I have such a high opinion of myself as a parent, but I do have a sense of my responsibility. Back on land, we decided not to tell George what had happened. I thought it would frighten him, as it was still frightening me. But while I was largely silent, he eagerly recounted his adventures of the morning – what he'd eaten for breakfast, where he and Sue had been digging, what washed-up shells and twigs he had found, and how far he'd swum all by himself. In the urgency of his speech, I found the complement to my mishap. I understood that the daredevilry of ordering eel for lunch or going skydiving or visiting war-torn lands pale in comparison to the adventurous domesticity of being a parent, which involves simultaneously reckoning with the vastness of the world and agreeing, at least for a little while, to be that vastness to one's children.

The Entrance of Brexit and a Last Word on America First

June 2017

Abook about travel is of necessity a book about the world. It traffics in how we perceive and are perceived. The histories upon which these essays reflect are of particular relevance in a society that has begun to turn inwards against itself. All of a sudden, many countries are dissociating from one another, and the importance of championing connections across borders and time zones has assumed a shocking urgency. The kind of tyranny against which so many of the people described in this book fought – in Afghanistan, Libya, Russia, South Africa, Cambodia, Rwanda, and many other places – now threatens parts of the world where until recently it had seemed unimaginable. Their stories are evidence that resistance and courage can be learned, and they must be. If we are to survive the autocracy burgeoning in the West, we would do well to study the recent history of beleaguered countries and listen to the people within those countries who defended freedom despite a constant siege against it.

Alexander von Humboldt, the great nineteenth-century naturalist, said, 'There is no worldview so dangerous as the worldview of those who have not viewed the world.' Recent political shifts have increasingly placed policy in the hands of people who openly disdain viewing the world, including many who travel without viewing. I am a dual U.K./U.S. national, and in 2016, I voted against Brexit and against Trump – and lost. The victories of Brexit and Trump are attempts to reject the way things are in favour of a fantasy of the way things used to be. But attempts to recapitulate the past are always reinterpretations of it; they resemble what they mimic only in roughest outline. This is a new nationalism, not a return to any actual policy of yesteryear. The winning tallies – including also the election of nationalist governments in Poland, Hungary, Turkey, Italy, Russia, and elsewhere – represent in part a rejection of human diversity and of the internationalism and open borders that have defined Western society since the Second World War. Each reflects frustration with the forces that have steadily pushed the modern world towards openness. Some people on the winning sides have been motivated by fear and some by personal economic frustration; others, by incursions on what they see as self-reliance. Voters who were neither racist nor nationalist grew to tolerate the racism and nationalism evinced in these campaigns. Unsurprisingly, incidents of nationalist and racist hatred have followed. Public displays of misogyny, homophobia and anti-Semitism are on the rise. In Britain, there was an abrupt escalation in hate crimes after the Brexit referendum, and the rate of such attacks has remained elevated ever since. In the United States, nearly a thousand incidents of hateful harassment were recorded in the three weeks after the November 2016 election. These unfortunate tendencies have been sustained through Theresa May's time as prime minister and Trump's as president.

Overt xenophobia began its recent surge in continental Europe. Though Poland has no significant Muslim population, in the wake of controversy over European refugee policy, anti-Muslim rhetoric emerged as a major feature of the 2015 Polish election campaign. During the campaign, Jarosław Kaczyński, leader of the Law and Justice Party, which ultimately won the elections, accused immigrants of carrying 'various parasites and protozoa, which don't affect their organisms, but could be dangerous here'. Social media and some press also promulgated anti-Muslim slogans and images. Several massive anti-refugee protests followed. Protesters have held marches, burned European Union flags, and chanted nationalist phrases. In a number of Polish cities, gangs have beaten up or taunted dark-skinned 'Arab' students or tourists. In the city of Wrocław, a far-right group staged an anti-immigrant demonstration and – moving rapidly from one form of intolerance to another – burned an effigy of an Orthodox Jew.

In Hungary, Prime Minister Viktor Orbán declared that migrants entering Europe were a 'poison'. A glossy, government-funded booklet distributed to 4.1 million households depicted migrants as terrorists, and immigration as a danger to Hungarian culture and customs. Government-sponsored billboards warn visitors, 'If you come to Hungary, don't take the jobs of Hungarians.'

In December 2016, Italian voters soundly rejected a constitutional referendum aimed at stabilising the country's famously volatile government by reducing the size of its parliament. The outcome, a victory for the country's far-right populist parties, prompted the resignation of reformist prime minister Matteo Renzi and put into question Italy's continued involvement in the European Union, of which it was a founding member. Though the votes were not directly for a far-right party, voters were well aware of the meaning of their choice, which was effectively a plebiscite on the liberal values of a united Europe.

Nationalist sentiment in Turkey has fuelled territorial ambition. President Recep Erdoğan has recently disparaged the 1923 Treaty of Lausanne, which established the boundaries of modern Turkey, arguing against the 'loss' of Mosul and of Greek islands in the Aegean Sea. Erdoğan's ruling Justice and Development Party also implicitly regards being Sunni Muslim as an essential component of 'Turkishness' – a prejudice that undermines the legitimacy of the country's Armenian, Alevi, Shiite and Jewish citizens. Deputy Prime Minister Numan Kurtulmus recently exhorted Turks 'to stand tall and call an infidel "an infidel"', encouraging discrimination and prompting human rights advocates to lodge a complaint accusing him of violating both national law and international treaties. Kurds are routinely demonised in the media with tropes that echo those deployed by American racists against Muslims: they are supposedly 'terrorists', 'traitors', 'jihadists' and 'enemies'. In the summer of 2015, the neo-fascist youth wing of Turkey's Nationalist Movement Party, the Grey Wolves, protested a Chinese ban on Ramadan fasting, attacking Chinese, Korean and even Turkic Muslim Uighurs; one of the group's leaders said that there was no way to distinguish among people with 'slanted eyes'. Erdoğan questioned the legitimacy of the Constitutional Court, and following the 2016 *coup d'état* attempt, declared a state of emergency in which civil rights were severely curtailed. An October 2016 analysis by the Council of Europe's Commission against Racism and Intolerance confirmed that hate speech was common and increasing in Turkey, both among the general population and among members of government. Constitutional reforms approved in April 2017 substantially increased Erdoğan's executive powers. International observers declared the election unfair, but U.S. President Donald Trump immediately called to congratulate his fellow autocrat on the outcome. The persecution of domestic diversity of thought or ethnic identity has become the norm in Turkey.

Similar reactive prejudice is bubbling up across the developed world, even where extremists have not assumed control. The *New York Times* reported from Copenhagen about Johnny Christensen, 'a stout and silver-whiskered retired bank employee, [who] always thought of himself as sympathetic to people fleeing war, and welcoming to immigrants. But after more than 36,000 mostly Muslim asylum seekers poured into Denmark over the past two years, Mr Christensen, 65, said, "I've become a racist."' Then he added, 'Just kick them out', and aimed a kick at an imaginary target. Julie Jeeg, a law student and advocate against racism in Denmark, said, 'Denmark is closing in on itself. People are retreating inwards.'

In June 2016, U.K. voters chose by a narrow margin to leave the European Union. Brexit reflected the growing worldwide aversion to multinational collaborative governmental entities. It drew heavily on the rhetoric of tribalism, which in turn relies on the perception of likeness. Some who voted Leave seemed to believe that they were like others of their nationality and unlike everyone else. But nativist arguments about sovereignty often play to the perception of common ground where actually little exists – and foment disaffection where real sympathies may lie. The belief that those middle-aged and older, working-class Englishmen who led the Leave voters have more in common with London bankers and members of the House of Lords than they do with middle-aged and older, working-class Spanish men reflects archaic, ethnic notions of allegiance, nationality and identity.

At the Conservative Party Conference in October 2016, U.K. prime minister Theresa May, who rode to power on the Brexit vote despite having campaigned for Remain, said 'If you believe you are a citizen of the world, you're a citizen of nowhere. You don't understand what the very word "citizenship" means.' There will be no resolution to the tensions manifest in the Brexit referendum so long as citizens feel they must make this choice. But one citizenship need not preclude another. If U.K. nationals are forced to select between being British and being European, of course being British will win, especially if being European is stigmatised as a quasi-treasonous betrayal. But patriotism is different from nationalism; you can be a patriotic citizen without being an exclusionary nationalist. If identity politics has taught us nothing else, it has given us the vocabulary of intersectionality – that you can be, for example, black and queer; or poor, white and feminist; or Asian and a Scottish nationalist; or gay and alt-right; or American and British and a world citizen, too. The ability to embrace and embody coinciding identities is a hallmark of sophistication; its absence, a mark of abjection. Leave was, ironically, a nostalgic vote to regain lost dominion that relinquished yet more power. Leave voters in many instances believed that Remainers were out to build global interests at the expense of their fellow citizens. Many felt they had little cause to attend to far-flung others when their own needs weighed so heavily on them. But internationalism is not a charity programme designed to save the unwashed hordes abroad; it is a pragmatic recognition that the fate of nations has grown ever more inexorably intertwined, and that exclusion often hurts those who exclude as much as those who are excluded. In the global world, even Albion is not an island, entire of itself.

On referendum day, the Demos Centre for Analysis of Social Media found more than three hundred thousand tweets that used the hashtag #stopislam. The National Police Chiefs' Council of England, Wales and Northern Ireland identified more than three thousand reports alleging racially and ethnically motivated harassment in the two weeks before and the two weeks after the vote, a nearly 60 per cent increase over the same period the previous year. Two weeks later, the number had risen to over six thousand; by the end of September, three months after the vote, Sir Bernard Hogan-Howe, then London's metropolitan police commissioner, referred to the escalation as a 'horrible spike in hate crimes'. The Stop Hate U.K. helpline recorded a 61 per cent increase in call volume in the month following the referendum. At that same time, dozens of calls were made to European embassies in the U.K. to report harassment. The upsurge of violence against Eastern Europeans has continued. Lithuania's deputy foreign minister, Mantvydas Bekešius, said that Lithuanian children in British schools had been verbally abused not just by other pupils but by parents and even teachers. Shots were fired at a Lithuanian home in Lurgan, Northern Ireland. Latvian immigrants reported being refused service at a London post office and at a Bristol mobile-phone shop on the days after the referendum. In July 2016, a Romanian-owned shop in Norwich was torched. The Polish embassy reported eight assaults, and seven attacks on Polish-owned businesses, as well as many instances of verbal hostility. In Essex, a man was killed by a single blow to the head in an altercation with teenagers that began when they overheard him speaking Polish with a friend. A family in Plymouth awoke to find their garden shed aflame; a note was left warning them to 'go back to your fucking country next time it will be your family'. A Melton woman pleaded guilty to racially aggravated assault after kneeing a pregnant Polish girl in the face, knocking her to the ground and – referring to both the girl and her unborn child – declaring, 'You two dogs need to die.' In Coventry, a thirty-four-year-old Polish woman walking home after a night out with her partner was taunted by a claque of racists, who broke her nose. In April 2017, a brick lobbed through the window of the home of a Polish family in Antrim landed in a baby's crib; although the child was sleeping elsewhere and was unharmed, the family felt compelled to move house.

Jon Burnett, a researcher at the Institute of Race Relations in the U.K., said, 'The upsurge in attacks against Eastern Europeans should come as no surprise, given the way that they have been portrayed repeatedly as scroungers, cheats and, ultimately, threats.' In the wake of the Brexit vote, some sociologists spoke of 'post-referendum racism and xenophobia', or PRRX. The use of this term points to the close connection between racism at home and an exclusionary nationalism – to the idea that as we cut ourselves off from the diversity in our own societies, we sever our relationship to the diversity of the larger world. Enemies beyond one's borders become enemies within one's borders and vice versa. Official figures released in January 2017 show at least one racially motivated assault on NHS staff every day – twice as many as the previous year. Official figures released in February 2017 showed a doubling in the number of hate crimes recorded by regional police forces. Metropolitan Police statistics released a month later demonstrate a worrying increase in offences targeting disabled individuals; racial, ethnic and religious minorities; and gays and lesbians.

The violence against Muslims has been legion. British racists have freely borrowed symbols originating with their counterparts across the pond. In January 2017, a Turkish family in North London was targeted by a mob chanting 'Ku Klux Klan'; the victims later found the initials 'KKK' scratched into the frost on the windscreen of their car. On New Year's Day 2017, a Muslim convenience store owner was assaulted, robbed and racially vilified at his shop in Dundee. In February, a Muslim solicitor and her young son travelling home to Glasgow by train were the targets of a racist tirade by a fellow passenger who swore at the child and insisted that he and his mother – both British citizens – did not 'belong' in the country, or 'deserve' to sit in first class. In March 2017, a Sikh shopkeeper from Stroud was attacked with crowbars and run over whilst defending a Polish teenager who was being assaulted by a gang of racists. That same month, a seventeen-year-old Kurdish-Iranian boy was beaten unconscious by a gang of men and women in their twenties; the assault followed the boy's admission that he was seeking asylum in the U.K. In June, following the terrorist attack in London Bridge, a south London Islamic centre was vandalised with racist graffiti: 'Terrorise your own country' and 'Go away'.

Theresa May called a snap election for June 2017 because she wanted a stronger mandate for Brexit, and believed that the prospect of dissociating from the E.U. had grown only more attractive since the referendum. The apparent chaos among leaders of both the Labour Party and the Liberal Democrats seemed to favour this consolidation of her grip on power, but a surge of resistance mounted as the vote drew nigh. Two terrorist episodes that occurred in the lead-up to the election – one at a pop concert in Manchester and another at London Bridge and Borough Market – seemed to escalate xenophobia. May swore she would ramp up security, though she had as Home Secretary made significant cuts in the police, a move that played very badly. In the end she lost her parliamentary majority. Her failure of puissance owed in part to young Britons who felt that that the Brexit referendum had sentenced them to a fate calculated by people with whom they had little in common. They rejected May's smug and hoary nationalism. Jeremy Corbyn's Labour Party did not gain many seats; its relative success depended on a broad platform that opposed a hard Brexit – and that seemed in part to reflect younger Britons' belief that there is such a thing as a citizen of the world.

Theresa May's provincialism has been upstaged by Donald Trump's relentless divisiveness and implicit promotion of prejudice and hatred. Among his most pernicious and effective campaign strategies in the lead-up to the November 2016 election was the promise of a return to a long-vanished fantasy of American uniformity – one envisioned by founding fathers who did not regard as American either those people who had lived on American land before colonisation or those who had been forcibly removed from Africa and enslaved in the colonies. The white voters who massed behind Trump have not liked sharing their waning hegemony in an increasingly diverse country. In addition, they bridle at the condescension of an educated elite who persist in telling them where their interests lie. Many people with employment woes blame outsourcing of some jobs to the developing world and giving of others to immigrants willing to accept lower wages. Trump's repeated campaign promise was that if you got rid of what he expediently called 'bad hombres', you could fix these problems. As for any authentic engagement with foreign countries, Trump said, 'I've got no time to travel – America needs my attention now.' Is it possible to pay attention to America while ignoring or offending everyone everywhere else? Can you *see* America if you don't sometimes gaze at the country from abroad? Trump's egomania reflects a commonplace American solipsism: the presumption that one nation holds all the cards. Neither military nor economic power confers genuine independence from other nations; neither bullying others nor distancing oneself from them makes for good defence. In an article published after the election, Yale historian Timothy Snyder wrote, 'He defined the world as a source of endless threat and other countries as cradles of countless enemies. Global conspiracies were supposedly directed at his country and its uniquely righteous people. His left-wing opponents and the national minorities, he insisted, were not individuals but expressions of implacable international enmity to the righteous demands of his own people.' Snyder was describing Hitler, but the resonance with the Trump presidency is irrefutable, as Snyder intended.

As it did in the U.K. after the Brexit referendum, prejudice exploded following the U.S. election. In the month of November alone, the Southern Poverty Law Center collected hundreds of reports of acts of hostility against immigrants, Muslims, blacks, gays and women, including extensive swastika vandalism. The Massachusetts attorney general set up a hotline to respond to post-election reports of harassment; it received four hundred calls in its first week of operation. Hate crimes more than doubled in New York City in the week after the election. Michigan reported a doubling of bias crimes, and a thirty-fold increase in hate incidents. The FBI reported a 67 per cent increase in hate crimes against Muslims in 2016, starting well before the election. Abuse occurred in primary and secondary schools, in colleges and universities. Both inside and outside educational institutions, it was targeted primarily at women, inter-racial families, Latinos, Asians, LGBTQ people, Muslims and immigrants.

A study of schools in the ten days after the election showed 'an explosion in students' use of derogatory and racist language and in the display of racist symbols, including swastikas, Nazi salutes and Confederate flags. Numerous accounts describe students taunting schoolmates of colour and immigrants with assurances that they and their families would be deported come Inauguration Day.' A twelve-year-old in Colorado was told by a fellow student, 'Now that Trump is president, I'm going to shoot you and all the blacks I can find.' In Texas, a thirteen-year-old of Filipino parentage was told on the school bus, 'When they see your eyes, you are going to be deported.' In California, classmates of a teenage girl adopted from Mozambique warned her, 'Now that Trump won, you're going to have to go back to Africa – where you belong.' The day after the election, a Muslim high school teacher in Georgia received an anonymous note saying that her headscarf 'isn't allowed any more', and suggesting that she 'tie it around your neck & hang yourself with it'; it was signed, 'America!' A high school Spanish teacher in Tennessee reported that a black student was blocked from entering the classroom by 'two white students chanting "Trump, Trump",' and that others told her that they no longer needed to learn Spanish because the then president-elect was 'sending all the Mexicans back'.

In June 2017, *Buzzfeed* chronicled the first school year of the Donald Trump presidency, describing educators' struggle 'to navigate a climate where misogyny, religious intolerance, name-calling, and racial exclusion have become part of mainstream political speech.' The article continued, 'At a time of thick political and racial tensions, and of heightened worries among people of color, what is a teacher to say when a student asks: *Why can the president say it but I can't?*' One commentator on the article wrote that quoting the president is never inappropriate, to which another wrote, 'I wonder if those parents would be just as okay with their kids choosing "grab them by the pussy" as their senior quote, since they are, after all, still quoting the president.'

School barbarism was not limited to students. A hidden audio recorder captured a Los Angeles teacher telling a student that she would have her parents deported using information from school records. She explained, 'I have your phone numbers, your address, your mama's address, your daddy's address; it's all in the system, sweetie.' A faculty member at a Pasco County, Florida, high school was accused of telling a group of African-American students standing in a hallway, 'Don't make me call Donald Trump to get you sent back to Africa.' In May 2017, a substitute teacher at a Bronx school ripped the hijab off of an eight-year-old student.

On college campuses, racism and unwanted sexual advances also exploded. The morning after the election, a Baylor University sophomore was shoved by another student who warned her, 'No niggers allowed on the sidewalk . . . I'm just trying to make America great again.' The same day, Jewish students at the New School in Manhattan found swastikas on their doors, as did LGBTQ women of colour. An Asian-American student at Wesleyan University received a note warning, 'Your time is up, chink.' Posters at Texas State University called for the torture of school administrators who support diversity initiatives.

Bigotry ran riot off campuses, too, much of it directed against women and in particular against African-American women. A young woman I know in Los Angeles exited her car, festooned with Clinton and Sanders bumper stickers, and a man walked up, snatched her crotch, and said, 'Nothing you can do about it in Trump's America, you liberal, nigger cunt.' A woman in Boston was told, 'You think that's funny, dirty bitch? I'll spit on you, you dirty bitch. I can smell the Africa on you.' When a saleswoman at a store in Kalamazoo, Michigan, asked a customer if he needed help, he replied, 'I don't need to ask you for shit; Donald Trump is president.' He called her a 'black bitch' and spat on her shoes. People who publicly socialise across races are targets of particular vitriol. Shortly after the election, an inter-racially married man in Louisville, Kentucky, received a letter from a neighbour that read, 'The most important thing is for our children to grow up in a pure white Christian environment. It's not clear why you would have a nigger bitch in your house. We believe all races should be separate in the United States of America.' In May 2017, arsonists torched the garage of a black family in Schodack, New York, festooning their home with scrawled swastikas and racial insults. The Los Angeles home of basketball star LeBron James was similarly vandalised. Princeton professor Keeanga-Yamahtta Taylor had to cancel public appearances after her outspoken opposition to Trump had been featured on Fox News. She explained, 'I have been repeatedly called "nigger", "bitch", "cunt", "dyke", "she-male" and "coon". I have been threatened with lynching and having the bullet from a .44 Magnum put in my head. I am not a newsworthy person. Fox did not run this story because it was "news", but to incite and unleash the mob-like mentality of its fringe audience.'

Latinos have fared no better. In West Springfield, Massachusetts, two days after the election, an army veteran woke to find the words 'Trump' and 'Go home' keyed into the hood of the family car. In May 2017, the warehouse of a Mexican food wholesaler in Clifton, New Jersey, was burgled and graffitied with swastikas and messages such as 'wetbacks', 'white power', 'KKK', 'Trump' and 'Hitler'. Nor were Asians safe. In Hartland, Michigan, an Indian-American woman reported that a stranger spat on her, called her a terrorist, and told her to leave the country. At a petrol station in Farragut, Tennessee, a white man greeted a Chinese-American teenager with, 'Can't wait for Trump to deport you or I will deport you myself, dyke yellow bitch.' In February 2017, Srinivas Kuchibhotla and Alok Madasani, electrical engineers living and working in Olathe, Kansas, were ordered to 'get out of my country', then shot by a stranger in a tavern. Kuchibhotla died; Madasani sustained serious injuries. Trump responded to the Kansas shootings only a week after they occurred, and only following mounting criticism of his silence. Jews have been targeted, too. A friend's eighty-seven-year-old mother was passing two men while crossing the street in New York City when one of them suddenly remarked, 'Heil Hitler, you filthy bitch.' In February 2017, vandals desecrated nearly two hundred headstones at Chesed Shel Emeth Cemetery in University City, Missouri; later that month, nearly one hundred Jewish headstones at Philadelphia's Mount Carmel Cemetery were overturned.

LGBTQ people are frequently targeted by Trump supporters, many cheered by Vice President Mike Pence's vigorous opposition to legislation and programmes that benefit gay citizens. In Sarasota, Florida, a seventy-five-year-old gay man was pulled from his car, assaulted, and told, 'You know my new president says we can kill all you faggots now.' In North Canton, Ohio, a lesbian couple who had lived in their community peacefully for years found their car door and bonnet defaced with 'DYKE' immediately after the election. In Rochester, New York, gay pride rainbow flags were torched as they hung from people's homes. A note appeared on the car of a gay Burlington, Iowa, minister: 'So father homo, how does it feel to have Trump as your president? At least he's got a set of balls. They'll put marriage back where God wants it and take yours away. America's gonna take care of your faggity ass.' February and March 2017 saw a wave of homophobic vandalism targeting LGBT community centres, including the Los Angeles LGBT Center, Milwaukee's Diverse & Resilient Center, Equality Florida in Orlando and Garden State Equality in Asbury Park, New Jersey. At the Tulsa, Oklahoma, Equality Center, shots were fired at the front door and windows; shortly thereafter, a man entered and began to verbally abuse the staff, volunteers and patrons. Casa Ruby, an LGBT community centre in Washington, D.C., was vandalised and its staff assaulted and threatened. In the first three months of 2017, eight transgender women of colour were murdered. In May, riders on the New York City subway's Q train watched as a rabid homophobe violently attacked a lesbian couple, pummelling one unconscious.

The worst invective has been directed against Muslims and immigrants. In the weeks following the election, ten California mosques received a letter addressed to the 'children of Satan', labelling Muslims 'vile and filthy', and calling for their extermination; it stated, 'There's a new sheriff in town – President Donald Trump', who will 'cleanse America and make it shine again. And, he's going to start with you muslims. He's going to do to you muslims what Hitler did to the jews. You muslims would be wise to pack your bags and get out of Dodge.' It closed, 'long live President Trump and God bless the U.S.A.' In Astoria, Queens, New York, a Moroccan-born Uber driver was pilloried by another driver: 'Trump is president, asshole, so you can kiss your visa good-bye, scumbag. They'll deport you soon, don't worry, you fucking terrorist.' In Grand Rapids, Michigan, a cabbie born in Ethiopia was punched by a passenger who repeatedly yelled 'Trump!' during the assault. In Iowa City, a note was tacked onto the door of a Sudanese-American family: 'You can all go home now. We don't want niggers and terrorists here. #trump.' In January 2017, the Islamic Center in Victoria, Texas, was destroyed by arson. In February, arsonists torched the Daarus Salaam Mosque in Tampa, Florida. In March, Deep Rai, a Sikh citizen of Kent, Washington, was shot by an assailant who ordered him to 'go back to your own country'. It is worth noting that undocumented immigrants who receive such threats almost never report them to police, as they are afraid of deportation – so these anecdotes and statistics certainly represent the very tip of the iceberg.

In Portland, Oregon, in May 2017, two men were killed and another injured when they attempted to shield a Muslim woman who was being verbally abused by a white supremacist. The President waited nearly three days to respond to the attack. In the interim, he issued twenty-one tweets touting his proposals, bragging about his recent European trip, crowing over a Republican election victory and denouncing the 'fake news media'. Eventually there came not an official statement from the White House, but a tepid tweet. The NAACP issued a statement criticising Trump's tardy response to the upsurge in incidents of racially-motivated violence, and his failure to refrain from the antagonistic, xenophobic rhetoric that disinhibits those who disdain minorities. His press secretary, Sean Spicer, denied any connection between Trump's rhetoric and the increase in violence and harassment targeting racial, religious and ethnic minorities, and LGBT citizens.

Virtually every time he mentions a minority group, Trump uses the definite article *the*, as in 'the Hispanics', 'the Muslims', 'the blacks' and 'the immigrants'. The insinuation is that individuals belonging to these groups can be described through a single, monolithic aspect of their identity. He repeatedly essentialises anyone who is different from him, declaring, for example, 'I've got black accountants at Trump Castle and at Trump Plaza. Black guys counting my money! I hate it. The only kind of people I want counting my money are short guys that wear yarmulkes every day. Those are the kind of people I want counting my money. Nobody else.' On another occasion, he criticised a member of his staff, observing, 'Laziness is a trait in blacks.' Often enough, Trump's targeted groups are falsely accused of reprehensible behaviour. 'I watched when the World Trade Center came tumbling down,' Trump bragged to a crowd in Birmingham, Alabama, at a rally in 2015. 'And I watched in Jersey City, New Jersey, where thousands and thousands of people were cheering as that building was coming down. Thousands of people were cheering'. Extensive research undertaken by the *Washington Post* confirmed that no such cheering mobs had been there. Trump's claim was a lie designed to terrify and vilify.

Trump's positions on immigration are based on just such generalisations, though his own mother and his paternal grandfather were immigrants and he has married two immigrants. In 2015, he tweeted, 'We must stop the crime and killing machine that is illegal immigration. Rampant problems will only get worse. Take back our country!' He explained how the United States would cease to admit immigrants in response to their desperate, life-or-death situations: 'Remember, under a Trump administration it's called America first. Remember that. To choose immigrants based on merit. Merit, skill, and proficiency. Doesn't that sound nice?'

Within days of his election, the new president proposed a travel ban for anyone from Iraq, Syria, Iran, Libya, Somalia, Sudan and Yemen – even for those who were legal U.S. residents or who were in the late stages of the multi-year refugee admission process. Protests broke out at airports across America and the ban was blocked by the courts, but Trump only introduced it in further iterations, giving no credence to the obvious truth that such manifest bigotry incites hatred for the United States, a hatred far more dangerous than anything that could be enabled by admitting Syrian refugees or letting Sudanese citizens with visas tour the country. When the case against a revamped edition of the travel ban was heard, Roger Gregory, Chief Judge of the United States Court of Appeals for the Fourth Circuit, wrote that the order 'in text speaks with vague words of national security, but in context drips with religious intolerance, animus, and discrimination'. This evident animus notwithstanding, at the end of June, the U.S. Supreme Court allowed a limited version of the ban to go into effect pending the court's consideration of executive discretion in immigration matters.

Donald Trump has changed the relationship America has with the world. He has antagonised and insulted numerous countries, calling into question the good faith of their leaders, citizens and governing bodies. In Trump's world of winners and losers, the primary value is monetary. In threatening to take American troops out of countries that don't pay for their presence, in announcing his contempt for treaties in which Americans are defending people he feels couldn't afford to defend us, he, like Theresa May, overlooks how the liberal world order has benefited Americans monetarily as well as morally. He shows a callow disregard for how the failure of that order, the spread of war, and the proliferation of nuclear weapons would likely spell the end of American economic and military dominance and would threaten the daily lives of people across this country – thereby making America weak again. The issue that has dominated Trump's thinking for almost three decades is his perception that the United States is getting a raw deal from its alliances with other nations. He is deeply hostile to international economic integration. Trump believes that the United States has been poorly served by the international alliances and institutions that emerged after the end of the Second World War and thereby brought a previously unimaginable stability to Western Europe. Writing in the conservative *Wall Street Journal*, George Melloan, a specialist in international affairs during his fifty-four-year career at the paper, commented, 'Trump seeks nothing less than ending the U.S.-led liberal order.' And though Trump enthused about free trade while campaigning, he has lashed out viciously against NAFTA, the Trans-Pacific Partnership and most other free-trade deals. Regarding this paradoxical opposition, Thomas Wright observed in *Politico*, 'He wants to slap tariffs on other countries – again harking back to 19th-century protectionism – and negotiate bi-lateral deals. Most economists believe this would create a downward spiral in the global economy, but Trump does not seem to care.'

In support of this agenda, Trump launched his 'America First' campaign, unapologetically adopting the term Charles Lindbergh had used when militating to keep America out of the Second World War. This phrase was linked to anti-Semitism, to admiration for the Nazis and the KKK, and to incipient white supremacism. Trump's version of America First entails disparaging other countries and the U.S. relationship to them. He said, 'Americanism, not globalism, will be our credo. As long as we are led by politicians who will not put America first, then we can be assured that other nations will not treat America with respect. The respect that we deserve.' What constitutes the respect America deserves is not clear, nor is how respect – a concept often invoked by gangsters to justify their honour killings – should suddenly feature in international relations as though it were a fungible, quantifiable asset. But hearing Trump's words, I was reminded of the moment in *Anna Karenina* when the heroine declares, 'Respect was invented to cover the empty place where love should be.'

Trump is an inveterate champion of strongmen. 'We were the big bully, but we were not smartly led. And we were the big bully who was – the big stupid bully and we were systematically ripped off by everybody,' he said, apparently less regretful about being a bully than about being ineffectual at bullying. He has held that attitude for a long time; in a 1990 *Playboy* interview, he described the Chinese government's massacre of demonstrators in Tiananmen Square as a successful example of 'the power of strength', explaining, 'When the students poured into Tiananmen Square, the Chinese government almost blew it. Then they were vicious, they were horrible, but they put it down with strength. That shows you the power of strength.' Trump treats tolerance as a sign of weakness. He has advocated the use of torture for alleged terrorists, flouting the Geneva Conventions, and despite ever-mounting evidence that torture is ineffective. 'If it doesn't work, they deserve it anyway, for what they're doing,' he has said.

The perception that government is broken – which appears to have been a major factor behind the Brexit referendum, Trump's election and parallel developments in Europe – reflects a fantasy of what functioning government should be: an institution that will do more for you while asking less of you. But voting against the norms of the establishment – philosophically speaking, a liberal position rather than a conservative one – seldom engenders more coherence; it often signals a descent into chaos. It ignores the speed with which liberators historically have come to resemble whomever they have displaced. The notion that national problems are best resolved by national sequestration harks back to an imagined time when the activities of one nation could be genuinely separated from those of others. Liberalism holds that a country's interests are contingent on the betterment of the world; today's radical conservatism, that those interests are in competition with the rest of the world. The United States has never before been a country in which a president has so lavishly praised dictators, championed torture, or mocked the disenfranchised. Britain has gone decades without pursuing such perverse seclusion as is manifest in Brexit.

After his 'historic' meeting with King Salman bin Abdulaziz of Saudi Arabia, Trump said to his European counterparts, 'Terrorism must be stopped in its tracks, or the horror you saw in Manchester and so many other places will continue forever. You have thousands and thousands of people pouring into our various countries and spreading throughout, and in many cases we have no idea who they are . . . We must be tough. We must be strong. And we must be vigilant.' Yet he has opposed that very vigilance in relation to his ties to Russia and Russia's manipulation of the U.S. election in which he rose to power. Trump has consistently used acts of terrorism to boost his programme, lambasting London Mayor Sadiq Khan following the tragic attacks in June 2017. He deliberately distorted Khan's words, implying that his injunction not to be alarmed by increased police presence on London streets was a direction not to be alarmed by the terrorist attack itself. Trump reverted to his attempt to re-instate the travel ban that the courts had blocked, writing, 'We need to be smart, vigilant and tough. We need the courts to give us back our rights. We need the Travel Ban as an extra level of safety!' Khan replied simply, 'Some people thrive on feud and division. We are not going to let Donald Trump divide our communities.' When the BBC reported on world leaders' reactions to the attack, Trump's tweets were mentioned as what the journalist and memoirist Cheryl Tan called the 'unbelievably ridiculous punchline'.

Trump's June 2017 withdrawal from the Paris Agreement on climate change represents a deplorable and narcissistic unconcern for the future – and for the rest of the world, an abandonment of the dignity inherent in mutuality. German chancellor Angela Merkel finally said, 'The time in which we could fully rely on others is a bit in the past. I have experienced that in the past several days. And, because of that, I can say now that we Europeans truly have to take our fate into our own hands – naturally, in friendship with the United States of America, in friendship with Great Britain, as good neighbours wherever that may work, with Russia and other countries. But we must understand that *we* must fight for our future, as Europeans, for our own fate.'

This is a book about boundaries: about both the beauty in our differences and the surprising symmetries among us that persist despite those differences. It is about the diversity and the intimacy of human experience. Theresa May's Brexit position and Donald Trump's executive orders and posturing tweets reflect a view that difference is threatening rather than beautiful, and thereby they disavow our shared humanity. This represents the opposite of the arguments contained in these pages. At a time of anti-liberalism such as this one, the interests of beleaguered minorities are subordinated, violently or carelessly. The secondary threat is fragmentation, and the inaccurate perception that minorities have completely disparate agendas: the Muslims; the poor; the LGBTQ range of alternative sexualities and gender identities; the Jews; the bi-racial and multi-racial people; the disabled and differently abled; the African-Americans and the Africans; the Latinos and the Asians; the intellectuals; those in mixed-race or mixed-faith relationships; the single parents; the prison inmates guilty of minor infractions serving inexplicably heavy sentences; the legal immigrants; those subject to oppression and tragedy at home, whether that be personal trauma within their families or social trauma within their communities; the undocumented immigrants; the refugees; the very young and the very old; the homeless; women who work because they want to; women who work because they have to; women who parent full time; women seeking abortions and the doctors who care for them.

The utter shock so many liberals evinced at the British referendum and at Trump's electoral success points to how unknown half of each of these countries is to the other half. Further, it reflects the failure of pollsters and undermines our trust in the supposedly neutral media. Accusations have been rampant that Facebook and Google's algorithms have created a 'filter bubble' that has left liberals seeing only liberal news and conservatives, only conservative reporting; reinforced their existing patterns of interest, sharpening the divide; and made each side believe in a fictitious unanimity on most essential issues. Under the world's shift away from tolerance, members of these groups must recognise their mutual affinities as they find themselves targets of similar hatred. Each category that is oppressed is weak so long as it remains isolated, but the collective body of people who are oppressed can be strong. Everyone who is terrified by swastikas has something in common. The need for a unifying confederation is acute. Democracy is a numbers game; so is most protest. Protest has reached new heights since Trump's inauguration, starting with the Women's March that brought together vast numbers of people not only in Washington, D.C. but also around the globe; the British snap election of June 2017 felt like a protest, too. The voice of belonging must hold its own against the voice of othering. The open plains of our shared humanity are broader and more welcoming than the citadel within which the temporarily empowered have sought to sequester us.

Conservatism has bifurcated. The traditional reactionary platform entails expanding borders to assimilate additional territory; the new one entails closing borders in order to sustain national purity. Queen Victoria's colonialism has given way to Theresa May's isolationism. The liberal idea of an open and welcoming society rather than a conquering or self-sequestering one has guided the powerful of most parties for the last seventy years, but it is now very much in question. Old maps reflect constantly evolving political divisions; those territories demarcated by mountains, seas and rivers can have a reassuring aura of permanence, but even these have been repeatedly breached. Walls volunteer to take over in the absence of muscular geography, and modern politicians aren't the only ones to have contemplated their fortressing singularity. The American poet Robert Frost proposed in his poem 'Mending Wall' that nature abhors these barricades:

> Before I built a wall I'd ask to know
> What I was walling in or walling out,
> And to whom I was like to give offence.
> Something there is that doesn't love a wall,
> That wants it down.

To which the man next door in the poem can only say, 'Good fences make good neighbours.' But history shows that in many instances, good fences make real enemies. Walls are concrete symbols of exclusion, and exclusion is seldom a wise diplomatic move. Nevertheless, more than a quarter of a century after the destruction of the Berlin Wall – the ultimate imprisoning symbol – walls are back in the headlines. Building walls, keeping foreigners out, trivialising the delicate peace forged in Europe after two world wars, and expressing overt prejudice towards immigrant populations are all increasingly presented as viable foreign policies and reasonable security procedures.

Trump has promised a wall between the United States and Mexico – paid for by the Mexicans. Britain has built 'the great wall of Calais', as it has been named by some areas of the press, in the hope of reducing illegal immigration from the continent. There has likewise been talk of retaining some of the 'peace walls' separating

Catholic and Protestant neighbourhoods in Northern Ireland. Plans are underway for a massive new fence along the Hungarian border. Israel is well on its way to being a walled nation even as it expands beyond its established borders. As long as the world is infected with war and starvation and massive inequity, some people will attempt to escape from troubled and impoverished places to apparently less troubled and more prosperous ones. The problem cannot be solved by walls; it relies on a perpetual renewal of the social contract.

Freedom is a verb. It is something you live and achieve, that you must relive and achieve again every day. It does not sit static; it is not an estate to be presumed continuous. It takes time and enormous commitment to build freedom, but hard-won freedom can evanesce with alarming rapidity. Nazism, apartheid, Hutu Power, Greater Serbia – each descended abruptly and swept away the justice that had preceded it. In each case, those who would become victims of targeted violence did not believe it was possible on such a scale. We may not be at the brink of such an extreme crisis in the United States and the U.K. – but we are at the very least in a wave of unprecedented bigotry. If there is to be any effective resistance to its institutionalisation, it will come from our sustained openness, the most radical possible act of opposition to governing bodies that would stifle rebellious voices.

My friend Hasan Agili was admitted to the United States as a refugee from Libya after I had lobbied on his behalf, and he now lives with my family in New York. He is bright, warm and deeply enthusiastic and figures especially large in the life of our seven-year-old son, George, to whom he is, even at thirty-three, effectively a longed-for elder brother. We have Hasan with us because he is a fine and fascinating person; because we enjoy his company; and because the lives we live as gay people in New York in this time reflect so many privileges unavailable to others, and we feel we have a moral obligation to help. I also believe that this is a time when having a gay, Muslim immigrant become part of our family sends a message to our children and to the people we know and even to ourselves that someone who has been called 'other' can become not only familiar but also loved.

When I was away for a few days this summer, not long after Hasan arrived in New York, he sent me an email one night about what had been for him an astonishing experience. He had been sitting on the steps in front of our house in New York when two men walked past, hand in hand. They stopped to kiss each other, then ambled on. In our neighbourhood, such mundane intimacies happen all the time; sometimes I've been the man who kissed the other man on the street. But for Hasan, the lack of shame came as a revelation. He wrote, 'My heart was beating so fast, out of excitement or euphoria . . . I don't know. I stayed there sitting for another thirty minutes waiting for something similar to happen again, but it didn't. I want to try it, to have that feeling of holding someone's hand and walking down the street. Can't wait to experience that feeling.' That same week, one of his teenage cousins was shot and critically injured when a gang tried to steal his car; two more cousins were shot and killed when they went to visit the victim in the hospital.

We ask so much of refugees and immigrants, who of necessity live in two different realities. My husband and I watched the presidential debates with Hasan, who commented on the numerous references to his homeland as Trump invoked the 2012 attack by Islamist militants on the U.S. embassy in Benghazi. The day after the election, his mother called. 'I guess I'll never be able to come and see you,' she said, weeping. She knew that our next president had said, 'Donald J. Trump is calling for a total and complete shutdown of Muslims entering the United States.' His hatred spanned the gulf. I was affected by her grief, even though I've never met her, just as I was affected by Hasan's fear. Our lives and identities overlap and diverge every day, and that is political even as it is personal. It was political for Miep Gies and her friends to hide Anne Frank and her family, though they did so at least in part because of personal affection. It was political for Mildred and Richard Loving to marry in 1958, and to spend nine years fighting Virginia's laws against racially mixed unions all the way to the U.S. Supreme Court, even though their originating motive was their love for each other. And it is political for us to have Hasan as a member of our household, even though he is coaching George in soccer, working in a hospital, baking wonderful cakes for special occasions and making us all laugh. I had hoped that the passage of time would divest his presence in our household of its politics, leaving only the primacy of our mutual esteem and affection. That eventuality slipped away from us on election night.

Identity and association used to be bound largely by geography and class; a farmer in Indiana was not going to cross paths with a student at Beijing University. The internet allows tribes to form outside previous social constraints. The contrast between community with neighbours and community with these far-flung friends is sharp. The Trump campaign, like Brexit, surged in response to some Americans' fear of the other, a fear that has escalated even when friendly online contact with such others has become a daily reality for many users of social media. The 'shrinking world' may allow Scotsmen to play backgammon with Indonesians, but it has not necessarily humanised across differences of nationality or even political affiliation. Meanwhile, people in the developing world who see the extent of Western luxury become outraged in response, alienated by glimpses of the privilege they will never enjoy. Not even Trump proposes that a wall can arrest the spread of global technology, robotics and the internet – advances that appear to escalate not only global inequalities, but also awareness of those inequalities.

Hatred and envy do not respect national boundaries. A Bosnian professor of critical theory, Damir Arsenijević, wrote to me in sympathy from Tuzla a few weeks after the 2016 U.S. election. When I replied that it wasn't as bad as what had happened in his country twenty years earlier, he replied, 'It is an appalling time and I imagine it is no sunshine even compared with Bosnia. When it hits hard and for the first time like this, as it did with Trump, those times are very traumatic. It's a start of a longer discussion and this discussion must be international.' Such a discussion cannot become international if people throughout the world are not open to it. I posted part of Damir's letter on Facebook and received outraged comments from several friends appalled that an 'unfortunate' election result could be compared to a genocide. Damir's letter had not suggested that the electoral outcome matched the genocide in Bosnia, nor the violence I had written about elsewhere, but I found his warning sobering. Violence tends to gather steam slowly – at least in its early phases – and those who have seen their own societies destroyed can perhaps more easily recognise its signposts.

In a much-quoted *New York Times* article headlined 'The End of Identity Liberalism', the political scientist Mark Lilla wrote, 'At a very young age our children are being encouraged to talk about their individual identities, even before they have them. By the time they reach college many assume that diversity discourse exhausts political discourse, and have shockingly little to say about such perennial questions as class, war, the economy and the common good. Fascination with the identity drama has even affected foreign reporting. However interesting it may be to read, say, about the fate of transgender people in Egypt, it contributes nothing to educating Americans about the powerful political and religious currents that will determine Egypt's future, and indirectly, our own.' Lilla continues, 'Identity politics is largely expressive, not persuasive. Which is why it never wins elections – but can lose them.'

In response, Katherine Franke, Lilla's colleague at Columbia University, wrote, 'Former Egyptian President Hosni Mubarak and current President Abdel Fattah el-Sisi have both used the spectacular persecution of gay men and trans women as a ploy to legitimize and strengthen the expansion of authoritarian state power to excise from Egyptian society a convenient symbol of British colonial contamination. In fact, President Sisi's mass arrests of LGBT people and infiltration of gay chat rooms are quite clearly the leading edge of a government effort to shut down freedom of expression and sites of resistance to authoritarian rule in Egypt. The persecution of LGBT rights has played a key role in crushing efforts to bring about liberal, democratic reform in Egypt. The Egyptian case quite clearly illustrates the essential connection between identity politics and authoritarian governance.'

Lilla presumes that some news is useful, while other news is comparatively insignificant, and that we can readily tell the difference; Franke asserts that you have to know the whole story. Our knowledge is always imperfect, so the omniscience to which Franke might aspire is impossible, but Lilla's suggestion that we can foretell which foreign news will turn out to be significant is dangerous. Identity politics is often lampooned as its own isolationism, a smug echo chamber within which dissenting voices go unheard. Identity rights should not upstage the right to an individual point of view, and an identity-based idealism that wins no votes is of limited usefulness in a democracy. Group identification, whether from the left or the right, does not excuse a loss of compassion for those outside that group. But the solution is not to abandon identity; it is to broaden it and render it inclusive, to let people define their relationship to one another's particularities. While individual identities may be highly specific, the self-actualisation rooted in identity politics is nearly universal. All identities are enriched through contact beyond the group.

Tennyson's Ulysses says, 'I am a part of all that I have met.' All that he met was part of him, too; Tennyson knew that crossing boundaries constituted a language. It is becoming an endangered one. When I researched disability, I was often drawn into debates about education for the disabled. Some people believe that intellectually disabled people should be put in separate schools focused on their specific needs. But since separate is never equal, others have proposed that these children be educated in inclusion classrooms where they interact with non-disabled students. People need both: they need to be with those who are like them, and they need to be part of the larger community. So, too, for internationalism: we need not associate exclusively with foreigners, but neither should we be cut off from them. We need to spend time with those who are similar to us and with those who are different. If you don't know anyone else like you, figuring out who and what you are is nearly impossible. But without the people who are unlike you, you become a caricature of yourself, provincial in the extreme. Fortunately, neither model needs to win; neither subverts the other. Stupid things are done and said in the name of identity politics: the rights of small groups are positioned above those of larger ones and issues are argued specifically rather than inclusively. But our advances in minority and civil rights will be jeopardised if we dismantle the institutions established to protect them. One can pull away from the excesses of identity politics without giving up on the value of inclusiveness.

Justice can appear in or vanish from nations surprisingly quickly. I visited South Africa in 1992 to write an article about how the country's black and white artists were struggling to make sense of apartheid (an article that is included in this collection). Just after the 2016 U.S. election, William Kentridge, the most prominent of the South African artists I had befriended a generation earlier, came to New York to give a lecture. When we had dinner afterwards, I asked him how it felt to visit the United States at such a pivotal time, and he said, 'It's as though you have found out that part of your family has been in a terrible car accident; you come to see who is still breathing.' Then he said, 'What is shocking is not how shocked you are now, but how unshocked you will be in six months.' I took a silent pledge that night to stay shocked. Staying shocked is a long game; our natural impulse is to have an adrenal response to crisis followed by normalisation. Staying shocked requires that you resist the ways in which repetition desensitises you. It entails the ability to remain alert to the value of connectedness, and not to enact what Sebastian Haffner, in his memoir of Hitler's rise to power, called, 'the hypnotic trance into which his public fell, succumbing with less and less resistance to the glamour of depravity and the ecstasy of evil'.

I have written in these pages about travelling to understand depression, but actually, travel is the opposite of depression. Depression is a curling inwards, and travel is an opening outwards. Witnessing a global world is a way to make a global world. Openness makes us safe. Internationalism is complicated and messy, a source of conflict as much as peace, but travelling and welcoming travellers makes for justice. At the same time, those who would champion internationalism must acknowledge its faults. It is large and confusing and difficult to negotiate. It exploits cheap labour in the developing world, which closes down jobs for skilled workers in the West. It favours management from the developed world, which often results in exploitation of the scattered poor. Language gaps can lead to awful misunderstandings, and systems of values are often challenged. But retreating to our various corners and building walls does not address these problems. Admittedly, it's a weak campaign slogan to say, 'Globalism is very imperfect, inevitably damaging to everyone – but we're better off with the existing system than without any system at all.' But say it we must, because isolationist xenophobia turns other people and nations against us. In the end, it is a weakness masquerading as a fortification. In saying that those who believe themselves to be citizens of the world don't know what citizenship means, Theresa May had it inside out. We must take action as citizens of our own countries yet embrace a larger whole. As soon as we believe that we cannot be citizens of the world, we lose the world of which we might have been citizens.

Acknowledgements

When I set out to assemble this book, I suffered under the gross misapprehension that an anthology would involve merely scanning some things I wrote a long time ago and sending them to my publisher. In fact, the process has entailed selecting the articles; writing the introduction to the collection; composing prologues and epilogues; and endlessly polishing essays I'd already written, some of which had to be reworked. F. Scott Fitzgerald once said that he didn't want to repeat his innocence, but that he'd like to repeat the pleasure of losing it, and putting together an anthology of this kind provided a chance to grow out of my naïveté all over again.

The trip down memory lane was a return not only to my bygone adventures but also to the editors with whom I'd worked on the original pieces. I have been fortunate both in being sent to fantastic places and in having my reports on them edited with exquisite care. I thank Nicholas Coleridge and Meredith Etherington-Smith at *Harpers & Queen*, who sent me out on my first big reporting trips, and believed in me before there was any apparent reason to do so. For their guidance at the *New York Times Magazine*, I thank Jack Rosenthal, Adam Moss, and Annette Grant, who helped me grow into myself and find an audience. At the *New Republic*, I was fortunate to work with David Shipley. In connection with my work for the *New Yorker*, I thank David Remnick, Henry Finder, Amy Davidson and Sasha Weiss for their sterling care. As soon as she took over *Travel + Leisure*, Nancy

Novogrod began sending me everywhere I'd always wanted to go; she gave me a bigger and better life than I would ever have had without her. Our decades of collaboration are among the bright spots of my professional and personal life. I also thank the editors with whom I worked at *T+L*, particularly Sheila Glaser and the wonderful Luke Barr. For her support at *Food & Wine*, I thank Dana Cowin; no one has ever had a better friend, and I'd gladly have given the world away in exchange for the joy her generous affection and steady wisdom have given me. I thank Catherine Burns and all her colleagues at the Moth for the steadfast good humour with which they helped me to craft stories.

As always, I am deeply grateful to my glorious editor at Scribner, Nan Graham, whose trademark mix of loyalty, integrity, genius and kindness has become an organising force for my work and beyond my work. Also invaluable on the Scribner team are Brian Belfiglio and the divine Kate Lloyd, my beloved publicists; Daniel Loedel, whose calm patience protected me from stressful bureaucracy time and again; and dear, dear Roz Lippel, who publishes with such big-hearted enthusiasm; also to the tireless Katie Rizzo, who filtered endless corrections with infinite patience. I am grateful to Steven Henry Boldt for his excellent copy-editing, and to Eric Rayman for his careful legal read. At Chatto & Windus, I thank my entirely splendid editor, Clara Farmer, and her perfectly delightful deputy, Juliet Brooke. I thank Matt Broughton for the richly imaginative cover design. I am grateful to my excellent publicist at Chatto, Mari Yamazaki, and to my wonderfully energised external publicist, Fiona McMorrough. I am grateful to Luca Trovato for the frontispiece photo.

My agent, Andrew Wylie, has been the guiding light of my career, and with each book, I appreciate anew how lucky I am to have him as my representative and friend. I am also grateful to the others at the Wylie Agency who have devoted themselves unstintingly to this work: Jeffrey Posternak, Sarah Chalfant, Charles Buchan, Percy Stubbs and Alba Ziegler-Bailey.

I am deeply indebted to Alice Truax, who does the equivalent of auto-body work on my writing, pounding every dented sentence to a high-gloss shine and replacing all the scratched and fogged glass of my arguments with breathtaking transparency. Kathleen Seidel has identified research errors and found the right answer to every query or uncertainty; she has combed through my prose with meticulous care and made it more lucid; she has organised footnotes, bibliography, website and anything else that could possibly be organised. Writing is a crazy trapeze act, and she is my net. Thanks also to Jane McElhone for assistance on fact-checking.

I wrote portions of this book at Yaddo, where I write faster and more clearly than anywhere else, and I am profoundly grateful for my time there. I am particularly indebted to Yaddo's enchanting president, Elaina Richardson, who adds a patina of joy to each of those productive visits.

I thank my colleagues at PEN, who have helped me to think more deeply about freedom and justice, in particular PEN's remarkable executive director, Suzanne Nossel.

I thank Bonnie Burnham, Henry Ng and George McNeely at the World Monuments Fund, who have been invaluable advisers time and again on far-flung corners of the world.

Christian Caryl has been something of a muse to me. He hosted me in Germany when I first began to write about Russia in the 1980s and the artists had started exhibiting in Berlin. I stayed with him when I went to Kazakhstan, and climbed mountains, both physical and ethnographic, in his company. I crashed with him and his family in Tokyo when he was living in Japan. He talked me into visiting Afghanistan when I was afraid to do so, and he made sure I had a place to stay and someone to guide me when I got there. Additionally, he read the manuscript of this book and provided invaluable feedback. *Far and Away* and my life would have looked very different without him.

I thank the people who appear within these various stories, too many to list again here: all those who allowed me to observe or interview them. Some of the people who helped me where I went or helped get me there deserve special acknowledgement: Beezy Bailey, Sara Barbieri, Janet Benshoof, Eliot Bikales, Bonnie Burnham, Mario Canivello, Hans van Dijk, Ashur Etwebi, Susannah Fiennes, Fred Frumberg, Maria Gheorghiu, Philip Gourevitch, Guo Feng, David Hecht, Harold Holzer, Roger James, Cheryl Johnson, Susan Kane,

Aung Kyawmyint, Francesca Dal Lago, Lee Yulin, Elvira Lupsa, I Gede Marsaja, Joan B. Mirviss, Freda Murck, Henry Ng, Brent Olson, I Gede Primantara, Michaela Raab, Emily K. Rafferty, Jack Richard, Ira Sachs, Hélène Saivet, João Salles, Gh. Farouq Samim, Gabriel Sayad, Andreas Schmid, Lisa Schmitz, Jill Schuker, Luiz Schwarcz, Julie Krasnow Streiker, Andrea Sunder-Plassmann, Corina Şuteu, Dina Temple-Raston, Farley Tobin, Ko Winters and Mauricio Zacharias.

I owe a debt also to my many companions in travel, among them Anne Applebaum, Jessica Beels, Chuck Burg, S. Talcott Camp, Meri Nana-Ama Danquah, Kathleen Gerard, Kathryn Greig, Han Feng, John Hart, Leslie Hawke, Cheryl Henson, Michael Lee, Sue Macartney-Snape, David Solomon, Claudia Swan and, always most of all, my beloved Alexandra K. Munroe, who has joined me on continent after continent.

My thanks to Richard A. Friedman and Richard C. Friedman, who have kept me sane through experiences that often felt insane, and to Jon Walton for providing spiritual guidance when life seemed less than heavenly. Judy Gutow arranged the travel year in and year out, finding discounted fares and emergency hotel bookings in the most far-fetched destinations. I pay tribute to Danusia Trevino, who helps gracefully with so many thankless tasks and never grows impatient, and to Tatiana Martushev, who helped similarly in the earlier years of this project. Tremendous thanks to Celso, Miguela and Olga Mancol, who have kept my household humming when I've been frantically writing and have coddled me when I've been too busy to coddle myself; to Sergio Avila, who gets me wherever I need to go; to Kylee Sallak and Ildikó Fülöp, who have brought both love and order to my son's life and hence to mine.

I thank my mother, who encouraged me to be adventurous. She

has been dead a quarter century, but she read and commented on the earlier work in this collection. She always wanted my writing to be clear; she always wanted it to be kind. Returning to that early work has reminded me of how she influenced everything that has come since. My father has slowly come around to the idea that I head off to places where he would never go and wishes I wouldn't go, either. He is still my first and most loyal reader, and has been there with arms outstretched whenever I've flown too close to the sun. My thanks also to my stepmother, Sarah Billinghurst Solomon, who has been an unflagging supporter of this project.

I thank Tamara Ward and Laura Scher for always being in my corner, full of both love and fun.

I thank Blaine Smith, whose radiant and judicious presence has kept me steady when things looked stormy, and whose quiet insights help me to grow in beautiful ways.

I thank Oliver Scher, Lucy Scher, Blaine Solomon and George Solomon. No one else could root me to the world as they have.

Finally, I thank my husband, John Habich Solomon, who has accompanied me on both outward and inward journeys. There's no one with whom I'd prefer to see the world, nor to live in it. He is my north and south poles, my equator, my Tropics of Cancer and Capricorn, my seven continents and seven seas.

Notes

Dispatches from Everywhere

2 The U.S. Army's Standards of Medical Fitness (Army Regulation 40-501) call for referral to a Medical Evaluation Board for 'pes planus, when symptomatic, more than moderate, with pronation on weight bearing which prevents the wearing of military footwear, or when associated with vascular changes'. Mild and moderate cases of flat feet would not disqualify one from military service.

4 Erika Urbach's obituary can be found on the Norwegian Bachelor Farmers website, at http://norwegianbachelorfarmers.com/lakewoodrock/stories/Erika.html.

4 This delightful collection is still in print: Frances Carpenter, *Tales of a Korean Grandmother* (1989).

8 The ruins of Ingapirca – also known as the 'Inca wall' – are currently being restored; see 'En Ingapirca continúa proceso de restauración en piedras,' *El Tiempo*, 8 April 2015.

11 The Chernobyl nuclear disaster is described in British Broadcasting Corporation, 'Chernobyl: 20 years on', BBC News, 12 June 2007. For a striking collection of photographs of the site at the time of the reactor fire and over the following twenty-five years, see Alan Taylor, 'The Chernobyl disaster: 25 years ago', *Atlantic*, 23 March 2011.

11 In Chekhov's 1900 play, *The Three Sisters*, youngest sister, Irina, yearns for the family's return to the city of her birth. Act 2 closes with her plaint 'Moscow . . . Oh, Lord. Could we go to Moscow'; see Anton Chekhov, *The Three Sisters: A Play by Anton Chekhov Adapted by David Mamet* (1992).

12 Sotheby's first auction of contemporary Soviet art, conducted 7 July 1988, was recounted in my first book, *The Irony Tower: Soviet Artists in a Time of Glasnost* (1991).

13 Nikita Alexeev's statement ('We have been preparing ourselves to be not great artists, but angels') occurs on page 283 of Solomon (1991), ibid.

14 For the Russian edition, see *The Irony Tower. Советские художники во времена гласности* (2013).

16 Tennyson's 'Ulysses' may be found on page 88 of *Poems by Alfred Tennyson in Two Volumes: Vol. 2* (1842).

16 The earliest known instance of the quote attributed to St Augustine ('The world is a book and those who do not travel read only one page') occurs on page 2 of John Feltham, *The English Enchiridion* (1799).

16 Christian Caryl is author of *Strange Rebels: 1979 and the Birth of the 21st Century* (2013), and dozens of insightful pieces of political journalism; see, e.g., 'The young and the restless', *Foreign Policy*, 17 February 2014; and 'Putin: During and after Sochi', *New York Review of Books*, 3 April 2014.

18 For more background on the shifts in Cuba's official stance regarding religion, see Rone Tempest, 'Pope meets with Castro, agrees to a Cuba visit,' *Los Angeles Times*, 20 November 1996; and Marc Frank, 'Cuba's atheist Castro brothers open doors to Church and popes', Reuters, 7 September 2015.

18 I reminisce about my Cuban New Year's Eve party at greater length in my article 'Hot night in Havana', *Food & Wine*, January 2002.

22 See Robert S. McNamara and Brian Van De Mark, *In Retrospect: The Tragedy and Lessons of Vietnam* (1996).

24 The Vilna Gaon Jewish State Museum continues to welcome visitors; its website is at http://jmuseum.lt.

24 The quote from John Ruskin ('It is merely being "sent" to a place . . .') appears in the essay 'The moral of landscape', anthologised in *The Works of John Ruskin, Vol. 5* (1904), pages 370–71.

25 The quote from E. M. Forster ('When I got away, I could get on with it') comes from an interview by P. N. Furbank and F. J. H. Haskell, 'E. M. Forster: The art of fiction no. 1', *Paris Review*, Spring 1953.

25 The quote from Samuel Johnson ('All travel has its advantages . . .') occurs in Boswell's *Life of Johnson* (1887).

27 The 'paper architects' were the subject of my article 'Paper tsars', *Harpers & Queen*, February 1990.

29 Walter Pater's advice can be found in the 'Conclusion' to *The Renaissance* and appears on page 60 of *Selected Writings of Walter Pater* (1974).

29 Zhou Enlai's quip about the French Revolution is disputed, but is nonetheless 'a misunderstanding that was too delicious to invite correction'; see Richard McGregor, 'Zhou's cryptic caution lost in translation', *Financial Times*, 10 June 2011.

32 See Andrew Solomon, *The Noonday Demon: An Atlas of Depression* (2001); and Andrew Solomon, *Far from the Tree: Parents, Children, and the Search for Identity* (2012).

33 For a recent tally of countries permitting same-sex marriage, see Freedom to Marry, 'The freedom to marry internationally', Freedom to Marry, 2015.

33 For an up-to-date summary of overseas legislation pertaining to homosexuality, see International Lesbian, Gay, Bisexual, Trans and Intersex Association, 'The lesbian, gay and bisexual map of world laws', ILGBTIA, May 2015.

34 News coverage of my wedding includes Eric Pfanner, 'Vows: Andrew Solomon and John Habich,' *New York Times*, 8 July 2007; Laurie Arendt, 'A toast to her brother', *Ozaukee Press*, 30 September 2007; and Geordie Greig, 'My big fab gay wedding', *Tatler*, October 2007.

34 For a report of the UN sessions on abuses committed by terrorists against gays, see Lucy Westcott, 'Gay refugees addresses [*sic*] U.N. Security Council in historic meeting on LGBT rights', *Newsweek*, 25 August 2015.

34 Terrorist atrocities against gay people in Syria and Iraq are documented in James Rush, 'Images emerge of "gay" man "thrown from building by Isis militants before he is stoned to death after surviving fall"', *Independent*, 3 February 2015; and Jamie Dettmer, 'The ISIS hug of death for gays', *Daily Beast*, 24 April 2015.

35 The execution of Makwan Moloudzadeh is reported in British Broadcasting Corporation, 'Iranian hanged after verdict stay', BBC News, 6 December 2007.

35 For background on the charges against twenty-six men arrested in a raid on a Cairo bathhouse, see John McManus, 'Egypt court clears men accused of bathhouse "debauchery"', BBC News, January 12, 2015.

35 The arrest of guests at a gay wedding in Egypt is reported in British Broadcasting Corporation, 'Egypt cuts "gay wedding video" jail terms', BBC News, 27 December 2014.

35 A Saudi Arabian court's draconian 2007 sentence of two men for sodomy is reported in Doug Ireland, '7000 lashes for sodomy', *Gay City News*, 11 October 2007.

35 On the deplorable situation in Russia, see Tanya Cooper, 'Licence to harm: Violence and harassment against LGBT people and activists in Russia', Human Rights Watch, 15 December 2014.

35 Entrapment of gay men in Kyrgyzstan is documented in Anna Kirey, '"They said we deserved this": Police violence against gay and bisexual men in Kyrgyzstan', Human Rights Watch, 28 January 2014. Recent proposals for anti-gay legislation in Kyrgyzstan are the subject of Hugh Ryan, 'Kyrgyzstan's anti-gay law will likely pass next month, but has already led to violence', *Daily Beast*, 18 September 2015.

35 Human consequences of the Indian court decision recriminalising homosexuality are discussed in Andrew Buncombe, 'India's gay community scrambling after court decision recriminalises homosexuality', *Independent*, 26 February 2014.

35 For a catalogue of homophobic laws in Africa, see Global Legal Research

Directorate, 'Laws on homosexuality in African nations', Library of Congress, 9 June 2015.

35 For an exhaustive review of persecution of gay people in Nigeria and elsewhere in Africa, see Thomas Probert et al., 'Unlawful killings in Africa', Centre for Governance and Human Rights, University of Cambridge, 2015. The chilling effects of Nigeria's anti-gay legislation are documented in Katy Glenn Bass and Joey Lee, 'Silenced voices, threatened lives: The impact of Nigeria's anti-LGBTI law on freedom of expression', PEN American Center, 29 June 2015.

35 The sentencing of Roger Jean-Claude Mbede and the ordeal of two other Cameroonian men jailed for allegedly engaging in homosexual acts are discussed in British Broadcasting Corporation, 'Cameroon "gay sex" men acquitted', BBC News, 7 January 2013; see also David Artavia, 'Cameroon's "gay problem"', *Advocate*, 7 July 2013.

35 For more details on Zimbabwe president Robert Mugabe's dramatic condemnation of homosexuals, see South African Press Association, 'Mugabe condemns Europe's gay "filth"' *IOL News*, 14 April 2011; Obey Manayiti, 'Mugabe chides homosexuals again', *NewsDay* (Bulawayo), 25 July 2013; and Dan Littauer, 'Mugabe promises "hell for gays" in Zimbabwe if he wins', *Gay Star News*, 17 June 2013.

35 The Ugandan legislature's crusade against gays has entered a further round; see Saskia Houttuin, 'Gay Ugandans face new threat from anti-homosexuality law', *Guardian*, 6 January 2015.

36 Protests against surreptitious censorship of translated works by Chinese publishers are covered in Alexandra Alter, 'China's publishers court America as its authors scorn censorship', *New York Times*, 28 May 2015; and PEN America, 'Publishers' pledge on Chinese censorship of translated works', PEN America, 15 October 2015.

36 See Bettina Zilkha, 'Andrew Solomon named President of PEN', *Forbes*, 5 March 2015.

37 'Words are no deeds' occurs in William Shakespeare's *Henry VIII*, act 3, scene 2, line 152.

37 Emma Lazarus's oft-quoted saying, 'Until we are all free, we are none of us free', originally appeared in 'Epistle to the Hebrews', a series of columns published in the *American Hebrew* from 3 November 1882, to 23 February 1883; see the centennial anthology, *An Epistle to the Hebrews* (1987), page 30.

37 Aung San Suu Kyi's entreaty served as the title to her 1997 op-ed, 'Please use your liberty to promote ours', *New York Times*, 4 February 1997.

38 In relation to Dima Prigov in the living room, I am thinking in particular of Luis Buñuel's brilliant 1972 film, *The Discreet Charm of the Bourgeoisie*.

38 See 'Reporter Daniel Pearl is dead, killed by his captors in Pakistan', *Wall Street Journal*, 24 February 2002.

39 Proposals by Republican presidential candidate Donald Trump and other conservatives to staunch the entry of Muslims into the United States and

routinely subject Muslim Americans to surveillance following the November 15 terrorist attacks in Paris are discussed in Jenna Johnson, 'Conservative suspicions of refugees grow in wake of Paris attacks', *Washington Post*, 15 November 2015; Jose DelReal, 'Donald Trump won't rule out warrantless searches, ID cards for American Muslims', *Washington Post*, 19 November 2015; and Patrick Healy and Michael Barbaro, 'Donald Trump calls for barring Muslims from entering U.S.', *New York Times*, 7 December 2015.

39 See Brigitte Vittrup Simpson's dissertation, 'Exploring the influences of educational television and parent-child discussions on improving children's racial attitudes', University of Texas at Austin, May 2007. I became aware of her work via Po Bronson and Ashley Merryman, 'Even babies discriminate: A NurtureShock excerpt', *Newsweek*, 4 September 2009.

40 The quote from Jung ('If one does not understand a person, one tends to regard him as a fool') occurs on page 125 of his alchemical treatise, *Mysterium Coniunctionis* (1977).

44 The quote from Rainer Maria Rilke ('We need, in love, to practise only this . . .') occurs in 'Requiem for a Friend', in *Selected Poetry of Rainer Maria Rilke* (1984), page 85.

The Winter Palettes

57 Recent surveys of the art scene in Russia include Anna Kaminski, 'In Russia, contemporary art explodes from Soviet shackles', BBC News, 23 February 2014; Kelly Crow, 'Moscow's contemporary art movement', *Wall Street Journal*, 4 June 2015; and Ekow Shun, 'Moscow's new art centres', *Financial Times*, 15 March 2013.

57 For more background on art fairs in Russia, see Alexander Forbes, 'Manifesta 10 succeeds despite controversy', *Artnet News*, 27 June 2014; Masha Goncharova, 'Cosmoscow: A fair for the Russian art collector', *New York Times*, 17 September 2015; Rachel Donadio, 'Museum director at Hermitage hopes for thaw in relations with West', *New York Times*, 14 May 2015; and Zoë Lescaze, 'An abbreviated Moscow Biennale unites scrappy performances, bourgeois spiders, and one former Greek finance minister', *ARTnews*, 16 October 2015.

57 Quotes from members of the 'art-anarch-punk gang' Voina come from Marion Dolcy, 'Russian art anarchists explain themselves', *Don't Panic*, 20 December 2010; see also Taryn Jones, 'The art of "War": Voina and protest art in Russia', *Art in Russia*, 29 September 2012.

57 The quote by Andrei Klimov occurs in Sasha Shestakova, 'Outcry: Ten recent art exhibitions that caused a storm in Russia', *Calvert Journal*, 29 July 2015.

57 This broad range of art controversies, including those relating to the

NOTES

exhibitions with LGBT content, are reviewed in Shestakova, op. cit.; and 'Moscow venue refuses to host pro-LGBT teen photo display, cites police pressure', *Queer Russia*, 13 June 2015.

58 For a comprehensive analysis of the art market in Russia, see Renata Sulteeva's dissertation, 'The market for Russian contemporary art: An historical overview and up-to-date analysis of auction sales from 1988 to 2013'
(Sotheby's Institute of Art, 2014).

58 Vladimir Ovcharenko's comment on artists in the kitchen was originally
published in Emma Crichton-Miller, 'Young Russian curators tap into country's recent art history', *Financial Times*, 27 June 2014.

Young Russia's Defiant Decadence

79 'A Stewardess Named Zhanna' was a 1996 hit for pop singer Vladimir Pres-
nyakov. These days, his fans can find him on Facebook, SoundCloud and
Instagram.

97 For obituaries of and memorials to deceased Russian artists featured in
'Young Russia's Defiant Decadence', see Kathrin Becker, 'In memoriam
Timur Novikov', *Art Margins*, 23 May 2002; 'Poslednyi Geroi: Georgy
Guryanov (1961–2013)', *Baibakov Art Projects*, 20 July 2013; and 'In
memory of Vlad Mamyshev-Monroe, 1969–2013', *Baibakov Art Projects*,
22 March 2013. Herwig Höller pays tribue to Petlyura in 'Aleksandr Ilich
Lyashenko known as Petlyura: A controversial protagonist of Russian contemporary art', *Report: Magazine for Arts and Civil Society in Eastern and
Central Europe*, June 2006. Petlyura participated in the One-Man Picket at
the 2015 Moscow Biennale; see Moscow Biennale of Contemporary Art,
'One-man picket.' The story of Garik Vinogradov's persecution at the hands
of the mayor of Moscow is told in Konstantin Akinsha, 'Art in Russia: Art
under attack', *ARTnews*, 1 October 2009. Valera Katsuba describes his most
recent project, 'Father and Child (Отцы и дети)', at http://katsuba.net.

97 Boris Grebenshchikov's musical career is the subject of Aleksandr Gorbachev,
'Meet Boris Grebenshchikov, the Soviet Bob Dylan', *Newsweek*, 25 May
2015; and Alexandra Guryanova, 'Boris Grebenshchikov: The founding
father of Russian rock', *Russia and India Report*, 19 October 2014.

97 MC Pavlov's observations on musical trends in Russia appear in Lisa Dickey,
'Moscow: Rap star MC Pavlov', Russian Chronicles, *Washington Post*, 2
November 2005.

97 Artyom Troitsky's sartorial protest against electoral fraud is described in
British Broadcasting Corporation, 'Moscow protest: Thousands rally against
Vladimir Putin', BBC News, 25 December 2011.

97 Yuri Begalov's business dealings are discussed in Nadezhda Ivanitskaya, 'As a
State Duma deputy and businessman Yuzhilin Kobzar built a billion-dollar

business', *Forbes Russia*, 22 October 2011; and his marital split in '*Татьяна Веденеева расстается с мужем* (Tatiana Vedeneeva has divorced)', *DNI*, 2 June 2008.

97 Aleksandr Kiselev's profitable resignation is reported in '*Киселев после увольнения из "Почты России" получит почти 3 млн руб* (Kiselev after the dismissal of "Mail of Russia" will receive nearly 3 million rubles)', *RIA Novosti*, 19 April 2013.

97 Sergei Stankevich's political career, and the graft charges that led him to flee to Poland, are described in Andrew Higgins, 'Putin and Orthodox church cement power in Russia', *Wall Street Journal*, 18 December 2007; and Sergey Strokan and Vladimir Mikheev, 'E.U.-Russia sanctions war to continue', *Russia Beyond the Headlines*, 26 June 2015.

98 *Pravda* touts the Russian club scene in Marcelo de Vivo, 'Experience the best of Russian nightlife', *Pravda*, 10 October 2013.

98 Avdotja Alexandrova's description of the aesthetic philosophy underpinning her innovative modelling agency appears in Maeve Shearlaw, '30 under 30: Moscow's young power list', *Guardian*, 8 June 2015.

98 The quote from independent publisher Sergey Kostromin comes from Sasha Pershakova, 'Zine scene: How Russia's long tradition of self-publishing is still thriving today', *Calvert Journal*, 28 October 2014.

98 Andrey Urodov's magazine *Russia Without Us* features in Michael Idov, 'No sleep till Brooklyn: How hipster Moscow fell in love with Williamsburg', *Calvert Journal*, 31 December 2013; this article is also the source of the quote 'Every Moscow restaurant is a theme restaurant . . .'

98 The censoring of musicians Andrei Makarevich and Noize MC for their expressions of support for the people of Ukraine is reported in Karoun Demirjian, 'Russian youths find politics as their pop icons face pressure', *Washington Post*, 2 December 2014.

99 Human Rights Watch has documented the oppression of Russia's LGBT population and their allies in considerable detail; see Cooper, op. cit.

99 Official and popular responses to Yelena Klimova's creative work are described in Alec Luhn, 'LGBT website founder fined under Russia's gay propaganda laws', *Guardian*, 29 July 2015.

99 The quotes from Dmitry Kuzmin come from his essay 'On the Moscow metro and being gay', trans. Alexei Bayer, *Words without Borders*, 2013.

99 The role of conservative religious authority figures in the contemporary Russian power structure, and allegations against Patriarch Kirill, are discussed in Peter Pomerantsev, 'Putin's God squad: The Orthodox Church and Russian politics', *Newsweek*, 10 September 2012. Churchgoing habits in post-Soviet Russia are documented in Alan Cooperman, Phillip Connor and Erin O'Connell, 'Russians return to religion but not to church', Pew Research Center, 10 February 2014. Quotes from Patriarch Kirill, Ivan Ostrakovsky, Georgi Mitrofanov and the Orthodox skinhead gangsters come from the *Newsweek* piece.

100 Alleged affiliations between Vladimir Putin and Russian criminal gangs are described in Tom Porter, 'Vladmir [*sic*] Putin allies named as "key associates of Russian gangsters" by Spanish prosecutors', *International Business Times*, 30 June 2015; Porter discusses the Russian mafia in depth in 'Gangs of Russia: Ruthless mafia networks extending their influence', *International Business Times*, 9 April 2015.

100 Freedom House's assessment of corruption in Russia appears in Freedom House, 'Nations in transit 2015: Russia', Freedom House, 2015.

101 Putin's offer of amnesty to criminals with assets abroad, and the quote from Andrey Makarov, are reported in Rob Garver, 'Putin lets criminals bring money back to Russia', *Fiscal Times*, 11 June 2015. Capital flight from Russia is put at $150 billion in Stephanie Saul and Louise Story, 'At the Time Warner Center, an enclave of powerful Russians', *New York Times*, 11 February 2015.

101 Russian authorities' crackdown on imports of foreign food is described in Shaun Walker, 'Russia swoops on gang importing £19m of banned cheese from abroad', *Guardian*, 18 August 2015.

101 Economic inequality in modern Russia is discussed and the wealthiest oligarchs are listed in Maria Hagan, 'The 10 richest Russians in 2014', *Richest*, 10 October 2014.

101 Russia's schools for aspiring tycoons are described in Alexandra Tyan, 'Classes aimed at raising a new generation of Russian businessmen', *Moscow Times*, 27 July 2015.

102 My discussion of the Russian economy relies heavily on Ian Bremmer's excellent 'These 5 facts explain Russia's economic decline', *Time*, 14 August 2015.

102 Max Katz, Isabelle Magkoeva, Roman Dobrokhotov and other young movers and shakers are the subject of Shearlaw, op. cit.

102 The modern Russian protest movement and official retaliation against its leaders are examined in Alexander Korolkov, 'Is the protest movement dead?', *Russia Beyond the Headlines*, 15 January 2015; this article is the source of quotes by Georgy Chizhov, Nikita Denisov and Yelena Bobrova.

Their Irony, Humour (and Art) Can Save China

135 The phenomenal prices realised for the works of contemporary Chinese artists are reported in Nazanin Lankarani, 'The many faces of Yue Minjun', *New York Times*, 5 December 2012; Ian Johnson, 'Some Chinese artists are testing their limits', *Wall Street Journal*, 2 October 2009, and Eileen Kinsella, 'Who are the top 30 Chinese artists at auction?', *Artnet News*, 8 September 2014.

135 The quotes from Lao Li (Li Xianting) come from Jackie Wullschager, 'No more Chinese whispers', *Financial Times*, 2 October 2004.

136 Quotes from Cao Fei and Huang Rui come from Christopher Beam, 'Beyond

Ai Weiwei: How China's artists handle politics (or avoid them)', *New Yorker*, 27 March 2015.

136 The history of Chinese artist villages is explored in Angela Lin Huang, 'Leaving the city: Artist villages in Beijing', *Media Culture Journal* 14, no. 4 (August 2011). The quote from Li Wenzi comes from Zhu Linyong, 'Art on the move', *China Daily*, 25 January 2010.

136 Fang Lijun's praise for Lao Li occurs in Andrew Cohen, 'Off the page: Li Xianting', *Art Asia Pacific* 71, November/December 2010.

136 The shuttering of the Beijing Independent Film Festival was reported in Jonathan Kaiman, 'Beijing independent film festival shut down by Chinese authorities', *Guardian*, 24 August 2014.

137 The ongoing ordeals of Yuanmingyuan 'mayor' Yan Zhengxue are described in William Wan, 'Chinese artist recounts his life, including the one time he painted "X" on Mao's face', *Washington Post*, 2 June 2014.

137 Ma Liuming's 1994 arrest and incarceration is noted in the artist's biography, 'Ma Liuming', *Chinese Contemporary*, 2002, at http://chinesecontemporary.com.

137 The uproar over Zhu Yu's video in the *Fuck Off* exhibition is described in Wullschlager, op. cit.

137 The quote from Wang Peng comes from William Wan, 'China tried to erase memories of Tiananmen. But it lives on in the work of dissident artists', *Washington Post*, 31 May 2014.

137 Chen Guang's work and the official reaction to it are described in Mallika Rao, 'Five Chinese dissident artists who aren't Ai Weiwei', *Huffington Post*, 10 June 2014.

137 Dai Jianyong's arrest is reported in Jamie Fullerton, 'Chinese artist who posted funny image of President Xi Jinping facing five years in prison as authorities crackdown [*sic*] on dissent in the arts', *Independent*, 28 May 2015.

137 The story of and quote from Zhao Zhao comes from Ulrike Knöpfel, 'Risky business: China cracks down on Ai Wei Wei protégé Zhao Zhao', *Der Spiegel*, 28 August 2012.

138 Wu Yuren is the subject of Arvind Dilawar, 'Teatime with Big Brother: Chinese artist Wu Yuren on life under surveillance', *Vice*, 15 June 2015. Wu's exchange with his arresting officers relies on a 4 November 2015, personal communication via Ysabelle Cheung, Klein Sun Gallery, New York.

138 The description of the arrest and torture of Wang Zang and the quote from his wife come from Wan, op. cit. Tan Jianying's observation on the limits to freedom of speech in modern China comes from Jack Chang, 'Chinese art colony's free-speech illusion shatters', *Asahi Shumbun*, 17 October 2014.

139 Quotes from Xi Jinping and other PRC officials on the role of art and artists in society come from Fullerton, op. cit.

139 My discussion of Ai Weiwei's work and Chinese officials' response to it relies on Emily Rauhala, 'Complete freedom, always just eluding the grasp of Chinese artist Ai Weiwei', *Washington Post*, 30 July 2015. The quote 'Chinese

art is merely a product . . .' comes from Ai Weiwei, 'Ai Weiwei: China's art world does not exist', *Guardian*, 10 September 2012; 'They always stand on the side of power' comes from Beam, op. cit. The comment from the Beijing curator critical of Ai Weiwei comes from Wan, op. cit.

140 The anonymous Chinese curator's and Ouyang Jianghe's words come from Lankarani, op. cit.

The Artists of South Africa: Separate and Equal

175 Observations on the South African art scene by National Gallery director Riason Naidoo come from Jason Edward Kaufman, 'South Africa's art scene is poised for a breakthrough – at home and abroad', *Huffington Post*, 19 February 2013.

175 For full text of the ANC's objections to *The Spear*, see Jackson Mthembu, 'ANC outraged by Brett Murray's depiction of President Jacob Zuma', African National Congress, 17 May 2012. Protesters' vandalisation of the painting is described in Alex Perry, 'South Africa: Over-exposing the President', *Time*, 23 May 2012. The Shembe Church leader's call to stone Brett Murray to death, and quotes from Steven Friedman, Aubrey Masango and Jonathan Jansen, come from Karen MacGregor, 'A spear to the heart of South Africa', *New York Times*, 5 June 2012. For the withdrawal of the classification of the painting as 'harmful', see South African Press Association, 'Appeal tribunal declassifies "The Spear"', *City Press*, 10 October 2012.

176 The withdrawal and reinstatement of Ayanda Mabulu's painting of Zuma is the subject of 'Zuma, Marikana painting pulled from Jo'burg Art Fair', *Mail & Guardian*, 27 September 2013; and the quote from Avanda Mabulu ('It's not the first time I've been censored . . .') comes from Matthew Krouse, 'Art Fair forced to reinstate Mabulu painting after Goldblatt threat', *Mail & Guardian*, 28 September 2013.

176 The controversy over South Africa's choice of curators and exhibitors for the 2015 Venice Biennale is chronicled in Stefanie Jason's reports, 'Venice Biennale: SA Pavilion finally announces artists', *Mail & Guardian*, 16 April 2015; and 'SA trips as Joburg lands on the steps of the Venice Biennale', *Mail & Guardian*, 30 April 2015 (source of the 'reputation of butchering foreigners' quote); see also Jeremy Kuper, 'Venice Biennale: View from the ground', *Mail & Guardian*, 20 May 2015.

Vlady's Conquests

177 The BBC's assessment of Vladimir Zhirinovsky appears in British Broadcasting Corporation, 'Profiles of Russia's 2012 presidential election candidates',

BBC News, 1 March 2012; Howard Amos's characterisation comes from Howard Amos, 'Russian publisher prints books about Putin under names of western authors', *Guardian*, 11 August 2015.

'Don't Mess with Our Cultural Patrimony!'

203 The renovation and reopening of Taiwan's National Palace Museum was reported in Keith Bradsher, 'Rare glimpses of China's long-hidden treasures', *New York Times*, 28 December 2006. Attendance figures come from 'Blackout hits Taipei's Palace Museum Thursday afternoon', *Want China Times*, 10 July 2015. The opening of the Chiayi branch is the subject of 'NPM southern branch to open with jadeite cabbage display', *Want China Times*, 18 September 2015.

203 The National Palace Museum's refusal to exhibit sculptures allegedly looted from the Summer Palace is described in British Broadcasting Corporation, 'Taiwan rejects "looted" China art', BBC News, 7 October 2009. The loan by the PRC of Qing dynasty relics and Taiwan's restrictions on loans to other countries are discussed in Tania Branigan, 'Chinese treasures to be reunited in Taiwan', *Guardian*, 19 February 2009. For more information on cooperation between the two museums, see Yin Pumin, 'Probing ancient mysteries', *Beijing Review*, 7 December 2009.

203 Quotes from White Shirt Army founder Liulin Wei come from William Wan, 'Taiwan's "white shirt army," spurred by Facebook, takes on political parties', *Washington Post*, 11 November 2013.

203 The Sunflower movement is described in '"Sunflower" protesters break on to political scene', *Economist Intelligence Unit*, 2 April 2014.

On Each Palette, a Choice of Political Colours

210 I reported on Cai Guo-Qiang's 'Golden Missile' project in Andrew Solomon, 'As Asia regroups, art has a new urgency', *New York Times*, 23 August 1998.

Enchanting Zambia

227 Recent developments favourable to the Zambian tourism industry are discussed in Matthew Hill, 'Yellow fever relaxation by South Africa helps Zambia tourism', Bloomberg, 5 February 2015.

NOTES

Phaly Nuon's Three Steps

229 The horrors of the Khmer Rouge are extensively documented. For a vivid if slightly fictionalised re-enactment of the atrocities, I would commend the 1984 film *The Killing Fields*.

235 The death of Phaly Nuon was announced in Rob Hail, 'Madame Nuon Phaly is gone', *Out of the Blog*, 27 November 2012; her funeral observance is described in Sophanna Ma, 'Funeral of our beloved Mum Phaly Nuon', Ezra Vogel Special Skills School, December 2012.

235 For in-depth analyses of the impact of human trafficking and forced displacement on the mental health of Cambodians, see Ligia Kiss et al., 'Health of men, women and children in post-trafficking services in Cambodia, Thailand and Vietnam', *Lancet Global Health* 3 (March 2015); and Jayson Richardson et al., 'Mental health impacts of forced land evictions on women in Cambodia', *Journal of International Development*, 27 September 2014.

235 Figures on Cambodia's suicide rate come from World Health Organisation, 'Mental health atlas 2011: Cambodia', Department of Mental Health and Substance Abuse, World Health Organisation, 2011.

235 Figures on the proportion of mentally ill Cambodians who are permanently restrained, and on the country's mental health budget, rely on Daniel McLaughlin and Elisabeth Wickeri, 'Mental health and human rights in Cambodia', Leitner Center for International Law and Justice, 31 July 2012.

235 Figures on the number of psychiatrists in Cambodia come from Tanja Schunert et al., 'Cambodian mental health survey', Royal University of Phnom Penh, Department of Psychology, 2012.

235 Proposals to relocate mentally ill citizens to pagodas are described in Radio Free Asia Khmer Service, 'Cambodian province plans campaign for monks to care for mentally ill', Radio Free Asia, 20 April 2015.

The Open Spaces of Mongolia

247 The decline of nomadism in Mongolia is described in World Health Organisation, 'WHO country cooperation strategy for Mongolia 2010–2015', World Health Organisation, 2010.

247 Figures on the Mongolian economy rely on the World Bank press release 'Poverty continued to decline, falling from 27.4 per cent in 2012 to 21.6 per cent in 2014', World Bank, 1 July 2015.

247 Riots over purported election fraud in Mongolia were reported in Tania Branigan, 'Mongolia declares state of emergency as riots kill five', *Guardian*, 2 July 2008; the conviction of former president Nambar Enkhbaya, in Xinhua News Agency, 'Former Mongolian president jailed for four years', *CRI English*, 3 August 2012.

247 The effects of overgrasing on the environment are analysed in Sarah Wachter, 'Pastoralism unraveling in Mongolia', *New York Times*, 8 December 2009; see also Troy Sternberg et al., 'Tracking desertification on the Mongolian steppe through NDVI and field-survey data', *International Journal of Digital Earth* 4, no. 1 (2011).

247 The decline of many over-harvested Mongolian species is discussed in Jeffrey Reeves, 'Mongolia's environmental security', *Asian Survey* 51, no. 3 (2011).

247 For more information on the impact of modern technology on daily life in Mongolia, see Jim Yong Kim, 'How Mongolia brought nomads TV and mobile phones', *Bloomberg View*, 14 October 2013; and Mark Hay, 'Nomads on the grid', *Slate*, 5 December 2014.

247 UNESCO's designation of Naadam as an Intangible Cultural Heritage of Humanity is documented in 'Naadam, Mongolian traditional festival', United Nations Educational, Scientific and Cultural Organisation, 2010.

247 The repurposing of the former Lenin Museum in Ulaanbaatar is the subject of Tania Branigan, 'It's goodbye Lenin, hello dinosaur as fossils head to Mongolia museum', *Guardian*, 27 January 2013.

Inventing the Conversation

250 The suicide rate in Greenland at the time of my original research there had been most recently published in Tine Curtis and Peter Bjerregaard's *Health Research in Greenland* (1995), page 31.

255 The descriptions of polar hysteria, mountain wanderer syndrome and kayak anxiety come from Inge Lynge, 'Mental disorders in Greenland', *Man & Society* 21 (1997). I must thank John Hart for providing the parallel to 'running amok'.

256 Malaurie's quote ('There is an often dramatic contradiction . . .') is from Jean Malaurie, *The Last Kings of Thule* (1982), page 109.

258 The high incidence of suicide in Greenland is explored in Jason George, 'The suicide capital of the world', *Slate*, 9 October 2009; and Lene Bech Sillesen, 'Another word for suicide', *Al Jazeera*, 21 November 2015. Sillesen's report is the source of Greenland's current suicide rates, and the quote from Astrid Olsen. For a scholarly discussion of the subject, see Peter Bjerregaard and Christina Viskum Lytken Larsen, 'Time trend by region of suicides and suicidal thoughts among Greenland Inuit', *International Journal of Circumpolar Health* 74 (2015).

259 Greenland's vote for independence from Denmark is reported in British Broadcasting Corporation, 'Self-rule introduced in Greenland', BBC News, 21 June 2009.

259 Expansion of hydroelectric power in Greenland is discussed in 'Greenland powers up fifth hydroelectric plant', *Arctic Journal*, 6 September 2013.

259 The dramatic calving of a Manhattan-size chunk from a Greenland glacier is reported in British Broadcasting Corporation, 'Greenland's Jakobshavn Glacier sheds big ice chunk', BBC News, 24 August 2015.

Naked, Covered in Ram's Blood, Drinking a Coke, and Feeling Pretty Good

262 For a discussion of the tradition of communicating with spirits among the Senegalese, see William Simmons, *Eyes of the Night: Witchcraft among a Senegalese People* (1971).

268 My comments on the state of mental health care in Senegal rely on World Health Organisation, 'WHO mental health atlas 2011: Senegal', Department of Mental Health and Substance Abuse, World Health Organisation, 2011.

268 The quote 'Without openness to Lebou beliefs and culture . . .' comes from William Louis Conwill's seminal academic study of the *n'deup* ritual: William Louis Conwill, 'N'deup and mental health: Implications for treating Senegalese immigrants in the U.S.', *International Journal for the Advancement of Counselling* 32, no. 3 (September 2010).

An Awakening after the Taliban

283 Statistics on the number of U.S. casualties in Afghanistan rely on U.S. Department of Defense, 'Casualty report', U.S. Department of Defense, 10 November 2015; numbers of troops remaining appear in Matthew Rosenberg and Michael D. Shear, 'In reversal, Obama says U.S. soldiers will stay in Afghanistan to 2017', *New York Times*, 15 October 2015.

283 Dominic Tierney's comment 'The popular narrative . . .' comes from his article 'Forgetting Afghanistan', *Atlantic*, 24 June 2015.

284 Murders of female journalists in Afghanistan are described in Declan Walsh, 'Second female Afghan journalist killed in five days', *Guardian*, 6 June 2007; and Associated Press, 'Women journalists targeted in Afghanistan', NBC News, 26 June 2007.

284 Kubra Khademi's performance art project and its aftermath are chronicled in Emma Graham-Harrison, 'Afghan artist dons armour to counter men's street harassment', *Guardian*, 12 March 2015.

284 For more on the Centre for Contemporary Art, see 'Introducing the Centre for Contemporary Art Afghanistan (CCAA)', ARCH International, no date, at http://archinternational.org.

284 The quote by Munera Yousefzada ('Before I opened the gallery . . .') comes from Peter Holley, 'In Afghanistan, the art of fighting extremism', *Washington Post*, 12 September 2015.

284 Turquoise Mountain's programmes are described on its extensive website, http://turquoisemountain.org, and in Daud Rasool, 'Rebuilding Afghanistan's creative industries', British Council, 14 October 2013.

284 A cofounder of Berang Arts discusses the situation of artists in Afghanistan in Francesca Recchia, 'Art in Afghanistan: A time of transition', *Muftah*, 6 August 2014.

284 Professor Alam Farhad's description of the explosion of interest in the arts programme at Kabul University is recounted in Mujib Mashal, 'Women and modern art in Afghanistan', *New York Times*, 6 August 2010.

284 Ali Akhlaqi's lament ('Kabul is a cursed city of night . . .') comes from Chelsea Hawkins, '9 artists challenging our perceptions of Afghanistan', *Mic*, 9 October 2014.

284 The quote from Shamsia Hassani comes from her interview with Lisa Pollman, 'Art is stronger than war: Afghanistan's first female street artist speaks out', *Art Radar*, 19 July 2013.

284 Azim Fakhri's philosophy ('My feeling is accept what you can't change . . .') comes from Hawkins, op. cit.

285 Kabir Mokamel's 'Art Lords' project is described in Fazul Rahim and Sarah Burke, 'Afghan artist Kabir Mokamel takes aim at corruption with blast wall art', NBC News, 19 September 2015.

285 Marla Ruzicka was well loved and widely mourned; see, e.g., Ellen Knickmeyer, 'Victims' champion is killed in Iraq', *Washington Post*, 18 April 2005; Robert F. Worth, 'An American aid worker is killed in her line of duty', *New York Times*, 18 April 2005; Simon Robinson, 'Appreciation: Marla Ruzicka, 1977–2005', *Time*, 18 April 2005; Jonathan Steele, 'Marla Ruzicka', *Guardian*, 19 April 2005; Janet Reitman, 'The girl who tried to save the world', *Rolling Stone*, 16 June 2005; and Sarah Holewinski, 'Marla Ruzicka's Heroism', *Nation*, 18 September 2013.

Museum without Walls

291 Up-to-date information about the Benesse Art Site can be found on its website, http://benesse-artsite.jp. For a recent review of Benesse, see Susan Adams, 'Treasure islands: Inside a Japanese billionaire's art archipelago', *Forbes*, 29 July 2015. The quote by Soichiro Fukutake comes from Lee Yulin's dissertation, 'Strategies of spatialisation in the contemporary art museum: A study of six Japanese institutions' (New York University, 2012).

Song of Solomons

302 For information about UNESCO's designation of the Marovo Lagoon, see 'Tentative lists: Marovo-Tetepare complex', United Nations Educational, Scientific and Cultural Organisation, 23 December 2008.

302 Reports of major seismic events in the Solomon Islands include Richard A. Lovett, 'Deadly tsunami sweeps Solomon Islands', *National Geographic News*, 2 April 2007; James Grubel, 'Tsunami kills at least five in Solomons after big Pacific quake', Reuters, 6 February 2013; Lincoln Feast, 'Strong quake hits near Solomon Islands; tsunami warning cancelled', Reuters, 12 April 2014; and Sandra Maler and Peter Cooney, 'Magnitude 6.6 quake hits Solomon Islands in the Pacific: USGS', Reuters, 12 August 2015.

303 The relocation of Choiseul is reported in Megan Rowling, 'Solomons town first in Pacific to relocate due to climate change', Reuters, 15 August 2014; and Adam Morton, 'The vanishing island', *Age*, 19 September 2015.

303 World Bank–funded efforts to upgrade infrastructure in order to withstand disasters better are announced in the press release 'World Bank, Govt. of Solomon Islands launch two new projects towards improved power supply, disaster & climate resilience', World Bank, 1 April 2014.

303 Tectonic phenomena endangering the Solomon Islands are discussed in Gerald Traufetter, 'Climate change or tectonic shifts? The mystery of the sinking South Pacific islands', *Der Spiegel*, 15 June 2012.

Children of Bad Memories

305 Unsourced quotations in my essay about Rwanda come from personal interviews conducted in Rwanda in 2004.

Books consulted on the Rwandan genocide include Alison Liebhafsky Des Forges, *'Leave None to Tell the Story': Genocide in Rwanda* (1999); Jean Hatzfeld, *Machete Season: The Killers in Rwanda Speak* (2005); Elizabeth Neuffer, *The Key to My Neighbour's House: Seeking Justice in Bosnia and Rwanda* (2002); Binaifer Nowrojee, *Shattered Lives: Sexual Violence during the Rwandan Genocide and Its Aftermath* (1996); Philip Gourevitch, *We Wish to Inform You That Tomorrow We Will Be Killed with Our Families: Stories from Rwanda* (1999), and Jonathan Torgovnik, *Intended Consequences: Rwandan Children Born of Rape* (2009). For journalistic coverage, see Donatella Lorch, 'Rape used as a weapon in Rwanda: Future grim for genocide orphans', *Houston Chronicle*, 15 May 1995; Elizabeth Royte, 'The outcasts', *New York Times Magazine*, 19 January 1997; Lindsey Hilsum, 'Rwanda's time of rape returns to haunt thousands', *Guardian*, 26 February 1995; Lindsey Hilsum, 'Don't abandon Rwandan women again', *New York Times*, 11 April

2004; and Emily Wax, 'Rwandans are struggling to love children of hate', *Washington Post*, 28 March 2004.

306 The role of Rwandan media in inciting genocide is discussed in Dina Temple-Raston's remarkable book *Justice on the Grass* (2005). See also Russell Smith, 'The impact of hate media in Rwanda', BBC News, 3 December 2003. Also, in his doctoral dissertation, 'Propaganda and conflict: Theory and evidence from the Rwandan genocide' (Stockholm University, 2009), political economist David Yanagizawa found a direct correlation between hate radio and violence by analysing locations of transmission towers and topographical impediments to transmission, and the locations and numbers of subsequent genocide prosecutions.

306 The Rwandan proverb 'A woman who is not yet battered is not a real woman' is reported in Nowrojee, op. cit., page 20.

306 General information sources on rape as a tool of war include Susan Brownmiller, *Against Our Will* (1975); Maria de Bruyn, *Violence, Pregnancy and Abortion: Issues of Women's Rights and Public Health* (2003); and the Global Justice Centre report *The Right to an Abortion for Girls and Women Raped in Armed Conflict* (2011).

307 The expression 'die of sadness' and the account that follows of atrocities committed against one rape survivor are documented in Nowrojee, op. cit.

307 Statistics on wartime rapes in Rwanda are supported by the UN Office for the Coordination of Humanitarian Affairs news report 'Our bodies, their battle ground: Gender-based violence in conflict zones', *IRIN News*, 1 September 2004. Estimates of the numbers of wartime rapes and births come from the introduction by Marie Consolée Mukagendo, 'The struggles of Rwandan women raising children born of rape', in Torgovnik, op. cit.

307 The expression 'children of bad memories' (*enfants de mauvais souvenir*) comes from Nowrojee, op. cit., but is used widely.

307 The phrase 'living legacy of a time of death' comes from Wax, op. cit.

308 The quote 'I could not even die with this baby inside me . . .' comes from Wax, op. cit.

308 The quote 'To be taken as a wife is a form of death . . .' comes from Nowrojee, op. cit.

308 The quote from Catherine Bonnet occurs in Nowrojee, op. cit., page 79, citing to Bonnet's paper 'Le viol des femmes survivantes du génocide du Rwanda', in *Rwanda: Un génocide du XXe siècle* (1995), page 18.

308 The quote from Godelième Mukasarasi ('The women who have had children after being raped are the most marginalised . . .') comes from Nowrojee, op. cit.

308 The work of Avega is described in Alexandra Topping, 'Widows of the genocide: How Rwanda's women are rebuilding their lives', *Guardian*, 7 April 2014.

309 Jean Damascène Ndayambaje examines psychological roots of the Rwandan genocide in his thesis, 'Le genocide au Rwanda: Une analyse psychologique' (National University of Rwanda, 2001).

310 The loaded baby names chosen by some Rwandan rape survivors are catalogued in Wax, op. cit.

319 Figures on annual growth of GDP and ease of doing business in Rwanda rely on 'Rwanda overview', World Bank, 6 October 2015; and 'Ease of doing business in Rwanda', World Bank, 2015.

319 Assassinations, atrocities, invasions and exploitation by Paul Kagame's regime are outlined in Howard W. French, 'Kagame's hidden war in the Congo', *New York Review of Books*, 24 September 2009; Judi Rever and Geoffrey York, 'Assassination in Africa: Inside the plots to kill Rwanda's dissidents', *Globe & Mail*, 2 May 2014; Siobhan O'Grady, 'Former Rwandan official worries that Kagame's administration is backsliding into mass murder', *Foreign Policy*, 29 September 2014; and Global Campaign for Rwandan Human Rights, 'Crimes and repression vs. development in Rwanda: President Paul Kagame's many shadows', Africa Faith & Justice Network, 13 July 2015.

319 Information on relative rates of political exclusion, and the reference to Rwanda as 'a country on lockdown' come from Marc Sommers, 'The darling dictator of the day', *New York Times*, 27 May 2012.

319 The claim that Paul Kagame sought to abolish term limits in Rwanda in response to 'popular demand' comes from Agence France-Presse, 'U.S. opposes third term for Rwanda's Kagame: Diplomat', *Guardian* (Nigeria), 5 June 2015. The success of his campaign is reported in Clement Uwiringiyimana, 'Rwandan parliament agrees to extend Kagame's rule', Reuters, 29 October 2015. The referendum required to approve extension of term limits is described in British Broadcasting Corporation, 'Paul Kagame's third term: Rwanda referendum on 18 December', BBC News, 9 December 2015.

319 The inability of Rwanda's Green Party to obtain legal counsel for a lawsuit challenging the abolition of term limits is reported in Agence France-Presse, 'Rwanda opposition says can't find lawyer for Kagame 3rd term case – one said "God was against it"', *Mail & Guardian*, 8 July 2015.

Circle of Fire: Letter from Libya

356 For contemporary reports on the attack on the U.S. consulate in Benghazi, see Associated Press, 'Assault on U.S. consulate in Benghazi leaves 4 dead, including U.S. Ambassador J. Christopher Stevens', Associated Press / CBS News, 12 September 2012; Luke Harding and Chris Stephen, 'Chris Stevens, U.S. ambassador to Libya, killed in Benghazi attack',

Guardian, 12 September 2012; and David Kirkpatrick and Steven Lee Myers, 'Libya attack brings challenges for U.S.', *New York Times*, 12 September 2012. In 2015, former secretary of state Hillary Clinton defended her actions prior to and following the attack before the U.S. Congress; see Byron Tau and Peter Nicholas, 'Hillary Clinton defends actions in Benghazi', *Wall Street Journal*, 22 October 2015; and Stephen Collinson, 'Marathon Benghazi hearing leaves Hillary Clinton largely unscathed', *CNN Politics*, 23 October 2015.

356 The capture of Sirte by ISIL (also known as ISIS or Daesh) forces is reported in 'ISIL "brutally" quells rebellion in Libya's Sirte', *Al Jazeera*, 17 August 2015.

356 The relationship between ethnic conflict and human trafficking is explored in Callum Paton, 'Libya: Scores killed in ethnic clashes for control of south's people-trafficking routes', *International Business Times*, 23 July 2015.

356 Amnesty International documented the assassination of hundreds of Libyan citizens by Islamist forces in 'The state of the world's human rights', Amnesty International, 11 March 2015.

357 The quote from the French foreign minister ('two governments, two parliaments, and complete confusion') comes from Nathalie Guibert, Yves-Michel Riols and Hélène Sallon, 'Libya's Tripoli and Tobruk dilemma no nearer to resolution', *Guardian*, 27 January 2015. Responses to proposals for a 'unity government' are discussed in Suliman Ali Zway and Carlotta Gall, 'Libyan factions reject unity government plan', *New York Times*, 20 October 2015. Khalifa Haftar's threats to form yet another government were reported in Mary Fitzgerald, 'Libyan renegade general Khalifa Haftar claims he is winning his war', *Guardian*, 24 June 2014.

357 Saif Qaddafi's troubling words ('There will be civil war in Libya . . .') are recorded in Lindsey Hilsum, 'Saif al-Islam Gaddafi: The prophet of his own doom', *Guardian*, 5 August 2015.

357 Saif Qaddafi describes the amputation of his fingers by his captors in Fred Abrahams, 'In his first interview, Saif al-Islam says he has not been given access to a lawyer', *Daily Beast*, 30 December 2012.

357 The conviction and sentencing of Saif Qaddafi is reported in Chris Stephen, 'Gaddafi's son Saif al-Islam sentenced to death by court in Libya', *Guardian*, 28 July 2015; and Hilsum, op. cit.

357 The chant of the August 2015 pro-Qaddafi demonstrators ('Zintan, Zintan, free Saif al-Islam') was described in Hilsum, ibid.

All the Food in China

370 Food-oriented television programming in China is described in Li Xiaoyu, 'A bite of food culture', *BJ Review*, 2 July 2015.

370 Statistics on the proportion of Chinese who regularly share photos of their

meals online rely on Angela Xu, 'China's digital powered foodie revolution', *Lab Brand*, 6 January 2015.

370 Efforts to persuade UNESCO to include Chinese cuisine on its list of Intangible Cultural Heritage of Humanity are described in Li, op. cit.

370 The growing popularity of organic food in China is the subject of Cai Muyuan, 'Eat green, think greener', *China Daily Europe*, 5 June 2015.

370 The apparent health benefits of spicy food are documented in Jun Lv et al., 'Consumption of spicy foods and total and cause specific mortality: Population based cohort study', *British Medical Journal* 351 (4 August 2015).

370 Shanghai's dominance in Asian restaurant ratings is reported in Jessica Rapp, 'Locavores, health food and celebrity chefs: The hottest trends in Shanghai's dining scene', *Jing Daily*, 24 August 2015.

370 The widespread contamination of Chinese soil is discussed in British Broadcasting Corporation, 'Report: One fifth of China's soil contaminated', BBC News, 18 April 2014.

370 Sources on food adulteration in China include Yanzhong Huang, 'The 2008 milk scandal revisited', *Forbes*, 16 July 2014; Peter Foster, 'Top 10 Chinese food scandals', *Telegraph*, 27 April 2011; Associated Press, 'Vinegar contaminated with antifreeze kills Chinese Muslims at Ramadan meal', *Guardian*, 22 August 2011; Patrick Boehler, 'Bad eggs: Another fake-food scandal rocks China', *Time*, 6 November 2012; Patrick Boehler, 'Police seize chicken feet in storage since 1967, smuggled from Vietnam', *South China Morning Post*, 8 July 2013; British Broadcasting Corporation, 'Chinese police arrest 110 for selling "contaminated pork"', BBC News, 12 January 2015; and Elizabeth Barber, '"Gutter oil" scandal raises food-safety fears once again in greater China', *Time*, 8 September 2014.

370 Chinese skepticism regarding the 'organic' label is noted in Dominique Patton, 'Cashing in on health scares, China online food sales boom', Reuters, 11 August 2013.

370 The popularity of imported food, particularly fruit, is the subject of Rebecca Kanthor, 'In China, imported fruit is the must-have luxury item for the New Year', *The World*, Public Radio International, 20 February 2015; and Nan Zhong, 'China has a healthy appetite for food imports', *China Daily*, 2 March 2015.

371 The secretive cultivation of organic food for the Chinese political elite is described in Barbara Demick, 'In China, what you eat tells who you are', *Los Angeles Times*, 16 September 2011.

371 For more information on the increasing popularity of alternatives to rice in the Chinese diet, see Te-Ping Chen, 'In latest mash-up, China puts spotlight on spuds', *Wall Street Journal*, 17 August 2015.

371 Recent increases in obesity and diabetes in China are discussed in Laurie Burkitt, 'Selling health food to China', *Wall Street Journal*, 13 December

2010; and Lily Kuo, 'By 2015, China will be the world's largest consumer of processed food', *Quartz*, 23 September 2013.

Adventures in Antarctica

395 Global warming's impact on the ability of scientists to reach their posts in Antarctica is the subject of Michael Safi, 'Antarctica's increasing sea ice restricting access to research stations', *Guardian*, 11 May 2015.

396 The deterioration of the West Antarctic ice sheet is discussed in Chris Mooney, 'Scientists declare an "urgent" mission – study West Antarctica, and fast', *Washington Post*, 29 September 2015.

396 The potential fate of the Totten Glacier is described in James Hamblin, 'How the most important glacier in east Antarctica is melting', *Atlantic*, 20 March 2015; this article is also the source of the quote from NASA.

396 Record temperatures in Antarctica are reported in Katia Hetter, 'Antarctic hits 63 degrees, believed to be a record', CNN News, 1 April 2015.

396 The effects of warmer temperatures on fungi, crustaceans, and penguins are discussed in Australian Associated Press, 'Temperature affects fungi in Antarctica', Special Broadcasting Service, 28 September 2015; Chelsea Harvey, 'Next up from climate change: Shell-crushing crabs invading Antarctica', *Washington Post*, 28 September 2015; and Chris Mooney, 'The melting of Antarctica is bad news for humans. But it might make penguins pretty happy', *Washington Post*, 13 August 2015.

396 China's intent to expand operations in Antarctica is detailed in Jane Perlez, 'China, pursuing strategic interests, builds presence in Antarctica', *New York Times*, 3 May 2015.

When Everyone Signs

397 Bengkala is the focus of I Gede Marsaja, *Desa Kolok: A Deaf Village and Its Sign Language in Bali, Indonesia* (2008). The first report in the medical literature of the strain of deafness prevalent there is S. Winata et al., 'Congenital non-syndromal autosomal recessive deafness in Bengkala, an isolated Balinese village', *Journal of Medical Genetics* 32 (1995). For a general, accessible discussion of syndromic deafness within endogamous communities, see John Travis, 'Genes of silence: Scientists track down a slew of mutated genes that cause deafness', *Science News*, 17 January 1998. Additionally, for an opinionated overview of the academic research on the subject, see Annelies Kusters, 'Deaf utopias? Reviewing the sociocultural literature on the world's "Martha's Vineyard situations"', *Journal of Deaf Studies & Deaf Education* 15, no. 1 (January 2010).

398 The complex webs of relations among the Balinese are the subject of Hildred and Clifford Geertz's oft-cited *Kinship in Bali* (1975).

403 'Deaf' with a lowercase *d* refers to hearing impairment; the same word, capitalised, refers to the culture of those who communicate with each other in sign language and identify themselves as part of a community. For an exploration of Deaf politics in the United States in the nineties, see my article 'Defiantly deaf', *New York Times Magazine*, 28 August 1994.

405 The postscript on the Kata Kolok language relies on the work of Connie de Vos of the Max Planck Institute for Psycholinguistics, who has emerged as the most prolific scholar of the language. See, for example, Connie de Vos and N. Palfreyman, 'Deaf around the world: The impact of language', *Journal of Linguistics* 48, no. 3 (November 2012), which describes the relative numbers of deaf and hearing users of Kata Kolok; Connie de Vos, 'Absolute spatial deixis and proto-toponyms in Kata Kolok', *NUSA: Linguistic Studies of Languages In and Around Indonesia* 56 (2014), which examines the relocation of Kata Kolok signers from Bengkala; and Connie de Vos, 'A signers' village in Bali, Indonesia', *Minpaku Anthropology News*, 2011, which chronicles the lack of new transmission of the language.

Rio, City of Hope

407 The 2014 World Cup finals are the subject of both domestic and international corruption investigations; see Lisa Flueckiger, 'Brazil's federal police to investigate after FIFA scandal', *Rio Times*, 29 May 2015; and Vincent Bevins, 'Coming "tsunami"? In Brazil, calls for reform in wake of FIFA scandals', *Los Angeles Times*, 12 June 2015.

407 Circumstances surrounding Brazil's selection as the site of the 2016 Olympics are also suspect; see Caroline Stauffer, 'Brazil's Petrobras corruption investigators to probe Olympic contracts', Reuters, 25 November 2015; and Tariq Panja and David Biller, 'Soccer icon Romario, Rio mayor Paes cited in corruption tape', Bloomberg, 25 November 2015.

408 For more on the work of Vik Muniz, see Carol Kino, 'Where art meets trash and transforms life', *New York Times*, 21 October 2010; and Mara Sartore, 'Lampedusa: Migration and desire, an interview with Vik Muniz', *My Art Guides*, June 2015.

409 For a comprehensive history of samba and Rio's Carnival, see Marlene Lima Hufferd, 'Carnaval in Brazil, samba schools and African culture: A study of samba schools through their African heritage', Retrospective Theses and Dissertations, Paper 15406, University of Iowa, 2007. Alas, not even the world's biggest party is free from allegations of corruption; see Anderson Antunes, 'When samba meets African dictators: The ugly side of Rio de Janeiro's Carnival', *Forbes*, 19 February 2015.

409 Lilia Moritz Schwarcz shares insights about her country's culture in an interview with Robert Darnton, 'Talking about Brazil with Lilia Schwarcz', *New York Review of Books*, 17 August 2010. For a sample of her academic work, see Lilia Moritz Schwarcz, 'Not black, not white: Just the opposite: Culture, race and national identity in Brazil', Working Paper CBS-47-03, Centre for Brazilian Studies, University of Oxford, 2003.

409 For an in-depth discussion of Brasília, see Benjamin Schwarz, 'A vision in concrete', *Atlantic*, July/August 2008.

409 A clinical description of the horrendous practise of execution with flaming tyres occurs in Carlos Durao, Marcos Machado and Eduardo Daruge Jr., 'Death in the "microwave oven": A form of execution by carbonisation', *Forensic Science International* 253 (August 2015).

409 The quote by Philip Alston ('A remarkable number of police lead double lives . . .') comes from Todd Benson, 'U.N. watchdog denounces police killings in Brazil', Reuters, 15 September 2008.

410 Figures on the proportion of arrestees killed by police in Rio and in the United States come from Fernando Ribeiro Delgado, 'Lethal force: Police violence and public security in Rio de Janeiro and São Paulo', Human Rights Watch, 8 December 2009.

410 Luiz Eduardo Soares has repeatedly called for a complete overhaul of Brazil's police structure; see Nashla Dahas, 'Luis Eduardo Soares', *Revista de Historia*, 11 January 2014; and Leandro Resende, ' "A nação está perturbada," define antropólogo Luiz Eduardo Soares', *O Dia Brasil*, 10 October 2015.

410 Figures on the number of people killed by police in Rio and São Paulo come from the Human Rights Watch report, Delgado, op. cit.

410 The arrest of Colonel Alexandre Fontenell Ribeiro, chief of special operations of the Rio de Janeiro military police, is reported in British Broadcasting Corporation, 'Brazil corruption: Rio police arrested over "extortion racket" ', BBC News, 16 September 2014.

410 The quote from Colonel José Carvalho ('We need fresh, strong minds, not a Rambo') comes from a 2009 diplomatic cable included in the WikiLeaks disclosures; see American Consul Rio de Janeiro, 'Counter-insurgency doctrine comes to Rio's favelas', 30 September 2009.

411 For discussion of the practise of offering pay raises for police demonstrations of 'bravery' against favela residents, see Steven Dudley, 'Deadly force: Security and insecurity in Rio', North American Congress on Latin America, November 1998.

411 Figures on the number of favelas served by UPPs come from Andrew Downie, 'Rio finally makes headway against its drug gangs', *Time*, 26 November 2010; and U.S. Department of State, 'Country reports on human rights practises for 2011: Brazil', U.S. Department of State, 2012.

412 The complaint of the Red Command's *patrão* ('It is fucking up our lives . . .')

comes from Jonathan Watts, 'Rio police tackle favelas as World Cup looms', *Guardian*, 10 June 2013.

413 The colonel sets forth his perspective on pacification in greater detail in Robson Rodrigues, 'The dilemmas of pacification: News of war and peace in the "marvelous city"', *Stability Journal*, 22 May 2014.

414 Thanks to official concerns over gang influence, unofficial *baile* funk parties have become an endangered species; see Beth McLoughlin, 'Rio's funk parties silenced by crackdown on gangs', BBC News, 5 May 2012; and Jillian Kestler-D'Amours, 'Silencing Brazil's baile funk', *Al Jazeera*, 5 July 2014.

414 For one example of more recent upscale accommodations in the favelas, see Joanna Hansford and Mary Bolling Blackiston, 'Luxury boutique hostel opens in Vidigal', *Rio Times*, 4 March 2014.

414 The work of the Museu de Favela is described in British Broadcasting Corporation, 'Rio de Janeiro's favelas reflected through art', BBC News, 29 May 2011.

414 On the reduction of bullet wounds in Rio, see Melissa Rossi, 'Gun wounds down in Complexo do Alemão', *Rio Times*, 3 July 2012. On comparative murder rates in Rio and D.C., see Richard Florida, 'Gun violence in U.S. cities compared to the deadliest nations in the world', *Citylab*, 22 January 2013.

414 For more of Christopher Gaffney's insights into his adoptive homeland, see Christopher Gaffney, 'Global parties, galactic hangovers: Brazil's mega event dystopia', *Los Angeles Review of Books*, 1 October 2014.

415 André Urani died shortly after publication of his book *Rio: A Hora da Virada* (2011); see his obituary, 'Die economist André Urani', *O Globo*, 14 December 2011.

416 When I originally interviewed Maria Silvia Bastos Marques, she was head of Empresa Olímpica Municipal. She has since stepped down from this position; see Nick Zaccardi, 'President of company preparing Rio for Olympics resigns', NBC Sports, 1 April 2014.

417 Controversy over forced evictions of favela dwellers to make way for Olympic commuter trains is discussed in Donna Bowater, 'Olympics bus route to displace 900 families from Rio favela', *Al Jazeera*, 1 September 2014; Matthew Niederhauser, 'Rio's Olympic inequality problem, in pictures', *Citylab*, 9 September 2015; and Bruce Douglas, 'Brazil officials evict families from homes ahead of 2016 Olympic Games', *Guardian*, 28 October 2015.

417 For a lengthier interview with Faustini, see Luiz Felipe Reis, 'As muitas redes do agitador da "perifa" Marcus Vinicius Faustini', *O Globo*, 21 July 2012.

418 Philip Alston's denouncement of the idea that 'occasional violent invasions can bring security' comes from the press release 'UN Special Rapporteur finds that killings by Brazilian police continue at alarming rates, government has failed to take all necessary action', United Nations Office of the High Commissioner for Human Rights, 1 June 2010. For his detailed analysis of the situation in Brazil, see Philip Alston, 'Report of the Special Rapporteur

on extrajudicial, summary or arbitrary executions: Follow-up to country recommendations – Brazil', United Nations Human Rights Council, 28 May 2010.

420 For a historical overview of racial identity politics in Brazil, see Antonio Sérgio and Alfredo Guimarães, 'The Brazilian system of racial classification', *Ethnic and Racial Studies* 35, no. 7 (2012).

420 The bewildering assortment of racial identities claimed by Brazilians is discussed in Melissa Block, 'Skin colour still plays big role in ethnically diverse Brazil', *All Things Considered*, National Public Radio, 19 September 2013; for a report of the study finding 136 varieties, see Cristina Grillo, 'Brasil quer ser chamado de moreno e só 39% se autodefinem como brancos', *Folha*, 25 June 1995.

420 The study examining attitudes towards racism of Brazilian urbanites and rural dwellers is described in Étore Medeiros and Ana Pompeu, 'Brasileiros acham que há racismo, mas somente 1.3% se consideram racistas', *Correio Braziliense*, 25 March 2014.

420 The study of São Paulo residents' perceptions of their own and others' racism is described in Lilia Moritz Schwarcz, 'Especificidade do racismo Brasileiro', in *História da vida Privada no Brasil* (1998).

421 Cíntia Luna describes her work in Rachael Hilderbrand, 'Conheça Cíntia Luna, Presidente da AMUST do Morro do Fogueteiro', *Rio On Watch*, 4 July 2014.

422 The Enraizados website is at http://enraizados.com.br.

422 For Fernando Gabeira's memoir, see *O Que É Isso, Companheiro?* (1979); the film based upon it is *Four Days in September* (1997).

422 For perspectives on the renovation of Estádio do Maracanã, see Tom Winterbottom, 'The tragedy of the Maracanã Stadium', *Rio On Watch*, 13 June 2014; and Mark Byrnes, 'A brief history of Brazil's most treasured World Cup stadium', *Citylab*, 16 June 2014.

423 The renovation of the Theatro Municipal is described in Sean Collins, 'City's theatre re-opens in style', *Rio Times*, 8 June 2010.

423 Sergio Mattos discusses trends in the modelling industry in Jenny Barchfield, 'Transgenders break into Brazil's modeling sector', *CNS News*, 6 December 2012.

424 See Vik Muniz's film *Waste Land* (2011); see also Kino, op. cit.

425 Tom Jobim's alleged pronouncement 'Morar em Nova Iorque é bom mas é uma merda, morar no Rio é uma merda mas é bom' has attained the status of urban legend in Brazil; references to it online abound. Cautious journalists identify the quote as 'attributed'; see, e.g., Antonio Carlos Miguel, 'Ser ou não ser carioca da gema não é a questão (To be or not to be carioca is the question)', *O Globo*, 28 February 2015 ('O conceito atribuído a Tom Jobim . . . é daqueles infalíveis'); and Fernando Canzian, 'É bom, mas é ruim (It's good, but it's bad)', *Folha*, 13 July 2009 ('A frase é atribuída a Tom Jobim . . .').

425 Statistics on the UPPs come from Clarissa Lins, 'Providing electricity to Rio de Janeiro's favelas', *Guardian*, 18 March 2014; and Janet Tappin Coelho, 'Brazil's "peace police" turn five. Are Rio's favelas safer?', *Christian Science Monitor*, 19 December 2013.

425 The drop in crime rates following implementation of the UPP programme is described in Simon Jenkins, 'Vision of the future or criminal eyesore: What should Rio do with its favelas?', *Guardian*, 30 April 2014; educational improvements are noted in Robert Muggah and Ilona Szabo de Carvalho, 'Fear and backsliding in Rio', *New York Times*, 15 April 2014.

425 Findings of research by the Institute of Social and Political Studies regarding criminal activity in Rio's favelas were reported in Coelho, op. cit.

426 The minuscule number of sanctions resulting from citizens' reports of police violence are discussed in Human Rights Watch, 'Letter: Brazil: Protect detainees in police custody', 25 July 2014.

426 For Amnesty International's report on homicides by police in Rio, see 'You killed my son: Homicides by military police in the city of Rio de Janeiro', Amnesty International, 3 August 2015.

426 For the report finding widespread displacement of favela residents and disappearance of street children during preparations for the 2016 Olympics, see Karin Elisabeth von Schmalz Peixoto et al., 'Rio 2016 Olympics: The exclusion games', World Cup and Olympics Popular Committee of Rio de Janeiro, 7 December 2015; see also Jonathan Watts, 'Rio Olympics linked to widespread human rights violations, report reveals', *Guardian*, 8 December 2015.

426 The demise of Amarildo de Souza while in police custody was widely reported and analysed; among the articles dealing with it is Jonathan Watts, 'Brazil: Rio police charged over torture and death of missing favela man', *Guardian*, 2 October 2013; see also Human Rights Watch, 'Brazil: Reforms fail to end torture', Human Rights Watch, 28 July 2014.

426 Douglas Rafael da Silva Pereira's death by beating provoked widespread protests; see Wyre Davies, 'Brazil: Protesters in Rio clash with police over dancer's death', BBC News, 23 April 2014.

426 Gunfights in 'pacified' favelas are described in Donna Bowater, 'Rio's police-occupied slums see an increase in drug-related violence', *Washington Post*, 19 February 2014.

426 The quote from Cleber Araujo ('It feels like we're in a war') comes from Loretta Chao, 'Rio faces surge of post–World Cup violence in slums', *Wall Street Journal*, 22 July 2014.

427 The Pew Research Trust found increasing distrust of police by Brazilian citizens; see Judith Horowitz et al., 'Brazilian discontent ahead of World Cup', Pew Research Global Attitudes Project, 3 June 2014.

427 The impact on local residents of police attempts to expel criminal gangs from the Maré favela is described in Jonathan Watts, 'Rio police tackle favelas as World Cup looms', *Guardian*, 10 June 2013. Pacification of the Rocinha

favela also had a devastating effect on law-abiding citizens; see Paula Ramon, 'Poor, middle class unite in Brazil protests', CNN News, 24 July 2013.

427 The quote from Atila Roque ('backfiring miserably') comes from 'You killed my son: Homicides by military police in the city of Rio de Janeiro', op. cit.

427 The quote from the anonymous favela resident ('They will run into each other on the way out') appears in Rodrigo Serrano-Berthet et al., 'Bringing the state back into the favelas of Rio de Janeiro: Understanding changes in community life after the UPP pacification process', World Bank, October 2012.

In Bed with the President of Ghana?

431 Speculation that I had figured in the death of the late president of Ghana was published in Daniel Danquah Damptey, 'Investigate Mills' death', *GhanaWeb*, 29 July 2015.

432 Moses Foh-Amoaning's prophecy that I would one day join the ministry was broadcast on Ghanaian radio; see Kweku Antwi-Otoo, 'Gay activist Andrew Solomon will be a pastor one day: Moses Foh-Amoaning', *Atinka 104.7 FM*, 13 July 2015. The quote 'God will meet him at a point and hit him to change' comes from another report that deals with my sexual identity at some length, ' "Prayer" is the key against "devilish" homosexuality worldwide: Moses Foh-Amoaning', *Daily Guide Ghana*, 14 July 2015.

432 For similar, albeit less hopeful, demagoguery, see Gyasiwaa Agyeman, ' "Mahama will soon mortgage Ghana to anti-Christ" ', *Adom Online*, 8 January 2016.

Gay, Jewish, Mentally Ill and a Sponsor of Gypsies in Romania

442 The sanction against National University of Theatre Arts and Cinematography professor Andrei Rus for allegedly 'ruining the University's image' with his 'gay propaganda and homosexual agenda' was reported in Dorina Calin, 'Decizie UNATC: Criticul de film Andrei Rus nu va fi dat afară din instituție, dar va fi sancționat', *Mediafax*, 2 July 2015.

Myanmar's Moment

443 All quotes in my essay on Myanmar come from personal interviews unless otherwise specified.

443 Myanmar's release of eleven hundred political prisoners was acknowledged in a 2014 report by Tomás Ojea Quintana, UN human rights rapporteur for Burma; see Samantha Michaels, 'Quintana releases final report on Burma human rights', *Irrawaddy*, 14 March 2014.

443 The initial U.S. relaxation of sanctions against Burma is reported in Karen De Young, 'Ban on U.S. investment in Burma is lifted', *Washington Post*, 11 July 2012.

444 Suu Kyi's release from house arrest is reported in Tracy McVeigh, 'Aung San Suu Kyi "released from house arrest"', *Guardian*, 13 November 2010; the NLD's victory in the 2012 general elections, in Esmer Golluoglu, 'Aung San Suu Kyi hails "new era" for Burma after landslide victory', *Guardian*, 2 April 2012.

445 Paradoxically, at least one Burmese commentator regarded Ma Thida's early release from prison as a cynical PR ploy on the part of the military junta; see Aung Zaw, 'The SPDC's diplomatic gambit', *Irrawaddy*, February 1999.

446 Aung San Suu Kyi, op. cit.

446 The artist Aye Ko discusses his work in Whitney Light, 'Pressing questions with Aye Ko', *Myanmar Times*, 18 May 2014.

446 Lu Maw and his brother, the late Par Par Lay, were imprisoned after a performance by their comedy troupe in 1996; see Philip Heijmans, 'Skirting comedy limits in Myanmar', *New York Times*, 29 July 2015.

446 In addition to his role as mayor, Ko Min Latt is also editor of the Mon-language newspaper *Than Lwin Times*; see Banyar Kong Janoi, 'Pushing for ethnic language media in a changing Burma', *Asia Calling*, 10 November 2012.

446 Moe Satt, too, has aroused official suspicion of his art; see Hillary Luong, 'Artists detained by Myanmar police', *Art Asia Pacific*, 8 June 2012.

447 Nay Phone Latt's journalistic bravery earned him a place on *Time* magazine's 2010 *Time 100* roster; see Salman Rushdie, 'Heroes: Nay Phone Latt', *Time*, 29 April 2010. For a recent interview, see 'Nay Phone Latt speaks', *Myanmar Times*, 3 March 2014.

447 Thant Myint-U, grandson of former UN secretary-general U Thant, is a prolific author on political topics and chairman of Yangon Heritage Trust, which seeks to document the history of historical architecture, establish zoning laws and preserve urban architecture in Yangon; the organisation's website is at http://yangonheritagetrust.org.

447 For a recent article featuring Sammy Samuels, see Joe Freeman, 'Myanmar's Jewish vote', *Tablet*, 9 November 2015. Sammy Samuels's travel agency, Myanmar Shalom, can be found online at http://myanmarshalom.com.

448 The dramatic expansion of the mobile-phone industry in Myanmar is discussed in Jason Motlagh, 'When a SIM card goes from $2,000 to $1.50', *Bloomberg Business*, 29 September 2014; Michael Tan, 'One million SIM cards sold in Myanmar', *CNET*, 2 October 2014; and Jared Ferrie, 'SIM sales soar as Myanmar races to catch up in telecoms', Reuters, 6 May 2015.

448 Responding to safety concerns, Myanmar has recently passed legislation requiring left-hand drive on new car imports; see Kyaw Hsu Mon, 'Govt to push left-hand steering wheels on future car imports', *Irrawaddy*, 25 November

2014; and Aye Nyein Win, 'Right-hand drives to remain on the roads', *Myanmar Times*, 23 October 2015.

449 Statistics on child nutrition in Myanmar come from UNICEF, 'Country statistics: Myanmar', UNICEF, 2015.

450 For a detailed analysis of the contribution of tourism to Myanmar's economy, see Rochelle Turner et al., 'Travel and tourism: Economic impact 2015: Myanmar', World Travel and Tourism Council, 2015.

450 More background on Burmese history can be found in Michael Aung-Thwin and Maitrii Aung-Thwin, *A History of Myanmar since Ancient Times* (2012).

451 For more detail on the 1988 student uprisings, see British Broadcasting Corporation, 'Burma's 1988 protests', BBC News, 25 September 2007; and Rodion Ebbighausen, 'Myanmar: The uprising of 1988', *Deutsche Welle*, 8 August 2013.

452 Full text of the 'Constitution of the Republic of the Union of Myanmar (2008)' can be found on the website of the World Intellectual Property Organisation, http://wipo.int/edocs/lexdocs/laws/en/mm/mm009en.pdf. For discussion of the constitution's problematic aspects and efforts to reform it, see Thomas Fuller, 'Myanmar's leader backs change to constitution', *New York Times*, 2 January 2014; Jared Ferrie, 'Myanmar president enacts law allowing referendum on disputed constitution', Reuters, 12 February 2015; and Thomas Fuller, 'Myanmar's military uses political force to block constitutional changes', *New York Times*, 15 June 2015.

453 The homesickness of Burmese refugees is described in Julia Lyon, 'Invited to escape to America, some refugees just say no', *St. Louis Tribune*, 14 September 2009; and Ron Corben, 'Burmese refugees in Thailand long to return home', *Deutsche Welle*, 13 December 2011.

453 Among dissidents demanding an apology from their former captors is Win Tin; see Kyaw Phyo Tha, 'Ex–political prisoner Win Tin demands apology from junta leaders', *Irrawaddy*, 30 October 2013.

453 See Aung San Suu Kyi, *The Voice of Hope: Conversations with Alan Clements* (2008).

453 Myanmar's low-occupancy capital is described in Matt Kennard and Claire Provost, 'The lights are on but no one's home in Myanmar's capital Naypyidaw', *Guardian*, 19 March 2015; and Katie Amey, 'Government-issued housing, super-highways that span 20 lanes but not a soul in sight: Inside Myanmar's haunting capital city', *Daily Mail*, 18 April 2015.

454 See U.S. Department of State, 'U.S. economic engagement with Burma', U.S. Embassy in Rangoon, June 2014.

454 Although many Burmese professionals have removed to Singapore, the tide is slowly turning; see Kyaw Zwa Moe, 'Burmese professionals earn good money in Singapore but still miss home', *Irrawaddy*, March 2007; and Joanna Seow, 'More Myanmar professionals in Singapore heading home to tap booming economy', *Straits Times*, 24 March 2014.

455 Shwe Mann's pragmatic alliance with Aung San Suu Kyi engendered misgivings among his fellow USDP members, including President Thein Sein, who staged Mann's dramatic ouster from his role as head of the party; see Thomas Fuller, 'Conservatives in Myanmar force out leader of ruling party', *New York Times*, 13 August 2015; British Broadcasting Corporation, 'Aung San Suu Kyi hails Shwe Mann as an "ally"', BBC News, 18 August 2015; and Hnin Yadana Zaw and Antoni Slodkowski, 'Myanmar's ousted ruling party head to work with Suu Kyi', Reuters, 5 November 2015.

455 See the highly regarded biography by Peter Popham, *The Lady and the Peacock: The Life of Aung San Suu Kyi* (2012).

456 Aung San Suu Kyi's Nobel Lecture can be found on the Nobel Prize website at http://nobelprize.org/nobel_prizes/peace/laureates/1991/kyi-lecture_en.html.

456 See previously cited sources on the Burmese constitution: Fuller (2014 and 2015), op. cit., and Ferrie, op. cit.

457 Robert San Pe discusses constitutional reform in the twenty-four-minute video 'Legal adviser to Aung San Suu Kyi, Robert Pe', Reliefweb Labs, 5 May 2015.

457 Donors to Myanmar's fledgling Parliamentary Library include Canada, the United States and the Asia Foundation; see 'Baird bears gifts', *Mizzima*, 9 March 2012; Malaysian Myanmar Business Council, 'U.S. contributes publications to parliamentary library', 24 October 2012; and Asia Foundation, 'The Asia Foundation donates books to parliamentary library in Burma', 24 October 2012.

457 For discussion of the impact and dynamics of Nargis, see Michael Casey, 'Why the cyclone in Myanmar was so deadly', *National Geographic News*, 8 May 2008.

458 Consul General Ye Myint Aung's outrageous statement appeared in a letter dated 9 February 2009 (available online at http://asiapacific.anu.edu.au/newmandala/wp-content/uploads/2009/02/the-consul-generals-letter.pdf), and was originally reported in Greg Torode, 'Myanmese envoy says Rohingya ugly as ogres', *South China Morning Post*, 11 February 2009.

458 For the Myanmar government's interpretation of the history of its Muslim population, see Republic of the Union of Myanmar, 'Final report of inquiry commission on sectarian violence in Rakhine State', 8 July 2013.

459 Several NGOs have prepared overviews of the history of the Rohingya; see, e.g., Euro-Burma Office, 'The Rohingyas: Bengali Muslims or Arakan Rohingyas?', EBO Briefing Paper No. 2, Euro-Burma Office, 2009; and Eliane Coates, 'Sectarian violence involving Rohingya in Myanmar: Historical roots and modern triggers', Middle East Institute, 4 August 2014.

460 Speculation that the Rohingya have links with terrorist groups is disputed by security experts and Burmese parliamentarians; see Paul Vrieze, 'Experts reject claims of "Rohingya mujahideen" insurgency', *Irrawaddy*, 15 July 2013.

460 Human Rights Watch has documented the persecution of Rohingya in

Matthew Smith et al., ' "All you can do is pray": Crimes against humanity and ethnic cleansing of Rohingya Muslims in Burma's Arakan State', Human Rights Watch, April 2013.

460 Ashin Wirathu's sermon that is thought to have provoked the massacre of Rohingya at Meiktila can be viewed online at 'Anti Muslim monk Wira thu talk about Meiktila before riot', YouTube, 24 March 2013; a summary translation is available at Maung Zarni, 'Racist leader monk Rev. Wirathu's speech', *M-Media*, 24 March 2013. Wirathu's exhortation to 'rise up' and 'make your blood boil' was quoted in Hannah Beech, 'The face of Buddhist terror', *Time*, 1 July 2013. The quote from the pamphlet distributed at one of Ashin Wirathu's sermons appears in Thomas Fuller, 'Extremism rises among Myanmar Buddhists', *New York Times*, 20 June 2013. Wirathu is compared to Hitler in Sarah Kaplan, 'The serene-looking Buddhist monk accused of inciting Burma's sectarian violence', *Washington Post*, 27 May 2015.

461 See Yassin Musharbash, 'The "Talibanisation" of Pakistan: Islamists destroy Buddhist statue', *Der Spiegel*, 8 November 2007.

461 The term 'savage Buddhists' is cited in Jonathan Pearlman, 'Jihadist group calls on Muslims to save Burmese migrants from "savage Buddhists" ', *Telegraph*, 20 May 2015.

462 The Rohingyas' flight from Myanmar is documented in David Mathieson, 'Perilous plight: Burma's Rohingya take to the seas', Human Rights Watch, 2009.

462 Suu Kyi's silence on the Rohingya issue has been widely noted; see, e.g., Moshahida Sultana Ritu, 'Ethnic cleansing in Myanmar', *New York Times*, 12 July 2012; and Charlie Campbell, 'Arakan strife poses Suu Kyi political problem', *Irrawaddy*, 13 July 2012.

462 Tensions between Arakanese Buddhists and foreign aid workers are described in Lawi Weng, 'Arakan monks boycott UN, INGOs', *Irrawaddy*, 6 July 2012.

462 The 2014 Mandalay riots were reported in 'Five injured in Mandalay unrest, damage limited', *Irrawaddy*, 2 July 2014.

463 For a scholarly discussion of the variety of Muslims residing in Myanmar, see Khin Maung Yin, 'Salience of ethnicity among Burman Muslims: A study in identity formation', *Intellectual Discourse* 13, no. 2 (2005).

465 For more information on the tattooed women of Chin state, see Sarah Boesveld, 'Stealing beauty: A look at the tattooed faces of Burma's Chin province', *National Post*, 15 July 2011.

466 The number of monks in Myanmar is put at four hundred thousand to five hundred thousand in Sarah Buckley, 'Who are Burma's monks?', BBC News, 26 September 2007.

467 The history of Jewish migration to and from South Asia is explored in Nathan Katz and Ellen S. Goldberg, 'The last Jews in India and Burma', *Jerusalem Letter*, 15 April 1988.

467 Moses Samuels died on 29 May 2015; see Jonathan Zaiman, 'Remembering Moses Samuels, the man who preserved Jewry in Myanmar', *Tablet*, 2 June 2015.

468 Moses Samuels himself stated, 'There is no problem with religion here'; see Seth Mydans, 'Yangon Journal; Burmese Jew shoulders burden of his heritage', *New York Times*, 23 July 2002. Also, see a touching remembrance of Moses Samuels and an account of Myanmar's Jewish community: Sammy Samuels, 'Hanukkah with spirit in Yangon', *BBC News*, 4 December 2015.

468 The outcome of cease-fire negotiations with armed rebel groups in Myanmar is reported in Shibani Mahtani and Myo Myo, 'Myanmar signs draft peace deal with armed ethnic groups', *Wall Street Journal*, 31 March 2015.

468 For more background on the remnants of the Kuomintang in Myanmar, see Denis D. Gray, 'The remaining veterans of China's "lost army" cling to old life styles in Thailand', *Los Angeles Times*, 7 June 1987.

469 Mong La's National Democratic Alliance and its leader, Sai Leun, figure in Michael Black and Roland Fields, 'Virtual gambling in Myanmar's drug country', *Asia Times*, 26 August 2006; and Sebastian Strangio, 'Myanmar's wildlife trafficking hotspot', *Al Jazeera*, 17 June 2014.

469 Kachin state's lucrative jade industry is investigated in Andrew Marshall, 'Myanmar old guard clings to $8 billion jade empire', Reuters, 1 October 2013. The escalating death toll in a landslide at a jadeite mine is reported in Kyaw Myo Min, Kyaw Kyaw Aung and Khin Khin Ei, 'Hopes fade for Myanmar landslide survivors as lawmakers urge greater safety for miners', Radio Free Asia, 24 November 2015.

471 Thant Thaw Kaung's story is told in Mary O'Shea, 'Journey of shelf discovery', *Post Magazine*, 14 October 2012.

473 Htein Lin's life and work are the subjects of Thomas Fuller, 'Back to a Burmese prison by choice', *New York Times*, 6 December 2014.

475 Htein Lin's project, *A Show of Hand*, is described on his website, at http://hteinlin.com/a-show-of-hand; and in Kyaw Phyo Tha, 'Hands of hardship; Artist Htein Lin spotlights political prisoners' travails', *Irrawaddy*, 27 July 2015.

475 The work of Wah Nu and Tun Win Aung is discussed in Mike Ives, 'Culling Myanmar's past for memories', *New York Times*, 16 October 2013; and Susan Kendzulak, 'Burma's flying circus', *Art Radar*, 18 October 2013.

476 Maung Tin Thit (also known as U Ye Mon) won a seat in the Hluttaw (the legislative assembly) in the 2015 general elections; see Pyae Thet Phyo, 'Ex-minister's agent denies seeking recount', *Myanmar Times*, 12 November 2015.

476 Ma Thanegi, *Nor Iron Bars a Cage* (2013).

476 Ma Thanegi articulated her opposition to sanctions in 'The Burmese fairy tale', *Far Eastern Economic Review*, 19 February 1998.

478 Misuu Borit's efforts to reestablish the Burmese cat in its native land are recounted in Kelly McNamara, 'Burmese cats return to a new Burma',

Bangkok Post, 14 September 2012; and Kyaw Phyo Tha, 'A purr-fect pedigree in Burma', *Irrawaddy*, 24 February 2014.

479 Figures on tourism in Myanmar come from Turner et al., op. cit.

479 The convicted *Unity Journal* staffers remain in prison; see San Yamin Aung, 'Supreme Court rejects appeal of Unity journalists', *Irrawaddy*, 27 November 2014.

479 Charges against some protesters were eventually dropped; see 'Charges dropped against 23 journalists', *Nation* (Bangkok), 25 August 2014.

479 The death of Aung Kyaw Naing (Par Gyi) in police custody is reported in Lawi Weng, Nyein Nyein and Kyaw Hsu Mon, 'Missing reporter killed in custody of Burma army', *Irrawaddy*, 24 October 2014. On the aftermath of the event, see British Broadcasting Corporation, 'Myanmar court "must investigate Aung Kyaw Naing death"', BBC News, 3 December 2014.

479 Zaw Pe's conviction for 'trespassing' while investigating a scholarship programme is described in Zarni Mann, 'DVB reporter jailed for one year', *Irrawaddy*, 7 April 2014.

479 The conviction and sentencing of the *Bi Mon Te Nay* staffers is reported in Nobel Zaw, 'Court sentences 3 journalists, 2 media owners to 2 years in prison', *Irrawaddy*, 16 October 2014.

479 Htin Kyaw's arrest and conviction are the subject of Nobel Zaw, 'Activist hit with additional sentence, totaling over 13 years', *Irrawaddy*, 31 October 2014.

479 Press freedom rankings come from Reporters Without Borders's annual World Press Freedom Index, 2015, at http://index.rsf.org.

480 The quotes from Yanghee Lee ('to criminalise and impede', 'disproportionately high') come from Yanghee Lee, 'Report of the Special Rapporteur on situation of human rights in Myanmar', United Nations Office of the High Commissioner for Human Rights, 23 September 2014.

480 The increasingly desperate plight of the Rohingya people is described in Rishi Iyengaar, 'Burma's million-strong Rohingya population faces "final stages of genocide" says report', *Time*, 28 October 2015; and Penny Green, Thomas MacManus and Alicia de la Cour Venning, 'Countdown to annihilation: Genocide in Myanmar', International State Crime Initiative, 2015.

481 The 969 movement is the subject of Andrew Marshall's reports 'The 969 catechism', Reuters, 26 June 2013; and 'Myanmar gives official blessing to anti-Muslim monks', Reuters, 27 June 2013. For discussion of the Ma Ba Tha political party, see Annie Gowen, 'Hard-line Buddhist monks threaten Burma's hopes for democracy', *Washington Post*, 5 November 2015.

481 The pending lawsuit against Burmese president Thein Sein is discussed in Agence France-Presse, 'Muslim groups sue Myanmar president for Rohingya "genocide"', *Guardian*, 5 October 2015.

481 The National League for Democracy's election victory is reported in Oliver Holmes, 'Aung San Suu Kyi wins outright majority in Myanmar election',

Guardian, 13 November 2015. U Win Htein's post-election comments on Muslims in Burma are drawn from Austin Ramzy, 'After Myanmar election, few signs of a better life for Muslims', *New York Times*, 18 November 2015.

481 The expansion of the Myanmar press, and its simultaneous suppression by the government, is the subject of Julie Makinen, 'Myanmar press freedom: Unprecedented but still subject to pressures', *Los Angeles Times*, 27 March 2015; Paul Mooney, 'Jail, lawsuits cast shadow over Myanmar media freedom', Reuters, 15 May 2014; and Amnesty International, 'Caught between state censorship and self-censorship: Prosecution and intimidation of media workers in Myanmar', Amnesty International, 16 June 2015.

482 The military's constitutionally enshrined dominance over Burmese politics is noted in 'A milestone for Myanmar's democracy', *New York Times*, 12 November 2015.

482 Suu Kyi's remarks on the constitution of Myanmar are reported in Claire Phipps and Matthew Weaver, 'Aung San Suu Kyi vows to make all the decisions in Myanmar's new government', *Guardian*, 10 November 2015; see also Fergal Keane, 'Myanmar election: Full BBC interview with Aung San Suu Kyi', BBC News, 10 November 2015.

Lost at the Surface

483 I would not have seemed such an adventurous eater had I been born forty years later. Eel has become so popular that both Japanese and American varieties have been added to the International Endangered Species List; see Frances Cha, 'Japanese eel becomes latest "endangered food"', *CNN Travel*, 5 February 2013; and Annie Sneed, 'American eel is in danger of extinction', *Scientific American*, 1 December 2014.

484 Dutch Springs Quarry in Lehigh, Pennsylvania, is the watery grave of not only a school bus, but also a fire truck, a trolley, three different aeroplanes, and a Sikorsky H-37 helicopter; see Julie Morgan, 'Keeping 'em diving in the Keystone State', *Sport Diver*, 21 April 2006.

485 My opening address at the Sydney Writers' Festival can be viewed on the festival website, at http://swf.org.au.

485 Orpheus Island Resort, a pleasant enough place when you aren't being abandoned at sea by its incompetent staff and then asked to pay for your trip by its impenitent manager, has a website at http://orpheus.com.au.

487 Although the Tarzan yell is unmistakable, its provenance is debatable; see Bill De Main, 'The disputed history of the Tarzan yell', *Mental Floss*, 22 August 2012.

490 The story 'In Which Piglet Is Entirely Surrounded by Water' is chapter 9 of A. A. Milne, *Winnie-the-Pooh* (1926).

493 This statement is widely attributed to Alexander von Humboldt, but a definitive source is elusive. Original German: 'Die gefährlichste Weltanschauung ist die Weltanschauung derer, die die Welt nie angeschaut haben.'

494 Instances of verbal and physical aggression toward ethnic and religious minorities following the Brexit referendum are described in National Police Chiefs' Council, 'Hate crime undermines the diversity and tolerance we should instead be celebrating', 8 July 2016; Matthew Weaver, '"Horrible spike" in hate crime linked to Brexit vote, Met police say', *Guardian*, 28 September 2016; and Hannah Corcoran and Kevin Smith, 'Hate crime, England and Wales, 2015/6', Home Office, 13 October 2016.

494 For the Southern Poverty Law Center's tally of postelection harassment in the United States, see Cassie Miller and Alexandra Werner-Winslow, 'Ten days after: Harassment and intimidation in the aftermath of the election', Southern Poverty Law Center, 29 November 2016. I have drawn heavily from this excellent report.

495 Jarosław Kaczyński's statement about the public-health threat supposedly posed by refugees was reported in Vanessa Gera, 'Right-wing Polish leader Kaczynski says migrants carry diseases to Europe', *U.S. News & World Report*, 14 October 2015.

495 Protests against refugees in Poland are described in Agence France-Presse, 'E.U. flag burned as tens of thousands join Warsaw national demo', *Daily Telegraph*, 12 November 2015; and Allgemeiner staff, 'Polish anti-refugee demonstrators burn effigies of Orthodox Jews at Wroclaw protest', *Allgemeiner Zeitung*, 18 November 2015.

495 Hungarian prime minister Viktor Orbán's pronouncements on immigrants are described in Caroline Mortimer, 'Hungarian PM Viktor Orbán says "all the terrorists are basically migrants" in response to Paris attacks', *Independent*, 24 November 2015; and Reuters and Agence France-Presse, 'Hungarian prime minister says migrants are "poison" and "not needed"', *Guardian*, 26 July 2016.

495 The propaganda booklet posted to Hungarian voters is reproduced in its entirety and translated into English in '"We must stop Brussels!" referendum booklet warns Hungarians', *Budapest Beacon*, 7 September 2016.

495 Hungary's poster war against refugees is described in Nick Thorpe, 'Hungary's poster war on immigration', BBC News, 14 June 2015.

495 The Italian referendum vote and its impact are considered in Richard Maher, 'As Austria rejects the far-right and Italy votes No, Europe's future hangs in the balance', *Conversation*, 5 December 2016; and Lauren Said-Moorhouse, 'Is Italy's referendum result the first step toward leaving the E.U.?', CNN, December 5, 2016. Italy's role in the creation of the European Union is discussed in Eric Reguly, 'Support for the E.U. is even dropping in Italy – the country that inspired its creation', *Globe & Mail*, 21 June 2016. For

in-depth analysis of the rise of nationalism in Italy, see Timothy Lindsay, 'Security implications of Italian nationalism', PhD diss., Naval Postgraduate School, March 2016.

495 Turkish president Recep Erdoğan's dissatisfaction with the Treaty of Lausanne and with Turkey's modern boundaries is the subject of Nick Danforth, 'Turkey's new maps are reclaiming the Ottoman Empire', *Foreign Policy*, 23 October 2016; and Associated Press, 'Erdoğan comments on historic treaty irk opposition, Greece', *Washington Post*, 30 September 2016.

495 For more on Turkish nationalism and the concept of Islam as a necessary component of Turkish identity, see Senem Aslam, 'Different faces of Turkish Islamic nationalism', *Washington Post*, 20 February 2015; and Tom Stevenson, 'The growing strength of Turkey's ultra-nationalists', *Middle East Eye*, 1 June 2016. The history of Turkey's crypto-Jews is described in Nick Ashdown, 'Public Muslims, secret Jews: A Turkish sect faces crackdown', *Forward*, 5 August 2016.

496 Numan Kurtulmus's exhortation to Turkish citizens to 'call an infidel an infidel' is reported in Agence France-Presse, ' "Infidel!" Ottoman slur raises hackles in Turkey', *Tribune* (Pakistan), 15 December 2016.

496 Verbal aggression against ethnic and religious minorities in Turkey is discussed in Pinar Sevinclidir, 'Hate speech on the rise in Turkish media', BBC News, 30 October 2014.

496 The leader of Turkey's Nationalist Movement Party referred to people with 'slanted eyes' as indistinguishable from one another in Amy Sawitta Lefevre and Yesim Dikmen, 'Thai PM defends decision to send Uighurs back to China', Reuters, 9 July 2015.

496 Turkey's recent drift toward authoritarianism is discussed in Steven A. Cook, 'How Erdoğan made Turkey authoritarian again', *Atlantic*, 21 July 2016; Lizzie Dearden, 'Turkey slides towards authoritarian rule as commission approves plan to increase powers for President Erdoğan', *Independent*, 30 December 2016; and Burcu Degirmen and Alperen Atik, 'Turkey: Authoritarianism and academic "closure" ', *Open Democracy*, 14 February 2017.

496 The upsurge in hate speech in Turkey is noted in European Commission against Racism and Intolerance, 'ECRI report on Turkey (fifth monitoring cycle)', Council of Europe, 4 October 2016.

496 Trump's speedy post-election congratulations to Erdoğan are reported in Carol Morello, 'Trump calls Erdoğan to congratulate him on contested referendum, Turkey says', *Washington Post*, 17 April 2017.

496 Quotes by Johnny Christensen and Julie Jeeg are taken from David Zucchino, ' "I've become a racist": Migrant wave unleashes Danish tensions over identity', *New York Times*, 6 September 2016.

497 At the October 2016 Conservative Party Conference, Theresa May disparaged the concept of global citizenship; see Theresa May, 'Theresa May's conference speech in full', *Daily Telegraph*, 5 October 2016.

497 The concept of intersectionality was pioneered by sociologist Kimberlé Crenshaw in 'Demarginalizing the intersection of race and sex', *University of Chicago Legal Forum* 1989, no. 1 (1989): article 8; see also Bim Adewunmi, 'Kimberlé Crenshaw on intersectionality', *New Statesman*, 2 April 2014.

497 Representative arguments for leaving the E.U. are set forth in Toby Young, 'Voting remain is an act of heartless snobbery', *Spectator*, 14 May 2016; 'We urge our readers to beLEAVE in Britain and vote to quit the E.U. on June 23', 13 June 2016; and Patrick Minford, 'The economic case for a Brexit', *Forbes*, 22 June 2016.

498 For the study of hostile tweets post-Brexit, see Carl Miller et al., 'From Brussels to Brexit: Islamophobia, xenophobia, racism and reports of hateful incidents on Twitter: Research prepared for Channel 4 Dispatches "Racist Britain"', Demos Centre for Analysis of Social Media, 11 July 2016.

498 For reports on ethnically motivated aggression post-Brexit, see National Police Chiefs' Council, op. cit.; and Caroline Mortimer, 'Post-Brexit increase in hate crimes continues as police promise crackdown', *Independent*, 22 July 2016.

498 The quote from Bernard Hogan-Howe comes from Weaver, op. cit.

498 The post-Brexit increase in calls to the Stop Hate UK helpline is documented in Rose Simkins, 'Stop Hate UK: Report on post-referendum hate crime', Stop Hate UK, 22 August 2016.

498 Post-Brexit threats reported to embassies and consulates within the UK are discussed in Matthew Weaver and Sandra Laville, 'European embassies in UK log more alleged hate crimes since Brexit vote', *Guardian*, 19 September 2016.

498 The murder of Arkadiusz Jóźwik is reported in Press Association, 'Man in Harlow assault died after single punch to the head, CCTV shows', *Guardian*, 6 September 2016.

498 The arson targeting the Banaszak family is described in 'Polish family's Plymouth home damaged in "race hate arson attack"', BBC News, 7 July 2016.

499 An assault on a pregnant teenager is reported in Suzy Gibson, 'Woman kicked pregnant 14-year-old schoolgirl in head during racist attack', *Leicester Mercury*, 17 December 2016.

499 The mugging of a Polish woman and her partner is reported in Katie Mansfield, 'Gang launch horror racist attack on woman in West Midlands during night out', *Express*, 14 March 2017.

499 See Rachel Martin and Jonny Bell, 'Antrim racist attack: "Scared" mother and baby leave home after brick lands in cot', *Belfast Telegraph*, 12 April 2017.

499 The quote from Jon Burnett comes from Weaver and Laville, op. cit.

499 See Priska Komaromi and Karissa Singh, 'Post-referendum racism and xenophobia: The role of social media activism in challenging the normalisation of xeno-racist narratives', PostRef Racism, 11 July 2016.

499 Figures on assaults of NHS staff rely on Peter Yeung, 'Racist assaults on hospital staff double in a year', *Times*, 24 January 2017.

499 See Jon Sharman and Ian Jones, 'Hate crimes rise by up to 100 per cent across England and Wales, figures reveal', *Independent*, 15 February 2017.

499 See Becca Meier, 'Huge rise in hate crime across London, new figures reveal', *Independent*, 7 March 2017.

499 See Emily Dugan, 'A racist mob chanting "Ku Klux Klan" targeted a Turkish family in North London', *BuzzFeed News*, 23 January 2017.

499 See Lindsey Hamilton, 'Dundee shopkeeper "still feels worried at work" after racist attack', *Evening Telegraph*, 6 April 2017.

500 See Rozina Sabur, ' "You don't belong here": Solicitor caught on film launching racist attack on woman and her young son', *Daily Telegraph*, 4 February 2017.

500 See Michael Purton, 'Stroud shopkeeper run over in vicious gang attack', *Stroud News & Journal*, 29 March 2017.

500 See Jamie Grierson and Lin Jenkins, 'Croydon "hate crime": three more held in hunt for teenager's attackers', *Guardian*, 2 April 2017.

500 See Charles White, 'Vandals paint racist graffiti on Islamic community centre after London Bridge attack', *Metro*, 4 June 2017.

500 For analysis of the impact of budget cuts on policing, see Alan Travis, 'Simple numbers tell story of police cuts under Theresa May', *Guardian*, 5 June 2017.

501 Donald Trump referred to immigrants from Mexico as 'bad hombres' during his 2016 presidential campaign debate with Hillary Clinton in Las Vegas, Nevada; see Maya Rhodan, 'Donald Trump raises eyebrows with "bad hombres" line', *Time*, 19 October 2016.

501 Re Donald Trump's taste for travel, see David Usborne, 'Donald Trump on foreign policy: "I've got no time to travel – America needs my attention now"', *Independent*, 27 August 2015.

501 The quote by Timothy Snyder comes from Timothy Snyder, 'Him', *Slate*, 18 November 2016.

501 For a countrywide tally of postelection aggression, see Miller and Werner-Winslow, op. cit.

501 The Massachusetts post-election hotline is described in 'AG Healey's hate crime hotline received 400 calls in first week', WBUR, 21 November 2016.

501 The increase in aggression in New York City after the 2016 presidential election is reported in Sarah Maslin Nir, 'Finding hate crimes on the rise, leaders condemn vicious acts', *New York Times*, 5 December 2016; and Will Bredderman, 'NYPD reports "huge spike" in hate crimes since Donald Trump's election', *Observer*, 5 December 2016.

502 The post-election experience in Michigan is documented in Niraj Warikoo, 'Hate crimes increase in Michigan post-election, drawing concern', *Detroit Free Press*, 20 November 2016.

502 For a summary of the FBI's findings on aggression against Muslim citizens, see Kevin Johnson, 'FBI: Hate crimes targeting Muslims up 67% in 2015', *USA Today*, 14 November 2016.

502 See Maureen Costello, 'The Trump effect: The impact of the presidential campaign on our nation's schools', Southern Poverty Law Center, 13 April 2016.

502 Ibid. For example, one child repeatedly asked his teacher, 'is the wall here yet?'

502 'Now that Trump is president, I'm going to shoot you and all the blacks I can find': Miller and Werner-Winslow, op. cit.

502 'When they see your eyes, you are going to be deported': Southern Poverty Law Center, 'Update: More than 400 incidents of hateful harassment and intimidation since the election', 15 November 2016.

502 'Now that Trump won, you're going to have to go back to Africa – where you belong': Miller and Werner-Winslow, op. cit.

502 Harassment of Muslim high school teacher in Georgia: Joshua Sharpe, 'Muslim Gwinnett teacher told to "hang yourself" with her headscarf', *Atlanta Journal-Constitution*, 11 November 2016.

502 Classroom incidents in Tennessee: Costello, op. cit.

503 For a survey of American schoolchildren's use of Trump's words and message to harass their classmates, see Albert Samaha, Mike Hayes and Talal Ansari, 'The kids are Alt-Right', *BuzzFeed News*, 6 June 2017.

503 Los Angeles teacher threatening student with deportation: Jen Carlson, 'Racist teacher who threatened student with deportation put on "Do Not Hire" list', *LAist*, 14 November 2016.

503 Racist Florida teacher: Adam Manno, 'Florida teacher tells black student that Trump will send her "back to Africa"', *Orlando Weekly*, 15 November 2016.

503 John Annese, 'Ex-substitute teacher slapped with hate crime charges after allegedly ripping hijab off 8-year-old Bronx student', *New York Daily News*, 25 May 2017.

503 Natasha Nkhama's ordeal and her classmates' response are described in Cleve R. Wootson Jr., 'A Baylor student was shoved and called the "n" word. This is how the school responded', *Washington Post*, 14 November 2016.

503 Incidents at the New School, NYU, and Wesleyan University are reported in Claire Cohen and Orlando Mendiola, 'Students wake up to doors vandalized with swastikas at Kerrey Hall', *New School Free Press*, 12 November 2016; Laura Bult, 'Vandal wrote "Trump!" on door to prayer room used by New York University's Muslim student organization', *New York Daily News*, 10 November 2016; and Devonaire Ortiz and Jenny Davis, 'Wave of post-election hate crimes hits Wesleyan', *Wesleyan Argus*, 14 November 2016.

503 Post-election hostilities at Texas State University are the subject of Denise Cervantes, 'Pro-Trump flyers on Texas State campus call for torture of school officials', *University Star*, 10 November 2016; and Rick Jervis, 'Texas campus tense with incidents since Donald Trump's election', *USA Today*, 18 December 2016.

503 Verbal harassment of woman in Boston: Southern Poverty Law Center, 'Update: Incidents of hateful harassment since Election Day now number 701', 18 November 2016.

504 Racist shopper in Kalamazoo insults and spits at female salesperson: Miller and Werner-Winslow, op. cit.

504 'We believe all races should be separate': Maira Ansari, 'Neighbor mails man typed letter laced with hate', WAVE 3 News, 15 November 2016.

504 See Emily Masters and Robert Gavin, 'Black family's garage torched, painted with racist graffiti in Schodack, police say', Times Union, 16 May 2017.

504 See Aria Bendix, 'LeBron James responds to racist vandalism of his L.A. home', Atlantic, 31 May 2017.

504 See Sara Bernard, 'Princeton Professor cancels Seattle talk following deluge of racist threats', Seattle Weekly, 31 May 2017.

504 Vandalism of veteran's car: Samara Abramson, 'Local business helps family that had "Trump", "Go Home" keyed into car', Western Mass News, 21 November 2016.

504 See Tony Gicas, 'Clifton police investigate hate crime against Mexican business', The Record, 26 May 2017.

504 Indian American woman spit on by a stranger: Warikoo, op. cit.

504 Harassment of Asian student at petrol station: Miller and Werner-Winslow, op. cit.

504 For reports on the shooting of Srinivas Kuchibhotla and Alok Madasani, and Donald Trump's tardy response, see Tony Rizzo, et al., 'First-degree murder charge filed in possible hate crime shooting at Olathe's Austins bar', Kansas City Star, 23 February 2017; and AOL.com Editors, 'Trump condemns anti-Semitic threats and Kansas City attack in major speech to Congress', AOL, 28 February 2017.

505 See Sam Clancy, Jimmy Bernhard and Kiya Edwards, '180+ headstones damaged at Jewish cemetery in University City', KSDK, 21 February 2017; and Ian Simpson, 'Philadelphia Jewish cemetery desecrated by vandals', Reuters, 27 February 2017.

505 Sarasota assault: Kera Mashek, '75-year-old Sarasota man says he was attacked for being gay', WFTS, 16 November 2016.

505 Defacement of car in North Canton, Ohio: Miller and Werner-Winslow, op. cit.

505 Arson of gay pride flags in Rochester, New York: Gary Craig, 'Gay pride rainbow flags burned in Rochester', Democrat & Chronicle, 10 November 2016.

505 Hateful note in Burlington, Iowa: Elizabeth Meyer, 'Burlington minister finds hateful note left on his car', Hawk Eye, 11 November 2016.

505 For reports on attacks on LGBT centres, see Mary Emily O'Hara, 'LGBT community centers in Los Angeles, Milwaukee vandalized with slurs', NBC News, 11 February 2017; and Michael Cook, 'Attacks on equality from

Orlando to Asbury Park', *Huffington Post*, 6 March 2017; Kyle Hinchey, 'Shots fired at Equality Center first act of serious vandalism in 12 years at downtown site, director says', *Tulsa World*, 7 March 2017; and Jeff Taylor, 'Police arrest man for attack on DC's Casa Ruby community center', *LGBTQ Nation*, 14 March 2017.

505 See Michael Rulli, '8 trans women of color have been murdered in 2017', *Out*, 23 March 2017.

505 See Rocco Parascandola and Thomas Tracy, 'Anti-LGBT bigot turns Q train ride into nightmare for couple, leaves woman with concussion and broken eye socket', *New York Daily News*, 24 May 2017.

506 Letter to mosques: Kristine Guerra, ' "It's a sickness": Letters calling for genocide of Muslims sent to mosques across the country', *Washington Post*, 29 November 2016.

506 Verbal assault on New York City Uber driver: Kristine Guerra, ' "Trump is president . . . They'll deport you soon": Man filmed unloading on Muslim Uber driver', *Washington Post*, 21 November 2016.

506 Assault on Ethiopian cabbie in Grand Rapids: John Tunison, 'Cab driver describes beating from man yelling "Trump" ', *Michigan Live*, 18 November 2016.

506 Note on door of Sudanese American family: Miller and Werner-Winslow, op. cit.

506 Mosque arsons: Jim Malewitz, 'Investigators: Fire that ravaged Victoria mosque was arson', *Texas Tribune*, 8 February 2017; and Tony Marrero, 'Worshippers relocate after arson fire damages Thonotosassa mosque', *Tampa Bay Times*, 24 February 2017.

506 The shooting of Deep Rai is reported in Sandi Doughton, 'FBI aids in investigation into shooting of Sikh man in Kent', *Seattle Times*, 5 March 2017.

506 See Jim Ryan, '2 killed in stabbing on MAX train in Northeast Portland as man directs slurs at Muslim women, police say', *Oregonian*, 26 May 2017.

506 See Elliot Hannon, 'President of United States waits nearly three days to condemn racist Portland murders', *Slate*, 29 May 2017.

506 NAACP, 'Inadequacy of President Trump and federal responses to hate crimes', press release, 6 March 2017.

506 During a conference with reporters, Trump's press secretary disavowed any connection between the shooting of two Indian software engineers and the president's anti-immigrant rhetoric; see Sean Spicer, 'Press gaggle by Press Secretary Sean Spicer, 2/24/2017', White House Office of the Press Secretary, 24 February 2017.

507 For examples of Donald Trump's collective references to ethnic groups, see 'Trump says he has good relationship with "the blacks" ', CNN, 14 April 2011; Associated Press, 'Trump at Mexico border: "Hispanics are going to love Trump" ', *Chicago Sun Times*, 23 July 2015; Jeremy Diamond, 'Donald Trump: Ban all Muslim travel to U.S.', CNN, 8 December 2015; Nicholas

Riccardi, 'Nevada becomes one of Trump's big hopes for swing state win', Associated Press, 27 August 2016; and Mark Abadi, ' "The blacks", "the gays", "the Muslims" – linguists explain one of Donald Trump's most unusual speech tics', *Business Insider*, 17 October 2016.

507 Donald Trump's disparagement of blacks is documented in John O'Donnell, *Trumped!* (1991), cited by David Emery, 'Race evasions', *Snopes*, 8 August 2016.

507 For discussion of Trump's false witness to 'cheering' at the attack on the World Trade Center, see Glenn Kessler, 'Trump's outrageous claim that "thousands" of New Jersey Muslims celebrated the 9/11 attacks', *Washington Post*, 22 November 2015.

507 Donald Trump's mother's immigration status is confirmed in Mary Pilon, 'Donald Trump's immigrant mother', *New Yorker*, 24 June 2016.

507 Donald Trump referred to illegal immigration as a 'killing machine' in a tweet: Donald J. Trump, 'Tweet (immigration killing machine)', *Twitter*, tweet no. 630906211790102528, 10 August 2015.

507 Donald Trump referred to 'merit, skill, and proficiency' as criteria for successful immigrants; see Philip Bump, 'Here's what Donald Trump said in his big immigration speech, annotated', *Washington Post*, 31 August 2016.

508 For background on Trump's originally-proposed ban on travel from seven Muslim-majority countries, see Steve Almasy and Darran Simon, 'A timeline of President Trump's travel bans', CNN, 10 February 2017. Protests against the ban are chronicled in Lauren Gambino, et al., 'Thousands protest against Trump travel ban in cities and airports nationwide', *Guardian*, 29 January 2017.

508 For the quote from Judge Robert Gregory, see Michael Bobelian, 'In latest rebuke, an appellate court minces no words in condemning Trump's travel ban', *Forbes*, 25 May 2017.

508 For details on the U.S. Supreme Court's approval of a modified, temporary ban, and on the scope of its pending review of presidential authority to enact such a ban, see Robert Barnes, 'Supreme Court allows limited version of Trump's travel ban to take effect, will consider case in fall', *Washington Post*, 26 June 2017.

508 For a comprehensive catalogue of insults lobbed by Donald Trump on Twitter, see Jasmine C. Lee and Kevin Quealy, 'The 282 people, places and things Donald Trump has insulted on Twitter: A complete list', *New York Times*, 23 October 2016.

508 The quote by George Melloan comes from George Melloan, 'Donald Trump, meet Herbert Hoover', *Wall Street Journal*, 3 November 2015.

509 The quote by Thomas Wright comes from Thomas Wright, 'Trump's 19th century foreign policy', *Politico*, 20 January 2016.

509 The history of Donald Trump's foreign policy proposals, and of the 'America First' slogan, are discussed in Thomas Wright, ibid; Rick Hampson, 'Donald Trump says "America First" like isolationists before World War II',

USA Today, 11 April 2016; and Michael Biesecker, 'Trump's "America First" echoes old isolationist rallying cry', Associated Press, 29 June 2016.

509 Donald Trump declared that 'Americanism, not globalism, will be our credo' in his speech to the Republican National Convention; see NPR staff, 'Fact check: Donald Trump's Republican convention speech annotation', National Public Radio, 21 July 2016.

509 Leo Tolstoy, *Anna Karenina*, tr. Richard Peaver and Larissa Volokhonsky (2004): part 7, chapter 24.

509 'We were the big bully': Maggie Haberman and David E. Sanger, 'Transcript: Donald Trump expounds on his foreign policy views', *New York Times*, 26 March 2016. 'When the students poured into Tiananmen Square': Glenn Plaskin, 'Playboy interview: Donald Trump', *Playboy*, March 1990, cited in Thomas Wright, 'The 2016 presidential campaign and the crisis of U.S. foreign policy', Lowy Institute for International Policy, 10 October 2016.

509 Donald Trump's views on torture are discussed in Jenna Johnson, 'Trump says "torture works", backs waterboarding and "much worse"', *Washington Post*, 17 February 2016. Trump bemoaned the inconvenience of the Geneva Conventions in 'Exclusive interview with Donald Trump', *Anderson Cooper 360°*, CNN, 9 March 2016.

510 'Terrorism must be stopped in its tracks': Donald J. Trump, 'Remarks by President Trump at NATO unveiling of the Article 5 and Berlin Wall Memorials, Brussels, Belgium', The White House Office of the Press Secretary, 25 May 2017.

510 Donald Trump's distortion of Sadiq Khan's advice to Londoners is discussed in James Masters and Karl de Vries, 'Trump criticized for tweet about London mayor after attack', CNN, 5 June 2017.

511 See Andrew Buncombe, 'London attack: Sadiq Khan hits back at Donald Trump and accuses him of "trying to divide communities"', *Independent*, 5 June 2017.

511 Cheryl Tan, Facebook post, 4 June 2017. Her post in full: 'On BBC News tonight, in the segment where they discuss world leaders' reactions to the London attack, they run through official responses from heads of Canada, Germany, Belgium, Australia, France, etc. U.S.A.? Trump's manipulative, inflammatory & self-serving Tweets are mentioned at the very end as the unbelievably ridiculous punchline – capped with London mayor Sadiq Khan saying he has more important things to do than respond to Trump's Tweets at this time. This is the U.S. in the world now, people – the ridiculous punchline.'

511 The quote from Angela Merkel comes from Amy Davidson, 'Angela Merkel and the insult of Trump's Paris climate-accord withdrawal', *New Yorker*, 1 June 2017.

512 The concept of the 'filter bubble; was pioneered by Eli Pariser; see Eli Pariser, *The Filter Bubble: What the Internet Is Hiding from You* (2011). Facebook's

curation of its news feed is discussed in Issie Lapowsky, 'Of course Facebook is biased; that's how tech works today', *Wired*, 11 May 2016; and Elle Hunt, 'Facebook to change trending topics after investigation into bias claims', *Guardian*, 23 May 2016.

513 'Mending Wall' can be found on page 11 of Robert Frost, *North of Boston* (1914).

513 Donald Trump promised to build a wall at the Mexican border in his announcement of his candidacy; see Donald J. Trump, 'Full text: Donald Trump announces a presidential bid', *Washington Post*, 16 June 2015.

513 See Matt Broomfield, 'Calais jungle wall is completed two months after all the refugees were driven out', *Independent*, 13 December 2016.

513 See Robbie Meredith, 'Northern Ireland interfaces: More residents want peace walls to stay', BBC News, 15 December 2015.

513 Hungary's border wall against refugees is described in Lizzie Dearden, 'Hungary planning "massive" new border fence to keep out refugees as PM vows to "hold them back by force"', *Independent*, 27 August 2016.

514 See Peter Beaumont, 'Israel builds wall deep underground to thwart Hamas tunnels', *Guardian*, 8 September 2016.

514 Hasan Agili's story is told at greater length in Paul P. Murphy and Samantha Guff, 'The Libyan refugee who made it into the U.S. before the ban', CNN, 3 February 2017.

516 Damir Arsenijević, personal communication.

517 See Mark Lilla, 'The end of identity liberalism', *New York Times*, 18 November 2016.

517 See Katherine Franke, 'Making white supremacy respectable. Again', *Los Angeles Review of Books*, 21 November 2016.

518 'I am a part of all that I have met' is line 18 of Alfred, Lord Tennyson's poem 'Ulysses'; the poem can be found on page 40 of *The Poetical Works of Alfred, Lord Tennyson* (1895).

519 Sebastian Haffner, *Defying Hitler: A Memoir* (2003). From pages 89–90: 'It was strange to observe how the behavior of each side reinforced that of the other: the savage impudence that gradually made it possible for the unpleasant little apostle of hate to assume the proportions of a demon; the bafflement of his tamers, who always realized just too late exactly what it was he was up to—namely, when he capped it with something even more outrageous and monstrous; then, also, the hypnotic trance into which his public fell, succumbing with less and less resistance to the glamour of depravity and the ecstasy of evil.'

Bibliography

Abadi, Mark. '"The blacks", "the gays", "the Muslims" – linguists explain one of Donald Trump's most unusual speech tics.' *Business Insider*, 17 October 2016.

Abrahams, Fred. 'In his first interview, Saif al-Islam says he has not been given access to a lawyer.' *Daily Beast*, 30 December 2012.

Abramson, Samara. 'Local business helps family that had "Trump", "Go Home" keyed into car.' *Western Mass News*, 21 November 2016.

Adams, Susan. 'Treasure islands: Inside a Japanese billionaire's art archipelago.' *Forbes*, 29 July 2015.

Adewunmi, Bim. 'Kimberlé Crenshaw on intersectionality.' *New Statesman*, 2 April 2014.

Agence France-Presse. 'Muslim groups sue Myanmar president for Rohingya "genocide."' *Guardian*, 5 October 2015.

——. 'Rwanda opposition says can't find lawyer for Kagame 3rd term case – one said "God was against it".' *Mail & Guardian*, 8 July 2015.

——. 'U.S. opposes third term for Rwanda's Kagame: Diplomat.' *Guardian* (Nigeria), 5 June 2015.

——. 'E.U. flag burned as tens of thousands join Warsaw national demo.' *Telegraph*, 12 November 2015.

——. '"Infidel!" Ottoman slur raises hackles in Turkey.' *Tribune* (Pakistan), 15 December 2016.

'AG Healey's hate crime hotline received 400 calls in first week.' WBUR, 21 November 2016.

Agyman, Gyasiwaa. '"Mahama will soon mortgage Ghana to anti-Christ."' Adom Online, 8 January 2016.

Ai Weiwei. 'Ai Weiwei: China's art world does not exist.' *Guardian*, 10 September 2012.

Akinsha, Konstantin. 'Art in Russia: Art under attack.' ARTnews, 1 October 2009.

Alston, Philip. 'Report of the Special Rapporteur on extrajudicial, summary or arbitrary executions: Follow-up to country recommendations – Brazil.' United Nations Human Rights Council, 28 May 2010.

Allgemeiner staff. 'Polish anti-refugee demonstrators burn effigies of Orthodox Jews at Wroclaw protest.' *Allgemeiner Zeitung*, 18 November 2015.

Almasy, Steve, and Darran Simon. 'A timeline of President Trump's travel bans.' CNN, 10 February 2017.

Alter, Alexandra. 'China's publishers court America as its authors scorn censorship.' *New York Times*, 28 May 2015.

American Consul Rio de Janeiro. 'Counter-insurgency doctrine comes to Rio's favelas.' 30 September 2009.

Amey, Katie. 'Government-issued housing, super-highways that span 20 lanes but not a soul in sight: Inside Myanmar's haunting capital city.' *Daily Mail*, 18 April 2015.

Amnesty International. 'Caught between state censorship and self-censorship: Prosecution and intimidation of media workers in Myanmar.' Amnesty International, 16 June 2015.

———. 'State of Libya.' In 'The state of the world's human rights.' Amnesty International, 11 March 2015.

Amos, Howard. 'Russian publisher prints books about Putin under names of western authors.' *Guardian*, 11 August 2015.

Anistia Internacional Brasil. 'You killed my son: Homicides by military police in the city of Rio de Janeiro.' Amnesty International, 3 August 2015.

Annese, John. 'Ex-substitute teacher slapped with hate crime charges after allegedly ripping hijab off 8-year-old Bronx student.' *New York Daily News*, 25 May 2017.

Ansari, Maira. 'Neighbor mails man typed letter laced with hate.' WAVE 3 News, 15 November 2016.

'Anti Muslim monk Wira thu talk about Meiktila before riot.' YouTube, 24 March 2013. http://youtube.com/watch?v=N7irUgGsFYw.

Antunes, Anderson. 'When samba meets African dictators: The ugly side of Rio de Janeiro's Carnival.' Forbes, 19 February 2015.

Antwi-Otoo, Kweku. 'Gay activist Andrew Solomon will be a pastor one day: Moses Foh-Amoaning'. *Atinka 104.7 FM Online*, 13 July 2015.

AOL.com Editors. 'Trump condemns anti-Semitic threats and Kansas City attack in major speech to Congress.' AOL, 28 February 2017.

Arendt, Laurie. 'A toast to her brother', *Ozaukee Press*, 13 September 2007.

Artavia, David. 'Cameroon's "gay problem."' *Advocate*, 7 July 2013.

Ashdown, Nick. 'Public Muslims, secret Jews: A Turkish sect faces crackdown.' *Forward*, 5 August 2016.

Asia Foundation. 'The Asia Foundation donates books to parliamentary library in Burma.' Asia Foundation, 24 October 2012.

Aslam, Senem. 'Different faces of Turkish Islamic nationalism.' *Washington Post*, 20 February 2015.

Associated Press. 'Assault on U.S. consulate in Benghazi leaves 4 dead, including U.S. Ambassador J. Christopher Stevens.' CBS News, 12 September 2012.

———. 'Vinegar contaminated with antifreeze kills Chinese Muslims at Ramadan meal.' *Guardian*, 22 August 2011.

———. 'Women journalists targeted in Afghanistan.' NBC News, 26 June 2007.

———. 'Erdoğan comments on historic treaty irk opposition, Greece.' *Washington Post*, 30 September 2016.

———. 'Trump at Mexico border: "Hispanics are going to love Trump." ' *Chicago Sun Times*, 23 July 2015.

Aung San Suu Kyi. 'Please use your liberty to promote ours.' *New York Times*, 4 February 1997.

Aung San Suu Kyi and Alan Clements. *The Voice of Hope: Conversations with Alan Clements*. New York: Seven Stories Press, 2008.

Aung-Thwin, Michael, and Maitrii Aung-Thwin. *A History of Myanmar since Ancient Times*. Chicago: University of Chicago, 2012.

Aung Zaw. 'The SPDC's diplomatic gambit.' *Irrawaddy*, February 1999.

Australian Associated Press. 'Temperature affects fungi in Antarctica.' Special Broadcasting Service, 28 September 2015.

Aye Nyein Win. 'Right-hand drives to remain on the roads.' *Myanmar Times*, 23 October 2015.

'Baird bears gifts.' *Mizzima*, 9 March 2012.

Barber, Elizabeth. ' "Gutter oil" scandal raises food-safety fears once again in greater China.' *Time*, 8 September 2014.

Barchfield, Jenny. 'Transgenders break into Brazil's modeling sector.' CNS News, 6 December 2012.

Barnes, Robert. 'Supreme Court allows limited version of Trump's travel ban to take effect, will consider case in fall.' *Washington Post*, 26 June 2017.

Bass, Katy Glenn, and Joey Lee. 'Silenced voices, threatened lives: The impact of Nigeria's LGBTI law on Freedom of Expression.' PEN American Center, 29 June 2015.

Beam, Christopher. 'Beyond Ai Weiwei: How China's artists handle politics (or avoid them).' *New Yorker*, 27 March 2015.

Beaumont, Peter. 'Israel builds wall deep underground to thwart Hamas tunnels.' *Guardian*, 8 September 2016.

Becker, Kathrin. 'In memoriam Timur Novikov.' *Art Margins*, 23 May 2002.

Beech, Hannah. 'The face of Buddhist terror.' *Time*, 1 July 2013.

Bendix, Aria. 'LeBron James responds to racist vandalism of his L.A. home.' *Atlantic*, 31 May 2017.

Benson, Todd. 'U.N. watchdog denounces police killings in Brazil.' Reuters, 15 September 2008.

Bernard, Sara. 'Princeton Professor cancels Seattle talk following deluge of racist threats.' *Seattle Weekly*, 31 May 2017.

Bevins, Vincent. 'Coming "tsunami"? In Brazil, calls for reform in wake of FIFA scandals.' *Los Angeles Times*, 12 June 2015.

Biesecker, Michael. 'Trump's "America First" echoes old isolationist rallying cry.' Associated Press, 29 June 2016.

Bjerregaard, Peter, and Christina Viskum Lytken Larsen. 'Time trend by region of suicides and suicidal thoughts among Greenland Inuit.' *International Journal of Circumpolar Health* 74 (19 February 2015): 26053.

Black, Michael, and Roland Fields. 'Virtual gambling in Myanmar's drug country.' *Asia Times*, 26 August 2006.

'Blackout hits Taipei's Palace Museum Thursday afternoon.' *Want China Times*, 10 July 2015.

Block, Melissa. 'Skin color still plays big role in ethnically diverse Brazil.' *All Things Considered*, National Public Radio, 19 September 2013.

Bobelian, Michael. 'In latest rebuke, an appellate court minces no words in condemning Trump's travel ban.' *Forbes*, 25 May 2017.

Boehler, Patrick. 'Bad eggs: Another fake-food scandal rocks China.' *Time*, 6 November 2012.

———. 'Police seize chicken feet in storage since 1967, smuggled from Vietnam.' *South China Morning Post*, 8 July 2013.

Boesveld, Sarah. 'Stealing beauty: A look at the tattooed faces of Burma's Chin province.' *National Post*, 15 July 2011.

Boswell, James. *Boswell's Life of Johnson*. Edited by George Birkbeck Hill. Oxford: Clarendon Press, 1887.

Bowater, Donna. 'Olympics bus route to displace 900 families from Rio favela.' *Al Jazeera*, 1 September 2014.

———. 'Rio's police-occupied slums see an increase in drug-related violence.' *Washington Post*, 19 February 2014.

Bradsher, Keith. 'Rare glimpses of China's long-hidden treasures.' *New York Times*, 28 December 2006.

Branigan, Tania. 'Chinese treasures to be reunited in Taiwan.' *Guardian*, 19 February 2009.

———. 'It's goodbye Lenin, hello dinosaur as fossils head to Mongolia museum.' *Guardian*, 27 January 2013.

———. 'Mongolia declares state of emergency as riots kill five.' *Guardian*, 2 July 2008.

Bredderman, Will. 'NYPD reports "huge spike" in hate crimes since Donald Trump's election.' *Observer*, 5 December 2016.

Bremmer, Ian. 'These 5 facts explain Russia's economic decline.' *Time*, 14 August 2015.

British Broadcasting Corporation. 'Aung San Suu Kyi hails Shwe Mann as an "ally."' BBC News, 18 August 2015.

———. 'Brazil corruption: Rio police arrested over "extortion racket."' BBC News, 16 September 2014.

———. 'Burma's 1988 protests.' BBC News, 25 September 2007.

———. 'Cameroon "gay sex" men acquitted.' BBC News, 7 January 2013.

———. 'Chernobyl: 20 years on.' BBC News, 12 June 2007.

———. 'Chinese police arrest 110 for selling "contaminated pork."' BBC News, 12 January 2015.

———. 'Egypt cuts "gay wedding video" jail terms.' BBC News, 27 December 2014.

———. 'Greenland's Jakobshavn Glacier sheds big ice chunk.' BBC News, 24 August 2015.

———. 'Iranian hanged after verdict stay.' BBC News, 6 December 2007.

———. 'Moscow protest: Thousands rally against Vladimir Putin.' BBC News, 25 December 2011.

———. 'Myanmar court "must investigate Aung Kyaw Naing death."' BBC News, 3 December 2014.

———. 'Paul Kagame's third term: Rwanda referendum on 18 December.' BBC News, 9 December 2015.

———. 'Profiles of Russia's 2012 presidential election candidates.' BBC News, 1 March 2012.

———. 'Report: One fifth of China's soil contaminated.' BBC News, 18 April 2014.

———. 'Rio de Janeiro's favelas reflected through art.' BBC News, 29 May 2011.

———. 'Self-rule introduced in Greenland.' BBC News, 21 June 2009.

———. 'Taiwan rejects "looted" China art.' BBC News, 7 October 2009.

Bronson, Po, and Ashley Merryman. 'Even babies discriminate: A NurtureShock excerpt.' Newsweek, 4 September 2009.

Broomfield, Matt. 'Calais jungle wall is completed two months after all the refugees were driven out.' Independent, 13 December 2016.

Brownmiller, Susan. Against Our Will: Men, Women and Rape. New York: Simon & Schuster, 1975.

Buckley, Sarah. 'Who are Burma's monks?' BBC News, 26 September 2007.

Bult, Laura. 'Vandal wrote "Trump!" on door to prayer room used by New York University's Muslim student organization.' New York Daily News, 10 November 2016.

Bump, Philip. 'Here's what Donald Trump said in his big immigration speech, annotated.' Washington Post, 31 August 2016.

Buncombe, Andrew. 'India's gay community scrambling after court decision recriminalises homosexuality.' Independent, 26 February 2014.

———. 'London attack: Sadiq Khan hits back at Donald Trump and accuses him of "trying to divide communities".' Independent, 5 June 2017.

Burkitt, Laurie. 'Selling health food to China.' Wall Street Journal, 13 December 2010.

Byrnes, Mark. 'A brief history of Brazil's most treasured World Cup stadium.' Citylab, 16 June 2014.

Cai Muyuan. 'Eat green, think greener.' *China Daily Europe*, 5 June 2015.

Calin, Dorina. 'Decizie UNATC: Criticul de film Andrei Rus nu va fi dat afară din instituţie, dar va fi sancţionat.' *Mediafax*, 2 July 2015.

Campbell, Charlie. 'Arakan strife poses Suu Kyi political problem.' *Irrawaddy*, 13 July 2012.

Canzian, Fernando. 'É bom, mas é ruim (It's good, but it's bad).' *Folha*, 13 July 2009.

Carlson, Jen. 'Racist teacher who threatened student with deportation put on "Do Not Hire" list.' *LAist*, 14 November 2016.

Carpenter, Frances. *Tales of a Korean Grandmother*. St. Louis, MO: Turtleback Books, 1989.

Caryl, Christian. 'Putin: During and after Sochi.' *New York Review of Books*, 3 April 2014.

———. 'The young and the restless.' *Foreign Policy*, 17 February 2014.

Casey, Michael. 'Why the cyclone in Myanmar was so deadly.' *National Geographic News*, 8 May 2008.

Cervantes, Denise. 'Pro-Trump flyers on Texas State campus call for torture of school officials.' *University Star*, 10 November 2016.

Cha, Frances. 'Japanese eel becomes latest "endangered food."' *CNN Travel*, 5 February 2013.

Chang, Jack. 'Chinese art colony's free-speech illusion shatters.' *Asahi Shumbun*, 17 October 2014.

Chao, Loretta. 'Rio faces surge of post-World Cup violence in slums.' *Wall Street Journal*, 22 July 2014.

'Charges dropped against 23 journalists.' *Nation* (Bangkok), 25 August 2014.

Chekhov, Anton. *The Three Sisters: A Play by Anton Chekhov Adapted by David Mamet*. New York: Samuel French, 1992.

Chen Te-Ping. 'In latest mash-up, China puts spotlight on spuds.' *Wall Street Journal*, 17 August 2015.

Clancy, Sam, Jimmy Bernhard and Kiya Edwards. '180+ headstones damaged at Jewish cemetery in University City.' KSDK, 21 February 2017.

Coates, Eliane. 'Sectarian violence involving Rohingya in Myanmar: Historical roots and modern triggers.' Middle East Institute, 4 August 2014.

Coelho, Janet Tappin. 'Brazil's "peace police" turn five. Are Rio's favelas safer?' *Christian Science Monitor*, 19 December 2013.

Cohen, Andrew. 'Off the page: Li Xianting.' *Art Asia Pacific* 71, November/December 2010.

Cohen, Claire, and Orlando Mendiola. 'Students wake up to doors vandalized with swastikas at Kerrey Hall.' *New School Free Press*, 12 November 2016.

Collins, Sean. 'City's theater re-opens in style.' *Rio Times*, 8 June 2010.

Collinson, Stephen. 'Marathon Benghazi hearing leaves Hillary Clinton largely unscathed.' *CNN Politics*, 23 October 2015.

Conwill, William Louis. 'N'deup and mental health: Implications for treating Senegalese immigrants in the U.S.' *International Journal for the Advancement of Counselling* 32, no. 3 (September 2010): 202–13.

Cook, Michael. 'Attacks on equality from Orlando to Asbury Park.' *Huffington Post*, 6 March 2017.

Cook, Steven. 'How Erdoğan made Turkey authoritarian again.' *Atlantic*, 21 July 2016.

Cooper, Tanya. 'License to harm: Violence and harassment against LGBT people and activists in Russia.' Human Rights Watch, 15 December 2014.

Cooperman, Alan, Phillip Connor and Erin O'Connell. 'Russians return to religion but not to church.' Pew Research Center, 10 February 2014.

Corben, Ron. 'Burmese refugees in Thailand long to return home.' *Deutsche Welle*, 13 December 2011.

Corcoran, Hannah, and Kevin Smith. 'Hate crime, England and Wales, 2015/6.' Home Office, 13 October 2016.

Costello, Maureen. 'The Trump effect: The impact of the presidential campaign on our nation's schools.' Southern Poverty Law Center, 13 April 2016.

Craig, Gary. 'Gay pride rainbow flags burned in Rochester.' *Democrat & Chronicle*, 10 November 2016.

Crenshaw, Kimberlé. 'Demarginalizing the intersection of race and sex.' *University of Chicago Legal Forum* 1989, no. 1 (1989): article 8.

Crichton-Miller, Emma. 'Young Russian curators tap into country's recent art history.' *Financial Times*, 27 June 2014.

Crow, Kelly. 'Moscow's contemporary art movement.' *Wall Street Journal*, 4 June 2015.

Curtis, Tine, and Peter Bjerregaard. *Health Research in Greenland*. Copenhagen: Danish Institute for Clinical Epidemiology, 1995.

Dahas, Nashla. 'Luis Eduardo Soares.' *Revista de Historia*, 11 January 2014.

Damptey, Daniel Danquah. 'Investigate Mills' death.' *GhanaWeb*, 29 July 2015.

Danforth, Nick. 'Turkey's new maps are reclaiming the Ottoman Empire.' *Foreign Policy*, 23 October 2016.

Darnton, Robert. 'Talking about Brazil with Lilia Schwarcz.' *New York Review of Books*, 17 August 2010.

Davidson, Amy. 'Angela Merkel and the insult of Trump's Paris climate-accord withdrawal.' *New Yorker*, 1 June 2017.

Davies, Wyre. 'Brazil: Protesters in Rio clash with police over dancer's death.' BBC News, 23 April 2014.

Dearden, Lizzie. 'Hungary planning "massive" new border fence to keep out refugees as PM vows to "hold them back by force".' *Independent*, 27 August 2016.

———. 'Turkey slides towards authoritarian rule as commission approves plan to increase powers for President Erdoğan.' *Independent*, 30 December 2016.

de Bruyn, Maria. *Violence, Pregnancy and Abortion: Issues of Women's Rights and Public Health*. 2nd ed. Chapel Hill, NC: Ipas, 2003.

Degirmen, Burcu, and Alperen Atik. 'Turkey: Authoritarianism and academic "closure".' *Open Democracy*, 14 February 2017.

Delgado, Fernando Ribeiro. 'Lethal force: Police violence and public security in Rio de Janeiro and São Paulo.' Human Rights Watch, 8 December 2009.

DelReal, Jose. 'Donald Trump won't rule out warrantless searches, ID cards for American Muslims.' *Washington Post*, 19 November 2015.

De Main, Bill. 'The disputed history of the Tarzan yell.' *Mental Floss*, 22 August 2012.

Demick, Barbara. 'In China, what you eat tells who you are.' *Los Angeles Times*, 16 September 2011.

Demirjian, Karoun. 'Russian youths find politics as their pop icons face pressure.' *Washington Post*, 2 December 2014.

Des Forges, Alison Liebhafsky. *'Leave None to Tell the Story': Genocide in Rwanda.* New York: Human Rights Watch, 1999.

Dettmer, Jamie. 'The ISIS hug of death for gays.' *Daily Beast*, 24 April 2015.

de Vivo, Marcelo. 'Experience the best of Russian nightlife.' *Pravda*, 10 October 2013.

de Vos, Connie. 'Absolute spatial deixis and proto-toponyms in Kata Kolok.' *NUSA: Linguistic Studies of Languages in and around Indonesia* 56 (2014): 3–26.

———. 'A signers' village in Bali, Indonesia.' *Minpaku Anthropology News*, 2011.

de Vos, Connie, and N. Palfreyman. 'Deaf around the world: The impact of language.' *Journal of Linguistics* 48, no. 3 (November 2012): 731–35.

De Young, Karen. 'Ban on U.S. investment in Burma is lifted.' *Washington Post*, 11 July 2012.

Diamond, Jeremy. 'Donald Trump: Ban all Muslim travel to U.S.' CNN, 8 December 2015.

Dickey, Lisa. 'Moscow: Rap star MC Pavlov.' Russian Chronicles, *Washington Post*, 2 November 2005.

'Die economist André Urani.' *O Globo*, 14 December 2011.

Dilawar, Arvind. 'Teatime with Big Brother: Chinese artist Wu Yuren on life under surveillance.' *Vice*, 15 June 2015.

Dolcy, Marion. 'Russian art anarchists explain themselves.' *Don't Panic*, 20 December 2010.

Donadio, Rachel. 'Museum director at Hermitage hopes for thaw in relations with West.' *New York Times*, 14 May 2015.

Doughton, Sandi. 'FBI aids in investigation into shooting of Sikh man in Kent.' *Seattle Times*, 5 March 2017.

Douglas, Bruce. 'Brazil officials evict families from homes ahead of 2016 Olympic Games.' *Guardian*, 28 October 2015.

Downie, Andrew. 'Rio finally makes headway against its drug gangs.' *Time*, 26 November 2010.

Dudley, Steven. 'Deadly force: Security and insecurity in Rio.' North American Congress on Latin America, November 1998.

Dugan, Emily. 'A racist mob chanting "Ku Klux Klan" targeted a Turkish family in North London.' *BuzzFeed News*, 23 January 2017.

Durao, Carlos, Marcos Machado and Eduardo Daruge Jr. 'Death in the "microwave oven": A form of execution by carbonisation.' *Forensic Science International* 253 (August 2015): e1–3.

Ebbighausen, Rodion. 'Myanmar: The uprising of 1988.' *Deutsche Welle*, 8 August 2013.

Emery, David. 'Race evasions.' *Snopes*, 8 August 2016.

Euro-Burma Office. 'The Rohingyas: Bengali Muslims or Arakan Rohingyas?' EBO Briefing Paper No. 2, Euro-Burma Office, 2009.

European Commission against Racism and Intolerance. 'ECRI report on Turkey (fifth monitoring cycle).' Council of Europe, 4 October 2016.

'Exclusive interview with Donald Trump.' *Anderson Cooper 360°*, CNN, 9 March 2016.

Feast, Lincoln. 'Strong quake hits near Solomon Islands; tsunami warning cancelled.' Reuters, 12 April 2014.

Feltham, John. *The English Enchiridion*. Bath: R. Crutwell, 1799.

Ferrie, Jared. 'Myanmar president enacts law allowing referendum on disputed constitution.' Reuters, 12 February 2015.

———. 'SIM sales soar as Myanmar races to catch up in telecoms.' Reuters, 6 May 2015.

Fitzgerald, Mary. 'Libyan renegade general Khalifa Haftar claims he is winning his war.' *Guardian*, 24 June 2014.

'Five injured in Mandalay unrest, damage limited.' *Irrawaddy*, 2 July 2014.

Florida, Richard. 'Gun violence in U.S. cities compared to the deadliest nations in the world.' *Citylab*, 22 January 2013.

Flueckiger, Lisa. 'Brazil's federal police to investigate after FIFA scandal.' *Rio Times*, 29 May 2015.

Forbes, Alexander. 'Manifesta 10 succeeds despite controversy.' *Artnet News*, 27 June 2014.

Foster, Peter. 'Top 10 Chinese food scandals.' *Daily Telegraph*, 27 April 2011.

Frank, Marc. 'Cuba's atheist Castro brothers open doors to Church and popes.' Reuters, 7 September 2015.

Franke, Katherine. 'Making white supremacy respectable. Again.' *Los Angeles Review of Books*, 21 November 2016.

Freedom House. 'Nations in transit 2015: Russia.' Freedom House, 2015.

Freedom to Marry. 'The freedom to marry internationally.' Freedom to Marry, 2015.

Freeman, Joe. 'Myanmar's Jewish vote.' *Tablet*, 9 November 2015.

French, Howard. 'Kagame's hidden war in the Congo.' *New York Review of Books*, 24 September 2009.

Frost, Robert. *North of Boston*. New York: Henry Holt, 1914.

Fuller, Thomas. 'Back to a Burmese prison by choice.' *New York Times*, 6 December 2014.

———. 'Conservatives in Myanmar force out leader of ruling party.' *New York Times*, 13 August 2015.

———. 'Extremism rises among Myanmar Buddhists.' *New York Times*, 20 June 2013.

———. 'Myanmar's leader backs change to constitution.' *New York Times*, 2 January 2014.

———. 'Myanmar's military uses political force to block constitutional changes.' *New York Times*, 15 June 2015.

Fullerton, Jamie. 'Chinese artist who posted funny image of President Xi Jinping facing five years in prison as authorities crackdown [sic] on dissent in the arts.' *Independent*, 28 May 2015.

Furbank, P. N., and F. J. H. Haskell. 'E. M. Forster: The art of fiction no. 1.'*Paris Review*, Spring 1953.

Gabeira, Fernando. *O Que É Isso, Companheiro?* Rio de Janeiro: Editora Codecri, 1979.

Gaffney, Christopher. 'Global parties, galactic hangovers: Brazil's mega event dystopia.' *Los Angeles Review of Books*, 1 October 2014.

Gambino, Lauren, et al. 'Thousands protest against Trump travel ban in cities and airports nationwide.' *Guardian*, 29 January 2017.

Garver, Rob. 'Putin lets criminals bring money back to Russia.' *Fiscal Times*, 11 June 2015.

Geertz, Hildred, and Clifford Geertz. *Kinship in Bali*. Chicago: University of Chicago Press, 1975.

George, Jason. 'The suicide capital of the world.' *Slate*, 9 October 2009.

Gera, Vanessa. 'Right-wing Polish leader Kaczynski says migrants carry diseases to Europe.' *U.S. News & World Report*, 14 October 2015.

Gibson, Suzy. 'Woman kicked pregnant 14-year-old schoolgirl in head during racist attack.' *Leicester Mercury*, 17 December 2016.

Gicas, Tony. 'Clifton police investigate hate crime against Mexican business.' *The Record*, 26 May 2017.

Global Campaign for Rwandan Human Rights. 'Crimes and repression vs. development in Rwanda: President Paul Kagame's many shadows.' Africa Faith & Justice Network, 13 July 2015.

Global Justice Center. The Right to an Abortion for Girls and Women Raped in Armed Conflict. New York: Global Justice Center, 2011.

Global Legal Research Directorate. 'Laws on homosexuality in African nations.' U.S. Library of Congress, 9 June 2015.

Golluoglu, Esmer. 'Aung San Suu Kyi hails "new era" for Burma after landslide victory.' *Guardian*, 2 April 2012.

Goncharova, Masha. 'Cosmoscow: A fair for the Russian art collector.' *New York Times*, 17 September 2015.

Gorbachev, Aleksandr. 'Meet Boris Grebenshchikov, the Soviet Bob Dylan.' *Newsweek*, 25 May 2015.

Gourevitch, Philip. *We Wish to Inform You That Tomorrow We Will Be Killed with Our Families: Stories from Rwanda*. New York: Picador, 1999.

Gowen, Annie. 'Hard-line Buddhist monks threaten Burma's hopes for democracy.' *Washington Post*, 5 November 2015.

Graham-Harrison, Emma. 'Afghan artist dons armour to counter men's street harassment.' *Guardian*, 12 March 2015.

Gray, Denis. 'The remaining veterans of China's "lost army" cling to old life styles in Thailand.' *Los Angeles Times*, 7 June 1987.

Green, Penny, Thomas MacManus and Alicia de la Cour Venning. 'Countdown to annihilation: Genocide in Myanmar.' International State Crime Initiative, 2015.

'Greenland powers up fifth hydroelectric plant.' *Arctic Journal*, 6 September 2013.

Greig, Geordie. 'My big fab gay wedding.' *Tatler*, October 2007.

Grierson, Jamie, and Lin Jenkins. 'Croydon "hate crime": three more held in hunt for teenager's attackers.' *Guardian*, 2 April 2017.

Grillo, Cristina. 'Brasil quer ser chamado de moreno e só 39% se autodefinem como brancos.' *Folha*, 25 June 1995.

Grubel, James. 'Tsunami kills at least five in Solomons after big Pacific quake.' Reuters, 6 February 2013.

Guerra, Kristine. ' "It's a sickness": Letters calling for genocide of Muslims sent to mosques across the country.' *Washington Post*, 29 November 2016.

———. ' "Trump is president . . . They'll deport you soon": Man filmed unloading on Muslim Uber driver.' *Washington Post*, 21, November 2016.

Guibert, Nathalie, Yves-Michel Riols and Hélène Sallon. 'Libya's Tripoli and Tobruk dilemma no nearer to resolution.' *Guardian*, 27 January 2015.

Haberman, Maggie, and David E. Sanger. 'Transcript: Donald Trump expounds on his foreign policy views.' *New York Times*, 26 March 2016.

Haffner, Sebastian. *Defying Hitler: A Memoir*. New York: Macmillan, 2003.

Hamilton, Lindsey. 'Dundee shopkeeper "still feels worried at work" after racist attack.' *Evening Telegraph*, 6 April 2017.

Hagan, Maria. 'The 10 richest Russians in 2014.' *Richest*, 10 October 2014.

Hail, Rob. 'Madame Nuon Phaly is gone.' *Out of the Blog*, 27 November 2012.

Hamblin, James. 'How the most important glacier in east Antarctica is melting.' *Atlantic*, 20 March 2015.

Hampson, Rick. 'Donald Trump says "America First" like isolationists before World War II.' *USA Today*, 11 April 2016.

Hannon, Elliot. 'President of United States waits nearly three days to condemn racist Portland murders.' *Slate*, 29 May 2017.

Hansford, Joanna, and Mary Bolling Blackiston. 'Luxury boutique hostel opens in Vidigal.' *Rio Times*, 4 March 2014.

Harding, Luke, and Chris Stephen. 'Chris Stevens, U.S. ambassador to Libya, killed in Benghazi attack.' *Guardian*, 12 September 2012.

Harvey, Chelsea. 'Next up from climate change: Shell-crushing crabs invading Antarctica.' *Washington Post*, 28 September 2015.

Hatzfeld, Jean. *Machete Season: The Killers in Rwanda Speak*. New York: Farrar, Straus & Giroux, 2005.

Hawkins, Chelsea. '9 artists challenging our perceptions of Afghanistan.' *Mic*, 9 October 2014.

Hay, Mark. 'Nomads on the grid.' *Slate*, 5 December 2014.

Healy, Patrick, and Michael Barbaro. 'Donald Trump calls for barring Muslims from entering U.S.' *New York Times*, 7 December 2015.

Heijmans, Philip. 'Skirting comedy limits in Myanmar.' *New York Times*, 29 July 2015.

Hetter, Katia. 'Antarctic hits 63 degrees, believed to be a record.' CNN News, 1 April 2015.

Higgins, Andrew. 'Putin and Orthodox church cement power in Russia.' *Wall Street Journal*, 18 December 2007.

Hilderbrand, Rachael. 'Conheça Cíntia Luna, presidente da AMUST do Morro do Fogueteiro.' *Rio On Watch*, 4 July 2014.

Hill, Matthew. 'Yellow fever relaxation by South Africa helps Zambia tourism.' Bloomberg, 5 February 2015.

Hilsum, Lindsey. 'Don't abandon Rwandan women again.' *New York Times*, 11 April 2004.

———. 'Rwanda's time of rape returns to haunt thousands.' *Guardian*, 26 February 1995.

———. 'Saif al-Islam Gaddafi: The prophet of his own doom.' *Guardian*, 5 August 2015.

Hinchey, Kyle. 'Shots fired at Equality Center first act of serious vandalism in 12 years at downtown site, director says.' *Tulsa World*, 7 March 2017.

Hnin Yadana Zaw and Antoni Slodkowski. 'Myanmar's ousted ruling party head to work with Suu Kyi.' Reuters, 5 November 2015.

Holewinski, Sarah. 'Marla Ruzicka's heroism.' *Nation*, 18 September 2013.

Höller, Herwig. 'Aleksandr Ilich Lyashenko known as Petlyura: A controversial protagonist of Russian contemporary art.' *Report: Magazine for Arts and Civil Society in Eastern and Central Europe*, June 2006.

Holley, Peter. 'In Afghanistan, the art of fighting extremism.' *Washington Post*, 12 September 2015.

Holmes, Oliver. 'Aung San Suu Kyi wins outright majority in Myanmar election.' *Guardian*, 13 November 2015.

———. 'Much still at stake in Myanmar after Aung San Suu Kyi's election victory.' Guardian, 13 November 2015.

Horowitz, Judith, et al. 'Brazilian discontent ahead of World Cup.' Pew Research Global Attitudes Project, 3 June 2014.

Houttuin, Saskia. 'Gay Ugandans face new threat from anti-homosexuality law.' *Guardian*, 6 January 2015.

Huang, Angela Lin. 'Leaving the city: Artist villages in Beijing.' *Media Culture Journal* 14, no. 4 (August 2011): 1–7.

Huang Yanzhong. 'The 2008 milk scandal revisited.' *Forbes*, 16 July 2014.

Hufferd, Marlene Lima. 'Carnaval in Brazil, samba schools and African culture: A study of samba schools through their African heritage.' Retrospective Theses and Dissertations, Paper 15406, University of Iowa, 2007.

Human Rights Watch. 'Brazil: Reforms fail to end torture.' Human Rights Watch, 28 July 2014.

————. 'Letter: Brazil: Protect detainees in police custody.' Human Rights Watch, 25 July 2014.

Hunt, Elle. 'Facebook to change trending topics after investigation into bias claims.' *Guardian*, 23 May 2016.

Idov, Michael. 'No sleep till Brooklyn: How hipster Moscow fell in love with Williamsburg.' *Calvert Journal*, 31 December 2013.

'In memory of Vlad Mamyshev-Monroe, 1969–2013.' Baibakov Art Projects, 22 March 2013.

International Lesbian, Gay, Bisexual, Trans and Intersex Association. 'The lesbian, gay and bisexual map of world laws.' International Lesbian, Gay, Bisexual, Trans and Intersex Association, May 2015.

'Introducing the Center for Contemporary Art Afghanistan (CCAA).' ARCH International, no date.

Ireland, Doug. '7000 lashes for sodomy.' *Gay City News*, 11 October 2007.

'ISIL "brutally" quells rebellion in Libya's Sirte.' *Al Jazeera*, 17 August 2015.

Ivanitskaya, Nadezhda. 'As a State Duma deputy and businessman Yuzhilin Kobzar built a billion-dollar business.' *Forbes Russia*, 22 October 2011.

Ives, Mike. 'Culling Myanmar's past for memories.' *New York Times*, 16 October 2013.

Iyengar, Rishi. 'Burma's million-strong Rohingya population faces "final stages of genocide," says report.' *Time*, 28 October 2015.

Janoi, Banyar Kong. 'Pushing for ethnic language media in a changing Burma.' *Asia Calling*, 10 November 2012.

Jason, Stefanie. 'SA trips as Joburg lands on the steps of the Venice Biennale.' *Mail & Guardian*, 30 April 2015.

————. 'Venice Biennale: SA Pavilion finally announces artists.' *Mail & Guardian*, 16 April 2015.

Jenkins, Simon. 'Vision of the future or criminal eyesore: What should Rio do with its favelas?' *Guardian*, 30 April 2014.

Jervis, Rick. 'Texas campus tense with incidents since Donald Trump's election.' *USA Today*, 18 December 2016.

Johnson, Ian. 'Some Chinese artists are testing their limits.' *Wall Street Journal*, 2 October 2009.

Johnson, Jenna. 'Conservative suspicions of refugees grow in wake of Paris attacks.' *Washington Post*, 15 November 2015.

————. 'Trump says "torture works", backs waterboarding and "much worse".' *Washington Post*, 17 February 2016.

Johnson, Kevin. 'FBI: Hate crimes targeting Muslims up 67% in 2015.' *USA Today*, 14 November 2016.

Jones, Taryn. 'The art of "War": Voina and protest art in Russia.' *Art in Russia*, 29 September 2012.

Jung, C. G. *Mysterium Coniunctionis: An Inquiry into the Separation and Synthesis of Psychic Opposites in Alchemy*. Princeton, NJ: Princeton University Press, 1977.

Kaiman, Jonathan. 'Beijing independent film festival shut down by Chinese authorities.' *Guardian*, 24 August 2014.

Kaminski, Anna. 'In Russia, contemporary art explodes from Soviet shackles.' BBC News, 23 February 2014.

Kanthor, Rebecca. 'In China, imported fruit is the must-have luxury item for the new year.' The World, Public Radio International, 20 February 2015.

Kaplan, Sarah. 'The serene-looking Buddhist monk accused of inciting Burma's sectarian violence.' *Washington Post*, 27 May 2015.

Katsuba, Valera. 'The roosters are coming.' *Independent*, 12 February 1997.

Katz, Nathan, and Ellen S. Goldberg. 'The last Jews in India and Burma.' *Jerusalem Letter*, 15 April 1988.

Kaufman, Jason Edward. 'South Africa's art scene is poised for a breakthrough – at home and abroad.' *Huffington Post*, 19 February 2013.

Keane, Fergal. 'Myanmar election: Full BBC interview with Aung San Suu Kyi.' BBC News, 10 November 2015.

Kendzulak, Susan. 'Burma's flying circus.' *Art Radar*, 18 October 2013.

Kennard, Matt, and Claire Provost. 'The lights are on but no one's home in Myanmar's capital Naypyidaw.' *Guardian*, 19 March 2015.

Kessler, Glenn. 'Trump's outrageous claim that "thousands" of New Jersey Muslims celebrated the 9/11 attacks.' *Washington Post*, 22 November 2015.

Kestler-D'Amours, Jillian. 'Silencing Brazil's baile funk.' *Al Jazeera*, 5 July 2014.

Khin Maung Yin. 'Salience of ethnicity among Burman Muslims: A study in identity formation.' *Intellectual Discourse* 13, no. 2 (2005): 161–79.

Kim, Jim Yong. 'How Mongolia brought nomads TV and mobile phones.' *Bloomberg View*, 14 October 2013.

Kino, Carol. 'Where art meets trash and transforms life.' *New York Times*, 21 October 2010.

Kinsella, Eileen. 'Who are the top 30 Chinese artists at auction?' *Artnet News*, 8 September 2014.

Kirey, Anna. ' "They said we deserved this": Police violence against gay and bisexual men in Kyrgyzstan.' Human Rights Watch, 28 January 2014.

Kirkpatrick, David, and Steven Lee Myers. 'Libya attack brings challenges for U.S.' *New York Times*, 12 September 2012.

'*Киселев после увольнения из "Почты России" получит почти 3 млн руб* (Kiselev after the dismissal of "Mail of Russia" will receive nearly 3 million rubles).' *RIA Novosti*, 19 April 2013.

Kiss, Ligia, et al. 'Health of men, women, and children in post-trafficking services in Cambodia, Thailand, and Vietnam: An observational cross-sectional study.' *Lancet Global Health* 3, no. 3 (March 2015): e154–e161.

Knickmeyer, Ellen. 'Victims' champion is killed in Iraq.' *Washington Post*, 18 April 2005.

Knöpfel, Ulrike. 'Risky business: China cracks down on Ai Wei Wei protégé Zhao Zhao.' *Der Spiegel*, 28 August 2012.

Komaromi, Priska, and Karissa Singh. 'Post-referendum racism and xenophobia: The role of social media activism in challenging the normalisation of xeno-racist narratives.' PostRef Racism, 11 July 2016.

Korolkov, Alexander. 'Is the protest movement dead?' *Russia Beyond the Headlines*, 15 January 2015.

Krouse, Matthew. 'Art fair forced to reinstate Mabulu painting after Goldblatt threat.' *Mail & Guardian*, 28 September 2013.

Kuo, Lily. 'By 2015, China will be the world's largest consumer of processed food.' *Quartz*, 23 September 2013.

Kuper, Jeremy. 'Venice Biennale: View from the ground.' *Mail & Guardian*, 20 May 2015.

Kusters, Annelies. 'Deaf utopias? Reviewing the sociocultural literature on the world's "Martha's Vineyard situations."' *Journal of Deaf Studies & Deaf Education* 15, no. 1 (January 2010): 3–16.

Kuzmin, Dmitry. 'On the Moscow metro and being gay.' Trans. Alexei Bayer. *Words without Borders*, 2013.

Kyaw Hsu Mon. 'Govt to push left-hand steering wheels on future car imports.' *Irrawaddy*, 25 November 2014.

Kyaw Myo Min, Kyaw Kyaw Aung, and Khin Khin Ei. 'Hopes fade for Myanmar landslide survivors as lawmakers urge greater safety for miners.' Radio Free Asia, 24 November 2015.

Kyaw Phyo Tha. 'Ex–political prisoner Win Tin demands apology from junta leaders.' *Irrawaddy*, 30 October 2013.

———. 'Hands of hardship; Artist Htein Lin spotlights political prisoners' travails.' *Irrawaddy*, 27 July 2015.

———. 'A purr-fect pedigree in Burma.' *Irrawaddy*, 24 February 2014.

Kyaw Zwa Moe. 'Burmese professionals earn good money in Singapore but still miss home.' *Irrawaddy*, March 2007.

Lankarani, Nazanin. 'The many faces of Yue Minjun.' *New York Times*, 5 December 2012.

Lapowsky, Issie. 'Of course Facebook is biased; that's how tech works today.' *Wired*, 11 May 2016.

Lawi Weng. 'Arakan monks boycott UN, INGOs.' *Irrawaddy*, 6 July 2012.

Lawi Weng, Nyein Nyein, and Kyaw Hsu Mon. 'Missing reporter killed in custody of Burma army.' *Irrawaddy*, 24 October 2014.

Lazarus, Emma. *An Epistle to the Hebrews*. New York: Jewish Historical Society, 1987.

Lee, Jasmine, and Kevin Quealy. 'The 282 people, places and things Donald Trump has insulted on Twitter: A complete list.' *New York Times*, 23 October 2016.

Lee, Yanghee. 'Report of the Special Rapporteur on situation of human rights in Myanmar.' United Nations Office of the High Commissioner for Human Rights, 23 September 2014.

Lee, Yulin. 'Strategies of spatialization in the contemporary art museum: A study of six Japanese institutions.' Dissertation, New York University, 2012.

Lefevre, Amy Sawitta, and Yesim Dikmen. 'Thai PM defends decision to send Uighurs back to China.' Reuters, 9 July 2015.

Lescaze, Zoë. 'An abbreviated Moscow Biennale unites scrappy performances, bourgeois spiders, and one former Greek finance minister.' *ARTnews*, 16 October 2015.

Li Xiaoyu. 'A bite of food culture.' *BJ Review*, 2 July 2015.

Light, Whitney. 'Pressing questions with Aye Ko.' *Myanmar Times*, 18 May 2014.

Lilla, Mark. 'The end of identity liberalism.' *New York Times*, 18 November 2016.

Lindsay, Timothy. 'Security implications of Italian nationalism.' PhD diss., Naval Postgraduate School, March 2016.

Lins, Clarissa. 'Providing electricity to Rio de Janeiro's favelas.' *Guardian*, 18 March 2014.

Littauer, Dan. 'Mugabe promises "hell for gays" in Zimbabwe if he wins.' *Gay Star News*, 17 June 2013.

Lorch, Donatella. 'Rape used as a weapon in Rwanda: Future grim for genocide orphans.' *Houston Chronicle*, 15 May 1995.

Lovett, Richard A. 'Deadly tsunami sweeps Solomon Islands.' *National Geographic News*, 2 April 2007.

Luhn, Alec. 'LGBT website founder fined under Russia's gay propaganda laws.' *Guardian*, 29 July 2015.

Luong, Hillary. 'Artists detained by Myanmar police.' *Art Asia Pacific*, 8 June 2012.

Lv, Jun, et al. 'Consumption of spicy foods and total and cause specific mortality: Population based cohort study.' *British Medical Journal* 351 (4 August 2015): h3942.

Lynge, Inge. 'Mental disorders in Greenland.' *Man & Society* 21 (1997): 1–73.

Lyon, Julia. 'Invited to escape to America, some refugees just say no.' *St. Louis Tribune*, 14 September 2009.

Ma, Sophanna. 'Funeral of our beloved Mum Phaly Nuon.' Ezra Vogel Special Skills School, December 2012.

MacGregor, Karen. 'A spear to the heart of South Africa.' *New York Times*, 5 June 2012.

Maher, Richard. 'As Austria rejects the far-right and Italy votes No, Europe's future hangs in the balance.' *Conversation*, 5 December 2016.

Mahtani, Shibani, and Myo Myo. 'Myanmar signs draft peace deal with armed ethnic groups.' *Wall Street Journal*, 31 March 2015.

Makinen, Julie. 'Myanmar press freedom: Unprecedented but still subject to pressures.' *Los Angeles Times*, 27 March 2015.

Malaurie, Jean. *The Last Kings of Thule*. Trans. Adrienne Foulke. New York: Dutton, 1982.

Malaysian Myanmar Business Council. 'U.S. contributes publications to parliamentary library.' Malaysian Myanmar Business Council, 24 October 2012.

Maler, Sandra, and Peter Cooney. 'Magnitude 6.6 quake hits Solomon Islands in the Pacific: USGS.' Reuters, 12 August 2015.

Malewitz, Jim. 'Investigators: Fire that ravaged Victoria mosque was arson.' *Texas Tribune*, 8 February 2017.

Manayiti, Obey. 'Mugabe chides homosexuals again.' *NewsDay* (Bulawayo), 25 July 2013.

Mann, Zarni. 'DVB reporter jailed for one year.' *Irrawaddy*, 7 April 2014.

Manno, Adam. 'Florida teacher tells black student that Trump will send her "back to Africa".' *Orlando Weekly*, 15 November 2016.

Mansfield, Katie. 'Gang launch horror racist attack on woman in West Midlands during night out.' *Express*, 14 March 2017.

Marrero, Tony. 'Worshippers relocate after arson fire damages Thonotosassa mosque.' *Tampa Bay Times*, 24 February 2017.

Marsaja, I Gede. *Desa Kolok: A Deaf Village and Its Sign Language in Bali, Indonesia*. Nijmegen, Netherlands: Ishara Press, 2008.

Marshall, Andrew. 'Myanmar gives official blessing to anti-Muslim monks.' Reuters, 27 June 2013.

————. 'Myanmar old guard clings to $8 billion jade empire.' Reuters, 1 October 2013.

————. 'The 969 catechism.' Reuters, 26 June 2013.

Martin, Rachel, and Jonny Bell. 'Antrim racist attack: 'Scared' mother and baby leave home after brick lands in cot.' *Belfast Telegraph*, 12 April 2017.

Mashal, Mujib. 'Women and modern art in Afghanistan.' *New York Times*, 6 August 2010.

Mashek, Kera. '75-year-old Sarasota man says he was attacked for being gay.' WFTS, 16 November 2016.

Masters, Emily, and Robert Gavin. 'Black family's garage torched, painted with racist graffiti in Schodack, police say.' *Times Union*, 16 May 2017.

Masters, James, and Karl de Vries. 'Trump criticized for tweet about London mayor after attack.' CNN, 5 June 2017.

Ma Thanegi. 'The Burmese fairy tale.' *Far Eastern Economic Review*, 19 February 1998.

————. *Nor Iron Bars a Cage*. San Francisco: Things Asian Press, 2013.

Mathieson, David. 'Perilous plight: Burma's Rohingya take to the seas.' Human Rights Watch, 2009.

Maung Zarni. 'Racist leader monk Rev. Wirathu's speech.' *M-Media*, 24 March 2013.

May, Theresa. 'Theresa May's conference speech in full.' *Telegraph*, 5 October 2016.

McGregor, Richard. 'Zhou's cryptic caution lost in translation.' *Financial Times*, 10 June 2011.

McLaughlin, Daniel, and Elisabeth Wickeri. 'Mental health and human rights in Cambodia.' Leitner Center for International Law and Justice, 31 July 2012.

McLoughlin, Beth. 'Rio's funk parties silenced by crackdown on gangs.' BBC News, 5 May 2012.

McManus, John. 'Egypt court clears men accused of bathhouse "debauchery."' BBC News, 12 January 2015.

McNamara, Kelly. 'Burmese cats return to a new Burma.' *Bangkok Post*, 14 September 2012.

McNamara, Robert S., and Brian Van De Mark. *In Retrospect: The Tragedy and Lessons of Vietnam*. New York: Times Books, 1995.

McVeigh, Tracy. 'Aung San Suu Kyi "released from house arrest."' *Guardian*, 13 November 2010.

Medeiros, Étore, and Ana Pompeu. 'Brasileiros acham que há racismo, mas somente 1.3% se consideram racistas.' *Correio Braziliense*, 25 March 2014.

Meier, Becca. 'Huge rise in hate crime across London, new figures reveal.' *Independent*, 7 March 2017.

Melloan, George. 'Donald Trump, meet Herbert Hoover.' *Wall Street Journal*, 3 November 2015.

Meredith, Robbie. 'Northern Ireland interfaces: More residents want peace walls to stay.' BBC News, 15 December 2015.

Meyer, Elizabeth. "Burlington minister finds hateful note left on his car." *Hawk Eye*, 11 November 2016.

Michaels, Samantha. 'Quintana releases final report on Burma human rights.' *Irrawaddy*, 14 March 2014.

Miguel, Antonio Carlos. 'Ser ou não ser carioca da gema não é a questão (To be or not to be carioca is the question).' *O Globo*, 28 February 2015.

'A milestone for Myanmar's democracy.' *New York Times*, 12 November 2015.

Miller, Carl, et al. 'From Brussels to Brexit: Islamophobia, xenophobia, racism and reports of hateful incidents on Twitter: Research prepared for Channel 4 Dispatches "Racist Britain".' Demos Centre for Analysis of Social Media, 11 July 2016.

Miller, Cassie, and Alexandra Werner-Winslow. 'Ten days after: Harassment and intimidation in the aftermath of the election.' Southern Poverty Law Center, 29 November 2016.

Milne, A. A. *Winnie-the-Pooh*. New York: Dutton, 1926.

Minford, Patrick. 'The economic case for a Brexit.' *Forbes*, 22 June 2016.

Mooney, Chris. 'The melting of Antarctica is bad news for humans. But it might make penguins pretty happy.' *Washington Post*, 13 August 2015.

———. 'Scientists declare an "urgent" mission – study West Antarctica, and fast.' *Washington Post*, 29 September 2015.

Mooney, Paul. 'Jail, lawsuits cast shadow over Myanmar media freedom.' Reuters, 15 May 2014.

Morello, Carol. 'Trump calls Erdoğan to congratulate him on contested referendum, Turkey says.' *Washington Post*, 17 April 2017.

Morgan, Julie. 'Keeping 'em diving in the Keystone State.' *Sport Diver*, 21 April 2006.

Mortimer, Caroline. 'Hungarian PM Viktor Orbán says "all the terrorists are basically migrants" in response to Paris attacks.' *Independent*, 24 November 2015.

———. 'Post-Brexit increase in hate crimes continues as police promise crackdown.' *Independent*, 22 July 2016.

Morton, Adam. 'The vanishing island.' *Age*, 19 September 2015.

Moscow Biennale of Contemporary Art. 'One-man picket.' Moscow Biennale of Contemporary Art, 2015.

'Moscow venue refuses to host pro-LGBT teen photo display, cites police pressure.' *Queer Russia*, 13 June 2015.

Motlagh, Jason. 'When a SIM card goes from $2,000 to $1.50.' *Bloomberg Business*, 29 September 2014.

Mthembu, Jackson. 'ANC outraged by Brett Murray's depiction of President Jacob Zuma.' African National Congress, 17 May 2012.

Muggah, Robert, and Ilona Szabo de Carvalho. 'Fear and backsliding in Rio.' *New York Times*, 15 April 2014.

Murphy, Paul P., and Samantha Guff. 'The Libyan refugee who made it into the U.S. before the ban.' CNN, 3 February 2017.

Musharbash, Yassin. 'The "Talibanisation" of Pakistan: Islamists destroy Buddhist statue.' *Der Spiegel*, 8 November 2007.

Mydans, Seth. 'Yangon Journal; Burmese Jew shoulders burden of his heritage.' *New York Times*, 23 July 2002.

NAACP. 'Inadequacy of President Trump and federal responses to hate crimes.' press release, 6 March 2017.

National Police Chiefs' Council. 'Hate crime undermines the diversity and tolerance we should instead be celebrating.' 8 July 2016.

Nay Phone Latt. 'Nay Phone Latt speaks.' *Myanmar Times*, 3 March 2014.

Ndayambaje, Jean Damascène. 'Le genocide au Rwanda: Une analyse psychologique.' Thesis, National University of Rwanda, Butare, 2001.

Neuffer, Elizabeth. *The Key to My Neighbour's House: Seeking Justice in Bosnia and Rwanda*. London: Bloomsbury, 2002.

Niederhauser, Matthew. 'Rio's Olympic inequality problem, in pictures.' *Citylab*, 9 September 2015.

Nir, Sarah Maslin. 'Finding hate crimes on the rise, leaders condemn vicious acts.' *New York Times*, 5 December 2016.

Nobel Zaw. 'Activist hit with additional sentence, totaling over 13 years.' *Irrawaddy*, 31 October 2014.

————. 'Court sentences 3 journalists, 2 media owners to 2 years in prison.' *Irrawaddy*, 16 October 2014.

Nowrojee, Binaifer. *Shattered Lives: Sexual Violence during the Rwandan Genocide and Its Aftermath*. New York: Human Rights Watch, 1996.

'NPM southern branch to open with jadeite cabbage display.' *Want China Times*, 18 September 2015.

NPR staff. 'Fact check: Donald Trump's Republican convention speech annotation.' National Public Radio, 21 July 2016.

O'Donnell, John. *Trumped!* New York: Simon & Schuster, 1991.

O'Grady, Siobhan. 'Former Rwandan official worries that Kagame's administration is backsliding into mass murder.' *Foreign Policy*, 29 September 2014.

O'Hara, Mary Emily. 'LGBT community centers in Los Angeles, Milwaukee vandalized with slurs.' NBC News, 11 February 2017.

O'Shea, Mary. 'Journey of shelf discovery.' *Post Magazine*, 14 October 2012.

Ortiz, Devonaire, and Jenny Davis. 'Wave of post-election hate crimes hits Wesleyan.' *Wesleyan Argus*, 14 November 2016.

Panja, Tariq, and David Biller. 'Soccer icon Romario, Rio mayor Paes cited in corruption tape.' *Bloomberg*, 25 November 2015.

Parascandola, Rocco, and Thomas Tracy. 'Anti-LGBT bigot turns Q train ride into nightmare for couple, leaves woman with concussion and broken eye socket.' *New York Daily News*, 24 May 2017.

Pariser, Eli. *The Filter Bubble: What the Internet Is Hiding from You*. New York: Penguin, 2011.

Pater, Walter. *Selected Writings of Walter Pater*. Edited by Harold Bloom. New York: Columbia University Press, 1974.

Paton, Callum. 'Libya: Scores killed in ethnic clashes for control of south's people-trafficking routes.' *International Business Times*, 23 July 2015.

Patton, Dominique. 'Cashing in on health scares, China online food sales boom.' Reuters, 11 August 2013.

Pearlman, Jonathan. 'Jihadist group calls on Muslims to save Burmese migrants from "savage Buddhists."' *Telegraph*, 20 May 2015.

Peixoto, Karin Elisabeth von Schmalz, et al. 'Rio 2016 Olympics: The exclusion games.' World Cup and Olympics Popular Committee of Rio de Janeiro, 7 December 2015.

PEN America. 'Publishers' pledge on Chinese censorship of translated works.' PEN America, 15 October 2015.

Perlez, Jane. 'China, pursuing strategic interests, builds presence in Antarctica.' *New York Times*, 3 May 2015.

Perry, Alex. 'South Africa: Over-exposing the President.' *Time*, 23 May 2012.

Pershakova, Sasha. 'Zine scene: How Russia's long tradition of self-publishing is still thriving today.' *Calvert Journal*, 28 October 2014.

Pfanner, Eric. 'Vows: Andrew Solomon and John Habich.' *New York Times*, 8 July 2007.

Phipps, Claire, and Matthew Weaver. 'Aung San Suu Kyi vows to make all the decisions in Myanmar's new government.' *Guardian*, 10 November 2015.

Pilon, Mary. "Donald Trump's immigrant mother." *New Yorker*, 24 June 2016.

Plaskin, Glenn. 'Playboy interview: Donald Trump.' *Playboy*, March 1990.

'Polish family's Plymouth home damaged in "race hate arson attack".' BBC News, 7 July 2016.

Pollman, Lisa. 'Art is stronger than war: Afghanistan's first female street artist speaks out.' *Art Radar*, 19 July 2013.

Pomerantsev, Peter. 'Putin's God squad: The Orthodox Church and Russian politics.' *Newsweek*, 10 September 2012.

Popham, Peter. *The Lady and the Peacock: The Life of Aung San Suu Kyi*. New York: Experiment, 2012.

Porter, Tom. 'Gangs of Russia: Ruthless mafia networks extending their influence.' *International Business Times*, 9 April 2015.

———. 'Vladmir [sic] Putin allies named as "key associates of Russian gangsters" by Spanish prosecutors.' *International Business Times*, 30 June 2015.

'Poslednyi Geroi: Georgy Guryanov (1961–2013).' Baibakov Art Projects, 20 July 2013.

'"Prayer" is the key against "devilish" homosexuality worldwide: Moses Foh-Amoaning.' *Daily Guide Ghana*, 14 July 2015.

Press Association. 'Man in Harlow assault died after single punch to the head, CCTV shows.' *Guardian*, 6 September 2016.

Probert, Thomas, et al. 'Unlawful killings in Africa.' Centre for Governance and Human Rights, University of Cambridge, 2015.

Purton, Michael. 'Stroud shopkeeper run over in vicious gang attack.' *Stroud News & Journal*, 29 March 2017.

Pyae Thet Phyo. 'Ex-minister's agent denies seeking recount.' *Myanmar Times*, 12 November 2015.

Radio Free Asia Khmer Service. 'Cambodian province plans campaign for monks to care for mentally ill.' *Radio Free Asia*, 20 April 2015.

Rahim, Fazul, and Sarah Burke. 'Afghan artist Kabir Mokamel takes aim at corruption with blast wall art.' NBC News, 19 September 2015.

Ramon, Paula. 'Poor, middle class unite in Brazil protests.' CNN News, 24 July 2013.

Ramzy, Austin. 'After Myanmar election, few signs of a better life for Muslims.' *New York Times*, 18 November 2015.

Rao, Mallika. 'Five Chinese dissident artists who aren't Ai Weiwei.' *Huffington Post*, 10 June 2014.

Rapp, Jessica. 'Locavores, health food, and celebrity chefs: The hottest trends in Shanghai's dining scene.' *Jing Daily*, 24 August 2015.

Rasool, Daud. 'Rebuilding Afghanistan's creative industries.' British Council, 14 October 2013.

Rauhala, Emily. 'Complete freedom, always just eluding the grasp of Chinese artist Ai Weiwei.' *Washington Post*, 30 July 2015.

Recchia, Francesca. 'Art in Afghanistan: A time of transition.' *Muftah*, 6 August 2014.

Reeves, Jeffrey. 'Mongolia's environmental security.' *Asian Survey* 51, no. 3 (2011): 453–71.

Reguly, Eric. 'Support for the E.U. is even dropping in Italy – the country that inspired its creation.' *Globe & Mail*, 21 June 2016.

Reis, Luiz Felipe. 'As muitas redes do agitador da "perifa" Marcus Vinicius Faustini.' *O Globo*, 21 July 2012.

Reitman, Janet. 'The girl who tried to save the world.' *Rolling Stone*, 16 June 2005.

'Reporter Daniel Pearl is dead, killed by his captors in Pakistan.' *Wall Street Journal*, 24 February 2002.

Reporters Without Borders. World Press Freedom Index, 2015. Paris: Reporters Without Borders, 2015.

Republic of the Union of Myanmar. 'Final report of inquiry commission on sectarian violence in Rakhine State.' Republic of the Union of Myanmar, 8 July 2013.

Resende, Leandro. ' "A nação está pertubada," define antropólogo Luiz Eduardo Soares.' *O Dia Brasil*, 10 October 2015.

Reuters and Agence France-Presse. 'Hungarian prime minister says migrants are "poison" and "not needed".' *Guardian*, 26 July 2016.

Rever, Judi, and Geoffrey York. 'Assassination in Africa: Inside the plots to kill Rwanda's dissidents.' *Globe & Mail*, 2 May 2014.

Rhodan, Maya. 'Donald Trump raises eyebrows with "bad hombres" line.' *Time*, 19 October 2016.

Riccardi, Nicholas. 'Nevada becomes one of Trump's big hopes for swing state win.' Associated Press, 27 August 2016.

Richardson, Jayson, et al. 'Mental health impacts of forced land evictions on women in Cambodia.' *Journal of International Development*, 27 September 2014.

Rilke, Rainer Maria. *Selected Poetry of Rainer Maria Rilke*. Trans. Stephen Mitchell. New York: Vintage, 1984.

Ritu, Moshahida Sultana. 'Ethnic cleansing in Myanmar.' *New York Times*, 12 July 2012.

Rizzo, Tony, et al. 'First-degree murder charge filed in possible hate crime shooting at Olathe's Austins bar.' *Kansas City Star*, 23 February 2017.

Robinson, Simon. 'Appreciation: Marla Ruzicka, 1977–2005.' *Time*, 18 April 2005.

Rodrigues, Robson. 'The dilemmas of pacification: News of war and peace in the "marvelous city." ' *Stability Journal* (22 May 2014): Article 22.

Rosenberg, Matthew, and Michael D. Shear. 'In reversal, Obama says U.S. soldiers will stay in Afghanistan to 2017.' *New York Times*, 15 October 2015.

Rossi, Melissa. 'Gun wounds down in Complexo do Alemão.' *Rio Times*, 3 July 2012.

Rowling, Megan. 'Solomons town first in Pacific to relocate due to climate change.' Reuters, 15 August 2014.

Royte, Elizabeth. 'The outcasts.' *New York Times Magazine*, 19 January 1997.

Rulli, Michael. '8 trans women of color have been murdered in 2017.' *Out*, 23 March 2017.

Rush, James. 'Images emerge of "gay" man "thrown from building by Isis militants before he is stoned to death after surviving fall."' *Independent*, 3 February 2015.

Rushdie, Salman. 'Heroes: Nay Phone Latt.' *Time*, 29 April 2010.

Ruskin, John. *The Works of John Ruskin, Vol. 5: Modern Painters*. Vol. 3. Edited by E. T. Cook and Alexander Wedderburn. London: G. Allen, 1904.

Ryan, Hugh. 'Kyrgyzstan's anti-gay law will likely pass next month, but has already led to violence.' *Daily Beast*, 18 September 2015.

Ryan, Jim. '2 killed in stabbing on MAX train in Northeast Portland as man directs slurs at Muslim women, police say.' *Oregonian*, 26 May 2017.

Sabur, Rozina. '"You don't belong here": Solicitor caught on film launching racist attack on woman and her young son.' *Daily Telegraph*, 4 February 2017.

Safi, Michael. 'Antarctica's increasing sea ice restricting access to research stations.' *Guardian*, 11 May 2015.

Said-Moorhouse, Lauren. 'Is Italy's referendum result the first step toward leaving the E.U.?' CNN, December 5, 2016.

Samaha, Albert, Mike Hayes, and Talal Ansari. 'The kids are Alt-Right.' *BuzzFeed News*, 6 June 2017.

Samuels, Sammy. 'Hanukkah with spirit in Yangon.' BBC News, 4 December 2015.

San Yamin Aung. 'Supreme Court rejects appeal of Unity journalists.' *Irrawaddy*, 27 November 2014.

Sartore, Mara. 'Lampedusa: Migration and desire, an interview with Vik Muniz.' *My Art Guides*, June 2015.

Saul, Stephanie, and Louise Story. 'At the Time Warner Center, an enclave of powerful Russians.' *New York Times*, 11 February 2015.

Schunert, Tanja, et al. 'Cambodian mental health survey.' Royal University of Phnom Penh, Department of Psychology, 2012.

Schwarcz, Lilia Moritz. 'Especificidade do racismo Brasileiro.' In *História da Vida Privada no Brasil*. Edited by Fernando Novais. São Paulo: Companhia de Letras, 1998.

———. 'Not black, not white: Just the opposite: Culture, race and national identity in Brazil.' Working Paper CBS-47-03, Centre for Brazilian Studies, University of Oxford, 2003.

Schwarz, Benjamin. 'A vision in concrete.' *Atlantic*, July/August 2008.

Seow, Joanna. 'More Myanmar professionals in Singapore heading home to tap booming economy.' *Straits Times*, 24 March 2014.

Sérgio, Antonio, and Alfredo Guimarães. 'The Brazilian system of racial classification.' *Ethnic and Racial Studies* 35, no. 7 (2012): 1157–62.

Serrano-Berthet, Rodrigo, et al. 'Bringing the state back into the favelas of Rio de Janeiro: Understanding changes in community life after the UPP pacification process.' World Bank, October 2012.

Sevinclidir, Pinar. 'Hate speech on the rise in Turkish media.' BBC News, 30 October 2014.

Shakespeare, William. *Henry VIII*. In *The Complete Works*. Edited by G. B. Harrison. New York: Harcourt, Brace & World, 1968.

Sharman, Jon, and Ian Jones. 'Hate crimes rise by up to 100 per cent across England and Wales, figures reveal.' *Independent*, 15 February 2017.

Sharpe, Joshua. 'Muslim Gwinnett teacher told to "hang yourself" with her headscarf.' *Atlanta Journal-Constitution*, 11 November 2016.

Shearlaw, Maeve. '30 under 30: Moscow's young power list.' *Guardian*, 8 June 2015.

Shestakova, Sasha. 'Outcry: Ten recent art exhibitions that caused a storm in Russia.' *Calvert Journal*, 29 July 2015.

Shun, Ekow. 'Moscow's new art centres.' *Financial Times*, 15 March 2013.

Simkins, Rose. 'Stop Hate UK: Report on post-referendum hate crime.' Stop Hate UK, 22 August 2016.

Simmons, William. *Eyes of the Night: Witchcraft among a Senegalese People*. Boston: Little, Brown, 1971.

Simpson, Brigitte Vittrup. 'Exploring the influences of educational television and parent-child discussions on improving children's racial attitudes.' Dissertation, University of Texas at Austin, May 2007.

Simpson, Ian. 'Philadelphia Jewish cemetery desecrated by vandals.' Reuters, 27 February 2017.

Smith, Matthew, et al. ' "All you can do is pray": Crimes against humanity and ethnic cleansing of Rohingya Muslims in Burma's Arakan State.' Human Rights Watch, April 2013.

Smith, Russell. 'The impact of hate media in Rwanda.' BBC News, 3 December 2003.

Sneed, Annie. 'American eel is in danger of extinction.' *Scientific American*, 1 December 2014.

Snyder, Timothy. 'Him.' *Slate*, 18 November 2016.

Solomon, Andrew. 'As Asia regroups, art has a new urgency.' *New York Times*, 23 August 1998.

———. 'Defiantly deaf.' *New York Times Magazine*, 28 August 1994.

———. *Far from the Tree: Parents, Children, and the Search for Identity*. New York: Simon & Schuster, 2012.

———. 'Hot night in Havana.' *Food & Wine*, January 2002.

———. *The Irony Tower: Советские художники во времена гласности*. Moscow: Garage, 2013.

———. *The Irony Tower: Soviet Artists in a Time of Glasnost*. New York: Knopf, 1991.

————. *The Noonday Demon: An Atlas of Depression*. New York: Simon & Schuster, 2001.

————. 'Paper tsars.' *Harpers & Queen*, February 1990.

Sommers, Marc. 'The darling dictator of the day.' *New York Times*, 27 May 2012.

South African Press Association. 'Appeal tribunal declassifies "The Spear."' *City Press*, 10 October 2012.

————. 'Mugabe condemns Europe's gay "filth."' IOL News, 14 April 2011.

Southern Poverty Law Center. 'Update: Incidents of hateful harassment since Election Day now number 701.' 18 November 2016.

————. 'Update: More than 400 incidents of hateful harassment and intimidation since the election.' 15 November 2016.

Spicer, Sean. 'Press gaggle by Press Secretary Sean Spicer, 2/24/2017.' White House Office of the Press Secretary, 24 February 2017.

Stauffer, Caroline. 'Brazil's Petrobras corruption investigators to probe Olympic contracts.' Reuters, 25 November 2015.

Steele, Jonathan. 'Marla Ruzicka.' *Guardian*, 19 April 2005.

Stephen, Chris. 'Gaddafi's son Saif al-Islam sentenced to death by court in Libya.' *Guardian*, 28 July 2015.

Sternberg, Troy, et al. 'Tracking desertification on the Mongolian steppe through NDVI and field-survey data.' *International Journal of Digital Earth* 4, no. 1 (2011): 50–64.

Stevenson, Tom. 'The growing strength of Turkey's ultra-nationalists.' *Middle East Eye*, 1 June 2016.

Strangio, Sebastian. 'Myanmar's wildlife trafficking hotspot.' *Al Jazeera*, 17 June 2014.

Strokan, Sergey, and Vladimir Mikheev. 'E.U.-Russia sanctions war to continue.' *Russia Beyond the Headlines*, 26 June 2015.

Sulteeva, Renata. 'The market for Russian contemporary art: An historical overview and up-to-date analysis of auction sales from 1988 to 2013.' Dissertation, Sotheby's Institute of Art, New York, 2014.

'"Sunflower" protesters break on to political scene.' Economist Intelligence Unit, 2 April 2014.

Tan, Cheryl. Post. Facebook post no. 10155335450332790, 4 June 2017.

Tan, Michael. 'One million SIM cards sold in Myanmar.' CNET, 2 October 2014.

'Татьяна Веденеева расстается с мужем (Tatiana Vedeneeva has divorced).' DNI, 2 June 2008.

Tau, Byron, and Peter Nicholas. 'Hillary Clinton defends actions in Benghazi.' *Wall Street Journal*, 22 October 2015.

Taylor, Alan. 'The Chernobyl disaster: 25 years ago.' *Atlantic*, 23 March 2011.

Taylor, Jeff. 'Police arrest man for attack on DC's Casa Ruby community center.' *LGBTQ Nation*, 14 March 2017.

Tempest, Rone. 'Pope meets with Castro, agrees to a Cuba visit.' *Los Angeles Times*, 20 November 1996.

Temple-Raston, Dina. *Justice on the Grass.* New York: Free Press, 2005.

Tennyson, Alfred. *Poems by Alfred Tennyson in Two Volumes.* Boston: William D. Ticknor, 1842.

———. *The Poetical Works of Alfred, Lord Tennyson.* London: Macmillan, 1895.

Thomas, Wright. 'The 2016 presidential campaign and the crisis of U.S. foreign policy.' Lowy Institute for International Policy, 10 October 2016.

Thorpe, Nick. 'Hungary's poster war on immigration.' BBC News, 14 June 2015.

Tierney, Dominic. 'Forgetting Afghanistan.' *Atlantic*, 24 June 2015.

Tolstoy, Leo. *Anna Karenina.* Tr. Richard Peaver and Larissa Volokhonsky. New York: Viking Penguin, 2004.

Topping, Alexandra. 'Widows of the genocide: How Rwanda's women are rebuilding their lives.' *Guardian*, 7 April 2014.

Torgovnik, Jonathan. *Intended Consequences: Rwandan Children Born of Rape.* New York: Aperture, 2009.

Torode, Greg. 'Myanmese envoy says Rohingya ugly as ogres.' *South China Morning Post*, 11 February 2009.

Traufetter, Gerald. 'Climate change or tectonic shifts? The mystery of the sinking South Pacific islands.' *Der Spiegel*, 15 June 2012.

Travis, Alan. 'Simple numbers tell story of police cuts under Theresa May.' *Guardian*, 5 June 2017.

Travis, John. 'Genes of silence: Scientists track down a slew of mutated genes that cause deafness.' *Science News*, 17 January 1998.

Trump, Donald J. 'Full text: Donald Trump announces a presidential bid.' *Washington Post*, 16 June 2015.

———. 'Remarks by President Trump at NATO unveiling of the Article 5 and Berlin Wall Memorials, Brussels, Belgium.' The White House Office of the Press Secretary, 25 May 2017.

———. 'Tweet (immigration killing machine).' *Twitter*, tweet no. 630906211790102528, 10 August 2015.

'Trump says he has good relationship with "the blacks".' CNN, 14 April 2011.

Tunison, John. 'Cab driver describes beating from man yelling "Trump".' *Michigan Live*, 18 November 2016.

Turner, Rochelle, et al. 'Travel and tourism: Economic impact 2015: Myanmar.' World Travel and Tourism Council, 2015.

Tyan, Alexandra. 'Classes aimed at raising a new generation of Russian businessmen.' *Moscow Times*, 27 July 2015.

UNICEF. 'Country statistics: Myanmar.' UNICEF, 2015.

United Nations Educational, Scientific and Cultural Organisation. 'Naadam, Mongolian traditional festival.' United Nations Educational, Scientific and Cultural Organisation, 2010.

———. 'Tentative lists: Marovo-Tetepare complex.' United Nations Educational, Scientific and Cultural Organisation, 23 December 2008.

United Nations Office for the Coordination of Humanitarian Affairs. 'Our bodies, their battle ground: Gender-based violence in conflict zones.' IRIN News, 1 September 2004.

United Nations Office of the High Commissioner for Human Rights. 'UN Special Rapporteur finds that killings by Brazilian police continue at alarming rates, government has failed to take all necessary action.' United Nations Office of the High Commissioner for Human Rights, 1 June 2010.

Urani, André, and Fabio Giambiagi. *Rio: A Hora da Virada*. Rio de Janeiro: Elsevier, 2012.

U.S. Department of Defense. 'Casualty report.' U.S. Department of Defense, 10 November 2015.

U.S. Department of State. 'Country reports on human rights practises for 2011: Brazil.' U.S. Department of State, 2012.

———. 'U.S. economic engagement with Burma.' U.S. Embassy in Rangoon, June 2014.

U.S. Department of the Army. 'Standards of medical fitness.' Army Regulation 40-501, 4 August 2011.

Usborne, David. 'Donald Trump on foreign policy: "I've got no time to travel – America needs my attention now".' *Independent*, 27 August 2015.

Uwiringiyimana, Clement. 'Rwandan parliament agrees to extend Kagame's rule.' Reuters, 29 October 2015.

Vrieze, Paul. 'Experts reject claims of "Rohingya mujahideen" insurgency.' *Irrawaddy*, 15 July 2013.

Wachter, Sarah J. 'Pastoralism unraveling in Mongolia.' *New York Times*, 8 December 2009.

Walker, Shaun. 'Russia swoops on gang importing £19m of banned cheese from abroad.' *Guardian*, 18 August 2015.

Walsh, Declan. 'Second female Afghan journalist killed in five days.' *Guardian*, 6 June 2007.

Wan, William. 'China tried to erase memories of Tiananmen. But it lives on in the work of dissident artists.' *Washington Post*, 31 May 2014.

———. 'Chinese artist recounts his life, including the one time he painted "X" on Mao's face.' *Washington Post*, 2 June 2014.

———. 'Taiwan's "white shirt army," spurred by Facebook, takes on political parties.' *Washington Post*, 11 November 2013.

Warikoo, Niraj. 'Hate crimes increase in Michigan post-election, drawing concern.' *Detroit Free Press*, 20 November 2016.

Watts, Jonathan. 'Brazil: Rio police charged over torture and death of missing favela man.' *Guardian*, 2 October 2013.

———. 'Rio Olympics linked to widespread human rights violations, report reveals.' *Guardian*, 8 December 2015.

———. 'Rio police tackle favelas as World Cup looms.' *Guardian*, 10 June 2013.

Wax, Emily. 'Rwandans are struggling to love children of hate.' *Washington Post*, 28 March 2004.

'"We must stop Brussels!" referendum booklet warns Hungarians.' *Budapest Beacon*, 7 September 2016.

'We urge our readers to beLEAVE in Britain and vote to quit the E.U. on June 23.' *Sun*, June 13, 2016.

Weaver, Matthew. '"Horrible spike" in hate crime linked to Brexit vote, Met police say.' *Guardian*, 28 September 2016.

Weaver, Matthew, and Sandra Laville. 'European embassies in UK log more alleged hate crimes since Brexit vote.' *Guardian*, 19 September 2016.

Westcott, Lucy. 'Gay refugees addresses [sic] U.N. Security Council in historic meeting on LGBT rights.' Newsweek, 25 August 2015.

White, Charles. 'Vandals paint racist graffiti on Islamic community centre after London Bridge attack.' *Metro*, 4 June 2017.

Winata, S., et al. 'Congenital non-syndromal autosomal recessive deafness in Bengkala, an isolated Balinese village.' *Journal of Medical Genetics* 32 (1995): 336–43.

Winterbottom, Tom. 'The tragedy of the Maracanã Stadium.' *Rio On Watch*, 13 June 2014.

Wootson, Cleve R., Jr. 'A Baylor student was shoved and called the "n" word. This is how the school responded.' *Washington Post*, 14 November 2016.

World Bank. 'Ease of doing business in Rwanda.' World Bank, 2015.

———. 'Poverty continued to decline, falling from 27.4 per cent in 2012 to 21.6 per cent in 2014.' World Bank, 1 July 2015.

———. 'Rwanda overview.' World Bank, 6 October 2015.

———. 'World Bank, Govt. of Solomon Islands launch two new projects towards improved power supply, disaster & climate resilience.' World Bank, 1 April 2014.

World Health Organisation. 'Mental health atlas 2011: Cambodia.' Department of Mental Health and Substance Abuse, World Health Organisation, 2011.

———. 'WHO country cooperation strategy for Mongolia 2010–2015.' World Health Organisation, 2010.

———. 'WHO mental health atlas 2011: Senegal.' Department of Mental Health and Substance Abuse, World Health Organisation, 2011.

Worth, Robert F. 'An American aid worker is killed in her line of duty.' *New York Times*, 18 April 2005.

Wright, Thomas. 'Trump's 19th century foreign policy.' *Politico*, 20 January 2016.

Wullschager, Jackie. 'No more Chinese whispers.' *Financial Times*, 2 October 2004.

Xinhua News Agency. 'Former Mongolian president jailed for four years.' CRI English, 3 August 2012.

Xu, Angela. 'China's digital powered foodie revolution.' Lab Brand, 6 January 2015.

Yanagizawa, David. 'Propaganda and conflict: Theory and evidence from the Rwandan genocide.' Dissertation, Stockholm University, 2009.

Yeung, Peter. 'Racist assaults on hospital staff double in a year.' *Times*, 24 January 2017.

Yin Pumin. 'Probing ancient mysteries.' *Beijing Review*, 7 December 2009.

Young, Toby. 'Voting remain is an act of heartless snobbery.' *Spectator*, 14 May 2016.

Zaccardi, Nick. 'President of company preparing Rio for Olympics resigns.' NBC Sports, 1 April 2014.

Zaiman, Jonathan. 'Remembering Moses Samuels, the man who preserved Jewry in Myanmar.' *Tablet*, 2 June 2015.

Zhong Nan. 'China has a healthy appetite for food imports.' China Daily, 2 March 2015.

Zhu Linyong. 'Art on the move.' *China Daily*, 25 January 2010.

Zilkha, Bettina. 'Andrew Solomon named President of PEN.' Forbes, 5 March 2015.

Zucchino, David. ' "I've become a racist": Migrant wave unleashes Danish tensions over identity.' *New York Times*, 6 September 2016.

'Zuma, Marikana painting pulled from Jo'burg Art Fair.' *Mail & Guardian*, 27 September 2013.

Zway, Suliman Ali, and Carlotta Gall. 'Libyan factions reject unity government plan.' *New York Times*, 20 October 2015.

Index

Absolutely Fabulous (TV), 214
abstract expressionism, 152
Abu Ghraib, 350
ACCEPT (Romanian gay-rights organisation), 437, 440
Acer America, 184, 195, 202
Aegis Trust, 305
Aeschylus, 214
Afghanistan:
    after the Taliban, 269–85
    artistic community in, 270–72, 273–74, 276, 284–85
    author's friends in, 38–39
    Contemporary Art Prize in, 284
    culture destroyed in, 29, 271–72
    dinner party in, 280–83
    ethnic groups in, 278–79, 461
    filmmakers in, 275–77
    music in, 277–80
    poets in, 274–75
    rebuilding, 272–73
    Soviet invasion of, 6, 11, 272, 275, 460
    Taliban in, 27, 37, 270–75, 278, 279–80, 460, 461
    television in, 272–73, 278
    update, 283–84
    women in, 27, 271, 276, 277, 284
Africa:
    antisodomy laws in, 34
    gay people in, 431
    'native art' in, 146
    tourism in, 23, 227
    transitional societies in, 249
    see also specific nations
African National Congress (ANC), 142, 148, 151, 157, 162–64, 175
Agili, Hasan, 34, 38, 335, 356, 514–16
Ahmida, Ali Abdullatif, 326, 345
Ainslie, Bill, 152
Ai Weiwei, 103, 129, 137, 138, 139–40
Akhlaqi, Ali, 284
Alborough, Alan, 146
Alexander, Jane, 151
Alexander the Great, 215, 217, 271
Alexandrova, Avdotja, 98
Alexeev, Nikita, 13
Al-Fateh, 340
Al Jazeera, 341
Alkikli, Omar, 335
al-Qaeda, 272, 325, 460
Al Shams (*The Sun*), Libya, 327, 339
Alston, Philip, 409
Alvarez, A., 250
Amach, Sanga, 284
Amazon rainforest, 425
Amin, Idi, 335
Amnesty International, 356, 426, 427
Amos, Howard, 177

Ando, Tadao, 288, 289, 290, 291
André, Marcus, 414–15
Antarctica, 385–96
    ban on polar mining in, 396
    blue snow of, 394
    Chinese research stations on, 396
    icebergs of, 393–94
    krill harvesting at, 396
    new fungi in, 396
    oil and mineral resources of, 396
    pack ice of, 388–95
    penguins of, 396
    Shackleton Centennial Expedition
        to, 385
    update, 395–96
    vulnerability of, 385
Antarctic Circle, crossing of, 388
Antarctic Treaty, 396
Anufriev, Sergey, 47, 48
Arab Spring, 448, 449
Arakan (Rakhine) State, 459,
        461–63
    author's visit to, 464–68
Araujo, Cleber, 426
Argumenty i Fakty, 72
Aris, Michael, 456
armaments, development of, 41
Arman (Hope), 274
Arsenijević, Damir, 516–17
art:
    for art's sake, 152
    auction world of, 53
    commercial expectations of, 13,
        54–55, 56, 112
    conceptual, 144, 206
    and controversy, 176, 181, 186
    and craft, 144–45, 146, 165,
        207, 284
    cultural vocabulary of, 186
    as entertainment, 13, 46–47
    figurative painting, 111
    formalism, 135
    interpretation of, 185–86
    minimalism, 135
    modernism, 135
    painted miniatures, 273

performance art, 47, 76–77, 137,
        210, 284
    and politics, 15, 140, 162–64,
        184–85, 191, 210
    power to change the world, 13, 152
    and protectionism, 184, 196
    purposes of, 14, 15, 54, 56
    purposes of museums, 189
    radical form in, 109
    realist, 108, 125
    trompe-l'oeil, 380
    and truth, 56, 59
    visual, 148
Asefi, Yousof, 270, 273–74
Asian democracies, U.S. support of, 185
Atatürk, Kemal, 337
Athens, Olympics in, 416
Attiga, Giumma, 335
Augustine of Hippo, 16
Aung Kyaw Naing, 479
Aung Min, 467
Aung San, 451, 455, 475
Aung San Suu Kyi, 37, 443–44, 446,
        447, 454–58, 476, 479
    background of, 455–56
    and elections, 455, 456–58, 462,
        475, 482
    and ethnic groups, 461, 462
    The Voice of Hope, 453
Australia, 483–92
Aye Ko, 446
Aye Lwin, 463, 468
Azerbaijan, organised crime in, 87–88
Baggio, Rodrigo, 415–16
Bahkstein, Josif, 64, 67
Bailey, Beezy, 147, 166, 169
Balanchine, George, 300
Baldwin, James, *Giovanni's Room,* 81
Bali, clan system in, 398
Baloyi, Vincent, 155
Bangladesh, 458, 465, 481
Bangweulu Swamps, Zambia, 222–24
Bank for International Settlements, 347
Barcelona, Olympics in, 416
Barker, Wayne, 147
Bashir, Omar al-, 339

Bastos Marques, Maria Silvia, 416, 418
Bastrykin, Alexander, 100
Baywatch (TV), 17
BBC, 130, 177, 511
Bebe Scott (nanny), 3–4
Begalov, Yuri, 84–85, 97
Beijing:
    ear massage in, 369
    food in, 367–69
    Forbidden City in, 187, 188,
        373–76, 378, 383
    Garden of the Palace of Established
        Happiness, 383
    Qianlong Garden in, 373–84
Beijing Independent Film Festival, 136
Bekešius, Mantvydas, 498
Beltrame, José Mariano, 410–14
Benesse Art Site, 288–91
Benesse Island, Japan, 287–91
    Art House Projects, 290
    Chichu Museum, 291
Benghazi, Libya, 345, 352–53, 356
Bengkala, Bali:
    alcohol abuse in, 402
    deafness in, 397–405
    government of, 398
Ben-Gurion, David, 468
Berlusconi, Silvio, 348
Bermuda, map of, 49
Bernhardt, Sarah, 423
Bester, Willie, 156–58
Bi Mon Te Nay, 479
bin Laden, Osama, 325, 347
Birch, James, 126
Birman, Yevgeny, 73–74, 78
Bisgaard, Poul, 251–52
Bite of China, A (TV), 370
Black, Robert, QC, 346
Blair, Gavin, 219–27
Blair, Marjorie, 220–27
Blair, Tony, 27, 348
Blake, William, 'Jerusalem', 40
Blignaut, Belinda, 146
Bobrova, Yelena, 102
Boltanski, Christian, *Les Archives du
    Coeur,* 291

Bolton, John, 348
Bonaparte, Napoléon, 5, 57
Bonnet, Catherine, 308
Borit, Misuu, 457, 463–64,
    477–78
Bosnia, 516–17
Botha, Andries, 150–51
Botswana:
    elephants in, 23–24
    travel in, 219
Botticelli, Sandro, 125
Bouazizi, Mohamed, 448
Bowman, Vicky, 446, 474
Bo Xiaobo, 128
Brady, Anne-Marie, 396
Brâncuși, Constantin, *Endless
    Column,* 287
Brasília, capital of Brazil, 409
Bratskii Krug, 100
Brazil, 407–28
    democracy in, 415, 421
    dictatorship in, 418, 421, 422
    economy of, 407, 415–17
    inequality in, 409
    models in, 423
    NGOs in, 422
    and offshore oil, 407
    rainforest in, 425
    see also specific cities
Bremmer, Ian, 101
Brexit:
    author votes against, 494
    general election (2017) and,
        500, 512
    internet and, 516
    perception that government is
        broken and, 510
    prejudice and hate crime surge
        within U.K. after, 494,
        498–500, 501
    Theresa May and, 497, 500, 508,
        511, 512–13, 520
    tribalism and, 38–9
Brezhnev, Leonid, 45–46, 47, 61, 92
Bronya, Pani, 76, 97
Brown, David J., 150

Bruskin, Grisha, 52
Buckingham Palace, 374
Buddha, living, 381
Buddhism:
    born in India, 459
    Chan, 381
    ideal of pure nature, 378, 381
    idea of forgiveness, 453
    monasteries, 288, 449–50
    religious structures of, 466
    Theravada, 450, 459, 462, 465,
        480, 481
    Tibetan, 381–82
Buhuceanu, Florin, 437, 440
Bulatov, Erik, 57
Bulgaria, travel in, 6, 25
Burma, 450–51
    Communists in, 469
    see also Myanmar
Burmese cats, 478
Burnett, Jon, 499
Burnett, Ricky, 171
Bush Senior, George, 347
Bush, George W., 27, 90, 326,
        347–48, 437
Butcher, Duane, 440
Buzzfeed, 502–3

Cahill, James, 201
Cai Guo-Qiang, 103
    Cultural Melting Bath, 290
    Golden Missile, 210
Calder, Alexander, 290
Cambodia:
    civil war in, 229–31
    depression in, 229–35
    Future Light Orphanage in,
        231, 235
    Khmer medicine in, 233
    Khmer Rouge in, 230–32, 468
    mental health in, 235
Cambridge Energy Research
        Associates, 344
Cameroon, homosexuality punished
        in, 34
Camp, S. Talcott, 23

Campbell Island, 384
Cao Fei, 135–36
Cardiff, Janet, 291
Carol I, king of Romania, 437
Cărtărescu, Mircea, 436, 440–41
Carvalho, José, 410–11
Caryl, Christian, 16–17
Casé, Regina, 425
Castiglione, Giuseppe ('Lang Shining'),
        380
Castro, Fidel, 18
Catherine the Great, 5, 376
Ceaușescu, Nicolae, 6, 119
Cele, Alois, 156
censorship:
    in China, 35–36, 104, 175
    in Myanmar, 443, 451, 461,
        470–73, 479–80, 481
    and PEN, 35–36
    in Russia, 57–58, 97, 98, 175
    in South Africa, 175–76
Central Academy, Beijing, 108, 131
Central House of Artists, Moscow,
        85–86
Cernea, Remus, 440, 441
Cézanne, Paul, 185, 213
Chang, Johnson, 120
Chang, K. C., Food in Chinese
        Culture, 363
change, unexpected effects of, 28–30
Chang Lin-sheng, 182, 190, 194,198
Charles, Prince of Wales, 213
Chechnya, organised crime in, 100
Chekhov, Anton, 11, 67
Chengdu, China, food in, 366–67
Chen Guang, 137
Chen Hui-chiao, 208
Chen Shaoping, 113
Chen Shih-meng, 198
Chen Yifei, 125
Chernobyl nuclear disaster, 11
Chiang Kai-shek, 183, 184, 188, 190,
        197–98, 468
China:
    advanced civilisation in, 128–29
    and Antarctica, 396

art of, *see* Chinese art
Buddhism in, 381
censorship in, 35, 104, 175
Communism in, 134, 188, 359, 360, 375
criticism of government punished in, 138
cultural heritage of, 375
Cultural Revolution, 28, 108, 113, 119–24, 139, 162, 193, 230, 468
Democracy Wall movement, 108, 111, 121, 123
food in, 359–71
Forbidden City in, 187, 188, 373–76, 378, 383
Great Wall, 375
hierarchical society of, 106
housing in, 117–18
Hygiene Campaign (1991), 117
idealism in, 119, 123
imperial rulers of, 375, 381, 382
intelligentsia in, 105
international trade of, 376
Internet use in, 138–39
language in, 128–29
last emperor (Pu Yi) of, 188, 376
life in, 28
and Myanmar, 449, 458, 476
nationalism in, 131, 192, 197, 247
New Policy in, 186
Olympic Games in, 126, 139
pollution in, 370
possibility of democracy in, 105, 121–22, 134
Qianlong Garden in, 373–84
radical individualism in, 105, 113–15, 134, 136–40
Red Guards in, 120, 124
and reunification, 202–4, 206
ruling the world, 132
Sichuan earthquake (2008), 139
social change in, 360
and Taiwan, 184, 185, 195, 196–98, 205, 206
Tiananmen Square, 26, 109, 110,

115, 121–22, 123, 137, 138, 374, 448, 509
tradition of conformity in, 105, 112, 113, 121, 131, 134, 139
two camps in, 141
updates, 135–40, 369–71
Warring States period (475–221 BC), 378
Western exhibitions in, 125–28
Chinati Foundation, Texas, 287
Chinese art, 103–39
abroad, 129
artist harassment and lawsuit, 132–34, 137
avant-garde, 105, 106–8, 109–10, 113–17, 118–23, 124, 125, 127, 131
brush-and-ink painting, traditional, 108, 112–13, 124–25, 128, 206
calligraphy, 187, 199–203, 378
categories of, 110
collections of, 186–88
contemporary, 135–40
Cynical Realism, 110–12, 118, 135, 140
and emphasis on past, 202
Gaudy Art, 135, 140
guohua styles, 125, 128
hidden meanings in, 138–39, 186, 205, 272, 378
Imperial Collection, 187–89, 192, 203, 379
Japanese influence on, 380
landscape paintings, 186, 378, 379
literati (scholar-artist ink painting), 108, 290, 379
moved to Taiwan (1949), 183, 185, 188, 198
New Revolutionaries, 119, 129
'No U-turn' symbol in, 109–10
official crackdown on, 136–40
paper cutting, 131
performance art, 137
Political Pop, 110, 112, 118, 475
Post-'89 influence on, 111, 112, 113, 115, 118–19, 122

Chinese (*cont.*)
   as propaganda vehicle, 140
   realism, 108, 125
   sales of, 135
   scrolls, 190
   'slender gold' calligraphy, 201
   history of, 108–10
   Soviet model for, 108
   U.S. tour (*Chinese Art Treasures*,
      1961), 188
   and Western art, 108, 109, 125,
      131–32, 135, 210, 381
Chin Hsiao-yi, 184, 190–91, 193
Chin women, tattoos of, 465
Chirac, Jacques, 348
Christensen, Johnny, 496
Chitambo, Chief, 224–25
Chizhov, Georgy, 102
Chopin, Frédéric, 366
Chou Chuan, 191, 192
Chou Hai-sheng, 206
Chou Kung-shin, 203
Christiansen, René Birger, 255
Chuck (friend), 294
Chu Hui-liang, 191, 194
Chu Ko, 191
Chuykov, Ivan:
   Fragment of a Fence, 52–53
   Noughts and Crosses, 53
citizenship, global ('citizen of the
     world' concept), 497–8,
     500, 520
CIVIC (Campaign for Innocent
     Victims in Conflict), 285
civil partnership, 33
Clements, Alan, 453
Clinton, Bill, 90, 193, 347
   My Life, 322
Clinton, Hillary, 356
CNN, 60, 66
Coetzee, J. M., 148
Collective Action Group (K/D), USSR,
     46–49, 52
Colombia, sexual identity in, 33
Confucius, 187, 381
Congreve, William, 327

Connoisseur, 45
Conservation International (CI), 294
conservatism, modern, 510, 512–13
Conservative Party Conference
     (October, 2017), 497
Conwill, William Louis, 268
Copacabana, 408
Coral Sea, 485
Corbyn, Jeremy, 500
Cosmoscow, 57
Cousteau, Jacques, 484
Crimmins, Pamela, 7–8
crossroads of history, 5–6, 22, 29
Cuba:
   autocracy in, 26
   celebrations in, 18
   changes in, 18
cultural dissonance, 20–23, 129–30
cultural exclusion, 38
Cultural Revolution, *see* China

Daesh (ISIS), 34
Dai Jianyong, 137
Dalai Lama:
   coining of the title, 238
   and living Buddha, 381
Danquah, Meri Nana-Ama, 429
da Silva Pereira, Douglas Rafael, 426
Dayan, Moshe, 468
deafness, 397–405
Dean I-mei, 207, 208
   Made in Hong Kong, 207
De Maria, Walter, 290, 291
democracy:
   arrival of, 27–28
   as euphemism for capitalism, 95,
     185, 327
   and freedom, 129
   identity politics and, 518
   local meanings of the word, 74,
     90–91, 93, 105, 121–22, 134,
     139, 336–37, 446, 451
   protest and, 512
de Montebello, Philippe, 184, 187,
     192, 193, 195, 196, 202
de Morro Agudo, Dudu, 422

Deng Xiaoping, 28, 105, 134, 375
Denisov, Nikita, 102
Denmark, immigration and, 496
depression:
    alternative treatments of, 262
    and distraction, 233
    and learning to forget, 233–34, 235
    and learning to love, 234–35
    and loneliness, 257
    Noonday Demon (Solomon), 31,
        36, 211, 229, 249, 261, 435,
        436–37
    rescue from isolation, 234, 257
    and suicide, 250, 257, 258
    talking about emotions, 253–54,
        256–58
    travel as opposite of, 519–20
    and trust, 234
    and working, 234, 235
    writing about recovery, 261–62
de Pury, Simon, 50, 51, 52, 53
de Souza, Amarildo, 426
de Wet, Barend, 150
Didenko, Tanya, 66, 75
Ding Fang, 132
Ding Yi, 127, 131
Diouf, Madame, 263–65
diplomacy, 40–42
disability:
    education and, 518
    social constructionist model of, 405
diversity, embracing, 41–42
Djebbar, Maître Saad, 323
Dmitri (ship captain), 389–90, 392–93
Dobrokhotov, Roman, 102
d'Offay, Anthony, 126
Donadio, Mr (teacher), 5
Drevin, Aleksandr, 50
Duchamp, Marcel, 185
Dumontt, Luiz Carlos, 422
Dupree, Nancy Hatch, 271
Dürer, Albrecht, 124

Ecuador, 8–9
Egypt, homosexuals imprisoned in,
    34, 517

ElBaradei, Mohamed, 347
Elkhair, Abdulgader, 343
elsewhere, idea of, 32
el-Sisi, Abdel Fattah, 517
Elton, Louise, 6
Enderby Island, 387
enemies from abroad, 41
England:
    author's affection for, 2–5, 10
    author's move to, 10–11
    civil partnership in, 33
    foreign habits in, 9–10
    see also United Kingdom
Enkhbaya, Nambar, 247
Enraizados (Brazilian educational
        organisation), 422
Erdoğan, Recep, 495, 496
Ernst, Max, 301
escape fantasies, 3, 4
Eskimos, *see* Inuit peoples
Esquire, 261
Etwebi, Ashur, 355, 356
E.U., 38–39, 495, 496–7
Eugenia, Unforgettable, 178
Evans, Nicholas, 397
evil:
    good vs. evil, 17, 79, 120, 122
    of the Holocaust, 1, 306
    rape-conceived children considered
        products of, 309–10
    in society, 230, 356, 432
evil spirits, 266

Facebook, 512, 516
Fakhri, Azim, 284
families, differences within, 40
Fang Lijun, 111, 112, 118, 120–21,
    133, 136
Fan Kuan, 181, 182, 185, 196
    *Travellers amid Streams and
        Mountains,* 186, 188, 189,
        194, 196
Fan Rong, 137
*Far from the Tree: Parents, Children, and
        the Search for Identity* (Solomon),
    32, 39–40, 305, 397

Farhad, Alam, 284
Farrakhan, Rev. Louis, 340
Faustini, Marcus Vinícius, 417, 420
Feith, Roberto, 410
Feldman, Ronald, 50
Fellows, Sir Charles, 215
Feng Boyi, 137
Feng Mengbo, 122
Fiennes, Susannah, 211, 212–13,
    215, 217
Fierau, Genevieve, 437
Fierce Animals (film), 123
Figaro Prize for Humanitarian
    Service, 231
Filippov, Andrei, 61, 63–65, 66
'filter bubble', 512
Fine Arts in China, 109
Fini, Gianfranco, 353
First World War, 448
Fitzgerald, F. Scott, 493
flat feet, 2, 499
Fluxus, 135
Foh-Amoaning, Moses, 433
Fong, Wen C., 183–84, 188, 191
    Beyond Representation, 184
    and Met exhibition, 185,
        187, 189, 192–95,
        200, 202
    Possessing the Past, 202
Food & Wine, 269
Foreign Policy in Focus (organisation),
    348
Forster, E. M., *A Passage to India*, 24
Four Days in September (film), 422
Fox News, 504
Frank, Anne, 515
Franke, Katherine, 517–18
Franz Ferdinand, Archduke, 448
Franz Josef, Emperor, 376
freedom, idea of, 26–28, 514
Freedom House, 100–101
French airliner UTA 772, 346
French Revolution, 28
French West Africa, menu in, 21
Friedman, Steven, 175
Frolov, Viktor, 72

Frost, Robert, 'Mending Wall', 513
Fugard, Athol, 148
Fukutake, Tetsuhiko, 288
Fuller, Buckminster, 301
Gabeira, Fernando, 415, 417, 422
Gable, Clark, 332
Gaffney, Christopher, 414
Gaidar, Yegor, 89
Gainsborough, Thomas, 212
Galápagos Islands, 8
Garage Museum of Contemporary Art,
    Moscow, 56–57
Gardner, Kevin, 81
Gatsinzi, Jean-Pierre, 309
Gauguin, Paul, 299
Gaultier, Jean Paul, 168
gay marriage, 32, 33, 35
gay people, 32–35
    atrocities against, 34–36, 98–99,
        494, 501, 502, 503, 505, 506,
        514–15, 517–18
    author's identity, 3, 10, 11, 33–34,
        430, 485
    freedom and, 514–15
    protection of, 33
gay rights, 33–36, 99, 430–32, 437
Geers, Kendell, 146–47
Gehry, Frank, 287
gender identity, 33–34
Geneva Conventions, 418, 509
Geng Jianyi, 114–15, 130, 361
genocide commemoratives, 305
George, Sister, 9
Gerasimov, Igor, 83–84
Getar (Balinese chief), 403–4
Ghana, 429–33
    gay rights in, 431, 432
    wedding ceremony in, 429
Ghanem, Shukri, 329–31, 341, 349,
    353–54
Ghaznavi, Aziz, 279, 280, 282
Gies, Miep, 515
Gilbert & George, 125–28, 140
'Girl from Ipanema, The' (song), 425
'Girls Just Want to Have Fun'
    (song), 8

glaciers, melting, 259, 395–96
global warming, 302–3, 385, 392, 396
globalism, 497–8, 509, 519–20
Gobi Desert, 237, 242–43
Godfather, The (film), 87
Goebbels, Joseph, 57
Goldblatt, David, 176
Goldfinger (film), 366
Golovin, Andrei L., 90–91, 92, 95
Goodhew, Steve, 299
Gorbachev, Mikhail, 45, 47, 66, 94, 177, 334
  and glasnost, 50, 448
  kidnapping of, 448
  and perestroika, 93
  resignation of, 59–60
Gordimer, Nadine, 148
Gottgens, Kate, 150
Graham, Dan, *Cylinder Bisected by Plane*, 290
Graham, Martha, 297
Grantseva, Arisha, 75
Great Barrier Reef, 301, 485
Grebenshchikov, Boris, 78, 79, 97
Greece, public protests in, 184
Greenland:
  beauty of, 252
  Danish colonisation of, 249, 253
  depression in, 249–58
  gay identity in, 34
  hard life in, 250
  Inuit in, *see* Inuit peoples
  language in, 249
  taboo against talking about yourself in, 251
  trauma as ever-present in, 254
  update, 258–59
Gregory, Chief Judge Roger, 508
Grey Wolves, 496
Guadalcanal, Battle of, 294
Guantánamo, 350
Guanyin (Buddhist goddess of mercy), 369
Guatamala City, La Limonada neighbourhood of, 24

Gu Dexin, 113–14
Guest, Michael, 437
Guggenheim Museum, Bilbao, 287
gun laws, 24
Guo Xi, 185
  Early Spring, 186, 188, 192, 196, 200, 202
Guryanov, Georgi, 73, 78, 97
Gu Wenda, 129, 131–32, 139

Haas, Aleksei, 73–74, 75
Habich, John, *see* Solomon, John Habich
Habyarimana, Juvénal, 306
Hadrian, 215
Haffner, Sebastian, 519
Haftar, Khalifa, 357
Hakimian, Timur, 275–77
Hamas, 352
Han Chinese, 197, 199
Han Feng, 360–65
Hangzhou, China, food in, 114, 363–64
Hangzhou gardens, 378
Haring, Keith, 288
Harpers & Queen, 12, 45
Harun, Happy, 383
Harvey, Mark, 221–22
Hasan (sailing ship captain), 215
Hassani, Shamsia, 284
hate crime, Brexit, Trump and rise in, 494, 498–506
hate speech, 36
Havel, Václav, 337
Hawke, Leslie, 436, 437, 438
Hearn, Maxwell, 182
Hecht, David, 262, 264
Hecht, Hélène, 262–63, 264
Helms, Jesse, 192
Helmsley, Leona, 127
Henrique Cardoso, Fernando, 416
Henriques, Ricardo, 412
Heritage Expeditions, 386–95
Heritage Foundation, 343
Hermitage, St Petersburg, 50, 57
Hitchcock, Alfred, 302

Hitler, Adolf, 57, 178, 460, 501, 504, 505, 506, 519
Hlungwani, Jackson, 160, 171–72
Hobbes, Thomas, 323
Hobson, Andrew, 212, 214, 216
Hogan-Howe, Bernard, 498
Holocaust, 1–2, 23, 25, 36, 306, 439
home, idea of, 15–16
homosexuality, *see* gay people; gay rights
Hong Kong, pro-democracy demonstrations in, 138–39
Honmura, Japan, 288, 290
hope, 15, 28–29, 140, 284, 407, 443
Houmaidi, Ahmed El, 8
Houston, Whitney, 112
Hsia I-fu, 210
Htein Lin, 473–75
    A Show of Hand, 474–75
Htin Kyaw, 479
Huaisu, 201
    Autobiographical Essay, 199
Huang Chih-yang, *Maternity Room,* 209
Huang Gongwang, *Dwelling in the Fuchun Mountains,* 201
Huang Rui, 136
Huizong, emperor of China, *Two Poems,* 201
Human Rights Watch, 479
Humboldt, Alexander von, 493
Hungary, immigration and nationalism in, 494, 495, 513
Hussein, Saddam, 335, 449

Ibrahim (sailing crew), 212, 216
Ibrahim, Ahmed, 326, 354
identity politics, 497, 517–19
Idris, king of Libya, 322
Ilimanaq, Greenland, 252, 253, 256–58
immigration:
    Brexit and, 498–500, 513
    effects of, 25
    restrictions on, 37–38
    Trump and, 501, 502, 505–8, 513, 514–16
    xenophobia in continental Europe and, 494–6, 513

Inca ruins, Ecuador, 8–9
India:
    British Raj in, 450
    gay culture in, 33, 432
    homosexual behaviour criminalised in, 34
    and Myanmar, 473
    partition of (1947), 460
Indonesia, 397–405, 461
Indonesian Sign Language (ISL), 405
Indyk, Martin, 347
Ingapirca ('Inca wall'), 9
Inkomtrust, 83
Institute of Race Relations, 499
International Atomic Energy Agency (IAEA), 347
International Criminal Court, 7, 357
internationalism, 39, 494, 497–8, 500, 518–20
International Monetary Fund (IMF), 348, 415, 416
Inuit peoples, 249
    depression in, 250–58
    hunters and fishermen, 250–51, 254
    kiviak (fermented auks) eaten in, 251
    large families of, 251
    living in igloos, 251
    mental illnesses in, 255
    storytellers, 251, 253
    suicide rate in, 250
    three sage women, 253–58
Inujima Island, 291
Ionesco, Eugène, 192
Ipanema beach, 408, 427
Iran:
    atrocities against gays in, 34
    and nuclear programme, 348
    and terrorists, 346
Iraq:
    atrocities against gays in, 34
    chaos in, 29
    refugees from, 38
    war in, 27, 269
irony, 14, 54, 217, 246, 330, 355
Irony Tower, The: Soviet Artists in a Time of Glasnost (Solomon), 14–15, 45

ISIL (Islamic State of Iraq and the Levant), 34
ISIS (Islamic State of Iraq and Syria), 34, 357
Islam, 351–53
    Sunni Mālikī (theological school), 331
Isle of Mull, 3
Israel, state of, 468, 513–14
Istratsov, Vasily N., 96
Italy:
    constitutional referendum (2016), 494, 495
    public protests in, 184
IT Park, Taipei, 206–8
Ivanov, Viktor, 100
Ivleva, Viktoria, 59–60, 65–66

Jahid, Abdul Raqib, 274
Jaipur Literature Festival, 432
Jakobshavn Glacier, 259
James, Le Bron, 504
James, Roger, 294–96
Jansen, Jonathan, 176
Januário, Márcio, 427–28
Japan, Benesse Art Site in, 287–91
Jason, Stefanie, 176
Jeeg, Julie, 496
Jessica (friend), 294, 298, 300
Jiang Wen, 123–24
Jianyi, Geng, 361
Jobim, Antônio Carlos (Tom), 424–25
Joburg Art Fair, 176
Joelson, Amalia, 254, 256–58
Johannesburg Art Foundation, 152, 153
Johansen, Karen, 254–58
John, Elton, 51, 53
John Paul, Pope, 18
Johns, Jasper, *White Alphabets*, 289
Johnson, Samuel, 25
Johnson, Scott, 281, 282
Johnson, Tom, 212, 214, 216
Judd, Donald, 287
Jung, Carl, *Mysterium Coniunctionis*, 40
Justice and Development Party (Turkey), 495

Kabakov, Ilya, 53
    Man Who Described His Life Through Characters, 50
    Man Who Flew into Space from His Apartment, 50
    Man Who Never Threw Anything Away, 50
Kabinet, 77–78
Kaczyński, Jarosław, 494–5
Kafue National Park, Zambia, 226
Kagame, Paul, 305, 306, 307, 319
Kalimba, Célestin, 310
Kamran, Baktash, 278
Kangerlussuaq ice fjord, 252–53
Kangxi Emperor, 377
Kanta (teacher), 398–401
Karzai, Hamid, 270, 271
Kasanka National Park, Zambia, 225
Kasparov, Garry, 102
Kata Kolok sign language, 398–401, 405
Katsuba, Valera, 81, 97
Katz, Max, 102
'kayak anxiety', 255
Kazakhstan, nomads in, 16–17
Kebyar (Balinese woman), 402–3
Kennedy, John F., 162
Kentridge, William, 149–50, 171, 173–74, 519
Kesyar (Balinese woman), 403
KGB (Russian intelligence agency), 12, 54, 63, 99
Khademi, Kubra, 284
Khan, Altan, 238
Khan, A. Q., 347
Khan, Genghis, 272
Khan, Sadiq, 510, 511
khanqah (Afghan holy building), 278
Khin Kyi, 455–56
Khmer Rouge, 230–32, 468
Khövsgöl Lake National Park, Mongolia, 244–46
Khrushchev, Nikita, 47, 61, 334
King, Alice, 128
Kirill, Patriarch, 99
Kiselev, Aleksandr A., 90, 91–92, 97

Kisevalter, Georgi, 47
Klimov, Andrei, 57
Klimova, Yelena, 99
Koloane, David, 145, 147–48, 152, 158, 173
Ko Minn Latt, 446, 453, 470
Kopystiyanskaya, Svetlana, 53
Korea, elections in, 455
Kostromin, Sergey, 98
Kounellis, Jannis, 289
Krylov, Romuald, 89
Kuan Kuan, 191
Ku Klux Klan, 36, 499, 509
Kuchibhotla, Srinivas, 504
Kuksinaite, Irina, 78, 79, 86
Kurds, 496, 500
Kurlyandtseva, Lena, 64
Kurtulmus, Numan, 495–6
Kusa, Musa, 326
Kusama, Yayoi, 290
Kuzmin, Dmitry, 99
Kvant International, 84
Kyi Zaw Lwin, 469
Kyrgyzstan, gay men entrapped by police in, 34

Labour Party, 500
Lake Iteshi-Teshi, Zambia, 226
Lalae (yacht), 298–301
Lange, Amelia, 254–55, 256–58
Lantos, Tom, 349
Lao Li (Li Xianting), 126, 128, 136
    on categories of Chinese art, 110
    and Chinese avant-garde, 106–8, 119, 127, 131
    and *Fine Arts in China*, 109
    and Gaudy Art, 135
    influence of, 107, 122
    moral purpose of, 107, 134
    and Yan's lawsuit, 133, 134
Lauder, Leonard, 329
Law and Justice Party (Poland), 494–5
Lazarus, Emma, 36
Leblon Beach, Rio de Janeiro, 408
Lee, Lily, 208
Lee Teng-hui, 187, 197, 206

Lee Yulin, 206, 208–9, 291
Legae, Ezrom, 145
Leidermann, Yuri, 63
Lenin, V. I., 50, 102, 151, 175, 246
Leonardo da Vinci, 125
Leshan Grand Buddha, 367
letting go, 44
LGBT issues, *see* gay people; gay rights
Liberal Democrats, 500
Libya, 7, 321–57
    atrocities against gay people in, 35–36
    Basic People's Congresses in, 322, 337–39, 354
    Bulgarian nurses in, 334–35, 348
    chaos in, 29, 355, 356–57
    Circle of Fire in, 354–56
    corruption in, 343–44
    economy of, 321–22, 330–31, 333, 341–43, 345, 353, 354
    fundamentalism in, 325, 331, 349, 352
    Green Square in Tripoli, 331–32
    growing population of, 331
    isolation of, 34
    Italian occupation of (1912–43), 324, 353
    literacy rate in, 333
    National Oil Company in, 326, 330, 341, 348
    and nuclear weapons, 347
    oil in, 321, 333, 341–43, 348
    possibility of democracy in, 327, 336–37, 350
    poverty in, 333
    prisons in, 334–35
    refugees from, 514–16
    social life in, 350–51, 355
    student visas to people from, 38
    surveillance in, 336
    television in, 341
    and terrorist groups, 346–47, 348, 354
    travel to, 327–29
    tribal structure in, 327, 337, 343, 355
    Trump and, 515

update, 356–57
U.S. and UN sanctions against, 326, 341, 346, 348
U.S. relations with, 345–50, 354
women in, 334, 351
Libyan Islamic Brotherhood, 357
Libyan Publishers' League, 322
Libyan Writers' League, 335
Lichtenstein, Roy, 109
Lilla, Mark, 'The End of Identity Liberalism' (*New York Times* article), 517–18
Lindbergh, Charles, 509
Lithuania, Jewish State Museum in, 23, 500
Lithur, Nana Oye, 430
Litichevsky, Zhora, 55
Litvinenko, Alexander, 100
Liu Anping, 121–22
Liulin Wei, 203
Liu Shenli, 396
Liu Wei, 111
Li Wenzi, 136
Li Xianting, *see* Lao Li
Locke, John, 323
Lockerbie air crash, 322, 326, 346, 347, 348
Long, Richard, 289
Longtime Companion (film), 81
Lord of the Flies (film), 473
Louis XIV, king of France, 376
Louvre Museum, Paris, 194, 375
Loving, Mildred, 515
Loving, Richard, 515
Lucy (Xhosa bead worker), 144–45
Lugar, Richard, 349
Lula da Silva, Luiz Inácio, 410, 416, 421
Lu Maw, 446
Lumpen modelling agency, 98
Luna, Cíntia, 421
Lusaka, Zambia, 225
Lu Shengzhong, 131
Luzhkov, Yuri, 97
Lycia, Turkey, 213–14
Lynge, Sara, 257

Mabasa, Noria, 166–67
Ma Ba Tha (Burmese Buddhist political group), 480–81
Mabulu, Ayanda, 176
Macartney-Snape, Sue, 485, 486, 489, 492
Mack, David, 348, 349
Macquarie Island, 387–88
Madasani, Alok, 504
Ma Desheng, 108
Maelaua, Wilson, 294
Magadlela, Fikile, 159
Maghur, Azza, 349–50
Magkoeva, Isabelle, 102
Mahama, John Dramani, 429–33
My First Coup d'État, 429
Mahmoudi, Baghdadi al-, 354
Makarevich, Andrei, 98
Makarov, Andrey, 101
Makoba, Trevor, 159–60
Malange, Nise, 164
Malaurie, Jean, 255–56
Ma Liuming, 137
Mamyshev-Monroe, Vladik, 74, 97
Manaka, Matsemela, 158
Manchu Qing dynasty, 376, 379, 381
Manchuria, Japanese invasion of (1931), 188
Mandela, Nelson, 142, 152, 158
Manjusri (bodhisattva), 381
Mansour, Abdul, 271, 272
Mao Zedong:
as art subject, 112, 122, 123
and Chinese art, 103, 108, 109, 272
and Cultural Revolution, 119–24, 162
death of, 120–21
and 'international friends', 109
legacy of, 375
and Revolutionary Model Operas, 122
Mapplethorpe, Robert, 192
Maqhubela, Louis, 148
Marie Antoinette, queen of France, 118, 384
Marleni (ballerina), 18

Marrakesh, Morocco, 8
Marsaja, I Gede, 398, 401
Marshall Plan, 42, 269, 411
Martin, Marilyn, 144–45, 149
Masango, Aubrey, 176
Masekela, Barbara, 142, 146, 174–75
Mashinee, Abdul Rashin, 280
Matamura, Marie Rose, 311–12
Ma Thanegi, 444, 448, 453, 455, 469,
    471, 475, 476–77
  Nor Iron Bars a Cage, 476
Ma Thida, 27, 444–45, 458, 464, 471,
    472, 480
Mathieson, Dave, 479
Matisse, Henri, 214
Matlock, Jack F., 51
Matshoba, Mtutuzeli, 162
Mattawa, Khaled, 323
Mattos, Sergio, 423
Maung Tin Thit, 446, 475–76
Mautloa, Pat, 145
May, Theresa, 494
  Brexit and, 497, 500, 508, 511,
    512–13, 520
  general election (2017), 500
Mayakovsky, Vladimir, 78
Mazin, Viktor, 78
McCarthyism, 22
McNamara, Robert S., 21–22
Medeiros, Luciana, 423
Medical Hermeneutics movement, 47
Mediterranean Sea, 211
Meherzad, Hafiz, 273
Meishugan (National Art Gallery),
    Beijing, 108
  China/Avant-Garde exhibit, 109
  Country Life Plan exhibit, 104–5
  Gilbert & George show in, 126–27
Melloan, George, 508
Melville, Herman, *Moby-Dick*,
    293–94, 302
Merkel, Angela, 41, 511
Merleau-Ponty, Maurice, 78
Metropolitan Museum, New York:
  Chinese collection in, 184, 203
  conservation of Asian art in, 193

and cultural exchange, 192, 203
exhibition of work from Taipei,
    181, 182–83, 184, 185, 189–91,
    193–96, 199–203
  King Tut exhibit (1978), 184–85
Mexico, public protests in, 184
Michelangelo, 109
Michener, James, 300
Miller, George Bures, 291
Mills, John Atta, 430, 432
Ming dynasty, 375, 379, 382
Minghella, Anthony, 361
Mironenko, Serioja, 64, 65, 66
Mironenko, Vladimir, 61, 64
Misiano, Viktor, 55
Mitchell, Derek, 448, 454, 455, 457,
    459, 461, 468
Mitrofanov, Georgi, 100
Miyajima, Tatsuo, 290
Moe Satt, 446–47
Mokamel, Kabir, 284
Moletsi, Andrew (pseud.), 147
Moloudzadeh, Makwan, 34
Molsami (Balinese woman), 403
Momba, Willie, 222, 224, 225
Mona Lisa (Leonardo), 194
Monastyrsky, Andrei, 47
Monet, Claude, *Water Lilies*, 291
Mongolia, 237–47
  airag (fermented horse milk) in,
    239, 240, 243
  Bayanzag Flaming Cliffs in, 243
  camels in, 243
  description of, 238
  elections in, 455
  gay identity in, 33–34
  gers (tent-like structures) in,
    238–39, 243–44
  irony in, 246
  and Manchus, 381
  monasteries in, 246
  Naadam celebration in, 239–41
  nomadism in, 242–44, 247
  ortz (tepee) in, 245
  Övörkhangai Province, 241, 242
  reindeer people in, 245–46

roads in, 241
shamans in, 245
as symbol of the remote, 237
train ride to, 237–38
yaks in, 241–42
Monitor Group, 344
Moriconi, Italo, 409, 414, 423
Morocco, author's visit to, 7–8, 9
Morrison, Toni, 27
Moscow:
artists in, 12, 13–15, 48–49, 54–58,
59, 60, 63, 69, 74–75, 85–86
billionaires in, 98
change in, 13, 15, 30, 56–58
First Gagarin party in, 73–74, 80
life in, 29
'paper architects' in, 26
Sotheby's first sale of Soviet art in,
45, 49–56
VDNKh, 73, 101
Moscow Biennale, 57
Moscow Exchange, 84
Moscow Museum of Modern Art, 56
Moth, The, 261, 483
'mountain wanderer syndrome', 255
Mount Wutai, 381
Mozart, Wolfgang Amadeus, 22
Mthembu, Jackson, 175
Mubarak, Hosni, 517
Muhammad (prophet), Danish
cartoons of, 352
Muhammad, Abdul Akbar, 340
Mukamakuza, Alphonsine, 315–17
Mukamana, Espérance, 308
Mukamana, Marianne, 312–14
Mukansanga, Beatrice, 311
Mukasarasi, Godelièvre, 308
Mukhuba, Nelson, 172–73
Multimedia Art Museum, Moscow, 56
Muniz, Vic, 408, 415, 424
Munyai, Albert Mbudzeni, 169–70
Murdoch, Rupert, 361
Murray, Brett, 175–76
Muslim Brotherhood, 351–52
Muslims:
Brexit and, 499–500

European nationalism and, 494–6
in Myanmar, 458–64, 468, 481
polygamy among, 460
Trump and, 501, 502, 505–6, 507,
514–15
see also Islam
Myanmar, 443–82
absence of basic services in, 447–48,
451–52, 461, 469
artists in, 446–47, 474–75
blogging in, 471–72
Buddhist majority in, 444, 449,
458–59, 462, 464, 466–68, 481
censorship in, 443, 451, 461,
470–73, 479–80, 481
and China, 449, 458, 476
constitution of, 452, 456,
457–58, 482
Cyclone Nargis in, 457–58
economy of, 454, 469
education in, 451, 452–53
88 Generation in, 452
elections in, 443, 454–55, 456–58,
480–82
ethnic groups in, 451, 453, 458–64,
465, 466–70, 479, 481
expatriates from, 454, 471–72
Golden Rock shrine in, 465–66
government move to Naypyidaw,
450, 453–54
hope in, 443, 444, 480
idea of freedom in, 27
independence of, 444, 451, 455,
468, 469
individual states in, 469–70
Inle Lake guesthouse in, 477–79
international sanctions in, 443,
448–49
Inthar Heritage House in, 478
Kyaiktiyo Pagoda in, 466
laws in, 457, 458, 463, 480
military junta in, 445–46, 448, 449,
451–52, 453, 455, 464, 465,
469, 472, 477, 481, 482
national identity in, 459, 463, 470
Plain of Temples (Bagan), 466–67

Myanmar (*cont.*)
  political prisoners in, 443–45, 457,
    469, 472–73, 474, 476–77, 481
  political reforms in, 445, 447,
    448–49, 472
  possible democracy in, 450, 451,
    452, 455, 480, 482
  poverty in, 449, 450, 463–64, 471
  Rohingya people in, 458–62, 464,
    468, 480–81
  Saffron Revolution (2007)
    in, 444, 447, 449, 452,
    462, 472
  Shwedagon Pagoda in, 449–50
  history of, 459, 480
  structures demolished in, 450
  student uprisings (1988) in, 444,
    456, 465, 470, 473, 475, 476
  threat of guerrilla warfare in,
    468–69
  tourism in, 450, 478–79
  update, 480–82
My Life as a Red Guard (documentary
  film), 124

NAACP, 506
NAFTA, 508
Naidoo, Riason, 175
Naito, Rei, 291
Namibia, national museum in, 144
NASCO (National Supply
  Corporation), 338, 342
National Cancer Institute, 343
National Endowment of the Arts
  (NEA), 162
National Gallery, Kabul, 270
National Gallery of Art, Washington,
  D.C., *Circa 1492* exhibition, 184
National Gallery of South Africa,
  143–45, 146, 175
National Palace Museum, Taipei,
  187–96, 198–99, 202–3, 209
  artworks reattributed by, 189
  balance needed against, 198
  Imperial Collection in, 187–89,
    192, 203

and Met exhibit, 182–83, 185,
    189–91, 193, 195, 196
  preview exhibition of, 189–90
  renovations in, 203
  restricted list of, 189, 190–91,
    194–95
  seventieth anniversary of, 185–86
Nation of Islam, 340
nationalism, rise of new, 494–520
Nationalist Movement Party
  (Turkey), 496
Nauman, Bruce, *100 Live and Die*, 289
Navalny, Alexei, 102
Nay Phone Latt, 447, 452–53, 461,
    471–72, 473, 480
Nazism, 230, 306, 501, 502, 504, 505,
    506, 509, 512, 514, 519
Ndayambaje, Jean Damascène, 309
Ndou brothers (Goldwin and Owen),
    167–68
  Sport for a Gentleman, 168
Nemtsov, Boris, 102
New Analysts Group, Beijing, 113
New Europe College, Bucharest, 440–41
Ne Win, 451
New Republic, 17
New Wave, 109
New Yorker, 321, 435
New York Times, 205, 269, 429,
    496, 517
New York Times Magazine, 59, 71, 103,
    139, 141, 181
Ngabonziza, Jean-de-Dieu, 316
Ngarda (Balinese man), 403
Ngcukana, Fitzroy, 164
Nhlengethwa, Sam, 145–46, 156
NHS (National Health Service), 499
Niazi, Mohammed Yasin, 274
Nicolaisen, Flemming, 22
Nigeria, gay people stoned to death in,
    34
Night Wolves (biker gang), 99
Ni Haifeng, 106, 117, 121, 124, 129
Nikolayev, Leonid, 57
Nimrod, 385–96
Nishizawa, Ryue, 291

Niyonsenga, Marcelline, 314–15
Nkosi, Charles, 152, 155
Nkotsi, Tony, 173
Noize MC, 98
Noonday Demon, The: An Atlas of Depression (Solomon), 31, 35, 211, 229, 249, 261, 435, 436–37
Norman, Jessye, 361
North, Oliver ('Ollie'), 177
Northern Ireland, 498, 513
Northern Song dynasty, 378
Norway, menu in, 20–21
Novikov, Timur, 78, 81, 97
Novogratz, Jacqueline, 319–20
nowhere to go, 1–2, 16, 23, 481
    always someplace to go, 36
    escape fantasies, 2, 3, 32
    refugees, 24, 39–42, 233–35
Ntobe, Joyce (pseud.), 147
Ntshangase, Alson, *The AIDS Doctors*, 153
Nyirahabimana, Alphonsine, 310

Offenbacher, Mrs, 4
Olsen, Astrid, 258
Olshvang, Anton, 60
Oppenheimer, J. Robert, 188
Oprah (TV), 341
Orbán, Viktor, 495
Orpheus Island, 485–86
Ostrakovsky, Ivan, 99–100
Ouyang Jianghe, 140
Ovcharenko, Vladimir, 58
Ovchinnikova, Masha, 82–83
OvidiuRo (NGO), 436, 440

Pachugin, Yaroslav, 83
Paes, Eduardo, 416
Pahlavi, Shah Mohammad Reza, 337
Pakistan:
    intelligence service (ISI), 271
    and Muslim guerrillas, 460
    nuclear weapons of, 347
    women wearing hijab in, 26
Palestine, 352

Pan Africanist Congress of Azania (PAC), 164
Panama Papers, 102
Pan Am Flight 103 (Lockerbie bombing), 322, 326, 346, 347, 348
Pan Dehai, 106
paper, origins of, 128
paranoia, 255
Paris:
    Garnier (theatre) in, 422
    Sots Art: Political Art from Russia exhibit, 58
Paris Agreement (2016), 511
Paris terrorist attacks (November 2015), 38
Parks, Rosa, 340
Pascoe, Lynn, 207
Pater, Walter, 28
Patricof, Alan, 329
Pavlov, MC, 75, 79–80, 97
Payne, Malcolm, 144, 145, 146, 150, 159
peace, 41
Pearl, Daniel, 37
Pearsall, Cornelia, 21
Peilman, Kirsten, 252
Pe Myint, 449
PEN:
    and censorship, 35–36
    Myanmar office of, 443
PEN American Center, author as president of, 35–36, 443
Pence, Mike, 505
Penkin, Sergei, 81
Perm, Russia, *Welcome to Sochi* exhibit in, 57
Peterson, Peter G., 329
Petlyura, 75–77, 97
Pew Research Trust, 427
Phaly Nuon, 229, 231–35
    death of, 235
photography, invention of, 185
phytoplankton, 396
Picasso, Pablo, 185
Pierneef, Henk, 144
Pinda (Balinese man), 401

Pindu, Nym, 403
Plutser-Sarno, Alex, 57
Poland, immigration and nationalism
    in, 494–5
'polar hysteria', 255
Politico, 508
Polo, Marco, 366
Pol Pot, 230, 231
Popov, Sergey, 53
'post-referendum racism and
    xenophobia (PRRX), 499
Powell, Ivor, 164, 173
Prague, cultural dissonance in, 22
Prigov, Dima, 38
Professor Khromov, 386–87, 390
propaganda, 36
Pushkin State Museum of Fine Arts,
    Moscow, 55
Pussy Riot (band), 57, 100
Putin, Vladimir, 15, 57–58, 71, 97,
    99–100, 102, 437
Pu Yi (the last emperor), 188, 376

Qaddafi, Muammar, 6, 28, 321–23,
    326–27, 329, 332–34, 335, 349,
    351–52, 354
  bedouin roots of, 323, 341, 343
  and Circle of Fire, 354–56
  and corruption, 343
  death of, 356, 449
  on elections, 336–37
  Green Book, 322, 330, 332–33
  hegemony of, 345
  Jamahiriya system of, 332–33, 334,
    337, 342
  legacy of, 357
  and Nation of Islam, 340
  possibility of meeting with,
    339–41
  Third Universal Theory of, 332
  and unrest, 345–48, 352–53
Qaddafi, Saif al-Islam, 6–7, 323–26,
    327, 329, 334, 337, 349, 354
  imprisonment of, 357
  Qaddafi Foundation of, 323, 335
  and unrest, 352–53

Qianlong Emperor, 374–84
  death of, 377
  idealism of, 384
  meditation of, 382
  poems written by, 377, 382
  reign of, 377
Qianlong Garden of Retirement,
    China, 373–84
  design of, 378–80, 382
  Juanqinzhai in, 373, 374, 376, 377,
    379–84
  restoration of, 383–84
Qing dynasty, 128, 187, 203, 375–77
Qudratullah (chef), 281–82

Radio Liberty, 61
Rados, Antonia, 281
Rafferty, Emily K., 192, 196
Rahim, Said Makhtoum, 271, 272
Rakhine (Arakan) State, 459, 461–63
  author's visit to, 464–68
Ramabulana, Freddy, 168–69
Reagan administration, 325, 345
Reed, Lou, 361
refugee camps, 25, 233–35, 307,
    461–62, 473, 481
refugees, 39–42
  and cultural exclusion, 39
  and immigration, 25, 494, 495,
    507–8, 514–16
Renaissance, 185, 380
Renzi, Matteo, 495
Resmini, Ni Md, 401
Rezayee, Shaima, 284
Rezun-Zvezdochetova, Larisa, 13, 60,
    65, 66–68
Richards, Colin, 163
Rilke, Rainer Maria, 44
Rio de Janeiro, Brazil, 407–28
  aesthetics of sensuality in, 423
  beach culture in, 423
  Carioca culture of, 409, 414–15,
    417, 422
  Carnival in, 408–9
  Christ the Redeemer statue in, 417
  deindustrialisation, 409

favelas in, 408–15, 417–22, 423,
    425–28
Museu de Favela in, 414
nightlife in, 423–24
Olympic Games in, 407, 410, 416–
    17, 418, 419, 422, 426, 427
pacification programme in, 415–17,
    420, 421, 426–28
police and crime in, 409–13, 418,
    421, 422, 425–27
rejuvenation of historic sites in,
    422–25
samba in, 408, 409, 420, 424
skin colour in, 419–20
social services in, 412–14, 418–19,
    422, 426, 427
sports competitions in, 413
street library in, 422
Theatro Municipal in, 422–23
update, 425–28
UPP (Unidade de Polícia
    Pacificadora) in, 410–14, 418,
    420–21, 422, 425–26
World Cup in, 407, 410, 418, 422
'Ríu Ríu Chíu' (song), 6
Rockefeller, David, 329
Rodchenko, Aleksandr, 50
    Line, 52
Roden Crater, Arizona, 287
Rodrigues da Silva, Robson, 413–14
Roiter, Andrei, 15
Rolpai, Dorje, 381
Romania, 435–42
    Brâncuşi's *Endless Column* in, 287
    depression in, 435, 436–39
    Dorohoi (home of author's
        ancestors), 436, 438–39
    gay rights in, 437, 440–42
    language of, 441
    Roma (Gypsy) settlements in, 436,
        440, 441
    social liberalisation in, 441
    travel in, 6, 25
Romanian National Radio, 437
Ronald Feldman Fine Arts, New York,
    50

Roque, Atila, 427
Rossouw, David, 169–70
Ross Sea, 385, 388–89, 392
royal albatross, 394
Rohingya people , 458–62, 464, 468,
    480–81
Rus, Andrei, 441–42
Ruskin, John, 24
Russ, Rodney, 386, 388–90, 392–94
Russia, 28, 71–102
    from 1917 to 1991, *see* USSR
    businessmen in, 83–86
    and capitalism, 74, 83–84, 95–96
    censorship in, 57–58, 97, 98, 175
    changing politics in, 89–96, 102
    constitution of, 92, 94, 97
    corruption in, 100–101
    despair in, 247
    drug use in, 73
    economy of, 101–2
    emerging social classes in, 71–72, 90
    expats in U.S., 177–79
    gay life in, 35, 58, 71, 80–82, 98–99
    ideology in, 82, 91, 93
    Imperial Porcelain from, 30
    interpretation of democracy in, 91–93
    magazines in, 77–78, 98
    manipulation of U.S. election
        (2016), 510
    nationalism in, 494
    organised crime in, 71, 73–74, 77,
        79, 81, 86–89, 100
    Orthodox Church in, 72, 82–83,
        99–100
    parties and nightclubs in, 73–74, 98
    popular music in, 78–80, 97, 98
    rave scene in, 72–74
    sanctions against, 101
    social scene in, 72–77
    spirit vs. bureaucracy in, 61
    tusovkis (social circles) in, 72–73,
        75, 77, 87
    update, 97–102
Russian Patriotic movement, 94
Russian Revolution (1917), 62
Russia Without Us (zine), 98

Rutskoi, Alexander, 178
Ruzicka, Marla, 27, 281, 285
Rwanda, 305–20
    Avega (widows' organisation) in,
        308, 310
    as Belgian colony, 305–6
    genocide in, 305–7
    HIV/AIDS in, 307, 308, 310–12,
        313, 315
    independence (1962), 306
    internal politics in, 306
    les enfants de mauvais souvenir in,
        307–19
    post-genocide years in, 310
    propaganda in, 36
    Radio Mille Collines in, 306
    update, 319–20
    women raped in, 305, 306–19

Saffron Revolution (2007), Myanmar,
        444, 447, 449, 452, 462, 472
St John, Ronald Bruce, 348
Sakharov, Andrei, 93
Sakharov Center Moscow, Forbidden
        Art exhibit, 57
Salakhova, Aydan, 85
Salman bin Abdul-aziz, king of Saudi
        Arabia, 510
Samim, Farouq, 37–38, 282, 283–84
Samuels, Sammy, 447, 467
Sandi (Balinese man), 402–3
San Pe, Robert, 457
San San Oo, 467
Santia (Balinese man), 401–2, 404
Santyar, Achmed Shekib, 'Epitaph', 275
São Paulo, Brazil, 409, 410, 420
Sarandon, Susan, 361
Saudi Arabia:
    assassination plot in, 341, 348
    capital punishment for gays in, 35
Sbeta, Abdulmonem M., 344
Scher, Lucy, 44, 489
Scher, Oliver, 44, 489
Schönfeldt, Joachim, 146
Schröder, Gerhard, 348
Schwarcz, Lilia Moritz, 409

Scott, Robert Falcon, 393
Scott Island, 392
scuba diving, 484–92
sea level, rising, 303, 396
seasonal affective disorder (SAD), 250
Sebidi, Helen, 159
Seck, Stephen, 153
Sediqi, Ismail, 273
Second World War, 2, 5, 188, 294,
        301–2, 494, 508, 509
    Burma in, 450–51
Sekete, Paul, 174
Selepe, Sydney, 152, 153
Senegal, 261–68
    immigrants to U.S., 268
    Lebou beliefs and culture in, 268
    mental health services in, 267–68
    n'deup ritual in, 262–67, 268
Senoussi, Abdallah, 326
September 11 terrorist attacks, 38, 269,
        339, 347, 453
Seuss, Dr (pseud. Theodore Geisel), 301
sexual identity, 33–36
Shackleton, Sir Ernest, 385–86, 388
Shakespeare, William, 385, 490
    Henry VIII, 36
Shakila, Zamzama, 276–77
Shalgham, Abdurrahman, 335, 345, 352
Shanghai, food in, 162–64, 360
Shaoxing, China, food in, 364–65
Shembe Church, South Africa, 175
Shenzong, emperor of China, 186, 200
Shia Yan, 191, 209–10
Shih, J. J., 207
Shih Shou-chien, 182
shoebill (elusive bird), 223
Shwe Mann, 455, 457, 458
Sichuan opera, 367
Sichuan province, food in, 365–67
sign language, 397–405
Sihlali, Durant, 145, 154–55, 159
Silence Number Nine (TV), 75
Silverstein, Mindy, 483, 485
Siopis, Penny, 149, 163
Siwedi, Linos, 158–59
Skotnes, Cecil, 152

Skotnes, Pippa, 150
Smith, Judith, 192
Snares islands, 386
Snowden, Edward, 102
Snyder, Timothy, 501
Soares, Luiz Eduardo, 410, 412, 421
Sobchak, Anatoly, Foundation, 97
social media, 495, 498, 516
socialisation, grooming in, 234
Solntsevskaya Bratva, 100
Solomon, Andrew:
    adventurousness of, 484, 492
    alone at sea, 488–92
    Anglophilia of, 2–5, 10
    Brexit and U.S. election (2016)
        voting, 494
    depression of, 211, 261–62,
        263, 439
    dual citizenship of, 16, 494
    emotions of, 43–44, 483–84
    first family trip abroad, 5
    forebears of, 26, 435–36,
        438–39, 441
    scuba diving, 484–92
    speaking in Romania, 437, 440–42
    wedding of John Habich and, 33
Solomon, Blaine, 42, 489, 490
Solomon, George, 42–43, 485, 486,
    489, 490, 492
Solomon, John Habich:
    in China, 359
    and discrimination against gays, 36
    scuba diving, 484, 485, 489, 490,
        491–92
    in Solomon Islands, 294
    wedding of Andrew Solomon
        and, 33
Solomon Islands, 293–303, 484
    Circumcision Island, 302
    coral atolls, 300
    discrimination against gays in, 35
    Hauta, 295–98
    island-hopping, 298–301
    Lake Tegano, 301–2
    languages in, 294
    Makira Island, 294–98

Malaita people in, 294
Marovo Lagoon, 300–301, 302
Polynesia life in, 301–2
provincial capital relocated, 302–3
rainforest in, 295
Uepi, 301
update, 302–3
Song dynasty, 181, 185, 187, 193, 199,
    201, 203, 379
Song Shuangsong, 104–5, 109,
    113–14, 130, 134
Songzhuang, China, 136, 138–39
Sotheby's (auction house):
    commercialism of, 54–55
    first sale of Soviet art by, 45, 49–56
    Soviet tour sponsored by, 49, 51, 52
South Africa, 141–76, 519
    absurd theatre of symbolic respect,
        163–64
    affirmative action in, 151, 161–62
    apartheid art centres in, 151–52, 154
    apartheid categories in, 156
    art appreciation, no tradition of, 161
    art competitions in, 159
    art dialogue in, 155–56
    art schools in, 152–53
    basket weaving in, 160–61
    black people invisible in, 142–43,
        145–46, 160, 161, 175
    black-white mutual influence in,
        173–75
    censorship in, 175–76
    coloured (mixed race) people in,
        156–57
    commercial galleries in, 158–59,
        172, 175
    conflicting priorities in, 143–49,
        153–54, 155, 175–76
    cultural boycott (1980s) in, 148–49
    elections in, 455
    end of apartheid in, 29, 141, 148, 162
    in the hinterlands, 161, 164–73
    Hottentots, 145
    National Arts Initiative (NAI), 143,
        162–64
    'necklacing' in, 409

South Africa (*cont.*)
  politics in, 162–64, 174
  public stoning ordered in, 175
  *sangoma*s (witch doctors), 153,
      166, 173
  shebeens in, 163
  townships in, 151–57
  transitional art in, 153
  travel in, 19–20
  Tributaries exhibition in, 171
  update, 175–76
  and Venice Biennale, 159–60, 176
  white art collectors in, 157–58
  white-directed programmes for
      blacks in, 160–62
  white liberal artists in, 148–51
  Xhosa beadwork, 144–45
South Seas fantasies, 293
Soviet art:
  Actions (happenings), 46–49, 52,
      55, 57
  avant-garde, 46–51, 53, 55, 56–58
  contemporary, 49–58
  hidden meanings in, 12, 54, 55, 56,
      103, 272
  influence of, 108
  The Irony Tower (Solomon), 14–15, 45
  market for, 45–58
  self-reference in, 56
  Sotheby's first sale of, 45, 49–56
  update, 56–58
  Western discovery of, 49–50, 135
Soviet Union, *see* USSR
Soweto, South Africa, travel in, 19–20
Spain, money laundering in, 100
Speedy Bag Factory, Johannesburg,
      145–47, 149
spirt (grain alcohol), 17
Spratt, Captain, 215
Sri Lanka, 459
Stalin, Joseph, 13, 17, 28, 54, 60, 118,
      178, 230, 246
Stankevich, Sergei B., 90, 92–95, 97
Stars group, China, 108, 109, 110, 123
Stepanova, Varvara, 50
Stevens, Christopher, 356

Stewart, Lucas, 447, 463
storytelling, 24, 30–33, 258, 261
Stravinsky, Igor, 423
Styazhkin, Denis, 58
Suara Putra (Balinese man), 402
Suarayasa (Balinese teenager), 400, 402
Sudarma (Balinese man), 403
Sugimoto, Hiroshi, 289
Suharto, 449
Sukesti, Cening, 402, 403–4
Su Shi:
  Ode to the Red Cliff, 200
  *Poems Written at Hangzhou on the
      Cold-Food Festival,* 200–201
Suu Kyi, *see* Aung San Suu Kyi
Suzhou gardens, 378, 379
Suzman, Helen, 162
Sviblova, Olga, 65, 86, 97
Swehli, Ahmed, 337, 344
Syria, 319, 336, 346
  atrocities against homosexuals in, 34
  chaos in, 28
  refugees from, 38

Taipei Fine Arts Museum, 206, 208, 210
Taiwan, 181–204
  American Institute in, 195, 207
  autonomous art for, 198–99
  calligraphy in, 199–203
  Chinese art moved to (1949), 183,
      185, 188, 198
  Chinese heritage in, 209
  contemporary art scene in, 205–10
  economy of, 198
  elections in, 455
  ethnic tensions in, 197–98
  identity crisis of, 183, 197, 198,
      204, 206, 207–9
  and mainland China, 184, 185,
      195, 196–98, 205, 206
  massacres (February 28, 1948), 208
  as model for democracy, 185
  nationalism in, 208
  nativist Taiwanese styles, 205
  New Paradise (artist-run space)
      in, 208

Palace Museum, *see* National Palace Museum

politics in, 191–94, 195, 202, 205, 206–7, 208–9, 210

and protectionism, 16, 184

protests of Met exhibit, 182, 183, 190–97, 202

public protests continuing in, 203–4

and reunification, 202–4, 206

self-definition in, 206

Sunflower Movement in, 204

U.S. relations with, 185, 196, 197

White Shirt Army, 203

Tales of a Korean Grandmother (Carpenter), 4

Taliban, 28, 38, 270–75, 278, 279–80, 347, 460, 461

Tambovskaya Prestupnaya Grupirovka, 100

Tan, Fiona, 291

Tang dynasty, 187, 193

Tang Hsiao-li, 190

Tang Jianying, 139

Tatlin, Vladimir, 289

    Monument to the Third International, 75

Taylor, Professor Keeanga-Yamahatta, 504

Tchenogramme (pseud.), 207

Tennyson, Alfred, Lord, 16, 518

Teresa, Mother, 127

terrorism, effects of, 38–39

Teshima Island, 291

Thant Myint-U, 447, 450, 459, 463, 469, 470

Thant Thaw Kaung, 456, 471

Thaton, reclining Buddha at, 466

Thein Sein, 448, 454, 455, 481

Thurber, James, 223

Thyssen-Bornemisza, Baron Hans Heinrich von, 50

Tiananmen Square, 122, 138, 374

Tiananmen Square massacre (1989), 26, 109, 110, 121–22, 137

    post-'89 influence of, 111, 112, 113, 115, 119, 122

Tibet, Buddhists in, 459

Tierney, Dominic, 283–84

Timin, Rose (great-aunt), 435–36, 439, 441

Tin Win Win (Ju), 471

Titomir, Bogdan, 79

Tolstoy, Leo, 96

Toscanini, Arturo, 422–23

tourism:

    disaster tourism, 385

    travel vs., 17, 23

Trans-Pacific Partnership, 508

Transparency International, 343

Travel + Leisure, 31, 219, 237, 287, 293, 359, 385, 407, 443

travel:

    with children, 42–43

    and death, 44

    decontextualised essence in, 20–23

    depression and, 519–20

    engagement and reciprocity in, 18–19

    expectations in, 20, 22

    legacy of, 43

    new perspectives gained in, 25–26

    observation vs. engagement in, 17–18, 23

    political importance of, 25–28

    and storytelling, 24

    time stopped in, 16

    tourism vs., 17, 23

    Trump and, 501

Treaty of Lausanne (1923), 495

Tremlett, David, 289

Troitsky, Artyom, 64–65, 79, 96, 97

Trudeau, Justin, 41

Trump, Donald, 39, 127

    election of (2016), 494, 500–19, 512, 515, 516

    immigration and minority groups, attitudes towards, 38, 507–8

    internet and, 516

    Paris Agreement, withdrawal from, 511

    prejudice and hate crime explode in U.S. after election of, 494, 501–7

strongmen, champion of, 496, 509
terrorism responses to, 510–11
travel ban, 38, 507–8, 510–11
wall between Mexico and United
  States, promises, 39, 513
world outside U.S. attitude towards,
  501, 508–9
Tsaatan (Mongolian shamanists), 245–46
Tsinghua University, Cultural Heritage
  Conservation Centre, 384
Tsong Pu, 208
Tsu Ming, 207
Tunisia, and Arab Spring, 448
Tun Win Aung, 475
Tupelo Workshops, Johannesburg, 152
Turkey:
  rise of nationalism in 494, 495–6
  sailing adventure in, 211–17
Turkina, Olesya, 78
Turrell, James, 287, 290, 291
Tuyisenge, Clémence, 315
Twombly, Cy, 289

Udaltsov, Sergei, 102
Ufan, Lee, 291
Uganda, homosexuality a capital offence
  in, 34
Ulaanbaatar, Mongolia, 33–34, 237,
  238, 244, 246, 247
UNESCO, 281, 282, 300
  Intangible Cultural Heritage List,
    247, 370
  World Heritage Sites, 247, 301–2
UNICEF, 449
United Arab Emirates, 343–44
Untited Kingdom:
  Brexit and, 494, 496–500, 501,
    510, 511, 512, 516
  general election (2017), 500, 512
United Nations (UN):
  and Brazil, 418, 419
  Convention against Torture, 335
  on extrajudicial executions, 409
  and human rights, 480
  on LGBT issues, 33
  and Libya, 340–41, 346, 357

and Myanmar, 480
and Rwanda, 306
and South Africa, 148
and Taiwan, 207
UN-HABITAT, 419
United States:
  election (2016), 494, 500–11, 512,
    513, 515–17, 519
  See also Trump, Donald
Urani, André, Rio: The Turning
  Point, 415
Urbach, Erika, 4
Urodov, Andrey, 98
USSR, 45–58
  art of, see Soviet art
  bureaucracy of, 61
  Communist system in, 89, 91–92,
    93, 94
  elusiveness in, 54
  end of Soviet Union, 448
  glasnost in, 29, 45, 50, 65, 126, 448
  Gorbachev resignation in, 59–60; see
    also Gorbachev, Mikhail
  Gulag in, 66
  ideology in, 95
  invasion of Afghanistan by, 6, 11,
    272, 275, 460
  irony in, 14, 54, 61, 65
  KGB in, 12, 54, 63, 99
  Komsomol in, 91
  people's resistance (1991) in, 13,
    61–69
  perestroika in, 49, 90, 93
  and revolution (1917), 30
  Stalin years in, 14, 54
  two camps in, 141
  underground rock musicians, 64–65
Utopia (zine), 98
Uwamahoro, Christine, 317–19
U Win Htein, 481

van Graan, Mike, 143, 162
Venda, South Africa, 164–73
Venice Biennale, 149, 159–60, 176
Versace, Gianni, 382
Vickers, Sveta, 74–75

Victoria, queen, of Great Britain and Ireland, 512
Vietnam, travel to, 22
Vietnam War, 2, 22, 468
Vinogradov, Garik, 76, 77, 97
Virginia (Xhosa bead worker), 144–45
Vittrup Christensen, Erik, 419
Voina (Russian 'art-anarch-punk gang'), 57
Volkov, Sergei, 80, 86
Vorotnikov, Oleg, 57

Wah Nu, 475
Waihuru, John, 295
Wall Street Journal, 508
walls, exclusion and building of, 513–14
Wandering Jew, legend of, 2
Wang Guangyi, 112
Wang Jiaqi, 133–34
Wang Jinsong, 111
Wang Luyan, 113
Wang Peng, 137
Wang Yin, 128
Wang Zang, 138–39
Warhol, Andy, 148
war on terror, 322, 325, 348
Washington Post, 507
Waste Land (film), 424
Watt, James C. Y., 191–92
Waugh, Evelyn, 214
Western art:
    aggressiveness of, 128
    Chinese emulation of, 108, 109
    Chinese exhibitions of, 125–31
    Chinese influence on, 381
    commercial expectations of, 13, 55, 56, 112
    contemporary, 108, 127
    forward focus of, 202
    influence of, 210, 287
    mixing Chinese art and, 125, 131–32, 135, 210
Western artists, egotism of, 114
Westminster Classic Tours, 212
Williamson, Sue, 149, 160, 161

Willis, Graham Denyer, 414
Wilson, Robert, 97
Win Min, 468, 470
Wirathu, Ashin, 460, 461, 481
Wolf, John, 347
Women's March, U.S. (2017), 512
World Bank, 303, 319, 348
World Monuments Fund (WMF), 373, 383
Wright, Thomas, 508–9
Wrocław, Poland, 495
Wu Tien-chang, *Portrait as a Sailor*, 209
Wu Wenguang, 124
Wu Yuren, 138
Wu Zhen, 201

xenophobia, 38, 122, 494–5, 499, 500, 520
Xi'an, China, nightlife in, 21–22
Xi Jinping, 137, 139
Xu Bing, 129, 139
Xu Hong, 130
Yang Feiyun, 125
Yanghee Lee, 480
Yang Shaobin, 118–19
Yang Xu, 119–20
Yang Yiping, 123
Yangzhou gardens, 378
Yan Zhengxue, 132–34, 137
Yashin, Ilya, 102
Yasuda, Kan, *Secret of the Sky*, 289
Yeltsin, Boris, 61–62, 63, 64, 66, 71, 91–96, 98
Yin Myo Su, *see* Borit, Misuu
Yokoo, Teshima, 291
Yongzheng Emperor, 382
Younge, Gavin, 150
Yousefzada, Munera, 284
Yuan dynasty, 193, 201
Yuanmingyuan (artists' village), China, 118–19, 128, 131, 132–34, 136, 137
Yue Minjun, 118–19, 135–36, 140
    Execution, 135
Yugoslavia, former, 470
Yu Youhan, 112, 120

Zacchi, José Maria, 409
Zagarev, Viktor, 64
Zaki, Zakia, 284
Zambia, 219–27
    Kapishya Hot Springs Lodge in,
        221–22
    safari in, 220–27
    Shiwa Ngandu house in, 222
    tourism in, 227
Zamzama (Shakila), 276–77
Zanabazar, king and sculptor
        (Mongolia), 246
Zarqawi, Abu Musab al-, 325
Zeng Fanzhi:
    The Last Supper, 135
    Mask Series 1996 No. 6, 135
Zhang Peili, 114–17, 122, 128, 130
    *The Correct Procedure for Washing a
        Chicken* (video), 117
Zhang Wei, 131
Zhang Xiaogang, 135
Zhao Bandi, 111, 124

Zhao Mengjian, 199
Zhao Zhao, 137–38
Zhejiang Academy, Hangzhou,
        108, 114
Zhirinovsky, Vladimir, 177–79
Zhou Enlai, 28
Zhou Tiehai, 119–20
Zhuangzi, 187
Zhu Qizhan, 124–25
Zhu Yu, 137
Zimbabwe:
    gay people threatened in, 34
    travel in, 18, 165
Zionists, 340
Zlitni, A. M., 327, 336, 342
Zulu people, 153, 156
Zuma, Jacob, 175, 176
Zuu, Erdene, 246
Zvezdochetov, Kostya, 14, 61, 63–65,
        66–69
Zvezdochetova, Larisa Rezun-, 13, 60,
        65, 66–68

penguin.co.uk/vintage